Lawn mo
page 155

Appliances

Home & yard

Home office

Autos

Product recalls

Reference

Consumer Reports
www.ConsumerReports.org

HOW THIS BOOK CAN HELP

On the verge of buying a cell phone but confused by the different service offers in the ads? Need to buy a new dishwasher but the thought of spending all that money makes your palms sweat? Been offered a used car at a good price, but worried that it will turn out to be a lemon?

The Buying Guide can help. It has solutions to all those problems of consumer life and more, giving you the best buying advice CONSUMER REPORTS has to offer. Our advice is based on years of experience and testing of cars, appliances, computers, home-entertainment gear, yard equipment, and other products.

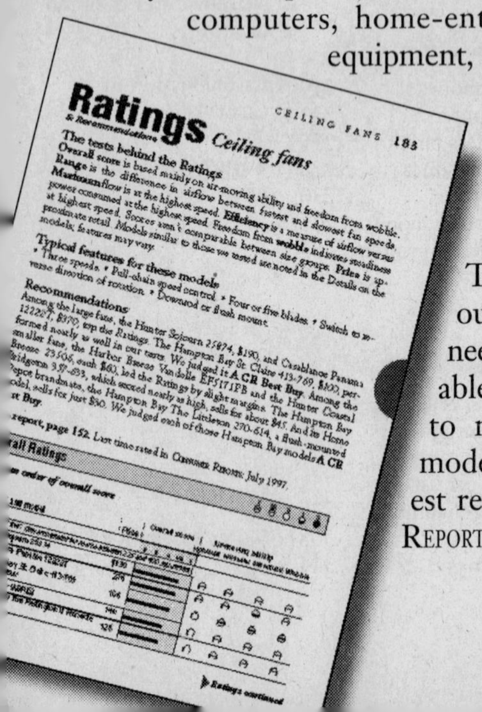

PRODUCTS FOR YOUR HOME

The reports in this book outline the essentials you need to know—what's available, key features, and how to make a choice among models. We include the latest results from the CONSUMER REPORTS test labs—Ratings of

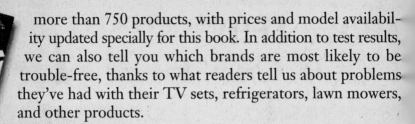

more than 750 products, with prices and model availability updated specially for this book. In addition to test results, we can also tell you which brands are most likely to be trouble-free, thanks to what readers tell us about problems they've had with their TV sets, refrigerators, lawn mowers, and other products.

CAR PREVIEWS

In these pages, you'll find previews of the 1999 cars, trucks, minivans, pickup trucks, and sport-utility vehicles. You'll also find CONSUMER REPORTS' unique reliability assessments for more than 200 vehicles and our guide to the best and worst used cars of the last eight years.

REFERENCE

The comprehensive reference section includes:

- Cars and household products recalled during the past year.
- An index of the last full test report in past issues of CONSUMER REPORTS magazine.
- A full list of manufacturers' telephone numbers and Web addresses.

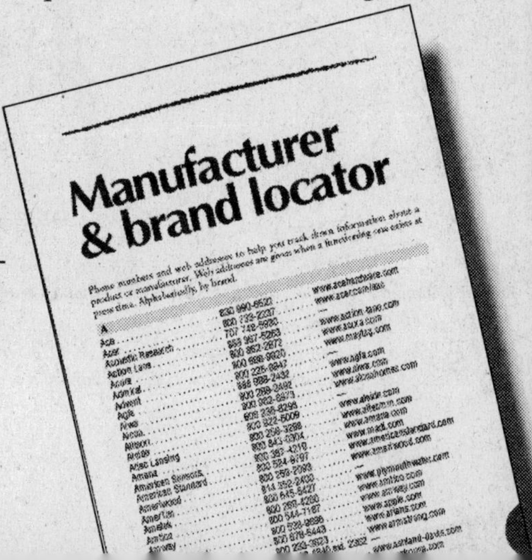

Manufacturer & brand locator

ABOUT CONSUMER REPORTS

CONSUMER REPORTS is published by Consumers Union, an independent, nonprofit testing and information organization. Founded in 1936, CU is the largest such organization anywhere in the world. We not only specialize in head-to-head, brand-name comparison tests of cars and other products, but we also provide informed, impartial advice on a broad range of topics of concern to consumers, such as health and nutrition, personal finance, and life and automobile insurance.

Consumers Union's mission has always been to test products, inform the public, and protect consumers. Our income is derived solely from the sale of CONSUMER REPORTS magazine and our other publications and services, and from nonrestrictive, noncommercial contributions, grants, and fees. We buy all the products we test, and accept no free samples. We take no advertising from outside entities, and do not let any company use our reports or Ratings for commercial purposes.

In the audio lab. The walls, floor, and ceiling of our anechoic chamber are covered with fiberglass wedges that deaden potential reflections from the walls, leaving only the direct sound coming from the speaker.

OTHER SERVICES FROM CONSUMER REPORTS

Consumer Reports Special Publications. We publish a series of specialty buying guides sold on newsstands and in bookstores, as well as books on finance, drugs, and other issues of consumer concern.

Consumer Reports Online. The CONSUMER REPORTS web site can be found at *www.ConsumerReports.org.* Free areas of the site give general buying guidance, a comprehensive list of product recalls, manufacturers' phone numbers, and other useful information. Members-only sections provide searchable Ratings of electronics, appliances, cars, and more, along with the current issue of CONSUMER REPORTS and participation in message boards. Membership is $2.95 per month or $24 year ($19 for CONSUMER REPORTS subscribers).

Consumer Reports On Health. Our monthly newsletter devoted to your health and well-being covers fitness, nutrition, medication, and more. To subscribe (12 issues, $24), write us at P.O. Box 56356, Boulder, Colo. 80322-6356.

Consumer Reports Travel Letter. Our monthly newsletter with money-saving travel information and the best travel deals. To subscribe (12 issues, $39), write us at P.O. Box 53629, Boulder, Colo. 80322-3629.

Zillions. Our bimonthly magazine for kids ages 8 and up, featuring toy tests, games, and "money smarts." To subscribe (6 issues, $16), write us at P.O. Box 54861, Boulder, Colo. 80322-4861.

Consumer Reports By Request. Specially edited reports from CONSUMER REPORTS are available by fax or mail. Call 800 896-7788 for an index of what's available. The index costs $1.

Consumer Reports New Car Price Service. Our comprehensive reports compare sticker price to dealer's invoice for a car or light truck and for factory installed options. Call 800 269-1139. Reports cost $12. See the back cover.

Consumer Reports Used Car Price Service. Find the market value and reliability summary for most 1989 to 1997 used cars and light trucks. Call 800 422-1079. Reports cost $10. See page 359.

Consumer Reports Auto Insurance Price Service. Compare the cost of insurance for the coverage you need; find the best price. Now available in 24 states. Call 800 944-4104. Reports cost $12. See page 360.

Consumer Reports Television. CRTV's nationally syndicated consumer news service appears on television stations all over the U.S.

Other media. Information from CONSUMER REPORTS is available on many radio stations around the country and in columns appearing in more than 500 newspapers.

Consumer Reports BUYING GUIDE

CONSUMER REPORTS (ISSN 0010-7174) is published 13 times a year by Consumers Union of U.S., Inc., 101 Truman Avenue, Yonkers, N.Y. 10703-1057. Second-class postage paid at Yonkers, N.Y., and at additional mailing offices. Canadian postage paid at Mississauga, Ontario, Canada. Canadian publications registration no. 2665247-98. Title CONSUMER REPORTS registered in U.S. Patent Office. CU is a member of the Consumers International. Mailing lists: CU occasionally exchanges its subscriber lists with those of selected publications and nonprofit organizations. If you wish your name deleted from such exchanges, send your address label with a request for deletion to CONSUMER REPORTS, P.O. Box 53029, Boulder, Colo. 80322-3029. Postmaster: Send address changes to the same address. Back issues: Single copies of 12 preceding issues, $5 each; Buying Guide, $10 each. Write Back Issues, CONSUMER REPORTS, P.O. Box 53016, Boulder, Colo. 80322-3016. For back issues in microform, write UMI, 300 N. Zeeb Rd., Ann Arbor, Mich. 48106.

Product reliability

GETTING THINGS FIXED

Our advice on handling breakdowns draws from the CONSUMER REPORTS 1997 Annual Questionnaire, inquiries to manufacturers, and tests in which our engineers, posing as regular consumers, had products repaired.

If an item breaks while under warranty, a repair (or in some cases, a replacement) is usually covered, although you must wait for a technician or deliver the product to a retailer or repair facility.

However, once a warranty expires, not every breakdown merits a repair. Here are the reasons why:

Dropping purchase prices versus rising repair costs. Chances are you can replace almost any major electronic item in your home today for considerably less than you paid for it. However, the solid-state assemblies and molded plastic construction that have lowered prices have also made repairs much more costly and difficult.

Changing technology. Major products are changing in ways that encourage upgrading. The most energy-efficient new refrigerators will cost hundreds of dollars less to run over their lifetime than older units, lawn mowers are less polluting, computers have increased in processing speed and versatility.

Parts availability. You can no longer assume as you once could that parts for major electronics products will remain available for at least five years, or that those for major appliances will be around for at least 10.

Busier lives. Many household items can be replaced more rapidly than they can be repaired and with less hassle.

A fix-it checklist

Is it really broken? The troubleshooting guide in the owner's manual may solve the problem. If that fails, consider calling the manufacturer for diagnostic help—especially for a major appliance or computer problem. General Electric (800 626-2000) and Sears (800 469-4663) offer full-fledged "help lines" for major appliances.

How much life is left? We provide an estimated lifespan for major appliances, audio and video products, and lawn mowers based on a survey of manufacturers and trade associations; see page 11.

Is the item still usable? You may choose to tolerate, say, a burned-out microwave light or a tractor seat that won't tilt all the way back.

What would a repair cost? Get an estimate. Then consider this rule of thumb: If the repair cost equals or exceeds half the price of a replacement, and you can afford that replacement, don't repair the item.

Would a newer model be a lot better? Even if a repair will cost less than half the price of a replacement, consider other factors—like what new models offer compared with yours and whether a replacement fits your budget.

Before you repair it

Establish the symptoms. The more you can tell a repairer about a product failure, the faster, better—and perhaps cheaper—it can be remedied.

Check warranty coverage. If a warranty is in effect, your choice of shops may be limited (see "Choose a Repairer," below). And a do-it-yourself repair may void the warranty coverage. If you don't have the sales receipt for an item under warranty, call the manufacturer to confirm the coverage.

Call the manufacturer, even about out-of-warranty repairs. You may receive an offer to fix or replace the item at no charge, sometimes as part of a program or "secret warranty" to quietly appease purchasers of a model the manufacturer knows to be trouble-prone. However, we have found that benefiting from these offers can often be frustrating.

Choose a repairer

Here are the main types of repairer:

Manufacturer-affiliated shops. As a rule, all in-warranty repairs must be done at these shops, whose staffers may receive special training from the manufacturer. *Factory service facilities* are generally owned by the manufacturer, bear its name, and meet its standards. Major-appliance companies generally rely on this type of service. *Authorized service shops* are privately run businesses that have a contractual agreement with manufacturers (usually a number of them) to fix their brands; certificates of authorization are usually displayed prominently in the shop. Though the manufacturer may hold authorized repairers to standards of performance, you can't always depend on them for honesty or reliability, our experience has shown.

Independent repair shops. Usually safe bets for routine maintenance and minor repairs, independent shops are worth considering for more demanding work, too, especially if their location is convenient and their reputation good. But try to check on its reputation with knowledgeable sources you trust and ask if the repairer belongs to a trade association like the International Society of Certified Electronic Technicians.

Repair cautions

Ask questions. Will labor be a flat fee or charged by the hour? When will the work be completed? Does the warranty cover parts? Labor? Both? Is there a "trip" charge (for house calls) or a charge for an estimate? If two appliances need repair, are there two "trip" charges?

Get it on paper. Try to identify everyone with whom you speak about the repair, and make notes on their comments or work. Ask for an estimate that states that no repair work will begin without your authorization. And remember, the cheapest repair isn't necessarily the best.

Once you do agree to have work done, demand an itemized list of services performed, parts installed, and warranties. If you leave the item at the shop, request a dated claim check that lists its brand, model, and serial number and a promised completion date.

Try to resolve problems directly with the shop that performed the work. If that's not possible and the shop is an authorized service provider, write or call the manufacturer's customer-service office. If that fails, contact the Better Business Bureau in your area, and notify any state or local consumer-protection office. Also notify the government licensing body, if accreditation is required where you reside. Keep the repairer apprised of any action you're taking.

Take further steps if necessary. If all else fails, contact your local small-claims court or a trade group. Unresolved problems with major appliances can be fielded by the Major Appliance Consumer Action Panel, a complaint-mediation group sponsored by the Association of Home Appliance Manufacturers. For information, write to MACAP at 20 N. Wacker Dr., Chicago, Ill. 60606. If you have a repair problem with a member of the National Electronics Service Dealers Association, the organization will investigate possible breaches of its code of ethics and enforce action as necessary. For information, write to NESDA at 2708 W. Berry St., Fort Worth, Texas 76109-2397.

EXTENDED WARRANTIES

As a rule, resist the offer of an extended warranty, which usually amounts to expensive and unnecessary insurance. Your cost by the time the item breaks may equal the average repair cost for that product. And in most categories of electronics products, less than one in four items has even required repair by the time it's four years old. Electronics retailers often make more money on "protection plans" or "service agreements" than they do on the sale of products they cover.

In its first year, an extended warranty mostly duplicates what the factory warranty already covers—and whatever extras it may add, such as routine maintenance, usually aren't needed. If you buy an item with certain credit cards (including most *Visa Gold* and *Platinum*, *MasterCard Gold* and *World*, and *American Express* and *Optima* cards), you may automatically double the factory warranty anyway; check with the card's issuer. A few manufacturers offer their own warranty extensions that allow you to continue coverage after the standard warranty has expired.

Electronics technology changes quickly, and you may not necessarily want, say, an old mono VCR repaired, even if you have an extended warranty on it.

Possible exceptions to the rule. There are a few products whose cost and troublesome nature might make a low-priced extended warranty worth considering. Projection TV sets are less reliable than big-screen direct-view sets, say repair experts. And virtually any repair to a projection set requires a home visit. Camcorders and notebook computers are also trouble-prone.

Warranty-shopping tips. Watch out for the fine print. Warranties invariably have a clause excusing repairs due to "abuse" or "misuse," and spokespeople said only that damage is reviewed "on a case-by-case basis." So you may or may not be covered for damage from dropping a camcorder.

Some plans have a stipulation that allows the company to cancel the contract and refund its price instead of paying for an expensive repair—which defeats the purpose of a service contract. And Montgomery Ward plans are automatically renewed unless you specify otherwise.

Check service convenience. It's better if you can drop off a camcorder at any of the store's branches rather than having to transport it to a far-off service center.

Shop around by price. Since high profit margins generally give salespeople room to move on price, consider bargaining.

GUIDE TO REPAIRS

This guide to repairing major appliances, audio and video products, lawn mowers and tractors, and other major household items can help you anticipate problems, make decisions when they occur, and avoid difficulties in the future. It draws on years of testing by CONSUMER REPORTS, real-life experiences from readers, and dozens of inquiries to manufacturers and repair experts.

Data are from the CONSUMER REPORTS 1997 Annual Questionnaire, in which readers reported on thousands of experiences with broken products.

In ***repair experience***, "bad repairs" refers to experiences in which the product was not working well after the repair. ***Typical price for new models*** is an estimate by our market analysts. ***Common problems*** are as identified by our experts; the ***likely culprits*** and estimates for how long products last are from a CONSUMER REPORTS questionnaire to major manufacturers regarding product longevity and failure. Data on ***replacement age*** are from a 1997 readers' survey. ***Rate of repairs/problems*** *and* ***brand reliability*** are from our most recent repair-history data, based on readers' experiences from 1992 to 1997, except where noted.

Major appliances

• Last an estimated 11 to 18 years. Replaced at 12 years, on average.

• Fixed more often than most other products.

• Fewer problems with the repair than with major audio and video products.

Refrigerators

Rate of repairs/problems by the time the product is five years old: The fewer features, the less trouble on average. The rates: 31 percent for side-by-side units with ice-maker and water dispenser; 22 percent for top-freezer units with ice-maker; 14 percent for units with neither ice-maker nor dispenser. ***Repair cost:*** Average, $105; typical range, $75 to $180. ***Typical warranty:*** One year, parts and labor. Fiv years on refrigeration components—generally the most expensive to fix.

Common problems (likely culprits) No cooling or reduced cooling (compressor, fan motor). No ice or water (icemaker or ice-water dispenser doesn' work). Leaking water (water valve). Excessive frost (defrosting components) ***Repair experience.*** About one in five re-

HOW LONG THINGS LAST

A product's useful life depends not only on its actual durability but also on such intangibles as your own desire for some attribute or convenience available only on a new model. These estimates are from manufacturers and trade associations.

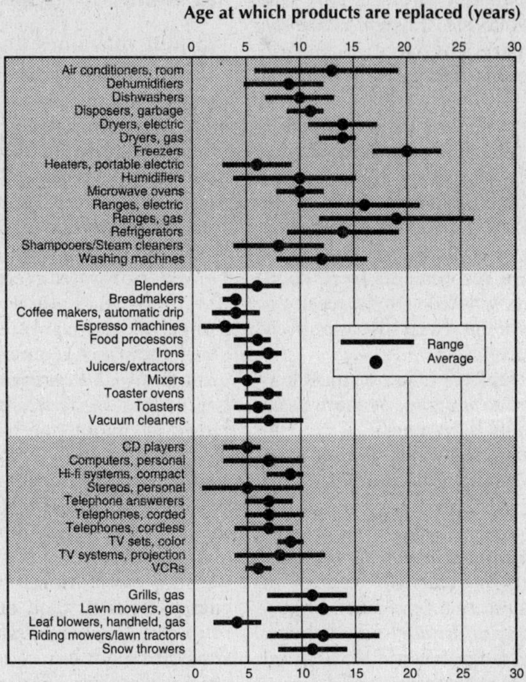

Reprinted by permission of Appliance magazine. © Dana Chase Publications, Inc. September 1998.

rigerators was repaired badly—more than most other appliances. But expect faster repair service than for many appliances. *Care tips.* Dust coils under or in back of unit. Inspect gasket around door seal for leaks, and keep the gasket and the surface it mates to free of debris.

Repair or replace? A new model will be kinder to the environment and consume less energy—at least $250 less in energy over its lifetime compared with older units. *Typical price for new model:* $400 to $1,200.

Dishwashers

Rate of repairs/problems by the time the product is five years old: 19 percent of units. *Repair cost:* Average, $95; typical range, $60 to $150. *Typical warranty:* One year, parts and labor; longer on typically trouble-free parts like tub and door liner.

Common problems (likely culprits). Won't run (door-lock assembly or motor assembly). Excessive water in unit (pump assembly). No water or water all over (water valve). *Repair experience.* Typical for an appliance; slightly more than half the respondents were completely or very satisfied with the repair experience. *Care tips.* Keep silverware away from spray arms.

Repair or replace? Question most big-ticket repairs to units six or more years old. New models are much quieter and use less energy and water. *Typical price for the new model:* $300 to $600.

Ranges

Rate of repairs/problems by the time the product is five years old. Varies a lot by type: 27 percent for gas units; 14 percent for electrics. *Repair cost:* Average, $100; typical range, $60 to $175. *Typical warranty:* One year, parts and labor.

Common problems (likely culprits). No heat (failed gas igniter or electric element). *Repair experience.* Compared with most appliances, costs more often described as excessive. Electric ranges had more problems with the repair than did most appliances. *Care tips.* Place heavy cookware gently on an electric smoothtop.

Repair or replace? Repairs are usually worthwhile, unless the unit is very old and the repair very expensive or you're redoing the kitchen. Except for adding sealed burners and electronic ignition, gas ranges have changed little in recent years. Electric ranges have added smoothtops, stylish but not necessarily better in performance or more reliable than a freestanding range. *Typical price for new model:* $300 to $800.

Washing machines (top-loaders)

Rate of repairs/problems by the time the product is five years old: 23 percent of units. *Repair cost:* Average, $100; typical range, $60 to $130. *Typical warranty:* One year, parts and labor; longer on parts—only for drive train.

Common problems (likely culprits). Won't run or runs continuously (timer). No water or water everywhere (pump, water valves). Poor washing performance (motor, transmission, or drive belt). Incorrect temperature (fill and mixing valves). *Repair experience.* Only one in four readers had any problem. However, about one in eight readers did complain of high repair costs. *Care tips.* Periodically check the screen for grit buildup where the hose attaches to the hot-water supply pipe.

Repair or replace? New front-loading washing machines are markedly more energy efficient than old models, but relatively expensive and have yet to establish a repair history, so a major repair often makes sense. *Typical price for new model:* $300-$500.

Dryers

Rate of repairs/problems by the time the product is five years old: 14 percent of units. ***Repair cost:*** Average, $80; typical range, $60 to $110. ***Typical warranty:*** One year, parts and labor.

Common problems (likely culprits). Won't run (drive motor). No heat (igniter or heating element). Poor performance, noisy (rollers and belts). ***Repair experience.*** Among the most satisfactory for all products; only one in four readers had a problem. ***Care tips.*** Clean a dryer's lint filter after each use to prevent the exhaust duct from clogging, which poses a fire hazard.

Repair or replace? Often a toss-up for major repairs. Dryers tend to be relatively inexpensive to fix and to replace. The least expensive replacement models offer little that's new; other models have a moisture sensor for better automatic drying. ***Typical price for new model:*** Electric models, $200-$500; gas models, $250 to $550.

Audio/video

- Last an estimated 5 to 15 years. Replaced at 7 years, on average.
- Many repairs are relatively difficult to do, which may explain why more people experienced repair problems with audio/video products than with appliances.
- Repairs to TV sets were more satisfactory and generally less problematic than those to camcorders, VCRs, or CD players—which were similar in incidence of problems.

The bigger the set, on average, the higher the price tag, the average hours used, and the likelihood and cost of repair.

TV sets

Rate of repairs/problems by the time the product is five years old: 10 percent for 19- and 20-in. sets; 20 percent for 25- and 27-in. sets; 24 percent for 31- to 35-in. sets. ***Repair cost:*** 19- and 20-in. sets: Average, $90; typical range, $65-$100. 25- and 27-in. sets: Average, $110; typical range, $80-$150. 31- to 35-in. sets: Average, $150; typical range, $100-$250. ***Typical warranty:*** One year, parts; three months, labor. Two years on the picture tube, the most expensive component.

Common problems (likely culprits). No picture or sound (power supply). Deteriorating picture quality (picture tube, tuner). Can't get channels (tuner). ***Repair experience.*** Repair satisfaction didn't differ by size. Readers were more likely to fix larger sets. Parts may be scarce for old sets.

Repair or replace? Unless the set is fairly large and fairly new, fixing may not pay, except for a small or cosmetic repair. A new set in almost any size will probably cost less and offer more than the one it's replacing. ***Typical price for new model:*** $200 to $300 for 19- and 20-inch sets; $350 to $600 for 25- and 27-inch sets; $500 to $1,000 for 31- to 36-inch sets.

Camcorders

Rate of repairs/problems by the time the product is five years old: 25 percent of units. ***Repair cost:*** Average, $125; typical range, $85 to $195. ***Typical warranty:*** One year, parts; three months, labor.

Common problems (likely culprits). Can't insert or eject tape (motors, loading mechanism). ***Repair experience.*** Forty percent of camcorders were in the shop for more than two weeks, and the cost of repair was deemed excessive for one in three units—the most for any product. Only about 1 in 3 readers who got a camcorder fixed was completely or very satisfied with the experience. ***Care tips.*** Check owner's manual for battery-care advice. Store tapes in their boxes and avoid changing them where it's dusty. Avoid using the camcorder where it's sandy. Remove lens debris with a soft-bristled brush only.

Repair or replace? Though a camcorder repair is often expensive and hassle-ridden, the cost seldom approaches one-third or even one-fourth the cost of a replacement, which may perform no better than the unit you own. ***Typical price for new model:*** $400 to $1,000.

VCRs

Rate of repairs/problems by the time the product is five years old: 24 percent of units. ***Repair cost:*** Average, $75; typical range, $50 to $100. ***Typical warranty:*** One year, parts; three months, labor.

Common problems (likely culprits). Can't insert or eject tape (loading mechanism). Deteriorating picture quality (video heads). Intermittent picture or sound, erratic or no tape movement (worn belt). ***Repair experience.*** VCR repairs were generally cheaper and faster than those for camcorders. ***Care tips.*** A loose tape-label could cause the tape to stick in the loading bay. Gently insert only clean and undamaged tapes, and store them in jackets or boxes. Consider a dust cover for when your VCR is not in use.

Repair or replace? Falling prices for VCRs and the relatively high cost and hassle of repairs make major repairs a dubious investment, except to a fairly new and expensive model. ***Typical price for new model:*** $150 to $450.

CD players

Rate of repairs/ problems by the time the product is five years old: 9 percent of carousel units; 17 percent of magazine units. ***Repair cost:*** Average, $80; typical range, $50 to $100. ***Typical warranty:*** One year, parts and labor.

Common problems (likely culprits). Won't work or skips (laser "reader," motors). Can't insert or eject disk (loading mechanism). ***Repair experience.*** Problems occurred with 60 percent of repairs; long waits and bad repairs topped the list.

Repair or replace? Even if a repair is possible, it often doesn't pay. CD players are relatively cheap to buy, and many new models hold more discs than older ones. Repairs are relatively problematic. ***Typical price for new model:*** $75 to $300.

Lawn mowers

- Last an estimated 7 to 20 years. Replaced at 8 years, on average.
- Repair satisfaction is on a par with that for audio and video products, below that for appliances.
- With many moving parts and seasonal use, lawn mowers (and other yard equipment) demand routine maintenance. Clean clippings from the underside. Annually, have the oil, air filter, and spark plug changed and the blades sharpened. Drain the fuel or run the engine dry at the end of the season.

Gasoline lawn mowers

Rate of repairs/problems by the time the product is five years old: Varies widely by type. 36 percent for self-propelled units; 19 percent for push mowers. ***Repair cost:*** Average, $65; typical range, $40 to $100. ***Typical warranty:*** Two years, parts and labor.

Common problems (likely culprits). Uneven cutting performance (blades). Noisy operation, mower won't move (belts). ***Repair experience.*** Nearly half of readers had problems. Their most frequent complaint, about one-fourth of the time: bad repairs. Readers chose to fix mowers less often than tractors or riding mowers. On average, repair costs were less than half as much as for tractors or riding mowers. ***Care tips.*** See general advice, page 14.

Repair or replace? Most repairs are cheap, so a repair often pays. But consider replacing a middle-aged mower (five or more years old), since new models run more cleanly and efficiently. ***Typical price for new model:*** $100 to $650 for a push-type; $300 to $850 for self-propelled.

Riding mowers and lawn tractors

Rate of repairs/problems by the time the product is five years old: 41 percent of units—the highest rate of any product for which we track repair histories. ***Repair cost:*** Average, $155; typical range, $100 to $300. ***Typical warranty:*** Two years, parts and labor.

Common problems (likely culprits). Uneven cutting performance (blades). Accessories won't work (PTO clutch, belts). Noisy operation, mower won't move (belts). ***Repair experience.*** Nearly half of readers had problems with a repair. The damage was apt to be serious, and the bill high—higher, on average, than for most other products. Expect to pay for a house call or transportation to haul the machine to the service center. ***Care tips.*** See general advice for lawn mowers, page 14. Change any oil filter annually. During cold winters, disconnect the battery and put it on a monthly trickle charge.

Repair or replace? The price of a new riding mower or lawn tractor usually makes a repair the best course, unless the unit is close to the end of its life and the repair is costly. Eighty-five percent of readers repaired their broken model. ***Typical price for new model:*** $900 to $4,000.

Other products

The data on vacuum cleaners and microwave ovens are drawn from the 1997 surveys used for this report.

Data on computers are drawn from our 1996 Annual Questionnaire and from tests in which we "spiked" computers and had them repaired under the factory warranty.

Vacuum cleaners

Rate of repairs/problems by the time the product is five years old: 34 percent of units. ***Repair cost:*** Average, $50; typical range, $35 to $75. ***Typical warranty:*** One year, parts and labor.

Common problems (likely culprits). Won't run (motor). Brush won't turn, self-propelled feature won't work (belts). Loud noise or vibration (broken impeller). ***Repair experience.*** About 1 in 4 readers expressed some degree of dissatisfaction, and problems occurred with about 1 in 3 repairs to vacuums. ***Care tips.*** Watch what you vacuum up. Hard objects like coins can damage fan blades. String can snarl the agitator. Avoid vacuuming outdoors or on any wet or damp surface. Running over the cord could fray it and expose you to live electrical wires.

Repair or replace? Even a simple repair to an inexpensive model may be worthwhile only if you can do the job yourself. An expensive vacuum that has served you well should last for years longer, so even a major repair may be worth undertaking. ***Typical price for new model:*** $70 to $300.

Microwave ovens

Rate of repairs/problems by the time the product is five years old: 13 percent of units. ***Repair cost:*** Average, $75; typical range, $50 to $100. ***Typical warranty:*** One year, parts and labor; longer for the magnetron.

Common problems (likely culprits). Oven stops working (power surge; try unplugging and replugging the power cord). ***Repair experience.*** Similar to vacuum cleaners and major appliances. Almost 4 in 10 repairs had some problems. The two biggest complaints: excessive repair costs (14 percent) and a long wait for the repair (15 percent). ***Care tips.*** Don't turn on an empty microwave oven or put anything metal inside it (except for racks that came with the oven). Either could cause arcing and damage the magnetron.

Repair or replace? With new oven prices steadily dropping, a repair to a small microwave oven usually won't pay. With a larger oven or an over-the-range unit, all but the biggest repairs may be worthwhile. ***Typical price for new model:*** $150 to $300.

Computers

Rate of repairs by the time the product is three years old: 19 percent of units (purchased from 1993 to 1996). ***Repair cost:*** Average, $100; typical range, $45 to $215. ***Typical warranty:*** One year, parts and labor; three months, in-home service. In our test of in-warranty repairs, service was excellent. But nearly every manufacturer replaced parts unnecessarily in completing the repair. One in 6 readers had purchased an extended warranty, but only 1 in 4 of them said it had saved money.

Common problems (likely culprits). Can't use a drive or peripheral (cables). Erratic cursor movement or no movement at all (mouse). Difficulty accessing outside telephone line (modem). System errors or halts, inability to restart (hard drive). Can't read disk (floppy drive). Can't access data on CD (CD-ROM drive). System crashes, inability to restart (motherboard). Software problems may also produce many of the above symptoms. ***Repair experience.*** Repairs typically begin with a call to the manufacturer's technical-support line. You can occasionally wait as long as 20 minutes to reach human help, in our experience, and a further 20 minutes to more than an hour trying to diagnose the problem. An authorized repairer, if needed, usually arrives at your home within a week; the alternative is to carry or ship the PC to a service center. ***Care tips.*** Turn off computer and monitor before you clean or dust screen. If possible, back up data from hard drive before taking computer for repairs. Periodically vacuum keyboard with a soft brush; remove and wash mouse or track ball.

Repair or replace? An expensive repair may not pay. New PCs offer dramatically improved features and technology, plus prices are dropping steadily. Our survey indicates that most people kept their PC an average of four years, and usually replaced it out of a desire to upgrade rather than because it failed. ***Typical price for new model:*** $1,000 to $3,000.

BRAND REPAIR HISTORIES

The repair histories that follow are for brands, not for specific models of these products. These histories can only suggest future trends, not predict them exactly. The reliability of a company's products can change for many reasons—company ownership changes, products are designed or manufactured in a new plant, quality-control procedures improve. Still, what readers report over the years has been consistent enough for us to be confident that using these repair histories can improve your chances of buying a trouble-free product.

The graphs represent the percent of each brand's products purchased new that have ever been repaired or had a serious problem that was not repaired, according to our 1997 Annual Questionnaire. Products covered by a service contract are excluded, since the repair rates for those products are much higher than for products without one. Histories for different product types are not directly comparable, since the histories cover products of different ages, and older products tend to break more often.

MICROWAVE OVENS

Based on more than 69,000 responses to our 1997 Annual Questionnaire. Readers were asked about repairs and serious problems with medium- and large-sized countertop microwave ovens bought new between 1993 and 1997. Data have been standardized to eliminate differences among brands due to age and usage. Differences of less than 3 points aren't meaningful.

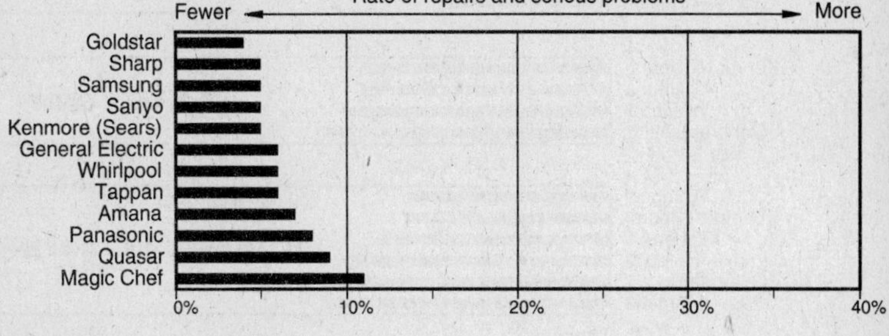

TOP-FREEZER REFRIGERATORS

Based on more than 51,000 responses to our 1997 Annual Questionnaire. Readers were asked about any repairs and serious problems with full-sized, top-freezer, two-door, no-frost refrigerators bought new between 1992 and 1997. Data have been standardized to eliminate differences among brands due to age. Differences of less than 4 points aren't meaningful.

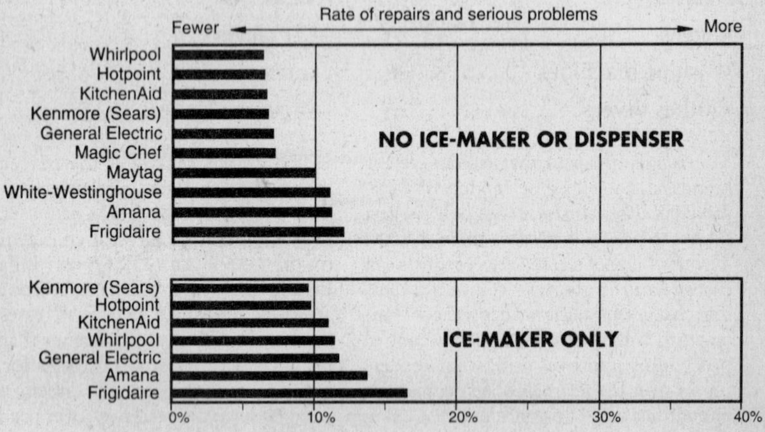

SIDE-BY-SIDE REFRIGERATORS

Based on more than 36,000 responses to our 1997 Annual Questionnaire. Readers were asked about any repairs and serious problems with full-sized side-by-side refrigerators bought new between 1992 and 1997. Data have been standardized to eliminate differences among brands due to age. Differences of less than 4 points aren't meaningful.

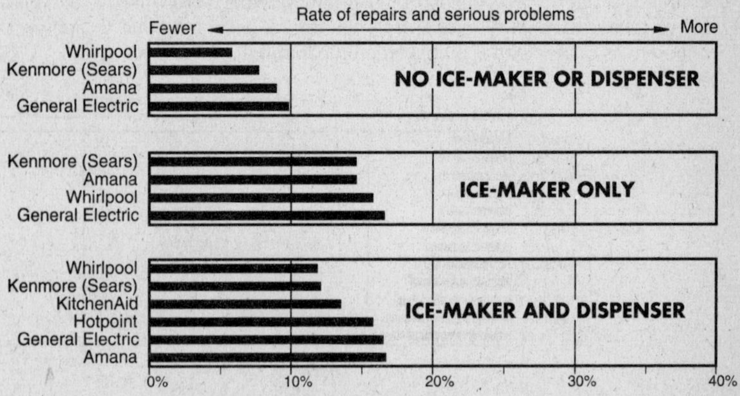

DISHWASHERS

Based on almost 118,000 responses to our 1997 Annual Questionnaire. Readers were asked about any repairs and serious problems with installed dishwashers bought new between 1992 and 1997. Data have been standardized to eliminate differences among brands due to age and usage. Differences of less than 3 points aren't meaningful.

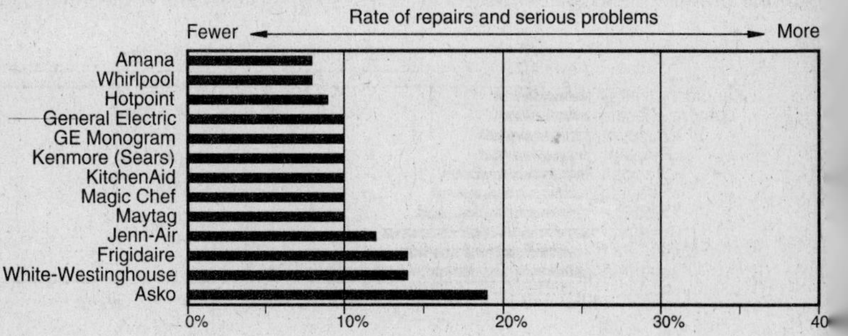

GAS RANGES

Based on more than 19,000 responses to our 1997 Annual Questionnaire. Readers were asked about any repairs and serious problems with freestanding, single-oven, self-cleaning gas ranges bought new between 1991 and 1997. Data have been standardized to eliminate differences among brands due to age. Differences of less than 3 points aren't meaningful.

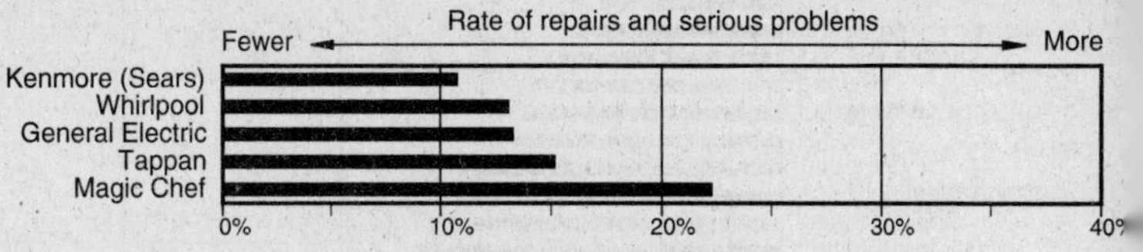

ELECTRIC RANGES

Based on more than 42,000 responses to our 1997 Annual Questionnaire. Readers were asked about any repairs and serious problems with freestanding, single-oven, self-cleaning electric ranges with a smoothtop or conventional coil burners bought new between 1992 and 1997. Data have been standardized to eliminate differences among brands due to age. Differences of less than 4 points aren't meaningful.

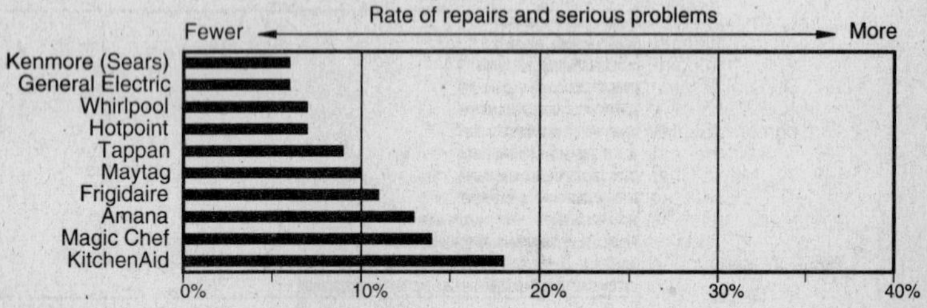

WASHING MACHINES

Based on more than 122,000 responses to our 1997 Annual Questionnaire. Readers were asked about any repairs and serious problems with full-sized washers bought new between 1991 and 1997. Data have been standardized to eliminate differences among brands due to age and usage. Differences of less than 4 points aren't meaningful.

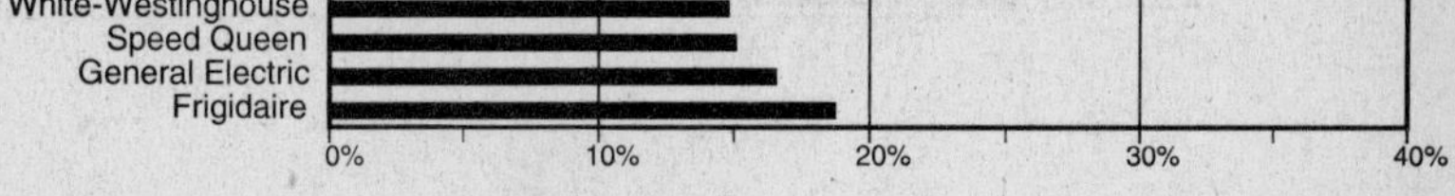

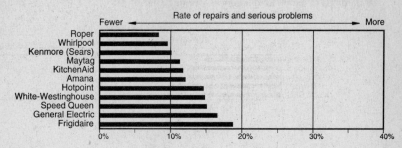

CLOTHES DRYERS

Based on more than 101,000 responses to our 1997 Annual Questionnaire. Readers were asked about any repairs and serious problems with full-sized electric and gas clothes dryers bought new between 1992 and 1997. Data have been standardized to eliminate differences among brands due to age and usage. Differences of less than 4 points aren't meaningful.

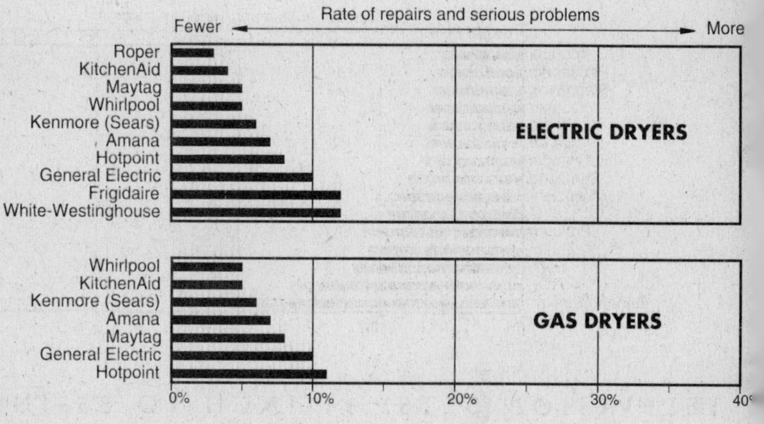

TELEVISION SETS: 19-INCH AND 20-INCH

Based on more than 60,000 responses to our 1997 Annual Questionnaire. Readers were asked about any repairs and serious problems with 19-inch and 20-inch color TV sets bought new between 1992 and 1997. Data have been standardized to eliminate differences among brands due to age and usage. Differences of less than 3 points aren't meaningful.

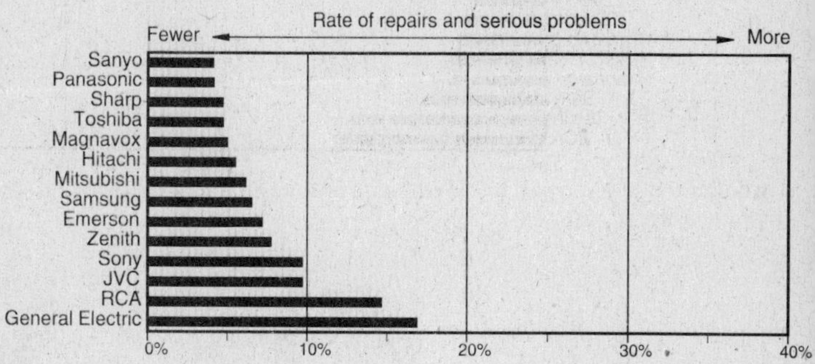

TELEVISION SETS: 25-INCH & 27-INCH

Based on more than 96,000 responses to our 1997 Annual Questionnaire. Readers were asked about any repairs and serious problems with 25- and 27-inch stereo color TV sets bought new between 1992 and 1997. Data have been standardized to eliminate differences among brands due to age and usage. Differences of less than 3 points aren't meaningful.

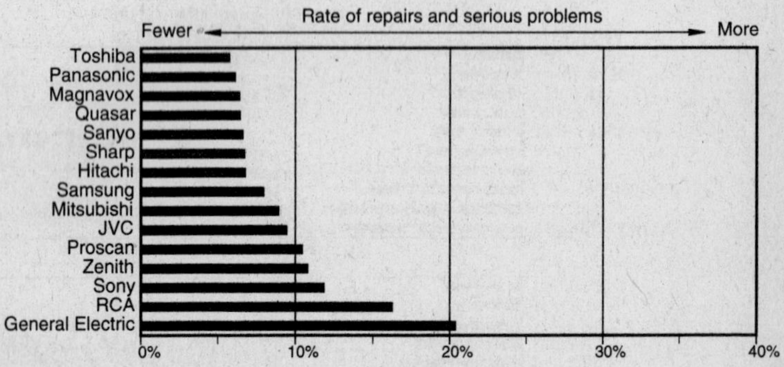

TELEVISION SETS: 31-INCH TO 35-INCH

Based on more than 30,000 responses to our 1997 Annual Questionnaire. Readers were asked about any repairs and serious problems with 31- to 35-inch stereo color TV sets bought new between 1993 and 1997. Data have been standardized to eliminate differences among brands due to age and usage. Differences of less than 3 points aren't meaningful.

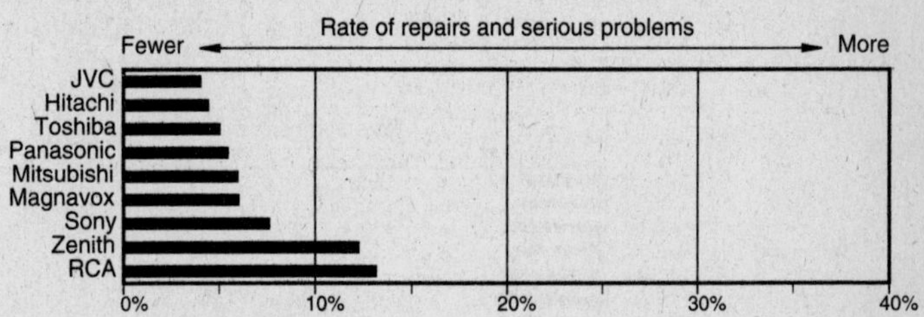

COMPACT CAMCORDERS

Based on about 46,000 responses to our 1997 Annual Questionnaire. Readers were asked about any repairs and serious problems with compact (8mm, Hi8, and VHS-C) camcorders bought new between 1992 and 1997. Data have been standardized to eliminate differences among brands due to age and usage. Differences of less than 4 points aren't meaningful.

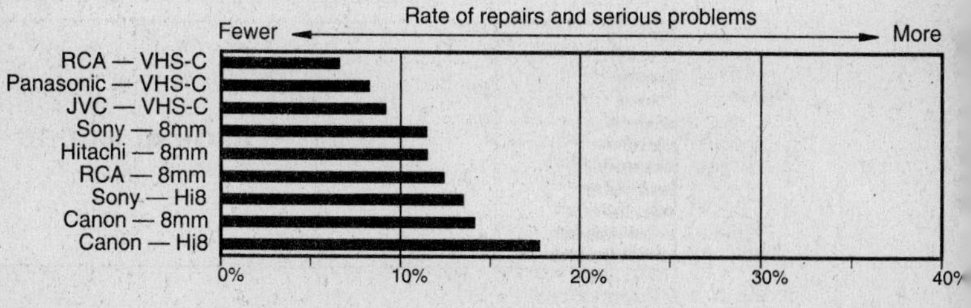

VCRs

Based on almost 200,000 responses to our 1997 Annual Questionnaire. Readers were asked about any repairs and serious problems with VHS VCRs bought new between 1992 and 1997. Data have been standardized to eliminate differences among brands due to age and usage. Differences of less than 4 points aren't meaningful.

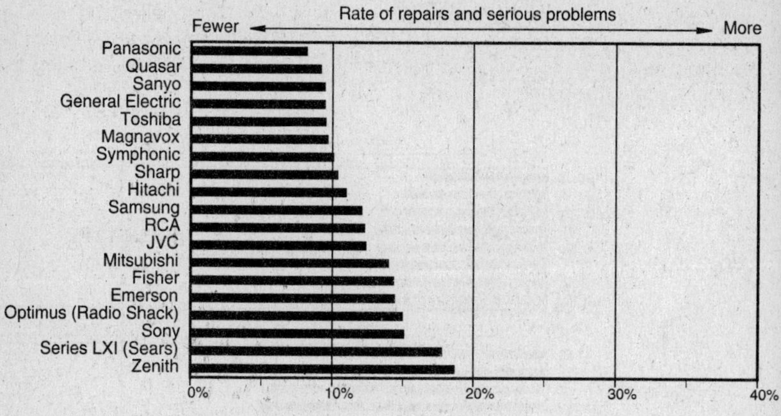

COMPACT-DISC PLAYERS

Based on more than 70,000 responses to our 1997 Annual Questionnaire. Readers were asked about any repairs and serious problems with changer tabletop models bought new between 1993 and 1997. Data have been standardized to eliminate differences among brands due to age and usage. Differences of less than 3 points aren't meaningful.

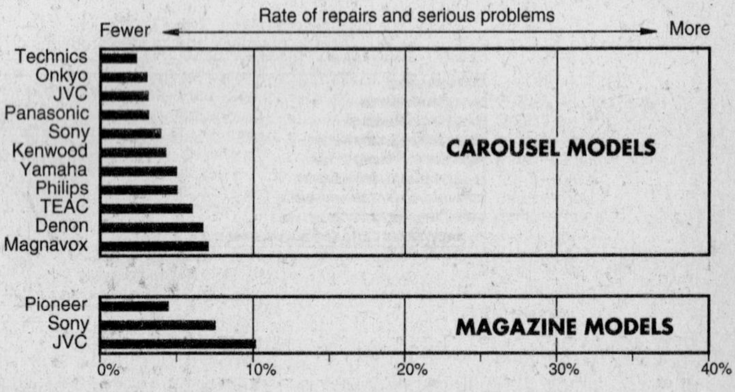

GASOLINE LAWN MOWERS

Based on more than 64,000 responses to our 1997 Annual Questionnaire. Readers were asked about any repairs and serious problems with self-propelled and push-type gasoline mowers bought new between 1992 and 1997. Data have been standardized to eliminate differences among brands due to age and usage. Differences of less than 5 points aren't meaningful.

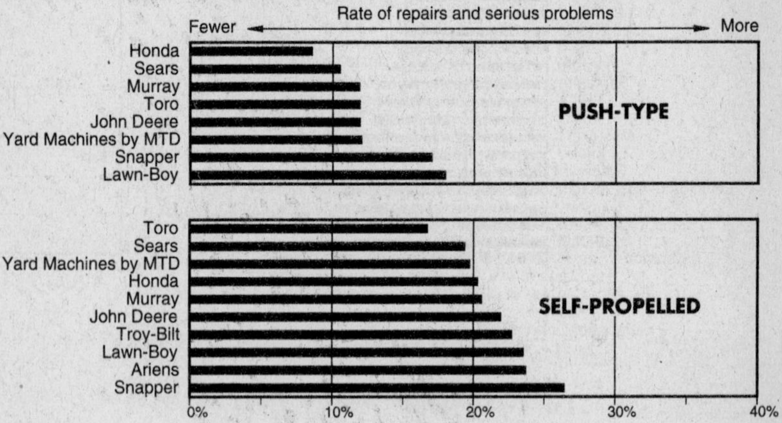

RIDING MOWERS AND LAWN TRACTORS

Based on more than 18,000 responses to our 1997 Annual Questionnaire. Readers were asked about any repairs and serious problems with tractors and riding mowers bought new between 1992 and 1997. Data have been standardized to eliminate differences among brands due to age and usage. Differences of less than 5 points aren't meaningful.

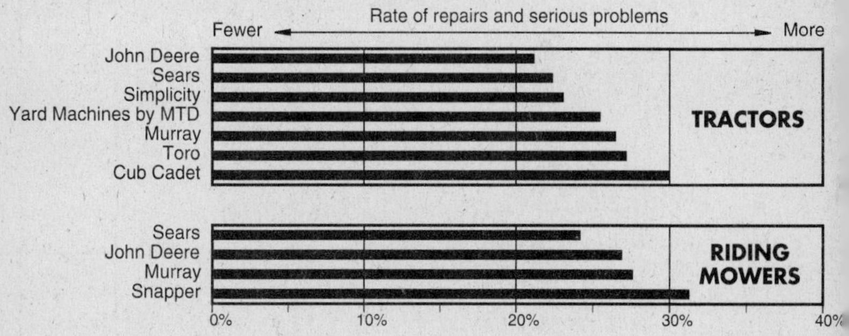

FULL-SIZED VACUUM CLEANERS

Based on more than 151,000 responses to our 1997 Annual Questionnaire. Readers were asked about any repairs and serious problems with full-sized upright and canister vacuum cleaners bought new between 1992 and 1997. Data have been standardized to eliminate differences among brands due to age and usage. Differences of less than 4 points aren't meaningful.

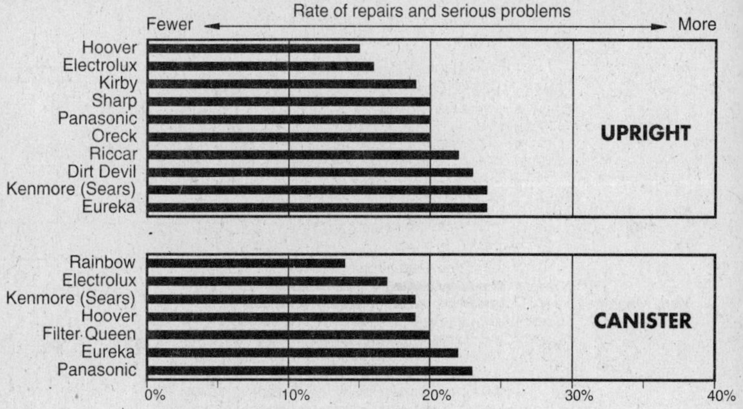

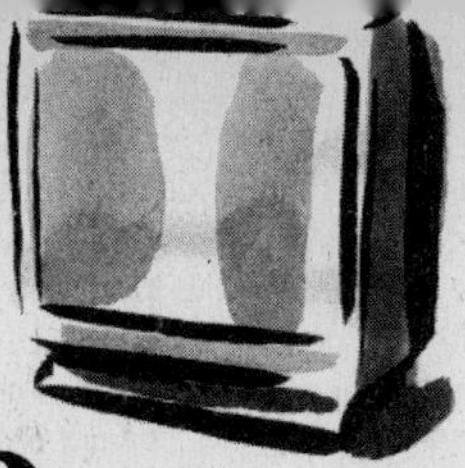

Home entertainment

THE BIG PICTURE

Good electronics gear on which to enjoy your favorite music, movies, and other entertainment has never been cheaper than it is today. Solid-state construction and more sophisticated assembly lines are among the factors that have improved most electronics goods, from TV sets to audio equipment to personal computers. The growing overlap between the technology and function of various information and entertainment devices in the home, called convergence, is also creating sweeping changes. Long ago, a digital format developed for computers—the compact disc—revolutionized the world of music and audio systems. Now, it's TV's turn. Convergence is bringing video images to computer screens and digital images to the TV screen. Digital signals can come from many directions: home satellite dishes; DVD (a CD that can hold movies); HDTV (high-definition television, a format due any time now); the new digital camcorders.

The convergence of all this technology means you can now have a home theater—an assemblage of audio and video equipment centered on the TV set that seeks, with increasing success, to mimic the experience of the movie house or concert hall, or you can get music from your TV set (satellite dish programs include commercial-free music channels) or home computer (via CDs or over the Internet). With the right electronics, you can get web access from your TV via services such as Web TV, and TV in your computer, via TV tuner cards.

For all the potential advantages new technology brings to home entertainment, it complicates the buying process. In virtually every new area, from digital TV to multichannel audio processing to recordable discs, the market is in transition. Several incompatible technologies are in competition, and it isn't clear which will prevail. Consumers who invest (often heavily) in the newest equipment and digital formats may wind up with the 1999 equivalent of quadraphonic sound or Betamax.

Our buying advice for electronics pays close attention to what's coming as well as what's here now. On the whole, we urge caution about taking up new technologies early, before prices have dropped and longevity is assured—advice that may not suit if you're an "early adopter" who craves new technology now and at almost any price. But we think it's wise in the current home-entertainment market, where most products are just fine as they are and many state-of-the-art newcomers are extremely expensive. A new digital TV set, for example, will cost at least $8,000.

SHOPPING STRATEGY

When to shop

Manufacturers of home-entertainment products commonly introduce new models once a year to stimulate sales and keep up with or stay ahead of competition. However, dealer inventories can't always keep pace with such rapid changes, so older models are carried over in the stores long after newer ones have arrived, perhaps remaining available for months or even years after the manufacturer says they have been discontinued. You can often save by waiting for sales on older models, as long as you don't mind equipment that may not be cutting-edge.

Sales are usually plentiful during the winter holiday season, when most home-entertainment gear is sold. In January, the Consumer Electronics Show introduces the latest models, which then make their way into the stores from April to October. In midwinter, as the previous year's models are cleared out, sales may be scarce but resume right before spring. For year-round good buys, consider the "open box" items sold at many stores for 20 percent or so below the regular price. These models, returned to the store by their original owners, generally work well but may have cosmetic blemishes. They usually carry the same warranty and return terms as the item sold new.

Where to shop

Where you shop not only affects the kind of service you can expect but also the brands you'll find. The following store descriptions draw on our own visits, a survey of readers, and a survey of price and availability for a specific list of products.

Specialty chains. The biggest retailers of electronics, like Circuit City, The Good

Guys, and Best Buy, often devote much space to computers, peripherals, music and movies. Sometimes these chains offer models unique to the chain. Readers tell us selection is outstanding. Prices are higher overall than at the warehouse clubs. You'll find listening rooms and home-theater salons but also heavy sales pressure (for extended warranties, particularly). Chains may charge a restocking fee for returns.

Department stores and mass merchandisers. As audio-video departments disappear from many department stores, they're growing at mass merchandisers like Wal-Mart. Such stores often emphasize lower-priced brands. They may not carry higher-priced categories, such as projection TV sets or digital camcorders, and readers report a middling selection. Prices are higher overall than at warehouse clubs, but return policies are often generous. Readers singled out Wal-Mart and Sears for lower product quality than other chains.

Warehouse clubs. Electronics is a growing presence in giant selling barns like Costco and Sam's Club. These emphasize value over convenience, ambience, or almost any other nicety. Selection is limited, according to readers. Prices are low, with little sales help or sales pressure. Extended warranties are rarely offered. An annual membership ($35 to $40) is required, though a free temporary membership may allow you to shop at prices 5 percent higher than members pay. Popular credit cards aren't accepted.

Catalog/online sellers. Vendors like Crutchfield and J&R Music World offer virtually everything you can buy at an electronics store. Web sites often provide interactive menus to help you tailor the choice of model to your needs. Prices can be low, especially if sales tax isn't charged (as it may not be out of state). Shipping adds up to 5 percent to the price of regular items, and can cost $100 or more for large TV sets or speakers. Returns can be expensive and inconvenient (Crutchfield arranges returns at its expense, whereas J&R pays for the shipping only if the product is defective).

Independent electronics stores. These are the most traditional ("Joe's TV Sales and Service") and most toney ("The Audio Salon") retailers. "Salons" specialize in expensive audio components, in brands that few other store types carry. The mom-and-pop retailers often emphasize repairs. Compared to all store types, independent retailers satisfied readers the most and had the most courteous and most knowledgeable staff. But readers spent more at independents, probably due to those audiophile brands.

Overall, Costco, Sam's Club, and Wal-Mart are the standout places to shop if price is paramount. But call ahead to check on the fairly limited selection those stores offer—or be more willing than at other chains to pick a model that may not be among your top choices.

The Good Guys and Circuit City are the surest places to find a particular model and to obtain knowledgeable sales help. At these chains, though, be prepared to bargain for a good price and, despite your best efforts, to possibly pay a little more than you might at a low-priced chain. Also, be particularly sure you want what you buy from Circuit City; the chain sometimes charges a 15 percent restocking fee on refunds if you've opened the box.

Our surveys turned up no particular reason to avoid or choose Service Merchandise (a catalog seller turned mass merchandiser), Sears, or Montgomery Ward when shopping for audio-video products. Indeed, the lack of distinction shown by Sears and Montgomery Ward may help explain why department stores are losing ground in today's cutthroat electonics marketplace.

SETTING UP A HOME THEATER

Home-theater systems have shifted from pricey equipment for videophiles to simple setups for any TV watcher. The secret of succesful home theater lies not in the picture but in its soundtrack. To make movies seem more real, theaters surround you with speakers that make you feel as if you're in the middle of the action. Moviemakers use various "ambience" techniques—Dolby Surround, Lucasfilm THX, Dolby AC-3, DTS Digital Surround—to shift the sound according to the action. Those effects are what home-theater systems try to re-create. Trouble is, most TV sets, even some new big-screen models, have small, tinny-sounding speakers that can't be separated to produce the surround-sound experience, so you usually need to connect the set to audio equipment. The ultimate connection is to a full home-theater setup, with a receiver that decodes Dolby Surround soundtracks (from broadcasts, videotapes, or laser discs) and sends separate signals to speakers to fairly faithfully reproduce the theater-like sound.

Building a home-theater system from scratch with separate components—receiver, VCR, speakers, TV set—can cost upward of $1,500. The system will take up plenty of space and can be a chore to wire together, although professional installation is available. While generally less powerful and less flexible than component systems, "home theater in a box" —usually five speakers and a receiver or processor that you connect to your existing TV set and hi-fi VCR for about $400 and up—makes setup simpler.

Gear for a basic setup

Receiver. Most home-theater systems use a Dolby Pro Logic-equipped receiver to process the sound. Look for a receiver with at least 80 watts for each of the three front channels. Other options: a TV set with built-in Dolby Pro Logic circuitry, or a stand-alone decoder to retrofit to your stereo system.

Speakers. The front speakers produce most of the sound and should be the best quality you can afford. The left and right speakers should sit to either side of your TV set, far enough apart to produce a noticeable stereo effect. Ideally, those two speakers and the listener should form an equilateral triangle. If you already own a decent set of stereo speakers, they will probably suffice.

The center speaker carries most of the dialogue and sounds that move across the screen and should come close to the sound quality of the left and right speakers. A center speaker should be placed above or below the set; many are designed to lie across the top of your TV. Because it's close to the set, the center speaker must be magnetically shielded so it won't interfere with the picture.

In a Dolby Pro Logic system, the rear speakers handle only ambient sounds—applause, the din of traffic—and so can be smaller and lower in quality than the front pair. They should go behind you, high on the wall and facing away from you, since reflected sound will enhance the surround effect. Almost any set of serviceable speakers will do. You can also use additional satellite speakers available with some three-piece satellite systems. A subwoofer for the bass, used in some systems, can be hidden behind furniture.

TV set. Your present set may do just fine as long as it has audio output jacks.

Video sources. You'll need at least a VCR with stereo hi-fi capability. Other video sources, including laser-disc players and the new DVD players, provide high-quality sound along with far better pictures than videotape. The newest computers with DVD drives usually have the outputs needed to drive a home-theater system. As with component DVD players, some have a Dolby AC-3 digital sound output for a decoder-equipped receiver.

Other home-theater options

Use fewer speakers. A home-theater system with fewer than five speakers still creates a semblance of surround sound by using a receiver's settings to electronically fill in some missing sound. *Phantom mode* on the receiver allows you to eliminate the center speaker. It distributes the center signal equally to the main left and right channels. Or you can use the TV set's internal speakers as the center channel if they're of acceptable quality. *Dolby 3 mode* uses only the three front speakers. Instead of rear speakers, delayed surround signals are sent to the front left and right channels.

Skip the Pro Logic. You can improve a TV set's stereo effect simply by connecting two external speakers. A plain stereo receiver can amplify the sound of any TV set. If your TV set doesn't have audio jacks, you can use a hi-fi VCR as the TV tuner. Some TV sets have ambience modes, such as SRS or SEq, that can create pleasing surround effects using the set's own speakers.

Deluxe home theater. Dolby Pro Logic receivers send the same signal to both rear surround speakers. *Dolby AC-3* receivers produce separate left and right surround channels. AC-3 models also produce a sixth, optional channel that directs low-frequency special effects to a separate, powered subwoofer. Such equipment is still quite expensive. Soundtrack titles are still limited.

Another enhancement to Dolby Pro Logic is *THX*, a movie-theater-quality sound reproduction format costing several thousand dollars.

DECIDING ON A SOUND SYSTEM

Until recently, if you bought a simple, all-in-one sound system, you sacrificed sound quality. Today, packaged systems, rack systems, minisystems, even some boom boxes can play music decently, even admirably. Speaker quality, amplifier power, and convenience features are the main items that push models up in price. To help determine the type of gear you'll need, ask yourself the following questions:

How do you listen to music? If you take your music seriously and want true high fidelity, your best bet is a system built of individual components. This kind of system lets you choose the best speakers. You will also get a receiver with plenty of power and a CD player with just the features you need.

For playing background music, consider an inexpensive rack system or a minisystem. For listening on the go, a good portable CD player costs less than $100, a radio/tape player less than $50. Or consider a good quality boom box.

How much can you spend? If you're on a limited budget and starting from scratch, consider a minisystem (about $300 for a decent one). Or start with a basic component system: a low-priced receiver ($250 or so), an inexpensive CD changer ($200 or less), and the best speakers you can afford. Shop around: Discounts of 20 or 30 percent are common.

Another option is to upgrade an existing system with new speakers (the simplest) or a new receiver with up-to-date features such as digital tuning, a remote control, and home-theater electronics. Unlike older cassette decks, some modern decks can make tapes with just a smidgen less fidelity than you'd find on a CD.

Where will you be listening? Room size and "liveness" (hard surfaces reflect sound and soft, upholstered ones absorb it) affect the quality of the sound. You'll need more receiver power to fill a large or plush room.

What kind of music do you listen to? If you like to listen to loud, deep bass, you'll need a more powerful receiver and bigger speakers than if your tastes run to quieter music.

Sound-system options

Minisystem. Small systems in all-in-one packages offer reasonably good overall performance, and compared with component systems, they're cheaper, more compact, and simpler to hook up. However, unlike a component system, minisystem parts are matched to each other, so you usually can't upgrade with bigger speakers or other components, or add a second pair of speakers to send music to another room. Minisystems also usually lack fully adjustable bass and treble controls, which help overcome speaker defects. Lower-priced models have limited power and anemic bass. **Price range:** $200 to more than $1,500. Higher-priced models have home-theater capabilities.

Boom box. This combines an AM/FM stereo radio with built-in antennas, one or two cassette decks, and, quite often, a CD player. Models weigh from less than 10 to more than 20 pounds. Small boxes usually have nondetachable speakers that can't reproduce sound faithfully. Larger ones often come with good-sized speakers that can be detached and moved for a better stereo effect. Bigger boxes produce decent sound—but not on a par with a decent rack or component system. Nor can boom boxes play as loudly or deeply into the bass range as minisystems. Models with a remote control or with speakers that have a better reach into treble and bass cost more. **Price range:** small, $50 to $150; larger, $150 to $250. (Price tends to correlate with size.)

Rack system. Like their smaller mini-

REMOTE CONTROLS

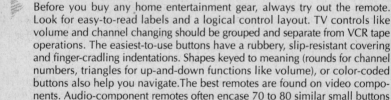

Before you buy any home entertainment gear, always try out the remote. Look for easy-to-read labels and a logical control layout. TV controls like volume and channel changing should be grouped and separate from VCR tape operations. The easiest-to-use buttons have a rubbery, slip-resistant covering and finger-cradling indentations. Shapes keyed to meaning (rounds for channel numbers, triangles for up-and-down functions like volume), or color-coded buttons also help you navigate.The best remotes are found on video components. Audio-component remotes often encase 70 to 80 similar small buttons in a rigid grip.

system cousins, rack systems are a package deal, but with full-sized components dressed in furniture-style cabinetry. Unlike minisystems, rack systems require assembly (the cabinet) and some wiring. They come with floor-standing speakers and with plenty to power them—at least 80 watts per channel (each channel corresponds to one speaker). A dual cassette deck, CD player, and remote control are standard. Higher-priced models include home-theater capabilities. Speaker size allows good bass reproduction, making rack systems a notch higher in quality than minisystems. The best rack systems match the performance and versatility of a decent component system but at a lower cost. Some manufacturers cut costs with cheaper cabinets, typically made of plastic-covered particleboard with thin back panels. **Price range:** $500 to more than $1,200, with good ones at $800.

Component system. This system delivers the most flexibility and highest sound quality. You can choose the best components from each manufacturer, upgrade individual elements, or add new ones. The downside: A component system costs more than a simpler system and takes some effort to set up.

A typical system includes a receiver, a CD player, one or two pairs of speakers, a cassette deck, maybe even your old turntable. Most receivers also allow you to hook up video equipment: a TV set, a VCR, and a DVD or a laser-disc player. If you'll be making tapes from CDs, consider getting a cassette deck and CD player of the same brand; look for synchronized starting to make taping easier. A receiver incorporates several components: an amplifier, a preamplifier, and a digital AM/FM tuner. Although purists insist that separate devices for each of those functions provide the best possible sound, we have found that while sensitive lab instruments may discern differences, human ears cannot. **Price range:** $900 to $1,100 for a budget system, $1,200 to $1,600 for a full-featured one. Spending more than $1,600 buys more features, not better sound quality: nice-looking speakers, a subwoofer for deep bass, a jukebox CD player, an ultrapowerful receiver. In audiophile land, the sky's the limit.

System setup

Boom boxes are the simplest to set up. They run on batteries, so you don't even need to plug them in. Minisystems, with speakers matched to the receiver, come next; just connect the speakers and antenna. Rack systems also come with compatible speakers but do require some assembly and stringing of cables.

Component systems require more decisions, including determining the power of the receiver and its compatibility with speakers. Once you've chosen your component, shop for the best price. If you can't install the system yourself, hire someone. Many stores, especially specialty stores and audiophile boutiques, offer this service.

Power decisions. Generally, the more power a receiver can deliver, the louder you can play music. Each doubling of loudness uses about 10 times as much power. To fill a good-sized living room with loud, undistorted sound, you usually need 65 to 100 watts per channel. If you play recordings at high volume with strong, deep bass or a wide dynamic range, or if your speakers require extra power, stay close to 100 watts.

For a small room—a bedroom or dorm room—you need about 35 or 40 watts per channel to play music loud. With less than 20 watts per channel, as found on some minisystems and boom boxes, don't expect loud bass. When the receiver's amplifier is supplying power to three or more channels, as it would in its Dolby Pro Logic modes, it supplies less power per channel than when it's powering only two channels in stereo mode. (Ads often show off the larger stereo-mode numbers.) Look for Pro Logic power that's even across the front channels—80-80-80, say. To meet federal guidelines, manufacturers are conservative in how they rate receivers' power. Our own measurements are often a bit higher.

Don't skimp on power. When a receiver runs short of power while playing peaks in the music, it produces a harsh distortion called clipping, which can damage speakers—and can occur even when the volume is only halfway up. Fortunately, even low-priced receivers usually have plenty of power these days.

Speaker/receiver compatibility. As a receiver runs, its power supply and amplifier heat up, due to the power the amplifier puts out and the resistance of the speakers—the impedance—measured in ohms. The lower the impedance, the higher the current draw and the hotter things get. So, a pair of four-ohm speakers will heat up the receiver more than an eight-ohm pair. Therein lies a problem in mating speakers with receivers.

Although a speaker's impedance has nothing to do with its quality, you'll find more four-ohm models among expensive speakers. Mass-market brands such as Sony, Pioneer, and Radio Shack generally include a mix of speakers rated at eight and six ohms. Companies like Bose and Cerwin-Vega market different lines for different retail venues, some with eight-ohm ratings, some six, some four. Many high-end salon speaker lines are made entirely of four-ohm models.

The labels on many receivers warn against four-ohm speakers. Ignoring the label can be risky. If the receiver cabinet gets uncomfortably hot to the touch after a half-hour's play of bass-heavy music, you're probably overheating internal parts. Turn the volume down and think seriously about getting a new receiver.

Positioning speakers. Ideally, two speakers should form an equilateral triangle at least six feet on each side, with you as the third point. With a system of two small speakers and a bass module, make the triangle with the two small satellites, and place the large bass unit wherever there's room. The ear can't tell which direction deep bass sounds come from. For a five- or six-speaker system, maintain that triangle with the front right and left speakers; put the center front speaker above or below the TV set, the two rear surround speakers pointed away from you and just behind you, and the bass module wherever it fits.

These speaker positions are the ideal. In many homes, you must put the speakers on the bookshelf or next to the couch. Experiment if possible—speaker placement can greatly affect the sound of your system.

For better bass: The closer a speaker is placed to the corner of a room, the stronger the bass—a boost for a small bass-light speaker. But putting a big bass-rich speaker right in the corner can make the bass sound muddy or boomy.

Adding a second pair. Most receivers provide outputs—labeled Main and Remote or A and B—for two pairs of speakers in stereo mode, so you can listen in a different room. If you want to play two pairs loudly, you need a receiver with 100 watts or more per channel, since two pairs need more power than one. In addition, some receivers are better suited to adding a second pair of speakers. If the remote speakers are on a separate circuit from the main speakers—in parallel—all four should sound as they were designed to. But if the extra pair are on the same circuit as the main speakers—in series—the sound will be altered and often degraded. The arrangement of the circuitry also affects impedance. Two pairs of speakers in parallel produce the equivalent of lower impedance, causing the same problem that four-ohm speakers do—overheating.

A receiver has the preferred parallel design if its switches and output jacks have labels that refer to three modes—A, B, and A+B—with a higher impedance noted for the A+B mode. Otherwise, you can't easily tell how the receiver is wired. A knowledgeable salesperson might be able to tell from the instruction manual.

THE DIGITAL FUTURE OF TV

TV technology is in transition. Broadcasters and cable companies are beginning to join satellite-TV providers in changing their transmissions from analog to digital signals. The result will be "cleaner," more detailed images, better sound, and such additional services as high-speed access to the Internet.

Existing digital programming, on satellite systems and some cable systems, offers the best TV pictures and sound that current equipment can handle. True digital television, or "DTV," is just starting to show up. But it may or may not be "HDTV," which offers striking movie-like clarity—a digital image of 16:9 compared with the 4:3 proportion of a standard TV image. Some broadcasters may instead use their new digital bandwidth for multiple channels of lower-resolution digital TV.

Our advice if you're buying a set now—weigh the prices and features against potential technological changes.

No TV sold now can take full advantage of high-definition television. At least initially, the few broadcasts may be restricted to prime-time programs on the major networks, and the sets will be priced at an estimated $8,000 or more. In time, programming should increase and prices of sets should decrease—but it's hard to say when.

Most people will enter TV's digital era less dramatically and much less expensively by connecting their conventional TV to a receiver or set-top box that will decode digital transmissions (in HDTV and other formats) into signals their set can display. Some viewers already use a satellite-dish system, DVD player, or digital cable box for this. Eventually, most cable systems will switch (only about 2 percent of cable customers now receive digital service), and so will broadcasters.

Buy or wait?

A moderately priced TV set is still worth buying if you need a set. If you plan to spend $2,000 or more, you may kick yourself in a few years.

Broadcasters are committed to simultaneously transmitting the same program in digital and conventional formats until at least the year 2006. After that, the old-style signals will continue in an area until 85 percent or more of viewers have a device to receive digital pictures. You may then be forced to buy a converter box for your old set.

Two features in a new TV set will help it make the most of digital signals:

Audio-output jacks. Current built-in sound systems cannot do justice to the multichannel audio of digital-TV signals, which need to be routed to external speakers or a sound system.

Input jacks for S-video and components. These allow the set to take better advantage of the higher quality of digital signals. More and more sets come with these jacks.

CABLE TV VS. SATELLITE

Seven million U.S. homes now sport a pizza-sized dish antenna that receives TV programming beamed from a satellite—more than three times as many as in 1995. With its hundreds of digitally-transmitted channels, satellite TV offers state-of-the-art picture and sound and a wide selection of programming, especially in movies and sports—but it's not cheap. You must buy equipment and pay monthly programming fees, and may still need a cable subscription or an antenna for local programming.

Here's a guide to evaluating the strengths and weaknesses of the two technologies.

Where cable TV has the edge

Access to service. Some 97 percent of American households now have the cable option. To receive satellite service, you need a clear sight from your home to the southern horizon toward Texas, along which the services' broadcast satellites are arrayed, which rules out a lot of urban dwellers as well as many residents of hilly terrains.

Getting equipped. Though they charge for cable connection, most systems don't make you buy or rent equipment unless you want premium or pay-per-view channels, which require renting (a cable-converter box).

Getting started with satellite TV is much less straightforward. First, you need to choose among the three satellite systems (DSS, Dish Network, and Primestar), each with its own satellite, programming, and other distinctions. Then you select your equipment, often from among several brands for that satellite system after you've decided how many TV sets you want to serve with satellite TV.

The three dish systems are technically incompatible; once you've chosen a setup, you can't later use it to subscribe to another. Satellite equipment may quickly show its age; every year, setups drop in price and become easier to use. Also, little equipment sold today will be able to take full advantage of new developments such as Dolby Digital sound processing and high-definition TV. So leasing equipment is an appealing alternative. Primestar equipment can be leased, and Bell Atlantic, GTE, and Southwestern Bell planned to lease DSS setups to their telephone customers beginning in fall 1998.

Local programming. Dish users who want to watch the local affiliates of ABC, CBS, Fox, NBC, and PBS must use an antenna or maintain a basic cable subscription. You can buy a satellite package (for $5 or so a month) of affiliates of those five major networks. But none of these stations will provide local content unless you happen to live in a city where satellite affiliates originate. One system, Dish Network, offers local affiliates to its subscribers in six major cities. But the service requires buying about $100 of equipment, including a second dish that must be positioned with a clear view to the southeast horizon (rather than the view the main dish requires).

Where satellite is superior

Picture and sound quality. Satellite systems don't reproduce images perfectly but they come very close, with only subtle visual flaws. Sound quality is excellent—much like a CD player. Cable systems, by contrast, often vary widely in signal quality from channel to channel. Larger cable companies such as Cablevision and TCI are now upgrading their service in selected markets to offer digital signals; smaller independent cable companies will lag in the transition. For now, so-called digital cable is usually a hybrid service, used only for premium and pay-per-view channels—and these signals may be digitally squeezed at the expense of visual clarity.

Breadth of programming. Satellite systems have double or more the number of channels found on a typical analog cable system, offering nearly everything else you'll find on cable. Satellite also has room for many of the networks cable systems often can't accommodate. Even multichannel digital cable systems can't match satellite for sheer diversity.

More choices in movies. Satellite's nonpremium movie networks run the gamut from classic cable fare (AMC, TCM) to the fairly esoteric (The Sundance Channel). On a satellite system, a premium network may occupy up to seven channels, each showing a different movie at a particular hour. Such "multiplexing" is also used for pay-per-view offerings. As many as 8 of DSS's 55 pay-per-view channels may be devoted to a popular movie—allowing, say, "Air Force One" to start every half-hour.

Audio-only music "stations." Satellite systems typically offer 30 or so services that play uninterrupted music, from rap to baroque, with CD quality sound making the services a good match with a home-theater setup. DSS setups display the song title and performer on the TV screen, along with an index number you can use to order the song on a CD; the other systems display only the music genre, usually after you press a button on the remote.

Sports programming. Though they lack broadcast-network sports programming, satellite systems generally offer the three ESPN services seen on cable. Mid- to high-priced satellite programming packages (costing about $30 and up) also typically include at least 15 regional sports channels. There are also special sports packages, such as NFL Sunday Ticket, with 13 games a week. Packages cost about $100 to $150 a season.

No clear advantage

Ease of use. Keeping track of regular cable programming is relatively easy. Satellite's programming, though, swamps you with wave after wave of channels. The systems have come up with different solutions to the problem: DSS and Dish Network Lifeline is an interactive programming guide that describes programs up to two and a half days in advance, sorted by areas of interest. Primestar's listings aren't interactive, but the system's unique remote does have 10 programming keys (labeled "movies," "sports," and the like). Expect to spend some time learning to navigate a system's menus—and becoming accustomed to scores of programs. (Satellite providers also publish monthly programming magazines.)

High-speed web access. Both cable and satellite deliver a fast path to the

World Wide Web. Subscribers to some cable systems now pay an additional $40 or $50 a month (plus installation of $180 or so) to use their cable line, along with a special cable modem. Satellite access may run from $299 to $899, plus a small monthly fee.

However, although a cable modem or satellite setup will allow you to download data much faster than a conventional phone line or even a high-speed ISDN phone line, neither yet provides a "return path" to the web. Instead, you need a phone line, using an Internet service provider—about another $20 a month.

Compatibility with HDTV. Neither technology will prepare you better for high-definition TV. The cable industry is resisting demands to carry HDTV transmissions. Current dish setups will require a new receiver to handle HDTV signals.

How to choose

If you must have it all in TV programming, or have the best picture and sound, a satellite dish may be your choice, especially if you can't get cable. Satellite TV will also appeal strongly to movie and sports aficionados.

For other consumers, cable is probably the better choice. Satellite TV requires you to buy equipment that may soon become outmoded and does not provide local stations.

Until it solves its local-programming problem, satellite TV will be more an expensive complement to cable than a replacement for it.

SATELLITE SYSTEMS

There are three small-dish satellite-TV systems—DSS, Dish Network, and Primestar—each with its own satellite and programming choices. When selecting a system, ask yourself these questions:

About the system

Is your location compatible with all the systems? Unless the view from your roof to the southern horizon toward Texas is completely unobstructed, ask the retailer for a professional site survey before you buy. Negotiate to have the survey fee—typically $25 or so—waived if you eventually buy a setup.

Does dish size matter? The standard size for DSS and Dish Network is 18 by 20 inches. Primestar dishes are larger—36 by 29 inches (soon to be replaced by a 27-inch version). For all systems, larger sizes still may be needed in Northern states.

Which offers the programs you want? DSS offers the most choice—especially for sports and movie buffs. Dish Network is strong on foreign-language programs, weaker than others on sports. Primestar's packages are a good value. DSS and Dish Network provide an on-screen program guide with listings up to a few days in advance; Primestar's guide shows only the next 1½ hours.

Which brands? A setup can mix components from different brands, providing all these components are of the same system. Hitachi, HNS, RCA, Sony, and Toshiba make equipment for the DDS system. EchoStar, JVC, and Philips Magnavox make gear for Dish Network. Primestar sells its own brand of satellite dish and receiver.

About the setup

A setup is a package of equipment comprising the dish and a VCR-sized receiver that decodes satellite broadcasts and is typically placed near the TV set.

How many TV sets do you want served—and how? To watch on more than one set may require extra equipment. To watch different channels on two sets will require an additional receiver and a monthly service fee. Serving three or more sets is possible with the purchase of additional receivers and a second dish.

How will you get local channels? If local channels are a priority, you'll probably need either a separate roof antenna or a basic cable subscription.

CAMCORDERS

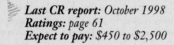

***Last CR report:** October 1998*
***Ratings:** page 61*
***Expect to pay:** $450 to $2,500*

Today's camcorders have evolved along with other electronic products: They work better, cost less, and have more automatic features. They're also smaller—the most popular types weigh about two pounds.

What's available

The biggest-selling brands are Sony, Panasonic, RCA, JVC, and Sharp. Sony is the major maker of 8mm camcorders, while Matsushita (maker of Panasonic) and JVC dominate the VHS world. Virtually all the models on the market now are a compact format:

8mm. These use cassettes about the size of an audio cassette. Most cassettes hold two hours. The tapes won't play in a standard VHS VCR; you must copy them onto a VHS cassette or connect the camcorder to a TV set for playback. The pictures produced by 8mm camcorders are of similar quality to those from VHS-C, but 8mm produces better sound than non-hi-fi VHS-C models. Price range: $400 to $800 for an 8mm camcorder.

Compact VHS (VHS-C). These models use cassettes about the size of a cigarette pack. Tapes typically hold 30 minutes on fast speed, 90 minutes on slow. VHS-C uses an adapter to play tapes in any VHS VCR. Price range: $450 to $1,000.

"High-band." Hi8 and S-VHS-C, premium variants of compact camcorders, deliver a sharper picture than 8mm or VHS-C models. You'll get the full benefit of that enhanced video resolution only if you watch the tape on a TV set with an S-video input and use Hi8 or S-VHS-C tape. Hi-band models cost $700 to $1,300.

Digital video (DV). The future of camcorders is digital, though digital camcorders are strictly a high-end product right now. This format can record very high-quality images—but in our tests they weren't always superior to analog models. At slow speeds, digital has the edge. With most analog camcorders, image quality worsens at the slower speeds. Digital camcorders use a unique tape cassette that's smaller than either a VHS-C or an 8mm cassette. For playback, the camcorder converts the data to an analog signal, so it can be played directly into a TV set. As with a Hi8 analog camcorder, you need a TV set with an S-video input to fully appreciate the image quality. These camcorders have a digital interface for connecting to a computer, most useful for editing. That requires an outlay of several hundred dollars for image-handling software, an interface for the computer, and special cables. DV models have been introduced by Sony, Panasonic, JVC, RCA, and Sharp. You'll pay $2,000 or more.

Key features

Every camcorder includes an **SP (standard-play) speed**. A few 8mm models have a **slower LP speed,** which doubles recording time. All VHS-C camcorders have an even slower **EP (extended-play) speed,** which triples recording time. The slower speeds almost always mean some loss of picture quality.

The **zoom** control is typically a rocker switch—you press one end to zoom in, the other to widen the view. On most camcorders, the zoom ratio ranges from 8:1 to 16:1. Some offer a digital zoom that extends the range to about 200:1 but with a fall-off in picture quality. Some models let you vary the zoom speed by how hard you press the switch.

Image stabilization, an increasingly common feature, aims to iron the jitters out of handheld shots. Effectiveness varies somewhat from brand to brand, according to our tests. Some versions can slightly mar picture clarity, we've found. At best, image stabilizers provide only a moderate improvement in steadiness. A video tripod is still the best tool for steady shots.

A **color viewfinder** is nice if you plan to watch an event from behind the camcorder, or if color aids your narration, say, when you're taping a tour of your garden. But it doesn't improve upon a black-and-white one for composing and focusing.

A **remote control** is handy when using the camcorder as a playback device. Remotes are not dependable at long distances or in sunlight. Some remotes are as small as a business card.

Shutter speeds faster than the "normal" $1/60$ of a second can be useful to study, say, a tennis serve in slow motion or frame by frame but don't enhance picture quality at normal speed. The fastest speeds require bright daylight. **Autofocus** adjusts for maximum sharpness; **manual focus** override is sometimes needed for problem situations, such as low light. With motorized manual focus, you may have to tap buttons repeatedly to focus just right. In many high-end camcorders, you can also control exposure, shutter speed, and white balance.

An **audio/video input** lets you record material from another camcorder or from a VCR—useful in copying part of someone else's video onto your own. Unlike the built-in microphone, an **external microphone,** plugged into a **microphone jack**, doesn't pick up noises from the camcorder itself, and typically improves audio performance. **A title generator** lets you use a built-in character generator to superimpose printed titles and captions.

Most models let you install a bigger **battery** than the original. Extra-capacity batteries typically run about twice as long as the one supplied. With some, you can use alkaline AA batteries if a charged nicad isn't available. **Refresh charging** lets you fully drain the battery before recharging to help maintain full running time. A nickel cadmium battery that's repeatedly recharged when not totally "empty" may lose the ability to "fill" itself.

How to choose

Performance differences. Any camcorder can do a decent job of recording in brightly and normally lit environments.

While overall picture color and quality vary, picture quality is only loosely related to price. In our most recent tests $400 models produced pictures as good as those costing $800.

The choice of format determines the maximum running time of the tape. Sound quality also separates the formats; 8mm is inherently superior to non-hi-fi VHS-C. The built-in microphone on most camcorders, however, would not do justice to a theater or concert performance. All are adequate for speech, and the best would be fine for a school recital.

What to spend. Features that used to be found only on high-end models—color LCD viewfinders, image stabilization, built-in video lights, a wide-range zoom—continue to migrate downward to the lower-priced models. A basic 8mm or VHS-C camcorder starts at about $400. Spending more gets you extra features that may make shooting more fun or more convenient but have little effect on basic performance. To get the added performance of a high-band model, you'll have to spend $700 or more. If you need the very best image quality (and can afford to pay a premium for it), then digital should be your first choice.

CAMERAS

Last CR report: *November 1998*
Ratings: *page 64*
Expect to pay: *$450 to $2,500*

Like many aspects of life, still photography is going digital, with a new kind of camera that looks much like a compact autofocus model but works more like a camcorder. Images are stored on a memory card instead of film. Transferred from the card to a computer, the images can be edited and manipulated using software supplied with the camera. You can print the photos on an ink-jet printer or send them by e-mail around the world.

There are still plenty of film-based "analog" cameras. Those using 35mm film outnumber models using new, smaller APS format film. APS hasn't caught on as its creators hoped.

Taking pictures involves the same actions, whether you use film or digital. You hold the camera and peer through a viewfinder (or look at an LCD panel) to compose a shot. Then you press the shutter release. With digital, the camera lens focuses light not on a strip of film but on an electronic sensor that records the picture as an electronic signal.

What's available

Major camera companies include Canon, Fuji, Kodak, Minolta, Nikon, and Olympus. Many of those companies also make digital cameras, as do computer companies like Hewlett-Packard and Epson.

Cameras these days, no matter the format, are highly automated. Flashes are built into all but the most expensive models. Low-priced film cameras are fixed-focus, like an old-fashioned box camera. Features that raise the price include autofocus, automatic exposure control, and a zoom lens.

35mm SLRs. Single-lens-reflex cameras with interchangeable lenses let you see what the camera sees. That gives a great deal of artistic control. SLRs are typically sold without a lens or bundled with a zoom lens. Price range: $200 and up for the camera body, $100 and up for a moderate-range zoom lens.

Compact 35mm cameras. Small and light compared with an SLR, these cameras are capable of producing very good, even excellent photos. Single-use and low-cost models have a fixed focus and no exposure adjustment. They're adequate for travel scenes and group shots. More expensive models include a zoom lens and many automated features. Some can shoot in panoramic mode, giving an expansive 4x12-inch photo. Price range: $5 to $50 for basic and single-use cameras; $50 and up for models with autoexposure; $140 and up for a zoom lens.

APS cameras. Since APS film is smaller than 35mm film, these cameras tend to be smaller and lighter still. Picture quality has been very good in our tests, and the format allows great flexibility: You can switch from regular to wide (a semi-panorama) to panoramic in midroll. Film handling is especially easy. Price range: $80 and up for an APS model with a fixed-focal-length lens; $120 and up for one with a zoom lens.

Digital cameras. These look and operate much like autofocus film cameras but produce files that can be loaded into a computer; there's no film involved. What we call megapixel models typically have a maximum resolution of 1,024x768 picture elements (pixels); low-resolution cameras have a resolution of 640x480 pixels. **Resolution** is the single most important property of a digital camera. Other things being equal, a megapixel camera will deliver a sharper image than one with a coarser resolution, and a sharper image means you can make larger prints. A 640x480 pixel image should be amply sharp for viewing on a computer monitor or sending via e-mail. Prices range from $300 to $800 or more, with megapixel models generally costing more. Digital cameras do come with about $60 worth of image-handling software. And they avoid the ongoing cost of film, at $4 to $6 a roll; one memory card can be reused indefinitely.

Key features

Automated features found on many models include **motorized film handling**. You drop the film in, pull out the leader, close the camera, and the camera automatically advances the film and rewinds it at the end of the roll.

Auto exposure regulates the shutter speed and lens opening to get a properly exposed photo, whether in bright light or low light. An **exposure-compensation** feature prevents underexposure when the background is bright or overexposure when the background is unusually dark compared with the subject. SLRs and more advanced compact models offer several **exposure modes** that let you fine-tune the exposure.

Autofocus frees you from having to focus the camera most of the time to ensure crisp pictures. Compact film cameras typically use an infrared beam. Digital cameras have shorter-focal-length lenses than film cameras, so they can keep a wider range in focus. Highly accurate focusing isn't very critical; some digital cameras get by with a fixed-focus lens.

Flashes cover various distances, from 4 or 5 feet to 20 feet or more. The smartest ones work with the zoom lens to broaden or narrow the beam. **Flash on demand** lets you fill in harsh shadows in bright, sunlit portraits. "Red eye" occurs when a flash reflects off people's retinas; **red-eye reduction** typically uses a light before the flash to constrict the subject's pupils. The **sensors** in digital cameras are about as sensitive as ISO 100 film, which usually requires a flash indoors. A handy override feature on the cameras allows you to cancel the flash to photograph night shots.

The digital cameras we tested have a maximum flash range of 8 to 13 feet—comparable with film cameras we've tested in the past using ISO 100 film.

Digital features include:

Compression. A way of mathematically removing redundant visual information from the image file to fit more images on the memory card. Most cameras give you a choice of two or three compression settings. Most images won't suffer from some compression. With an overcompressed image, fine details won't be reproduced accurately and the quality of large prints will suffer.

Memory card. The number of pictures each memory card holds depends on the camera, the capacity of the card, and even on the images themselves. There are several types of card: CompactFlash, which is less than half the size of a credit card and about three times as thick; the thinner SmartMedia cards; computer PCMCIA memory cards, which are much bigger than CompactFlash cards; or a standard floppy disk. Cards differ in their

OTHER WAYS TO MAKE PHOTOS DIGITAL

You don't have to buy a digital camera to get images into the computer.

The scanner option. Consider buying a scanner if you plan to use a lot of your own photos or drawings in documents that you produce. A flatbed scanner, the most practical type, resembles a photocopier and can scan individual photos or pages from a book. Scanners can cost several hundred dollars, though you can find some for less than $100.

Be sure any scanner you buy has the following minimum specifications:

- SCSI, USB, or parallel computer interface.
- A TWAIN driver and TWAIN-compliant software packages. The driver lets the scanner be used with any image-handling software.
- At least 24-bit color depth—30-bit is preferable—and 300 x 300 dot-per-inch optical resolution; 600 x 600 is preferable.

The photofinishing option. Camera stores and mail-order photofinishing labs offer digital processing as well as standard prints. The lab has the entire roll of film scanned onto a Photo CD, a computer-readable compact disc containing high-resolution (3,072x2,048 picture element) image files. Most labs can also scan much lower-resolution images onto a conventional floppy disk or send them to you over the Internet. One service called PhotoNet *(www.photonet.com)* loads the photos onto a web site you can access with a password. Costs range from $4 to $8, in addition to the normal cost of processing a roll of film.

To see how well the services stack up to digital cameras, we had a Photo CD, floppy disks, and an Internet download made and we printed the results on the same high-resolution printer used for the camera tests. Overall, prints from the Photo CD images appear to have slightly better detail than pictures from the digital cameras. The Photo CD images, including those taken under incandescent or fluorescent lighting, were all properly color-balanced. The images we received over the Internet were disappointing. The low-resolution photos (592x400 picture elements) were marred by digital artifacts and weren't well corrected for lighting.

maximum capacity—the megabytes of memory available to hold your images.

Color LCD screen. This is one of the handiest digital-camera features. It lets you check that the picture you just took is composed well and exposed properly (if it isn't, you can delete it from memory). The screen is often used to display prompts and commands for changing the resolution or the amount of digital compression. On many models, there's a viewfinder, too. Cameras that have only a screen and no viewfinder can be more difficult to use—especially in bright sunlight, which can wash out the LCD image. A screen guzzles battery power and can quickly drain a set of AA alkaline batteries.

Software. Every digital camera comes with software to link the camera and the computer and to let you manipulate the images—to control print size, correct colors, or eliminate the "red eye" look from people in a flash photo. A TWAIN driver allows the camera to work with virtually any image-handling software, not just the package provided with the camera. None of the packages was perfect. Most suffered from being too basic, the price of making the software easy to use. We preferred Adobe PhotoDeluxe, which was included with five cameras. Its "instant fix" function was easy and effective, and it included red-eye correction. But it won't let you gang different images on the same piece of paper.

Other features. These include video outputs for connecting the camera directly to a TV set to display images without using a computer. A few cameras can also record short video and audio clips.

How to choose

Digital photography will gain in popularity as the process of downloading and outputting images becomes simpler and the cameras come down in price. Right now, it takes time and the inclination to fiddle with computerized images. If you're uncomfortable with computers, a digital camera may not be right for you.

Performance differences. Our tests through the years have shown the optical quality of all the major brands of SLR to be consistently high. Compact 35mm and APS cameras are also capable of taking very good or excellent photos.

The results of our tests of digital cameras were surprisingly good. Photos from digital cameras won't look as sharp as photos shot on regular film, but some come awfully close. The better cameras can produce very good 5x7-inch prints—even very good 8x10-inch prints. All were easy to use, and all produced bright colors and well-exposed photos in any light. They differed in their ability to correct for incandescent and fluorescent lighting. But most were better than the average film-processing lab at correcting difficult cases. However, models varied considerably in the time the camera needs to digitize, compress, and store the image on the memory cards—from 2 seconds to 37 seconds. Megapixel models typically made you wait the longest. If you often shoot candid photos in rapid succession, look for a camera with a short delay.

What to spend

With film cameras, spending more gets you more features and often better optics. With digital cameras, spending more gets you higher resolution for your images. "Megapixel" cameras offer high resolution for making large prints and lower resolution for sending photos via e-mail. Low-resolution cameras are cheaper—OK for just sending images by e-mail or over the Internet.

Web sites like *www. shopper.com* are good places to price-shop. You can buy digital cameras at major electronics chains, computer stores, camera stores, and office superstores. Prices are dropping regularly and new models are introduced frequently. Promotional deals usually peak at year's end.

CASSETTE DECKS

***Last CR report:** February 1996*
***Expect to pay:** $100 to $1,000*

Cassette decks have probably gotten as good as they are going to get. They remain the medium of choice for recording and playing music at home. The best decks can satisfy all but the most critical ear, despite tape's inherent limitations—slow access to individual tracks, background hiss, and a limited ability to capture the whole audible spectrum. In fact, a deck that has Dolby S, the most advanced noise-reduction circuitry, sounds nearly as clean as a CD player.

What's available

Sony, JVC, and Pioneer are the biggest-selling brands.

Single-deck models. The tape drive in single-tape decks used to be a cut above that found in comparably priced dual-deck machines, but dual-decks are catching up. Price range: $100 to $1,000.

Dual-deck models. The most commonly sold type of deck, also called a "dubbing" deck, is useful for copying tapes and playing cassettes in sequence for long stretches of uninterrupted music. **Single-record models** allow playback

TIPS ON TAPE

Which tape to buy depends on how good it needs to sound. Avoid bargain tapes with nonbrand names, but don't overbuy—using expensive tape for making party tapes for a boom box is a waste of money.

Type I ("Normal bias"). This type has a relatively narrow dynamic range—the span between the loudest and softest sounds. The loudest sounds can overload the tape and cause distortion, particularly in the high frequencies; without Dolby noise reduction, the softest sounds suffer severely from background hiss, which is the residual noise on the tape that's heard during playback. Best uses: recording speech, copying pop music from LPs or the radio, creating recordings for a boom box or an inexpensive automobile tape player.

Type II ("high bias"). This type can reproduce both midrange and treble frequencies better, so it provides a wider dynamic range. Best uses: recording FM broadcasts, making copies of CDs, cassettes, or high-quality LPs, and making tapes for walkabout tape players or a good car tape player.

Type IV ("metal tape"). This type has the widest dynamic range. It won't record well on some rack and minisystem tape decks and most portable systems. Best uses: recording live music and copying audiophile-quality CDs for listening at home.

from both cassette wells but can record from only one; **dual-record models** allow playback and recording from both wells. Price range: $100 to $500.

Key features

Dolby Noise suppression is standard these days on most components. Dolby S, a step up from Dolby B and C, enhances the dynamic range—the ability to reproduce noiseless loud and soft passages.

Autoreverse automatically plays the flip side of the tape when you reach the end. **Adjustable bias control** helps adjust the deck to the brand of tape you're using. **Automatic bias control** sets itself. **Autoplay** will start playing the tape when it's fully rewound. **Autoreturn** lets you cancel a recording and return to the tape's starting point.

Intro scan plays the first few seconds of a track to help you decide which selections you want to hear. **Music search** lets you move the tape directly to a particular track. A **real-time tape counter**

TURNTABLES: GOING BUT NOT GONE

Mindful of all the people who still treasure their collections of vinyl platters, major home-electronics manufacturers, including Kenwood, Onkyo, Sony, and Technics, make single-play turntables. Many models are priced at less than $200; a few sell for under $100—not too different from when we last tested turntables, in the early 1980s. Some of the brands that consistently performed well in the past are still available. Look for models from Technics and Sony, and don't spend more than about $150.

Many modern turntables come with the cartridge—the part that holds the needle, or stylus—already installed. A "P-mount" cartridge, a common type, plugs in and avoids the need for a detachable headshell. The tone arm's vertical tracking force is typically preset, allowing good tracking and at the same time keeping record wear to a minimum.

The units work the same way they did years ago, rotating the turntable by direct drive or belt drive. Neither design holds an advantage, in our experience. The once-ubiquitous phono input on the back of a receiver is now missing on some component receivers and on almost all minisystems. To compensate, some turntables are now designed with their own preamplifier. That allows you to connect them to the receiver via the aux line input, as you would an extra CD player or cassette deck.

You can reduce record wear by cleaning the cartridge's stylus from time to time. Accumulations of dust and dirt accelerate record wear, and cause distortion and mistracking.

You should be able to use a phono cartridge stylus for at least 400 hours, or the time it takes to play about 600 LP records. If you don't know when to change the stylus, ask an audio technician to examine it with a microscope. If it shows little wear, check it again after another 200 hours.

If you damage the stylus, or if its cantilever—the thin bar that supports the diamond tip—looks bent out of its original shape, replace it immediately. It costs much less to replace a stylus than a cantilever.

is especially useful if it shows elapsed time in minutes and seconds and the tape time that remains. Most have an electronic display. **CD sync** links the cassette deck to a CD player of the same brand to simplify recording. **Recording mute** inserts momentary silence between cuts when you record continuously; the silences can act as a marker for search and scan features.

Features that make it easier to make tapes include **three-head design,** found on many single-deck machines, which lets you monitor the music off the tape as you record. **Two-button recording and dubbing** helps avoid inadvertent taping by requiring two button-presses instead of one.

How to choose

Performance differences. Dual-deck models usually give up a little in audio performance compared with comparably priced single-deck machines. They tend to suffer slightly more from flutter (a wavy, watery sound defect), and their frequency response is slightly less accurate.

On any deck, controls should be logically laid out and clearly labeled, displays should be informative and readable from just about any angle, and the cassette wells should be lighted so you can see the cassette inside. Look for a deck that lets you separately adjust the recording level and the balance between left and right channels. Recording-level meters (typically, lighted displays that work like animated bar graphs) should present a clear indication of the sound levels, not just a coarse approximation. Playback controls should let you skip easily from one selection to the next, repeat a selection, play both sides of the cassette automatically (or even play the cassette endlessly), and rewind rapidly.

Decide what to spend. All but the cheapest decks should be capable of producing good or very good sound. Expect to pay anywhere from $200 to $500 for a deck that performs well. More money buys more features but may not improve the sound.

You can spend less by opting for a portable unit. Portables include boom boxes and walkabouts. Boom boxes record, most walkabouts don't. You can hook up most walkabouts to a stereo system and get decent playing performance, although the small controls may be inconvenient. Boom boxes sell for about $40 and up; walkabouts, $20 and up.

CD PLAYERS

Last CR report: *November 1997*
Expect to pay: *$80 to $500*

Component CDs are a mature product, with little real innovation and change. Jukeboxes and portables are another story. For hundreds of dollars less than you'd spend even a year ago, you can buy a CD jukebox that holds 100 to 300 discs. Prices for portables are dropping, too. According to our most recent tests, portables now use batteries more efficiently, and better resist skipping when bumped or jolted.

What's available

Component CD players are marketed under more than 40 brand names. Six brands account for most sales: Sony, Pioneer, Magnavox, JVC, Technics, and Kenwood. Sony makes the largest number of portable CD players with its Discman line. Other big portable brands include Panasonic, RCA, and Aiwa.

There are three types of component CD players:

Single-disc players. There are a few inexpensive single-disc models left on the market, but CD changers have gotten so cheap that most have disappeared. Increasingly, this category is being left to audiophiles, with very high-end single-disc players. Price: Often less than $100.

Carousel and magazine changers. Multiple-disc changers, which hold 5 to 10 discs, can play hours of music nonstop. A **magazine** changer uses a slide-in cartridge the size of a small, thick book. Capable of holding 6 to 10 discs, each cartridge doubles as a convenient disc storage box. A **carousel** changer, which holds 5 or 6 discs on a platter, is easier to load and unload than the magazine type; most let you change discs that aren't playing without interrupting the music. Carousel players that use a slide-out drawer can fit in a stack of components; top-loaders must be positioned on top. Price range: $200 to $500.

CD jukeboxes. Also known as megachangers, jukeboxes can store 25 to 300 discs. Marketed as a way to manage and store an entire music collection, most models let you segment a collection by musical genre, composer, artist, and so forth; the unit flashes album titles as you hunt through the discs. Inputting all the necessary data can be tedious—models that connect to a computer keyboard make it easier—but then you can set a jukebox to shuffle and play random selections all night or play discs only from your choice of genre. There are some drawbacks: CD jukeboxes can be cumbersome (many may not fit the typical stereo rack), inconvenient to load, or noisy and slow in selecting CDs. Price range: $200 to $500, close to standard-capacity changers.

Portable players. These small players hold only one disc and have simple controls. Most can be connected to other audio gear, where they can play music as excellently as any console can. Early models often skipped or had poor-quality headphones—newer ones tested better. Portables now average several hours more playing time on a pair of AA batteries than just a few years ago. (Most portable players take two AA batteries, but some require four.) Battery use can be prodigious and varies considerably from model to model, according to our tests. Most come with an AC adapter. Many come

HEADPHONES FOR PORTABLES

Good headphones are the most important determinant of overall sound quality in a portable.

If the headphones that come with your walkabout or CD player are uncomfortable, you can replace them. The replacement headphones we've tested have reproduced sound more accurately, often providing better sound than the headphones that came with the walkabout.

The ones that are likely to give you the best sound are muff-style headphones, which sit on or over the ear, or ball-style, which pivot to better contact the ear.

Bud or bud-band headphones, which sit inside the ear, can be better than on-the-ear types at insulating you from outside noises.

with a built-in rechargeable battery pack. Price range: $80 to $200.

Key features

For component models. A **remote control,** still not standard equipment, is useful. Buttons should be grouped by function or color-coded and be visible in dim light. CD remotes are typically fairly simple and work only the player. A **calendar display** shows a block of numbers representing the tracks on the active disc and highlights the track that's playing. As the disc plays, numbers for previous tracks disappear—and you can see at a glance how many selections are left. A **numeric keypad** on the remote and on the console is a faster way to reach a particular track than pressing Up and Down buttons.

Some changers and jukeboxes have a handy **single-play drawer or slot**, which lets you play a single disc without disturbing the ones already loaded.

Features that make track selection easy include **delete track**, which allows you to mark music you don't like, then play the rest of the disc from start to finish; **favorite track** program memory, which lets you mark favorites for when discs are reinserted; and **music sampling**, which plays a few seconds of each selection. **Shuffle play** mixes the playing order in a random sequence. Look for nonrepeat shuffle.

People who tape will appreciate features like **auto edit**, which lets you enter the cassette's recording time; the CD player lays out the disc's tracks, usually in sequence, to fill both sides of your tape. **Comprehensive time display** lets you flip among time elapsed and time remaining for the current track and for the entire disc. **Running-time total** lets you total the time of tracks you're recording so you can fit the maximum on a tape. **Music-peak finder** scans for the loudest passage in a track you're going to record, so you can adjust the tape deck's recording level correctly and quickly. **Fade out/fade in** performs the audio equivalent of a movie fade for less abrupt starts and endings.

A **synchronizing jack** lets you connect a cable to a tape deck of the same brand so you can run both machines simultaneously. Those recording digitally on a minidisc recorder or a digital tape deck need a **digital output jack** to attach a fiber-optic or coaxial cable.

For portables. Most models have a **bass-boost** control to compensate for the thin bass that poorer headphones deliver. Some have digital signal processing (DSP), which electronically simulates the ambience of live music heard in a concert hall.

Most models have an **LCD display** that shows which track is playing and a **battery level indicator**, usually a flashing light, that warns you when batteries are low. The best have a shrinking scale that reflects power remaining. An **AC adapter,** standard with nearly every portable, not only runs the player on house current, it typically can also charge rechargeable cells. Sometimes the **rechargeable battery pack** is an extra-cost accessory.

Most models can be **programmed** to play tracks in sequence, to **shuffle play**, or to play a track over and over. Some offer **music sampling.** A few even come with a **remote control.** A few have **lighted displays,** helpful if the player is used in the car or other dark places.

A **car kit,** standard with many models, is an option on many others. It consists of an adapter that powers the unit through a car's cigarette lighter and a cassette adapter that pipes the player's sound into a car's tape player and, from there, into its amplifier and out the speakers. Our tests found most worked well, though on a few the cassette adapter added background noise or compromised a player's otherwise good performance. (You can also buy retrofit kits at electronics or auto-supply stores.)

A **line-out jack** is a better choice than the headphone jack when connecting a portable to other gear.

How to choose

Performance differences. Virtually any CD player can produce superb hi-fi sound—accurate and free of coloration or distortion. The sound reproduction differences that we've found in our years of testing are apparent only to a trained listener or a laboratory instrument. One big difference, however, is how well the players handle adverse conditions, like being bumped or playing a damaged disc.

Advertising for portable players often implies that a special memory feature called a "buffer" will prevent skipping. Ranging from 10- to 40-second capacities, a buffer scans the disc, continuously storing more music so it can "fill" if a bump throws the player off. However, our tests show that what's needed instead is a player design that helps prevent movement from disrupting the reading of data from the disc. Without such good design, even the longest buffer can smooth out only occasional bumps, not the more typical constant jolts.

What to spend. You needn't spend a lot to get a very good CD player, component, or portable. Cost reflects the number of features you get, not performance. Among component models, prices track with disc capacity, with single-disc models the cheapest and high-capacity jukeboxes the most expensive. Expect to spend less than $100 for a basic portable, $20 to $25 more for one with a car kit.

MINISYSTEMS

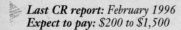

***Last CR report:** February 1996*
***Expect to pay:** $200 to $1,500*

A minisystem offers ease of use and reasonably good overall performance without the cost, clutter, and wiring headaches of a component sound system. It's also an easy, fairly inexpensive way to convert your TV into a small home theater.

These bookshelf-sized systems usually come with a remote control and the following components: a digital AM/FM tuner powered by an amplifier, which can vary from less than 20 watts per channel to more than 100; a CD changer that holds 3, 6, or even 50 discs; a dual-well cassette deck; and small detachable speakers.

However, you can't upgrade most systems with bigger speakers or other components. Nor does a minisystem allow you to add a second pair of speakers to send music to another room.

What's available

Sony, Aiwa, and JVC are the biggest-selling brands of minisystems.

Most minisystems have cabinets that measure about 11 inches wide and 14 inches high, with a molded facade that looks like several individual components in a stack, though most are one unit. (Standard-sized components are 17 inches wide.) A few minisystems are truly separate components; others can be divided in two and placed side by side on a shelf.

More compact minisystems, or microsystems, are as narrow as ½ inch. Price range: $200 to $1,500.

Key features

Minisystems have many of the same features found in full-sized components and rack systems—although controls are more integrated and displays are often more vivid, even hyperactive. These systems also add some capabilities of their own.

A **clock** lets you program the system to turn on at a predetermined time. Some systems allow you to set the cassette deck to record from the radio, just as you time-shift with a VCR. The **remote control** is usually simply designed, but buttons often perform two or more functions, sometimes confusingly. And there are no buttons to work video components, such as those on component receivers' remotes. **Karaoke capability** allows users to hear and record themselves singing along to specially made CDs that play without the vocal track.

How to choose

Performance differences. Even the best minisystems are apt to be a notch below low-priced component systems in quality because of subpar speakers and cassette decks. Adjustable bass and treble controls can help overcome some speaker defects, but many minisystems lack them.

Look for features you need, including amplifier power. Minisystems are often not capable of filling even a moderate-sized room with sound. A large living room (15 by 25 feet or more) needs 80 to 100 watts per channel; an average living room (10 by 25 feet) requires 40 to 80 watts per channel; and a bedroom or dorm room (12 by 14 feet), 20 to 40 watts per channel.

Decide what to spend. Minisystems costing less than $300 are little more than glorified boom boxes. Systems in the $350 to $500 price range begin to look and feel more like hi-fi separates. They typically include a CD changer, a receiver with more power (20 to 50 watts per channel), and a good complement of features.

SPEAKERS

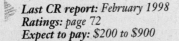

Last CR report: *February 1998*
Ratings: *page 72*
Expect to pay: *$200 to $900*

Good speakers are the key to good sound. And, fortunately, impressive-sounding ones don't have to be expensive.

Your listening needs will determine what kind of speakers to get. You'll find speakers marketed in two ways: as pairs or sets of audio speakers for traditional stereophonic listening; and singly, or in sets of three or five video speakers, for equipping a home theater. (Video speakers typically have magnetic shielding so they can be close to a TV screen without the magnets at their core distorting the TV picture.)

What's available

Of the hundreds of speaker brands on the market, Bose is the biggest seller. The story of speakers in recent years has been good performance in smaller and smaller sizes. For all but audiophiles (and conspicuous pretenders), the following types of speakers should more than satisfy most listeners:

Bookshelf. Speakers in this class can

reproduce sound reasonably accurately but won't deliver much bass or fill a large room with loud sound. They're fine for a medium-sized room or as the rear speakers in a home-theater setup. Price range: $200 to $300.

Conventional speakers. These will reproduce sound very accurately and deliver plenty of bass. Although not huge, speakers in this strata may nevertheless dominate the decor in some rooms. Price range: $300 to $600.

Three-piece speaker systems. This system performs on a par with conventional mid-priced speakers but is much less obtrusive. It consists of two small satellite speakers for the left and right treble and midrange sounds, and a larger, separate bass module for the woofer that can be kept out of sight. The satellites are small and light, so they can be wall-mounted or put on a shelf. You can use all three pieces for an audio setup alone or as the main speakers for a home theater.

A few companies prepackage their systems, but most satellites and bass units are sold separately. Price range: $300 to $600.

How to choose

Key characteristics. Power and controls. Most speakers need only to be connected to the receiver, with no need for electrical power or controls. But many satellite systems are active units, with an AC-powered amplifier to drive the bass module.

Whether a system is active or passive (no amplifier) makes no difference to the quality of the sound. Active systems do draw less power from the receiver, which allows you to drive speakers with a lower-powered receiver than would otherwise be required. These systems have one or more controls on the bass module, which you can usually set once and then leave alone.

Impedance. This term describes the speaker's resistance to electric current from the receiver. Though unrelated to sound quality, impedance matters because it determines a speaker's compatibility with a particular receiver. Some receivers may overheat when powering low-impedance speakers of 4 or 5 ohms. If you're considering low-impedance speakers, check your receiver's instruction manual or back panel for its impedance recommendations, to insure compatibility. If you choose to try low-impedance speakers with a receiver not recommended for use with 4-ohm speakers, periodically check that the receiver cabinet doesn't get too hot, especially if it's playing loudly.

Performance differences. Our tests show that, except for the bass part of the sound spectrum, even inexpensive speakers can reproduce sound accurately. But since even models of equal accuracy will sound different, listen to speakers before you buy. At the least, make sure you can return or exchange the speakers if they don't sound as good at home as you expected or heard in the showroom.

If you can audition speakers in a listening room at the store, compare only two pairs at a time and make sure they're equally loud; each time, judge the pair you prefer against the next pair. Take along a recording you know well that gives the bass and treble ranges a good workout.

What to spend. For a budget system, you may not want to spend more than $200 per pair or set, especially if your music isn't bass-heavy. Spending $300 to $600 buys speakers that should satisfy most listeners, even in the bass. Spending more—$700 to $900—buys the ability to play louder, and a nicer cabinet, but that's it.

For home-theater speakers, a center-channel speaker or pair of surround speakers costs $80 to $250; three-piece sets range from $100 to $300. In general, we've found that price correlates with accurate sound reproduction.

RECEIVERS

***Last CR report:** February 1998*
***Ratings:** page 75*
***Expect to pay:** $200 to $500*

The receiver is the brain of an audio/video system, providing AM and FM tuners, an amplifier, and switching capabilities. Also standard equipment: the connections to accommodate a CD player, a cassette deck, a turntable, two pairs of speakers, and the audio signal from a TV or VCR. Today's audio receivers can deliver an accurate frequency response (essential for the faithful reproduction of music) and enough power to fill an average-sized living room with sound.

In the past few years, however, we've noticed slippage in quality across the board in most of the receivers we've tested. We also noted many shortcomings in convenience and ease of use, such as eliminating certain controls and displays and having the remaining ones do double duty.

What's available

Receivers sell under more than 30 brand names. Five companies—Sony, Pioneer, Kenwood, Technics, and JVC—sell more than 80 percent of the models.

Stereo only. These receivers provide two channels that power a pair of stereo speakers. Price: for a respectable stereo-only model, less than $200. (Adding a tape deck or CD player and two speakers is all you need to enjoy recorded music and radio broadcasts, and system setup is fairly simple.)

Dolby Pro Logic. These receivers can decode the additional center and surround channels encoded on the stereo tracks of many movies and TV shows. They can feed five loudspeakers with four channels of audio—one each to the left and right speakers, which provide the main sound; one to the center speaker, which generally handles dialogue; and one to both rear speakers, which provide ambience. Price: Very good Pro Logic receivers sell for less than $400, some for less than $200. (Prices have been dropping.)

Dolby Digital Surround. Also known as AC-3, this is a six-channel system, adding separate channels for each rear speaker and for a subwoofer. To get the true impact from this type of system, you'd want to use a DVD player or other digital video source—along with top-notch speakers.

Both Dolby Pro Logic and Digital Surround put you in the middle of the action, with sounds seeming to move from side to side and front to rear. The three front speakers follow action across the screen, the center speaker plays most of the dialogue. Two rear speakers add sounds behind you—crowd noises, action sounds—and this ambient sound moves from side to side as well. Digital Surround also can accommodate a powered subwoofer that can provide low-frequency sound. Price range: $400 to $500.

Key features

Controls and outputs should be easy to use. None are—but some are much worse than others. Look for a front panel layout that groups displays and controls by function and provides clear labels. Clear labeling and logical grouping of the many jacks on the receiver's rear panel can help avert many setup glitches such as reversed speaker polarities and mixed-up inputs and outputs.

Many **remote controls** were better in years past. Clear labels and different-shaped and color-coded buttons grouped by function are the seldom-achieved goal.

Digital radio tuning is now standard, along with features such as **seek** (automatic searching for the next listenable station) and 20 to 40 **presets** to call up your favorite stations at the touch of a button. To catch stations too weak to pick up in the seek mode, most receivers also have a **manual stepping** knob or buttons. It's convenient in one-channel increments, but most models creep in half- or quarter-steps, meaning a lot of unnecessary button taps. **Direct frequency radio-tuning** lets you enter a station's frequency on a keypad.

Tone controls let you adjust bass and treble. Easiest to use are knobs—one for bass and one for treble. A **graphic equalizer** breaks the sound spectrum into more sections, conferring either greater control or greater confusion, depending on the receiver design and your mechanical aptitude. It's not much more effective than **bass and treble controls** unless it has at least seven frequency bands. Instead of tone controls, some receivers come with "tone styles" such as jazz, classical, or rock, each accentuating a different frequency pattern; often you can craft your own styles, too. Since tone controls are most useful in correcting for room acoustics and listening preferences, not musical genre, the tone-style approach seems needlessly indirect.

How to choose

Performance differences. In recent tests, none of the receivers met our criteria for overall excellence. But all were at least good, with ample power to drive two speakers to very loud levels. None provided excellent FM reception, which is easily attainable with today's technology. Many models scored only fair on AM reception, and some were poor. When you spend a few hundred dollars, the FM tuner should be top-notch, and the AM tuner should work better than a cheap portable radio.

What to spend. Unless you intend to incorporate video components, a stereo-only system is all you need. Almost all CD discs, tape cassettes, and radio broadcasts are produced for just two channels.

Upgrading to a full-fledged home theater, whether Pro Logic or Digital Surround, requires five or six speakers. But you needn't buy the complete system all at once. A subwoofer is optional with both Pro Logic and Digital Surround. A Dolby 3 stereo setting eliminates the need for the rear speakers. A Dolby phantom mode redirects the center speaker's to channel to the front right and left sides, so you can manage without the center speaker. These are compromises—but still better than plain stereo.

Investing in Digital Surround may be premature right now. Despite the superb sound, the price and complexity, the uncertainty of future programming, and the video-disc format complications all say wait and see.

TV SETS

> ***Last CR report:** March 1998*
> ***Ratings:** pages 78 & 81*
> ***Expect to pay:** $100 to $8,500*

The choice in TV sets has never been more varied—nor confusing. It isn't just set size. It's sweeping technology changes. Your TV may also function as a display monitor for the Internet, electronic mail, or other services. TV signals are received in traditional analog form via antenna or a cable connection—and they may also be beamed digitally to a satellite dish or piped digitally to a special cable box. With the coming of digital TV transmissions, an image will be dramatically sharper than what you get today—that is, if you buy a new TV set with an entirely different screen shape.

As if selecting a TV set isn't challenge enough, manufacturers and retailers are reducing both the number of models they offer and the available inventory. As a result, the fall and early winter are the best buying seasons. In spring and summer, manufacturers are readying their new models and the supply of TV sets tends to be tight.

There are, however, some encouraging trends for consumers:

• Lower prices for larger sets. TV sets have never been better or cheaper than they are today. In most size categories, good or better performance is the norm, and your choice of model may be driven most by the special features you want or need. In particular, prices are dropping for larger sets, especially those in the 32-inch size.

• Better features for less money. Comb filter, picture-in-picture, on-screen menus, MTS stereo—once found on top-of-the-line models—are now common on smaller and less expensive sets.

What's available

Small sets. Sets with a 13-inch screen are deemed as "second" sets, usually equipped with only monophonic sound and sparse features. Price range: $100 to $400.

Those with a 19- or 20-inch screen are also often considered second sets. Most lack high-end picture refinements such as a comb filter (which can largely eliminate extraneous colors, increasing visible detail). Models with stereo sound usually have extra inputs for plugging in a VCR or a laser-disc or digital video disc player, but sound is usually only mediocre. Price range: $150 to $500.

Midsized sets. Sets with a 27-inch screen, once considered large, are now called "standard size." Those with a 25-inch screen are their economy-minded cousins. Sets with a 27-inch screen are usually priced higher and frequently offer more features, including picture-in-picture, special sound systems, a universal remote control and, commonly, a comb filter. Price range: $350 to $600.

Large sets. Sets with 32-inch screens represent the entry level for big-screen TV. For proper viewing, you'll need about 10 feet of space from the screen to the seating. The largest direct-view sets (36-inch sets and up) can weigh hundreds of pounds, and are too wide and too high for conventional component shelving. Price range: $600 to $3,000.

Projection sets. These offer 40 to 80 diagonal inches of picture area but typically can't match the quality of a conventional picture tube. You'll want a viewing distance of about 15 feet for a 50-inch set, even more for larger ones. Brightness and, to some extent, color vary at the sides of the screen. Large sets and rear-projection sets come with plenty of features, such as ambient sound and custom settings. Price range: $1,500 to $8,500.

Key features

Virtually all TV sets have a **remote control** that lets you change channels, adjust sound volume, and fiddle with color balance. These features aren't yet universal: **Stereo sound** is virtually required for use with a home-theater setup but of little use if you're using only the set's built-in speakers. **Audio output jacks** let you connect the audio signal to a receiver or external speakers a must for top-quality sound. **Surround sound** is typically a simulated effect you may like or not. A **comb filter,** more common in large-screen sets, increases apparent picture detail and minimizes extraneous colors. **Video input jacks** are useful to plug in a camcorder or video game (front-mounted jacks make that the easiest) and to improve picture quality somewhat by connecting the set to, say, a VCR or cable box with the video jack rather than the standard coaxial cable jack. **Flesh-tone correction** can be set to automatically adjust color balance for Caucasian skin tones that are too green or red. Another feature, **white-balance**, lets you shade the picture toward the blue or red.

TV features that are useful to some people but won't necessarily improve the set's performance: A **universal remote** lets you control all or most of your video (and some audio) devices with one remote. Some sets have a "smart" version, so you don't have to enter a code for each device. (You can buy this remote separately for about $20.) **Picture-in-picture,** more common in larger sets, lets you watch two channels at once—one on a small picture inserted in the full-screen one. Unless the set has two tuners (more common in expensive sets), you have to connect to the tuner in a VCR or cable box to use PIP. A **commercial-skip timer** can spare you from commercials by switching to another channel for selected time periods, in 30-second increments, after which the set goes back to the original channel. **Automatic volume control** at least compensates for the volume jump when the commercials start (or when you change channels). All sets have manual **closed-captioning,** but **closed captioning when muted** automatically displays the dialogue on-screen while the sound is muted—say, so you can answer the phone. **Handles** on 13- to 27-inch sets make carrying the set easier if you'll carry something weighing upwards of 40 pounds. A **headphone jack** lets you watch silently.

Separate audio program lets you receive a second soundtrack, typically in another language, along with multilingual menus. With **channel blockout,** parents can render selected channels inaccessible to a child. (On a few sets, you can watch blocked channels without the remote, not so good if you misplace it.) The long-heralded V-chip, due to arrive in 1999, will go further by letting you block specific shows. An **S-video input jack** can take advantage of the superior picture quality from a high-band camcorder or VCR or from a digital source such as a satellite-dish system or digital cable box. **Video noise reduction** lowers the picture-degrading noise that comes from poor reception, interference, or other signal problems.

More flash than true utility: **Active-channel scan** starts the set surfing through the channels automatically, pausing at each for a few seconds, until you stop it. When you see a show you want, you stop scanning. Sets with **preference**

programming remember a second viewer's audio or video preferences; he or she punches one button instead of several. **Channel labeling** lets you enter a channel's name (say, ESPN, CNN, MTV) so you'll know you've landed on it when you change channels. If you use a universal remote, **auto code-entry** can be a marginal labor-saver; instead of punching in a code for each device you want the universal remote to operate, the remote searches for the device's code by itself.

How to choose

Performance differences. Our tests show such improved picture quality that most sets deliver good images. Sound quality varies more—in general, as the set gets bigger, sound gets better. (A hookup to external speakers or a home theater improves sound.)

What to spend. The best value for basic, midsized TV sets are 25-inch models, which sell for as little as $200 (mono) or $250 (stereo). Such sets are relatively inexpensive, in part, because they often lack many features common on 27-inch models. But to get a high-quality picture and many useful features, a 27-inch model offers the best deal.

You can buy a 31- or 32-inch set for less than $600. Spend more and you get picture-in-picture (PIP) and sound-enhancing features. For $1,000 and up, you may add such features as a higher-grade picture tube and a more advanced type of comb filter.

VCRs

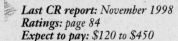

Last CR report: *November 1998*
Ratings: *page 84*
Expect to pay: *$120 to $450*

Basic capabilities haven't changed much in recent years, so manufacturers have been adding features, many aimed at ease of use. Even mid-line models are loaded with things like hi-fi audio, VCR Plus, and auto clock set. VCRs with four video heads, allowing cleaner-looking freeze-frames, are now the norm.

What's available

RCA and Magnavox are the biggest-selling brands. Magnavox, the best-selling low-end brand, is likely to be available from mass merchandisers and price clubs. Sony tends to price its products on the high side, as do some smaller brands such as Mitsubishi.

Almost all VCRs sold are VHS models. Other formats—8mm, S-VHS, Hi8—are scarce (only Sony currently offers Hi8 VCRs). Monophonic models record sound decently and typically cost $100 to $200. For little more—$140 to $450—hi-fi VCRs record near-CD quality sound.

Key features

All VCRs can be programmed via on-screen menus. **VCR Plus,** developed as a separate product, is now featured on many models that cost $20 to $50 extra. You use the remote to enter a program code found in TV listings. VCR Plus automatically switches to the set channel at the set time. If you use a cable box and want to program your VCR to record shows on more than one channel, without your intervention, you'll need a

cable channel changer, sometimes called C^3. Typically, an enhancement to VCR Plus, called **VCR Plus with C^3,** will also control a cable box and aid in recording. **Plug and play** automatically sets the channels and the time as soon as you plug in the VCR and attach it to a cable or antenna.

A universal remote, which works TV sets, VCRs, and cable boxes of various brands, is now common. A VCR universal remote features tape controls; channel selection is secondary.

Auto clock set adjusts the VCR's clock from broadcast signals. Some models have an **automatic Daylight Savings control**; others can add or subtract one hour at the press of a button.

Commercial Advance, a feature found on some General Electric, Hitachi, Panasonic, ProScan, and RCA models, lets the VCR bypass all commercials during playback by locating and fast-forwarding past such "cues" as fades-to-black and changes in sound level. **Go-to** searches the tape by time to find the passage you want to watch. **Index search** places an electronic "bookmark" on the tape each time you begin to record so the VCR can quickly skip to that segment on playback. **One-button skip** lets you fast-forward 30 seconds or a minute with each press of the

OTHER WAYS TO PLAY A MOVIE

Videotape, like cassette tape or vinyl platters, is an analog medium. Played in even the best VCR, it cannot match the picture quality of digital media. There are two, one coming and one fading:

DVD. This type has the potential to do for prerecorded movies what the CD did for music. These discs can contain far more data than a CD. For now, you can only play back DVDs; recordable discs are still not widely available. Picture quality is excellent, we've found in our tests—the best of any format currently available on the consumer market—flaws are difficult to detect, and picture resolution was far superior to conventional VHS videotape.

DVD is used for prerecorded movies and as a high-capacity storage medium for computers (DVD once stood for "digital video disc, nomenclature that became obsolete after the technology was used by computers). DVD-ROMs are now included in many PCs instead of the older CD-ROMS. DVD recorders are available for computer use. (The recorders are very new, expensive, and largely incompatible with each other.)

Nor has the technology settled down in DVD's home-entertainment incarnation. DivX, introduced this year, is a pay-per-play version of DVD being pushed by Circuit City, the big electronics chain, and others. DivX is designed mainly for video renters, not video collectors. In this system, you keep the DVD you buy, but it won't play after a certain amount of time. DivX players will be able to play current DVD movies, but current DVD players won't be able to play DivX fare.

Either DVD format is designed to make excellent use of a home-theater setup. The discs have a Dolby AC-3 soundtrack that splits sound into five full-range discrete channels plus a deep-bass channel. To get the full benefit of movie sound effects, you need an AC-3 stereo receiver.

button. **Auto rewind** automatically rewinds the tape when it reaches the end, and **auto speed-switching** slows recording from SP to EP if too little tape is left to complete a programmed recording.

A **dimming display** turns down the console's display brightness. **Front-mounted audio and video jacks** allow quick-and-easy hookup of a camcorder, a second VCR, or a video game. **Quasi S-VHS playback** lets you play higher-resolution S-VHS tapes but without improved S-VHS picture quality.

Useful in editing tapes: **Audio dub** lets you add music or narration to existing recordings. A **flying erase head** lets you insert segments without noticeable video glitches. A **jog-shuttle** is a two-part control—one part to let you shuttle quickly, the other to slowly jog frame by frame.

Auto head-cleaning is not worth the extra money. Machines without it have worked fine for thousands of hours.

How to choose

Performance differences. Expect good picture quality. But features vary widely. Decide what you want, and resist the temptation to buy more than you need. Paying more does not necessarily buy a better picture, although it buys

---

Sound quality is top-notch—what you'd expect from digital recording. Players let you also play audio CDs; a few even play laser discs as well.

Standard features on DVD players include: *Quick searching* in "chapters," listed on the movie jacket, that allow you to skip forward or back rapidly. *Multiple-screen formats* that allow you to view a movie in both "standard" (an aspect ratio—picture width to height—of 4:3) and "widescreen" (16:9) formats. The widescreen version, which appears letterboxed on a regular TV set, more closely matches the proportions of movie screens and DTV sets. *Parental control codes* prevent movies with certain ratings form being played back.

DVD players now cost about twice as much as a good hi-fi VCR. You'll also have to spend over $600 for a new Dolby Digital receiver or AC-3 receivers. Movies on DVD are becoming more plentiful after a slow start. Discs are priced at $10 to $30.

Laser disc. These players can provide better picture quality than a VCR, but their inability to record and the lack of a disc-rental market has kept them from being much more than a specialty item for movie buffs. The discs themselves are double-sided and come in two formats: *Constant angular velocity (CAV)* allows very stable, noise-free slow motion and still frames but needs two discs to hold a full-length movie. *Constant linear velocity (CLV)* requires a premium player for still frames but can get a whole movie on one disc. Players can often play both types, as well as audio compact discs, and "CD videos" (CD-Vs).

There are not many laser disc players in this fading market. The ones that are left are priced at $400 to $1,000. Features that add to the price include the ability to play both sides of one disc automatically, special effects, digital frame storage, and video game capability. The newer laser-disc players can supply the signal needed to reproduce Dolby AC-3 sound.

conveniences like VCR Plus.

What to spend. A basic VCR is sufficient for taping TV programs for viewing later. For watching stereo movies, choose a hi-fi model—well worth the extra $10 to $40 if you connect it to a stereo system or TV with great sound. If you have trouble programming a VCR, consider VCR Plus, a programming aid for $20 to $50 extra.

HOW TO USE THE RATINGS

- Read the Recommendations for information on specific models and general buying advice.
- Note how the rated products are listed—in order of performance and convenience, price, or alphabetically.
- The overall score graph gives the big picture in performance. Notes on features and performance for individual models are listed in the "Comments" column or "Details on the models."
- Use the key numbers to locate the details on each model.
- Before going to press, we verify model availability for most products with manufacturers. Some tested models listed in the Ratings may no longer be available. Discontinued models are noted in "Comments" or "Details on the models." Such models may still be available in some stores for part of 1999. Models indicated as successors should perform similarly to the tested models, according to the manufacturer. Features may vary.
- Models similar to the tested models, when they exist, are indicated in "Comments" or "Details on the models."
- The original date of publication is noted for each Ratings.

Ratings *Camcorders*

& Recommendations

The tests behind the Ratings

Overall score is based on picture and sound quality at the standard (SP) speed, as well as ease of use. **Picture** scores are based on judgments of trained viewers. The judgments cover picture clarity and color accuracy. **Audio** scores measure accuracy and degree of flutter, using each camcorder's built-in microphone. For both picture and audio, the standard rating is for the SP speed; the slow rating is for the slow speed. **Ease of use** covers design and placement of controls, clarity of operating menus, removing battery and tape, and battery life. **Price** is the estimated average, based on a survey.

Typical features for these models

• Variable-speed zoom. • Automatic and manual focus. • Tally light. • Tape counter. • Image stabilizer • Quick review of just-taped footage. • Audio fade, video fade, or both. • Built-in titling. • Backlight compensation. • Warranty of 12 months on parts and CCD (the image sensor), 3 months on labor.

Recommendations

The digital Sony DCR-PC10 delivered the best image, but it's still extremely expensive (it's been discontinued but is still available, according to the manufacturer). Less expensive but also capable of excellent image quality were the digital Panasonic PV-DV710 and the Hi8 Sony CCD TRV65. The Panasonic PV-D308, $490, is a very good value and would be just fine for documenting one's life. Panasonic has also been among the more reliable brands of camcorders.

See report, page 39. Last time rated in CONSUMER REPORTS: October 1998.

Overall Ratings

E VG G F P

Listed in order of overall score

Key no.	Brand and model	Price	Overall score (0–100; P F G VG E)	Picture STANDARD	Picture SLOW	Audio STANDARD	Audio SLOW	Ease of use
	DIGITAL CAMCORDERS							
1	**Sony** DCR-PC10	$2,700		E	E	G	G	G
2	**Panasonic** PV-DV710	2,000		E	E	VG	VG	G
	ANALOG CAMCORDERS							
3	**Sony** CCD-TRV65	780		E	G	VG	VG	VG
4	**Panasonic** PV-D308	490		VG	G	F	P	E
5	**Panasonic** PV-L658	680		VG	G	F	P	VG

Ratings continued

Key no.	Brand and model	Price	Overall score (0–100; P F G VG E)	Picture STANDARD	Picture SLOW	Audio STANDARD	Audio SLOW	Ease of use
	ANALOG CAMCORDERS *continued*							
6	**Sony** CCD-TRV25	$ 680		○	●	⊖	⊖	⊖
7	**Sharp** VL-E665U	550		○	—	○	—	⊖
8	**Hitachi** VM-E540A	500		○	—	⊖	—	○
9	**JVC** GR-AX930U	530		○	○	○	●	○
10	**RCA** Pro-V730	450		○	—	○	—	○
11	**Sony** CCD-TR67	490		○	●	⊖	⊖	⊖
12	**JVC** GR-AX430U	400		○	◒	○	◒	○
13	**Canon** ES970	570		○	—	○	—	⊖

Details on the models

Digital camcorders

1 Sony DCR-PC10 $2,700

• MiniDV • SP, LP speeds • 12:1 zoom • 1½ lb. • Color eyepiece viewfinder plus 2.5-in. color panel viewfinder • Battery life, 50 to 85 min.

Effective image stabilizer. Can capture still images. **But:** Lens cap is tethered, not built-in. **Features:** Stereo audio, built-in titling, manual focus and white balance, audio and video fades. **Availability:** Discontinued, but may still be available. **Recommendation:** Excellent overall. The best picture we tested, but also the most expensive camcorder.

2 Panasonic PV-DV710 $2,000

• MiniDV • SP, LP speeds • 10:1 zoom • 2 lb. • Color eyepiece viewfinder plus 3.8-in. color panel viewfinder • Battery life, 85 to 120 min.

Effective image stabilizer. Can capture still images. **But:** Lens cap is tethered, not built-in. Has only 6-mo. warranty on CCD. **Features:** Stereo audio, microphone jack, manual shutter speed, manual focus, manual white balance, audio and video fades. **Recommendation:** Very good but expensive.

Analog camcorders

3 Sony CCD-TRV65 $780

• Hi8 • SP, LP speeds • 18:1 zoom • 2¼ lb. • Black-and-white eyepiece viewfinder plus 2.5-in. color panel viewfinder • Battery life, 120 to 150 min.

Effective image stabilizer. Can use six AA batteries for alternative power. Records black-and-white picture without light (zero lux). **Features:** Stereo audio, microphone jack, built-in titling, manual shutter speed, manual focus, audio and video fades. **Recommendation:** Very good overall. Comparable to (2), but much less expensive.

4 Panasonic PV-D308 $490

• VHS-C • SP, EP speeds • 23:1 zoom • 2¾ lb. • Color eyepiece viewfinder only • Battery life, 235 min.

Makes good images in low light. **But:** Image stabilizer not very effective. Has only 6-mo. warranty on CCD. **Features:** Built-in titling, manual shutter speed, manual focus, audio and video fades. **Similar model:** PV-A208, $430. **Recommendation:** Good overall, and moderately priced.

5 Panasonic PV-L658 $680

• VHS-C • SP, EP speeds • 23:1 zoom • 3¼ lb. • Black-and-white eyepiece viewfinder plus 3.2-in. color panel viewfinder • Battery life, 145 to 210 min.

Makes good images in low light. **But:** Image stabilizer not very effective. Has only 6-mo. warranty on CCD. **Features:** Microphone jack, built-in titling, manual shutter speed, manual focus, built-in light, video fade. **Similar model:** PV-L558, $590. **Recommendation:** Good overall.

6 Sony CCD-TRV25 $680

• 8mm • SP, LP speeds • 16:1 zoom • 2¼ lb. • Black-and-white eyepiece viewfinder plus 2.5-in. color panel viewfinder • Battery life, 115 to 125 min.
Effective image stabilizer. Can use six AA batteries for alternative power. **Features:** Built-in titling, microphone jack. **Recommendation:** Good overall.

7 Sharp VL-E665U $550

• 8mm • SP speed • 16:1 zoom • 2 lb. • 3-in. color panel viewfinder only • Battery life, 125 min.
Image stabilizer somewhat effective. Can capture still images. **But:** Audible motor noise in audio track. Only one recording speed. Lens cap is tethered, not built-in. Only 3-mo. warranty on parts, CCD, labor. **Features:** Built-in titling, manual focus, audio and video fades. **Recommendation:** Good overall.

8 Hitachi VM-E540A $500

• 8mm • SP speed • 16:1 zoom • 2 lb. • Color eyepiece viewfinder only • Battery life, 125 min.
Image stabilizer somewhat effective. Makes good images in low light. **But:** Lacks slow recording speed and multispeed zoom. **Features:** Manual focus, audio and video fades. **Recommendation:** Good overall.

9 JVC GR-AX930U $530

• VHS-C • SP, EP speeds • 22:1 zoom • 2½ lb. • Color eyepiece viewfinder only • Battery life, 90 min.
Picture jitter may be distracting. Image stabilizer not very effective. **Features:** Full auto switch, built-in titling, manual shutter speed, manual focus, manual white balance, built-in light, video fade. **Recommendation:** Good overall.

10 RCA Pro-V 730 $450

• 8mm • SP speed • 16:1 zoom • 2¼ lb. • Black-and-white eyepiece viewfinder plus 2.9-in. color panel viewfinder • Battery life, 110 to 135 min.
Lacks slow recording speed, multispeed zoom, image stabilizer. **Features:** Manual focus, audio and video fades. **Similar model:** Pro-V742, $700. **Recommendation:** Good overall.

11 Sony CCD-TR67 $490

• 8mm • SP, LP speeds • 16:1 zoom • 2 lb. • Color eyepiece viewfinder only • Battery life, 105 min.
Makes good images in low light. Can use six AA batteries as alternative power. **But:** Lacks image stabilizer. **Features:** Microphone jack, full auto switch, built-in titling, built-in light. **Recommendation:** Good overall.

12 JVC GR-AX430U $400

• VHS-C • SP, EP speeds • 22:1 zoom • 2¼ lb. • Color eyepiece viewfinder only • Battery life, 75 min.
Picture jitter may be distracting. Poor low-light performance. Lacks image stabilizer. **Features:** Full auto switch, built-in titling, manual shutter speed, manual focus, manual white balance, audio and video fades. **Recommendation:** Good overall.

13 Canon ES970 $570

• 8mm • SP speed • 22:1 zoom • 2¼ lb. • Color eyepiece viewfinder only • Battery life, 65 min.
Effective image stabilizer. **But:** Lacks slow recording speed. Poor low-light performance. Lens cap is tethered, not built-in. **Features:** Stereo audio, microphone jack, full auto switch, manual shutter speed, manual focus, manual white balance, audio and video fades. **Recommendation:** Good overall, but some noticeable drawbacks. There are better values.

Ratings *Compact cameras*

& Recommendations

The tests behind the Ratings

The **overall score** is based on performance and convenience. Differences of less than 15 points were judged not significant. **Weight** includes batteries and film. **Focal length:** A 30-60-mm APS zoom gives coverage similar to that of a 40-to-80-mm 35mm zoom. **Image quality** is based on image sharpness and freedom from flare, from distortion, and from chromatic aberration. **Film handling** is the ease of loading and unloading. **Flash range** is the maximum distance with ISO 100 print film. **Pocketability** indicates compactness. **Price** is approximate retail.

Typical features for these models

For 35mm and APS models: • Automatic fim loading and handling. • Autofocus. • Autoexposure. • Automatic film-speed setting. • Focus hold. • Exposure lock. • Built-in flash with fill-flash capability and red-eye reduction. • Self-timer. **Except as noted, all have:** • A slowest shutter speed of ¼ second or longer. • Built-in lens cover. **For 35mm models:** • Warning if subject is too close. • Window that shows the type of film. **For APS models:** • Easy automatic film loading • Choice of three print shapes, which can be switched in mid-roll. • Date and time recording on film. • Lack window for checking film type.

Recommendations

Among 35mm models, the Olympus LT Zoom 105, $305, is an excellent but expensive choice. Among nonzoom 35mm models, the Yashica T4 Super Weatherproof, $200, from a previous report is still the top choice. Among nonzoom APS models, the Kodak Advantix 3700ix , $120, and Konica Super Big Mini BM-S100, $110, are excellent choices. The Canon Elph 490Z, $380, is an excellent but expensive zoom. A less expensive alternative is the Vivitar Z360ix, $120.

See report, page 41. Last time rated in CONSUMER REPORTS: November 1997.

Overall Ratings

E = Excellent, VG = Very good, G = Good, F = Fair, P = Poor

Listed in order of overall score

Key no.	Brand and model	Price	Overall score (0–100; P F G VG E)	Weight	Focal length(s)	Image quality	Film handling	Flash range	Pocketability
	COMPACT 35mm MODELS								
1	**Olympus** LT Zoom 105	$335		10oz.	38-105 mm	E	VG	14 ft.	VG
2	**Canon** Sure Shot 105 Zoom	200		10	38-105	E	VG	16	VG
3	**Ricoh** RZ105SF (zoom)	90		12	38-105	E	VG	12	G

Key no.	Brand and model	Price	Overall score (0–100: P F G VG E)	Weight	Focal length(s)	Image quality	Film handling	Flash range	Pocket-ability
	COMPACT 35mm MODELS *continued*								
4	**Leica** Mini 3	$190		7 oz.	32 mm	⊜	○	11 ft.	⊜
5	**Fujifilm** Discovery 290 Zoom	140		10	38-90	⊖	⊖	12	○
6	**Pentax** IQZoom 90MC	190		8	38-90	⊖	⊖	12	⊖
7	**Samsung** Maxima Evoca 115 (zoom)	200		11	38-115	⊖	⊖	16	⊖
8	**Yashica** Microtec Zoom 90	200		11	38-90	⊖	⊖	15	⊖
	COMPACT APS MODELS								
9	**Kodak** Advantix 3700ix	120		7	24	⊖	⊜	10	⊜
10	**Canon** Elph 490Z (zoom)	380		11	22.5-90	⊖	⊜	11	⊖
11	**Konica** Super Big Mini BM-S100	110		6	28	⊖	⊖	11	⊜
12	**Nikon** Nuvis 125 i (zoom)	280		10	30-100	⊖	⊜	11	⊖
13	**Vivitar** Z360ix (zoom)	120		7	30-60	⊖	⊖	13	⊜
14	**Fujifilm** Endeavor 400ix Zoom	360		9	25-100	⊖	⊜	9	⊖
15	**Minolta** Vectis 40 (zoom)	370		12	30-120	⊖	⊖	18	◒
16	**Minox** CD 25	110		6	25	⊖	⊖	8	⊜
17	**Yashica** Acclaim 100	95		6	25	⊖	⊖	8	⊜
18	**Fujifilm** Endeavor 100	90		6	25	⊖	⊖	8	⊜
19	**Nikon** Nuvis Mini i	140		6	25	⊖	⊖	8	⊜
20	**Olympus** Newpic AF200	80		7	27	⊖	⊖	5	⊜

Details on the models

Framing accuracy is the percentage of the actual picture area you see in the viewfinder. Above 80 percent is reasonably accurate. **Smallest field** is the width of the smallest subject that fills the frame at the closest regular (not macro) focus; the smaller the better for tight close-ups.

35mm models

1 Olympus LT Zoom 105 $335

• Framing accuracy: 82% • Smallest field: 5 in. A fine zoom model, light and compact. **Features:** Choice of panoramic or regular format pictures. Optional wireless shutter release. Spot-metering mode. Weatherproof. Has date/time imprinting. **Recommendation:** An excellent but expensive choice in a zoom model.

2 Canon Sure Shot 105 Zoom $200

• Framing accuracy: 86% • Smallest field: 7 in. A fine zoom model, light and compact. **Features:** Versatile multiarea autofocus. **But:** Flash illuminates less uniformly than most. Self-timer doesn't cancel automatically. **Recommendation:** An excellent choice in a zoom model.

3 Ricoh RZ105SF $190

• Framing accuracy: 83% • Smallest field: 7 in. A zoom model. **Features:** Warns when subject exceeds flash range. Choice of panoramic or regular format pictures. Versatile multiarea autofocus. Infinity focus lock. Backlight compensation. Self-timer can take more than one picture. Switch for continuous advance mode. Optional wireless shutter release. **But:** Self-timer doesn't cancel automatically. **Recommendation:** Excellent, but relatively bulky.

4 Leica Mini 3 $190

• Framing accuracy: 83% • Smallest field: 25 in. Very compact and light. **Features:** Infinity focus lock. Backlight compensation. **But:** Lacks lens cover. Less convenient than most for eyeglass wearers. Has continuous-advance mode only; may waste a shot now and then. **Recommendation:** An excellent but expensive nonzoom camera.

5 Fujifilm Discovery 290 Zoom $140

• Framing accuracy: 80% • Smallest field: 9 in. **Features:** Prewinds film to end, advances back into cartridge. Optional wireless shutter release. **But:** Lacks low-battery warning. **Recommendation:** Excellent but relatively bulky.

6 Pentax IQ Zoom 90MC $190

• Framing accuracy: 68% • Smallest field: 9 in. **Features:** Choice of panoramic or regular format. Versatile multiarea autofocus. Optional wireless shutter release. **But:** Self-timer doesn't cancel automatically. **Recommendation:** Excellent except for framing inaccuracy.

7 Samsung Maxima Evoca 115 $200

• Framing accuracy: 79% • Smallest field: 5 in. A wide zoom range. **Features:** Choice of panoramic or regular-format pictures. Infinity focus lock. Exposure-compensation. Automatic zoom modes. Self-timer can take more than one picture. Can make multiple exposures. Switch for continuous-advance mode. Optional wireless shutter release. Has date/time imprinting. **But:** May leak light in bright sun. **Recommendation:** Very good; has many features.

8 Yashica Microtec Zoom 90 $200

• Framing accuracy: 82% • Smallest field: 6 in. **Features:** Flash zooms to maintain range on telephoto shots. Versatile multiarea autofocus. Infinity focus lock. Self-timer can take more than one picture. Backlight compensation. Automatic zoom mode. Switch for continuous-advance mode. **But:** May leak light in bright sun, fogging fast film. **Recommendation:** Very good.

APS models

9 Kodak Advantix 3700ix $120

• Framing accuracy: 84% • Smallest field: 21 in. Very compact and light. **Features:** Warns when subject exceeds flash range. Large lens/flash separation helps reduce red-eye. Infinity focus lock. Film-compartment interlock prevents accidental opening. **But:** Flash illuminates less uniformly than most. **Recommendation:** An excellent choice in a nonzoom APS camera.

10 Canon Elph 490Z $380

• Framing accuracy: 75% • Smallest field: 7 in. A pricey model with a 4x zoom. **Features:** Has separate "macro" setting for close-ups. Versatile multiarea autofocus. Large lens/flash separation helps reduce red-eye. Warns when subject is too close. Spot-metering mode. Optional wireless shutter release. Exposure-compensation. Automatic zoom modes. Switch for continuous-advance mode. Film-compartment interlock prevents accidental opening. **But:** Self-timer doesn't cancel automatically. **Recommendation:** Excellent but pricey.

11 Konica Super Big Mini BM-S100 $110

• Framing accuracy: 79% • Smallest field: 11 in. One of the lightest, most compact models tested. **Features:** TV mode for shots of TV screen. Warns when subject is too close. Infinity focus lock. Backlight compensation. **But:** Short lens/ flash separation worsens red-eye. Rewinds film in midroll when you change battery. **Recommendation:** An excellent nonzoom model.

12 Nikon Nuvis 125 i $280

• Framing accuracy: 69% • Smallest field: 7 in. **Features:** Warns when subject is too close. Infinity focus lock. Optional wireless shutter release. Film-compartment interlock prevents accidental opening. **Recommendation:** An excellent nonzoom model except for framing inaccuracy.

13 Vivitar Z360ix $120

• Framing accuracy: 74% • Smallest field: 7 in. The lightest, most compact zoom model tested. **Features:** Warns when subject is too close. Infinity focus lock. **But:** Rewinds slowly. **Recommendation:** Excellent and very portable.

14 Fujifilm Endeavor 400ix Zoom $360

• Framing accuracy: 71% • Smallest field: 5 in. Wide zoom range. **Features:** Warns when subject is too close. Flash zooms to maintain range for telephoto shots. Infinity focus lock. Self-timer can take more than one picture. Optional wireless shutter release. Film-compartment interlock prevents accidental opening. **But:** Rewinds slowly. **Recommendation:** Pricey, but excellent.

15 Minolta Vectis 40 $370

• Framing accuracy: 73% • Smallest field: 12 in. A feature-laden camera with 4x zoom. **Features:** Has separate "macro" setting for close-ups. Can reload partially used film. Weatherproof. Flash zooms to maintain range for telephoto shots. Infinity focus lock. Rewinds quickly. Auto zoom mode. Switch for continuous-advance mode. Optional wireless shutter release. **But:** Lacks built-in lens cover. **Recommendation:** Very good, with lots of features, but pricey and bulky.

16 Minox CD 25 $110

• Framing accuracy: 75% • Smallest field: 13 in. A no-frills, nonzoom camera. **Features:** Short lens/flash distance worsens red-eye. Rewinds slowly. **Recommendation:** Very good but basic.

17 Yashica Acclaim 100 $95

• Framing accuracy: 75% • Smallest field: 15 in. Similar to (15).

18 Fujifilm Endeavor 100 $90

• Framing accuracy: 76% • Smallest field: 11 in. Similar to (15).

19 Nikon Nuvis Mini i $140

Framing accuracy: 75% • Smallest field: 11 in. Similar to (15).

20 Olympus Newpic AF200 $80

• Framing accuracy: 77% •Smallest field: 33 in. A no-frills nonzoom camera. **Features:** Bare-bones viewfinder makes accurate framing difficult, especially for eyeglass wearers. Rewinds slowly. Slowest shutter speed is 1/30 sec. Flash range only 5 feet. **Recommendation:** Very good except for viewfinder. There are better choices.

Ratings *Digital cameras*
& Recommendations

The tests behind the Ratings

Overall score combines our print-quality judgments, flash range, and ease of use. **Weight** is for a camera with battery and a memory card. **Print quality** is based on the judgments of a trained panel that inspected glossy 5x7-inch prints made on a Hewlett-Packard PhotoSmart color ink-jet printer. **Next-shot delay** is our measurement of the time it takes for the camera to store one shot on its memory card and ready itself for the next shot. Print quality and next-shot delay are for camera's best-photo made. **Flash range** is manufacturer's claim of the greatest distance from the camera that would produce a well-lit flash picture. **Price** is approximate retail.

Typical features for these models

• Come with image-handling software (the program we used is listed in Details on the models). • Come with AA alkaline batteries but can also use rechargeables. • Autofocus. • Both optical viewfinder and LCD screen on back. • Video output for viewing stored images on TV set. • Built-in lens cover. • 1-yr. warranty on parts and labor. **Except as noted, all megapixel models:** • Come with 4-megabyte (MB) memory card. **Except as noted, all low-resolution models:** • Come with 2-MB card.

Recommendations

The highest-rated cameras tend to have the highest resolution, but they also tend to be the most expensive. If all you want is to send pictures by e-mail or to upload photos onto a web site, it's OK to choose a cheaper low-resolution camera. But if your goal is to get high-resolution prints, choose a megapixel camera. The top-rated Nikon Coolpix 900, $800, had excellent picture quality and was easy to use. But it's the most expensive model we tested. The Olympus D-340L, $600, also had excellent picture quality; it lacks a zoom lens, though. Among 640x480-pixel cameras, the Fujifilm DX-9 Zoom, $500, and Ricoh RDC-300Z, $450, edged out the others. However, the Ricoh has only a flip-up LCD screen, whereas the Fujifilm has both a screen and an optical viewfinder.

See report, page 41. Last time rated in CONSUMER REPORTS: November 1998.

Overall Ratings

E = Excellent, VG = Very good, G = Good, F = Fair, P = Poor

Within types, listed in order of overall score

Key no.	Brand and model	Price	Overall score (0–100; P F G VG E)	Weight	Print quality	Next-shot delay	Flash range
	MEGAPIXEL CAMERAS						
1	**Nikon** Coolpix 900	$800		16 oz.	E	7 sec.	10 ft
2	**Olympus** D-340L	600		12	E	8	10
3	**Konica** Q-M100	600		14	VG	13	10
4	**Kodak** Digital Science DC210	600		15	VG	12	10
5	**Casio** QV-5000SX	500		12	VG	13	7
6	**HP** PhotoSmart C20	500		14	VG	12	10
7	**Sanyo** VPC-X300	500		13	VG	10	8
8	**Kodak** Digital Science DC200	500		14	VG	12	10
9	**Epson** PhotoPC 600	500		14	VG	12	8
10	**Agfa** ePhoto 1280	600		17	VG	18	9
11	**Panasonic** PV-DC1580	500		11	G	14	8
12	**Vivitar** ViviCam 3100	380		14	G	37	8
	LOW-RESOLUTION CAMERAS						
13	**Fujifilm** DX-9 zoom	500		12	F	7	11
14	**Ricoh** RDC-300Z	450		13	F	7	10
15	**Sony** Mavica MVC-FD7	665		25	F	12	13
16	**Casio** QV-700	400		13	F	2	10
17	**JVC** GC-S1	400		13	F	5	7
18	**Casio** QV-770	400		10	F	2	10

Details on the models

Megapixel cameras

1 Nikon Coolpix 900 $800

• 1,280x960-pixel resolution • CompactFlash memory card • Adobe PhotoDeluxe 2.0 for Windows 95, Mac OS 7.2

Yields excellent prints. Has 3:1 zoom lens. Video output also displays live image from camera. **But:** Lacks lens cover. Viewfinder includes less picture area than it should at wide end of zoom range; LCD is better. **Recommendation:** Excellent.

2 Olympus D-340L $600

• 1,280x960-pixel resolution • SmartMedia memory card (3.3-volt) • Adobe PhotoDeluxe 2.0 for Windows 95, Mac OS 7.2

Yields excellent prints. Video output can also display live image from camera. **Recommendation:** Excellent.

3 Konica Q-M100, $600

• 1,152x872-pixel resolution • CompactFlash memory card • Adobe PhotoDeluxe 2.0 for Windows 95, Mac OS 7.2

Yields very good prints. Comes with case. **Availability:** Discontinued; replaced by Q-M100V, $650. **Recommendation:** Very good.

4 Kodak Digital Science DC210 $600

• 1,152x864-pixel resolution • CompactFlash memory card • Adobe PhotoDeluxe 2.0 for Windows 95, Mac OS 7.2

Yields very good prints. 2:1 zoom lens has fixed focus with close-up setting. Comes with case. **But:** Lacks a lens cover. **Availability:** Discontinued; replaced by DC210 Plus, $600. **Recommendation:** Very good.

5 Casio QV-5000SX $500

• 1,280x960-pixel resolution • Built-in memory (8 MB) • Adobe PhotoDeluxe 2.0 for Windows 95, Mac OS 7.2

Yields very good prints. Has manual and autofocus settings. Comes with case. **But:** Built-in memory constrains number of pictures you can take before downloading. Records images in proprietary format; must convert file to use it with other software. Lacks lens cover. **Recommendation:** Very good overall, but can't use a memory card, a limitation.

6 HP PhotoSmart C20 $500

• 1,152x872-pixel resolution • CompactFlash memory card • HP PhotoSmart 1.0 for Windows 95

Similar to (3). **But:** Battery cover not attached and can be lost. **Recommendation:** Very good.

7 Sanyo VPC-X300 $500

• 1,024x768-pixel resolution • SmartMedia memory card (3.3-volt) • MGI PhotoSuite SE for Windows 3.1, 95

Yields very good prints. Can record audio clip along with a picture. Video output also displays live image from camera. Comes with case. **But:** Only 3-mo. warranty on labor. **Recommendation:** Very good.

8 Kodak Digital Science DC200 $500

• 1,152x864-pixel resolution • CompactFlash memory card • Kodak PictureEasy 2.0 for Windows 95

Similar to (4), but has fixed-focus, nonzoom lens. **But:** Has a separate lens cap, which can be misplaced. **Recommendation:** Very good.

9 Epson PhotoPC 600 $500

• 1,024x768-pixel resolution • Built-in memory (4 MB), CompactFlash memory card optional • Sierra Imaging Image Expert 1.1.2f for Windows 3.1, 95, Mac OS 7.1

Yields very good prints. Video output also displays live image from camera. **Availability:** Discontinued but may be available; PhotoPC 700, $700, is similar. **Recommendation:** Very good.

10 Agfa ePhoto 1280 $600

• 1,024x768-pixel resolution • SmartMedia memory card (3.3-volt) • Only LCD screen • Agfa Photowise 1.5 for Windows 95, Mac OS 7.0

Yields very good prints. 3:1 zoom lens. Has manual and autofocus settings. Video output can also display live image from camera. Comes with four rechargeable batteries, charger. **But:** Composing photos with LCD can be awkward. Lens and battery covers not attached; can be lost. **Recommendation:** Very good; some drawbacks.

11 Panasonic PV-DC1580 $500

• 1,025x768-pixel resolution • CompactFlash memory card 8 MB • Adobe PhotoDeluxe 2.0 for Windows 95, Mac OS 7.2

Yields good prints. Comes with case and rechargeable battery that recharges in camera; charger included. **But:** Flash battery cover not attached; can be lost. 3-mo. warranty on labor, 6 mo. on sensor. **Recommendation:** Good.

12 Vivitar ViviCam 3100 $380

• 960x800-pixel resolution • PCMCIA memory card (2 MB) or CompactFlash with adapter • Simple optical viewfinder • Vivitar ViviCam 3100 2.0028 for Windows 95

Yields good prints. Fixed-focus lens. Can record audio clip along with picture. Includes case. **But:** Viewfinder frames photos imprecisely. No video output. Very long delay between photos. Display indicates memory left, not images left; can be confusing. **Recommendation:** Fair.

Low-resolution cameras

(All have 640x 480-pixel resolution)

13 Fujifilm DX-9 Zoom $500

• SmartMedia memory card (3.3 or 5-volt) • Fujifilm PhotoEnhancer 3.2 for Windows 3.1, 95, Mac OS 7.1.2
Yields fair prints. 3:1 zoom lens. Has manual and autofocus settings. Video output also displays live image from camera. Comes with lithium battery that recharges in camera, plus AC adapter. **But:** Lacks lens cover. **Recommendation:** Good.

14 Ricoh RDC-300z $450

• SmartMedia memory card (3.3 or 5-volt) • Only LCD screen • Ricoh PhotoStudio Lite 1.0 for Windows 3.1, 95, Mac OS 7
Yields fair prints. 3:1 zoom lens. Has manual and autofocus settings. Video output also displays live images from camera. Includes case. **But:** Composing pictures with flip-up LCD can be awkward. **Recommendation:** Good.

15 Sony Mavica MVC-FD7 $665

• Standard 1.4-MB diskette • Only LCD screen • ArcSoft PhotoStudio 2.0SE for Windows 3.1, 95
Yields fair prints. Has manual and autofocus settings, 10:1 zoom lens. Comes with rechargeable lithium battery and charger. **But:** Flash must be operated manually and tends to cause overexposure at short distances. Display indicates memory left, not images left; can be confusing. No video output. Composing photos with LCD can be awkward. Lens cap attached with string. 3-mo. warranty on labor. **Availability:** Discontinued; replaced by MVC-FD71, $700. **Recommendation:** Good, but diskette storage can be a drawback.

16 Casio QV-700 $400

18 Casio QV-770 $400

• QV-700: CompactFlash memory card; QV-770: onlybuilt-in memory (4MB) • Only LCD screen • Adobe PhotoDeluxe 2.0 for Windows 95, Mac OS 7.2
Yields fair prints. Fixed-focus lens with close-up setting. Video output can also display live image from camera. Comes with case. **But:** Lacks lens cover. Records in proprietary format; must convert file to use it with other software. Composing photos with LCD screen can be awkward. **Recommendation:** QV-700 is good; QV-770, fair.

17 JVC GC-S1 $400

• Built-in memory (3 MB) CompactFlash memory card optional • Only LCD screen • MGI PhotoSuite SE 1.04 for Windows 3.1, 95
Yields fair prints. Has 10:1 zoom lens. Comes with case. **But:** Composing photos with LCD can be awkward. Lacks lens cover. Flash must be operated manually. 3-mo. warranty on labor. **Recommendation:** Fair.

Ratings *Loudspeakers*

& Recommendations

The tests behind the Ratings

Overall score sums up the way the speakers fared in our accuracy tests and our judgment of bass capability. **Accuracy**, measured for tones ranging from deep bass to very high treble, is given greatest weight in the overall performance. The first score is the speakers' accuracy with the receiver's tone controls set at zero; the second score is with controls adjusted as noted in the Details on the models. **Impedance** is an electrical characteristic, unrelated to quality, that helps match speakers with receiver. Our measurement is listed first, then the manufacturer's. Our figure is a practical minimum for the midbass, which usually draws the most power. **Power** is our estimate of the minimum receiver power needed to play loud, full-range music in a medium-sized room. **Price** is the total approximate price for the bass and satellites; separate prices for the bass and satellites are given in the Details on the models.

Typical features for these models

• Spring-loaded connectors or binding posts for the speaker wires, which aren't included. • Bass-module amplifier and volume control. • Magnetically shielded satellite speakers.

Recommendations

Many of these models would make a fine choice. The Bose Acoustimass-5 Series II, $650, leads the pack by a couple of points overall. These speakers, with their subwoofer and very small satellites, have excellent bass capability and should be compatible with any receiver. The best value is the Cambridge Soundworks Ensemble III, **A CR Best Buy** at $350. However, with impedance at 4 ohms, it won't be compatible with every receiver, and its bass is a bit weak, a problem if you like very loud, brassy music. The Yamaha system, $560, is very accurate and has excellent bass capacity (the satellite is discontinued).

See report, page 51. Last time rated in CONSUMER REPORTS: February 1998.

Overall Ratings

E VG G F P

Listed in order of overall score

Key no.	Brand and model	Price	Overall score (0–100; P F G VG E)	Accuracy	Impedance CU	Impedance MFR.	Power
1	**Bose** Acoustimass-5 Series II	$650		92/87	7 ohms	8 ohms	17 watts
2	**Cambridge Soundworks** Ensemble III **A CR Best Buy**	350		92/92	4	6	29

Key no.	Brand and model	Price	Overall score (0–100; P F G VG E)	Accuracy	Impedance CU	Impedance MFR.	Power
3	**Yamaha** YST-SW150 (bass), NS-A325 (sat.)	$ 560		90/86	7	6	7
4	**NHT** SW1P (bass), SuperZero (sat.)	730		90/82	8	8	24
5	**Phase Technology** Power 10 Octave Series(bass), 2.5T (sat.)	600		87/87	5	8	11
6	**Bose** Acoustimass-3 Series III	400		90/86	4	4	7
7	**Polk Audio** RM3300	750		88/82	5	8	18
8	**Acoustic Research** S8HO (bass), The Edge (sat.)	590		86/80	5	6	15
9	**Boston Acoustics** Micro90	800		87/80	5	8	17
10	**Infinity** BU-1 (bass), Reference 2000.1 (sat.)	500		81/70	6	8	4

Details on the models

We give optimum **bass placement**, the ideal distance from the rear and side walls for positioning the bass unit. Use the measurements to help position the bass in your own room. **Tone settings** show the receiver and bass-unit settings we used. The details also list the cabinetry finish for what we tested; other colors may be available.

1 Bose Acoustimass-5 Series II $650

• Bass unit: 14x7½x19 in., 20 lb.; black veneer finish • Satellites: 6¾x3x5 in., 2 lb., with black plastic finish, cloth grilles • 5-yr. warranty
Doesn't have its own amplifier. Each satellite has two components that can be turned to direct sound for best effect. Comes with speaker wire. Optional wall-mounting brackets available. **Tone settings:** Bass, +2; treble, +4. **Best bass placement:** 60 in. from side, 24 in. from back. **Availability:** Only through 12/98. **Recommendation:** A top performer, but pricey.

2 Cambridge Soundworks Ensemble III $350

• Bass unit: 15¼x8x8¼ in., 11 lb.; black veneer finish • Satellites: 6½x4¼x3¼ in., 2 lb., die-cast metal with metal grilles • 7-yr. warranty
Doesn't have its own amplifier. Falls a bit short on bass, but only with music that has a lot of bass played at unusually high levels. Screw slots for hanging satellites on wall. **Tone settings:** Bass, 0; treble, 0. **Best bass placement:** 60 in. from side, 48 in. from back. **Recommendation:** A top performer that's a good value. **A CR Best Buy.**

3 Yamaha YST-SW150/NS-A325 $560 (bass $400, sat. $160)

• Bass unit: 24½x10x17 in., 40 lb.; black veneer finish • Satellites: 8x4½x4¼ in., 3 lb., black plastic finish with cloth grilles • 2-yr. warranty
The satellites, which can be purchased separately as small bookshelf speakers, have slots for wall mounting. Optional wall brackets available. **Tone settings:** Bass, 0; treble, –3; bass unit crossover/volume, 90Hz/3.25. **Best bass placement:** 54 in. from side, 48 in. from back. **Availability:** Satellite is not available. **Recommendation:** An excellent midpriced performer.

4 NHT SW1P/SuperZero $730 (bass $500, sat. $230)

• Bass unit: 16x11¾x12½ in., 22 lb. • Satellites: 6x5½x5½ in., 6 lb. • All have black laminate finish, cloth grilles • 5-yr. warranty
The satellites can be purchased separately as small bookshelf speakers. Optional wall brackets available. The bass module has a separate external amplifier, which adds clutter. **Tone settings:** Bass, +1; treble, +5; bass unit crossover/volume, 100 Hz/10 o'clock. **Best bass placement:** 54 in. from side, 36 in. from back. **Availability:** Satellite is not available. **Recommendation:** Very good but pricey.

5 Phase Technology Power 10 Octave Series/2.5T $600 (bass $400, sat. $200)

• Bass unit: 15½x14½x15 in., 30 lb. • Satellites: 10½x6½x8¼ in., 9 lb. • All have black veneer finish, cloth grilles • 5-yr. warranty
Satellites, not magnetically shielded, can't be used next to TV set. The satellites, which can be purchased separately as small bookshelf speakers, have screw slots for hanging. **Tone settings:** Bass, 0; treble, +1; bass unit crossover/volume, 100 Hz/8 o'clock. **Best bass placement:** 30 in. from side, 36 in. from back. **Recommendation:** Very good performance at a moderate price.

6 Bose Acoustimass-3 Series III $400

• Bass unit: 7¾x14¼x8 in., 11 lb.; black veneer finish • Satellites: 3x3x4¾ in., 1 lb.; black plastic finish with cloth grilles • 5-yr. warranty
Doesn't have its own amplifier. Tiny satellite speakers. System falls a bit short on bass, but only with music that has a lot of bass played at unusually high levels. Comes with speaker wire. Optional wall brackets available. **Tone settings:** Bass, 0; treble, +3. **Best bass placement:** 48 in. from side, 36 in. from back. **Recommendation:** A very good choice at a reasonable price.

7 Polk Audio RM3300 $750

• Bass unit: 14½x11x20 in., 31 lb., with black veneer finish • Satellites: 6¾x4¼x5¼ in., 4 lb., of die-cast metal with cloth/plastic grilles • 5-yr. warranty
Satellites include hardware for wall mounting. **Tone settings:** Bass, +2; treble, +4; bass volume, 2.5. **Best bass placement:** 54 in. from side, 30 in. from back. **Availability:** Only through 1/99. **Recommendation:** Very good but expensive.

8 Acoustic Research S8HO/The Edge $590 (bass $320, sat. $270)

• Bass unit: 12¾x12½x13¾ in., 23 lb.; black veneer finish • Satellites: 9¾x6¾x7 in., 6 lb.; black plastic finish with metal grilles • 5-yr. warranty
The satellites, which can be purchased separately as small bookshelf speakers, include hardware for wall mounting. Bass module has user-accessible fuse, a plus. **Tone settings:** Bass, +2; treble, +5; bass unit crossover/volume, 100 Hz/12 o'clock. **Best bass placement:** 60 in. from side, 48 in. from back. **Recommendation:** There are better choices that cost less.

9 Boston Acoustics Micro90 $800

• Bass unit: 14¾x14½x16½ in., 32 lb.; black veneer finish • Satellites: 6¾x4x5¼ in., 5 lb.; die-cast metal with metal grilles • Bass warranty, 1-yr.; satellites, 5-yr.
Satellites include hardware for wall mounting. Bass module has user-accessible fuse, a plus. **Tone settings:** Bass, +2; treble, +4; bass unit crossover/volume, 120 Hz/9:30 o'clock. **Best bass placement:** 60 in. from side, 36 in. from back. **Recommendation:** Expensive for what you get. Noticeably less accurate than top-rated models.

10 Infinity BU-1/Reference 2000.1 $500

• Bass unit: 12¾x11½x12½ in., 23 lb.• Satellites: 10½x6½x8¼ in., 9 lb. • All have black veneer finish, metal grilles • 5 yr. warranty
The satellites can be purchased separately as small bookshelf speakers. **Tone settings:** Bass, –1; treble, +5; bass unit crossover/volume, 50 Hz/min. **Best bass placement:** 60 in. from side, 36 in. from back. **Availability:** Satellite is not available. **Recommendation:** Noticeably less accurate than top-rated models. There are better choices.

Ratings *Receivers*

& Recommendations

The tests behind the Ratings

Overall score is based on tuner and amplifier performance, on ease of use, and design features. **FM** and **AM** detail our findings on tuner performance and include tests of station sensitivity and selectivity, among others. **Amplifier** scores the effectiveness of the tone controls and the presence of background noise. **Features** taps our judgment of advantageous and disadvantageous items offered on various models. **Controls/displays** evaluates the front and rear panels, remote, and overall ease of operation. **Price** is approximate retail.

Typical features for these models

• Accommodate at least a CD player and either two tape decks or a tape deck and VCR or TV audio. • Have enough power for loud, undistorted sound in a large room. • Provide FM/AM tuning with 30 to 40 presets. • Come with a remote control that operates other components of the same brand. • Have at least one switched AC outlet for other components. • Can power 6- or 8-ohm speakers, but aren't recommended with 4-ohm speakers. • Have an input for a turntable. • Have a 1-yr. warranty.

Recommendations

Spending more buys features, but not necessarily any improvement in sound. Expect to spend $200 or less for a fine stereo-only receiver. The Technics SA-EX110, $150, performed best. The Sony STR-DE310, $180, was the runner-up. To set up a home theater with surround sound, you'll need a Dolby Pro Logic receiver, which costs $200 to $400. The Technics SA-AX710, $380, is especially convenient, and its AM and FM tuners were among the best.

See report, page 53. Last time rated in CONSUMER REPORTS: February 1998.

Overall Ratings

E VG G F P

Listed in order of overall score

Key no.	Brand and model	Price	Overall score (0–100; P F G VG E)	FM	AM	Amplifier	Features	Controls/displays
	STEREO ONLY							
1	**Technics** SA-EX110	$150		G	F	VG	G	G
2	**Sony** STR-DE310	180		G	F	VG	F	F
3	**Onkyo** TX-8511	290		G	F	G	G	G
4	**Pioneer** SX-255R	160		VG	F	G	F	F

Ratings continued

Key no.	Brand and model	Price	Overall score (0–100; P F G VG E)	FM	AM	Amplifier	Features	Controls/ displays
	STEREO ONLY *continued*							
5	**Kenwood** 104AR	$170		○	●	○	○	◒
	DOLBY PRO LOGIC							
6	**Technics** SA-AX710	380		⊖	○	⊖	⊖	⊖
7	**Yamaha** RX-V492	360		⊖	○	⊖	○	○
8	**JVC** RX-552VBK	190		⊖	◒	⊖	◒	○
9	**Technics** SA-EX310	190		○	○	○	○	○
10	**Sony** STR-DE615	340		⊖	●	⊖	○	◒
11	**Onkyo** TX-SV444	380		○	◒	⊖	○	○
12	**Sony** STR-DE315	190		⊖	◒	⊖	◒	◒
	DOLBY DIGITAL SURROUND							
13	**Pioneer** VSX-D606S	800		○	●	⊖	◒	◒

Details on the models

Power is our measurement of watts per channel for the main left and right channels, for 8-ohm and 6-ohm speakers. (Center channels for all Dolby Pro Logic models are capable of delivering roughly equivalent power. Rear channels are typically one-fourth to one-third of the front channel, sufficient for surround-sound effects.)

Stereo-only models

1 Technics SA-EX110 $150

Remote can tune frequency directly. Very good console layout. **Power:** 108/118 watts. **But:** Fair remote layout. Lacks loudness compensation to boost bass when the volume is turned down. **Recommendation:** A good choice overall.

2 Sony STR-DE310 $180

Better than most at resisting interference from adjacent FM stations. 2-yr. warranty. **Power:** 104/120 watts. **But:** Lacks tape monitor. Lacks loudness compensation to boost bass when the volume is turned down. Fair console layout. **Recommendation:** A good choice overall.

3 Onkyo TX-8511 $290

Display can show station call letters. Allows 4-ohm speakers. Good features and controls, displays. 2-yr. warranty. **Power:** 66/79 watts. **Recommendation:** A good but pricey receiver.

4 Pioneer SX-255R $160

Very good FM performance. **Power:** 111/125 watts. **But:** Lacks loudness compensation to boost bass when the volume is turned down. Mute can't be turned off from console. Fair console and remote layout. **Recommendation:** Fair overall, though a good choice for FM listeners.

5 Kenwood 104AR $170

Allows 4-ohm speakers. **Power:** 113/132 watts. **But:** Poor AM performance. Amplifier has slight background hiss, audible at normal listening levels. Fair console and remote layout. **Recommendation:** A fair choice overall.

Dolby Pro Logic models

6 Technics SA-AX710 $380

Allows 4-ohm speakers. Has universal remote to control components from other manufacturers. Remote can tune frequency directly. Has help button. Very good console and remote layout. DVD ready (has jacks and amplifier for adding DVD Digital Surround). **Power:** 136/154 watts. **Availability:** Discontinued. **Successor:** SA-AX720,

$300. **Recommendation:** The best overall combination of tuner, amplifier, features, controls, and displays in this group makes this a very good choice.

7 Yamaha RX-V492 $360

Allows 4-ohm speakers. Very good FM performance. Tuner is better than most at resisting interference from adjacent stations. Has universal remote control to control components from other manufacturers. 2-yr. warranty. **Power:** 83/98 watts. **But:** Lacks loudness compensation to boost bass when the volume is turned down. **Availability:** Discontinued. **Successor:** RX-V493, $400. **Recommendation:** A very good choice overall.

8 JVC RX-552VBK $190

Very good FM performance. Better than most at resisting interference from adjacent stations. 2-yr. warranty. **Power:** 90/100 watts. **But:** Lacks tape monitor. **Availability:** Discontinued. **Successor:** RX-554VBK, $230. **Recommendation:** Good, and relatively inexpensive.

9 Technics SA-EX310 $190

Remote can tune frequency directly. Very good console layout. DVD ready (has jacks and amplifier for adding DVD Digital Surround). Lacks "B" speaker output terminals. **Power:** 83/91 watts. **But:** Lacks loudness compensation to boost bass when the volume is turned down. **Availability:** Discontinued. **Successor:** SA-EX320, $180. **Recommendation:** Good and relatively inexpensive.

10 Sony STR-DE615 $340

Allows 4-ohm speakers. Very good FM performance. Display can show station call letters. Remote can tune frequency directly. Better than most at resisting interference from adjacent FM stations. DVD ready (has jacks and amplifier for adding DVD Digital Surround). 2-yr. warranty. **Power:** 108/126 watts. **But:** Poor AM performance. Lacks tape monitor. Lacks loudness compensation to boost bass when the volume is turned down. Fair console and remote layout. **Availability:** Discontinued. **Recommendation:** A good performer.

11 Onkyo TX-SV444 $380

Has display dimmer. DVD ready (has jacks and amplifier for adding DVD Digital Surround). 2-yr. warranty. **Power:** 80/96 watts. **But:** Lacks loudness compensation to boost bass when the volume is turned down. **Availability:** Discontinued. **Successor:** TX-SV454, $430. **Recommendation:** A good receiver, but expensive for what you get.

12 Sony STR-DE315 $190

Very good FM performance. 2-yr. warranty. **Power:** 74/85 watts. **But:** No video inputs or outputs, so you must run external video sources directly to the TV. No turntable input. Lacks tape monitor. Lacks loudness compensation to boost bass when the volume is turned down. Fair console and remote layout. **Availability:** Only through 9/98. **Recommendation:** Good overall, but some drawbacks.

Dolby Digital Surround models

13 Pioneer VSX-D606S $800

Remote can tune frequency directly. Better than most at resisting interference from adjacent FM stations. Universal remote control can control components from other manufacturers. Has inputs on front panel for camcorder. 2-yr. warranty. **Power:** 117/133 watts. **But:** Poor AM performance. Can't turn off mute from console. Fair console layout. **Availability:** Discontinued. **Successor:** VSX-D607S, $600. **Recommendation:** A fair receiver with lackluster convenience.

Ratings *19- & 20-inch TV sets*

& Recommendations

The tests behind the Ratings

To measure the quality of the **picture**—the main component of the **overall score**—a trained viewing panel assessed each set's clarity and color accuracy. Contrast, distortion, and other factors were also measured. We judged the sound delivered by each set's built-in speaker(s). If you want better **sound,** choose one of the two models with audio-output jacks and connect the set to self-powered speakers or a sound system. **Cable** is how well the set, without a cable box, would prevent adjacent channels from interfering with the one you are watching. **Ease of use** includes how easy the remote control and on-screen menus are to use; no sets were particularly difficult. **Price** is approximate retail.

Typical features for these models

• Cable ready. • Numeric keypad and previous-channel button on remote control. • Sleep or "off" timer. • Alarm or "on" timer. • Multilingual menus. • Monophonic sound. • 12-mo. parts warranty. • 24-mo. picture-tube warranty. • 3-mo. labor warranty.

Recommendations

Almost all the sets we tested have a fine picture. The Samsung TXG2045, $220, with its excellent picture and reasonable price, deserves first consideration despite its mediocre sound. If audio is a priority, look first for the Sanyo AVM-1907, $190 (discontinued, but still available according to the manufacturer). Those who receive cable without the use of a cable box should limit their choices to models that were very good for such reception: the Samsung TXG2045, Sanyo AVM-1907, GE 19GT317, RCA F19251GY, and GE 19GT356. If you use an antenna in an area of fringe reception, select from among the Samsung TXG2045, Toshiba CF19G22, Zenith Z19A11S, and GE 19GT317.

See report, page 55. Last time rated in CONSUMER REPORTS: February 1998.

Overall Ratings

E VG G F P

Listed in order of overall score

Key no.	Brand and model	Price	Overall score (0–100; P F G VG E)	Picture	Sound	Cable WITHOUT BOX	Ease of use
1	**Samsung** TXG2045	$220		E	F	VG	VG
2	**Sanyo** AVM-1907	190		VG	VG	VG	VG
3	**Toshiba** CF19G32	220		VG	G	F	VG

Key no.	Brand and model	Price	Overall score (0–100; P F G VG E)	Picture	Sound	Cable WITHOUT BOX	Ease of use
4	**Zenith** Z19A11S	$210		⊖	◒	◒	⊖
5	**RCA** F19205GY	175		⊖	⊖	○	⊖
6	**Samsung** TXD1972	180		⊖	◒	○	⊖
7	**Zenith** Z19A02G	180		⊖	○	○	⊖
8	**GE** 19GT317	180		⊖	◒	⊖	⊖
9	**Orion** TV1926A	180		⊖	○	●	○
10	**Toshiba** CF19G22	200		⊖	○	○	○
11	**RCA** F19251GY	200		⊖	●	⊖	⊖
12	**Philips Magnavox** PR1902C	175		○	◒	◒	⊖
13	**GE** 19GT356	180		○	◒	⊖	⊖

Details on the models

Dimensions are HxWxD. We identify sets with audio- and video-input jacks (A/V inputs)—for connection to a VCR, camcorder, or cable box—and those that can be connected to external speakers or a sound system.

1 Samsung TXG2045 $220

• Stereo • A/V inputs, front and rear (only one set can be used at a time) • 18¼ x19¼ x19½ in. • 20-in. screen
Excellent detail and color reproduction; only tested set with a comb filter. One of the best remotes. Very good for off-the-air reception. Fine-tuning adjustment. Has audio output jacks for connection to a stereo system. Commercial-skip timer, antenna for channels 2-13, built-in handles, and headphone jack. Active-channel scan. 12-mo. labor warranty. **Similar model:** TXG2046, $230, adds universal remote. **Availability:** Through 12/98. **Recommendation:** Though there are better-sounding models, a very good set—the only one tested that has an excellent picture. Among the best choices for cable without a box.

2 Sanyo AVM-1907 $190

• 17¾x19¼ x18½ in. • 19-in. screen
Excellent color reproduction. Can automatically display closed captions when muted. No alarm or "on" timer. **But:** Picture distorts during even modest electrical fluctuations. Warranty doesn't cover pattern "burned" into picture tube—from a computer game, for example. **Availability:** Discontinued but available. **Recommendation:** A very good set, despite minor drawbacks. Among the best choices for sound quality or for cable without a box.

3 Toshiba CF19G32 $220

• Universal remote • Stereo • Channel block-out • A/V inputs • 18¼ x20x18½ in. • 19-in. screen
Excellent color reproduction. Very good for off-the-air reception. One of the best remotes. Tone controls and ambience sound enhancement. Can automatically display closed captions when muted. Can be turned on from light switch. Has extended-data-services decoder. No alarm or multilingual menus. **Availability:** Discontinued. **Successor:** CF19H32, $220. **Recommendation:** A very good set, with a lot of features—but only a fair choice for cable without a box.

4 Zenith Z19A11S $210

• Stereo • 18½x19¾x18½ in. • 19-in. screen
Excellent color reproduction. Very good for off-the-air reception. **But:** Picture distorts during even modest electrical fluctuations, as when an air conditioner turns on. **Availability:** Discontinued. **Successor:** A19A11D, $210. **Recommendation:** A

very good set, though somewhat spartan and only a fair choice for cable without a box.

5 RCA F19205GY $175

• Channel block-out • 18x19¼x18¾ in. • 19-in. screen

Automatic flesh-tone correction. Can indicate programs with closed captions and can automatically display closed captions when muted. Has extended-data-services decoder. **Similar model:** F19207BC, $185. **Recommendation:** A very good performer at a very good price, and among the best-sounding sets. But RCA is one of the two least reliable brands.

6 Samsung TXD1972 $180

• A/V inputs, front and rear (only one set may be used at a time) • 17½x19¼ x18¼ in. • 19-in. screen

Has fine-tuning adjustment. Commercial-skip timer, antenna for channels 2-13, built-in handles, and headphone jack. Active-channel scan. 12-mo. labor warranty. **Similar model:** TXD1986, $190, adds universal remote. **Availability:** Discontinued. **Recommendation:** A very good set.

7 Zenith Z19A02G $180

• 18½x20x18½ in. • 19-in. screen

Excellent color reproduction. **But:** Picture distorts during even modest electrical fluctuations, as when an air conditioner turns on. **Availability:** Discontinued. **Successor:** A19A02D, $250. **Recommendation:** Spartan, but very good.

8 GE 19GT317 $180

• Channel block-out • 18x20x18¾ in. • 19-in. screens

Automatic flesh-tone correction. Very good for off-the-air reception. Can indicate programs with closed captions and can automatically display closed captions when muted. Has extended-data-services decoder. **But:** Only fair at rendering fine detail. **Availability:** Only through 3/99. **Similar model:** 19GT319, $175. **Recommendation:** A very good performer, and one of the best for cable reception without a box. But GE is one of the two least reliable brands.

9 Orion TV1926A $180

• 16¼ x19x18¼ in. • 19-in. screen

Sold mainly in Wal-Mart stores. 12-mo. labor warranty. No alarm. **But:** Picture distorts during even modest electrical fluctuations, as when an air conditioner turns on. Somewhat noisy off-the-air reception of channels 2-13. Side-firing speakers may limit set's placement. Without the remote, you can't adjust picture or sound. **Recommendation:** A very good set, despite minor drawbacks, but the worst choice for cable without a box.

10 Toshiba CF19G22 $200

• Channel block-out • 17¼x20¼x18½ in. • 19-in. screen

Can be turned on from light switch. No alarm or multilingual menus. **But:** Picture distorts during even modest electrical fluctuations, as when an air conditioner turns on. Side-firing speaker may limit set's placement. **Availability:** Discontinued but available. **Successor:** CF19H22, $200. **Recommendation:** A very good set, providing its minor limitations don't bother you.

11 RCA F19251GY $200

• Stereo • A/V inputs • 18½x20x18 in. • 19-in. screen

Automatic flesh-tone correction. Tone control (but poor sound quality). Commercial-skip timer. **Recommendation:** A good performer, and one of the best for cable without a box. But the worst sound quality of any set tested for this report, and RCA is one of the two least reliable brands.

12 Philips Magnavox PR1902C $175

• 17¾x19½x19 in. • 19-in. screen

Can automatically display closed captions when muted. Built-in handles. **But:** Somewhat noisy off-the-air reception of channels 2-13. **Recommendation:** A good set, though only a fair choice for cable without a box.

13 GE 19GT356 $180

• Stereo • Channel block-out • 18½x20x18¼ in. • 19-in. screen

Automatic flesh-tone correction. Can indicate programs with closed captions, and can automatically display closed captions when muted. Has extended-data-services decoder. **But:** Ability to render fine detail is only fair. **Recommendation:** A good performer, but from one of the two least reliable brands. One of the best for cable without a box.

Ratings *27-inch TV sets*

& Recommendations

The tests behind the Ratings

A viewing panel assessed each set's **picture** quality (the main component of the **overall score**) by judging clarity, color accuracy, and other factors. We judged **sound** quality from the built-in speakers; most sets can yield better sound by being connected to external speakers. **Cable** is a measure of how well the set connected to a cable-TV system (but not using a converter box) would prevent adjacent channels from interfering with the one you're watching. **Ease of use** includes such factors as how easy the remote control and on-screen menus are to use, in dim light and without referring to the manual. **Price** is approximate retail.

Typical features for these models

• Stereo sound. • Sleep or "off" timer. • Multilingual menus. • Comb filter. • Universal remote control. • Alarm or "on" timer. • S-video-input jack. • Picture and audio-tone controls, both on the set and on the remote control. • Separate audio program, for receiving audio soundtracks in a second language. • Channel block-out. • 12-mo. parts warranty. • 24-mo. picture-tube warranty. • 3-mo. labor warranty.

Recommendations

All the tested models have at least very good picture quality. Sound quality varies widely. If you watch a lot of movies or music programs and don't plan to connect your set to external speakers or a sound system, choose the Philips Magnavox MX2790B, $500, which has excellent sound, or one of the five models with very good sound. If you plan to connect the set to other audio equipment, consider the Samsung TXG2746, the best value at $350. If you use an antenna and live in an area with weak TV signals, consider the Toshiba. If you don't use a cable box, the Zenith Z27H32D, $450, offers the best insurance against interference between adjacent cable channels.

See report, page 55. Last time rated in CONSUMER REPORTS: March 1998.

Overall Ratings

E VG G F P

Listed in order of overall score

Key no.	Brand and model	Price	Overall score (0–100; P F G VG E)	Picture	Sound	Cable (WITHOUT BOX)	Ease of use
1	**Toshiba** CF27G50	$400		E	VG	G	VG
2	**RCA** F27681GY	500		E	VG	G	VG
3	**RCA** F27679BC	490		E	VG	G	VG

Key no.	Brand and model	Price	Overall score (0–100; P F G VG E)	Picture	Sound	Cable (WITHOUT BOX)	Ease of use
4	**Sony** KV-27V26	$580		⊜	⊖	○	⊖
5	**JVC** AV-27890	580		⊜	⊖	●	⊖
6	**Philips Magnavox** MX2790B	500		⊖	⊜	○	⊜
7	**Sony** KV-27S26	540		⊖	○	⊖	⊖
8	**Samsung** TXG2746	350		⊜	●	○	⊖
9	**GE** 27GT622	350		⊖	○	⊖	⊖
10	**Zenith** Z27H32D	450		⊖	○	⊜	⊖
11	**Panasonic** CT-27G32	500		⊖	○	○	⊖
12	**Hitachi** 27CX21B	400		⊖	○	◒	○

Details on the models

Dimensions are HxWxD.

1 Toshiba CF27G50 $400

• Picture-in-picture • 1 video input • 1 audio input, 1 output • Ambience sound • 24¼x26¾x22 in.
Excellent at displaying detail; the best color rendering of all the tested sets. Among the most frugal models for standby power consumption. Can set color "warmth." Has extended-data-services (EDS) decoder. Can be turned on with a light switch and automatically displays closed captions when muted. 12-mo. labor warranty (longer than most). No alarm or "on" timer; no clock. **Availability:** Discontinued but available. **Recommendation:** Excellent, and very good reception of weak over-the-air broadcasts.

2 RCA F27681GY $500

3 RCA F27679BC $490

• Picture-in-picture (2 tuners on (2)) • 2 video inputs • 2 audio inputs, 1 output • Ambience sound on (2) • 231¼x25¾x18¾ in.
Excellent detail reproduction. Automatic flesh-tone adjustment; can set color "warmth." Video-noise-reduction switch. (2) has automatic volume control and extended-data-services (EDS) decoder, and can automatically display closed captions when muted. (3) has TV Guide Plus and 12-mo. labor warranty (longer than most). **But:** Picture-tube warranty has restrictions. **Availability:** (3) is discontinued but available. **Recommendation:** Very good, but RCA's brand repair record is among the worst in recent years.

4 Sony KV-27V26 $580

• Picture-in-picture • 3 video inputs, 1 output • 3 audio inputs, 2 outputs • Ambience sound • 22½x27¼x19¾ in.
Side-firing speakers; may enhance stereo effect, but can restrict position of set. Front input jacks. Can be turned on with a light switch. Has extended-data-services (EDS) decoder. **But:** Picture and audio-tone controls on remote only. **Availability:** Discontinued. **Recommendation:** Very good.

5 JVC AV-27890 $580

• Picture-in-picture (2 tuners) • 3 video inputs • 3 audio inputs, 1 output • Ambience sound • 23¼x25¾x20¼ in.
Video-noise-reduction switch. Front input jacks. Has TV Guide Plus. 12-mo. labor warranty (longer than most). Can be turned on with a light switch. **Availability:** Discontinued. **Recommendation:** Very good, but poor cable reception without a box, and only fair reception of weak over-the-air broadcasts.

6 Philips Magnavox MX2790B $500

• Picture-in-picture (2 tuners) • 1 video input • 2 audio inputs, 2 outputs • Ambience sound • 22¾x28¼x20¼ in.
Video-noise-reduction switch. Side-firing speak-

ers; may enhance stereo effect, but can restrict position of set. Automatic volume control. Has beeper that helps find a lost remote. "Smart" remote. Can automatically display closed captions when muted. **But:** Lacks channel block-out. **Availability:** Discontinued. **Recommendation:** Very good, and the best-sounding set.

7 **Sony KV-27S26** $540

• Picture-in-picture • 2 video inputs • 2 audio inputs, 1 output • Ambience sound • $23\frac{3}{4}$x26x$20\frac{1}{2}$ in.
Has extended-data-services (EDS) decoder. Can be turned on with a light switch. **But:** Picture and audio-tone controls on remote only. **Availability:** Discontinued but available. **Recommendation:** Very good, both overall and for reception without a cable box.

8 **Samsung TXG2746** $350

• 1 video input • 1 audio input, 1 output • $23\frac{1}{2}$x26x20 in.
Excellent detail reproduction. Among the most frugal for standby power consumption. Video-noise-reduction switch. Front input jacks. Commercial skip-timer. 12-mo. labor warranty (longer than most). **But:** Lacks S-video-input jack, audio-tone controls, and channel block-out. **Availability:** Discontinued. **Recommendation:** Very good, and excellent value. But poor sound quality may be a drawback.

9 **GE 27GT622** $350

• Picture-in-picture • 1 video input • 1 audio input, 1 output • Ambience sound • $23\frac{1}{4}$x$25\frac{1}{2}$x$18\frac{3}{4}$ in.
Automatic flesh-tone adjustment. Commercial skip-timer. **But:** Lacks channel block-out. **Recommendation:** Very good, both overall and for cable reception without a box. But GE's brand repair record is among the worst in recent years.

10 **Zenith Z27H32D** $450

• Picture-in-picture • 1 video input • 1 audio input, 1 output • Ambience sound • 19x$26\frac{1}{4}$x$23\frac{3}{4}$ in.
Can set color "warmth." Automatic volume control. "Smart" remote. Can automatically display closed captions when muted. **Availability:** Discontinued. **Recommendation:** Very good, and excellent for cable reception without a box.

11 **Panasonic CT-27G32** $500

• Picture-in-picture (2 tuners) • 2 video inputs • 2 audio inputs, 1 output • Ambience sound • $23\frac{1}{4}$x$26\frac{1}{4}$x$21\frac{1}{4}$ in.
Among the most frugal for standby power consumption. Automatic volume control. Can be turned on from light switch. **But:** Lacks channel block-out. **Availability:** Discontinued. **Recommendation:** Very good.

12 **Hitachi 27CX21B** $400

• 1 video input • 1 audio input, 1 output • $22\frac{3}{4}$x$26\frac{3}{4}$x$20\frac{1}{2}$ in.
Can set color "warmth," automatically display closed captions when muted. Commercial skip-timer. 12-mo. labor warranty (longer than most). Can be turned on from light switch. **But:** Picture-tube warranty has restrictions. Remote is very difficult to use in dim light. **Availability:** Discontinued but available. **Recommendation:** Very good, though only fair for cable reception without a box.

Ratings *VCRs*
& Recommendations

The tests behind the Ratings

Overall score is based mainly on picture quality, but reflects measurements of tuner selectivity and judgments of ease of use as well. To assess picture quality, trained panelists viewed side-by-side images, recorded on each VCR at both standard-play (SP) and extended-play (EP) speeds and played back on the same machine. SP performance is given greater weight than EP performance. **Ease of use** is a composite judgment, reflecting programming, operating the remote, and the presence of important features. **Tuner selectivity** indicates how well a VCR filters out unwanted signals from channels next to the one being watched or recorded. This is especially important if you use cable without a cable box. **Price** is an estimated average based on a national survey; for (13) price is approximate retail.

Typical features for these models

• Can receive at least 125 cable channels. • Four video heads. • Warranty of 1yr. on video heads and parts and 3mo. on labor. • Childproof lock. • Energy Star compliance • Front audio-video jacks. • Universal remote control. • VCR Plus programming.

Recommendations

It's safe to expect good picture quality. But features vary widely. Decide what you want, and resist buying more than you need. The excellent Panasonic PV-8662, $240, is a fine all-around performer that offers features for a range of family uses. Panasonic has also been among the more reliable VCR brands. The JVC HR-A54U, $180, also delivers top picture quality, although it's not as easy to use and has fewer features. Two Zeniths scored very well, but the brand has been among the less reliable.

See report, page 51. Last time rated in CONSUMER REPORTS: November 1998.

Overall Ratings

E VG G F P

Listed in order of overall score

Key no.	Brand and model	Price	Overall score (0–100; P F G VG E)	Picture quality SP	Picture quality EP	Ease of use	Tuner selectivity
1	**Panasonic** PV-8662	$240		E	G	VG	VG
2	**JVC** HR-A54U	180		E	G	F	G
3	**Zenith** VRA424	200		VG	VG	G	VG

Key no.	Brand and model	Price	Overall score (0–100; P F G VG E)	Picture quality SP	Picture quality EP	Ease of use	Tuner selectivity
4	**Zenith** VRA422	$170		⊖	○	○	⊖
5	**Quasar** VHQ860	155		⊖	○	○	⊖
6	**Sony** SLV-778HF	245		⊖	○	○	⊖
7	**Sony** SLV-798HF	290		⊖	○	○	○
8	**JVC** HR-VP654U	220		⊖	○	○	⊖
9	**RCA** VR622HF	170		⊖	○	○	⊖
10	**RCA** VR692HF	225		⊖	○	⊖	○
11	**Panasonic** PV-8451	180		⊖	○	○	⊖
12	**Toshiba** M-674	180		○	○	⊖	⊖
13	**Samsung** VR8708	170		○	○	○	○
14	**Sharp** VC-H986U	190		○	○	⊖	⊖
15	**RCA** VR636HF	190		⊖	◒	○	○
16	**Toshiba** M-764	265		○	○	⊖	○
17	**GE** VG4268	200		○	○	○	⊖
18	**Hitachi** VTFX633A	200		○	○	○	⊖
19	**Sharp** VC-H982U	155		○	◒	⊖	◒
20	**Philips Magnavox** VRZ262AT	170		○	◒	○	⊖

Details on the models

1 Panasonic PV-8662 $240

Auto clock set. Cable channel-changer. Excellent picture quality at SP tape speed, and very nearly top marks in other Ratings categories. **Added features:** Commercial advance, movie advance, index search, and backlit buttons on remote. **But:** Lacks power backup. **Recommendation:** Our first choice, made even more attractive by Panasonic's repair record.

2 JVC HR-A54U $180

Backup power. Picture quality on a par with that of (1), but not as easy to use. Added features: Auto speed-switching and index search. **But:** Lacks auto clock set, cable channel-changer, childproof lock, and universal remote control. **Recommendation:** An excellent choice.

3 Zenith VRA424 $200

Auto clock set. Cable channel-changer. Auto SP and EP picture quality are very good. **Added features:** Auto speed-switching, warning of programming conflicts, and jog and shuttle on remote. **But:** Lacks power backup, childproof lock. **Recommendation:** An excellent choice, especially for those who time-shift a lot, but Zenith has been among the less reliable brands.

4 Zenith VRA422 $170

Auto clock set. Very good SP picture quality. Added features: Auto speed-switching, warning of programming conflicts. **But:** Lacks power backup, cable channel-changer, childproof lock, front audio-video jacks, and VCR Plus. **Recommendation:** Very good overall and priced attractively, but note Zenith's repair history.

5 Quasar VHQ860 $155

Very good SP picture quality; excellent tuner selectivity should keep neighboring channels well separated. **Added feature:** Index search. **But:** Lacks auto clock set, power backup, cable channel-changer, and front audio-video jacks. **Recommendation:** Very good overall and priced attractively, with one of the better brand repair records.

6 Sony SLV-778HF $245

Backup power. Auto clock set. Very good SP picture quality. Added features: Jog and shuttle on console. **But:** Lacks cable channel-changer. **Similar model:** SLV788HF, $270; adds mouse cable channel-changer. **Recommendation:** Very good overall, but expensive.

7 Sony SLV-798HF $290

Backup power. Auto clock set. Cable channel-changer. Not quite as clear-cut tuner selectivity as that of (6). **Added features:** Auto speed-switching, index search, VCR Plus Gold, jog and shuttle on console, and quick rewind and fast forward. **But:** Lacks universal remote control. **Recommendation:** Very good, but expensive.

8 JVC HR-VP654U $220

Backup power. Auto clock set. Cable channel-changer. Very good SP picture quality. **Added feature:** Index search, plug and play. **But:** Lacks childproof lock. **Similar model:** HR-VP650U, $195; lacks cable channel-changer. **Recommendation:** Very good overall, but there are better values.

9 RCA VR622HF $170

Very good SP picture quality. **Added features:** Index search, warning of programming conflicts. **But:** Lacks auto clock set, power backup, cable channel-changer, front audio-video jacks, and universal remote control. **Recommendation:** Very good overall.

10 RCA VR692HF $225

Auto clock set. Very good for ease of use. **Added features:** Warning of programming conflicts, commercial advance, movie advance, "go to" and index search, and backlit buttons on remote. **But:** Lacks power backup and cable channel-changer. **Recommendation:** Very good overall, but not a good value.

11 Panasonic PV-8451 $180

Auto clock set. Very good SP picture quality and tuner selectivity. **Added feature:** Index search. **But:** Lacks power backup and cable channel-changer. **Similar model:** PV-8450, $170; lacks VCR Plus. **Recommendation:** Very good overall.

12 Toshiba M-674 $180

Very good for ease of use. **Added features:** Auto speed-switching and on-screen warning of programming conflicts. **But:** Lacks auto clock set, power backup, cable channel-changer, childproof lock, and universal remote control. Higher standby power consumption than others tested. **Recommendation:** Very good overall.

13 Samsung VR8708 $170

Auto clock set. Average marks all around. **Added features:** Auto speed-switching, warning of programming conflicts. **But:** Lacks power backup, universal remote control, and VCR Plus. **Similar model:** VR8608, $150; lacks auto clock set, cable channel-changer. **Recommendation:** Very good overall, and from one of the more reliable brands.

14 Sharp VC-H986U $190

Auto clock set. Cable channel-changer. Very good for ease of use. Added feature: Plug and play, quick rewind and fast forward. **But:** Lacks power backup. **Similar model:** VC-H988U, $200. **Recommendation:** Good overall.

15 RCA VR636HF $190

Auto clock set. Cabble channel-changer. Very good SP picture quality, but EP picture quality is only fair. **Added features:** Warning of programming conflicts, and "go to" and index search. **But:** Lacks power backup and universal remote control. **Recommendation:** Good overall.

16 Toshiba M-764 $265

Auto clock set. Cable channel-changer. Very good for ease of use. Added features: Auto speed-switching, warning of programming conflicts, and index search. **But:** Lacks power backup and childproof lock. **Recommendation:** Good overall, but expensive.

17 GE VG4268 $200

Auto clock set. Good picture quality. **Added features:** Warning of programming conflicts, commercial advance, and "go to" and index search.

But: Lacks power backup, cable channel-changer, front audio-video jacks, and universal remote control. **Recommendation:** Good overall, but expensive.

18 Hitachi VTFX633A $200

Backup power. Auto clock set. Cable channel-changer. Good picture quality. **Added feature:** Index search. **But:** Lacks childproof lock. **Recommendation:** Good overall, but there are better choices.

19 Sharp VC-H982U $155

Only fair EP picture quality. Added features: Index search, quick rewind and fast forward. **But:** Lacks auto clock set, power backup, cable channel-changer, front audio-video jacks, and VCR Plus. **Recommendation:** Good overall, but there are better choices.

20 Philips Magnavox VRZ262AT $170

Only fair EP picture quality. **Added features:** Warning of programming conflicts and "go to" search. **But:** Lacks auto clock set, power backup, cable channel-changer, and childproof lock. **Recommendation:** Good overall, but there are better choices.

HOW TO USE THE RATINGS

- Read the Recommendations for information on specific models and general buying advice.
- Note how the rated products are listed—in order of performance and convenience, price, or alphabetically.
- The overall score graph gives the big picture in performance. Notes on features and performance for individual models are listed in the "Comments" column or "Details on the models."
- Use the key numbers to locate the details on each model.
- Before going to press, we verify model availability for most products with manufacturers. Some tested models listed in the Ratings may no longer be available. Discontinued models are noted in "Comments" or "Details on the models." Such models may still be available in some stores for part of 1999. Models indicated as successors should perform similarly to the tested models, according to the manufacturer. Features may vary.
- Models similar to the tested models, when they exist, are indicated in "Comments" or "Details on the models."
- The original date of publication is noted for each Ratings.

Appliances

THE BIG PICTURE

Truly new appliances—a food processor, a breadmaker—happen only now and then. More often, appliances are improved in small ways or are simply restyled. Here are some current trends affecting what's now on store shelves.

• Some features are improved. Moisture sensors more accurately time clothes drying than do thermostats, for instance.

• European design sells. Its characteristics: Bauhaus-inspired white housings and clear, functionally arranged controls. In addition, high energy costs at home have given the European companies an incentive to design washing machines and diswashers that are extra stingy with water. Now, American makers are coming out with washers and dishwashers that not only pick up on the cachet of the imports but help American brands anticipate government energy efficiency goals.

• The "commercial kitchen" look. It's showing up even on less expensive lines. For many years now, a tiny trend-setting part of the kitchen-appliance market has been devoted to restaurant-level equipment. Now, industrial-strength cookware is in every department store, and the appliance majors are adding "professional look" models—refrigerators 24 inches deep so they don't protrude beyond kitchen cabinets, ranges with beefy knobs and heavy grates—all sheathed in stainless steel.

• The retro look. Small appliances such as toasters and blenders often don the rounded-chrome designs of the past.

• Electronic controls are spreading. Touchpads are found on appliances from ranges to blenders. Energy- and water-monitoring devices improve washing-appliance efficiency.

• Energy efficiency is improving. Since 1980, the U.S. government has required major appliances to carry a yellow " Energy Guide" label to help shoppers compare the likely cost of operation. Following prescribed formulas to calculate the annual energy bill, manufacturers note on the label the annual cost for operating each product, along with the typical range for similar products.

The labels are useful for comparison, not as a guide to what you'll actually pay, since energy costs and usage patterns differ so much. Be careful that the products you're comparing are labeled on the same basis. For example, the government uses one scale to rate front-loading wash-

APPLIANCE FAMILIES

Although there are many brand names, just a handful of companies manufacture major appliances. Many of these companies also make specific models for other manufacturers to fill gaps in their lines. For instance, we know from examining products in our lab that Frigidaire makes GE's front-loading washer and Amana makes GE's bottom-freezer refrigerator. Similarly, the Kenmore brand is made for Sears entirely by others. (These relationships change continually, as manufacturers redesign their products and refine their marketing strategies.)

Amana

• Amana

The fifth largest maker of large kitchen appliances in the U.S., Amana's presence is most prominent in the ranks of refrigerators. Amana makes bottom-freezer models in addition to top-freezer, side-by-side, and built-in models. In other product categories, this brand is a smaller player. The Amana family once included Speed Queen, Caloric, and Modern Maid, but those brands are not currently being manufactured.

Frigidaire

• Frigidaire • Gibson • Kelvinator • Tappan • White-Westinghouse

The flagship Frigidaire brand is generally higher-priced—especially models in the upscale Frigidaire Gallery and Gallery Professional lines. Tappan is a leading brand of gas range. The family's other brands are generally lower priced, with fewer features. With small market shares, they may be hard to find in stores.

General Electric

• GE • GE Monogram • Hotpoint • RCA

General Electric and Whirlpool are the largest U.S. appliance makers, with GE particularly strong in cooking appliances. GE is a midrange brand, with the GE Profile and GE Profile Performance lines pitched to more affluent buyers. The Monogram brand, distributed separately, focuses on high-style, commer-

ing machines—inherently more efficient—and another to rate top-loaders. Among refrigerators, models that are nearly identical in external dimensions but slightly different inside may fall into in different energy-label categories with different guidelines. For now, the best way to read the sticker is to focus on the kilowatt-hours of electricity used per year and the estimated annual cost.

Our recent tests of dishwashers turned up another problem with Energy Guides. The Energy Guide protocol for dishwashers calls for them to be loaded with clean dishes and run on the normal cycle. But since new "smart" models have a dirt sensor that adjusts water level according to how dirty the dishes are, the clean load elicits an unrealistically low amount of water. That, in turn, creates an Energy Guide figure that may underestimate the machine's true running cost by $20 or more a year. A Department of Energy spokesperson told us last winter that work is under way to solve the problem.

---

cial-look appliances for the kitchen, both freestanding and built-in. Hotpoint is a "value" brand. The RCA brand may be hard to find.

Kenmore

• *Kenmore*

The store brand for Sears, Kenmore is one of the best-selling brands of major appliances. Sears has its models manufactured to its specifications by other companies. For instance, Whirlpool has long been the principal manufacturer of Kenmore laundry equipment and GE its principal manufacturer of cooking appliances.

Maytag

• *Maytag* • *Admiral* • *Jenn-Air* • *Magic Chef*

In most product categories, Maytag pursues a premium image with its flagship brand, although Maytag refrigerators are fairly inexpensive given the features they offer. Maytag made its name first in laundry appliances. The Maytag Neptune is a new line of premium washers and dryers. Performa is Maytag's low-priced line. Jenn-Air, best known for modular ranges and cooktops, is the family's premium brand. Admiral and Magic Chef are budget brands.

Whirlpool

• *Whirlpool* • *KitchenAid* • *Roper*

Whirlpool and General Electric are the largest U.S. appliance makers, with Whirlpool particularly strong in laundry appliances. In most major appliance categories, Whirlpool is the leading manufacturer. Whirlpool, the flagship brand, covers a wide range of prices, with Whirlpool Gold the premium line. KitchenAid is the family's upscale brand and Roper its basic, budget brand.

European brands

• *Asko* • *Bosch* • *Miele*

Aimed at the premium end of the market, these brands are low on market share but long on influence. In the dishwasher and washing machine categories, they've led the way toward more water-efficient designs and cleaner-looking controls.

SHOPPING STRATEGY

Don't rush to buy a new type of product. Later versions may have often-significant flaws ironed out and cost a lot less.

Skip extras manufacturers use to create a range of price points, such as lots of cycles or speeds on electronic controls. You may not need or use them.

Where to shop. Two chains—Sears and Circuit City—sell more than 37 percent of all major appliances. Other places to buy appliances include superstores such as Home Depot or Circuit City, warehouse clubs such as Costco, and department stores. The big stores may have a wider selection, while small, local stores may have more helpful service. Prices for major appliances vary widely and, like car prices, are sometimes negotiable.

Brand families. Just a handful of companies manufacture major appliances. Between them, General Electric and Whirlpool make more than half. Maytag and Frigidaire are the other big names. These companies sell appliances under many more brand names as each tries to fill as many market "niches" as possible. A recent trend: gilding the prime brand name with a premium line like Whirlpool Gold or General Electric Profile.

Manufacturers make many but not all of the appliances they sell, since setting up manufacturing facilities is a big capital investment. So the companies often fill in gaps in their lines with machines made by another.

In the box on pages 90 and 91, we trace these relationships, since they can point the way to good buys. Related models may share features or design approaches. If you like a feature, you may be able to find it on a less expensive relation. Relationships can also shift from year to year, so the families may have changed since we published this book.

Deciphering model numbers. Major appliances usually come in a small selection of colors, such as white, black, white-on-white, or almond. Most manufacturers designate each color as a suffix in the model number: JGBP30WEWWW for white-on-white, JGBP30WEWB for black. In our appliance Ratings, we show such codes with empty brackets—JGBP30WEW[ ]—so you know that our Ratings apply to any model with the "base" model number.

BLENDERS

***Last CR report:** February 1997*
***Expect to pay:** $25 to $100*

A blender is basically a set of rotating blades in a covered jar. After the food proessor was introduced, the blender became an inexpensive commodity appliance. Then "professional" models with lots of power—enough to chip ice without liquid—were introduced, followed by a new breed of blender, with the base, not the container or jar, dominant and electronic touchpad controls. None of this changes the fact that blenders are good at some tasks but not others—say, pureeing vegetables, but not whipping cream.

What's available

The traditional blender brands—Hamilton Beach, Waring, Osterizer, Sunbeam—have lately been joined by Cuisinart, KitchenAid, and Krups. Old-style blenders are priced at $25 to $30. The new, powerful designs are typically $50 to $100 or more.

Key features

You need a range of **speeds** but not a zillion buttons, since adjacent speeds will likely be almost identical. A **Pulse feature** helps avoid overblending. A **power boost** (or "burst") lets you momentarily increase blade speed. **Electronic controls** are no easier to use than **push buttons** but easier to clean.

Many blenders claim that their **jars** have a "unique design" to increase effectiveness, but others did just as well in our tests. A **wide mouth** makes loading food easier; **clear markings** aid measuring. A **pouring spout** is standard. **Glass containers** are heavy—usually 3 to 3½ pounds—but more stable and keep their good appearance. **Plastic containers** may wobble in their bases, and they may scratch. A **chrome base** shows fingerprints.

How to choose

First make sure a blender is the right appliance for the tasks you have in mind. It excels at pureeing vegetables, making milkshakes and smoothies, and grating lemon peel. A food processor is better at grating hard cheese like Parmesan or Romano and grinding peanuts into butter. Neither can whip cream very well—for that you need a mixer.

Performance differences. Design changes don't necessarily improve performance. In our tests, two expensive blenders choked on basic tasks or lacked a dishwasher-safe container and top. Some cheap blenders leaked food when operated full, and others finished our tests with slightly rusty blades.

What to spend. More money typically buys a fancy model with touchpad controls or lots of of speeds, but that won't necessarily improve performance.

BREADMAKERS

***Last CR report:** November 1997*
***Ratings:** page 110*
***Expect to pay:** $60 to $250*

What's available

A breadmaker is essentially a mixer, kneader, proofing oven, and mini-oven rolled into one appliance. There are more than two dozen brands of breadmakers, but the major players in the marketplace are Oster, Regal, Welbilt, and West Bend. Breadmaker size indicates maximum loaf size: 1, 1½, 2, or 2½ pounds. Larger machines may cost more but generally offer extra cycles such as whole-wheat and "dough" for rolls, croissants, or pizza you bake in a conventional oven. Most make a tall, square column-shaped loaf with a rounded top; several now produce a more traditional rectangular one. Prices for the smaller, less featured models can start as low as $60. Larger models cost $100 to $250.

Key features

A **digital display** indicates preparation stage and time left. A few touchpad buttons and a start button set controls. A

delay-start timer lets you assemble ingredients in the pan up to 13 hours ahead. A **mix-in signal** lets you know when to add raisins, caraway seeds, and so forth. (If your machine has no mix-in signal, add such ingredients before the end of the knead cycle.)

Most have a **rapid cycle** that cuts an hour or so but may sacrifice height and a light texture. A **dough cycle** mixes and kneads. You can then remove the dough to shape it, then bake it in a conventional oven. **Programmed cycles** let you adjust the time, temperature, or handling for special breads, such as fruit and nut or batter breads.

Other features include a control to lighten or darken the crust; a yeast dispenser; power-outage protection; an automatic stop if the room temperature is too hot or cold for the yeast to rise.

How to choose

Performance differences. All breadmakers we've tested made good or very good bread as long as the ingredients were correctly measured and fresh. Well-designed controls plus simple loading and cleanup make the task easier. Most have a simple, color-coded keypad with large, easy-to-read keys. Comparison-shop if you can, and don't settle for manufacturer's list price.

What to spend. Basic machines of all sizes can be found priced at less than \$100. A higher price buys extra features and special cycles.

CLOTHES DRYERS

Last CR report: *June 1998*
Ratings: *page 118*
Expect to pay: *\$250 to \$650*

The most sophisticated machines let you select the degree of dampness for clothes that need ironing. They can keep the drum tumbling to prevent wrinkles from setting if you can't remove dry clothes right away. And they treat delicate fabrics more gently than dryers that rely on thermostat-controlled heat—saving time and energy, and offering more convenience.

What's available

Kenmore (Sears), Whirpool, General Electric, and Maytag are the leading brands in this market.

Full-sized models. They vary only slightly in width, the critical dimension for fitting into cabinetry and closets—27 to 29 inches. Full-sized models vary in drum capacity from 5½ to 7 cubic feet. Some can be stacked with a washer. The larger the drum, the more easily a dryer can handle bulky items and the less likely big loads will come out wrinkled. Gas models, which contain more hardware, cost about \$50 more than electric models. Price range: electric, \$250 to \$550; gas, \$300 to \$600.

Compact models. All electric, these are typically 24 inches wide, with a drum capacity roughly half that of full-sized models—about 3½ cubic feet. They can be stacked, using additional hardware, atop a companion washer. Compacts take longer than full-sized models to dry clothes—they don't gauge dryness as well—and they offer few conveniences. Some models operate on 120 volts, others on 240. Typically, the lint filter is inconveniently located in the rear of the drum. Price: $350 or so.

Key features

Useful to all. As clothes tumble by a **moisture sensor,** electrical contacts in the drum test surface dampness and relay signals to electronic controls, which adjust the automatic cycles. Dryers with a **thermostat,** by contrast, measure moisture indirectly by taking the temperature of exhaust air from the drum. A moisture sensor is more accurate, sparing your laundry unnecessary drying—and you needless energy costs.

In response to energy-efficiency standards that the Department of Energy issued in May 1994, manufacturers now produce dryers that have at least one cycle in which the dryer automatically shuts off when the clothes are done. Full-sized dryers often have two or three **auto-dry cycles**; each cycle has a More Dry setting to dry clothes completely and a Less Dry setting, which is supposed to provide damp clothes ready for ironing. Most also have a separate temperature control so you can, say, keep the heat lower for delicate fabrics.

Most models have a **cool-down** feature—such as "Press Care" or "Finish Guard"—to prevent wrinkles from setting in if you don't remove clothing when the drying cycle is over. Some models continue to tumble without heat, and others cycle the drum on and off intermittently.

Most dryers have straightforward **dials** for choosing the cycle, temperature, and other options. A few are more complicated. Markings may be small and hard to line up to the desired setting. Some more expensive models, in addition to a cycle-selector dial, have **mechanical touchpad buttons** for setting other functions. But when set they're hard to make out from a distance.

A top-mounted **lint filter** is generally easier to clean than a filter that fits inside the drum. Some models have a signal to warn you when the lint filter is blocked.

Useful to some. Most full-size models have a **drum light**, which makes it easy to spot stray socks. Some offer a **drying rack**, which remains stationary while the drum rotates around it, for delicate or heavy, noisy items. On some models you can adjust the **end-of-cycle signal** volume or shut it off altogether.

How to choose

Performance differences. Nearly all the dryers we've tested in recent years have dried ordinary laundry loads well. Models with a moisture sensor don't overdry as much as models controlled by a thermostat, saving a little energy as well as fabric wear and tear.

If the dryer will go near the kitchen or a bedroom, consider noise level. Some models are loud enough to drown out conversation.

What to spend. Moisture-sensing dryers are priced between $350 and $650, but spending more doesn't necessarily buy you more features or better performance. Thermostat-regulated dryers generally cost $30 less. If you have gas service, opt for a gas dryer. Although priced about $50 more than electric ones, they typically cost about 30 cents less per load to operate, making up the price difference in a year or two of use. However, all the extra plumbing usually makes repairing gas dryers more expensive.

DISHWASHERS

Last CR report: *March 1998*
Ratings: *page 113*
Expect to pay: *$250 to $2,000*

A new dishwasher is likely to be quieter and more energy efficient than the one you now own, especially if yours is more than a few years old. New models typically use only 7 or 7½ gallons versus 14 gallons on older models. Stainless steel is currently fashionable inside and out but adds as much as $200 or $300 to the price. Pricey machines may also be very quiet and very energy efficient. But some may also have a filter that needs to be manually cleaned.

New technology, which adjusts water use to the dirtiness of the loads, is supposed to improve the water-and-energy efficiency. But you can conserve with any model—run it at the lightest cycle. Using as little as half the water of a normal cycle, this cycle may well suffice for many loads.

What's available

Whirlpool, Maytag, and General Electric account for most of the dishwashers sold. The biggest-selling brand is Kenmore (Sears). Most models fit into a 24-inch-wide space under the kitchen countertop, where they are permanently attached to a hot-water pipe, a drain, and an electrical line. Compact models require less width. Portable models are functionally similar to built-ins, in a finished cabinet on rollers so they can be brought over to the sink. Price range: $250 to $800 for domestic brands; $550 to $2,000 for European models.

Key features

Most models offer a choice of at least three **wash cycles**—light, normal, and heavy. Light may be good enough. Normal is usually a compromise between wash quality and water usage. The heaviest cycle cleans the best but uses the most water. Rinse-and-hold lets you wait for a full load. Other cycles—"pot scrubber," "soak and scrub," "china and crystal"—aren't worth the extra expense. Dishwashers typically let you choose a heated dry cycle or an electricity-saving, no-heat dry. Pricier dishwashers often distribute water from more places—or "levels"—in the machine. We haven't found a significant cleaning difference based solely on the number of wash levels or number of cycles.

The way a dishwasher keeps food it has removed off cleaned dishes does make a difference. Many of the best-performing machines use two **filters** to keep wash water free of food particles: a coarse outer filter for trapping large bits and a fine inner one to catch minute grit. In most models, the coarse filter is self-cleaning; a spray arm washes residue off it during the rinse cycle. In the others, the filter must be cleaned by hand from time to time. A **food-disposal grinder** in some machines cuts up large food particles into smaller ones.

Some models give you the option of heating rinse water, which doesn't clean better but might be useful if you want to sanitize baby bottles. It could prove a little expensive if used routinely—as much as $14 or so a year in electricity.

Better **soundproofing** is a step-up feature in many lines.

Mechanical controls, usually operated by a dial and push buttons, are found on the least expensive dishwashers; other models have **electronic touchpad controls**. Neither works better, though touchpads are easier to clean. Dial movement helps you chart progress through a cycle. Some electronic models provide a digital display showing time left in the cycle. Others merely show a "clean" signal. Some models with mechanical controls require you to set both dial and push buttons. If they don't match, you may not get the right combination of water quantity and temperature. A delayed-start control lets you run the washer at night when utility rates may be lower.

Most models put cups and glasses on top, plates on the bottom, and silverware in a basket. If your dishes are an unusual size or shape, take a couple of plates along when shopping to see if they fit. Features that enhance flexibility include **adjustable and removable tines**, which can flatten areas to accept bigger dishes, pots, and pans; **removable racks** to let you load and unload items outside the dishwasher; **stemware holders** to keep wine glasses steady; **fold-down shelves** for stacking cups in a double-tiered arrangement; and **adjustable and terraced racks** to accommodate tall items.

Stainless-steel tubs may last virtually forever, whereas plastic ones can discolor or crack, but most plastic tubs are backed with a 20-year warranty—much longer than most people keep a dishwasher. In our tests, stainless-steel-lined models did have a slightly shorter drying time but did not wash any better.

How to choose

Performance differences. Manufacturers typically make a few different wash systems, with different arrays of "levels" and filters. Most do an excellent or very good job of washing dishes, with little or no spotting or redepositing of food. Avoid the lowest-priced models, those without a filtering system, which tends to redeposit tiny bits of food. Otherwise, the main differences are water and energy usage and noise level.

A dishwasher uses some electricity to run its motor and drying heater or fan. But about 80 percent goes into heating water in the water heater and the machine. In the long run, differences in water efficiency noticeably affect the cost of owning a new dishwasher. The models in our most recent tests used between $4\frac{1}{2}$ and $10\frac{1}{2}$ gallons per normal cycle. The annual cost of operation might range from about \$35 to \$50 if you have a gas water heater, or \$50 to \$80 if it's electric.

Most good-performing models took at least 90 minutes to complete a cycle; a few models even ran for about two hours. Though most models are fairly noisy, especially when filling, the quietest are so unobtrusive you might barely hear them. Most models with the word "quiet" in their name were among the noisiest machines in our tests.

What to spend. You can buy a very good dishwasher for less than \$400. Higher-priced machines are more likely to come with electronic controls and a stainless-steel tub, and be notably quiet. Many are European imports, which conserve water and energy and may be very good (but not excellent) at washing. But they are generally expensive, sometimes astonishingly so.

Compare store prices for delivery and installation. Expect to pay about \$100; removing your old machine may cost \$25 to \$50 more.

FOOD PROCESSORS

***Last CR report:** August 1997*
***Ratings:** page 122*
***Expect to pay:** $35 to $230*

Food processors can take vegetables from grocery bag to salad bowl in record time, quickly puree a batch of baby food, mix dough, or even chop meat. But they aren't for everyone. While many owners have relegated them to an out-of-the-way cupboard, others find them indispensable.

What's available

Processors vary by bowl capacity, ranging from less than a cup to nine cups or so (that's dry capacity; the bowl's open-topped tube for the drive shaft limits liquid capacity to about half that). Large processors are useful for ambitious menus or the large quantities required for feeding many. Midsized models handle four to seven cups, good for most uses. The mini models—essentially just choppers with accessories—can dice an onion, shred a carrot, or chop a cup of nuts.

Price range: Mini models, $30 to $40. Midsized models, $35 to $90. Large, $50 to $100 for basic models, up to $230 for more powerful, versatile models.

Key features

All standard food processors have **a clear plastic bowl** and lid and a **plastic food-pusher.** And some provide a chute to expel shredded or sliced food into a separate container. Some **feed tubes** are wide enough to fit a medium-sized tomato. Some also incorporate a slender inner tube for holding narrow foods like carrots.

A simple housing is easier to wipe clean. **Touchpad** controls also expedite cleanup. One **speed** is usually enough.

An S-shaped metal chopping **blade** and a slicing-shredding **disk** are standard for large and midsized models. Some models come with separate slicing and shredding disks.

How to choose

Performance differences. Most models we've tested can puree and shred without problems. Chopping and slicing are more demanding. Kneading dough takes power. Large models handled moveable dough effortlessly. With less powerful machines, we had to split the dough into two batches.

Cooking enthusiasts may want to consider a large model. A midsized model may suit you if you simply want the basics—pureeing, chopping and shredding. Mini food processors save space but don't do much.

A food processor can't handle all tasks. An electric mixer is better for mashed potatoes or whipped cream, a standard blender for pureeing baby food or concocting drinks.

What to spend. You needn't pay top dollar. Spending more than $70 for a midsized model or more than $100 for a large model buys features such as an extra, small bowl, wide feed tube, or special attachments for whipping cream or mixing dough. In our tests, the more expensive models were typically better slicers and quieter in use, however.

Mass merchandisers like Kmart and kitchen stores like Lechter's usually carry brands like Betty Crocker, Black & Decker, and Hamilton Beach. Look for top-of-the-line brands in department stores, gourmet shops, and mail-order sources.

FREEZERS

Last CR report: October 1997
Expect to pay: $300 to $650

Bulk freezing lets you buy or cook food in quantity and freeze it for later use. You can also buy fresh foods in season to enjoy all year round.

What's available

Nearly all freezers sold in the U.S. are made by two companies: Frigidaire and W.C. Woods, a Canadian manufacturer. Frigidaire sells under its name as well as Gibson, Kelvinator, Kenmore (Sears), Tappan, and White-Westinghouse. Woods makes Admiral, Amana, Magic Chef, Maytag, Roper, and Whirlpool models. General Electric models are made by both companies.

Chest freezers. These are best for lots of bulk purchases, long-term storage, and large, bulky items.

Because of their design, chests excel in almost every aspect of cold storage, and they run very efficiently. Their walls encase cooling coils that surround the stacked frozen food (there are no shelves). The top-open door allows only the warmest air to escape; when the door is closed, its weight helps seal the unit. Their design also helps chests do better than uprights when the power goes off.

However, chests take up more floor area than uprights and, with only some hanging baskets, the space is hard to organize. Finding specific food packages may take hunting. Defrosting has to be done manually; automatic defrost is not available. Some have a "flash defrost" that circulates hot refrigerant through the coils. But you still have to empty the unit, store the food, and drain the water. Price range: $300 for a 7-cubic-foot model to $550 for one that's 25 cubic feet.

Manual-defrost uprights. Similar in size and shape to refrigerators, these provide eye-level storage on the upper shelves and door storage. Uprights are good if you buy smaller quantities more often. Manual-defrost models are cheaper to buy and run than self-defrosters. This type comes with four or five fixed shelves (they contain cooling coils), which make it easy to organize food, but it may not hold bulky items.

When the door is opened, cool air spills out at the bottom and warm air sneaks in at the top. Ice forms on the coldest surfaces—the wire-covered cooling coils. So defrosting is a chore—and often needed more frequently than with a chest model. Price range: $300 to $550.

Self-defrost uprights. These have been the fastest growing type, despite costing the most to buy and run. They perform very well and are as convenient as refrigerators. Most of their main shelves are adjustable or removable and are further organized by wire racks, bins, and baskets. As with manual-defrost uprights, door shelves abound, although they're not the greatest spots for long-term storage. Cooling coils are hidden, as in a refrigerator; their effect is enhanced by fan action that circulates chilled air, keeping temperatures fairly uniform despite cold-air losses inherent in the vertically opening door. Price range: $500 to $650.

Key features

You don't need to adjust a freezer's **controls** often. But it's still easier if they're in the front. Chest models have a useful **power-on light** atop the unit. Less useful features: a "temperature alarm," which doesn't work in a power outage, and "quick freeze," which you can do with any model by using the coldest setting. Most freezers have at most only one **light**, not enough if they're full. Chest freezers have a hanging **basket** or two. A few manual-defrost uprights have an **adjustable shelf** in addition to the fixed ones. Self-defrost uprights have lots of removable **shelves**, baskets, bins, and a few adjustable shelves—some with a front "gate" to secure food.

How to choose

Performance differences. Within a type, we found, most models are similar in performance, efficiency, and conveniences—or inconveniences. Choose by freezer type and size, price and features.

What to spend. To make the investment in a freezer worthwhile, you would need to save $50 to $125 on food a year over, say, a 12-year period. The smallest, cheapest freezers, chest or manual-defrost models, cost about $300. Expect to pay extra for the convenience of an upright. Automatic defrost can add $150.

MICROWAVE OVENS

Last CR report: *March 1998*
Ratings: *page 125*
Expect to pay: *$100 to $200*

The microwave oven has come a long way since it was introduced 30 years ago. Today's models are easier to use than those we tested as recently as 5 years ago, and they're less expensive. For less than $200, you can get a large, high-powered machine with one-touch settings for popping popcorn, warming leftovers, defrosting meat, and more.

What's available

Microwave ovens come in a range of sizes, from subcompacts to family-sized models. Most are designed to sit on a countertop. Some medium-sized models are specifically designed to be mounted over the range. The main difference between large and small ovens is the power produced by the magnetron, which generates the high-energy microwaves. The higher the wattage, the more powerful the oven and the more quickly it heats food, most noticeable when cooking large quantities.

Key features

A **turntable** promotes uniform heating. In some models, you can turn it off so you can use a dish that's too big to rotate in the oven, but the results won't be as even.

In addition to the **numeric keypad** used to set cooking times and power levels, ovens typically have **shortcut keys** for cooking particular foods, reheating, or defrosting. Often, you press the touchpad, then enter the quantity or weight. Some models have you press the shortcut key and the start touchpad—a guard against children turning on the oven. Other ovens start immediately with the shortcut key itself. A **one-minute (or 30-second) key** runs the oven at full power or extends current cooking time.

Models typically have several **power levels**. Six are more than adequate. Some models have a **sensor** to shut off the oven when food is cooked. In reheat tests, we found that ovens with a sensor left foods hotter than those with an automatic timed setting.

Some useless features: Stacking food on **racks** produces uneven results. With **delay start,** you can program some ovens hours in advance. But most food left in an oven can spoil. **Two-stage cooking** defrosts, then cooks, but you still must stir, turn, and check between cycles.

How to choose

Performance differences. Most of the ovens we've tested are easy to use and handle general microwaving tasks well. The higher the rated output wattage, the faster the cooking. Compact models typically produce 600 to 700 watts (about as much as large models did less than 10 years ago); midsized and large models, between 800 and 1000 watts.

What to spend. Look for a model whose dimensions will fit available counter space, and allow a few inches of clearance in back for oven vents. Bigger ovens obviously hold more, but even small ones will hold quite a lot of food. Some countertop ovens can also be mounted into a wall or cabinet with an optional kit, which costs about $80 to $160. For stainless-steel exteriors, add $50 to $100.

An over-the-range microwave oven is a good choice if you lack counter space—but costs about twice as much as a large countertop model. In recent tests, most performed microwave functions very well, but since the microwave ovens don't reach over the front range burners, their exhaust fans were less effective than those on typical range hoods. Such ovens are heavy—54 to 62 pounds—taking two people to install, and, if you lack a dedicated outlet, an electrician too.

STAND MIXERS

***Last CR report:** November 1994*
***Expect to pay:** $25 to $270*

Not everyone needs a stand mixer. An inexpensive hand mixer might suit you just fine if you mostly mix cake batter, whip cream, mash potatoes, or handle other moderate to light chores. But if you often make bread and cookies from scratch, a stand mixer is useful and convenient.

What's available

KitchenAid and Sunbeam are the leading brands in this market. Other sizable brands include Oster, Krups, Hamilton Beach, and Waring.

Stand mixers come in various sizes:

Heavy-duty models. These offer the most power and the largest mixing bowls, typically have a dough hook and a whisk, and can handle at least six cups of flour. On most models, the beater head can be tipped up to remove the bowl. Price range: $200 to $270.

Medium-duty models. This category (our designation) is lighter and less powerful, can handle less bread dough—3½ cups of flour at most—and typically comes with one large and one small bowl, a pair of beaters, and a pair of dough hooks.

Light-duty models. These are essentially hand mixers resting on a stand. You can detach them and use them that way. Price range: $25 to $120.

Other ways to mix. *Hand mixers,* small

enough to store in a drawer, may be all you need for light chores like mashed potatoes and cake batter. Price range: $20 to $50. *Multipurpose food fixers* combine stand mixer, blender, food processor, and salad maker. Price: $200 or so.

Key features

Medium- and heavy-duty mixers typically have two sizes of **bowls**, a **beater** or pair of **beaters**, a **wire whisk**, and a pair of **dough hooks**. A heavy-duty stand mixer offers attachments for separate purchase, such as a meat grinder and pasta maker. The bowls rotate automatically as the beaters spin.

Expect three or more **speeds** (three are plenty). Speed dials or switches should be easy to read. Ideally, a stand mixer's **head** can be locked in the up or down position so it won't slip in use or between mixings.

How to choose

Performance differences. Choose a heavy-duty model, the size that performed best overall in our tests, from kneading dough to whipping cream. Medium-duty mixers outperformed the heavyweights at mashing potatoes. They also mixed cookie dough and kneaded bread fairly well.

The heavier the mixer, the steadier it is while mixing. Of course, heavy machines are harder to handle. Some heavy-duty stand mixers can weigh over 20 pounds while medium-duty and light-duty mixers weigh from 4½ to 8½ pounds. Keep weight in mind when you consider how you'll keep your mixer—leave it on your counter or store it—when not in use.

What to spend. Heavy-duty models cost more than $200. But they can handle heavy baking chores that hand mixers can't touch. Medium-duty mixers are better at potato-mashing than dough-kneading, but they do all that many cooks need at about half the price of a heavy-duty model. Hand mixers are low-priced, $20 to $50, and small enough to keep in a drawer.

Warranties typically cover parts and labor for one or two years.

RANGES

Last CR report: *May 1998*
Expect to pay: *$200 to $1,500*

Many of the choices to make in buying a range are probably dictated by your kitchen. If your home is plumbed for natural gas or propane, you can avail yourself of the instant response preferred by serious cooks. If you must choose electric, those ranges offer new cooktop heating technologies and typically superior baking performance. Your cabinetry and kitchen floorplan will probably dictate the width and position of your range.

What's available

General Electric, Whirlpool, and Kenmore (Sears) account for more than half the freestanding electric ranges sold. Kenmore and General Electric are the top-selling brands of gas ranges, with Tappan, Magic Chef, and Whirlpool clustered in the second tier.

Freestanding models. These can fit in

the middle of a kitchen counter or at the end. Depending on whether you choose gas or electric, widths range from 20 to 40 inches, but most are 30 inches. Price range: $200 to $1,500.

Built-in models. *Slide-ins* fit into a space between cabinets. *Drop-ins* fit into cabinets connected below the oven (at the toe-kick level). Both types look built-in and cost about the same as comparable freestanding models. A *stand-alone cooktop* paired with a *wall oven* allows more flexibility in layout. Most stand-alone cooktops are 30 inches wide and made of porcelain-coated steel or ceramic glass, with four elements or burners. Some are 36 inches wide, with space for an extra burner. Modular cooktops may have a pop-in grill, a rotisserie, or other options. Wall ovens come in 24-, 27-, and 30-inch widths. You can install an oven at eye level, nest the oven under a cooktop, or stack two ovens. A cooktop and wall oven typically cost considerably more than an all-in-one range—up to $800 for the cooktop and $2,000 for the oven.

Gas models. Gas cooktops can be porcelain-coated steel or stainless steel, and for freestanding cooktops, even glass. Gas burners are easy to adjust and shut off instantly. But even so-called high-speed burners tend to heat more slowly than electric coil elements. *Sealed burners*, with no space for spills to seep below the cooktop, are almost universal and are a bit easier to clean than the older, unsealed burners. Most ranges have several burner sizes, often one or two medium ones (9,000 British thermal units per hour), a small one (5,000 Btu/hr.) for simmering, and one or two large ones (up to 12,500 Btu/hr.) for fast heating. Gas ovens often have the broiler inside instead of underneath. Oven capacity is typically slightly smaller than that of electric models.

Electric models. Electric elements offer quick heating and the ability to maintain low heat levels. *Coil elements*, the most common and least expensive type, are fairly forgiving of warped and dented pots. If they break, they're an easy and inexpensive do-it-yourself repair job. Spills go into easily cleaned bowls and residue burns off coils; heavy spills may go into wells under the prop-up cooktop.

In smoothtop electric ranges, a sheet of ceramic glass conceals *radiant* or *halogen* elements. Smoothtops are easy to clean, since no burners block the way. The surface can also double as a temporary counter when the heat is off. To get the best performance, you should use flat-bottom cookware. To keep it sleek, you must wipe up sugary spills immediately, or they'll pit the ceramic surface. Manufacturers also recommend the regular use of a special cleansing cream that comes with each new unit. Although the top is hard to break, it's not invincible. Replacement can cost as much as half the range's original price, labor not included. Electric ovens are typically spacious and heat evenly.

"Commercial" models. The "commercial" or "professional" look—burnished chrome or stainless-steel panels set off by brawny black grates and knobs—is making its way from high-end product lines like Viking into more traditional lines like General Electric, Kenmore, and Frigidaire.

Key features

Hot-surface **indicator lights** on an electric range warn against touching the cooktop. Ovens with a **12-hour shutoff** turn off automatically, but most models allow you to disable this feature—a useful option for people who, for religious reasons, can't turn on their oven on certain days. **Child lockout** lets you disable the oven controls.

Dial controls are still standard for cooktops. Freestanding electric ranges have them on the backguard; freestanding gas ranges, in front of the cooktop. On electric ranges, controls may be divided left and right, with the oven controls in between, giving you a quick sense of which control works which element. Controls clustered in the center of the backguard stay visible even with tall pots on back elements. **Dual-element burners,** on many smoothtops, allow you to switch between a large, high-power burner and a small, lower-power burner.

A **warm zone** or **simmer feature** will keep just-cooked food warm. **Porcelain-coated drip bowls** on coil-burners keep their luster longer than chrome ones.

Easy-cleaning features include **porcelain drip pans**, a **glass** or **porcelain backguard** instead of a painted one, and a design that includes **seamless corners and edges,** especially where the cooktop joins the backguard—a **raised edge** around the cooktop to contain spills, like chrome. On a conventional cooktop, look for **deep wells** to contain spills, and, for electric cooktops, minimal clutter under the cooktop and a top that props up for cleaning.

Usable **oven capacity** is sometimes not much more than half of what the manufacturer claims because they don't take protruding broiler elements and such into account. The largest ovens by our most recent measurements are found on Magic Chef and Whirlpool electrics; they're more than 25 percent larger than the smallest ovens, on the Hotpoints and the Kenmores.

A **dial** is faster to use and more straightforward than a microwave-type **touchpad,** although touchpad controls are easier to clean. A dial costs about $80 to $90 to replace; touchpad controls might cost twice that. Pricier models generally have touchpads. **Variable broil,** found on some electric ranges, offers adjustable settings for foods such as fish or thick steaks that require slower or faster cooking.

Cook-time/delay-start lets you set a time for the oven to start and stop cooking. But avoid leaving most foods in a cold oven for long. A **self-cleaning cycle** is well worth the extra cost, even if you don't use the oven a lot. It generally does a better job on walls than on the window. The feature adds about $50 to $75 to the price of a coil-burner; it's included in the price of most smoothtop ranges. **An automatic door lock,** on most self-cleaning models, is activated during the high-temperature self-cleaning cycle. The door unlocks when the oven has cooled. An **automatic oven light** comes on when you open the door. Some ovens have only a switch-operated light.

How to choose

Performance differences. Virtually every range we've tested of late does a fine job of heating, baking, and broiling. Decide on a type of cooktop first, and then let features, styling, price, and repair history guide your choice.

What to spend. Freestanding ranges generally offer the best value. You can buy a very basic electric or gas range for less than $300. Sealed burners add $50 to $100 to the price of a gas range, while a self-cleaning oven adds $150 to $200 to any model. We recommend both of these labor-saving features. Smoothtops generally cost $100 more than electrics with conventional coil elements. Spending more than $1,000 on a range buys lots of extras, like electronic controls and a "professional" design. A model's price typically varies by $25 to $75, depending on the color combination. Stainless steel is usually expensive.

REFRIGERATORS

Last CR report: *January 1998*
Expect to pay: *$450 to $2,150*

Refrigerators come in all sizes, from inexpensive cubes for offices or dorms to built-ins approaching restaurant proportions. "Built-in-look" models are the newest type. Less deep than regular models, they can be almost flush with kitchen cabinets and faced with cabinetry-matching door panels. Useful features such as glass shelves, once found only on expensive models, are practically standard on mid-priced ones. Stainless-steel doors, the latest kitchen fashion, are an expensive extra.

New refrigerators no longer use environmentally damaging chlorofluorocarbon (CFC) refrigerants; all models now use hydrofluorocarbons (HFCs) and hydrochlorofluorocarbons (HCFCs), chemicals that have far less potential impact on the ozone layer than CFCs.

What's available

Top-freezer models. The most common type, these are generally less expensive to buy and run than comparably sized side-by-side models. Width, the critical measurement, ranges from about 24 to 36 inches. The eye-level freezer offers easy access. Fairly wide shelves in the refrigerator compartment make it easy to reach the back, but you must bend to get at bottom shelves. Nominal capacity ranges from about 10 to almost 26 cubic feet, but we find usable capacity to be about 25 percent less. Price range: $450 to $1,300 or more, depending on size and features.

Bottom-freezer models. These are only offered in a few brands—Amana, GE, Kenmore, and KitchenAid. The design puts the items you use most at eye level, with fairly wide shelves in the refrigerator compartment. Despite a pullout freezer basket, you must still bend to locate most items. Bottom-freezer models are a bit more expensive than top-freezer models, with somewhat less capacity for their external dimensions. Price range: $850 to $1,100.

Side-by-side models. Part of both the main compartment and the freezer is at eye level and easy to reach. Narrow doors are handy where clearance is tight. High, narrow compartments make finding stray items easy in front (but harder in the back) and may not hold such items as a big turkey or large platter. Compared with top- and bottom-freezer models, there's more freezer space. Side-by-sides are typically large—30 to 36 inches wide, with nominal capacity of 19 to 30 cubic feet. They are much more expensive than similar-size top-freezer models and typically less energy-efficient than other types. Price range: $800 to $2,150 or more.

Key features

Glass shelves are easier to clean than the wire racks on "base model" refrigerators—but also easier to break. Shelves on most models have a **spill-guard,** a sealed and raised rim that keeps small spills from dripping downward. **Split shelves** (half shelves that span the main space) can be independently adjusted for height.

Pullout shelves make food easier to get at. **Adjustable door bins** allow you to arrange door storage space as you like. In the freezer, **pullout freezer shelves** or **bins** provide easier access to frozen foods.

A **temperature-controlled chiller** keeps meat or fish a few degrees cooler but can also be left unchilled for other foods. (All the temperature-controlled chillers we've tested recently performed very well.) **See-through compartments**—transparent crispers, meat drawers—let you tell at a glance what's inside. An **interior light** is standard. A **freezer light** is handy.

Once a refrigerator's set, there's little need to reach the controls. Still, **accessible controls** are an added convenience.

Most models come with an **ice-maker** installed in the freezer (or the option to install it yourself). They typically produce three or four pounds of ice a day but reduce freezer space by about a cubic foot. Many side-by-sides have an **ice and water dispenser** on the outside of the door. Though convenient, these extras add to the base cost and increase the repair risk. Some models offer a **water filter** on the line that serves the ice-maker and water dispenser. Assess your need for filtration before you buy it.

Shelf snuggers are sliding brackets that attach to door shelves to hold bottles and jars. A **wine rack** allows you to chill a bottle on its side.

Crispers with controls keep fruits and vegetables in the right humidity range. But so did the crispers without controls in our tests.

How to choose

Performance differences. Except for some small, basic models, modern refrigerators do a good job of keeping things cold. Many models are pretty quiet, too—some exceptionally so. Energy efficiency, configurations, and convenience features vary considerably, our tests show. The low-rated refrigerators are likely to be less satisfying to live with long-term than the best. Most lack niceties such as simple-to-use crispers and chillers or easily-arranged shelves. While many low-rated models are relatively inexpensive to buy, they also tend to be fairly inefficient.

Your refrigerator probably accounts for as much as one-fifth of your annual electricity bill. In response to federal regulations, new refrigerators use less power. Our tests show an energy-efficiency variation of as much as 65 percent, even among top-freezer models, the most efficient type. A highly efficient model that costs $200 or $300 more than an inefficient model is the better buy in the long run.

What to spend. A top-freezer model gives you the most refrigerator for the money. But your kitchen layout or personal preferences may send you to another type. In general, larger refrigerators have more features. An ice-maker adds $70 to $100, and an in-door ice dispenser adds $100 to $200 or so.

Before you shop, measure your space carefully, including room to open the doors. Some models can be flush against a side wall, and others need space for the doors to swing open. Top- and bottom-freezer models have reversible hinges so that they can open to either right or left. Overall, the narrow doors on side-by-side models require the least amount of space to open.

TOASTERS & TOASTER OVEN/BROILERS

Last CR report: *August 1998*
Ratings: *page 129*
Expect to pay: *$20 to $100*

Toasters, like a lot of small appliances, have become commodity items. For less than $20, you can buy a toaster that has a control for light or dark toast, a push-down lever to lower the bread, and not much else. And it will make decent toast, two slices at a time.

Appliance manufacturers have also been working on reinventing the toaster, inspired by newly popular foods, like bagels, and other kitchen appliances, notably the microwave oven, and the luxe/retro school of design that has also given us heavy-duty blenders and commercial-style espresso machines. For some of these toasters, you can pay $70, even $100.

Toaster oven/broilers also range from the simple small box that can toast four slices or bake a couple of potatoes to large models capable of standing in for certain kinds of oven cooking.

What's available

Longtime toaster brands like Sunbeam, Black & Decker, Proctor-Silex, and Toastmaster have been joined by names made familiar by other kitchen equipment: Cuisinart, KitchenAid, Krups, Oster, and Breadman. Other brands you will find include Rival, Kenmore (Sears), and DeLonghi.

Most toasters have an easy-to-clean plastic body that stays cool to the touch. Most brands are available in two-slice and four-slice versions, with slots wide enough to accommodate a bagel or English muffin half. Some have one or two long slots instead of two or four.

Small toasters can hold four slices; large ones, six. Some four-slice models have separate controls for each pair. Most toaster ovens broil and have a "top brown" element for melting cheese and the like.

Key features

Most toasters still have a dial or lever to set for darkness. **Electronic controls** allow you to control shadings and settings with a touchpad. **Indicator lights** show the settings. A **toast boost** allows you to raise smaller items like English muffins. A **pop-up control** you push is now a touchpad or a button rather than a lever. A **cord wrap** feature keeps the cord out of the way. Most models have a hinged **crumb tray.** Cleaning is easier if the tray is removeable.

Toaster ovens have an **indicator light** to show they're heating. They come with a removable **metal pan.** The best kind: a deep oven pan that moves toward you on the rack when the door is opened. Some models have an under-cabinet **installation kit** as an option.

How to choose

Performance differences. For even, golden toast, choose a toaster. Even the best toaster oven produced toast with a stripe on one side, and many can't toast evenly at all. But ovens can cook many other things.

Most toasters make adequate toast. But few, we found, toast to perfection. Our tests revealed some whose controls wouldn't allow light toasting.

What to spend. If you just want a few slices of toast now and then, practically any toaster will suit your needs. For $70 or more, you also get an elegantly designed appliance, but it doesn't guarantee better toast.

WASHING MACHINES

***Last CR report:** July 1998*
***Ratings:** page 133*
***Expect to pay:** $300 to $1,100*

Manufacturers, anticipating new federal regulations that may require washing machines to use less energy, are increasingly offering front-loading washers. Since they fill with water only partially (the inner tub spins on its side like a dryer, plunging the clothes in and out of a small pool of suds), front-loaders use less hot water—and hence less energy—than top-loading machines. (Because front-loaders relieve electrical demand, some utilities, mostly in the West, are offering rebates of $40 to $300 to customers who buy the machines.) Also, most front-loading washers fit where no full-sized top-loader will go—under a counter, for example, or stacked below a clothes dryer.

But front-loading machines cost at least twice what many top-loading washers cost. And to get the best results, you need to use special detergent

What's available

The biggest-selling brands are Kenmore (Sears), Whirlpool, Maytag, and General Electric.

Top-loaders. In a top-loader, the clothes are circulated by an agitator, providing some advantages over front-loaders. They're less expensive to buy, easier to load, often handle larger loads, have faster cycles, and you can add items mid-cycle. Price range: $300 to $700.

Front-loaders. Front-loaders clean clothes by tumbling them so they rise near the top of the tub and then drop into the water below. The design handles unbalanced loads better than do top-loaders. Older designs used to hold significantly less laundry, but American-made front-loaders are now comparable with top-loaders—14 pounds of laundry or more. Price range: American brands, $700 to $1,100; European brands, $1,000 or more.

Compact models. Selection is limited. Tub capacity is about two cubic feet. Some are portable, and can be stored in a closet, rolled out, and hooked up to the kitchen sink for use. Price range: $450 to $550.

Key features

Most washers have a **porcelain-coated steel inner tub** that can rust if the porcelain chips or water stands too long. **Stainless-steel or plastic tubs** won't rust. A **porcelain top and lid** resist scratching better than paint.

Look for dials and buttons that are legible, easy to push or turn, and logically arranged. A plus: **cycle-indicator lights** or **signals**. On a top-loader, the **automatic lock during spin cycle** keeps children from opening the lid. Front-loaders must lock at the beginning of a cycle but can usually be opened by interrupting the cycle, although some doors stay shut for a minute or so after the machine stops.

Front-loaders automatically set **wash speed** according to fabric cycle selected, and some also set the spin speed. Many top-loaders we tested offer more flexibility. Most provide at least three wash/spin speed combinations, generally for "regular" (also called "cotton"), "permanent press," and "delicate" (also called "gentle") cycles. A few also allow an **extra rinse** or a longer final spin.

Front-loaders set **water levels** automatically, ensuring efficient use of water.

Next best are top-loaders that can be set for four or more levels, probably providing as much flexibility as anyone would need. (If you always wash a full load set to the maximum water level, fewer water-level settings are no problem.)

Most machines establish **wash and rinse temperatures** by mixing hot and cold water in preset proportions. If your incoming cold water is especially cold, **automatic temperature controls** adjust the flow to get the desired temperature.

Dispensers for detergent and fabric softener automatically release powder or liquid at the optimum time. **Bleach dispensers** can prevent spattering or premature leakage.

How to choose

Performance differences. All washers can get clothes clean. In our tests, we've found both front-loaders and top-loaders that did an excellent cleaning job. The noisiest machines, all top-loaders, made a racket through the whole cycle. Front-loaders are generally quieter but make the most noise when draining and spinning.

The efficiency of any washing machine rises with larger loads, but overall, front-loaders still use much less water per pound of laundry and excel in energy efficiency. Using electricity to heat water for six eight-pound loads a week, the most efficient top-loader would cost $35 a year to run; the least efficient, $44. The most frugal front-loader, by contrast, would cost about $17. (Those costs are based on national average utility prices; the differences would narrow if you used gas to heat your water, or if you consistently washed only a full load.)

What to spend. Unless you live in an area of very high water or energy rates, a top-loading washer is likely to be less expensive overall than a front-loading model. Best values are mid-priced top-loaders with few features—less than $500, sometimes a lot less. Features like extra wash/spin options, a porcelain top and lid, or an automatic detergent dispenser add some convenience but don't significantly improve washing performance.

Even though front-loaders are expensive, they could cost significantly less to operate, a saving that could, over time, help make up the difference. So could a utility company rebate. European front-loaders are expensive and small; none could handle much more than an eight-pound load. However, consumers who don't have space for a full-sized washer may want to consider one. They're about the same size as compact washing machines, but they perform much better.

Ratings Breadmakers
& Recommendations

The tests behind the Ratings

The **overall score** is based on bread quality, convenience (including quiet operation during kneading cycle), and versatility, which we judged based on the number of useful features. **Number of cycles** gives an idea of versatility. **Cycle times** are for a basic white loaf on the regular cycle and on the rapid cycle. The dough cycles are usually shorter; the whole-wheat, longer. **Price** is approximate retail.

Typical features for these models

• 14 in. high, 14 wide, and 11 deep. • Cycles for basic, basic rapid, and whole-wheat bread, and for basic bread dough. • Bakes a loaf that is shaped like a square column. • Lid that's removable, for easier cleaning. • Bakes a 2-lb. loaf. • Has a delay-start timer. • Has an "add ingredients" signal for fruit. • Bread pan and paddle that will cost from $40 to $60 to replace. • 1-yr. warranty for parts and labor.

Recommendations

Any breadmaker should bake good bread, but some make it easier or are quieter than others. The two top-rated models—the Panasonic SD-YD205, $190, and the Breadman TR800, $100—made the best bread and boast lots of special cycles that make them versatile. A simpler machine that is easier to use and very quiet: the Goldstar HB202CE, $100.

See report, page 93. Last time rated in CONSUMER REPORTS: November 1997.

Overall Ratings

E VG G F P

Listed in order of overall score

Key no.	Brand and model	Price	Overall score (0–100; P F G VG E)	No. of cycles	Cycle times, hrs. BASIC	RAPID
1	**Panasonic** Bread Bakery SD-YD205	$190		12	4:00	3:00
2	**Breadman** TR800	100		14	3:00	2:30
3	**Zojirushi** Home Baker Super BBCC-Q20	150		5	3:50	2:00
4	**Goldstar** HB202CE	100		7	3:40	2:00
5	**Toastmaster** Breadbox 1188	100		7	3:40	2:00
6	**Regal** Kitchen Pro K6743	100		6	2:40	—
7	**Breadman** Ultra TR700	100		7	2:40	—
8	**Pillsbury** Automatic Bread/ Dough Maker 1021	120		6	3:40	—

Key no.	Brand and model	Price	Overall score (0–100; P F G VG E)	No. of cycles	Cycle times, hrs. BASIC	Cycle times, hrs. RAPID
9	**West Bend** Baker's Choice Plus 41090	$200		8	3:40	3:20
10	**Black & Decker** All in One Deluxe B1630	110		6	3:50	2:00
11	**West Bend** Automatic Bread/ Dough Maker 41044	100		7	3:40	3:00
12	**Welbilt** The Bread Machine ABM4100T	95		6	3:00	2:30

Details on the models

1 Panasonic Bread Baker SD-YD205 $190

Extra cycles: Basic and whole-wheat (each with regular, rapid, "sandwich," and raisin bread and dough settings); multigrain bread and dough.
Better bread, even on rapid cycle. Rectangular loaf. Lots of useful features: "on" light, 10-min. power-outage protection, measuring cup and spoon, yeast dispenser. **But:** Less convenient than others—no window, timer sets in only 1 direction, "ready" signal too quiet, lid not removable. **Recommendation:** A very good, versatile bread-lover's machine—but pricey.

2 Breadman TR800 $100

Extra cycles: French, sweet, whole-wheat regular and rapid breads; "quick" breads; pizza and bagel dough; jam; "Bake-only."
Better bread. Rectangular loaf. Lots of cycles. Useful features: independent crust setting, cycle-progress timer light, 1-hr. power-outage protection, warning when ambient temperature is too low to bake bread, instructional video. **But:** Raucous motor, "ready" signal too quiet, only 90-day warranty on bread pan, paddle. Complaints about customer service. **Recommendation:** A very good but noisy machine.

3 Zojirushi Home Baker Super BBCC-Q20 $150

Extra cycles: Mixed and whole-grain breads.
Very fast rapid cycle. Useful features: independent crust settings, "on" light, 20-sec. power-outage protection, instructional video, measuring cup and spoon. Clear display. Loud "ready" signal. **But:** New pan is $67. **Recommendation:** A very good machine with no big drawbacks.

4 Goldstar HB202CE $100

Extra cycles: French and specialty bread, cake.
Programs easily. Very convenient to use. Very quiet. Fast rapid cycle. Independent crust settings, measuring cup. **But:** LED display is barely visible in bright light. **Recommendation:** A very good machine at a very nice price.

5 Toastmaster Breadbox 1188 $100

Extra cycles: French and sweet breads; jam.
Similar to (4) in looks, programming layout, accessories, and results. Has a 3-yr. warranty. **But:** Keypad, in French and English, is cluttered. **Availability:** Discontinued. **Recommendation:** A very good machine at a very nice price.

6 Regal Kitchen Pro K6743 $100

Extra cycles: French, sweet, and "quick" breads.
Basic cycle is fast; no rapid cycle. Programs easily. Slightly smaller "footprint" than other machines. Useful features: cycle-progress display, 10-min. power-outage protection, warning when ambient temperature is too low to bake bread, instructional video. **But:** Lid not removable, "ready" signal too quiet. **Availability:** Discontinued. **Recommendation:** A very good machine, and very fast.

7 Breadman Ultra TR700 $100

Extra cycles: French bread; fruit and nut bread; cake; jam.
Basic cycle is fast; no rapid cycle. Programs easily and has a clearer, more intuitive keyboard lay-

out than others. Useful features: warning when ambient temperature is too low to bake bread, instructional video. **But:** Very noisy. **Availability:** Discontinued. **Recommendation:** A very good, fast machine—but noisy.

8 Pillsbury Automatic Bread/Dough Maker 1021 $120

Extra cycles: French, sweet, and "quick" breads. Useful features: independent crust settings, cycle-progress display, warns when ambient temperature is too low to bake bread, 10-min. power-outage protection. **But:** Controls not clearly coded, "ready" signal too quiet, lacks keep-warm feature and "add ingredients" signal. **Recommendation:** Good.

9 West Bend Baker's Choice Plus 41090 $200

Extra cycles: Whole-wheat rapid bread; French, sweet, and quick breads.
Opens from front; shorter but much wider than others. Clear LED display. Useful features: independent crust settings, cycle-progress display, "on" light, 10-min. power-outage protection, warning when ambient temperature is too low to bake bread, interior light, loud "ready" signal, extended rise settings. **But:** Bread tended to be pale and sometimes lopsided. Harder to clean. Controls not clearly color coded. **Recommendation:** Only good—at a hefty price tag.

10 Black & Decker All in One Deluxe B1630 $110

Extra cycles: Sweet and whole-grain breads; pasta.
Generic recipe made bread of lower quality. Timer hard to set. Has independent crust settings on most cycles, "on" light, timer light, 20-sec. power-outage protection, instructional video, loud "ready" signal, fast rapid cycle. Slightly smaller footprint than others. Has 2-yr. warranty. **Similar model:** B1620, $100. **Recommendation:** Good, but finicky with recipes other than its own.

11 West Bend Automatic Bread/Dough Maker 41044 $100

Extra cycles: French and sweet breads; whole-wheat rapid bread.
Claims to make a 2-lb. loaf, but makes a 1½-lb. loaf. Noisy. Keypad layout not clear. Pan hard to insert, remove. Harder to clean. Has independent crust settings, cycle-progress display, warning when ambient temperature is too low to bake bread, "on" light. New pan only $25. **Recommendation:** Only good. There are better choices.

12 Welbilt The Bread Machine ABM4100T $95

Extra cycles: Sweet regular and sweet rapid breads; sweet dough. (No whole-wheat.)
Keyboard layout is less intuitive than others. Harder to clean than other machines. Lid not removable. No warranty. Has independent crust settings, cycle-progress displays, loud "ready" signal, quiet motor. **Recommendation:** Only good. There are better choices.

Ratings *Dishwashers*

& Recommendations

The tests behind the Ratings

Overall score stresses washing performance, but also considers energy efficiency, noise, and convenience. **Washing** performance reflects how well each model coped with a very tough challenge: regular loads (see **loading**) of food-smeared china, glasses, and flatware. **Energy use** reflects consumption on the normal cycle calculated annually at national average rates—61.9 cents per gas therm, 8.4 cents per kilowatt-hour—and running about six loads per week at the normal cycle. **Loading** reflects how easily a **regular** load could be placed into the dishwasher and how readily the model could handle **special** loads—including extra place settings and oversized items. **Ease of use** takes into account controls, features, and maintenance. **Price** is approximate retail.

Typical features for these models

• At least three wash cycles. • Automatic self-cleaning filter. • Plastic tub and door liner, warrantied for at least 20 yr. • Telescoping or fixed spray tower in the center of the lower rack. • Front panel that's replaceable or can be reversed to display another color. • Show progress through a cycle. • Programmable for a delayed start. • Boost wash-water temperature and supply heat for drying.

Recommendations

Most of the dishwashers tested do an excellent or very good job at the basic task. Energy efficiency, noise level, and features vary, however, as do brand reliability and, of course, price. The Kenmore models, sold by Sears, stood out on the strength of excellent washing performance. According to the manufacturer, though, the tested Dirt Sensor and QuietGuard models are being replaced by models with the same designation but different water-delivery systems, which we have not tested. Of the remaining models, all but the seven lowest-rated would make fine choices.

See report, page 96. Last time rated in CONSUMER REPORTS: March 1998.

Overall Ratings

E = Excellent, VG = Very good, G = Good, F = Fair, P = Poor

Listed in order of overall score

Key no.	Brand and model	Price	Overall score (0–100; P F G VG E)	Washing	Energy use	Loading: Reg.	Loading: Special	Ease of use
1	**Kenmore** (Sears) Dirt Sensor 1595	$580		E	F	E	F	E
2	**Kenmore** (Sears) QuietGuard 1579	420		E	VG	VG	P	G
3	**Kenmore** (Sears) Dirt Sensor 1583	450		E	F	VG	F	E

Ratings continued

Key no.	Brand and model	Price	Overall score (0–100: P F G VG E)	Washing	Energy use	Loading REG.	Loading SPECIAL	Ease of use
4	**Frigidaire** Gallery FDB949GF	$490		⊖	⊖	○	◓	⊜
5	**Kenmore** (Sears) QuietGuard 1568 **A CR Best Buy**	350		⊜	⊖	⊖	●	○
6	**Maytag** Quiet Plus II MDB6000A	470		⊜	○	⊖	◒	○
7	**GE** Profile Performance GSD4920Z	550		⊖	⊖	⊖	◒	⊜
8	**Miele** Turbothermic Plus G865	950		⊖	⊖	⊖	○	◒
9	**Asko** 1585	850		⊖	⊜	○	○	◒
10	**KitchenAid** Whisper Quiet Ultima Superba KUDS24SE	700		⊖	⊖	⊜	○	⊜
11	**Maytag** Quiet Pack MDB4000A	390		⊖	⊖	⊖	◒	○
12	**Asko** 1375	660		⊖	⊜	○	◒	◒
13	**Whirlpool** Quiet Wash Plus DU927QWD	400		⊖	⊖	⊖	◒	⊖
14	**Whirlpool** Quiet Wash Plus DU940QWD	450		⊖	⊖	⊖	◒	⊖
15	**Amana** Stainless Series ASU8000	730		⊖	◒	⊖	○	◒
16	**KitchenAid** Quiet Scrub KUDI24SE	540		⊖	⊖	⊖	●	⊖
17	**White-Westinghouse** QuietClean I MDB531RF	300		○	⊜	⊖	◒	○
18	**General Electric** Profile Quiet Power GSD4320Z	430		○	⊜	⊖	◒	⊜
19	**Whirlpool** Clean Wash DU840CWD	300		○	⊖	⊖	◒	◒
20	**Frigidaire** Ultra Quiet II Precision Wash FDB635RF	360		○	⊜	⊖	◒	⊜
21	**Magic Chef** Tri Power Wash System DU6500	350		○	⊖	⊖	◒	○
22	**GE** Monogram ZBD4600X	660		◒	⊜	⊖	○	◒
23	**Bosch** SHU300	580		◒	⊜	⊖	◒	◒

Details on the models

Normal-cycle data is for same conditions as for the energy-use column in the Ratings.

1 Kenmore (Sears) Dirt Sensor 1595
$580

3 Kenmore (Sears) Dirt Sensor 1583
$450

• Normal cycle: 7 to 9.5 gal., 116 min. • Electronic touchpad controls

Among the best models for both washing and convenience. (1) is one of the best models for regular loading. Both are among the noisiest. **Features:** Dirt sensor. Digital, time-remaining display. End-of-cycle indicator. Child lock-out on controls. Lack interchangeable front panels. (1) has a high-temperature rinse option. **Warranty:** 3 yr.; 2 and 5 yr. on some parts (1); 1 yr.; 2 yr. on some parts (3). **Availability:** Tested models discontinued; different models with same designations are being sold. **Recommendation:** Though relatively noisy and costly to operate, very good overall. (3) is the better value.

2 Kenmore (Sears) QuietGuard 1579 $420

5 Kenmore (Sears) QuietGuard 1568 $350

• Normal cycle: 7 gal., 100 min. • Dial and mechanical touchpad controls (2); dial and push-button controls (5)

Among the best models for washing. Less convenient, but more energy efficient than their brandmates (1) and (3). Both are among the noisiest. **But:** Among the worst for oversized loads. You must adjust the dial and button to same setting for cycle to work properly. (2) lacks an interchangeable front panel. (5) can't be set to run at a later time. **Warranty:** 1 yr.; 2 yr. on some parts. **Availability:** Tested models discontinued; different models with same designations are being sold. **Recommendation:** Though relatively noisy, very good overall. (5) is **A CR Best Buy**.

4 Frigidaire Gallery FDB949GF $490

• Normal cycle: 7.5 gal., 116 min. • Electronic touchpad controls

Among the quietest and most convenient models and the best model for oversized loads. **Features:** Broken-glass trap. Digital, time-remaining display. End-of-cycle indicator. Child lock-out on controls. **But:** Lacks a built-in food disposer and interchangeable front panel. Failed to restart after an electrical interruption. **Warranty:** 2 yr.; 5 yr. on some parts. **Similar model:** FDB989GF, $600. **Recommendation:** Very good performance, though Frigidaire has been among the less reliable brands.

6 Maytag Quiet Plus II MDB6000A $470

11 Maytag Quiet Pack MDB4000A $390

• Normal cycle: 5 to 10 gal., 104 min. (6); 7 gal., 102 min. (11) • Dial and mechanical touchpad controls

(6) is among the best models for washing; it washes glasses and flatware a little better than (11), but may use more water for many loads. Both are among the noisiest. **Features:** (6) has a dirt sensor, end-of-cycle indicator, and high-temperature rinse option. **But:** You must adjust the dial and button to same setting for cycle to work properly. Lack interchangeable front panels. **Warranty:** 1 yr.; 2 and 5 yr. on some parts. **Availability:** Tested model (6) discontinued; different model with same designation is being sold. **Recommendation:** Very good. (11) is the better value.

7 GE Profile Performance GSD4920Z $550

18 GE Profile Quiet Power GSD4320Z $430

• Normal cycle: 7.5 to 10.5 gal., 96 min. (7); 9 gal., 92 min. (18) • Electronic touchpad controls

Among these two, both very quiet and very convenient, (7) washes slightly better. (18) is among the most energy efficient; (7) has a dirt sensor that we found to be ineffective in conserving water for light loads. **Features:** End-of-cycle indicator. High-temperature rinse option. Child lock-out on controls. **But:** Lack interchangeable front panels. (7) lacks option to enable or disable water-temperature boost. (18) cannot indicate progress of the cycle. **Warranty:** 1 yr.; 2 and 5 yr. on some parts. **Similar models:** GSD4610Z, $520; GSD4620Z, $500;GSD4630Z, $520; GSD4910Z, $570; GSD4930Z, $570; GSD4940Z, $670; GSD4310Z, $450; GSD4330Z, $450. Sold at Sears only: 1847, $650; 1859, $550. **Availability:** Tested model (18) discontinued; different model with same designation is being sold. **Recommendation:** Among the quietest models tested. (7) is very good; (18), only good.

8 Miele Turbothermic Plus G865 $950

• Normal cycle: 6.5 gal., 93 min. • Dial controls • Stainless-steel tub and door liner

Among the best models for oversized loads. Among the quietest. **Features:** Broken-glass trap. Child lock-out on door. **But:** Lacks a built-in food disposer, requires periodic cleaning of the filter, cannot be set to run at a later time, and has no option to enable or disable heated-dry. **Warranty:** 1 yr. (2 yr. with authorized installation). Lacks tub and liner warranty. **Availability:** Tested model discontinued; different model with same designation is being sold. **Recommendation:** Very good but very pricey. Among the safest models if children are around.

9 Asko 1585 $850

12 Asko 1375 $660

• Normal cycle: 4.5 gal., 93 min. • Electronic push-button controls (9); dial and push-button controls (12) • Stainless-steel tub and door liner

Among the most frugal models with both water and energy, and (9) is among the best for oversized loads. Both are among the quietest. **Features:** Broken-glass trap. Child lock-out on door (12); door and controls, (9). End-of-cycle indicator. High-temperature rinse option (9). **But:** Lack a built-in food disposer and interchangeable front panel, require periodic cleaning of filter and cannot be set to run at a later time. (9) cannot indicate progress of the cycle. **Warranty:** 1 yr.; 5 yr. on some parts. **Recommendation:** Very good performance, among the safest models if children are around. But pricey, and Asko has the worst brand repair record.

10 KitchenAid Whisper Quiet Ultima Superba KUDS24SE $700

16 KitchenAid Quiet Scrub KUDI24SE $540

• Normal cycle: 6.5 gal., 108 min. • Electronic touchpad controls • Stainless-steel tub and door liner

Compared with (16), (10) is a little better for loading, noise, and convenience (for which it is among the best overall). (16) is among the noisiest. **Features:** End-of-cycle indicator. Child lock-out on controls. (10) has a high-temperature rinse option. Both lack interchangeable front panels. **Warranty:** 1 yr.; 5 yr. on some parts. **Availability:** Tested models discontinued; different models with same designations are being sold. **Recommendation:** Very good. (10) is convenient, but (16) is the better buy.

13 Whirlpool Quiet Wash Plus DU927QWD $400

14 Whirlpool Quiet Wash Plus DU940QWD $450

• Normal cycle: 7.5 gal., 103 min. • Electronic touchpad controls

Solid performers; virtually identical except for some minor features. Both are among the noisiest. **Features:** End-of-cycle indicator. Child lock-out on controls. **Warranty:** 1 yr.; 2 and 5 yr. on some parts. **Availability:** Discontinued. **Recommendation:** Very good. (13) is the better value.

15 Amana Stainless Series ASU8000 $730

• Normal cycle: 9 gal., 132 min. • Dial and push-button controls • Stainless-steel tub and door liner

Quiet, and among the best for oversized loads. **Features:** Broken-glass trap. **But:** Longest cycle time. Didn't dry flatware as effectively as most other models. Lacks built-in food disposer and interchangeable front panel, requires periodic cleaning of filter and cannot be set to run at a later time. **Warranty:** 1 yr.; 2 yr. on some parts. **Availability:** Discontinued. **Recommendation:** Very good, but very slow and costly to operate.

17 White-Westinghouse Quiet Clean I MDB531RF $300

20 Frigidaire Ultra Quiet II Precision Wash FDB635RF $360

• Normal cycle: 6 gal., 76 min. (17); 93 min. (20) • Dial and push-button controls (17); dial and mechanical touchpad controls (20)

Though (20) is among the most convenient models, it's a bit noisier than (17). Both are among the most energy-efficient models. **Features:** Broken-glass trap. (20) has an end-of-cycle indicator and high-temperature rinse option. **But:** Lack built-in food disposer. (17) has no option to enable or disable water-temperature boost, and you must adjust the dial and button to the same setting for the cycle to work properly. **Warranty:** 1 yr.; 2 yr. on some parts (and only 10 yr. on tub and door liner). **Similar models:** (17): MDB631RF, $330; (20): FDB435RF, $300. **Recommendation:** Good performance, though Frigidaire and White-Westinghouse have been among the less reliable brands.

19 Whirlpool Clean Wash DU840CWD $300

• Normal cycle: 7 gal., 100 min. • Dial and mechanical touchpad controls

Less adept at washing and much less convenient than its brandmates, (13) and (14). Among the noisiest. **Features:** Broken-glass trap. **But:** Lacks many features and conveniences. **Warranty:** 1 yr. **Recommendation:** Good.

21 Magic Chef Tri Power Wash System DU6500 $350

• Normal cycle: 9 gal., 110 min. • Dial and push-button controls
A basic model. Among the noisiest. **Similar model:** DU 4500, $300. **Warranty:** 1 yr. **Recommendation:** Good.

22 GE Monogram ZBD4600X $660

• Normal cycle: 6.5 gal., 78 min. • Dial and push-button controls • Stainless-steel tub and door liner
The shortest cycle time, and among the most energy-efficient models. **But:** Lacks many features and conveniences. **Warranty:** 1 yr.; 2 and 5 yr. on some parts. **Recommendation:** Good, but only fair at washing, and pricey.

23 Bosch SHU300 $580

• Normal cycle: 5.5 gal., 95 min. • Dial and push-button controls • Stainless-steel tub and door liner
Among the most energy-efficient models, and fairly miserly with water. **But:** Lacks many features and conveniences. **Warranty:** 5 days for cosmetic damage; 1 and 5 yr. on some parts. **Availability:** Discontinued. **Recommendation:** Good, but only fair at washing.

HOW TO USE THE RATINGS

• Read the Recommendations for information on specific models and general buying advice.

• Note how the rated products are listed—in order of performance and convenience, price, or alphabetically.

• The overall score graph gives the big picture in performance. Notes on features and performance for individual models are listed in the "Comments" column or "Details on the models."

• Use the key numbers to locate the details on each model.

• Before going to press, we verify model availability for most products with manufacturers. Some tested models listed in the Ratings may no longer be available. Discontinued models are noted in "Comments" or "Details on the models." Such models may still be available in some stores for part of 1999. Models indicated as successors should perform similarly to the tested models, according to the manufacturer. Features may vary.

• Models similar to the tested models, when they exist, are indicated in "Comments" or "Details on the models."

• The original date of publication is noted for each Ratings.

Ratings *Clothes dryers*

& Recommendations

The tests behind the Ratings

Drying is a composite judgment based on the results of drying tests with 4 kinds of load: a large (12-lb.) mixed load of towels, jeans, and shirts; a small (6-lb.) mixed load; a 6-lb. load of cotton shirts; and a 3-lb. load of delicate-fabric items. **Drum volume** ranges from less than 5½ cu. ft. to about 7 cu. ft. **Ease of use** reflects our judgments on such matters as the ease of loading laundry and using the controls. **Noise** indicates how loud each machine sounded as it dried a 6-lb. load. **Price** is approximate retail.

Typical features for these models

• Mechanical rotary control with 2 or 3 automatic drying cycles. • Separate start control. • Separate rotary temperature control with at least 3 heat settings. • Timed-dry and air-fluff (without heat) cycles of at least 60 min. (though such lengthy cycles aren't very useful). • Optional end-of-cycle buzzer. • Raised edges on top to contain spills. • Lint filter located in the drum opening. • Drum light. • Door that can be adjusted to open left or right. • Venting options from 3 or 4 places. • 1-yr. warranty on parts and labor.

Recommendations

To spare your laundry unnecessary drying time and save yourself needless energy costs, choose a model with a moisture sensor. Among those, you can safely expect to get fine drying performance. While the Kenmores earned top scores, lower-rated models are nearly as good and, sometimes, cheaper. The best choices among models with a thermostat: the top four electric models and the Hotpoint NWXR473GT (gas).

See report, page 94. Last time rated in CONSUMER REPORTS: March 1997, June 1998.

Overall Ratings

E VG G F P

Listed in order of overall score

Key no.	Brand and model	Price	Overall score (0–100; P F G VG E)	Drying	Drum volume	Ease of use	Noise
	Models with a moisture sensor						
	ELECTRIC						
1	**Kenmore** 6893	$580		E	E	VG	E
2	**Frigidaire** FDE648GF	360		E	VG	G	G
3	**Kenmore** 6790	500		VG	E	VG	VG

Key no.	Brand and model	Price	Overall score (0–100; P F G VG E)	Drying	Drum volume	Ease of use	Noise
4	**Kenmore** 6681	$440		◓	⊜	◓	◓
5	**General Electric** Profile DPSQ495ET	480		◓	⊜	◓	◓
6	**Whirlpool** Gold GEC9858E	490		◓	⊜	◓	◓
7	**GE** Profile Performance DPSF495EV	470		◓	⊜	◓	◓
8	**Whirlpool** LEL8858E	500		◓	⊜	◓	●
9	**KitchenAid** Superba KEYS677E	430		◓	⊜	○	◓
10	**Maytag** MDE9606	490		◓	◓	◓	◓
11	**Amana** LEA80AW	470		○	⊜	○	◓
12	**Whirlpool** LER5848E	420		◓	⊜	○	◓
	GAS						
13	**Kenmore** 7893	630		⊜	⊜	◓	◓
14	**Kenmore** 7790	550		◓	⊜	◓	◓
15	**Kenmore** 7681	490		◓	⊜	◓	◓
16	**General Electric** Profile DPSQ495GT	510		◓	⊜	◓	◓
17	**KitchenAid** Superba KGYS677E	480		◓	⊜	○	◓
18	**GE** Profile Performance DPSF495GV	500		◓	⊜	◓	◓
19	**Maytag** MDG9606	530		◓	◓	◓	◓
20	**Whirlpool** LGR5848E	480		◓	⊜	○	◓
	Models with a thermostat (previously tested)						
	ELECTRIC						
	Roper RES7648E	330		○	⊜	○	◓
	Hotpoint NWXR473ET	320		○	◓	◓	◓
	Admiral LDEA200	300		○	⊜	○	◓
	Magic Chef YE225	310		○	⊜	○	◓
	White-Westinghouse MDE436RE	320		○	○	○	○
	Frigidaire FDE546RE	350		○	○	○	○
	GAS						
	Hotpoint NWXR473GT	350		○	◓	◓	◓
	Frigidaire FDG546RE	360		○	○	○	○
	White-Westinghouse MDG436RE	350		○	○	○	○

Details on the models with moisture sensors

Note: The following details pertain only to models with a moisture sensor. For details on models with a thermostat, see the March 1997 issue of Consumer Reports.

When electric models match up with otherwise similar gas counterparts, the corresponding pairs are listed together. **Dimensions**, in order of height, width, and depth, are to the nearest quarter-inch. Height includes the control panel; depth is also measured with the door open 90 degrees. More space may be needed for vent piping.

1 Kenmore 6893 (electric) $580

13 Kenmore 7893 (gas) $630

42½x27x28¼ in. (42½ in. with door open)
Rated best at recognizing when loads had been dried to the desired level, and fastest in reacting to already dry loads. Equipped with the Evenheat feature, they kept temperatures cooler than most with delicate loads. A single automatic drying cycle serves well for all fabric loads. An extended period of no-heat tumbling can be selected with all cycles. The volume of the end-of-cycle signal can be adjusted. The door opens down. Drying rack included. **Similar models:** 6894 and 6897 (electric), $580; 7894 and 7897 (gas), $630. **Recommendation:** Excellent overall.

2 Frigidaire FDE648GF (electric) $360

42x27x25¾ in. (48 in. with door open)
Kept temperatures cooler than most with delicate loads. But this model has less capacity and was noisier than most. An extended period of no-heat tumbling is automatic with permanent-press and delicate cycles. The volume of the end-of-cycle buzzer can be adjusted. The door won't clear tall basket. 2-yr. warranty on parts and labor. **Recommendation:** A very good performer at an attractive price, but Frigidaire has been among the less reliable brands of electric dryer.

3 Kenmore 6790 (electric) $500

14 Kenmore 7790 (gas) $550

42½x27x28¼ in. (42½ in. with door open)
The electric version kept temperatures cooler than most with delicate loads. On both models, a single automatic drying cycle serves for all fabric loads. An extended period of no-heat tumbling can be selected with all cycles. The air-fluff cycle runs for just 30 min. The volume of the end-of-cycle buzzer can be adjusted. The door opens down. Drying rack included. **Similar models:** 6690 and 6691 (electric), $500; 7690 and 7691 (gas), $550. **Recommendation:** Very good and less expensive alternatives to (1) and (13).

4 Kenmore 6681 (electric) $440

15 Kenmore 7681 (gas) $490

43x29x28 in. (41¾ in. with door open)
A single automatic drying cycle serves for all fabric loads. An extended period of no-heat tumbling is automatic with all cycles. The volume of the end-of-cycle buzzer can be adjusted. The lint filter is accessed from top of cabinet. The door opens down. Drying rack included. Vents only from the rear. **Recommendation:** Very good performers.

5 General Electric Profile DPSQ495ET (electric) $480

16 General Electric Profile DPSQ495GT (gas) $510

42¼ x27x28¼ in. (51½ in. with door open)
An extended period of no-heat tumbling can be selected with all cycles. Additional 5-yr. parts-only warranty on the drum. Drying rack included. But the mechanical touchpad-button temperature controls are rather inconvenient. **Availability:** Discontinued. **Recommendation:** Very good performers, but GE has been among the less reliable brands.

6 Whirlpool Gold GEC9858E (electric) $490

41¾x27x28¼ in. (42½ in. with door open)
A single automatic drying cycle serves for all

fabric loads. An extended period of no-heat tumbling can be selected with all cycles. The membrane-covered push-button controls are rather inconvenient.The door opens down. The air-fluff cycle runs for just 30 min. **Recommendation:** A very good performer, but there are better buys.

7 GE Profile Performance DPSF495EV (electric) $470

18 GE Profile Performance DPSF495GV (gas) $500

41½x27x28¼ in. (51½ in. with door open)
An extended period of no-heat tumbling can be selected with all cycles. But membrane-covered (and color-coded) push-button controls are rather inconvenient, and the door won't clear a tall basket. Drying rack included. Additional 5-yr. parts-only warranty on the drum. **Availability:** Discontinued. **Successors:** DPSF495EW (electric), $470; DPSF495GW (gas), $500. **Recommendation:** Very good performers, but GE has been among the less reliable brands.

8 Whirlpool LEL8858E (electric) $500

42½x29x28 in. (41¾ in. with door open)
This was by far the noisiest model we tested. A single automatic drying cycle serves for all fabric loads. An extended period of no-heat tumbling can be selected with all cycles. The membrane-covered push-button controls are rather inconvenient. The lint filter has a 5-yr. warranty, and it need not be cleaned after every cycle. The door opens down. Vents only to the rear. **Recommendation:** A very good performer.

9 KitchenAid Superba KEYS677E (electric) $430

17 KitchenAid Superba KGYS677E (gas) $480

42¾x29x28 in. (41¾ in. with door open)
An extended period of no-heat tumbling is automatic with all cycles. The air-fluff cycle runs for only 20 min. There's a blocked-lint-filter signal on the console. Membrane-covered push-button controls are inconvenient, and edges along the top are not raised to contain spills. The door opens down, and the machine vents only to the rear. 2-yr. warranty on parts and labor; 5-yr. (limited) on the element or burner, motor, and controls; and 10-yr. on the drum and against cabinet rust. **Availability:** Discontinued. **Recommendation:** Very good performers.

10 Maytag MDE9606 (electric) $490

19 Maytag MDG9606 (gas) $530

43x27x28¼ in. (50½ in. with door open)
The electric version kept temperatures cooler than most with delicate loads. On both models, an extended period of no-heat tumbling is automatic in permanent-press and delicate cycles. Large, clearly marked push-buttons set temperature. Porcelain top. Unique door and drum opening allow for easier loading. The end-of-cycle signal can't be turned off or adjusted. Additional 2-yr. parts-only warranty, 5-yr. on the drum, and 10-yr. against cabinet rust. **Similar models:** MDE9806 (electric), $530; MDG9806 (gas), $560. **Recommendation:** Very good performers.

11 Amana LEA80A (electric) $470

42½x27x28¼ in. (51½ in. with door open)
Has a variable temperature control and offers an extended period of no-heat tumbling with all cycles. Kept temperatures lower than most with delicate loads. The start control is part of the rotary cycle selector; but the selector turns only clockwise, making it harder than most to correct a false start. The control panel may be difficult to read in low light. The air-fluff cycle runs for only 20 min. The volume of the end-of-cycle signal can be adjusted. Drying rack included. Door won't clear a tall basket. Drum isn't well lit. **Recommendation:** A very good performer.

12 Whirlpool LER5848E (electric) $420

20 Whirlpool LGR5848E (gas) $480

42¼x29x28 in. (41¾ in. with door open)
An extended period of no-heat tumbling can be selected with all cycles. Color-coded dial is hard to set, and edges along the top are not raised to contain spills. The air-fluff cycle runs for only 30 min. The door opens down. Vents only to the rear. **Recommendation:** Very good performers.

Ratings *Food processors*

& Recommendations

The tests behind the Ratings

Overall score is based mainly on our judgment of how the machines performed key processor chores—chopping, slicing, shredding, and pureeing. We also considered **noise, features,** and convenience (ease of setup, use, and cleaning). **Price** is approximate retail. Models similar to those we tested are noted in the Details on the models; features may vary.

Typical features for these models

• Excellent or very good at routine chopping. • Clear plastic bowl and lid and plastic food pusher. • S-shaped chopping blade and at least one slicing disk. • One motor speed that's adequate for most tasks (the motor is powerful enough for heavy chores like brioche dough only in some large models). • Come with a 1-yr. warranty.

Recommendations

For basic tasks we recommend the midsized Cuisinart Little Pro Plus, $90. For heavy-duty tasks like kneading dough, the clear choice is the top-rated KitchenAid Professional KFP650, $230. It's well equipped, capable, convenient to use, and quiet. For chopping or shredding small amounts, the Sunbeam 4817-8 mini processor, $40, was capable and efficient.

See report, page 98. Last time rated in CONSUMER REPORTS: August 1997.

Overall Ratings

E VG G F P

Listed in order of overall score

Key no.	Brand and model	Price	Overall score (0–100; P F G VG E)	Performance: SLICING	Performance: SHREDDING	Performance: PUREEING	Noise	Features
	LARGE MODELS							
1	**KitchenAid** Professional KFP650	$230		E	VG	E	E	E
2	**Cuisinart** Pro Custom 11 DLC-8S	190		E	VG	E	E	VG
3	**Braun** UK11	85		G	E	VG	G	G
4	**Black & Decker** FP1000	55		G	VG	VG	F	G
5	**Krups** 706	100		G	VG	G	G	G
	MIDSIZED MODELS							
6	**Cuisinart** Little Pro Plus	90		G	VG	E	E	VG

Key no.	Brand and model	Price	Overall score (0–100; P F G VG E)	Performance: Slicing	Performance: Shredding	Performance: Pureeing	Noise	Features
7	**Krups** 704	$70		⊖	⊖	○	⊖	○
8	**Hamilton Beach** 70700	55		○	⊖	○	◒	○
9	**Hamilton Beach** 70100	35		○	⊖	◒	◒	○
10	**Regal** K813	40		◒	⊖	⊖	◒	○
	MINI PROCESSORS							
11	**Sunbeam** 4817-8	40	[1]	◒	⊖	⊖	●	–
12	**Betty Crocker** Micro Food Processor BC-1424	25	[1]	◒	○	○	◒	–

[1] *The mini processors are not comparable to the full-sized models and couldn't be rated on the same scale.*

Details on the models

Dimensions (HxWxD) are to the nearest inch. **Bowl capacity** is based on the amount of dry ingredients it holds when not in use and may not agree with manufacturer's rated capacity; actual capacity is lower when machine is running. **Weight** is to the nearest pound.

Large models

1 KitchenAid Professional KFP650 $230

• 15x9x11 in. • 9½-cup capacity • 17 lb.
Easy to use, very powerful, quiet. Has very useful mini bowl, effective dough blade, so-so whipping paddle, extra slicing/shredding disks, storage box for disks and blades. **Similar model:** KFP600, has plastic housing instead of metal and lacks whipping paddle. **Recommendation:** Excellent—does it all very well.

2 Cuisinart Pro Custom 11 DLC-8S $190

• 15x8x11 in. • 9¼-cup capacity • 13 lb.
Very powerful and quiet. Easy-to-use controls. Assembling the large feed tube, shredding blade, and slicing disk can be tricky. Dough blade works well. Has extra thin-slicing disk. 3-yr. overall warranty; 5-yr. motor warranty. **Recommendation:** Excellent—does everything very well. But it could be a bit more convenient to use.

3 Braun UK11 $85

• 14x14x7 in. • 10¾-cup capacity • 7 lb.
Very powerful two-speed machine. Whipping attachment is effective. Has extra thin-slicing/shredding disk, but its slicing didn't work well. Manufacturer recommends hand-washing components. **Recommendation:** Very good. And a good value, if you don't mind convenience compromises.

4 Black & Decker FP1000 $55

• 13x11x8 in. • 9-cup capacity • 5 lb.
Powerful, user friendly, and lightweight—but noisy. Not great at chopping beef cubes or almonds. But very good at pureeing and shredding. 2-yr. warranty. **Recommendation:** Good. Lots of machine for the money.

5 Krups 706 $100

• 13x15x8 in. • 9¼-cup capacity • 9 lb.
Powerful two-speed motor. But didn't turn out tidy thin slices, very smooth purees, or voluminous whipped cream. **Recommendation:** Good—but too little for too much.

Midsized models

6 Cuisinart Little Pro Plus $90

• 13x6x9 in. • 4-cup capacity • 7 lb.
Very good, very quiet performer. Continuous-feed chute. Easy-to-use controls. Has juicer attachment that spins disconcertingly fast and

sprays droplets on you and the countertop. 3-yr. overall warranty; 5-yr. motor warranty. **Recommendation:** Very good. Best and smallest of the midsized batch.

7 **Krups 704** $70

• 11x12x7 in. • 6-cup capacity • 5 lb.
Variable-speed motor is noisy. Performance is good, although purees weren't as smooth as they could be. Plastic parts have to be hand-washed. **Recommendation:** Good. Worth considering.

8 **Hamilton Beach 70700** $55

• 13x16x9 in. • 7½-cup capacity • 7 lb.
Continuous-feed chute. Two-speed motor is noisy. **Recommendation:** Good. A decent, no-frills machine.

9 **Hamilton Beach 70100** $35

• 13x7x13 in. • 7¼-cup capacity • 5 lb.
Came up short in a couple of basic skills. Tricky to assemble. Noisy. Blades must be hand-washed. **Recommendation:** Good. There are better—though not cheaper—choices.

10 **Regal K813** $40

• 15x7x11 in. • 6-cup capacity • 6 lb.
Noisy. Not a good slicer. Lid shifts easily in the middle of a chore, shutting off motor. **Recommendation:** Good, but there are better choices.

Mini processors

11 **Sunbeam 4817-8** $40

• 15x8x8 in. • 2½-cup capacity • 4 lb.
Bowl mounted on tall, narrow base. Good for shredding and thick purees (hummus, for example) but not liquids, which leaked with less than ¼ cup of water. You must twist the lid to operate. Very noisy. Inconvenient to operate slicer/shredder chute. 2-yr. warranty. **Recommendation:** Best of the minis tested.

12 **Betty Crocker Micro Food Processor BC-1424** $25

• 11x9x8 in. • 3-cup capacity • 3 lb.
Looks like a miniversion of a standard food processor. Not quite as noisy as others. 2-yr. warranty.

Ratings *Microwave ovens*

& Recommendations

The tests behind the Ratings

Overall score is based mainly on **ease of use** and how well a model will **defrost** ground beef. All ovens performed comparably in tests to heat and reheat various foods. Countertop ovens are categorized based on claimed capacity. Over-the-range models fit above a standard-width range. Exterior dimensions are in order of height, width, and depth (**HxWxD**), rounded to the next-higher inch. Countertop models have rear vents and need extra clearance from a wall. **Price** is approximate retail.

Typical features for these models

• Turntable. • Door that opens left. • Shortcut keys for popping popcorn and defrosting and other functions. • A light bulb that must be replaced by a technician. • 1-yr. warranty on parts and labor, a 5-yr. warranty on the magnetron (the oven's energy source). **Over-the-range models:** • In-home service for the warranty. • A light bulb that owner can replace.

Recommendations

Most of the ovens we tested are easy to use and handle general microwaving tasks well. Bigger ovens work faster than smaller, less powerful ovens. If you have a big kitchen and heat large batches of food, choose among the top seven large ovens. You'll find the best value among midsized ovens like the Samsung MW5574, $130, or Sharp R310, $135. They're not much bigger than a compact, but often have the same power as a large oven and cost about $50 less. Compact models like the Samsung MW4371, $100, are fine for heating water for tea and popping popcorn. The over-the-range models save counter space but are pricey. Any of the tested models would be a fine choice.

See report, page 100. Last time rated in CONSUMER REPORTS: December 1997, March 1998.

Overall Ratings

E VG G F P

Listed in order of overall score

Key no.	Brand and model	Price	Overall score (0–100; P F G VG E)	Ease of use	Defrost	HxWxD
	LARGE COUNTERTOP MODELS					
1	**Panasonic** NN-S787	$185		E	VG	14x24x17 in.
2	**Sharp** R-430	165		VG	E	13x22x18
3	**General Electric** JE1540	200		E	VG	14x24x18

Ratings continued

Key no.	Brand and model	Price	Overall score (0–100; P F G VG E)	Ease of use	Defrost	HxWxD
	LARGE COUNTERTOP MODELS *continued*					
4	**Sharp** Multiple Choice R-490	$220		⊖	⊖	13x22x18
5	**Panasonic** NN-S667	150		⊖	⊜	12x22x17
6	**Sharp** R-510	170		⊖	⊖	14x24x20
7	**Kenmore** (Sears) 6830	130		⊖	○	13x22x18
8	**Panasonic** NN-S757	155		⊖	⊖	14x24x17
9	**General Electric** JE1235	140		○	○	13x23x17
	MIDSIZED COUNTERTOP MODELS					
10	**Whirlpool** MT9102SF	200		⊖	⊖	13x22x17
11	**Sanyo** EM-P340	120		⊖	○	12x21x17
12	**Goldstar** MA-900	130		⊖	○	12x21x16
13	**Samsung** MW5574	130		⊜	○	12x21x16
14	**Sharp** R-310	135		⊖	⊖	12x21x16
15	**General Electric** JE835	120		○	⊖	12x20x16
16	**Emerson** MW8985	100		○	⊖	12x20x15
17	**Panasonic** NN-S557	130		⊖	○	12x21x16
	COMPACT COUNTERTOP MODELS					
18	**Samsung** MW4371	100		⊜	○	11x20x14
19	**General Electric** JE635	100		○	⊖	11x19x14
	OVER-THE-RANGE MODELS					
20	**General Electric** JVM1350	415		⊜	⊖	17x30x15
21	**Kenmore** (Sears) 20-6768	370		⊖	○	18x30x17
22	**Sharp** R147[]A [1]	380		⊖	⊖	16x30x14

[1] *Brackets in model number indicate color code.*

Details on the models

Large countertop models

1 Panasonic NN-S787 $185

• 1,000 watts • 1.5 cu. ft. claimed/0.9 cu. ft. usable • 13-in. turntable • Sensor feature
Display prompts are very easy to follow. You always press start, even when using shortcut keys. **But:** One sample malfunctioned during the sensor-reheat test. **Availability:** Discontinued but available. **Recommendation:** Excellent, and a good value.

2 Sharp R-430 $165

• 1,000 watts • 1.3 cu. ft. claimed/0.7 cu. ft. usable • 12½-in. turntable • Sensor feature
With an optional kit, the oven can be mounted into a wall or a cabinet. **But:** The warranty excludes the turntable, accessories, light bulbs, and parts made of rubber, plastic, or glass. **Availability:** Discontinued but available. **Recommendation:** Excellent, and a good value.

3 GE JE1540 $200

• 1,000 watts • 1.5 cu. ft. claimed/1.0 cu. ft. usable • 14½-in. turntable

The oven is quieter than most and displays the power level during use. With an optional kit, it can be mounted into a wall or a cabinet. The magnetron warranty is 10 yrs. **But:** Reheat and auto-popcorn settings aren't intuitive. **Successor:** JE1640, $190. **Availability:** Discontinued but available. **Recommendation:** Very good overall.

4 Sharp Multiple Choice R-490 $220

• 1,000 watts • 1.3 cu. ft. claimed/0.7 cu. ft. usable • 12¾-in. turntable • Sensor feature

Controls and the interactive display may take getting used to. **Warranty:** 1-yr. parts and labor; additional 4 yrs. (parts only) on the magnetron (excludes turntable, light bulb, rubber or plastic parts). **Recommendation:** Very good model, though somewhat expensive.

5 Panasonic NN-S667 $150

• 1,000 watts • 1.3 cu. ft. claimed/0.7 cu. ft. usable • 13-in. turntable • Sensor feature

You always press start, even when using shortcut keys. **But:** The manual says to input weight of an auto-defrost item in pounds and tenths of pounds; the display (correctly) prompts you for pounds and ounces. **Availability:** Discontinued but available. **Recommendation:** Very good overall.

6 Sharp R-510 $170

• 1,000 watts • 1.8 cu. ft. claimed/1.1 cu. ft. usable • 14¾-in. turntable

With an optional kit, the oven can be mounted into a wall or a cabinet. **But:** The warranty excludes the turntable, accessories, light bulbs, and parts made of rubber, plastic, or glass. **Availability:** Discontinued but available. **Recommendation:** Very good overall.

7 Kenmore (Sears) 6830 $130

• 1,000 watts • 1.3 cu. ft. claimed capacity/0.8 cu. ft. usable •11½-in. turntable

Recessed turntable automatically stops at its starting position. **Warranty:** 1-yr. parts and labor; additional 4 yr. on the magnetron. **Availability:** Discontinued. **Recommendation:** Very good overall.

8 Panasonic NN-S757 $155

• 1,000 watts • 1.5 cu. ft. claimed/0.9 cu. ft. usable • 13-in. turntable

You always press start, even when using shortcut keys. **But:** The manual says to input weight for an auto-defrost item in pounds and tenths of pounds; the display (correctly) prompts you for pounds and ounces. **Availability:** Discontinued but available. **Recommendation:** Very good overall.

9 GE JE1235 $140

• 900 watts • 1.2 cu. ft. claimed/0.6 cu. ft. usable • 11¾-in. turntable

There's no recall feature to show which power level is in use. The light doesn't switch on when the door is opened. The shortcut key doesn't extend cooking in progress. There's no timer. **Availability:** Discontinued but available. **Recommendation:** Good overall; basic.

Midsized countertop models

10 Whirlpool MT9102SF $200

• 1,000 watts • 1.0 cu. ft. claimed/0.6 cu. ft. usable • 12-in. turntable

Has a "Micro Sizzler" pan. **Warranty:** 1-yr. parts and labor; additional 4 yr. (parts only) on the magnetron. **Recommendation:** Very good, but "Micro Sizzler" feature makes model expensive.

11 Sanyo EM-P340 $120

• 1,000 watts • 1.0 cu. ft. claimed/0.7 cu. ft. usable• 12¼-in. turntable

Turntable automatically stops at its starting position. **Warranty:** 1-yr. parts and labor; additional 4 yr. (parts only) on the magnetron. **Availability:** Discontinued. **Successor:** EM-P471, $185. **Recommendation:** Very good overall.

12 Goldstar MA-900 $130

• 850 watts • 0.9 cu. ft. claimed/0.6 cu. ft. usable • 10¼-in. turntable

Recessed turntable. Can program special settings. **Warranty:** 1-yr. parts and labor; additional 7 yr. (parts only) on the magnetron. **Recommendation:** Very good overall.

13 Samsung MW5574 $130

• 900 watts • 0.9 cu. ft. claimed/0.6 cu. ft. usable • 11½-in. turntable

You can program your own settings. The view through the window is better than most. The magnetron warranty is 8 yr. **Availability:** Discontinued but available. **Recommendation:** Very good overall.

14 Sharp R-310 $135

• 1,000 watts • 1.0 cu. ft. claimed/0.6 cu. ft. usable • 12-in. turntable

The turntable is bigger than some large ovens' turntables. **But:** The warranty excludes the turntable, accessories, light bulbs, and parts made of rubber, plastic, or glass. **Availability:** Discontinued but available. **Recommendation:** Very good overall.

15 GE JE835 $120

• 800 watts • 0.8 cu. ft. claimed/0.5 cu. ft. usable • 10¼-in. turntable

There's no recall feature to show which power level is in use. The light doesn't switch on when the door is opened. The shortcut key doesn't extend cooking in progress. There's no timer. **Availability:** Discontinued but available. **Recommendation:** Very good overall; basic.

16 Emerson MW8985 $100

• 800 watts • 0.9 cu. ft. claimed/0.5 cu. ft. usable • 10¼-in. turntable

The magnetron warranty is 7 yr. **But:** One sample failed the surge test. There's no recall feature to show which power level is in use. The light doesn't switch on when the door is opened. The shortcut key doesn't extend cooking in progress. There's no timer. **Recommendation:** Very good overall; basic, and a good price.

17 Panasonic NN-S557 $130

• 1,000 watts • 1.0 cu. ft. claimed/0.6 cu. ft. usable • 11½-in. turntable

You always press start, even when using shortcut keys. **But:** The manual (correctly) says to input weight for an auto-defrost item in pounds and tenths of pounds, but the display prompts for pounds and ounces. Some popcorn burned with the auto-popcorn feature. **Availability:** Discontinued but available. **Recommendation:** Very good overall.

Compact countertop models

18 Samsung MW4371 $100

• 700 watts • 0.7 cu. ft. claimed/0.4 cu. ft. usable • 10¼-in. turntable

It displays the power level during use. The view through the window is better than on any other model tested. The magnetron warranty is 8 yr. **Recommendation:** Very good overall.

19 GE JE635 $100

• 600 watts • 0.6 cu. ft. claimed/0.4 cu. ft. usable • 9-in. turntable

There's no recall feature to show which power level is in use. The light doesn't switch on when the door is opened. The shortcut key doesn't extend cooking in progress. There's no timer. Auto reheat isn't adjustable for different amounts of food. **Availability:** Discontinued but available. **Recommendation:** Good overall; basic.

Over-the-range models

20 GE JVM1350 $415

• 900 watts • 1.3 cu. ft. claimed/0.6 cu. ft. usable • 10¾-in. turntable • Sensor feature

The view through the window is better than most. The magnetron warranty is 10 yr. The oven comes with a cookbook. **But:** Two samples failed the surge test. **Availability:** Discontinued but available. **Recommendation:** Excellent, unless you live in an area prone to power surges.

21 Kenmore (Sears) 20-6768 $370

• 900 watts • 1.3 cu. ft. claimed/0.6 cu. ft. usable • 11¾-in. turntable • Sensor feature

The oven is quieter than most. **But:** There's no recall feature to show which power level is in use. **Availability:** Discontinued. **Recommendation:** Very good overall.

22 Sharp R147[1]A $380

• 900 watts • 1.1 cu. ft. claimed/0.5 cu. ft. usable • 10¾-in. turntable • Sensor feature

The magnetron warranty is 7 yr. **But:** The vent is even less effective than the other over-the-range oven vents. You can barely see through the window. The warranty excludes the turntable, accessories, light bulbs, and parts made of rubber, plastic, or glass. **Availability:** Discontinued but available. **Recommendation:** Very good overall.

Ratings *Toasters & toaster ovens*

& Recommendations

The tests behind the Ratings

Overall score covers toasting performance and convenience. **One slice** shows how well they produced a single slice of medium-brown toast. (All were judged good or very good at making a full batch of toast. And most were good or very good at producing four full batches, consistently the same shade of brown.) **Range** shows how well the toasters could make very light and dark toast. **Ease of use** is based on ease of setting controls, lowering bread in the toast wells, removing toast, disposing of crumbs, cleaning, and extra features and annoyances. **Price** is approximate retail.

Typical features for these models

Most toasters: • Hinged crumb tray. • "Slot adjustment," typically a set of metal jaws that closes in on bread as it's lowered. • Easy-to-use dial or lever to set the toast shade. • White plastic body that's easy to wipe clean. • 2-yr. warranty. **All toaster-oven/broilers:** • Indicator light. • Toast and oven controls, with marked temperature settings between low and broil on the oven dial. • One removable oven rack and pan. • Metal housing.

Recommendations

For a few slices of toast now and then, an inexpensive toaster like the Proctor-Silex 22205, $11, will suit your needs. If features and styling matter, the top-rated two-slice Cuisinart CPT-60, $70, is an excellent choice. If you need a four-slice toaster, the Kenmore (Sears) 238.48339, $45, is a standout. For an appliance that does more than toast, consider the Black & Decker toaster-oven TRO400, $35, **A CR Best Buy**, or the larger T670, $80, which has useful features.

See report, page 107. Last time rated in CONSUMER REPORTS: August 1998.

Overall Ratings

E VG G F P

Listed in order of overall score

Key no.	Brand and model	Price	Overall score (0–100; P F G VG E)	One slice	Range	Ease of use
	TWO-SLICE TOASTERS					
1	**Cuisinart** CPT-60	$70		VG	VG	E
2	**Sunbeam** 3802	28		E [1]	VG	E
3	**KitchenAid** KTT251	77		E	G	E
4	**Black & Decker** T270	25		G	VG	VG
5	**Cuisinart** CPT-30	40		VG	F	E

Ratings continued

Key no.	Brand and model	Price	Overall score (0–100; P F G VG E)	One slice	Range	Ease of use
	TWO-SLICE TOASTERS *continued*					
6	**Breadman** TR201	$35		⊖	◒	⊖
7	**Proctor-Silex** 22425	15		◒	⊖	⊜
8	**Krups** 155	32		○	○	⊖
9	**Oster** Designer 3826	45		○	○	⊖
10	**Toastmaster** B1021	16		○	⊖	○
11	**Proctor-Silex** 22415	35		◒	◒	⊜
12	**Toastmaster** B1035	21		○	⊖	○
13	**Betty Crocker** BC1611	25		◒	○	○
14	**Proctor-Silex** 22205	11		◒	○	⊖
15	**Rival** TT9215	13		◒	○	○
	FOUR-SLICE TOASTERS					
16	**Kenmore** (Sears) 238.48339	45		⊖	⊖	⊜
17	**Proctor-Silex** 24415	20		○	◒	⊖
18	**Rival** TT9415	20		○	○	○
19	**Toastmaster** D1050	20		⊖	○	○
20	**Black & Decker** T440	45		○	◒	○
	TOASTER-OVEN/BROILERS					
21	**Black & Decker** T670	80		○	⊖	⊜
22	**Black & Decker** TRO400 **A CR Best Buy**	35		⊖	⊖	○
23	**DeLonghi** XU-23STD	100		○	◒	⊖
24	**Toastmaster** 316	30		⊖	◒	○

[1] *If bread is in slot without window.*

Details on the models

1 Cuisinart CPT-60 $70

Single slot with deep toast well. Made 4 perfectly consistent batches of medium-brown toast. Electronic touchpad controls, with lights that are always on. 3-yr. warranty, with $7 charge for return shipping.

2 Sunbeam 3802 $28

2 slots. Must be plugged in for toast to be lowered. Glass window, designed to let you see toasting progress, leaves light spot on the bread. Window not covered in warranty. Compensates for voltage fluctuations. **Similar models:** Oster Designer 3804, 3805, 3807; Sunbeam 3806, $30 to $50.

3 KitchenAid KTT251 $77

Single slot. Must be plugged in for toast to be lowered. Power shuts off quickly if toast gets stuck. Marking on toast-shade dial lacks contrast for readability. 1-yr. warranty. **Similar model:** KTT241, $70.

4 Black & Decker T270 $25

2 slots. Shallow toast wells; large slices don't toast evenly.

5 Cuisinart CPT-30 $40

Single very wide slot with deep toast well. Made uneven batch of light toast. 3-yr. warranty, with $7 charge for return shipping.

6 Breadman TR201 $35

Single slot with deep toast well that's long enough for 3 slices. Must be plugged in for toast to be lowered. Hard to set for consistent toasting, and can't make very light toast. 1-yr. warranty. **Similar model:** TR200, $40.

7 Proctor-Silex 22425 $15

2 slots. Must be plugged in for toast to be lowered. Marking on toast-shade dial lacks contrast for readability. Compensates for voltage fluctuations.

8 Krups 155 $32

2 slots. Must be plugged in for toast to be lowered. Made uneven batch of light toast. 1-yr. warranty.

9 Oster Designer 3826 $45

Single slot. Toasts single slice very fast. Very narrow range on dial from light to dark.

10 Toastmaster B1021 $16

2 slots. Metal housing doesn't get hot, but ridges on outside are hard to clean. 3-yr. warranty.

11 Proctor-Silex 22415 $35

2 slots. Toasts single slice very fast. Marking on toast-shade dial lacks contrast for readability. Made too light a batch of dark toast.

12 Toastmaster B1035 $21

2 slots. Marking on toast-shade dial lacks contrast for readability. Chrome housing doesn't get hot, but is hard to keep clean. 3-yr. warranty.

13 Betty Crocker BC1611 $25

2 slots. Warranty specifies return toaster for refund or replacement.

14 Proctor-Silex 22205 $11

2 slots. Toasts single slice very fast. Metal housing gets hot. Made too-light a batch of dark toast.

15 Rival TT 9215 $13

2 slots. Must be pluggd in for toast to be lowered. Marking on toast-shade dial lacks contrast for readability. Shallow toast wells; large slices don't toast evenly. Metal housing gets hot. Made uneven batch of dark toast. 1-yr. warranty. **Similar models:** TT9222, TT9220, TT92218, each $13.

Four-slice toasters

16 Kenmore (Sears) 238.48339 $45

2 slots. Must be plugged in for toast to be lowered. Made 4 perfectly consistent batches of medium-brown toast. Marking on toast shade dial lacks contrast for readability. 1-yr. warranty.

17 Proctor-Silex 24415 $20

4 slots. Dual controls need different settings to get 4 slices of toast the same shade of brown. Marking on toast-shade dial lacks contrast for readability. Made uneven batch of light toast.

18 Rival TT9415 $20

4 slots. Must be plugged in for toast to be lowered. Marking on toast-shade dial lacks contrast for readability. Shallow toast wells; large slices don't toast evenly.

19 Toastmaster D1050 $20

4 slots. Made too-light a batch of dark toast. Chrome housing gets hot and is hard to keep clean. Bagels hard to fit in narrow slots. 3-yr. warranty. **Similar model:** D1051, $22.

20 Black & Decker T440 $45

4 slots. Dual controls need different settings to get 4 slices of toast the same shade of brown. Shallow toast wells; large slices don't toast evenly. Bagels hard to fit in narrow slots. Made uneven batches of light and dark toast.

Toaster-oven/broilers

21 Black & Decker T670 $80

6 slices. Automatically shuts off, and food rack advances, when door is open. Quicker at broiling hamburgers than others. Has deep oven pan. Beeps when toast is done. Door can be removed and put in dishwasher. Chromed parts of housing are hard to keep clean. One slice of bread must be placed over thermostat. Continuous-clean finish inside. 2-yr. warranty.

22 Black & Decker TRO400 $35
4 slices. Toasts single slice fast. Automatically shuts off when door is opened. Plastic sides don't get hot, but metal parts do. Bare-metal interior hard to clean. Heat warped oven pan. Under-cabinet installation kit available. 2-yr. warranty. **A CR Best Buy. Similar models:** TRO405, $40; TRO200 toaster-oven, $32.

23 DeLonghi XU-23STD $100
6 slices. 2-position rack. Stays on when door is opened. Beeps when toast is done. Porcelain-coated metal exterior easy to clean, but gets hot. Toast dial is a timer; harder to set than others. Toasts single slice slowly. Made uneven batch of light toast. Heat warped deep oven pan. Continuous-clean finish inside. 1-yr. warranty. **Similar model:** XU-28, $80.

24 Toastmaster 316 $30
4 slices. Stays on when door is opened. Nonstick finish inside. metal housing gets hot. Made uneven batch of light toast. Slower at broiling burgers than others. 3-yr. warranty. **Similar models:** 309, $30; 317 toaster-oven, $25.

HOW TO USE THE RATINGS

- Read the Recommendations for information on specific models and general buying advice.
- Note how the rated products are listed—in order of performance and convenience, price, or alphabetically.
- The overall score graph gives the big picture in performance. Notes on features and performance for individual models are listed in the "Comments" column or "Details on the models."
- Use the key numbers to locate the details on each model.
- Before going to press, we verify model availability for most products with manufacturers. Some tested models listed in the Ratings may no longer be available. Discontinued models are noted in "Comments" or "Details on the models." Such models may still be available in some stores for part of 1999. Models indicated as successors should perform similarly to the tested models, according to the manufacturer. Features may vary.
- Models similar to the tested models, when they exist, are indicated in "Comments" or "Details on the models."
- The original date of publication is noted for each Ratings.

Ratings *Washing machines*

& Recommendations

The tests behind the Ratings

Overall score is based on washing ability, capacity, efficiency, and noise. By scanning the washed swatches, we gauged **washing** performance. **Capacity,** as opposed to simple tub volume, is based on how well the washers could circulate clothes in increasingly heavy loads. We determined **water efficiency** by measuring the water it took to wash our eight-pound load and each machine's maximum load. **Energy efficiency** is based on the energy needed to heat the water and the electricity used to run the washer with both eight-pound and maximum loads. **Price** is approximate retail.

Typical features for these models

• Bleach and fabric-softener dispenser. • Painted cabinet top and lid. • 120-volt outlet requirement. • 1-yr. warranty on parts and labor. **Most front-loaders:** • Handle unbalanced loads better than top-loaders. • Automatic water-level setting. • Automatic wash and spin speeds. • Lock while in operation. • Stainless-steel tub. • Detergent dispenser. **Most top-loaders:** • Continuously variable water-level control. • 3 wash/spin combinations. • Porcelain-coated steel tub. • Lid that opens toward the back.

Recommendations

Most of the front-loaders and top-loaders did an excellent job of cleaning laundry, but the front-loaders as a group were more energy efficient. The Frigidaire Gallery FWT445GE, $700, and similar General Electric WSXH208T, $760, were the best front-loaders overall. Among the top-loaders tested, the Kenmore 2891, 2693, and 2683, $460 to $600, and the GE Profile Performance WPSF4170V, $490, were standouts.

See report, page 108. Last time rated in CONSUMER REPORTS: July 1998.

Overall Ratings

E ⊜ VG ⊖ G ○ F ◒ P ●

Listed in order of overall score

Key no.	Brand and model	Price	Overall score (0–100; P F G VG E)	Washing	Capacity	Efficiency: WATER	Efficiency: ENERGY
	FRONT-LOADING MODELS						
1	**Frigidaire** Gallery FWT445GE	$700		⊜	⊜	⊖	⊜
2	**General Electric** WSXH208T	760		⊜	⊜	⊖	⊜
3	**Miele** W1918A	1,600		⊜	◒	⊜	⊖
4	**Maytag** Neptune MAH3000AW	1,100		○	⊜	⊜	⊜

Ratings continued

Key no.	Brand and model	Price	Overall score (0–100; P F G VG E)	Washing	Capacity	Efficiency: WATER	Efficiency: ENERGY
	FRONT-LOADING MODELS *continued*						
5	**Equator** EZ3600C	$1,000		⊜	◒	⊖	⊖
6	**Asko** 11505	1,100		⊖	◒	○	⊜
	TOP-LOADING MODELS						
7	**Kenmore** (Sears) 2891	500		⊜	⊜	⊖	○
8	**Kenmore** (Sears) 2693	600		⊜	⊜	○	◒
9	**GE** Profile Performance WPSF4170V	490		⊜	⊜	○	○
10	**Kenmore** (Sears) 2683	460		⊜	⊜	○	◒
11	**Amana** LWA60A	470		⊖	⊜	○	○
12	**Whirlpool** LSS9244E	600		⊜	⊜	○ [1]	◒
13	**Whirlpool** LSL9345E	510		⊜	⊜	◒	◒
14	**Whirlpool** LSL9244E	420		⊜	⊜	○	◒
15	**Speed Queen** LWS55A	430		⊖	⊖	○	◒
16	**Maytag** LAT9706AA	570		⊖	⊖	◒	○
17	**Roper** RAS8245E	430		⊜	⊜	◒	◒
18	**Kenmore** (Sears) 2670	380		⊜	⊜	◒	◒
19	**Whirlpool** LSR5233E	500		⊜	⊜	◒	◒
20	**Maytag** LAT9406AA	520		⊖	⊖	◒	○
21	**Hotpoint** VWSR4100V	380		⊖	⊖	◒	◒
22	**White-Westinghouse** MWS445RE	350		⊖	⊜	○	○
23	**Frigidaire** FWS645GF	370		⊖	⊜	○	○
24	**Admiral** LATA300AA	440		⊜	⊖	◒	◒
25	**Magic Chef** W227L	430		⊜	⊖	◒	◒
26	**White-Westinghouse** MWX645RE	350		⊖	○	●	◒
27	**General Electric** WBXR2060T	360		⊖	○	◒	◒
28	**Kenmore** (Sears) 1820	300		⊖	◒	●	◒

[1] *With its optional spray rinse in use, this model would receive an excellent water-efficiency score.*

Details on the models

Comparable models are listed together. **Size** (HxWxD) is rounded up to the nearest inch. **Water used** is for a machine's maximum load at the maximum water setting.

Front-loading models

1 Frigidaire Gallery FWT445GE $700

2 GE WSXH208T $760

• 36x27x28 in. (43 in. with door open) • Water used: 33 gal. • Noise ◒ (1, 2)

These similar machines excelled in almost every category. They have an extra-rinse setting, a door-locked light, and an end-of-cycle signal that can be turned off. "Warm rinse" doesn't provide warm water in all rinses. The timed bleach dispenser, if overfilled, could spill bleach on dry clothes. 2-yr. warranty. **Similar models:** Frigidaire 39012 and 39022 (available only at Sears stores), each $700; Frigidaire Gallery FWTR445RF, FWT449GF, each $700. **Recommendation:** Excellent machines, and less expensive than most front-loaders.

3 Miele W1918A $1,600

• 33x24x25 in. (39 in. with door open) • Water used: 16 gal. • Noise ●

It has a gentler wash action than most, but takes 1¾ hours to complete a normal wash. It excelled at extracting water during the final spin. It has cycle-indicator lights, a display showing time left in a cycle, a delay-start setting, 7 selectable spin speeds, porcelain sides and front, and a plastic-coated top. It heats water up to 170° F. Lacks a bleach dispenser. Requires a 240-volt outlet. 2-yr. warranty, if installed by a Miele-certified installer. **Recommendation:** Excellent and quiet, but expensive and small.

4 Maytag Neptune MAH3000AW $1,100

• 44x27x29 in. (51 in. with door open) • Water used: 28 gal. • Noise ◒

The inner tub is angled up like a concrete mixer for easier access. It has extra-spin, extra-rinse, and delay-start settings, automatic temperature control, a timed bleach dispenser, a door-locked light, a porcelain top, and an end-of-cycle signal that can be turned off. The door stays locked for about a minute after the cycle ends. "Warm rinse" doesn't provide warm water in all rinses. **Recommendation:** Very good overall, but falls short in its cleaning ability.

5 Equator EZ3600C $1,000

• 33x24x24 in. (39 in. with door open) • Water used: 23 gal. • Noise ○

This is a washer and dryer. It's slow, taking 1¼ hours to complete a normal wash. As a dryer, it performed worse than other compacts tested in the past; even when it was set on high heat for 2 hours, clothes came out damp. It excelled at extracting water during the final spin. It has a timed bleach dispenser and 2 selectable spin speeds. The top lacks a lip. **Similar model:** EZ3600CEE, $1,000. **Recommendation:** A very good small washer but a pretty bad dryer.

6 Asko 11505 $1,100

• 32x24x25 in. (41 in. with door open) • Water used: 24 gal. • Noise ○

Has a gentler wash action than most, and excelled at extracting water during the final spin. It uses only cold water, but heats it up to 160° F. It's hard to unlock the door while the machine is running; the door stays locked several minutes after the cycle ends. It lacks a top lip and a bleach dispenser. Requires a 240-volt outlet. **Recommendation:** Very good, but small.

Top-loading models

7 Kenmore (Sears) 2891 $500

8 Kenmore (Sears) 2693 $600

10 Kenmore (Sears) 2683 $460

• 43x27x27 in. • Water used: 40 gal. (7), 42 gal. (8), 41 gal. (10) • Noise ◒ (7, 8); ○ (10)

These comparable models have automatic temperature control, an extra-rinse setting, and very easy-to-use controls. The lid opens left and doesn't lie flat. (7) has 4 selectable wash/spin combinations. (8) has 5 selectable wash/spin combinations, an automatic detergent dispenser, a timed bleach dispenser, a porcelain top and lid. (10) has 5 water-level settings, 4 selectable wash/

spin combinations, a porcelain top and lid. **Similar models:** 2890, $500; 2892, $520; 2684, $460. **Availability:** (8) has been replaced by 2893, 2894, 2897, each $600. **Recommendation:** Very good machines from one of the more reliable brands.

9 GE Profile Performance WPSF4170V $490

• 42x27x26 in. • Water used: 41 gal. • Noise ◓
Has automatic temperature control, extra-rinse setting and extended-spin settings, an end-of-cycle signal that can be turned off, mechanical touchpad controls, and a plastic inner tub. **Availability:** Discontinued but still available; replaced by WPS4170W, $490. **Recommendation:** A very good machine, but from one of the less reliable top-loader brands.

11 Amana LWA60A $470

• 43x26x28 in. • Water used: 43 gal. • Noise ○
Extra-rinse setting, a stainless-steel inner tub, and 4 selectable wash/spin combinations. 2-yr. warranty. **Similar models:** LWA50A, $450, LWA40A, $430. **Recommendation:** A very good machine.

12 Whirlpool LSS9244E $600

• 42x27x27 • Water used: 43 gal. • Noise ◓
Optional water-saving rinse, an extra-rinse setting, 4 water-level settings, and 4 selectable wash/spin combinations. It lacks a top lip and a fabric-softener dispenser. **Recommendation:** A very good machine from one of the more reliable top-loader brands, but expensive.

13 Whirlpool LSL9345E $510

14 Whirlpool LSL9244E $420

• 42x27x27 in. • Water used: 42 gal. (13), 41 gal. (14) • Noise ○ (13, 14)
Have an extra-rinse setting, some mechanical touchpad controls, and an end-of-cycle signal that can be turned off. The top lacks a lip. (13) has 5 water-level settings; (14) has 4. **Similar model:** LSQ9244E, $420. **Availability:** (13) has been replaced by Whirlpool Gold GSL9365E, $580. **Recommendation:** Very good machines from one of the more reliable top-loader brands.

15 Speed Queen LWS55A $430

• 43x26x28 in. • Water used: 42 gal. • Noise ○
Extra-rinse setting and a stainless-steel inner tub. **Recommendation:** A very good machine.

16 Maytag LAT9706AA $570

20 Maytag LAT9406AA $520

• 43x26x27 in. • Water used: 39 gal. • Noise ○ (16, 20)
Have a porcelain top and lid. The bleach dispenser is easier to pour into than others. (16) has extra-rinse and extended-spin settings, and cycle-indicator lights. (20) has 5 water-level settings. **Similar model:** LAT9356AA, $480. **Recommendation:** Very good machines.

17 Roper RAS8245E $430

• 42x27x27 in. • Water used: 41 gal. • Noise ○
Has 5 water-level settings. The top lacks a lip. **Recommendation:** A very good machine from one of the more reliable top-loader brands.

18 Kenmore (Sears) 2670 $380

• 43x27x27 in. • Water used: 41 gal. • Noise ○
Has very easy-to-use controls, but the lid opens left and doesn't lie flat. Has just 3 water-level settings. **Recommendation:** A very good machine and a good value from one of the more reliable top-loader brands.

19 Whirlpool LSR5233E $500

• 42x27x26 in. • Water used: 43 gal. • Noise ○
Has an extra-rinse setting and just 3 water-level settings. The top lacks a lip. **Similar models:** LSR7233E, LSR8233E, each $430. **Recommendation:** A very good machine from one of the more reliable top-loader brands.

21 Hotpoint VWSR4100V $380

• 42x27x26 in. • Water used: 41 gal. • Noise ○
Has an extra-rinse setting, 4 water-level settings, and 4 selectable wash/spin combinations. The inner tub is plastic. The lid opens left and doesn't lie flat. **Similar model:** RCA YWSR4100V, $380. **Recommendation:** A good machine.

22 White-Westinghouse MWS445RE $350

23 Frigidaire FWS645GF $370

• 43x27x27 in. (22), 42x27x27 in. (23) • Water used: 44 gal. • Noise ○ (22, 23)
The door locks during the spin cycle. The inner tub is plastic. The top lacks a front lip. (23) has 4 selectable wash/spin combinations and a 2-yr. warranty. **Availability:** (22) has been replaced

by MWS445RF, $350. **Recommendation:** Good machines, but Frigidaire is one of the less reliable top-loader brands.

24 **Admiral LATA300AA** $440

25 **Magic Chef W227L** $430

• 44x27x27 in. • Water used: 41 gal. (24), 42 gal. (25) • Noise ○ (24, 25)
The bleach dispenser is hard to pour into and allows bleach to flow into the inner tub, which is plastic. (25) has 4 selectable wash/spin combinations. **Similar model:** LATA200AA, $420. **Recommendation:** Good machines.

26 **White-Westinghouse MWX645RE** $350

• 43x27x27 in. • Water used: 39 gal. • Noise ○
The door locks during the spin cycle. Has 4 selectable wash/spin combinations. The inner tub is plastic. **Similar model:** Frigidaire FWX645RF, $350. **Recommendation:** A good machine.

27 **GE WBXR2060T** $360

• 42x27x26 in. • Water used: 38 gal. • Noise ◒
Has just 3 water-level settings and 2 automatic wash/spin combinations. Lacks a bleach dispenser. The inner tub is plastic. **Recommendation:** A good machine, but from one of the less reliable top-loader brands.

28 **Kenmore (Sears) 1820** $300

• 43x24x27 in. • Water used: 34 gal. • Noise ○
Has very easy-to-use controls, but the lid opens left and doesn't lie flat. Has just 2 water-level settings. Lacks a bleach dispenser. **Recommendation:** A good machine from one of the more reliable top-loader brands.

Home & yard

BUYING HEATING & COOLING SYSTEMS

Most furnaces or central air-conditioning systems are sold through contractors usually trained to install and repair the brands they sell. The contractor typically helps you choose the right size unit for your home, will install it, and, in most cases, also service the equipment.

So the contractor will make the biggest difference in how well the furnace, heat pump, or central air conditioning replacement goes. Ask friends, co-workers, or your local gas or electric utility for recommendations (some utilities install and maintain furnaces themselves). Check the Yellow Pages for additional names.

Get bids from at least three contractors, especially if you don't have a strong reference for one company. If state or local laws require it, make sure the contractor has a valid heating or cooling contractor's license, and ask for proof of insurance. The contractor's qualifications should blend training, certification, and on-the-job experience. Ask if any of the contractor's technicians are certified to install a furnace, heat pump, or central air conditioning, or if they plan to get certification from national programs such as North American Technician Excellence (NATE) or Air Conditioning Excellence (ACE).

Be wary of very low bids; the contractor may be cutting corners in ways that compromise the system's effectiveness. Before you sign a contract, ask for and check references, and find out if there are any complaints with the Better Business Bureau.

HEATING SYSTEMS

***Last CR report:** November 1998*

In this era of relatively low energy prices, replacing or improving a furnace may not pay off as handsomely as it did in, say, the energy crisis of the late 1970s. But it may deliver steady, modest savings. And efficient heating isn't only about money. Because they burn less fuel to generate heat, today's furnaces produce less carbon dioxide than their predecessors. They also tend to distribute heat more evenly and continuously, making your home more comfortable.

What's available

Two-thirds of people who buy a new central-heating system now buy a gas furnace, the focus of this report.

Gas furnaces. The two major manufacturers are United Technology (Carrier and Bryant brands) and Goodman (Janitrol and Amana). Other companies include Rheem (Ruud), American Standard (Trane), Lennox (Lennox, Armstrong), and International Comfort Products (Heil, Tempstar, Comfortmaker). All offer furnaces in a range of rated capacities and efficiencies (we think manufacturers generally deliver on their specifications), and each brand offers a generally similar array of key features. More important than brand-to-brand differences: ensuring that the unit's specifications fit your needs; that it is bought from a contractor who installs it well; and that it's adequately maintained. Our survey of 575 specialists in residential heating and air conditioning that elicited their experiences in installing and maintaining equipment confirmed our view: When asked about the most common reasons for service calls, about two-thirds of respondents cited human error—inadequate maintenance or improper installation—versus defective equipment.

Other central heating systems are also available:

Heat pumps. These predominantly electric appliances wring heat from outdoor air or the ground and pump it into your home. In summer, they run in reverse to act as an air conditioner, drawing heat from indoor air and pumping it outdoors. They're the preferred way to heat in the South and Southwest, where winters are temperate and electricity is generally cheap. In colder climates, or during cold snaps in temperate zones, the pump's heat must be supplemented, often with built-in electric elements that kick in automatically—providing rapid but expensive heat. As with furnaces, the main choices are size (or capacity), measured in British thermal units per hour (Btu/hr.), and efficiency, reflected in the unit's HSPF (for heating seasonal performance factor). HSPF ratings for new heat pumps range from 6.8, the minimum allowed, to about 10. Heat pumps cost more than many furnaces (though you do also get a central air-conditioning system in the bargain). Higher-efficiency models are more expensive, and the highest-efficiency models are more prone to require repair, according to the contractors we surveyed.

Oil furnaces and boilers. These heating appliances draw oil to burn from a tank located in the basement or underground. Probably only homeowners who already own an oil unit and who live in the Northeast or Midwest, where oil is widely distributed, should consider this option. As with gas furnaces, the main choices are in size and efficiency. It's safest to install a tank in the basement; in-ground models may eventually leak, posing an environmental hazard and requiring an expensive cleanup. Some oil dealers sell insurance against tank leakage; we recommend its purchase.

In-floor radiant heating systems. This system heats via hot water run through special plastic tubing imbedded in a room's concrete floor. It's worth considering if you plan to renovate a living area, especially one with high ceilings, in a house that already uses a hot-water-based central heating system. Though radiant systems are relatively slow to heat a cold room, they can provide even heat with no drafts. The water from radiant systems may be heated by an oil, gas, or electrically fired boiler, or, in some states, by the home's hot-water heater.

Key considerations for gas furnaces

Replace or repair? If your furnace falters or fails, try some simple troubleshooting first:

• If you're getting low airflow, check the air filter on the furnace; a clogged filter could cut airflow to a trickle.

• See if there are loose wires or a malfunction in the thermostat. If an electronic thermostat runs on batteries, try changing them.

• Check to see if fuses burned out or breaker switches tripped. If so, power may have been cut to the fan or circuit board.

If that doesn't work, call a heating contractor. Despite the improved efficiency and comfort of most new furnaces, it's generally more cost-effective to repair a furnace than to replace it. However, if a key component such as the heat exchanger or control module fails, you're probably better off replacing the furnace than repairing it, especially if the unit is more than about 15 years old (furnaces typically last about 18 years).

How large? A furnace that's too small won't heat adequately during extreme cold, so contractors sometimes sell furnaces that are too large for a particular home. However, an overly large unit won't work properly either: It will cycle on and off more frequently, putting wear on its components, wastes energy, and may cause the temperature to vary uncomfortably. Also, upgrading to a larger furnace may require the installation of wider ducts to accommodate increased airflow.

To be sure of correct sizing, choose a contractor who agrees to take time to calculate heating demand using an industry-standard calculation, such as the Air Conditioning Contractors of America's Manual J, which takes into account the climate, plus the house's size, design, and construction.

How efficient? How efficiently a furnace converts gas into heating energy is reflected in its annual fuel utilization efficiency (AFUE) rating, measured as a percentage. The higher that percentage, the more heat the furnace can wring from each therm of gas—and the lower the environmental impact of its emissions. Furnaces have generally become more efficient. A typical gas furnace made in the early 1980s has an AFUE of about 65 percent. Today, the lowest efficiency allowed by law for new gas furnaces is 78 percent, and the most efficient models have an AFUE as high as 97 percent—or near-total efficiency.

The more efficient a furnace, generally, the lower your energy bill for heating. But you must also figure in other costs: electricity to run the blowers, thermostats, and other components; and special installation requirements, such as new, revised, or special vents (needed for a furnace with an AFUE of 90 percent or more or if other appliances such as a gas-fired water heater share a vent or chimneys with a furnace). All this can easily add several hundred dollars to the installed cost of a new furnace.

One-third of the contractors we surveyed said the most efficient furnaces (those with, say, an AFUE of 95 or more) tend to need more repair than other models because they tend to have more components that can break down and are more likely to use new, less-tried-and-true designs. (More than half of the contractors we surveyed also cited new furnace designs as prone to needing more repair.)

Key features for gas furnaces

These features, among those most often highlighted in product literature or sales pitches for furnaces, are also more likely to be found on higher-efficiency furnaces.

Variable-speed blowers can deliver air more slowly (and often more quietly) when less heat is needed, meaning fewer uncomfortable swings in temperature and airflow. **Variable heat output,** available on some furnaces that have variable blower speed, can further increase efficiency and comfort by automatically varying the amount of heat the furnace delivers, usually between two levels, again resulting in steadier temperatures. **Zone heating** employs a number of thermostats, a central controller, and a series of dampers that control airflow to deliver different heating or cooling "loads" to different parts of the home. As a rule, the larger the home, and the more its different sections vary in their heating needs, the more useful zoning is. However, contractors said that furnaces connected to zoned ductwork required more repair than those connected to single-zone systems.

Furnaces with **intermittent, direct spark,** or **hot surface ignition** do away with the continuous pilot light, increasing efficiency—and usually earn a higher AFUE rating. To draw more heat from the air they burn, furnaces with an AFUE of 90 percent or higher have a **second heat exchanger**—the component that draws heat from the burned gas. Because the exhaust is cooler when it leaves the second exchanger, it may yield an acidic condensate. To prevent that acid from causing corrosion, the second exchanger is made of stainless steel, lined with PVC plastic, or otherwise protected.

Fitting a furnace with an **electrostatic filter,** which uses an electrical charge to help trap particles, or a **high-efficiency particulate arresting (HEPA) filter** can reduce the dust blown through the heating system, which may help people with asthma or other chronic lung diseases possibly aggravated by airborne particles. But there's little evidence that other people need such filtration. An air cleaner can't prevent airborne particles from entering a home in the first place. Nor can it significantly reduce the sources of allergens in the house, such as pet dander.

How to choose a gas furnace

Performance differences. System size and efficiency and the contractor's competence matter more than brand names.

What to spend. The price of a furnace

generally rises with its gas efficiency. A furnace with a 90 percent AFUE can cost $1,000 more than a similarly sized unit with an 80 percent AFUE. However, that additional cost can generally be recouped over the lifetime of the furnace. Just how quickly the expenditure is recovered depends not only on the unit's AFUE but also on its electrical consumption, how well your home retains heat, and your climate. In regions where winters are especially harsh—including most of the Northeast and Midwest—the payback time may be only a decade or so.

When comparing models, make sure the contractor's estimate for each choice includes the cost of any changes to venting. And insist that the contractor estimate annual operating costs using the unit's AFUE and electrical consumption, information on your home, and the region where you live. (Salespeople can make these calculations easily and accurately.)

Weigh operating-cost differences against the prices for various units, along with their features. If a model that fits your needs and priorities has an AFUE in the mid-90 percent range or above, pose additional questions to the contractor. Is the model fairly new, and thus relatively untested? Has the contractor noticed any reliability problems?

Some manufacturers' basic (usually low-efficiency) models may have less generous warranties than their premium models. For example, Lennox Value furnaces have a one-year warranty (10 years on the heat exchanger), compared with the five-year warranty (lifetime on the heat exchanger) offered on Lennox Elite furnaces.

CENTRAL COOLING SYSTEMS

Last CR report: June 1998

In the South and Southwest, central air is a feature of virtually every new house that's built.

There are two basic types of central cooling—**split-system air conditioners** and **heat pumps**. A split cooling system should last about 15 years. If a system that's more than a decade old begins to falter, consider total replacement of inside and outside units rather than a major repair. Usually only one of the system's major components—coil or compressor—fails, but it's usually more cost-effective to replace the whole system at once. Unmatched major components can compromise efficiency and lead to added repairs.

Though a central-cooling system is expensive, you could easily spend as much—and more—to equip every room in your home with its own air conditioner. Room units are practical in climates that get hot only a few months a year.

What's available

A central air-cooling system comprises cooling equipment (usually a central air conditioner) connected to a network of ducting that distributes air throughout the home. The most common such systems are "split"—they have both indoor and outdoor components. Refrigerant flows from the outdoor unit to the indoor one, where it cools warm household air and dispenses the cooled air throughout the house. The warm refrigerant is returned to the outdoor unit, where it releases its heat before being returned to the indoor unit.

Ideally, the outdoor unit is placed

where there's good airflow, close to the house and in a spot where operating noise doesn't disturb you or your neighbors (a shady, well-ventilated location can improve cooling performance).

The indoor unit is often mounted on the furnace of a forced-air heating system. If that's lacking, the unit is then typically placed in an attic or crawl space. The location should permit access to the unit's interior for cleaning and inspection.

In areas where winters are mild, a heat pump is often installed to move refrigerant between its indoor and outdoor units, cooling the house in summer by removing heat from indoor air and warming it in winter by drawing heat from outdoor air or the ground.

With either type of system, the design and installation of the ductwork are critical. Improper designs, such as ductwork that's too small, can result in poor cooling or excessive noise in one or more rooms. The U.S. Department of Energy estimates that a typical system wastes 20 to 40 percent of its energy through ducts that leak or lack insulation. Have the contractor seal any leaks along seams and insulate sections of ducting that run through uncooled or unheated spaces, such as attics or crawl spaces.

Some of the best-selling brands of central-air systems are Carrier (the same company manufactures Bryant and several other brands), Lennox, and Trane. Most contractors carry several brands. As with furnaces, the brand has only a minimal effect on the system performance. More important: how well the contractor sizes and installs the system, the efficiency level you choose, and how well you maintain it.

Key considerations

Size. Cooling capacity is expressed in "tons"; one ton equals 12,000 British thermal units per hour (Btu/hr.). A unit with too little cooling capacity may not keep the whole house cool. But the more common contractor error is an oversized system, not only more expensive to buy and run, but not fully effective. Although it may cool a warm house very quickly, the unit will shut off before it has completed the slower work of reducing humidity, leaving the air sticky and uncomfortable. An oversized air conditioner will also cycle on and off frequently, causing noticeable temperature swings and putting more wear on the equipment.

Oversizing often results when a contractor uses a rule of thumb to estimate capacity—one ton for every 500 square feet of floor space, say—instead of relying on a more detailed assessment. Unless you are replacing a system that worked well with another system of the same capacity, make sure that the contractor makes these calculations. If you want your system to cool the house before you get home, consider a programmable thermostat too.

Energy efficiency. The energy appetite of a central air-cooling system is expressed in its seasonal energy-efficiency rating (SEER). The higher an air conditioner's SEER, the less power it will use to cool your home each summer. Whereas 10-year-old systems might have an average SEER of 9, Department of Energy standards now require a minimum SEER of 10 for typical split systems. The most efficient units have a rating as high as 18.

Mid-efficiency models—those with a rating of between 11 and 14—may be the least expensive to own overall because they're cheaper to buy and are less likely to need repair. Minimum-efficiency units and no-frills models known as "builder's models" are often installed in new homes or as replacements. When bought for an existing home, they'll typically cost a couple of hundred dollars less than a mid-efficiency system. But those savings may be short-lived.

Based on average usage patterns and electricity rates across the country, a unit with an SEER of 10 will cost about $50 more, on average, to run each year than a unit with an SEER of 12. As a further financial incentive for investing in an efficient system, some utilities offer rebates to people who install high-efficiency air conditioners. Check with your utility company to see what's offered.

The contractors we surveyed said low-efficiency units (with an SEER of 10) are more likely to need repair than mid-efficiency models. And builder's models almost invariably have shorter warranties—typically 5 years on parts and labor, compared with 7 or 10 years for most mid- and high-efficiency units.

Going for the highest-efficiency model may not be the most economical choice, either. In our survey, contractors said that very high efficiency models are more prone to repair than mid-efficiency ones. That's probably because mid-efficiency units can use existing designs that have benefited from years of troubleshooting.

Type of compressor. The compressor is among the most expensive parts to replace in a central-air system. Many models—especially builder's models—use a *reciprocating* design that has many moving parts. But the contractors we surveyed said that newer *scroll compressors*, which have fewer moving parts, need less repair. They can also be more efficient, which is why they are often found on mid- and high-efficiency models.

Zoned cooling. "Zoned" systems, which cool (or heat) different parts of the house to different temperatures by controlling airflow, are becoming more prevalent. Such systems can help ensure that temperatures will remain comfortable throughout a home whose cooling demands can vary from room to room and by time of day.

But zoning has its drawbacks. It makes a system more expensive to buy and more expensive to repair. An improperly installed system can be noisy. Contractors we surveyed said the cooling equipment in zoned systems needed more repair. Zoning should not be used as a substitute for a properly sized and installed system.

Caring for your cooler

At least 40 percent of surveyed contractors said that service calls were primarily the result of improper maintenance. These steps will help keep a central air-cooling system running well for years to come.

What you can do. Keep air-supply outlets and return inlets clear of obstructions. Clear leaves, brush, and dirt as they accumulate on the outside unit. If there's a pipe for draining condensed water, check it for blockage. Check the air filter once a month during the operating season. Replace it if it looks dirty (some are washable).

What a contractor can do. Check the system initially for the proper amount of refrigerant in the system—too much or too little hurts efficiency and reliability. The refrigerant level should not need further service unless a problem develops.

Then, annually: Clean and flush the coils, drain pan, and drainage system. Vacuum dust and dirt from inside the blower compartments. On an older unit, check any drive belts and lubricate motors (newer models have no belts and do not require lubrication). Check all electrical connections and controls, and inspect wiring for signs of damage.

Service plan. Consider purchasing a service plan, particularly if it combines cooling and heating functions. Most cost about $80 to $200 a year and include two visits, which may allow the contractor to spot problems before they lead to a breakdown. You may also get discounts on repairs and receive priority service—a blessing if your cooling system breaks down during a heat wave.

How to choose

Performance differences. Because so many performance factors are specific to the house being cooled and the way the system has been installed and maintained, we have not reported on the performance of specific brands.

What to spend. Cost depends in part on the heating and cooling equipment you already own. If you have a central-cooling system or a forced-air heating system, you already have the ductwork required to distribute cool air throughout the house. All you'll need to add or replace are the basic hardware components of the central-cooling system. According to R. S. Means, a company that publishes construction-cost data, the national average price for replacing a common-size (36,000 Btu/hr.) system is about $2,800.

However, new ducts installed in a typical new house (2,100 square feet) can add thousands of dollars to a system's cost. And ducts that already serve a heating system may have to be upgraded to accommodate the higher airflow that a central-cooling system requires.

ROOM AIR CONDITIONERS

***Last CR report:** June 98*
***Ratings:** page 169*
***Expect to pay:** $200 to $850*

Room air conditioners work best to chill one or two rooms in climates that get hot only a few months a year. Consider two key variables: cooling capacity, measured in British thermal units per hour (Btu/hr.), and efficiency, reflected in its energy-efficiency rating (EER); the higher it is, the more efficient the unit. As a rule, the larger the capacity and the higher the EER, the more the unit costs.

The yellow Energy Guide tag on every new air conditioner lists its EER, which may range from 8, the minimum, to a superefficient 12. (A new standard further raising the minimum EER for models like those in the Ratings on page 169 will go into effect in October 2000.) A unit with an EER of 11 will cost 18 percent less to operate than a similar sized one with an EER of 9.

What's available

Fedders, Kenmore (Sears), General Electric, and Whirlpool account for more than half the room air conditioners sold. Fedders makes the Emerson Quiet Kool brands. Other makers include Frigidaire (maker of Gibson and White-Westinghouse models), Matsushita (maker of Panasonic and Quasar models), Carrier, and Friedrich.

All room air conditioners contain pretty much the same components. The outdoor-facing portion contains a compressor, fan, and condenser; the indooor part, a fan and an evaporator. Most room models are designed to be installed in double-hung windows. Some can also be adapted for through-the-wall installation. If you have casement windows, check with the store for units built especially for that type. Some models have a low-profile design, which blocks less of the window.

The smallest models have a cooling capacity of about 5,000 Btu/hr., which is suitable for a small bedroom. Price range: $200 to $350.

Medium-sized models have a cooling capacity of about 6,000 to 10,000 Btu/hr., right for a living room or master suite. Price range: $300 to $700.

Large models, those rated at 11,000 to 12,000 Btu/hr., can cool about 500 square feet—a large room, or areas that run together, such as a living room and dining room. Price range: $500 to $850. Models rated larger than 12,000 Btu/hr. usually require a 240-volt line instead of the normal 120-volt line.

Key features

Look for a **thermostat** with clear markings. Controls should be logically arranged and easy to operate. Some models have a digital readout, showing the temperature you've set and that power is on. A **built-in timer** can turn on an air conditioner before you get home. Most timers are the elapsed kind (much like a cooking timer); Friedrichs have a 24-hour timer that's programmable in 1 hour in-

HOW MUCH COOLING?

This chart can help you to determine how much cooling you'll need for living space with an eight-foot ceiling. Or refer to our web site *(www.ConsumerReports.org)*, where an interactive worksheet can help you more precisely figure out the size of air conditioner you need and how much it will cost to operate models with different EERs.

1. At the bottom of the chart, find the square footage of the space.

2. Choose the band for what's above the room: the thickest band for an occupied area above; medium-width for an insulated attic above; the thinnest for a noninsulated attic.

3. Within the band, move down for rooms facing mostly north or east, up for mostly south or west.

4. Read across to find the Btu/hr.

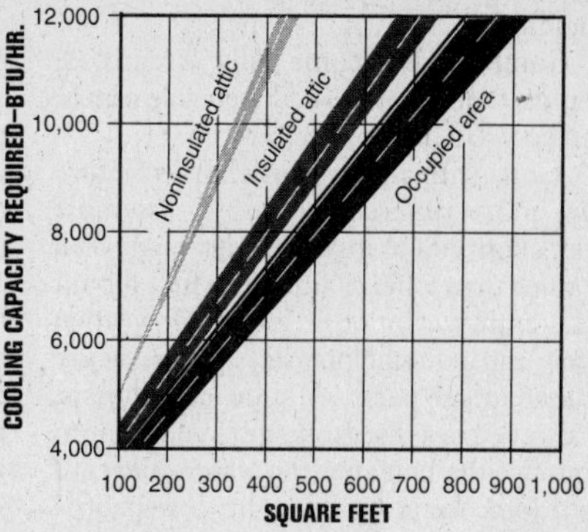

5. From that Btu/hr. figure, subtract up to 15 percent if you live in a Northern climate; add up to 10 percent for a Southern climate. Subtract 30 percent if the unit will be used only at night. If more than two people regularly occupy the area, add 600 Btu/hr. of cooling capacity for every additional person. Add 4,000 Btu/hr. if the area includes the kitchen.

crements. **Louvers** adjust side to side or up/down, and add versatility to airflow direction, but they can't correct it entirely. Most units direct air more to one side of the room than to the other because of the position of interior ducts and the direction of the fan rotation.

A low fan speed is ideal when you're asleep or the room is occupied; a high speed provides quick cooling. Three speeds should meet most needs; more than three is unnecessary. An **energy-saver mode** saves little, making a jarring sound as the unit cycles on and off.

A **remote control** is helpful if the unit is mounted high on a wall or for a disabled user. A **slide-out, washable filter** makes cleaning and maintenance easier. An **exterior support bracket** helps distribute weight to the window sash, sill, and outside wall. An **upper sash lock** secures the air conditioner to the window to deter break-ins.

Except for the most lightweight models, we recommend that installation be done by two people (weights range from 40 to 110 pounds).

Some models come fully assembled; others require you to add their side panels, an easy job on most brands.

Units with a **slide-out chassis** feature are more time-consuming to assemble but allow you to install a lightweight shell rather than a heavy unit. You first mount the empty cabinet to the window; then you and your helper slide in the heavy mechanical parts. A slide-out chassis, however, is a disadvantage if you want to remove the unit after the season is over. If so, look for a lightweight, low-profile unit with a handle.

Most air conditioners, including all those we tested, are designed to be installed in double-hung windows. (The Ratings include the size of the window the tested model should fit.) Some can also be adapted for through-the-wall installation. If you have casement windows, check with the store for units built especially for that type.

How to choose

Performance differences. Our recent tests have shown fine performance to be the norm. Only a few models in our latest test group were less than very good at maintaining comfortable temperature and humidity on a simulated hot, muggy day.

Models do differ in noise level, although the low settings, often used at night, were quiet overall.

What to spend. Cost depends on cooling needs and the model's energy efficiency. How much capacity you need depends on the size of your room, the number of windows, its exposure, and your climate. To figure out what you need, use the chart on page 147 or the interactive worksheet at our web site *(www.ConsumerReports.org)*. Too little capacity won't cool adequately. A unit that's too big will tend to cycle off before it can adequately dehumidify the room, leaving the air clammy.

Buying a high-efficiency model, of course, contributes to the national goal of reducing overall energy consumption. It may also make economic sense for you, especially if you're buying a fairly large unit that will see a lot of use. A good rule of thumb is to shop for the most efficient model that's competitively priced. If you face a choice between models of different efficiencies that vary widely in price, weigh such factors as your energy rate and how heavily you'll use the machine.

The best selection occurs during May, June, and July and falls off sharply thereafter. Prices are more likely to be discounted during the off-season.

BARBECUE GRILLS

Last CR report: *June 1998*
Ratings: *page 189*
Expect to pay: *$100 to $1,000*

With any outdoor grill, you'll want chicken that's seared outside yet moist inside, and burgers that give off that smoky cookout aroma that makes the neighbors wish they'd been invited over. And you don't need a "cooking system" roughly the size of a Hyundai to get it.

What's available

Char-Broil and Sunbeam, part of the same company, are the most widely sold brands of gas barbecue grills. The company also makes some Sears grills. Char-Broil makes Coleman and Thermos grills. Other popular brands: Weber and Ducane.

Gas grills. More convenient to use than charcoal grills, these are easy to start; warm up fast; cook predictably, as a rule; have niceties like shelves and side burners; and can be cleaned up fairly fast. They give meat a full, browned flavor that's less smoky than a charcoal flavor. Special wood chips deliver a smokier flavor but are tricky to use: You must soak them first, then add them continually as you cook. Price range: $100 to more than $1,000. More money may buy sturdiness, more burners (as many as five), and such options as a wok ring, smoker, or griddle.

Charcoal grills. First, the drawbacks: You'll spend about $1 for charcoal each time you cook, versus about 65 cents per cookout for a gas grill and 7 cents for an electric grill. However, natural lump charcoal gives food an intense, smoky flavor prized by many barbecuers. Standard charcoal briquettes impart a milder smoky flavor. Price range: $100 or less. Coals don't always light easily, need about 20 minutes to develop the proper ashen color, and burn less cleanly than gas. Regulating heat takes practice, and cleanup can be messy.

Electric grills. On the market for more than 10 years, these began to catch on a few years ago. You can start them easily, control their temperature precisely, keep the temperature low, and since there's no fire involved, cook on a nonstick surface. They can also smoke wood chips. However, the ones we tested took a long time to warm up, never got hot enough to cook steaks properly, and were hard to clean. Price range: $100 to $300.

Key features

The **cooking grate** should have wide bars, closely spaced to sear food well. Porcelain-coated steel grates are easy to clean, and the porcelain protects against rust. Bare cast-iron grates sear beautifully but will rust unless regularly seasoned with a light coat of cooking oil. Most grills come with separately controlled steel **burners**—porcelain-coated steel or stainless-steel are best.

Food drippings that fall into the **heat distributor** are vaporized to add flavor to whatever you're grilling. To reduce the possibility of flame flair-ups, choose a design that channels drippings down and away from the cooking grate, as do Weber's metal triangles. Heat can also be distributed by ceramic briquettes, charcoal-looking briquettes, or lava rocks. Briquettes and lava rocks used as heat distributors will need to be turned over to be cleaned every so often, and eventually replaced.

Most gas grills come with an **igniter**, either a knob or a button that produces a spark. Knobs emit two or three sparks per turn; push-button igniters emit a single spark per push of the button. Electronic igniters require a 9-volt battery, but one push of the button produces continuous sparks until you release it. Some grills have lighting holes on the side or beneath the grill in case the igniter fails.

The **lid and firebox** typically are painted aluminum, which tends to become weather-beaten. Porcelain-coated steel holds up better. Some grills have a **window**, quickly clouded by spatters.

Carts are made of steel tubing assembled with nuts and bolts (higher priced Weber grills have welded joints). Carts with two large wheels and two smaller casters are easiest to move around. Two wheels and two feet mean you have to lift one end to move the grill.

Gas grills generally have one or more **shelves**. Some flip up from the front or side, many are fixed on the side. Some grills come with interior **racks** that let you keep food warm without futher cooking time.

Easy-cleaning features include **removable bottoms** or **specially designed grates** that catch and vaporize drippings before they accumulate into a mess at the bottom of the heat distributor area.

Most grills come with a **propane tank**. There are also a few available in **natural-gas versions**. Generally the tank is easier to hook up than before—good news, since a loaded tank weighs about 38 pounds.

Grill makers offer a wealth of **accessories**: electric rotisseries, smokers, woks, steamer pans, nonstick grill baskets, covers, even recipe books. Decide if you want a **side burner**. It resembles a gas-stove burner, has its own heat control, and is handy to cook sauce as you grill.

How to choose

Performance differences. Many grills can heat evenly, sear steak on the outside while leaving it rare inside, and slow roast a chicken or even a turkey. Don't go by a grill's Btu/hr. rating (a measure of heating power)—higher isn't necessarily better.

What to spend. Our tests show that some midpriced grills costing $275 or less are excellent values for the money. Models that cost $350 to $570 have more features—wide bars, ample warming shelves, stainless-steel burners and grates, electronic igniters, longer warranties, and sturdier carts on casters. Some models may require you to buy the tank separately from the grill, adding as much as $40.

Assembly. Warning: Even our engineers took 50 minutes to over four hours to assemble some grills. Especially easy were the Weber grills. You may be able to buy a factory-assembled grill—or have the store put it together.

TIPS FOR GRILLING SAFELY

New grills are safer thanks to a feature that prevents overfilling the tank. Even so, it still pays to take certain precautions:

- Read the instructions supplied with the grill.
- Never store a tank indoors.
- Light the grill with the lid open.
- If the grill fails to light within about five seconds, shut off the gas and wait a few minutes before trying again.
- At the start of the grilling season, use a pipe cleaner to unclog the tubes that send gas to the burners.

CARPET CLEANERS

***Last CR report:** July 1997*
***Ratings:** page 177*
***Expect to pay:** $75 to $400*

Manufacturers claim that pricey deep cleaners, meant for occasional use, get deep down to the grime and leave soiled carpeting clean and fresh. Brisk sales tell us that many consumers have been convinced.

The Carpet and Rug Institute, a trade group, recommends that people deep-clean every 12 to 18 months, depending on the type and color of the carpeting, how much it's walked on, and the carpet manufacturer's recommendations. But you don't have to buy a machine: You can rent one for about $20 a day, or pay for a professional carpet-cleaner. And, of course, small rugs can simply be rolled up and sent to a rug-cleaning company. Expect to pay $1 to $2 a foot.

What's available

Carpet deep-cleaners are sold by Bissell, Eureka, Hoover, Regina and Sears, and are also available to rent at supermarkets and home-care centers.

Regular vacuum cleaners remove loose dirt but hardly touch the dirt and oils that stick to carpet fibers. **Deep-cleaners** or **extractors** are supposed to go a step further: They typically spray on a solution of detergent mixed with hot water, sometimes working it in with moving brushes, then vacuum up the dirty solution. With **rug shampooers** or other scrubbers, you wait until the carpet is dry, then use a regular vacuum cleaner to pick up the residue and fluff the pile.

The newer extractors for the home market are lighter and less bulky than typical rental machines, and look like conventional upright or canister vacuums. Most come with attachments for cleaning upholstery. Some can be used as a wet/dry vacuum.

Upright extractors combine into a single unit a tank for dispensing cleaning solution, a tank for holding the dirty solution, a vacuum to pick up the dirty solution, and a fixed or moving brush. When full, they typically weigh about 30 pounds and are cumbersome to push around. Several of the machines have attachments for cleaning upholstery, stairs, and tight spots between furniture. In general, uprights are easier to store than bulky canisters. Most uprights hold one gallon of cleaning solution (the rental we tested holds two gallons), enough to clean a small- to medium-size room. Price range: $100 to $300.

Canister extractors have a light wand and a generally longer hose, which make them much easier to work with—although their large handle may get in the way in tight spots. Carpet-cleaning attachments may have moving or fixed brushes—clear plastic provides good control and visibility. Changing tools can be a chore. Canisters hold about two gallons of cleaning solution (the rental we tested holds three gallons), enough for a large room. Price range: small canisters, about $75; large, $100 to $200.

Scrubbing machines have no vacuum power. They simply work the solution (or, in the case of the Windsor Dri-Matic, a moist powder) into the carpeting, then you pick up the loosened dirt with a regular vacuum cleaner. They're lighter than the extractors, and a little easier to keep clean because you don't have to deal with a dirty solution tank or suction hose. Compared with other uprights, they're less bulky but will probably take about the same amount of closet space. Price range: $100 to $400.

How to choose

Performance differences. Our tests showed that most of the machines don't perform very well. A few picked up soil pretty well, and some lightened the appearance of stains. But most models did neither task effectively. For $90 to nearly $400 per machine—plus cleaning solutions that cost about $1 to $5 per room—we expected more.

What to spend. Rent first to see if you like what a deep-cleaner does for your carpeting. Then consider whether you'll use it enough to justify buying one.

But cheaper, simpler methods may work better:

Shop vac ($5 to $7 for a bottle of stain pretreatment, about $100 for the machine). This method worked better than any of the tested machines for spot cleaning, though it isn't practical for cleaning large areas. Apply pretreatment to a stained area; vacuum with the wet/dry vac; repeat. Take care not to use so much solution at once that you soak carpeting to the point of damaging its backing or the floor underneath it.

A carpet-cleaning professional (about $75 for two rooms). This no-sweat method produced results similar to our best machines used with large amounts of cleaning solution.

Carpet stain cleaners, liquid dish detergent (less than $5). Cleaning manually with off-the-shelf products removed stubborn stains better than deep-cleaning machines did. Dilute the dish detergent 1 teaspoon to 1 cup of water. Before applying any cleaner to a prominent place, try it on an inconspicuous spot to make sure it won't hurt the carpeting or affect its color. To avoid damaging carpet fibers, pat with brush bristles; do not scrub. And be sure to rinse out and blot up residual detergent with clean cloths and sponges.

Aerosol foam cleaners ($5 for about 150 square feet of carpet). This was the most grueling and least effective way to clean heavy dirt. When we tried both Resolve Foam Carpet Cleaner and Woolite Heavy Traffic Foam Carpet Cleaner, according to their instructions, we found that the sponge floated on top of the foam without reaching down into the carpet. Even after we added more foam than recommended, the results were no better than with the worst-performing machines we tested.

Check the carpet manufacturer's recommendations to see what method of deep cleaning is best for your carpeting.

CEILING FANS

***Last CR report:** June 1997*
***Ratings:** page 183*
***Expect to pay:** $30 to $400*

A ceiling fan can make a room feel six or seven degrees cooler—enough to provide comfort on a moderately hot day. On a very hot or humid day, it can supplement an air conditioner set at a higher temperature.

What's available

The Hampton Bay brand is sold by Home Depot; Harbor Breeze, by Lowe's stores; Kenmore, by Sears stores. Ceiling fans are marketed as a decorative item as well as an appliance, and come in a vast array of styles and finishes to complement any decor. They range from 32 to 60 inches in diameter, measured from blade tip to blade tip. The two most widely sold are 42-inch models, weighing 10 to 15 pounds and recommended for rooms up to 225 square feet, and 52-inch models, weighing 15 to 40 pounds, for rooms up to 400 square feet. For larger spaces, you might consider installing multiple fans.

Key features

Fans typically come with a **lighting kit** or offer one for $15 to $150 extra, depending on style. Various types of **wall switches** are also available, as are **remote controls**, either as part of the unit or as an aftermarket option.

Most models can be installed in one of two ways: hanging from a swiveling downrod or mounted flush with the ceiling. A **downrod** provides better air circulation but accentuates any tendency to wobble. (A ceiling fan shouldn't hang lower than seven feet above the floor, especially in areas where people may raise their arms, as when dressing.) All the fans come with instructions on how to balance the assembly to minimize wobbling—typically, by interchanging the blades. Some have small weights with adhesive tabs to balance the blades. Balancing isn't difficult, but some models we've tested required more tedious trial and error than others.

A fan is often easiest to install in place of an existing overhead light, which already has wiring and is generally near the center of the room. Most fans use a **J-hook mount** that requires lifting the fan twice—once to hang it on the hook and connect the wiring, and a second time to attach it permanently. Some fans have a convenient **hanger bracket** that immediately secures the downrod. Installing a ceiling fan is more complex than putting in a ceiling-light fixture, perhaps making it a job for a licensed electrician. Whoever installs it should replace the existing outlet box with one that's UL-listed and labeled "acceptable for fan support." If the box is to go between ceiling joists, use a hanger bar or cross-brace. Secure the box with lag bolts or a U-bolt.

How to choose

Performance differences. Our tests of 42- and 52-inch fans have shown that both sizes can move air adequately. The number of blades does not significantly affect airflow, although an extra blade made the fan run a bit slower in our tests. Bigger isn't necessarily better. Choose the right size for the room.

What to spend. A very good large fan runs about $100. A very good smaller one may cost less than $50. Spending more buys "designer" styles and options such as a wall-mounted control or a remote. You'll find the best selection in May, June, and July, with prices more likely to be discounted in the off-season.

DECK TREATMENTS

***Last CR report:** June 1998*
***Ratings:** page 180*
***Expect to pay:** $10 to $50*

A deck treatment needs to protect from all types of weather. The sun's ultraviolet rays break down the lignin that holds wood together. Rain and sun alternately swell and dry the wood, eventually making it crack and split. Moisture promotes the growth of mold and mildew. Dirt infiltrates and lodges between wood fibers. Our tests, launched in 1996, show that many products can't handle the job.

What's available

You'll find many brands from familiar paint manufacturers—Glidden, Benjamin Moore, Behr, Pratt & Lambert. Other brands include Thompson, ZAR, DAP, and Sears.

Linseed oil and tung oil, once common in wood coatings, have been supplanted by new formulations described as preservatives, protectors, stabilizers, repellents, sealers, cleaners, restorers, and rejuvenators. Manufacturers claim that these products can be used on fences and siding, not just decks, and will retard, if not prevent, all the typical effects of weathering.

Deck treatments may be solvent-based or water-based. Some involve a two-step process, requiring application of a base coat followed by a top coat within a year.

Clear finishes. These are generally water-repellent and have no color to mask any of the wood grain. Often, a clear finish will let the wood turn gray. They must be renewed every year.

Toned finishes. This finish contains a little transparent pigment to help block ultraviolet radiation but hardly masks wood grain and may allow the wood to gray.

Semitransparent finishes. This type contains pigment to help block ultraviolet and visible light, and will mask the wood grain.

How to choose

Performance differences. Tests at our Yonkers headquarters and in the Miami area show a great range of performance. In fact, some products don't work at all.

Here's what we found:

• The more pigmented semitransparent products on the market are the best overall performers.

• The clear finishes are the worst performers by far.

• Solvent-based products generally did better at the beginning of the test but eventually lost their advantage over water-based ones.

• The ability to make water bead on the surface is not a sign of good water-repellency, despite ad claims.

• The ultimate result of water repellency is wood that isn't cracked.

• No treatment could prevent dirt from accumulating.

• Few clear finishes resisted mildew effectively.

Our findings aren't encouraging for clear finishes. Most semitransparent and toned products survived better.

What to spend. The best semitransparent and toned products are expensive—around $20 a gallon up to more than $50 a gallon. A cheaper product probably won't protect the wood as well.

LAWN MOWERS

***Last CR report:** June 1998*
***Ratings:** page 192*
***Expect to pay:** $100 to $4,000*

Your best buy depends very much on the size and shape of your lawn: large or small, hilly or flat, full of hard-to-reach spots—or not.

Most mowers allow you to mulch the clippings, reducing the disposal part of the chore, yielding a neat appearance, and reducing the need for chemical fertilizers. However, most mowers don't mulch well if you try to cut more than one-third the length of the grass, so mulching requires diligent mowing.

Compared with car engines, small engines like those in mowers produce a disproportionate amount of air pollution. As of September 1997, the Environmental Protection Agency instituted the first phase of regulations aimed at cutting these engines' emissions. The California Air Resources Board has required similar standards for yard equipment sold in California since 1995. Expect even tougher standards in the future.

What's available

Home centers and discount stores tend to have the best selection. Outdoor power-equipment dealers usually carry upscale mowers such as Honda, John Deere, Lawn-Boy, Snapper, and Toro—and often provide better service.

Manual reel mowers. These are practical for small, flat lawns. Although it's been brought up-to-date with lightweight alloys and plastic parts, this mower works as it always has: a series of blades linked to wheels slice the grass. Manual reel mowers are quiet, inexpensive, relatively safe to operate, don't pollute, and provide exercise. They require no maintenance aside from occasional sharpening or blade adjustment. Most can't cut grass higher than 1½ inches—those we've tested had a hard time plowing through thick, high grass—nor cut closer than three inches around obstacles. The cutting swath ranges from 14 to 18 inches. Price range: about $100.

Electric mowers. These use an electric motor to drive a rotary blade—but you usually do the pushing. They're quiet, require little maintenance, and run on standard house current. The motors are less powerful than gasoline-powered engines, but many electric mowers tackle tall and thick grass or weeds as well as most gasoline-powered mowers. Many also mulch.

Electrics are quiet and require little maintenance. They also start with the push of a button. Such models are practical for lawns of about a quarter-acre—typically, what can be reached by the 100-foot cord. Price range: $125 to $250.

Gasoline-powered mowers. These roam as long as there's fuel in the tank. Many can gobble up tall and thick grass or weeds. Most can mulch. "Hybrid" models have the catcher at the rear and the discharge chute on the side. Generally, handling ranges from easy to very easy. But gas-powered mowers are noisy and require regular maintenance.

The *push type* is practical for lawns of up to a half-acre and for trimming larger lawns. Their engines are typically a one-cylinder, four-stroke design that spins a 20-inch to 22-inch blade; power ranges from 3.5 to 6.5 hp. More and more of these engines have overhead valves for added efficiency and lower emissions. (A few models use a two-stroke engine, which uses a gasoline/oil fuel mixture and emits more pollutants.) Price range: from $100 for basic units to $500 for full-featured premium models.

Self-propelled models are worthwhile if your lawn is larger than a half-acre or hilly. The engine powers either the front or rear wheels. Front-wheel-drive models are sometimes easier to maneuver; rear-wheel-drive models have better traction for climbing hills, plus better steering control. Price range: $100 to $225 above push-type models.

Riding mowers and lawn tractors. Consider these for lawns about a half-acre and larger. A lawn tractor is the better buy, unless your lawn has lots of obstacles such as trees and rocks. There, a riding mower's small size is an advantage.

Tractors have a front-mounted engine, while riding mowers typically have a rear-mounted engine. Both usually have five to seven forward speeds and one reverse speed. Many tractors have a convenient hydrostatic transmission with continuously variable speed adjustment, which frees you from having to use a clutch. Most riding-mower decks range from 28 to 33 inches. Tractor decks are larger—anywhere from 36 to 48 inches. Tractors also accept a variety of add-ons that riding mowers can't—attachments that enable them to plow, throw snow, or tow a cart.

With either type of machine, you need a measure of mechanical ability and strength to cope with the controls and upkeep. Figure on a storage space of at least four feet wide and seven feet deep. Prices range: $900 to $4,000, with tractors more expensive.

Key features

Being tethered to the power cord of an electric mower is inconvenient. A **sliding clip** that lets the cord flip from side to side minimizes that better than a handle you flip every time you reverse direction.

On gasoline-powered mowers, a **blade-brake clutch safety system** provides the safety of a "deadman" handle. When you release the safety handle, the clutch releases the blade and a brake stops it from turning. But the engine keeps running, so you don't have to restart it every time. More common—and less expensive—is a simple **engine-kill system**.

A **four-stroke engine** tends to be less polluting than a **two-stroke engine,** which burns a mixture of oil and gasoline. The most convenient **choke** design is set

SAFETY TIPS

Mow only when and where it's safe. Don't mow when the grass is wet; your foot could slip under the mower. Push a mower across a slope, not up and down it (but ride a mower up and down, not across). If the slope is more than about 15 degrees, don't mow at all; on slopes that steep, a push mower can get away from you, and a riding mower can tip over.

- Wear sturdy shoes and close-fitting clothes. Consider wearing eye and ear protection.
- Before mowing, pick up toys, hoses, rocks, and twigs. Make sure no people or pets are nearby; a mower can hurl objects.
- Keep hands and feet away from moving parts.
- Don't defeat safety devices.
- Don't let children operate or ride a mower.

by simply adjusting the throttle control. Most mowers use a simpler device to help start the engine—a **primer** (a little rubber bulb located on the engine), which you press several times before you pull the starter rope. An **electric start** is much easier than tugging on a rope, but adds $50 to $100 to the price.

Some self-propelled mowers have one **speed**, usually about 2½ mph; others have several; still others have a continuous range, typically from 1 to 3 mph. One speed is fine, but two let you adjust to the terrain and the grass. Extra speeds are nice, but note that some six-speed mowers aren't as versatile as they seem—low speeds may be virtually the same.

Most mowers have spring-loaded **height adjusters** on each wheel. They're easy enough to use, but easier yet is a single lever or crank handle that adjusts all four wheels at once.

The most convenient design for changing from bagging to mulching mode lets you remove the bag and insert a plate or plug. Watch out for models that make you change the blade; you'll need a wrench.

The **rear-bag** design enhances maneuverability and makes close trimming easier than does a **side-bag** design. Make sure the bag is easy to install, remove, and empty.

A **hydrostatic transmission** on a lawn tractor frees you from the need to use a clutch, and it lets you continuously adjust the speed of the tractor, but it adds $200 to $400 to the price. **Zero-turn-radius** riding mowers promise better maneuverability, reducing mowing and trimming time. Often, rather than turning a steering wheel, you push or pull two control levers, each of which controls a rear drive wheel; you can make one wheel turn forward and the other wheel backward, for example. At the end of each run, you can turn 180 degrees for the next row without swinging wide or making several partial turns. You can also mow close to and around obstacles like trees and rock gardens. This agility comes at a steep price: about $3,500.

How to choose

Performance differences. Our tests regularly turn up a wide range of performance in lawn mowers. Few manufacturers balance power, handling, and convenience well. Our tests show no correlation between power and mowing ability.

What to spend. You'll find decently performing reel mowers for under $100. For an electric mower, expect to spend $200 or more, depending on features. While gasoline-powered mowers may go for as little as $100, expect to spend $150 to $200 for a decent model. You can spend up to $4,000 for a lawn tractor, but competent machines cost between $1,200 and $1,500.

HOW TO USE THE BUYING GUIDE

- Read the article for general guidance about types, features, and how to buy. There you'll find a discussion of the choices you'll face in the marketplace, what's new, and key buying advice.
- The Ratings graph the overall score so you can quickly understand the big picture in performance. Details on features or performance are also noted. For many products, we also have information on how reliable a brand is likely to be. See page 17.
- To find our last full report on a subject, refer to the article or the Ratings, or check the eight-year index, page 347.

PAINT

***Last CR report:** May 1998*
***Ratings:** page 197*
***Expect to pay:** $10 to $30*

The ideal paint goes on easily, covers the old paint thoroughly, and is reasonably priced. Exterior paint (or stain) should resist dirt, mildew, sun, and rain. Interior paint must meet particular needs—resist fading in a sunny room, for example, or hold its own in a busy hallway.

What's available

Major brands include Behr, Benjamin Moore, Dutch Boy, Glidden, Pittsburgh, Pratt & Lambert, and Sherwin-Williams. Sears and Ace hardware stores also sell paint under their labels. Wal-Mart brands include House Beautiful and ColorPlace. Paint prices typically range from $10 to $30 a gallon.

Exterior. Paint is the traditional and most widely used coating for exterior surfaces, providing a fairly tough film of resins and pigments that covers small blemishes and shields the surface from weathering. It can be applied over primer or old paint. Stain, on the other hand, penetrates wood, leaves hardly any surface film, and allows the texture of the wood to show through to varying degrees (stains come in transparent, semitransparent, and opaque varieties). Some stains should be applied only over unfinished wood; others can be used over sealed wood—that is, over an earlier coat of stain, paint, or primer.

Paints and stains come in water-based (latex) and oil-based (alkyd) versions. Latex paints and stains are easier to apply than oil-based formulas and can be applied to a damp surface. (You can use them the day after a rain but shouldn't use them if rain is forecasted; a brisk shower can wash off fresh latex paint or stain.) They dry quickly with little odor. And you can clean up drips and spatters—as well as hands, roller, and brush—with soap and water. Latex paints also contain lower amounts of volatile organic compounds (VOCs) than most alkyd paints.

Due to tighter solvent-emission laws, oil-based paints are increasingly rare. They must be applied to a totally dry surface, need about a day to dry between coats, smell like solvent while drying, and require mineral spirits for cleanup. They are, however, especially adept at adhering to old chalky painted surfaces, although latexes are catching up.

Generally, it's best to use the type of paint or stain that was used last time—oil over oil, latex over latex—to minimize stresses in the coating that can lead to blistering and peeling. On new wood, you can use either an alkyd or latex primer and a latex top coat.

Interior. Because latex paint is so much easier to work with—and because it doesn't smell—almost all interior paint sold is water-based. Wall paints are all-purpose and can be used in just about any room. Glossier trim enamels are meant for windowsills, woodwork, and the like. "Kitchen and bath" wall paints are usually fairly glossy (sometimes very glossy) and are formulated to hold up to water and scrubbing, withstand mildew, and let go of stains readily. A regular interior enamel or trim paint can do all this, but it may not resist mildew.

Key features

Colors are usually custom-mixed by adding colorant to one of several tint bases—pastel for lighter colors, medium for deeper colors, and so on. The tint base, not the specific hue, largely determines a paint's performance: its toughness, resistance to dirt and stains, and ability to withstand scrubbing. Most brands of paint come in several tint bases to create a full range of colors.

Some manufacturers claim that their products are one-coat paints, but our tests over the years have shown that few paints, especially whites, really are.

Colorfastness matters for exterior paints and for interior paints in sunny rooms, where sunlight can quickly blanch the wall's original color. The colorants added to tint the paint determine how much fading you'll see. Whites and browns don't fade; red and blue colorants fade somewhat; bright green and yellow pigments fade a lot. In a mixture of pigments, the other colors will begin to stand out as the greens and yellows fade. White paint can turn yellow. Often, white exterior paint is designed to **chalk** or turn to powder on the extreme surface, which can help shed dirt. However, chalking occurs to a small extent in almost any aging paint.

Paint typically comes in a variety of **sheens**—flat, satin, and semigloss. Names and the degree of glossiness aren't uniform from one manufacturer to another. **Flat paint** keeps reflections to a minimum and hides surface imperfections but as a rule is harder to clean and picks up more dirt than does a glossier formula. A semigloss paint is easier to clean than a flat paint but may be too shiny for larger surfaces. In addition, some semigloss paints can remain sticky long after the paint feels dry to the touch, making them poor choices for painting trim and shelving. A low-luster finish—often called eggshell or satin—is the middle ground between semigloss and flat. It's easy to clean and reflects less light than semigloss.

In response to government anti-smog regulations limiting the amount of volatile organic compounds (VOCs) in paints—VOCs from applied paint contribute to ground-level ozone—paint manufacturers are producing more **low- or zero-VOC paints,** which also claim to produce little or no odor.

How to choose

Performance differences. We have always found a fairly wide spread in paint toughness, ability to hide, and ease of application. Many brands offer a premium paint that should provide superior performance, along with two or three lines of paint with a lower price and, usually, lesser quality.

What to spend. In our tests, premium paints (those costing $20 or more per gallon) haven't always been the best performers. But although you will find paint for less, the manufacturer's top line should give best long-term value.

Whether you buy paint from an independent paint retailer that stocks several brands, a company store like Sherwin-Williams, a home center, or a mass merchandiser like Wal-Mart, ask about discounts or deals on high-quantity purchases—in our experience, as much as 10 to 15 percent. All else being equal, you can expect better service from a local paint store but better prices from a home center.

Before you paint

Prepare the surface. Wash the surface to remove grease and grime. Fill blemishes, chipped areas, and cracks with spackling compound. Sand the patches, along with other rough areas, and do spot prime repairs.

Outdoors, it's easiest to remove chalk

with a power-washer, which you can rent from many painting-supply or tool-rental outlets. A power washer should also dislodge most flaking or blistered paint; peel off the remaining bits with a scraper. Scrub the surface with detergent and a stiff brush and rinse thoroughly. Wash any mildewed areas with a solution of one part household bleach to three or four parts water, then rinse quickly with lots of water. (Wear goggles and rubber gloves to protect eyes and skin, cover plants with drop cloths.) After it's washed or bleached, the surface should be allowed to dry thoroughly, particularly if you plan to use an oil-based paint. Sand smooth areas where paint was dislodged to lessen surface imperfections.

Prime, if necessary. Spot-prime repairs or stubborn stains. If you're covering a very dark color or a very old or glossy surface, plan on priming the entire wall first to reduce the contrast between the old color and the new and to provide a sound surface for the new paint. Any bare wood must be primed before it's painted. A coat of primer is especially important when you're trying to seal knotty woods to prevent tannin bleed-through. There's no reason to prime before using stains—they're supposed to sink into the wood.

Have the right tools. Buy high-quality brushes and rollers. When working with latex paints, use synthetic-bristle brushes; they won't absorb water as natural-bristle brushes will. A roller should have a quarter-inch nap. A good-quality brush or roller will last a long time and is less likely to shed bristles or lint that can dry into the paint.

SNOW THROWERS

***Last CR report:** October 1997*
***Ratings:** page 199*
***Expect to pay:** $300 to $2,000*

Although faster and less physically taxing than shoveling snow, using a snow thrower is neither effortless nor without its annoyances. Snow throwers demand some awkward maneuvering of a heavy machine—and a sizable space for storage.

What's available

MTD, Sears Craftsman, and Toro are the most-purchased brands, accounting for about two-thirds of all snow-thrower sales. Most snow throwers use a gasoline-powered engine to propel a metal or rubber-tipped auger that paddles snow through a discharge chute. The chute can be rotated so you can cast snow left, right, and straight ahead, and adjusted to determine the height of snow discharge.

Single-stage throwers. These models pull snow from the ground and blow it out the discharge chute in one motion; they can clear snowfalls of only six to eight inches. They generally come with a 3-hp to 5-hp two-stroke engine that requires an oil-and-gasoline mixture. The rubber-tipped auger touches the ground, helping to move the non-self-propelled machine forward and leaving a cleaner surface than will a two-stage model. However, because the auger contacts the ground, this type shouldn't be used on gravel or stone drives or walks. It also has a deadman control similar to that on many lawn mowers, one that disengages the auger once you release the handle. Single-stage throwers are relatively easy to handle and compact to store. Price range: $300 to $750.

Two-stage throwers. Bigger and more powerful than single-stage models, this type can clean snow about 1½ feet deep. A 5-hp to 9-hp four-stroke engine runs on gasoline alone. The metal auger picks up snow and moves it to a fast-spinning impeller that sends the snow out the chute—the two "stages" that give this type its name. Most two-stage machines are self-propelled, with at least four forward and two reverse speeds (the range of speeds matters more than the number of speed settings).

Two-stage machines have independent deadman controls: One lever governs power to the auger, another power to the wheels. Initially you must squeeze both, but with most you then can operate the machine one-handed, which lets you adjust the discharge chute, and in some cases the snow deflector, as you go. Adjustable skid shoes let you determine how close to the ground the machine cleans—still not as close as single-stage models. Plan on plenty of storage space for this bulky unit. Price range: $600 to $1,000 or more.

Key features

Both types either have an **electric starter** or offer one as an option for about $100. (We had no trouble manually starting the machines in our tests; an electric starter isn't essential.)

Typical knobby **tires** provide good traction. Some models also come with **tire chains**, which may help on ice. Bulldozer-style **tracks** may also help on ice, though they hamper handling.

A **discharge deflector** governs how far and high the snow is thrown from the chute. To change its angle and send snow higher or lower into the air, you usually have to stop the machine and loosen a wing nut or a knob. Several two-stage models have an easy-to-reach lever that lets you change the deflector angle while continuing to throw snow.

Some two-stage models allow you to move the **wheels** to shift more of the machine's weight to the front, pushing the auger firmly into dense or compacted snow to help clear it.

How to choose

Performance differences. Horsepower matters. In our tests, the best of each type tended to have a more powerful engine that let them clear a wider swath and handle deep or wet snow.

What to spend. Single-stage models range from about $300 to $750; two-stage models, from around $600 to more than $2,000. Spending more usually buys a more powerful engine, which can clear a wider swath. An electric starter, if optional, is about $100 extra.

STRING TRIMMERS

Last CR report: *May 98*
Ratings: *page 204*
Expect to pay: *$20 to $300*

If you have a good-size lawn and you're finicky about the way it looks, a string trimmer can finish the job a lawn mower starts. Plus, a trimmer can go where mowers fear to tread.

What's available

Discount outlets like Kmart and Wal-Mart, mass merchants like Sears, and home centers like Builder's Square and Home Depot have the widest selection. Lawn-equipment and garden stores sell Echo, Husqvarna, Stihl, and some high-end models not sold in the big chains.

Gas-powered trimmers. These go anywhere, are better than electrics at cutting weeds and brush, and are often better at edging. They cut the biggest swath—up to 18 inches. Some accept a metal blade (typically an extra-cost option), mounted in place of the string spool, that can cut brush about ¼-inch thick or more. But these are noisy, and most weigh between 10 and 16 pounds. Mixing and adding fuel can be messy. The engine sometimes needs lots of pulls to start. On models that lack a clutch, the string is always spinning while the engine is running, an inconvenience and a hazard. Price range: A few cost less than $100, most from $100 to $230; heavy-duty models, more than $300.

Corded electrics. These are the least expensive and lightest (many weigh less than five pounds). They emit no pollution and, in our tests, handle some tasks nearly as well as gas models. They're less noisy than gas models and easy to start and stop.

But the extension cord limits their range and can be annoying to drag around. The weight of the motor at the bottom makes them hard to handle (some do have their motor at the top of the shaft). Especially lightweight models can be used with one hand, but our tests showed most to be weak. Price range: $20 to $65.

Battery-powered electrics. They combine the free range of gas models with some pluses of corded models: less noise, easy starting and stopping, lack of fuel, lack of pollution. But they're weak at cutting and unsuitable for edging. They're heavy (about 10 pounds), and some have poor balance. If the job lasts longer than 15 to 30 minutes, you must recharge the battery before finishing—which takes a day. Spent batteries must be taken to a municipal hazardous-materials site. Price range: $50 to $100.

Key features

Most gas models are powered by a small two-stroke, one-cylinder **gasoline engine** mounted at the top of a four- to six-foot shaft. Corded and battery models use a 1.8- to 5-amp **motor**, usually at the bottom of the shaft. For most types, the engine or motor is linked to a **spool** wrapped with plastic string, and the shaft may be curved (more common) or straight (better for getting under bushes and other obstacles). Two pieces of string, threaded through the trimmer head to stick out about four to seven inches, spin around fast enough to cut grass.

Some models have a **split shaft** that lets you replace the trimmer head with a leaf-blower, tiller, or metal edging blade.

Most gas engines run on a mixture of oil and gasoline; you add it to a small, generally translucent **tank**, so you can see the fuel level. To start a gas engine, you set the **choke**, push a primer bulb, then pull a cord. On most gas models, a **centrifugal clutch** lets the engine idle without spinning the string, a safety factor. Electrics don't spin until you press the trigger switch.

To replace the string, most trimmers have a "bump feed" **string-advance system**: When you bump the spinning trimmer head on a hard surface, the spool feeds out new string and a knife on the safety shield cuts it to the right length. Even more convenient is a system that feeds out new line automatically by sensing a change in the centrifugal force exerted by a shortened line. When a spool is empty, you remove it (generally by unscrewing a knob), replace it with a new spool, and thread the new string through the head. Some newer designs eliminate the spool—

simply push in or snap on a length of line—though you'll have to do it often.

Do look for switches that are easy to reach and adjust, comfortable handles, and for gas models, a translucent fuel tank.

How to choose

Performance differences. With gas models, we found no correlation between engine size and performance; with electrics, as a rule, the higher the amperage, the better they cut. Even the most anemic machines we've tested can trim a small, well-maintained lawn. But trimmers varied widely in their ability to slice through weeds and brush.

Trimmers can spin their string perpendicular to the ground, cutting downward to create a grass-free line between lawn and pavement in one of two ways: with a head or shaft that can be rotated or, less conveniently, with a handle that can be rotated to turn the whole trimmer. A few corded models and all the battery-powered ones in our most recent tests proved poor at edging—they were weak, and most were awkward to hold.

Noise. Most electrics are about as loud as an electric lawn mower. But most gas models are as noisy as a leaf-blower, warranting earplugs or muffs.

Safety. A trimmer's string can give you a painful sting, even through clothing. On bare skin, it can draw blood. It can also fling dirt and debris. While you're trimming, wear gloves, long pants, sturdy shoes, and safety glasses. Some gas trimmers require extra caution. Although most have a clutch to keep the string from spinning as you walk from one spot to another or check on string length, eight of the models we tested lack a clutch and must be turned off to stop the string.

What to spend. You can keep edges neat without a string trimmer by putting mulch around tress and posts, and between lawn and garden. Your mower will cut up to the mulch, leaving no grass that needs trimming. Or you can use hand-powered grass clippers to trim a very small lawn or garden border. They're nearly silent, use no fuel, and cost about $6.

If you need a trimmer and your needs are modest, consider a corded model—around $50 or so. If you plan to trim weeds as well as grass, want to create neat edges between grass and pavement, and are pretty picky about your yard, choose a gas-powered model—$100 or more.

TOILETS

Last CR report: *May 1998*
Ratings: *page 208*
Expect to pay: *$75 to $1,000*

A federal law, now four years old, requires new toilets to use no more than 1.6 gallons of water per flush, less than half as much as older models. Many of the first new designs didn't work very well—and they saved less water than intended because the toilets often had to be flushed more than once to do the job well.

Fortunately, that's changing. Some of the newer designs work just fine—almost always on one flush.

What's available

Biggest-selling brands include American Standard, Kohler, Eljer, and Crane. Prices range from $75 or so to more than $500. Toilets are sold in home-center stores, plumbing-supply stores, and also through contractors.

There are four basic varieties of low-flush toilets:

Gravity-flush. This type works very much like a traditional toilet, using the weight of water flowing down from the tank to clear the toilet bowl. These toilets are less effective at removing solid waste than pressure-assisted models, but they're generally the cheapest to buy and install. They're also the cheapest to maintain; most use standard, widely available parts, though some require a special flapper valve (the part that releases water out of the tank and into the bowl).

Pressure-assisted. Air compressed by pressure in the household water lines forces water into the bowl, blasting waste down the drain. This type tends to be the most effective, but it's also expensive to buy and maintain because its parts are more specialized. Pressure-assisted toilets tend to do their work noisily, and they need water pressure of at least 25 pounds per square inch to run well.

Pump-assisted. A hybrid of gravity-flush and pressure-assisted toilets uses an electrical pump under the tank to blast water into the bowl. But if the power goes out, it won't work.

Vacuum-assisted. This design relies on vacuum chambers inside the toilet tank to pull water and waste from the toilet bowl. Installation and upkeep are similar to gravity-flush toilets.

How to choose

Performance differences. Pressure-assisted toilets were best at flushing away solid waste. Most gravity-flush models paled in comparison, often requiring two flushes to do the same job. Most of these toilets—especially the gravity-flush ones—leave a rather small amount of water in the bowl after a flush. The smaller that patch of water, the more often you'll have to clean the part of the toilet bowl not covered by water.

If you're happy with your existing toilet, consider modifying it to use less water. You can displace some water in the tank using a plastic bottle filled with water. Or install an early-closing flapper valve, which will cut the flush short. "A dual flusher" valve delivers a full flush for solids, a half-flush for liquids.

Otherwise, decide which features are most important to you: The toilet we rated A CR Best Buy represents the best value and highest performance among toilets we tested—a pressure-assisted toilet that did an outstanding job of clearing waste and cleaning the bowl with each flush. But it's noisy. If you can't tolerate a noisy toilet, check the ratings for a quieter pressure-assisted model or one of the higher-rated gravity-flush models.

What to spend. We found no correspondence between price and performance in our tests. The top-scoring models cost $270, $420, and $940.

VACUUM CLEANERS

Last CR report: *March 1998*
Ratings: *page 211*
Expect to pay: *$100 to $1,500*

An ideal vacuum cleaner would leave carpeting and floors free of debris, have an assortment of useful attachments, and be sturdy enough for frequent use, yet light and flexible enough to maneuver. There would be no dust clouds from the exhaust, no dirtbag to change, no annoying whine or roar. All that, and be reasonably priced.

Our tests show that manufacturers have figured out how to do it all—just not combined in one machine

What's available

Full-sized vacuum cleaners may cost less than $100 or more than $1,000. Hoover, America's oldest and largest vacuum manufacturer, sells about 100 different models, priced up to $400. Many models are very similar; the "variety" is mainly marketing. Some models are made exclusively for one retail chain. You'll see about 50 different models from Eureka, a traditionally low-priced brand; many from Dirt Devil, also a low-priced brand better known for stick brooms and hand vacs; and Kenmore, the Sears brand that accounts for about 30 percent of all canister vacs sold in the U.S. Oreck, the biggest vacuum-cleaner advertiser, sells its lightweight models direct through an 800 number or by mail order and through independent vacuum stores. Kirby, the heavyweight, is sold door to door.

Once, there were two vacuum-cleaner choices—upright or canister. These lines have blurred in recent years. **Uprights,** more popular now, are easier to store than canisters, and their rotating brush efficiently removes dirt buried in carpet pile. **Canisters** generally are better under a bed or around chair legs, and are especially good for bare floors, where a rotating brush would merely spread the dirt around.

But many canisters come with a power nozzle—a rotating brush that can rival the performance of a good upright on carpeting. And most uprights have a clip on the back or side for on-board storage of a hose and other attachments. Some even allow you to turn off the rotating brush to vacuum bare floors or rugs.

Key features

The most common **attachments** are a dusting brush, a crevice tool, and an upholstery tool. Extension wands are a must for high places such as moldings. For carpeted stairs and other tight areas, a small power nozzle that attaches to the hose cleans more thoroughly than a simple suction nozzle. A long, flexible, sturdy **hose** also helps.

Most machines have at least a 20- to 30-foot **cord**; some run longer than 35 feet. Most uprights require you to manually wrap the cord for storage. Canisters usually have a retractable cord that you control with a slight tug or a push button.

Many vacs we tested have a full-dirtbag **indicator.** An overstuffed bag impairs cleaning ability, but at $1 to $3 per bag, you don't want to change until necessary. In general, bag-cleaning is easier with an upright than a canister, and in a hard-body vacuum than a soft-body one. Lately, many uprights have adopted a no-bag configuration, with a clear dirt collection area.

In soft-body and some hard-body uprights, dirt sucked into the vac first passes through the blower fan and then enters the dirtbag. Most blower fans are plastic, making them prone to damage from hard objects. With canisters and many hard-body uprights, dirt is pulled into and filtered through the dirtbag before it reaches the fan, so although hard objects can still lodge in the motorized brush, they are unlikely to break the fan. Vacuums with this system have a vent or filter at the bottom of the dirtbag compartment.

A vac's normal suction can pull in lightweight fabrics, so a **suction control** is useful for vacuuming drapes or throw rugs. It's common on canisters, less so on uprights. Some heavy uprights have a **self-propelled** feature that makes pushing easy, but they're still hard to carry up or down stairs.

How to choose

Performance differences. Choose a vacuum cleaner based on how well it cleans the kinds of floors you have and on the features that help you handle stairs, drapes, and other above-the-floor or hard-to-reach surfaces. All the uprights we've tested recently do at least a good job overall. The canisters are all very good. Some claims matter more than others. Among those you can safely ignore:

• Special emissions filters. Fine particles you vacuum up—such as fragments of pet dander and pollen—may escape a motor's filter and be released into the air through the exhaust. Many models claim "microfiltration" capabilities, which may mean smaller pores in the dirtbag or a second electrostatic filter in addition to the standard motor filter. Some have a high-efficiency particulate-arresting (HEPA) filter. But many models without a HEPA filter performed as well in our emissions test, because the amount of dust emitted depends as much on the design of the whole machine as on its filter system.

• Amps and suction. Amps are the amount of current a vac draws when the power is on; they don't measure cleaning power. Suction alone does not determine a vac's ability to lift dirt from carpeting. That is also a function of the configuration of the bristles on the rotating brush. (Suction power through the hose, however, does make a difference when you use attachments.)

• Nook-and-cranny power. Most models we tested have a power nozzle that manufacturers claim will pick up debris along a baseboard or in a corner. But few are standouts in edge-cleaning.

• Dirt-sensing. Some machines have a sensor that triggers a light indicator when the concentration of dirt particles in the vacuum cleaner's airstream approaches zero. But the sensor only lets you know when the vacuum is no longer picking up dirt, not if there's dirt left in your rug.

• What to spend. Some vacuum cleaners are extremely expensive—$800 or $900 or even $1,500. Our tests show that high-price brands like Miele, Electrolux, and Kirby have performed well—but so have many $200 and $300 models.

Avoiding repairs. According to a recent reader survey, the most commonly repaired part is the belt, usually a fairly simple repair. The owner's manual has instructions. Replacement belts and bulbs generally cost about $1 to $2, new brushes as much as $25.

Careful vacuuming helps you avoid some repairs altogether. A vacuum cleaner is made for basic household dirt like dustballs or soil and sand. Hard objects like coins or paper clips can damage the fan; string can wrap around the agitator. With no tolerance for wetness, it should never be used outdoors—even moisture in a recently shampooed carpet may be enough to damage the motor.

If your vac swallows something hard or stringy, turn off the power and try to dislodge the foreign object. A motor-overload protection feature automatically turns off the vac if a clog occurs. After the path is cleared and the motor cools, you can turn it on again.

To avoid catching the cord, turn off the rotating brush while you use an upright's attachments, or at least keep the cord out of the power nozzle's path.

WHIRLPOOL BATHTUBS

***Last CR report:** May 1998*
***Ratings:** page 216*
***Expect to pay:** $750 to $2,000*

These days, whirlpool bathtubs command pride of place in nearly 4 out of 10 renovated bathrooms. Some homeowners install a whirlpool and hope it will enhance the resale value of the house. Others buy a whirlpool for more immediate needs—to soothe sore muscles or simply have a place for a relaxing soak.

Before you buy a whirlpool, consider the implications of installation and use. Whirlpools use several times more water than you'd use in a five-minute shower, and perhaps twice as much as a typical bathtub holds. That's a lot of hot water—a whirlpool may drain the typical 40-gallon water heater each time you draw a bath.

A tub could be too heavy. A fiberglass tub, generally the lightest type, weighs a little more than 90 pounds with its pump and piping; a cast-iron whirlpool can weigh 400 pounds or more. A deep whirlpool tub filled with water and a bather could be too heavy for the floor to support. Widely followed federal construction guidelines require floors to support at least 40 pounds per square foot. If you're unsure how much weight your floor can support, hire an engineer or contractor to make an assessment.

Whirlpools are also noisy. Ads and brochures for whirlpool tubs promise serene luxury. In reality, some whirlpools are loud enough to drown out a conversation. Neither the size of the pump nor its price made a difference in noise, we found in our tests.

What's available

American Standard, Jacuzzi, and Kohler are the industry leaders. Tubs are designed to fit into the five- and six-foot spaces occupied by a standard bathtub, as well as in a variety of larger sizes and shapes. Prices start at about $750. Most tubs are made of acrylic or fiberglass, a few of cast iron or porcelain-coated steel. They come with a variety of motor sizes—½ hp to more than 1 hp.

Don't buy on pump size alone. A whirlpool manufacturer that rates a home-sized unit at more than 1 hp—we found some examples from Jacuzzi—may be using an inflated horsepower-rating system.

Using the tubs

Whirlpools require servicing. To us, the handiest to service are those with a removable apron on the long side that faces the room. Snap off the apron, and you can access the pump and major plumbing fittings. Pumps are usually positioned beneath the backrest. If the tub lacks a removable apron, you'll have to build a hatch at one end so you can access the pump.

Whirlpools also require regular maintenance. Water left in a whirlpool's pipes can allow harmful organisms to multiply. If you don't use a tub often, flush it with a bleach solution occasionally. If you have hard water, flush the system with a white-vinegar solution to clear away mineral deposits. Avoid using bath oils and salts, which can stay in the pipes and feed bacteria, and bubble bath—the whirlpool will froth it to a fare-thee-well.

Safety. The biggest risk for bathers is hyperthermia, an elevated body temperature that can cause a drop in blood pressure, making you feel weak. In extreme cases, hyperthermia can be fatal. Never stay in a recirculating hot bath for more than 15 minutes. Some models automatically shut off the pump after 15 or 20 minutes.

The typical whirlpool is deeper than a regular tub and may demand more agility getting in and out of the water. Many tubs come with grab bars or, at least, a place to attach them. If you have small kids, don't let them use a whirlpool unattended.

Be sure the tub's wiring is connected to a ground-fault circuit interrupter, which will reduce the admittedly remote risk of electrical shock. Most tubs use a dedicated 15-amp circuit; some need 20 amps.

Key features

The panelists who tested the tubs didn't much care for ones that were narrow, short, or shallow. They liked models with a large, deep interior. Price and size don't always travel together. Some high-priced tubs were especially uncomfortable, our panelists said.

The tubs our testers preferred tended to have six **jets**, including two at the feet or back. Some tubs have water jets all around, while others concentrate jets on the sides. Our panelists liked water jets at the back. The angle of the backrest molded into the tub mattered much less. Likewise, tubs with front jets were more comfortable and stimulating to the feet and legs than were tubs without front jets.

All things being equal, a **bigger pump** will produce higher water flow and more turbulence. Two **speeds** are enough. **On/off switches** and the like are easiest to use and reach if they're on the tub's long side. Our panelists didn't like reaching forward or twisting backward to reach controls at the end of a tub. The whirlpool jets on Jacuzzi tubs were the easiest to adjust for airflow, water flow, and direction. Kohler jets were the hardest to adjust for airflow without also changing their direction. If **handles** and **armrests** aren't standard, they're usually available as an option.

An **inline heater** is designed to keep already-heated bathwater warm. It had little noticeable effect in our tests. Some tubs have a **neck rest** with built-in jets. Panelists didn't like it; the jets sprayed water everywhere.

How to choose

A lot of the choice depends on personal factors—the size of your bathroom, the size of your body, whether you like the solid feel of cast iron or favor the look and feel of acrylic. Overall, we think 60-inch-long tubs priced between $1,200 and $1,600 represent the best value. Our panelists gave the highest overall marks to tubs in that price range. Cheaper tubs have fewer features and tend to be less comfortable, while the tubs priced at $2,000 and up come loaded with features, some of dubious value.

Ratings *Room air conditioners*

& Recommendations

The tests behind the Ratings

Overall score gives the most weight to performance and noise. **EER** is the energy-efficiency rating, as stated by the manufacturer. The higher the EER, the lower the operating cost. Comfort reflects both cooling and dehumidification in our environmental chambers, running on low speed. **Noise** was measured and judged indoors on low speed. We also indicate the presence of a built-in **timer** and **side-to-side** or **up/down louvers. Price** is approximate retail.

Typical features for these models

• Rating for a 115-volt circuit protected by a time-delay fuse or circuit breaker. • Design for installation in a double-hung window. • Removable, washable air filter. • R-22 HCFC refrigerant, which has relatively low ozone-depleting potential. • 3 cooling speeds and two fan-only speeds. • Energy-saver mode. • Adjustable louvers. • Power cord at least 60 in. long. • Vent control for exhausting room air. • No exterior support or leveling provision. • 1-yr. parts-and-labor warranty on entire unit, 5-yr. parts-and-labor warranty on sealed refrigeration system.

Recommendations

All the tested models were good to excellent performers overall. Match cooling capacity (measured in Btus per hr.) to your space using the chart on page 147 or the interactive worksheet at our web site *(www.ConsumerReports.org)*. Then shop for the most efficient model that's competitively priced. If the cooling capacity is what you need, consider one of the **CR Best Buys**—Fedders A4Q05F2AG (5,200 Btu/hr.), $230; Frigidaire FAB077Y7B (7,000 Btu/hr.), $290; Fedders A3Q08F2BG (8,000 Btu/hr.), $300.

See report, page 146. Last time rated in Consumer Reports: June 1998, August 1998.

Overall Ratings

E ⊜ VG ⊖ G ○ F ◒ P ●

Listed in order of overall score

Key no.	Brand and model	Price	Overall score (0–100; P F G VG E)	EER	Comfort	Noise	Timer	Louver SIDE	Louver UP/DOWN
	5,000 TO 5,800 BTU/HR.								
1	**Amana** Quiet Zone 5QZ21RC	$320		9.7	⊜	⊜	—	✔	—
2	**Panasonic** CW-606TU	360		10.0	⊜	⊜	—	✔	✔
3	**General Electric** Deluxe Series AMH06LA	300		10.0	⊜	⊜	—	✔	✔
4	**Fedders** Portable Series A4Q05F2AG **A CR Best Buy**	230		10.0	⊜	⊖	—	✔	✔

Ratings continued

Key no.	Brand and model	Price	Overall score (0–100) P F G VG E	EER	Comfort	Noise	Timer	Louver SIDE	Louver UP/DOWN
	5,000 TO 5,800 BTU/HR. *continued*								
5	**Sharp** Mechanical Series AF-505M6B	$285		9.7	⊜	⊜	—	—	✔
6	**Carrier** UCA051B	320		10.0	⊖	⊜	—	✔	✔
7	**Friedrich** Q-star SQ05J10	340		10.0	○	⊖	—	✔	✔
8	**Emerson** Quiet Kool Compact Q Series 5GC51	295		8.0	⊜	⊖	—	✔	—
9	**Sharp** Mechanical Series AF-500X	220		8.0	⊜	⊖	—	—	✔
10	**Whirlpool** Value Series ACM492XF	280		8.0	●	⊖	—	✔	—
	6,000 TO 6,600 BTU/HR.								
11	**Amana** Quiet Zone 7QZ21RC	350		10.0	⊜	⊜	—	✔	—
12	**Kenmore** (Sears) Innovative Line 78079	400		10.0	⊜	⊜	✔	✔	✔
13	**Gibson** Panorama GAB067F7B	395		10.0	⊜	⊖	—	✔	✔
14	**Friedrich** Q-star SQ06J10	370		10.0	○	⊖	—	✔	✔
15	**Carrier** VisionAire LCA061P	370		9.1	○	⊖	—	✔	✔
16	**General Electric** Value Line AQV06LA	300		9.0	⊜	⊖	—	—	✔
	7,000 TO 7,800 BTU/HR.								
17	**Panasonic** CW-806TU	420		10.0	⊜	⊜	—	✔	✔
18	**General Electric** Deluxe Series AGH08FA	380		10.0	⊖	⊖	—	✔	✔
19	**Kenmore** (Sears) Value Line 78073	330		9.2	○	⊜	—	—	✔
20	**Friedrich** Q-star SQ07J10	410		10.3	○	⊖	—	✔	✔
	8,000 TO 8,600 BTU/HR.								
21	**Friedrich** Quietmaster Electronic SS08J10A	670		10.8	⊜	⊖	✔	✔	✔
22	**Sharp** Comfort Touch Series AF-R908X	440		10.0	⊜	⊖	✔	✔	✔
23	**Whirlpool** Designer Style ACQ082XD	410		9.6	⊜	⊖	—	✔	✔
24	**Carrier** Siesta Series TCA081P	400		10.0	⊖	○	—	✔	✔
25	**Fedders** Portable Series A3Q08F2BG **A CR Best Buy**	300		9.5	⊖	⊖	—	✔	✔
26	**Carrier** Siesta Series TCA081D	380		9.2	⊖	○	—	✔	✔
27	**Frigidaire** Custom Series FAC083W7A	340		9.5	⊖	⊖	—	✔	✔
28	**Amana** Cool Zone 9P2MY	390		9.0	⊖	○	—	✔	—
	9,100 TO 9,200 BTU/HR.								
29	**Kenmore** (Sears) Innovative Line 78098	450		10.0	⊜	⊖	✔	✔	✔
30	**Amana** Quiet Zone Line 9M12TA	460		10.0	⊜	⊖	✔	✔	✔
31	**Amana** Quiet Zone 9QZ22RC	420		10.8	⊜	○	—	✔	✔
32	**Friedrich** Quietmaster Electronic SS09J10A	700		11.5	⊜	⊖	✔	✔	✔

Key no.	Brand and model	Price	Overall score (0–100; P F G VG E)	EER	Comfort	Noise	Timer	Louver SIDE	Louver UP/DOWN
	10,000 TO 10,500 BTU/HR.								
33	**Friedrich** Quietmaster Electronic SS10J10A	$840		11.7	⊜	⊖	✔	✔	✔
34	**Amana** Quiet Zone 10QZ22RC	470		10.1	⊜	⊖	—	✔	✔
35	**Whirlpool** DesignerStyle ACQ102XD	420		9.0	⊜	○	—	✔	✔
36	**White-Westinghouse** Continental Series WAL103Y1A	440		9.5	⊖	⊖	—	✔	✔
37	**Carrier** Siesta Series TCA101D	440		9.0	⊜	○	—	✔	✔
	11,500 TO 12,000 BTU/HR.								
38	**Friedrich** Quietmaster Electronic SS12J10A	700		10.5	⊜	⊖	✔	✔	✔
39	**Gibson** Air Sweep GAX128Y1A	600		9.5	⊖	⊖	—	✔	✔
40	**Amana** Quiet Zone 12QZ22RC	520		10.0	⊖	⊖	—	✔	✔
41	**Kenmore** (Sears) Value Line 78122	430		9.5	○	⊖	—	—	✔
42	**Fedders** Regency Series A3J12E2AG	390		9.0	⊖	○	—	✔	✔
43	**Whirlpool** DesignerStyle ACQ122XD	440		9.0	○	○	—	✔	✔

Details on the models

Note that similar models judged comparable in capacity and performance may differ by color or a few minor features.

5,000-5,800 Btu/hr. models

1 Amana Quiet Zone 5QZ21RC $320

• 5,400 Btu/hr. • 1.1 pints/hr. moisture removal. • 61 lb. • Fits 23- to-40-in. window. Highly efficient and excellent comfort control. Quiet. Exterior support bracket with leveling provision. 2-yr. warranty on the entire unit. 3rd through 5th year parts-and-labor warranty on refrigeration system. **But:** No up/down louver control. No slide-out filter. **Recommendation:** An excellent choice.

2 Panasonic CW-606TU $360

• 5,800 Btu/hr. • 0.9 pints/hr. moisture removal. • 67 lb. • Fits 22- to-37-in. window. Highly efficient and excellent comfort control. Quiet. Slide-out chassis. **But:** Mediocre at dehumidifying. Hard to install. No upper sash lock. Only 2 fan speeds on cool. **Similar models:** General Electric Deluxe Series AMH06LA, Quasar HQ2062KH. **Recommendation:** A very good choice.

3 General Electric Deluxe Series AMH06LA $300

• 5,800 Btu/hr. • 0.9 pints/hr. moisture removal. • 66 lb. • Fits 18- to-35-in. window. Highly efficient. Quiet. Slide-out chassis. Through-the-wall installation instructions provided. **But:** Mediocre at dehumidifying. Hard to install. Only 2 fan speeds on cool. **Similar models:** Panasonic CW-606TU, $360; Quasar HQ2062KH, $330. **Recommendation:** A very good choice.

4 Fedders Portable Series A4Q05F2AG $230

• 5,200 Btu/hr. • 1.6 pints/hr. moisture removal. • 59 lb. • Fits 21- to-39-in. window. Highly efficient and excellent comfort control. Exterior support bracket with leveling provision. 2-

yr. parts-only warranty on fan motor. **But:** No upper sash lock. Only parts warranty on sealed system 2nd through 5th yr. **Similar model:** Emerson Quiet Kool Compact Q Series 5HC53. **Recommendation:** A very good choice.

5 Sharp AF-505M6B $285

• 5,100 Btu/hr. • 1.2 pints/hr. moisture removal. • 46 lb. • Fits 23- to-36-in. window. Highly efficient, excellent comfort control, and quiet. **But:** Poor at directing air to either direction. No upper sash lock. Only 1 fan-only setting. No left/right louver. No vent. Only parts warranty on sealed system 2nd through 5th yr. **Recommendation:** A very good choice.

6 Carrier UCA051B $320

• 5,200 Btu/hr. • 2.1 pints/hr. moisture removal. • 73 lb. • Fits 25- to-38-in. window. Highly efficient. Quiet. Slide-out chassis. Through-the-wall installation instructions provided. **But:** Hard to install. No upper sash lock. Only 2 fan speeds on cool. Filter pulls out from bottom; may hit sill. No vent. Only parts warranty on sealed system 2nd through 5th yr. **Recommendation:** A very good choice.

7 Friedrich Q-star SQ05J10 $340

• 5,600 Btu/hr. • 1.5 pints/hr. moisture removal. • 70 lb. • Fits 26- to-42-in. window. Highly efficient. Slide-out chassis. Through-the-wall installation instructions provided. **But:** Hard to install. No upper sash lock. Thermostat settings not marked with numbers. **Recommendation:** A very good choice.

8 Emerson Quiet Kool Compact Q Series 5GC51 $295

• 5,000 Btu/hr. • 1.6 pints/hr. moisture removal. • 54 lb. • Fits 21- to-39-in. window. Excellent comfort control. Exterior support bracket with leveling provision. 2-yr. parts-only warranty on fan motor. **But:** May cost more to operate than others. No upper sash lock. Only 2 fan speeds on cool. No up/down louver control. No slide-out filter. No vent. Only parts warranty on sealed system 2nd through 5th yr. **Similar model:** Fedders Portable Series A1Q05F2AL, $230. **Recommendation:** A very good choice.

9 Sharp Mechanical Series AF-500X $220

• 5,000 Btu/hr. • 1.2 pints/hr. moisture removal. • 44 lb. • Fits 20- to-35-in. window. Excellent comfort control. **But:** May cost more to operate than others and poor at directing air to the left. No upper sash lock. Only 1 fan speed on cool. No fan-only setting. No left/right louver. No vent. Only parts warranty on sealed system 2nd through 5th yr. **Recommendation:** A very good choice.

10 Whirlpool Value Series ACM492XFO $280

• 5,000 Btu/hr. • 1.1 pints/hr. moisture removal. • 46 lb. • Fits 19- to-38-in. window. Poor comfort control and may cost more to operate than others. Poor at directing air to the right. No expandable side panels. Only 1 fan speed on cool. No fan-only setting. No up/down louver control. Thermostat settings not marked with numbers. No slide-out filter. No vent. **Recommendation:** There are better choices.

6,000-6,600 Btu/hr. models

11 Amana Quiet Zone 7QZ21RC $350

• 6,600 Btu/hr. • 2.0 pints/hr. moisture removal. • 65 lb. • Fits 23- to-40-in. window. Highly efficient and excellent comfort control. Quiet. Exterior support bracket with leveling provision. 2-yr. warranty on the entire unit. 3rd through 5th year parts-and-labor warranty on refrigeration system. **But:** No up/down louver control. No slide-out filter. **Recommendation:** An excellent choice.

12 Kenmore (Sears) Innovative Line 78079 $400

• 6,600 Btu/hr. • 2.0 pints/hr. moisture removal. • 72 lb. • Fits 23- to-40-in. window. Highly efficient and excellent comfort control. Quiet. Exterior support bracket with leveling provision. Digital temperature readout (also indicates that power is on in energy-saver mode). Built-in timer. Auto-fan speed. **Recommendation:** An excellent choice.

13 **Gibson Panorama GAB067F7B1** $395

• 6,100 Btu/hr. • 1.4 pints/hr. moisture removal. • 53 lb. • Fits 26- to-38-in. window. Highly efficient and excellent comfort control. Low profile design. Exterior support bracket with leveling provision. Handles to ease carrying. Extra 6th through 10th yr. parts-only warranty on compressor. **But:** No upper sash lock. Thermostat settings not marked with numbers. **Similar model:** Frigidaire FAB067W7B, $400. **Recommendation:** A very good choice.

14 **Friedrich Q-star SQ06J10** $370

• 6,600 Btu/hr. • 73 lb. • Fits 26- to-42-in. window.
Highly efficient. Slide-out chassis. Through-the-wall installation instructions provided. **But:** Mediocre comfort control on energy-saver mode. Hard to install. No upper sash lock. Thermostat settings not marked with numbers. **Recommendation:** A very good choice.

15 **Carrier VisionAire LCA061P** $370

• 6,050 Btu/hr. • 2.0 pints/hr. moisture removal. • 55 lb. • Fits 26- to-41-in. window. Low profile design. Exterior support bracket with leveling provision. Handles to ease carrying. **But:** Poor at directing air flow to the right. Only 1 fan-only setting. No vent. Only parts warranty on sealed system 2nd through 5th yr. **Recommendation:** A very good choice.

16 **General Electric Value Line AQV06LA** $300

• 6,000 Btu/hr. • 1.5 pints/hr. moisture removal. • 46 lb. • Fits 24- to-35-in. window. Excellent comfort control. **But:** Poor at directing air to the left. Only 1 fan-only setting. No left/right louver. No vent. 2nd through 5th yr. on compressor only. **Recommendation:** A good choice.

7,000-7,800 Btu/hr. models

17 **Panasonic CW-806TU** $420

• 7,800 Btu/hr. • 2.3 pints/hr. moisture removal. • 69 lb. • Fits 22- to-37-in. window. Excellent comfort control. Quiet. Slide-out chassis. **But:** Hard to install. No upper sash lock. Only 2 fan speeds on cool. **Similar model:** Quasar HQ2082KH, $400. **Recommendation:** A very good choice.

18 **General Electric Deluxe Series AGH08FAG1** $380

• 7,800 Btu/hr. • 2.5 pints/hr. moisture removal. • 69 lb. • Fits 21- to-36-in. window. Slide-out chassis. Exterior support bracket with leveling provision. **But:** Mediocre comfort control on energy-saver mode and poor at directing air to the left. Hard to install. Only 2 fan speeds on cool. No slide-out filter. **Recommendation:** A very good choice.

19 **Kenmore (Sears) Value Line 78073** $330

• 7,000 Btu/hr. • 2.3 pints/hr. moisture removal. • 69 lb. • Fits 25- to-36-in. window. Quiet. Slide-out chassis. Exterior support bracket with leveling provision. **But:** Poor at directing airflow to the left. Hard to install. Only 2 fan speeds on cool. No left/right louver. No slide-out filter. **Recommendation:** A good choice.

20 **Friedrich Q-star SQ07J10** $410

• 7,100 Btu/hr. • 2.5 pints/hr. moisture removal. • 78 lb. • Fits 26- to-42-in. window. Highly efficient. Slide-out chassis. Through-the-wall installation instructions provided. **But:** Mediocre comfort control on energy-saver mode. Poor performance in a brownout. Hard to install. No upper sash lock. Thermostat settings not marked with numbers. **Recommendation:** A good choice.

8,000-8,600 Btu/hr. models

21 **Friedrich Quietmaster Electronic SS08J10A** $670

• 8,200 Btu/hr. • 1.5 pints/hr. moisture removal. • 101 lb. • Fits 28- to-42-in. window. Highly efficient and excellent comfort control. Slide-out chassis. Exterior support bracket with leveling provision. Through-the-wall installation instructions provided. Digital temperature readout (also indicates that power is on in energy-saver mode). Built-in timer. Four fan speeds on cool. Auto-fan speed. Dirty filter indicator. Fresh air intake. 5-yr. warranty on electronics. **But:** Hard to install. No expandable side panels. No slide-out filter. **Recommendation:** A very good choice.

22 **Sharp Comfort Touch Series AF-R908X** $440

• 8,500 Btu/hr. • 88 lb. • Fits 23- to-38-in. window.
Excellent comfort control. Slide-out chassis. Through-the-wall installation instructions provided. Digital temperature readout (also indicates that power is on in energy-saver mode). Built-in timer. **But:** Hard to install. No upper sash lock. Only 1 fan-only setting. Short power cord. Only parts warranty on sealed system 2nd through 5th yr. **Similar model:** Sharp AF-T908X, $460. **Recommendation:** A very good choice.

23 **Whirlpool DesignerStyle ACQ082XD** $410

• 8,250 Btu/hr. • 1.7 pints/hr. moisture removal. • 88 lb. • Fits 28- to-48-in. window.
Excellent comfort control. Slide-out chassis. Through-the-wall installation instructions provided. **But:** Poor at directing air to the right. Only 1 fan-only setting. Thermostat settings not marked with numbers. **Recommendation:** A very good choice.

24 **Carrier Siesta Series TCA081P** $400

• 8,600 Btu/hr. • 2.1 pints/hr. moisture removal. • 66 lb. • Fits 26- to-38-in. window.
Excellent comfort control on energy-saver mode. Exterior support bracket with leveling provision. Handles to ease carrying. **But:** Only 1 fan-only setting. Only parts warranty on sealed system 2nd through 5th yr. **Recommendation:** A very good choice.

25 **Fedders Portable Series A3Q08F2BG** $385

• 8,000 Btu/hr. • 2.5 pints/hr. moisture removal. • 64 lb. • Fits 21- to-39-in. window.
Exterior support bracket with leveling provision. 2-yr. parts-only warranty on fan motor. **But:** Noisy outdoors. No upper sash lock. Only parts warranty on sealed system 2nd through 5th yr. **Similar model:** Emerson Quiet Kool Compact Q Series 8GC73, $370. **Recommendation:** A very good choice.

26 **Carrier Siesta Series TCA081D** $380

• 8,000 Btu/hr. • 2.0 pints/hr. moisture removal. • 63 lb. • Fits 26- to-38-in. window.
Exterior support bracket with leveling provision. Handles to ease carrying. **But:** Only 2 fan speeds on cool. No vent. Only parts warranty on sealed system 2nd through 5th yr. **Recommendation:** A good choice.

27 **Frigidaire Custom Series FAC083W7A** $340

• 8,000 Btu/hr. • 2.0 pints/hr. moisture removal. • 61 lb. • Fits 22- to-36-in. window.
Only parts warranty on sealed system 2nd through 5th yr. **Similar model:** White Westinghouse WAC083W7A, $350. **Recommendation:** A good choice.

28 **Amana Cool Zone 9P2MY** $390

• 8,600 Btu/hr. • 3.0 pints/hr. moisture removal. • 76 lb. • Fits 23- to-39-in. window.
Excellent at dehumidifying. Exterior support bracket with leveling provision. **But:** May cost more to operate than others. No up/down louver control. No slide-out filter. **Recommendation:** A good choice.

9,100-9,200 Btu/hr. models

29 **Kenmore (Sears) Innovative Line 78098** $450

• 9,100 Btu/hr. • 3.0 pints/hr. moisture removal. • 97 lb. • Fits 28- to-42-in. window.
Excellent at dehumidifying and comfort control. Slide-out chassis. Exterior support bracket with leveling provision. Digital temperature readout (also indicates that power is on in energy-saver mode). Built-in timer. Auto-fan speed. **But:** Hard to install. **Recommendation:** A very good choice.

30 **Amana Quiet Zone Line 9M12TA** $460

• 9,100 Btu/hr. • 2.5 pints/hr. moisture removal. • 97 lb. • Fits 28- to-42-in. window.
Excellent at dehumidifying and comfort control. Slide-out chassis. Exterior support bracket with leveling provision. Digital temperature readout (also indicates that power is on in energy-saver mode). Built-in timer. Auto-fan speed. 2-yr. war-

ranty on the entire unit. 3rd through 5th year parts-and-labor warranty on refrigeration system. **But:** Hard to install. **Recommendation:** A very good choice.

31 Amana Quiet Zone 9QZ22RC $420

• 9,100 Btu/hr. • 2.5 pints/hr. moisture removal. • 94 lb. • Fits 30- to-45-in. window. Excellent at dehumidifying and comfort control. Slide-out chassis. Exterior support bracket with leveling provision. **But:** Mediocre in a brownout. Only 1 fan-only setting. No slide-out filter. **Recommendation:** A very good choice.

32 Friedrich Quietmaster Electronic SS09J10A $700

• 9,200 Btu/hr. • 1.7 pints/hr. moisture removal. • 108 lb. • Fits 28- to-42-in. window. Highly efficient and excellent comfort control. Slide-out chassis. Exterior support bracket with leveling provision. Through-the-wall installation instructions provided. Digital temperature readout (also indicates that power is on in energy-saver mode). Built-in timer. Four fan speeds on cool. Auto-fan speed. Dirty filter indicator. Fresh air intake. 5-yr. warranty on electronics. **But:** Mediocre at dehumidifying and poor performance in a brownout. Hard to install. No expandable side panels. No upper sash lock. No slide-out filter. **Recommendation:** A good choice.

10,000-10,500 Btu/hr. models

33 Friedrich Quietmaster Electronic SS10J10A $840

• 10,200 Btu/hr. • 2.6 pints/hr. moisture removal. • 112 lb. • Fits 28- to-42-in. window. Highly efficient and excellent comfort control. Slide-out chassis. Exterior support bracket with leveling provision. Through-the-wall installation instructions provided. Digital temperature readout (also indicates that power is on in energy-saver mode). Built-in timer. 4 fan speeds on cool. Auto-fan speed. Dirty filter indicator. Fresh air intake. 5-yr. warranty on electronics. **But:** Hard to install. No expandable side panels. No upper sash lock. No slide-out filter. **Recommendation:** A very good choice.

34 Amana Quiet Zone 10QZ22RC $470

• 10,200 Btu/hr. • 3.0 pints/hr. moisture removal. • 102 lb. • Fits 30- to-45-in. window. Excellent comfort control. Slide-out chassis. Exterior support bracket with leveling provision. **But:** Only 1 fan-only setting. No slide-out filter. **Recommendation:** A very good choice.

35 Whirlpool DesignerStyle ACQ102XD $420

• 10,000 Btu/hr. • 2.6 pints/hr. moisture removal. • 96 lb. • Fits 28- to-46-in. window. Excellent comfort control. Slide-out chassis. Through-the-wall installation instructions provided. **But:** May cost more to operate than others. Only 1 fan-only setting. Thermostat settings not marked with numbers. Short power cord. **Recommendation:** A good choice.

36 White-Westinghouse Continental Series WAL103Y1A $440

• 10,000 Btu/hr. • 2.5 pints/hr. moisture removal. • 84 lb. • Fits 29- to-40-in. window. Slide-out chassis. Exterior support bracket with leveling provision. Through-the-wall installation instructions provided. **But:** Mediocre at dehumidifying and in a brownout. Noisy outdoors. Short power cord. **Similar models:** Frigidaire Custom Series FAL103Y1A, $410. **Recommendation:** A good choice.

37 Carrier Siesta Series TCA101D $440

• 10,000 Btu/hr. • 3.2 pints/hr. moisture removal. • 67 lb. • Fits 27- to-36-in. window. Excellent at dehumidifying and comfort control. Poor performance in a brownout. **But:** Noisier outdoors and may cost more to operate than others. Only 2 fan speeds on cool. No vent. **Recommendation:** A good choice.

11,500-12,000 Btu/hr. models

38 Friedrich Quietmaster Electronic SS12J10A $700

• 12,000 Btu/hr. • 3.5 pints/hr. moisture removal. • 111 lb. • Fits 28- to-42-in. window. Highly efficient and excellent comfort control. Slide-out chassis. Exterior support bracket with leveling provision. Through-the-wall installation instructions provided. Digital temperature readout (also indicates that power is on in energy-saver mode). Built-in timer. Four fan speeds on cool.

Auto-fan speed. Dirty filter indicator. Fresh air intake. 5-yr. warranty on electronics. **But:** Hard to install. No expandable side panels. No upper sash lock. No slide-out filter. **Recommendation:** A very good choice.

39 Gibson Air Sweep GAX128Y1A $600

• 12,000 Btu/hr. • 3.5 pints/hr. moisture removal. • 93 lb. • Fits 29- to-45-in. window. Slide-out chassis. Exterior support bracket with leveling provision. Through-the-wall installation instructions provided. Powered louvers sweep side to side. Extra 6th through 10th yr. parts-only warranty on compressor. **But:** No fan-only setting. Filter pulls out from bottom; may hit sill. Short power cord. **Recommendation:** A good choice.

40 Amana Quiet Zone 12QZ22RC $520

• 11,800 Btu/hr. • 3.3 pints/hr. moisture removal. • 104 lb. • Fits 30- to-45-in. window. Slide-out chassis. Exterior support bracket with leveling provision. **But:** Noisy outdoors and poor performance in a brownout. Only 1 fan-only setting. No slide-out filter. **Recommendation:** A good choice.

41 Kenmore (Sears) Value Line 78122 $430

• 12,000 Btu/hr. • 3.3 pints/hr. moisture removal. • 88 lb. • Fits 27- to-39-in. window. Slide-out chassis. Exterior support bracket with leveling provision. **But:** Mediocre at dehumidifying and poor at directing airflow to the left. Hard to install. No left/right louver. No slide-out filter. **Recommendation:** A good choice.

42 Fedders Regency Series A3J12E2AG $390

• 12,000 Btu/hr. • 3.9 pints/hr. moisture removal. • 97 lb. • Fits 25- to-39-in. window. Slide-out chassis. Exterior support bracket with leveling provision. 2-yr. parts-only warranty on fan motor. **But:** Noisier outdoors and may cost more to operate than others. Poor at directing air to the right. Hard to install. No expandable side panels. No upper sash lock. Only parts warranty on sealed system 2nd through 5th yr. **Similar model:** Emerson Quiet Kool Modulaire S/O Series 12GJ14. **Recommendation:** A good choice.

43 Whirlpool DesignerStyle ACQ122XD $440

• 12,000 Btu/hr. • 4.0 pints/hr. moisture removal. • 99 lb. • Fits 28- to-46-in. window. Slide-out chassis. Through-the-wall installation instructions provided. **But:** Noisier outdoors and may cost more to operate than others. Only 1 fan-only setting. Thermostat settings not marked with numbers. Short power cord. **Recommendation:** A good choice.

Ratings *Carpet deep-cleaners*

& Recommendations

The tests behind the Ratings

Overall score gives greatest weight to results of our **soil** test—how well a machine cleaned ground-in potting soil from carpeting. **Stains** shows how well the machine cleaned coffee, red wine, tomato sauce, and mud. **Ease of use** is a judgment of 14 factors, including setup and storage. **Dryness** indicates how damp the carpet was after cleaning; it was measured by weighing the carpet before and after each test. **Price** is approximate retail. Models similar to those we tested are noted in the Details on the models; features may vary.

Typical features for these models

• 17-ft. or longer power cord. • Hose that isn't long enough to clean a whole flight of stairs. • Shut off automatically when the dirty-water tank is full. • 1-yr. warranty. **Most canisters:** • Capacity of 2 gal. of cleaning solution. • Weigh 33 to 43 lb. (with solution). • Shut off automatically when the dirty-water tank is full. **Most uprights:** Capacity of 1 gal. of cleaning solution. • Weigh 25 to 31 lb. (with solution).

Recommendations

Before you buy a machine, consider renting one. The canister-style Rinse 'N Vac/Carpet Magic or the upright-style Rug Doctor Mighty Pack will give you a feel for what the machines can do, for $20 a day. If you do decide to buy one, the Bissell Big Green Powerbrush canister, $210, and the Kenmore Cleaning Machine scrubber, $170, did the best job.

See report, page 151. Last time rated in CONSUMER REPORTS: July 1997.

Overall Ratings

E VG G F P

Listed in order of overall score

Key no.	Brand and model	Price	Overall score (0–100; P F G VG E)	Cleaning: Soil	Cleaning: Stains	Ease of use	Dryness
	LARGE CANISTER EXTRACTORS						
1	**Bissell** Big Green Powerbrush 1680-3	$210		VG	G	VG	G
2	**Bissell** Powerlifter 16603	129		P	F	VG	VG
3	**Bissell** Big Green 1671	150		P	F	VG	VG
	UPRIGHT EXTRACTORS						
4	**Hoover** Steam Vac Deluxe F5857	230		G	G	G	VG
5	**Rug Doctor** Mighty Pack EZ MP-R (rental)	$20/day		G	F	F	P

Ratings continued

Key no.	Brand and model	Price	Overall score (0–100; P F G VG E)	Cleaning: SOIL	Cleaning: STAINS	Ease of use	Dryness
	UPRIGHT EXTRACTORS *continued*						
6	**Eureka** Dream Machine 2450B	$180		◒	●	○	⊖
7	**Hoover** Steam Vac F5805	130		●	◒	◒	⊖
	SMALL CANISTER EXTRACTORS						
8	**Kenmore** (Sears) 3-in-1 86603	100		●	●	⊖	○
9	**Hoover** Steam Vac Jr. F5411	90		●	◒	○	⊖
	SCRUBBING MACHINES						
10	**Kenmore** (Sears) Cleaning Machine 88973	170		⊖	◒	●	●
11	**Windsor** Dri-Matic	390		◒	●	○	⊜

Details on the models

Large canister extractors

1 Bissell 1680-3 $210

The machine works effectively, using moving brushes to scrub. The brushes can jam on shag carpeting. 2-yr. warranty. **Recommendation:** Good; the best of an unimpressive group of cleaners.

2 Bissell 16603 $129

The machine lacks the moving brush found on (1). It has a clear nozzle. 2-yr. warranty. **Recommendation:** Fair; there are better choices.

3 Bissell 1671 $150

Similar in performance to (4). It can also be used as a wet/dry (shop) vac and has an attachment for bare floors. 2-yr. warranty. **Similar model:** Bissell Big Green 1672, $150. **Recommendation:** Fair; there are better choices.

Upright extractors

4 Hoover F5857 $230

The machine's moving brushes give a good scrub. Its long power cord is convenient. It has an attachment for bare floors. **Availability:** Discontinued. **Recommendation:** Good overall performance; (1) rated better.

5 Rug Doctor EZ MP-R $20/day

This rental's brushes give a good scrub, but the machine is hard to use. It has twice the capacity of other uprights; it's also twice as heavy as some. The spray won't turn off while the brushes are on. The upholstery attachment should reach up a flight of stairs. **Recommendation:** A good way to see if you want to buy a deep-cleaner.

6 Eureka 2450B $180

The machine's moving brushes are soft and barely touch the carpeting. In our soil test, it left streaks. It converts easily to clean upholstery. It has an attachment for bare floors. **Availability:** Discontinued but available. **Similar model:** 2450D, $170. **Recommendation:** Fair; choose one of the few better choices.

7 Hoover F5805 $130

It has no moving brushes, and can't handle heavy dirt. It has an attachment for bare floors. **Availability:** Only through 12/98. **Recommendation:** Fair; there are better choices.

Small canister extractors

8 Kenmore (Sears) 86603 $100

Convenient but not effective, and the dirty-solution tank can overflow. **Availability:** Discontinued. **Recommendation:** Fair; there are better choices.

9 Hoover F5411 $90

It does a little better with stains than other portables, but its power cord is shorter than most, making it inconvenient. **Availability:** Only through 12/98. **Recommendation:** Fair; there are better choices.

Scrubbing machines

10 Kenmore (Sears) 88973 $170

This old-style shampooer is one of the best soil-removers tested. But it doesn't vacuum, and takes two hands to control. It has attachments for bare floors but no tools for cleaning in tight spots. The solution tank can fall off during use. **Recommendation:** Very good for heavy soil, but inconvenient. Barely ranked good overall.

11 Windsor $390

The machine's moist powder doesn't wet carpeting. But it doesn't clean carpeting either, unless you use a lot more powder than recommended. You sprinkle the powder, use the machine to scrub it in, then pick up the dirt with a regular vacuum. The brushes can jam on shag carpeting. **Recommendation:** There are better, less expensive choices.

HOW TO USE THE RATINGS

- Read the Recommendations for information on specific models and general buying advice.
- Note how the rated products are listed—in order of performance and convenience, price, or alphabetically.
- The overall score graph gives the big picture in performance. Notes on features and performance for individual models are listed in the "Comments" column or "Details on the models."
- Use the key numbers to locate the details on each model.
- Before going to press, we verify model availability for most products with manufacturers. Some tested models listed in the Ratings may no longer be available. Discontinued models are noted in "Comments" or "Details on the models." Such models may still be available in some stores for part of 1999. Models indicated as successors should perform similarly to the tested models, according to the manufacturer. Features may vary.
- Models similar to the tested models, when they exist, are indicated in "Comments" or "Details on the models."
- The original date of publication is noted for each Ratings.

Ratings *Exterior deck-treatments*

& Recommendations

The tests behind the Ratings

We built a large deck frame to support several hundred pieces of pressure-treated deck lumber, then coated each with a deck treatment, following manufacturer's instructions. To judge mildew resistance, we applied the treatments to plain pine boards and left them exposed to the weather in New York and in Florida. The **overall score** summarizes performance in our four main tests after 20 months' exposure to the elements. We judged resistance to the following: **dirt** accumulation; **color** change, a measure of the coating's color change (for semitransparent products) or graying of the wood (for clear and toned products); and mildew in our New York test. **Price** is the approximate retail.

Recommendations

Most of the treatments are solvent-based; the rest are water-based. After 20 months, only five clear treatments could still be deemed effective. DAP Woodlife Premium, $13 a gallon, is holding up the best. Among semitransparent and toned products, the Cabot product and the Akzo Nobel Sikkens Cetol DEK toned base coat are the best choices. But those products are expensive—$24 a gallon for the Cabot and $51 a gallon for the Akzo Nobel. You could use a cheaper product, but it probably won't protect the wood as well.

See report, page 154. Last time rated in CONSUMER REPORTS: June 1998.

Overall Ratings

E VG G F P

Listed in order of overall score

	Product	Price	Overall score (0–100; P F G VG E)	Resistance to... DIRT	COLOR CHANGE	MILDEW
	SEMITRANSPARENT TREATMENTS					
1	**Cabot** Decking Stain	$24/gal.		G	E	E
2	**Glidden** Endurance Deck and Siding Oil Stain	22		G	E	VG
3	**Olympic** Water Repellent Deck Stain	17		VG	VG	VG
4	**Wolman** Deck Stain with Water Repellent	21		G	VG	G
5	**Behr** Plus 10 Deck & Siding Stain	17		VG	VG	VG
6	**Tru-Test** Woodsman Deck Stain	19		VG	VG	G
7	**Pratt & Lambert** Stainshield Oil Deck Stain	24		G	G	VG
8	**Wolman** Rain Coat With Natural Wood Toner	15		G	G	VG

	Product	Price	Overall score (0–100; P F G VG E)	Resistance to . . . DIRT	COLOR CHANGE	MILDEW
	'TONED' (LIGHTLY TINTED) TREATMENTS					
9	**Akzo Nobel** Sikkens Cetol DEK (base coat)	$51		○	⊜	⊜
10	**Olympic** Natural Look Protector Plus	14		○	○	⊜
11	**Benjamin Moore** Moorwood Clear Finish	21		○	◒	○
12	**Behr** #81 Waterproofing Sealer, Finish and Stabilizer	16		○	◒	◒
	CLEAR TREATMENTS					
13	**DAP** Woodlife Premium Wood Preservative	13		○	○	⊜
14	**Olympic** Clear Wood Preservative	13		○	◒	⊜
15	**Olympic** Water Guard Wood Clear	10		○	◒	○
16	**Flood** Seasonite (base coat)	12		○	◒	◒
17	**ZAR** Clear Wood Sealer	17		○	◒	◒
18	**Thompson's** Water Seal	10		○	◒	●
19	**Thompson's** Water Seal Ultra	14		◒	◒	●
20	**Wolman** Raincoat Water Repellent VOC Compliant	21		◒	◒	◒
21	**Tru-Test** Clear Tru-Seal	11		○	◒	◒
22	**Behr** #92 Waterproofing Sealer, Finish and Stabilizer	17		◒	●	●
23	**Sears** Weatherbeater 18065	9		●	●	●

Details on the models

Semitransparent treatments

1 Cabot Decking Stain $24

Solvent based. 30 colors available. Resisted Florida mildew best.

2 Glidden Endurance Deck and Siding Oil Stain $22

Solvent based. 9 colors available. Resisted Florida mildew better than most.

3 Olympic Water Repellent Deck Stain $17

Solvent based. 12 colors available. Color tended to scrub out when being cleaned. Resisted cracking better than most.

4 Wolman Deck Stain with Water Repellent $21

Water based. 4 colors available. Resisted Florida mildew better than most. Resisted cracking better than most.

5 Behr Plus 10 Deck & Siding Stain $17

Water based. 40 colors available. Color tends to scrub out when being cleaned.

6 Tru-Test Woodsman Deck Stain $19

Solvent based. 26 colors available. Resisted Florida mildew better than most. Color tended to scrub out when being cleaned.

7 Pratt & Lambert Stainshield Oil Deck Stain $24

Solvent based. 6 colors available. Resisted Florida mildew better than most. Colors tended to scrub out when being cleaned.

8 Wolman Rain Coat With Natural Wood Toner $15

Water based. 3 colors available. Color tended to scrub out when being cleaned.

'Toned' treatments

9 Akzo Nobel Sikkens Cetol DEK (base coat) $51

Solvent based. 3 colors available. Two-coat system, topcoat to be applied within 1 yr. of base coat. Resisted Florida mildew better than most. Best at letting dirt wash off and resisting cracking.

10 Olympic Natural Look Protector Plus $14

Solvent based. Available in 4 wood tones. Color tended to scrub out when being cleaned.

11 Benjamin Moore Moorwood Clear Finish $21

Solvent based. Not available in different colors.

12 Behr #81 Waterproofing Sealer, Finish and Stabilizer $16

Solvent based. Not available in different colors. Color tended to scrub out when being cleaned.

Clear treatments

13 DAP Woodlife Premium Wood Preservative $13

Solvent based.

14 Olympic Clear Wood Preservative $13

Solvent based. Worse than most at letting dirt be washed off. Resisted cracking better than most.

15 Olympic Water Guard Wood Clear $10

Water based.

16 Flood Seasonite (base coat) $12

Water based. Two-coat system; topcoat to be applied after base coat.

17 ZAR Clear Wood Sealer $17

Solvent based.

18 Thompson's Water Seal $10

Solvent based. Resisted cracking better than most.

19 Thompson's Water Seal Ultra $14

Water based. Resisted cracking better than most.

20 Wolman Raincoat Water Repellent VOC Compliant $21

Water based.

21 Tru-Test Clear Tru-Seal $11

Solvent based.

22 Behr #92 Waterproofing Sealer, Finish and Stabilizer $17

Solvent based. Worse than most at letting dirt wash off.

23 Sears Weatherbeater 18065 $9

Water based. Worst at letting dirt wash off. Better than most at resisting cracking.

Ratings *Ceiling fans*
& Recommendations

The tests behind the Ratings

Overall score is based mainly on air-moving ability and freedom from wobble. **Range** is the difference in airflow between fastest and slowest fan speeds. **Maximum** flow is at the highest speed. **Efficiency** is a measure of airflow versus power consumed at the highest speed. Freedom from **wobble** indicates steadiness at highest speed. Scores aren't comparable between size groups. **Price** is approximate retail. Models similar to those we tested are noted in the Details on the models; features may vary.

Typical features for these models

• Three speeds. • Pull-chain speed control. • Four or five blades. • Switch to reverse direction of rotation. • Downrod or flush mount.

Recommendations

Among the large fans, the Hunter Sojourn 25874, $190, and Casablance Panama 12222T, $370, top the Ratings. The Hampton Bay St. Claire 413-769, $100, performed nearly as well in our tests. We judged it **A CR Best Buy**. Among the smaller fans, the Harbor Breeze Vandelle EF5171PB and the Hunter Coastal Breeze 23506, each $60, led the Ratings by slight margins. The Hampton Bay Bridgeton 357-633, which scored nearly as high, sells for about $45. And its Home Depot brandmate, the Hampton Bay The Littleton 270-614, a flush-mounted model, sells for just $30. We judged each of those Hampton Bay models **A CR Best Buy**.

See report, page 152. Last time rated in CONSUMER REPORTS: July 1997.

Overall Ratings

E VG G F P

Listed in order of overall score

Key no.	Brand and model	Price	Overall score (0–100; P F G VG E)	Air-moving ability: RANGE	MAXIMUM	EFFICIENCY	Wobble
	LARGE FANS *(Recommended for rooms between 225 and 400 square feet)*						
1	**Hunter** Sojourn 25874	$190		VG	E	VG	E
2	**Casablanca** Panama 12222T	370		E	E	F	VG
3	**Hampton Bay** St. Claire 413-769 **A CR Best Buy**	100		G	E	E	E
4	**Patton** 978A-WBR [1]	140		G	VG	VG	E
5	**Hampton Bay** The Redington II Pinnacle 175-718	125		G	E	VG	VG

Ratings continued

Key no.	Brand and model	Price	Overall score (0–100; P F G VG E)	Air-moving ability: RANGE	Air-moving ability: MAXIMUM	Air-moving ability: EFFICIENCY	Wobble
	LARGE FANS *continued*						
6	**Hunter** Infiniti 25286	$125		○	⊖	⊖	⊜
7	**Harbor Breeze** Colonial EF5006PB Item 37774	90		○	⊖	⊜	⊜
8	**Kenmore** (Sears) 99024	100		○	⊖	⊖	⊜
9	**Patton** 994BR[2]	200		⊖	⊜	◒	⊖
10	**Kenmore** (Sears) 99013	50		○	⊖	⊖	⊖
11	**Hunter** The Original 23856	200		⊖	⊜	◒	○
12	**Casablanca** Clairemont 5192D	220		○	⊜	⊜	○
13	**Kenmore** (Sears) 99022	80		◒	⊖	⊖	⊜
14	**Hunter** Studio Series Remote 25736	200		◒	⊖	⊖	⊜
15	**Encon** Empress 5EM-52PBE	90		◒	○	⊜	⊜
16	**Windmere** UL52W	60		○	⊖	○	○
17	**Lasko** Preferred Design & Light 6505L	90		○	⊜	⊖	◒
18	**Emerson** Northwind Designer CF755AB	140		◒	◒	●	⊜
	SMALL FANS *(Recommended for rooms up to 225 square feet)*						
19	**Harbor Breeze** Vandelle EF5171PB Item 37813	60		○	⊜	⊜	⊜
20	**Hunter** Coastal Breeze 23506	60		○	⊜	⊜	⊜
21	**Hampton Bay** Bridgeton 357-633 **A CR Best Buy**	45		○	⊜	⊜	⊜
22	**Hunter** Low Profile II 23800	85		○	⊖	⊖	⊜
23	**Hampton Bay** The Littleton 270-614 **A CR Best Buy**	30		○	⊜	⊖	⊜
24	**Lasko** Decor 4205L America with Light	75		○	⊜	○	⊜
25	**Casablanca** Four Seasons 75U11D	95		○	⊜	⊜	⊖
26	**Encon** Traditional 5TD-42WHC	60		○	⊜	⊖	⊜
27	**Hunter** Summer Breeze 23684	100		○	⊖	⊖	⊜
28	**Hampton Bay** The Landmark 460-249	35		◒	⊜	⊜	⊜
29	**Emerson** Northwind Snugger CF704SPB	110		○	⊖	○	⊜
30	**Patton** 979A-42BR[3]	95		●	⊖	○	⊜
31	**Windmere** MD42AW5C3TL	50		◒	○	●	●

[1] *Previously named Fasco Gulf Stream 978A-WBR.*
[2] *Previously named Fasco Gilespie 994BR.*
[3] *Previously named Fasco The Snugger 979A-42BR.*

Details on the models

Large fans (about 52 inches)

1 Hunter Sojourn 25874 $190

• Weight: 20 lb. • 40 to 160 rpm • 5 reversible blades

A very efficient fan with excellent air-moving ability and a wide range in airflow. Comes with a blade-balance kit. **But:** Judged harder to assemble and install than most. **Options:** Light kit, handheld remote, wall-mount control, different-length downrod, slanted-ceiling adapter. **Warranty:** 1-yr. full on fan, 25-yr. limited on motor. **Similar models:** 25875; 25876; 25879. Kenmore (Sears) 99412. Lowe's Item 84996. **Recommendation:** A very good overall performer—our top choice among the large fans.

2 Casablanca Panama 12222T $370

• 50-in. diameter • Weight: 21 lb. • 25 to 180 rpm • Choice of 4 or 5 blades • Downrod-mount only

Excellent air-moving ability and a wide range of airflow, with 6 fan speeds. Wall-mounted control can be programmed to turn lights on and off and change fan speeds at preset times. Attaches with a convenient hanger bracket. Blades are packaged and sold separately. **Options:** Light kit, flush-mount kit, different-length downrod, slanted-ceiling adapter. **Warranty:** 90-day in-home service, 1-yr. on fan, lifetime on motor. **Recommendation:** Very good overall, but expensive and not as energy-efficient as most others.

3 Hampton Bay St. Claire 413-769 $100

• Weight: 22 lb. • 55 to 170 rpm • 5 reversible blades • 4-globe light assembly • Available only at Home Depot stores

A highly efficient fan with excellent air-moving ability. Attaches with a convenient hanger bracket. Comes with a blade-balance kit and different-length downrods. **But:** Fan and light-switch pull chains are hard to tell apart. **Option:** Wall-mount control. **Warranty:** 1-yr. limited on fan, 30-yr. limited on motor. **Similar model:** 270-449; 390-114. **Recommendation:** A very good choice. **A CR Best Buy.**

4 Patton 978A-WBR $140

• Weight: 14 lb. • 55 to 160 rpm • 5 reversible blades • Downrod-mount only • Previously named Fasco Gulf Stream 978A-WBR

A very efficient fan. Attaches with a convenient hanger bracket. **Options:** Light kit, flush-mount kit, different-length downrod, slanted-ceiling adapter. Warranty: 1-yr. full on fan, 10-yr. limited on motor. **Availability:** Only through 12/98. **Recommendation:** Very good overall.

5 Hampton Bay The Redington II Pinnacle 175-718 $125

• Weight: 23 lb. • 50 to 140 rpm • 5 reversible blades 4-globe light assembly • Available only at Home Depot stores

A very efficient fan with excellent air-moving ability. Attaches with a convenient hanger bracket. Comes with a blade-balance kit, different-length downrods, and handheld remote speed and light control. **But:** Blades harder to balance than most. **Warranty:** 1-yr. limited on fan, lifetime limited on motor. **Similar models:** 175-620; 175-652; 175-702. **Recommendation:** A very good choice.

6 Hunter Infiniti 25286 $125

• Weight: 16 lb. • 55 to 155 rpm • 5 blades

A very efficient fan. Comes with a blade-balance kit. **Options:** Light kit, handheld remote, wall-mount control, different-length downrod, slanted-ceiling adapter. **Warranty:** 1-yr. full on fan, 20-yr. parts on motor. **Similar models:** 25280; 25284; 25285; 25289. Kenmore (Sears) models 99406; 99407. Lowe's Item 31768. **Recommendation:** A very good choice.

7 Harbor Breeze Colonial EF5006PB Item 37774 $90

• Weight: 20 lb. • 65 to 155 rpm • 5 reversible blades • 4-globe light assembly • Available only at Lowe's stores

A highly efficient fan. Attaches with a convenient hanger bracket. **Options:** Wall-mount control, handheld remote, different-length downrod, slanted-ceiling adapter. **Warranty:** 15-yr. limited on fan and motor. **Recommendation:** A very good choice.

8 Kenmore (Sears) 99024 $100

• Weight: 24 lb. • 55 to 150 rpm • 6 reversible blades • 5-globe light assembly
A very efficient fan. Comes with a blade-balance kit. **But:** Blades were harder to balance than most. **Options:** Different-length downrod, slanted-ceiling adapter. **Warranty:** 20-yr. replacement on fan and motor. **Recommendation:** A very good performer overall.

9 Patton 994BR $200

• Weight: 18 lb. • 40 to 185 rpm • Choice of 4 or 5 reversible blades • Downrod-mount only • Previously named Fasco Gilespie 994BR
Excellent air-moving ability and a wide range in airflow. Attaches with a convenient hanger bracket. **Options:** Light kit, flush-mount kit, different-length downrod, slanted-ceiling adapter. **Warranty:** 1-yr. full on fan, plus limited lifetime on fan and motor. **Availability:** Only through 12/98. **Recommendation:** A very good performer, though less efficient and a little noisier than most at high speed.

10 Kenmore (Sears) 99013 $50

• Weight: 16 lb. • 70 to 210 rpm • Choice of 4 or 5 reversible blades
A very efficient fan with very good air-moving ability. Comes with a blade-balance kit. **Options:** Light kit, different-length downrod, slanted-ceiling adapter. **Warranty:** 20-yr. replacement on fan and motor. **Similar models:** 99014; 99015. **Recommendation:** A very good and relatively inexpensive choice, though faster and a little noisier than most at high speed.

11 Hunter The Original 23856 $200

• Weight: 39 lb. • 45 to 200 rpm • Choice of 4 or 5 blades • Downrod-mount only
Excellent air-moving ability and a wide range in airflow. Attaches with a convenient hanger bracket. Comes with a blade-balance kit. **But:** Its weight makes it harder than most to assemble and install. Blades were harder to balance than most. The motor requires lubrication. **Options:** Light kit, handheld remote, wall-mount control, different-length downrod, slanted-ceiling adapter. **Warranty:** 1-year full on fan, lifetime parts on motor. **Similar models:** 23850; 23852; 23854; 23855. **Recommendation:** A very good performer, but less efficient and noisier than most at high speed, and less convenient.

12 Casablanca Clairemont 5192D $220

• Weight: 24 lb. • 85 to 180 rpm • 5 blades • Downrod-mount only
A highly efficient fan with excellent air-moving ability. Attaches with a convenient hanger bracket. Blades are packaged and sold separately. Comes with a blade-balance kit. **But:** Blades were harder to balance than most. **Options:** Light kit, wall-mount control, different-length downrod, slanted-ceiling adapter. **Warranty:** 1-yr. on fan, lifetime on motor. **Recommendation:** A very good performer, although a little noisier than most at high speed.

13 Kenmore (Sears) 99022 $80

• Weight: 19 lb. • 80 to 175 rpm • 5 reversible blades • 4-globe light assembly
A very efficient fan. **Warranty:** 20-yr. replacement on fan and motor. **Recommendation:** Very good overall, but with a limited range in airflow.

14 Hunter Studio Series Remote 25736 $200

• Weight: 17 lb. • 75 to 170 rpm • 5 reversible blades
A very efficient fan. Comes with a blade-balance kit and handheld remote speed (and light) control. **Options:** Light kit, wall-mount control, different-length downrod, slanted-ceiling adapter. **Warranty:** 1-yr. full on fan, 20-yr. parts on motor. **Similar models:** 25730; 25734; 25739. Kenmore (Sears) 99416. Lowe's Items 37157; 37158, 37159. **Recommendation:** Very good, but with a limited range in airflow.

15 Encon Empress 5EM-52PBE $90

• Weight: 19 lb. • 70 to 150 rpm • Choice of 4 or 5 reversible blades • 5-globe light assembly
A very efficient fan. **But:** Judged harder to assemble and install than most. **Options:** Different-length downrod, slanted-ceiling adapter. **Warranty:** 1-yr. full on fan, 10-yr. on motor. **Availability:** Discontinued. **Successor:** 5EMR-52PBE, $90. **Recommendation:** Good overall, but with a limited range in airflow.

16 **Windmere UL52W** $60

• Weight: 17 lb. • 55 to 160 rpm • Choice of 4 or 5 blades • Swiveling 4-globe light assembly
Comes with a blade-balance kit. **Warranty:** 1-yr. full on fan, 5-yr. on motor. **Availability:** Discontinued. **Recommendation:** A good performer.

17 **Lasko Preferred Design & Light 6505L** $90

• Weight: 20 lb. • 60 to 165 rpm • 5 reversible blades • 3-globe light assembly.
A very efficient fan. **But:** Blades were harder to balance than most, and the reverse switch, above the housing, is inconvenient. **Warranty:** 1-yr. limited on fan, 25-yr. limited on motor. **Similar models:** 6502L; 6507L. **Recommendation:** A good performer, but wobbled more than most.

18 **Emerson Northwind Designer CF755AB** $140

• Weight: 18 lb. • 55 to 180 rpm • 5 reversible blades • Downrod-mount only
Mediocre air-moving ability for a large fan. Attaches with a convenient hanger bracket. Comes with a blade-balance kit. **Warranty:** 1-yr. full on fan, 20-yr. limited on motor. **Similar models:** CF755BK; CF755DB; CF755G; CF755H; CF755NW; CF755OB; CF755PB; CF755TG; CF755TWW; CF755V; CF755W; CF755WPB; CF755WW. **Recommendation:** A good performer, but there are better choices.

Small fans (about 42 inches)

19 **Harbor Breeze Vandelle EF5171PB Item 37813** $60

• Weight: 14 lb. • 65 to 200 rpm • 6 reversible blades • 3-globe light assembly • Available only at Lowe's stores
A highly efficient fan with excellent air-moving ability. Attaches with a convenient hanger bracket. Comes with a blade-balance kit. **Options:** Handheld remote, wall-mount control, different-length downrod, slanted-ceiling adapter. **Warranty:** 10-yr. limited on fan and motor. **Recommendation:** A very good performer, and our top-rated small fan.

20 **Hunter Coastal Breeze 23506** $60

• 44-in. diameter • Weight: 11 lb. • 75 to 230 rpm • 4 blades
A highly efficient fan with excellent air-moving ability. Comes with a blade-balance kit. **Options:** Light kit, handheld remote, wall-mount control, different-length downrod, slanted-ceiling adapter. **Warranty:** 1-yr. full on fan, 20-yr. parts on motor. **Similar models:** 23500, 23504, 23509. **Recommendation:** A very good performer.

21 **Hampton Bay Bridgeton 357-633** $45

• Weight: 14 lb. • 110 to 210 rpm • Choice of 4 or 5 reversible blades • 3-globe light assembly • Available only at Home Depot stores
A highly efficient fan with excellent air-moving ability. Comes with a blade-balance kit and an extra downrod. **Option:** Wall-mount control. **Warranty:** 1-yr. limited on fan, 30-yr. limited on motor. **Recommendation:** A very good performer at an exceptional price. **A CR Best Buy.**

22 **Hunter Low Profile II 23800** $85

• Weight: 10 lb. • 85 to 225 rpm • 4 reversible blades • Flush-mount only
A very efficient fan. Attaches with a convenient hanger bracket. Comes with a blade-balance kit. **Option:** Light kit. **Warranty:** 1-yr. full on fan, 20-yr. limited on motor. **Similar models:** 23804; 23806. **Recommendation:** A very good choice for low ceilings.

23 **Hampton Bay The Littleton 270-614** $30

• Weight: 11 lb. • 100 to 230 rpm • 4 reversible blades • 1-globe light assembly • Flush-mount only • Available only at Home Depot stores
A very efficient fan with excellent air-moving ability. Comes with a blade-balance kit. **Option:** Wall-mount control. **Warranty:** 1-yr. limited on fan, 15-yr. limited on motor. **Recommendation:** A very good, very inexpensive choice for low ceilings. **A CR Best Buy**.

24 **Lasko Decor 4205L America with Light** $75

• Weight: 15 lb. • 85 to 230 rpm • 4 reversible blades • 3-globe light assembly

An excellent air-mover. Attaches with a convenient hanger bracket. **But:** Reverse switch, above the housing, is inconvenient. **Warranty:** 1-yr. limited on fan, 10-yr. limited on motor. **Similar models:** 4202L; 4207L. **Recommendation:** A very good performer overall.

25 Casablanca Four Seasons 75U11D $95

• Weight: 11 lb. • 105 to 220 rpm • 5 reversible blades • Downrod-mount only
A highly efficient fan with excellent air-moving ability. Attaches with a convenient hanger bracket. Comes with extra downrod and a blade-balance kit. **Options:** Light kit, handheld remote, wall-mount control, flush-mount kit, different-length downrod, slanted-ceiling adapter. **Warranty:** 1-yr. parts on fan, 25-yr. parts on motor. **Availability:** Only through 12/98. **Recommendation:** A very good performer.

26 Encon Traditional 5TD-42WHC $60

• Weight: 15 lb. • 80 to 195 rpm • Choice of 4 or 5 reversible blades • 3-globe light assembly.
A very efficient fan with excellent air-moving ability. **Options:** Handheld remote, wall-mount control, extra downrod, slanted-ceiling adapter. **Warranty:** 1-yr. full on fan, 10-yr. full on motor. **Recommendation:** A very good performer.

27 Hunter Summer Breeze 23684 $100

• Weight: 12 lb. • 75 to 225 rpm • 5 reversible blades
A very efficient fan. Comes with a blade-balance kit. **Options:** Light kit, handheld remote, wall-mount control, different-length downrod, slanted-ceiling adapter. **Warranty:** 1-yr. full on fan, 20-yr. limited on motor. **Similar models:** 23680; 23686. **Availability:** Discontinued. **Recommendation:** Very good overall.

28 Hampton Bay The Landmark 460-249 $35

• Weight: 10 lb. • 120 to 180 rpm • 4 reversible blades • Available only at Home Depot stores
A highly efficient fan with excellent air-moving ability. Comes with a blade-balance kit and extra downrod. **Options:** Light kit, wall-mount control. **Warranty:** 1-yr. limited on fan, 15-yr. limited on motor. **Similar models:** 460-281; 460-303. **Recommendation:** Very good, but limited airflow range, and faster than most at low speed.

29 Emerson Northwind Snugger CF704SPB $110

• Weight: 11 lb. • 80 to 205 rpm • 5 reversible blades • Flush-mount only
Comes with a blade-balance kit. **Options:** Light kit, wall-mount control. **Warranty:** 1-yr. full on fan, 15-yr. limited on motor. **Similar models:** CF704SAB; CF704SW; CF704SWW. **Recommendation:** Very good, suitable for low ceilings.

30 Patton 979A-42BR $95

• Weight: 11 lb. • 130 to 205 rpm • Choice of 4 or 5 reversible blades • Flush-mount only • Previously named Fasco The Snugger 979A-42BR
A very good air-mover. Attaches with a convenient hanger bracket. **Option:** Light kit. **Warranty:** 1-yr. full on fan, 10-yr. limited on motor. **Availability:** Only through 12/98. **Recommendation:** A good fan for low ceilings, but limited range in airflow, and faster than most at low speed.

31 Windmere MD42AW5C3TL $50

• Weight: 12 lb. • 110 to 210 rpm • 5 reversible blades • 3-globe light assembly
Warranty: 1-yr. on fan, 5-yr. on motor. **Availability:** Discontinued. **Recommendation:** A generally poor performer that wobbled more than most.

Ratings *Gas grills*
& Recommendations

The tests behind the Ratings

Overall score is based mainly on performance, convenience, and features. **Heating evenness** (with heat turned high or low) is most important when you cook for a crowd. **Grilling** scores reflect performance at low temperatures—necessary for chicken and fish, and for hamburgers after they've been seared. (All models grill well at high temperatures.) **Roasting** requires even lower temperatures, for indirect heating. Grills scoring very good or excellent here are fine for both regular roasting (a turkey) and slow-roasting (ribs); grills scoring good are fine for regular roasting only; the other grills could be too hot for roasting. Price is approximate retail.

Typical features for these models

• 2 separate steel burners. • Push-button igniter that emits a single spark with each push. • No viewing window. • Tank, included. • Cooking grate of porcelain-coated steel. • 2 wheels and 2 casters.

Recommendations

For basic grilling, consider three grills with friendly prices: the Coleman Powerhouse Plus 4858762, $250, the Thermos Texas Grill 4613800, $175, and the Sunbeam Grillmaster HG455EP, $200. For serious cooking, try one of the Webers or the Ducane. Of the three, the Weber Spirit 500, $360, provides the best value.

See report, page 149. Last time rated in CONSUMER REPORTS: June 1998.

Overall Ratings

Legend: E (Excellent), VG (Very good), G (Good), F (Fair), P (Poor)

Listed in order of overall score

Key no.	Brand and model	Price	Overall score (0–100; P F G VG E)	Heating evenness HIGH	Heating evenness LOW	Grilling	Roasting
1	**Weber** Genesis 1000	$480		VG	E	E	VG
2	**Weber** Spirit 500	360		VG	E	E	VG
3	**Ducane** 1504SHLPE	570		VG	E	E	VG
4	**Sunbeam** Grillmaster HG850C	450		E	E	VG	VG
5	**Kenmore** (Sears) 15875	350		G	E	VG	VG
6	**Coleman** Powerhouse Plus 4858762	250		G	VG	VG	VG
7	**Thermos** Texas Grill 4613800	175		VG	E	E	G

Ratings, continued

Key no.	Brand and model	Price	Overall score (0–100; P F G VG E)	Heating evenness HIGH	Heating evenness LOW	Grilling	Roasting
8	**Sunbeam** Grillmaster HG455EP	$ 200		⊜	⊖	⊖	○
9	**Char-Broil** Precision Flame 4638872	270		◒	⊖	⊖	○
10	**Thermos** Quantum 4613821	200		⊜	⊖	⊖	○
11	**Kenmore** (Sears) 15660	200		◒	⊖	⊖	○
12	**Sunbeam** Grillmaster GG540EPB	180		⊖	○	○	◒

Details on the models

Dimensions are of the whole grill, its cooking surface, and its front and side shelves. **Warranty** is for firebox and lid/burners/other parts. Scores for **convenience** assess sturdiness, shelf space, igniter, assembly, and features.

1 Weber Genesis 1000 $480

• HxWxD: 44x50x23 in. • 430 sq. in. cooking area • 590 sq. in. shelf space • Warranty: 10/-/5 yr. **Convenience:** ⊜. Porcelain-coated metal bars distribute heat. Very sturdy, easy to assemble. Lots of features, including three separately controlled stainless-steel burners, porcelain-coated steel grate with wide bars, utensil hooks, ample shelf space, accurate fuel gauge, air temperature/meat thermometer, and removable base for easy cleanup. Comes partially assembled. Available in a natural-gas version. **Similar models:** Genesis 1000LX, $490; 1100, $510. **Recommendation:** Excellent but pricey.

2 Weber Spirit 500 $360

• HxWxD: 40x46x21 in. • 338 sq. in. cooking area • 149 sq. in. shelf space • Warranty: 10/-/5 yr. **Convenience:** ⊜. Performance as good as (1), and less expensive. Very sturdy, easy to assemble. Available in a natural-gas version. **But:** Smaller than (1), has less shelf space, and lacks a third burner. Cart has two wheels; lift one end to move it. **Similar model:** Spirit 500LX, $370. **Recommendation:** Excellent performance and price.

3 Ducane 1504SHLPE $570

• HxWxD: 47x45x25 in. • 426 sq. in. cooking area • 216 sq. in. shelf space • Warranty: -/-/5 yr. **Convenience:** ⊖. Ceramic briquettes distribute heat. Very sturdy cart; stainless-steel burners and grate with wide bars. Rotary igniter, glowing wire indicator to show when burners are lit, plastic side shelf that doubles as a cutting board. Comes partially assembled. Available in a natural-gas version. Lifetime warranty for $15 surcharge. **But:** Limited shelf space, and you have to buy the tank separately. **Similar model:** 5004SHLPE, $1,000, with rotisserie system. **Recommendation:** Excellent but pricey.

4 Sunbeam Grillmaster HG850C $450

• HxWxD: 46x63x25 in. • 446 sq. in. cooking area • 750 sq. in. shelf space • Warranty: 10/5/1 yr. **Convenience:** ⊖. Metal bars distribute heat. Three stainless-steel burners, very sturdy cart, grate with wide bars of porcelain-coated cast-iron for superior searing, rotary igniter, removable base for easy cleanup, utensil hooks. **But:** Flimsy folding shelves and tank door, small center grate that often stuck when we tried to remove it, and interior components prone to rattling. One sample of igniter knob wore down and had to be replaced. Heavy and awkward to move on its two wheels. Bolt holes don't line up properly, so assembly is difficult. **Similar models:** Grillmaster 800 Series, $420; Grillmaster 850 Series, $470. **Recommendation:** Very good overall, annoying design quirks.

5 Kenmore (Sears) 15875 $350

• HxWxD: 49x64x23 in. • 465 sq. in. cooking area • 715 sq. in. shelf space • Warranty: -/-/1 yr. **Convenience:** ⊖. Charcoal-like briquettes distribute heat. Lots of features including side burner, wide bars on grate, ample warming shelves, electronic igniter with 10-yr. warranty, utensil hooks. Sturdy cart, on casters. **But:** Hard to light manually, and you must buy the tank separately. Assembly is complicated and time-consuming. **Recommendation:** Very good, but a little more money buys better performance in (2).

6 **Coleman Powerhouse Plus 4858762** $250

• HxWxD: 49x64x25 in. • 372 sq. in. cooking area • 607 sq. in. shelf space • Warranty: 50/-/1 yr. **Convenience:** ⊖. Charcoal-like briquettes distribute heat. Rotary ignition, rotisserie equipment, smoke tray, side burner, and utensil hooks. Grate has wide cast-iron bars. Sturdy cart, on casters. **But:** Hard to light manually, and you must buy the tank separately. Three-part rotisserie spit broke the first time we used it; replacement was sturdier. **Recommendation:** Very good performance, but not from the original rotisserie spit.

7 **Thermos Texas Grill 4613800** $175

• HxWxD: 46x52x22 in. • 305 sq. in. cooking area • 396 sq. in. shelf space • Warranty: life/3/1 yr. **Convenience:** ◒. Lava rocks distribute heat. **But:** Limited space on warming rack. The cart feels flimsy, assembly instructions are confusing, and parts don't line up properly. **Recommendation:** Despite these flaws, very good performance and price.

8 **Sunbeam Grillmaster HG455EP** $200

• HxWxD: 47x66x24 in. • 403 sq. in. cooking area • 609 sq. in. shelf space • Warranty: 10/5/1 yr. **Convenience:** ○. Ceramic briquettes distribute heat. Porcelain-steel burners. **But:** Hard to light manually. Confusing assembly instructions. **Similar models:** Grillmaster 455 Series, $200; Grillmaster 550 Series, $200. **Recommendation:** Very good performance and price.

9 **Char-Broil Precision Flame 4638872** $270

• HxWxD: 48x65x22 in. • 389 sq. in. cooking area • 662 sq. in. shelf space • Warranty: life/3/1 yr. **Convenience:** ⊖. Charcoal-like briquettes distribute heat. Utensil hooks, electronic igniter, sturdy cart, rotisserie burner, side burner. Grate has wide cast-iron bars. **But:** You have to buy rotisserie motor and spit separately, about $25. Bolt holes don't line up properly, so assembly is difficult. **Recommendation:** Good performance, poor value.

10 **Thermos Quantum 4613821** $200

• HxWxD: 48x51x23 in. • 306 sq. in. cooking area • 410 sq. in. shelf space. • Warranty: life/3/1 yr. **Convenience:** ◒. Charcoal-like briquettes distribute heat. Heavy wire cooking grate and side burner. **But:** Cart felt flimsy, and glass window broke during testing. Confusing instructions and ill-fitting parts make assembly difficult. **Similar model:** Quantum 4613820, $180. **Recommendation:** Good, but (7) performs better for less money.

11 **Kenmore (Sears) 15660** $200

• HxWxD: 49x55x23 in. • 424 sq. in. cooking area • 423 sq. in. shelf space • Warranty: -/-/1 yr. **Convenience:** ○. Charcoal-like briquettes distribute heat. Available in natural-gas version. **But:** You have to buy the tank separately. Cart has two wheels; lift one end to move it. **Recommendation:** Good overall, but there are better choices.

12 **Sunbeam Grillmaster GG540EPB** $180

• HxWxD: 45x53x24 in. • 309 sq. in. cooking area • 480 sq. in. shelf space • Warranty: 10/3/1 yr. **Convenience:** ○. Ceramic briquettes distribute heat. Comes with covered side burner. **But:** Hard to light manually. Confusing assembly instructions. **Similar model:** Grillmaster 540 Series, $180; Grillmaster 440 Series, $180. **Recommendation:** Good overall, but there are better choices.

Ratings *Push-type mowers*

& Recommendations

The tests behind the Ratings

Overall score is based mainly on performance in whichever cutting modes—bagging, side discharge, mulching—the mower's design permits. After trimming the test lawn to four inches, we set the mowers to cut as close to the top third of the grass as the wheel adjusters would permit. In **mulching** mode, dispersal is how well the mower got the clippings under the lawn's surface. In **bagging** mode, **vacuuming** is how well the mower sucked up clippings; capacity is the amount of clippings the catcher collected before it had to be emptied or its chute clogged. In **side discharge** mode, **dispersal** is how evenly the mower spread the clippings. A mower that cut **tall grass** well should be able to handle a typical two-week growth; a poor score means the mower stalled in as little as 20 feet. Except as noted, **price** is the approximate retail for the basic mower.

Typical features for these models

• 20- to 22-inch deck. • Deadman safety control that stops the engine and blade in less than two seconds when you release the handle. • 2-yr. warranty on the mower and engine. • Four-stroke, side-valve Briggs & Stratton or Tecumseh engine developing 3½ to 6½ hp. • Ability to mow in three modes. • No throttle control. **Most mowers with mulching capability:** • Mulching kit standard or $25 to $30 option. **Most hybrids:** • Optional discharge chute, $18 to $23, and optional catcher, $49 to $90. **Most rear-baggers:** Standard catcher and optional discharge chute, $27 to $40. **Most side-discharge models:** • Standard discharge chute and optional catcher, $30 to $40.

Recommendations

For mulching, the top choices are the John Deere JS60 hybrid, $340, and its lower-priced Sabre brandmate, $310. The Yard Machines 11A-428C and 11A-413A rear baggers, $235 and $180, also mulched very well, as did the Honda Harmony II HRS216PDA side-discharge model, $310. The high-wheel Scotts 21495X8 hybrid, $280, sold in Home Depot stores, is the top choice if you bag clippings. Though a bit hard to handle, it vacuums the clippings superbly, and the capacity of the catcher was unsurpassed. If you disperse clippings, choose a hybrid or a side-discharge model. The Lawn-Boy 10200 hybrid, $350, did especially well, but Lawn-Boy push mowers have been among the least reliable brands. If you cut in all three modes, the John Deere and Sabre hybrid and the two rear-bagging Yard Machines were the most versatile.

See report, page 155. Last time rated in Consumer Reports: May 1998.

Overall Ratings

E VG G F P

Listed in order of overall score

Key no.	Brand and model	Price	Mulching: DISPERSAL	Bagging: VACUUMING	Bagging: CAPACITY	Side discharge: DISPERSAL	Side discharge: TALL GRASS
	HYBRID MOWERS (REAR-BAGGING, SIDE-DISCHARGE)						
1	**John Deere** JS60	$340	VG	VG	VG	G	VG
2	**Sabre** M10 by John Deere	310	VG	VG	VG	G	VG
3	**Lawn-Boy** 10200	350	G	VG	VG	VG	E
4	**Scotts** 21495X8	280	VG	E	E	G	G
5	**Murray** Select 20456X8	235	VG	VG	VG	G	P
6	**Snapper** MR215014B	335	G	VG	E	F	E
	REAR-BAGGING MOWERS						
7	**Yard Machines** by MTD 11A-428C	235	VG	VG	VG	G	E
8	**Yard Machines** by MTD 11A-413A	180	VG	VG	VG	G	E
9	**Toro** Recycler 20449	320	VG	VG	VG	G	G
10	**Poulan** HD4QN20R	169	VG	VG	VG	F	F
11	**Murray** 20406X92	170	G	VG	VG	—	P
	SIDE-DISCHARGE MOWERS						
12	**Honda** Harmony II HRS216PDA	310	VG	[1]	[1]	G	VG
13	**Yard-Man** by MTD 11A-106C401	200	G	E	F	G	E
14	**Sears** Craftsman 38720	130	—	F	P	G	G
15	**Yard Machines** by MTD 11A-021C	105	—	—	—	F	VG
16	**Murray** 20102X92	100	—	—	—	F	G
17	**Rally** R2035G	110 [2]	—	F	P	F	G
18	**Yard Machines** by MTD 11A-084A	140	P	VG	F	F	P
19	**Murray** 22405X92	140	P	F	P	F	G

[1] *Accessory not available at time of tests.* [2] *Price CU paid.*

Ratings continued

Details on the models

Evenness is uniformity of cut. **Handling** includes pushing, pulling, and turning. **Convenience** includes starting, adjusting, and operating details that make a mower easy to use or a pain in the grass.

Hybrid mowers

1 John Deere JS60 $340

• Catcher, $49 • Chute, $18 • 6-hp Briggs & Stratton engine • Weight, 75 lb.
Evenness ⊖; handling ○; convenience ⊖. Big and heavy, but easy to handle. Handle height and cutting height easy to adjust. Catcher easy to empty. **But:** Lots of clippings drop from bottom of housing when you finish mulching. **Recommendation:** Very good overall, works well in all three mowing modes.

2 Sabre M10 by John Deere $310

• Essentially similar to (1), and performed the same in all our tests. • Weight, 75 lb.
Evenness ⊖; handling ○; convenience ⊖.

3 Lawn-Boy 10200 $350

• 6-hp Tecumseh engine • Weight, 63 lb.
Evenness ○; handling ○; convenience ⊖. U-turns easier than with most. Throttle control easy to reach. Catcher easy to empty. Cutting height easy to adjust. Evenness of cut very good in bagging mode, good in other modes. **But:** Switching modes can be difficult. Hard to jockey from side to side. If mulching plate or catcher isn't installed, clippings can blow at user. **Availability:** Discontinued but available. **Similar model:** 10249, $329. **Recommendation:** Very good cutting performance, but staggered front wheel makes some aspects of handling difficult. This brand has been among the least reliable of push mowers.

4 Scotts 21495X8 $280

• 6.5-hp Briggs & Stratton overhead-valve engine • Weight, 82 lb.
Evenness ○; handling ◒; convenience ⊖. Catcher very easy to remove, empty, and install. Handle height easy to adjust. Throttle control easy to reach. Reversible blade needs less frequent sharpening. **But:** Hard to push. Starter cord hard to pull. Blade needed sharpening when new. **Recommendation:** Very good overall, and excellent at bagging—but high-wheel design and weight hurt handling.

5 Murray Select 20456X8 $235

• 5.5-hp Briggs & Stratton engine • Weight, 61 lb.
Evenness ○; handling ○; convenience ○. Throttle control hard to reach. Lots of clippings drop from bottom of deck after mulching. Blade needed sharpening when new. Evenness of cut fair in mulching mode, good in other modes. **Recommendation:** Good overall performance at a good price, but cuts unevenly when mulching.

6 Snapper MR215014B $335

• Catcher, $90 • Discharge chute, $23 • 5-hp Briggs & Stratton engine • Weight, 65 lb.
Evenness ○; handling ◒; convenience ○. Handle height easy to adjust. Catcher easy to empty. **But:** Very hard to push. When mulching, use mulching plate for extra safety and performance. Tools needed to change modes. Blade needed sharpening when new. **Recommendation:** An excellent bagger, but one of the worst handlers we tested. This brand has been among the least reliable of push mowers.

Rear-bagging mowers

7 Yard Machines by MTD 11A-428C $235

• Chute, $30 • 5-hp Briggs & Stratton engine • Weight, 60 lb.
Evenness ◒; handling ○; convenience ○. Throttle control easy to reach. Catcher easy to empty. Evenness of cut good in discharge mode, very good in other modes. **Recommendation:** Very good overall; not bad in side-discharge mode for a rear-bagger.

8 Yard Machines by MTD 11A-413A $180

• Chute, $30 • 4-hp Tecumseh engine • Weight, 55 lb.
Evenness ⊖; handling ○; convenience ○. Throttle

control easy to reach. Catcher easy to empty. Evenness of cut good in discharge mode, very good in other modes. **But:** Only 1-yr. warranty on engine. Blade needed sharpening when new. **Recommendation:** Very good overall; not bad in side-discharge mode for a rear-bagger.

9 **Toro Recycler 20449** $320

• Catcher, $80 • Chute, $40 • 5-hp Briggs & Stratton engine • Weight, 67 lb.
Evenness ○; handling ○; convenience ⊖. Throttle control easy to reach. Handle height and cutting height easy to adjust. **But:** Catcher hard to empty. Tools needed to install bagging chute. **Availability:** Discontinued but available. **Successor models:** 20450 or R-21P, $240. **Recommendation:** Very good overall.

10 **Poulan HD4QN20R** $169

• Chute, $27 • 4-hp Briggs & Stratton engine • Weight, 60 lb.
Evenness ○; handling ○; convenience ○. Relatively quiet. Catcher very easy to remove and install. **But:** Lots of clippings drop from bottom of deck after mulching. Catcher hard to empty. Throttle control hard to reach. Fuel-filler opening hard to reach. **Recommendation:** Very good except in side-discharge mode.

11 **Murray 20406X92** $170

• 4-hp Briggs & Stratton engine • Weight, 55 lb.
Evenness ○; handling ○; convenience ○. Throttle control easy to reach. Evenness of cut fair in mulching mode, good in bagging mode. **But:** Lots of clippings drop from bottom of deck after mulching. Catcher hard to empty. Fuel-filler opening hard to reach. Blade needed sharpening when new. **Recommendation:** Generally good, but no side-discharge mode.

Side-discharge mowers

12 **Honda Harmony II HRS216PDA** $310

• 5.5-hp overhead-valve Honda engine • Weight, 64 lb.
Evenness ○; handling ○; convenience ⊖. Engine has choke for starting, slightly more convenient than primer bulb found in other models. Throttle control easy to reach. Relatively quiet. **But:** Lots of clippings drop from bottom of deck after mulching. Handle height not adjustable. **Recommendation:** A very good mower. Catcher will be available later this year.

13 **Yard-Man by MTD 11A-106C401** $200

• Catcher, $40 • 5-hp Briggs & Stratton engine • Weight, 59 lb.
Evenness ○; handling ○; convenience ⊖. Catcher sticks out much less than on other side-baggers. Throttle control easy to reach. Evenness of cut very good in side-discharge mode, good in other modes. **But:** Catcher hard to empty. **Similar model:** 11B-106C401, $240. **Recommendation:** Very good overall.

14 **Sears Craftsman 38720** $130

• Catcher, $40 • 3.5-hp Tecumseh engine • Weight, 50 lb.
Evenness ○; handling ⊖; convenience ○. U-turns easier than with most. Easy to push. **But:** Only 1-yr. warranty on mower and engine. Chute clogged quickly when bagging. Blade needed sharpening when new. **Availability:** Discontinued. **Recommendation:** Good mower, good price. Doesn't mulch.

15 **Yard Machines by MTD 11A-021C** $105

• 3.5-hp Tecumseh engine • Weight, 43 lb.
Evenness ○; handling ⊖; convenience ◒. U-turns easier than with most. Easy to push. **But:** Only 1-yr. warranty on mower and engine. Handle height not adjustable. Difficult assembly. Adjusting cutting height entails unbolting wheels. Need tools to fold handle. **Recommendation:** Very good handling can't make up for lackluster side-discharge performance. Can't mulch or bag.

16 **Murray 20102X92** $100

• 3.5-hp Briggs & Stratton engine • Weight, 44 lb.
Evenness ○; handling ⊖; convenience ◒. Pushing and U-turns easier than with most. **But:** Handle height not adjustable. Fuel-filler opening hard to reach. Difficult assembly. Adjusting cutting height entails unbolting wheels. Need tools to fold handle. Blade needed sharpening when new. **Recommendation:** A good handler and a rock-bottom price, but can't mulch or bag.

17 Rally R2035G $110 (price CU paid)

• Catcher, $40 • 3.5-hp Briggs & Stratton engine • Weight, 45 lb.

Evenness ○; handling ⊖; convenience ◒. Easy to push. U-turns easier than with most. **But:** Only 1-yr. warranty on mower. Chute clogged quickly during bagging. Throttle control hard to reach. Need tools to fold handle. Handle height not adjustable. Fuel-filler opening hard to reach. Difficult assembly. Adjusting cutting height entails unbolting wheels. **Availability:** Discontinued. **Successor model:** R35N20S, $99; mulching kit, $27. **Recommendation:** Fair overall; doesn't mulch.

—

18 Yard Machines by MTD 11A-084A $140

• Catcher, $30 • 4-hp Briggs & Stratton engine • Weight, 54 lb.

Evenness ○; handling ○; convenience ○. Throttle control easy to reach. **But:** Bogged down in mulching test. Fuel-filler opening hard to reach. **Similar models:** 11A-084B and 11A-084C, $140 each; catcher, $30. **Recommendation:** Fair. There are better choices.

19 Murray 22405X92 $140

• Catcher, $35 • 4-hp Briggs & Stratton engine • Weight, 59 lb.

Evenness ◒; handling ○; convenience ○. Throttle control easy to reach. Evenness of cut good in discharge mode, fair in other modes. **But:** Chute clogged quickly when bagging. Catcher hard to empty. Fuel-filler opening hard to reach. Blade needed sharpening when new. **Recommendation:** A poor performer.

Ratings Kitchen & bath paints
& Recommendations

The tests behind the Ratings

Overall score summarizes performance across our tests. All were judged good or very good in ease of application. **Mildew** shows how well the paints resisted the growth of four different types of fungus. **Tough** summarizes performance in tests of water resistance; the ability to withstand scrubbing; blocking (sticking to other surfaces after it's dry); gloss change from rubbing; ease of stain removal; and marring. **Hiding** shows how well these paints can cover old colors; the higher the score, the higher the contrast in color that you can cover in two coats. Only five of these paints did extremely well when we used a second coat. **Price** is the average per gallon, based on a survey taken in early 1998.

Recommendations

Most of the paints were quite good overall. The best value overall is Wal-Mart's House Beautiful Kitchen & Bath Semi-Gloss, $14 a gallon. We've judged it **A CR Best Buy**. Some products are best suited to certain uses than others. The best choices for window and door trim are Sears Best Easy Living Kitchen, Bath & Trim Enamel, Behr Premium Plus Interior Semigloss, and Benjamin Moore Moore's K&B for Kitchen & Baths Satin. For the highest gloss, choose Ace Royal Hi Gloss Latex Enamel. For a very smooth finish, choose either Zinsser Perma-Whites or Pratt & Lambert Accolade Interior Semi-Gloss.

See report, page 158. Last time rated in CONSUMER REPORTS: May 1998.

Overall Ratings

E VG G F P

Listed in order of overall score

Brand and model	Price	Overall score (0–100; P F G VG E)	Mildew	Tough	Hiding	Comments
Sears Best Easy Living Kitchen, Bath & Trim Enamel	$22		E	E	E	Good for door and window trim.
House Beautiful Kitchen & Bath Semi-Gloss (Wal-Mart) **A CR Best Buy**	14		E	VG	E	Excellent water resistance.
Behr Premium Plus Interior Semigloss (Home Depot)	20		E	E	F	Good for door and window trim. Very good water resistance.
Zinsser 2711 Perma-White Satin Mildew-Proof Bathroom Paint	18		E	VG	G	Leaves a smooth coating.
Dutch Boy Kitchen & Bath Semigloss Enamel	18		E	VG	VG	—

Ratings continued

Brand and model	Price	Mildew	Tough	Hiding	Comments
Behr Premium Plus Interior Satin (Home Depot)	$19	⊜	⊜	◒	Excellent water resistance.
Zinsser 2761 Perma-White Semigloss Mildew-Proof Bathroom Paint	18	⊜	⊖	◒	Resists marring.
Benjamin Moore Moore's K&B for Kitchen & Baths Satin	23	⊜	⊖	◒	Good for door and window trim.
Ace Royal Hi Gloss Latex Enamel (interior/exterior)	22	⊜	◒	⊜	Resists marring. Can form bubbles and runs as it dries. Sags. Scrubability is only fair.
Pratt & Lambert Accolade Interior Semi-Gloss	31	⊖	○	⊖	Very good water resistance.
Dutch Boy Fresh Look Kitchen & Bath (Kmart) Gloss	16	○	⊖	⊖	Very good water resistance. Resists marring.
Pratt & Lambert Accolade Interior Satin	30	◒	⊖	⊖	—
Pittsburgh Manor Hall Premium Semigloss	26	◒	⊖	⊜	Excellent water resistance.
Ace Royal Touch Satin Latex Wall & Trim	18	◒	⊖	⊜	—
Lucite Interior Kitchen & Bath Latex Semi-Gloss	17	○	○	◒	—
Ace Royal Touch Semi-Gloss Latex Wall & Trim	19	◒	⊖	⊖	—
Pittsburgh Kitchen, Bath & Trim Semigloss	19	⊖	○	◒	—
Glidden Interior Spred Kitchen Bath & Trim Semi-Gloss	18	●	⊜	◒	—
California Kitchen & Bath Eggshell Enamel	22	◒	⊖	○	—
Glidden Interior Spred Enamel Semi-Gloss	15	●	⊜	◒	—
ColorPlace Our Best Interior Latex Semi-Gloss Enamel (Wal-Mart)	10	●	○	○	—

Ratings *Snow throwers*

& Recommendations

The tests behind the Ratings

The **overall score** covers both snow removal and convenience. In scoring single-stage models, we considered the fact that they aren't self-propelled and can't clear deep snow. **Clearing** reflects how quickly each machine could move snow. The two-stage machines were tested in 9 to 11 inches of dry snow and again in deeper snow; single-stage machines, in 4 to 5 inches of snow. **Throwing** reflects how high and how far each machine threw dry snow. **Surface cleaning** indicates how thoroughly each machine could remove snow in its path. We judged the **handling** of each machine as it was throwing snow. **Ease of use** covers starting, handle height, discharge-chute adjustment, and the like. **Price** is approximate retail.

Typical features for these models

• Electric start, powered by plugging into a wall outlet. • Handle that's 36 to 40 inches high. • Crank on the side to turn the discharge chute. • Chute deflector that must be adjusted by first loosening a knob or wing nut. **Most two-stage models:** • 4-stroke engine. • 1-gal. fuel tank. • Interlock between the drive and auger deadman controls for one-hand operation. • A release to depower one wheel, to make turning easier in light snow. • Adjustable, replaceable skid shoes and steel scrapers. • Fuel shutoff valve. **Most single-stage models:** • 2-stroke engine. • 1.2- to 1.5-qt. fuel tank. • Handle that can be folded without tools. • Replaceable plastic scraper.

Recommendations

The two-stage machines outperformed the single-stage models in snow-clearing and throwing. Any of the two-stage models would make a fine choice. Among them, the Toro 824 Power Shift, $1,350, was the best all-around snow thrower. The powerful Honda HS828K1TAS, $2,050, scored next highest, but it's very expensive and hard to handle. The MTD E640F, $770, offers the best combination of performance and value; we've judged it **A CR Best Buy.** The John Deere TRS21, $640, and the Honda HS621A, $740, were our top-scoring single-stage models. The John Deere is the better value, and **A CR Best Buy.**

See report, page 160. Last time rated in CONSUMER REPORTS: October 1997.

Overall Ratings

Legend: E (excellent) · VG (very good) · G (good) · F (fair) · P (poor)

Listed in order of overall score

Key no.	Brand and model	Price	Overall score (0–100; P F G VG E)	Clearing	Throwing	Surface cleaning	Handling	Ease of use
	TWO-STAGE MODELS							
1	**Toro** 824 Power Shift	$1,350		E	E	G	F	E
2	**Honda** HS828K1TAS	2,050		VG	E	VG	P	E
3	**MTD** E640F **A CR Best Buy**	770		E	VG	VG	G	VG
4	**Noma** Performance G2794010	920		VG	E	G	F	VG
5	**Yard-Man** E623D	750		G	VG	G	G	E
6	**Ariens** ST824DL	1,500		VG	VG	F	F	E
7	**Sears** Craftsman 247.88569	1,200		VG	VG	G	F	E
8	**Troy-Bilt** 42010	1,200		G	VG	G	G	VG
9	**Toro** 622 Power Throw	850		G	VG	P	G	G
10	**Simplicity** 860E	1,420		G	VG	VG	F	VG
11	**John Deere** 826D	1,240		G	VG	P	G	E
12	**Snapper** I5223	900		G	VG	G	G	G
13	**Sears** Craftsman 536.88612	750		G	VG	F	G	G
14	**Simplicity** 555M	960		G	VG	G	G	G
15	**MTD** 611D	600		G	VG	VG	G	G
	SINGLE-STAGE MODELS							
16	**John Deere** TRS21 **A CR Best Buy**	640		G	VG	E	E	G
17	**Honda** HS621A	640		G	VG	E	VG	F
18	**Toro** CCR3000GTS	750		G	G	E	VG	G
19	**Murray** Ultra G2145060	410		G	F	E	VG	VG
20	**MTD** 140	310		F	F	E	E	G
21	**Sears** Craftsman 536.88468	550		F	G	VG	VG	VG
22	**White** Snow Boss 50	500		F	F	VG	VG	VG
23	**Snapper** LE317R	420		F	F	G	E	VG
24	**Sears** Craftsman 536.88458	450		F	F	G	VG	VG

Details on the models

Performance in wet snow was judged on 6 to 7 in. of loose granular snow and on the same depth of freshly fallen wet and heavy packed snow.

Two-stage models

1 Toro 824 Power Shift $1,350

• 8 hp • 235 lb. • 24-in. swath • 4 forward speeds, 0.5 to 2.7 mph • 2 reverse speeds, 1.1 and 1.8 mph • 2-yr. warranty • 40x26x55 in.

Better than most in deep snow and clearing wet snow. Has a weight-forward setting to handle dense, compact snow. Chute deflector can be adjusted without loosening hardware. Partial guard helps keep hands out of the discharge chute. Electric start optional. **But:** Slightly noisier than most. **Recommendation:** Excellent overall. A good first choice if you need a big snow thrower.

2 Honda HS828K1TAS $2,050

• 8 hp • 211 lb. • 28-in. swath • Continuously adjustable speeds, from 0.3 to 2.1 mph forward and from 0.4 to 1.3 mph in reverse • 1.6-gal. gas tank with gauge • 2-yr. warranty • 41x28x59 in.

No other model could throw snow as far or match the smoothness of the hydrostatic transmission. Better than most in deep snow and clearing wet snow. Has weight-forward settings for dense, compact snow. Quiet. Moves on tracks instead of tires. Convenient lever controls chute deflector. **But:** Very hard to handle; nearly impossible to move when engine is off. The 35-in.-high handle is a bit low for tall users. **Similar model:** HS828K1TA, $1,900. **Recommendation:** Excellent performance, but unwieldy and expensive.

3 MTD E640F $770

• 8 hp • 194 lb. • 26-in. swath • 6 forward speeds, 0.7 to 3.2 mph • 2 reverse speeds, 1.1 and 1.4 mph • 2-yr. warranty, plus 90-day no-fault coverage • 43x27x53 in.

We found little to fault in this fine machine. **But:** Scraper isn't adjustable. **Similar model:** MTD Gold 31A-E640F-382, $800. **Recommendation:** Excellent performance, low price. **A CR Best Buy.**

4 Noma Performance G2794010 $920

• 9 hp • 217 lb. • 27-in. swath • 6 forward speeds, 0.9 to 2.7 mph • 2 reverse speeds, 0.9 and 1.1 mph • 2-yr. warranty • 48x29x58 in.

Cleared wet snow very well. Convenient lever controls chute deflector. **But:** Had trouble with deep snow. Slightly noisier than most. Deadman controls are stiff and relatively hard to hold down. Handle may be too high even for tall users. **Availability:** Discontinued. **Successor:** 627104X8, $950. **Recommendation:** Very good overall.

5 Yard-Man E623D $750

• 5.5 hp • 166 lb. • 22-in. swath • 6 forward speeds, 0.8 to 2.3 mph • 2 reverse speeds, 0.7 and 1.1 mph • 2-qt. gas tank • 2-yr. warranty; 90-day no-fault coverage • 43x23x53 in.

A small, moderately powered machine that gives away little in performance. Better than most in deep snow and clearing wet snow. Slightly quieter than most. Convenient lever controls chute deflector. **But:** Scraper isn't adjustable. **Recommendation:** Very good overall, and a very good value.

6 Ariens ST824DL $1,500

• 8 hp • 246 lb. • 24-in. swath • 6 forward speeds, 1 to 2.9 mph • 2 reverse speeds, 1.2 and 1.3 mph • 5-yr. warranty on parts, 2-yr. on labor • 41x26x60 in.

This very heavy machine cleared and threw snow well. Better than most in deep snow and clearing wet snow. Handling left something to be desired. Chute-turning crank conveniently mounted atop the console. Chute deflector can be adjusted without loosening hardware. Comes with wheel chains. Electric start optional. **Recommendation:** Very good, but expensive.

7 Sears Craftsman 247.88569 $1,200

• 9 hp • 210 lb. • 26-in. swath • 6 forward speeds, 0.4 to 1.8 mph • 2 reverse speeds, 0.7 and 1 mph • 2-yr. warranty • 44x27x53 in.

Performed better than most in deep snow. Has weight-forward settings for dense, compact snow. Moves on tracks instead of tires. Convenient lever controls the chute deflector. **But:** Hard to handle. Control-cable adjustment mechanism is hard to get at. No fuel-shutoff valve. Scraper isn't adjustable. **Availability:** Discontinued: **Recommendation:** Very good, but it takes muscle.

8 Troy-Bilt 42010 $1,200

• 8 hp • 270 lb. • 24-in. swath • 5 forward speeds, 0.8 to 2 mph • 2 reverse speeds, 0.1 and 0.7 mph • 7-yr. warranty • 41x25x61 in.

Better than most at clearing wet snow. Unusual features include a heated handle, an easily adjusted chute deflector, and an automatic differential to make turning easier, although it tended to lose traction in deep or icy snow. Included wheel chains may help improve traction in those conditions. Electric start optional. **But:** Auger often stayed engaged even though we released the handlebar controls, which poses a safety hazard; mechanical adjustment can remedy the problem. Console-mounted chute-turning crank didn't move very smoothly. Handle is a bit low for tall users. **Recommendation:** Very good performance, but some annoying and dangerous quirks.

9 Toro 622 Power Throw $850

• 6 hp • 158 lb. • 22-in. swath • 3 forward speeds, 0.8 to 1.9 mph • 1.2-mph reverse speed • 2-yr. warranty • 44x24x55 in.

Chute deflector can be adjusted without loosening hardware. Partial guard helps keep hands out of the discharge chute. Slightly quieter than others. Electric start optional. **But:** Deadman controls aren't interlocked for one-hand operation, and they're rather stiff and hard to hold down. Scraper isn't adjustable. **Recommendation:** Very good overall.

10 Simplicity 860E $1,420

• 8 hp • 253 lb. • 24-in. swath • 5 forward speeds, 0.3 to 2.3 mph • 2 reverse speeds, 1 and 1.5 mph • 2-yr. warranty • 42x26x56 in.

Cleared wet snow very well. Chute-turning crank conveniently mounted atop the console. Partial guard helps keep hands out of the discharge chute. Comes with wheel chains. **But:** Deadman controls are rather stiff and hard to hold down. Slightly noisier than most. **Recommendation:** Very good overall.

11 John Deere 826D $1,240

• 8 hp • 192 lb. • 26-in. swath • 6 forward speeds, 0.6 to 2 mph • 2 reverse speeds, 0.5 and 0.8 mph • 2-yr. warranty • 42x28x51 in.

Performed better than most in deep snow. Convenient console-mounted lever controls chute deflector. **But:** Deadman controls aren't interlocked for one-hand operation. No provision to free a drive wheel for easier turning. Chute-turning crank sticks out from the back and can get in your way. Scraper isn't adjustable. **Recommendation:** Very good overall.

12 Snapper I5223 $900

• 5 hp • 139 lb. • 22-in. swath • 4 forward speeds, 0.8 to 2.1 mph • 0.7-mph reverse speed • 2-qt. gas tank • 2-yr. warranty • 44x24x52 in.

Handle height can be adjusted somewhat. Engine is slightly quieter than most. Comes with wheel chains. **But:** Deadman controls aren't interlocked for one-hand operation. No provision to free a drive wheel for easier turning. Speed-control lever is low and hard to reach. Scraper isn't adjustable. **Availability:** Only through 12/98. **Successor:** I55223, $900. **Recommendation:** Very good overall.

13 Sears Craftsman 536.88612 $750

• 5 hp • 142 lb. • 22-in. swath • 6 forward speeds, 0.7 to 2.7 mph • 2 reverse speeds, 1.1 and 1.9 mph • 2-qt. gas tank • 2-yr. warranty • 45x23x47 in.

Slightly quieter than most. **But:** Performance in deep snow was worse than most. Deadman controls aren't interlocked, but inconvenient one-hand operation is still possible. Speed-control lever is low and hard to reach. No fuel-shutoff valve. **Availability:** Discontinued. **Successor:** 88614, $750. **Recommendation:** Very good overall, but there are better choices.

14 Simplicity 555M $960

• 5 hp • 173 lb. • 22-in. swath • 5 forward speeds, 0.6 to 2.5 mph • 2 reverse speeds, 1.1 and 1.6 mph • 2-qt. gas tank • 2-yr. warranty • 42x25x49 in.

Chute-turning crank conveniently mounted atop the console. Partial guard helps keep hands out of the discharge chute. Slightly quieter than others. Comes with wheel chains. Electric start optional. **But:** Performance in deep snow was worse than most. Deadman controls aren't interlocked for one-hand operation, and they're rather stiff and hard to hold down. Scraper isn't adjustable. **Recommendation:** Good, but there are better choices.

15 MTD 611D $600

• 5 hp • 147 lb. • 22-in. swath • 5 forward speeds, 0.7 to 2.4 mph • 2 reverse speeds, 0.7 and 1.1 mph • 2-qt. gas tank • 2-yr. warranty, plus 90-day no-fault coverage • 43x24x52 in.
Slightly quieter than most. **But:** Performance in deep snow was worse than most. Deadman controls aren't interlocked for one-hand operation. Speed-control lever is low and hard to reach. Scraper isn't adjustable. **Recommendation:** Good, but there are better choices.

Single-stage models

16 John Deere TRS21 $640

• 5 hp • 83 lb. • 21-in. swath • 2-yr. warranty • 37x22x46 in.
Auger propels this model briskly. Very easy to handle, threw snow quite far. **But:** Slightly noisier than most. Chute-turning crank didn't turn smoothly. Lacks fuel-shutoff valve. **Similar model:** TRS21 without electric start, $540. **Recommendation:** Good overall. **A CR Best Buy.**

17 Honda HS621A $640

• 5.5 hp • 91 lb. • 20-in. swath • 2-yr. warranty • 38x23x47 in.
Threw snow farthest of all single-stage units. Has four-stroke engine. Auger propels the machine briskly. Slightly quieter than most. Adjustable scraper. Chute deflector can be adjusted without loosening hardware. Has fuel-shutoff valve. Electric start optional. **But:** Chute-turning crank became stiff during use. Folding the handle requires tools. **Similar model:** HS621AS, $830. **Recommendation:** Good but expensive.

18 Toro CCR3000GTS $750

• 5 hp • 75 lb. • 20-in. swath • 2-yr. warranty • 41x21x42 in.
Auger propels this machine briskly. Chute deflector can be adjusted without loosening hardware. **But:** Extremely stiff chute-turning crank (even when we installed a new gear). Folding the handle requires tools. **Recommendation:** Good, but expensive.

19 Murray Ultra G2145060 $410

• 4.5 hp • 65 lb. • 21-in. swath • 2-yr. warranty • 37x22x39 in.
A notch below the top single-stage machines. Auger propels machine weakly. Slightly noisier than others. Hard to access spark plug. **Availability:** Discontinued. **Successor:** 621450X4, $430. **Recommendation:** Fair.

20 MTD 140 $310

• 3 hp • 54 lb. • 21-in. swath • 1-qt. gas tank • 2-yr. warranty plus 90-day no-fault coverage • 35x21x41 in.
Adjustable and reversible scraper. Electric start optional. **But:** Engine is slightly noisier than most. Handle a bit low for tall users. Auger control-cable adjuster is hard to get at. **Similar model:** MTD Gold 31A-142-382, $320. **Recommendation:** Fair overall.

21 Sears Craftsman 536.88468 $550

• 5 hp • 65 lb. • 21-in. swath • 1.6-qt. gas tank • 2-yr. warranty • 39x22x42 in.
Hard to access spark plug. **Availability:** Discontinued. **Successor:** 88521, $450. **Recommendation:** Fair overall.

22 White Snow Boss 50 $500

• 5 hp • 73 lb. • 20-in. swath • 2-yr. warranty • 40x22x42 in.
Chute deflector can be adjusted without loosening hardware. Handle can be adjusted to three positions. Engine slightly quieter than most. Electric start optional. **But:** Auger provides weak propulsion. Chute-turning crank didn't turn very smoothly. Cover must be unscrewed to adjust control cables. **Recommendation:** Fair overall.

23 Snapper LE317R $420

• 3 hp • 49 lb. • 17-in. swath • 2-yr. warranty • 35x19x44 in.
Cleared wet snow poorly. Auger provides weak propulsion. Chute-turning crank inconveniently mounted on the chute itself. Handle is a bit low for tall users. Slightly noisier than others. Electric start optional. **Recommendation:** Fair overall.

24 Sears Craftsman 536.88458 $450

• 3 hp • 52 lb. • 21-in. swath • 1-qt. gas tank • 1-yr. warranty • 35x22x39 in.
Cleared wet snow poorly; nearly stalled. Handle is a bit low for tall users. Hard to access spark plug. **Availability:** Discontinued. **Recommendation:** Fair overall. There are better choices.

Ratings *String trimmers*
& Recommendations

The tests behind the Ratings

Overall score is based mainly on cutting weeds, trimming near a wall, edging, and handling. **Cut** gauges cutting power in overgrown weeds. **Trim** indicates how well the machines do when used next to a wall—how neatly they cut and how easy they are to control. **Edge** scores reflect the machines' ability to cut a neat line along the lawn's border with a road. **Handling** assesses responsiveness and balance. **Ease of use** includes ease of starting the engine and feeding out more string, handle comfort, and the location of controls. **Price** is the approximate retail for the trimmer, and typically includes one spool of string. A new spool costs less than $10.

Typical features for these models

• "Bump feed" string advance. • Curved shaft. • Spool that's at least fairly easy to change. • 2-yr. warranty. **Most gasoline-powered models:** • 2-stroke 18- to 31-cc. engine that uses gas-oil mix for fuel and produces more noise than most electric models. • Engine at top of shaft, an aid to balance. • Clutch; string spins only when you rev the engine. • Translucent fuel tank. • 2 cutting strings that create a 15- to 18-inch swath. **Most corded models:** • 1.8- to 5.2-amp motor at the bottom of the shaft, a design that makes them hard to balance. • 1 cutting string that creates an 8- to 15-inch swath. **Battery-powered models:** • 12-volt rechargeable battery that runs about 15 to 30 minutes, takes 24 hours to recharge, lasts about 3 to 5 years, and costs about $25 to $40 to replace. • 1 cutting string that creates a 9- to 10-inch swath.

Recommendations

Any of the top six gas-powered models should satisfy a demanding user. Of those six, the best values—both **CR Best Buys**—are the Ryobi 725r TrimmerPlus, $100, and the Stihl FS-36, $140. If your demands or funds are more modest, consider the corded Ryobi 132r TrimmerPlus or Toro 51450, $65 each. Battery-powered trimmers aren't powerful enough for any but the lightest work: the Toro 51559, $105, and Ryobi 150r, $95, are fairly easy to handle.

See report, page 161. Last time rated in CONSUMER REPORTS: May 1998.

Overall Ratings

E = Excellent, VG = Very good, G = Good, F = Fair, P = Poor

Listed in order of overall score

Key no.	Brand and model	Price	Cut	Trim	Edge	Handling	Ease of use
	GASOLINE MODELS						
1	**Stihl** FS-75	$200	E	E	E	E	VG
2	**Echo** GT-2000SB	180	E	VG	E	E	G
3	**Echo** SRM-2100	230	E	VG	E	E	E
4	**Ryobi** 725r TrimmerPlus **A CR Best Buy**	100	E	E	VG	E	G
5	**Stihl** FS-36 **A CR Best Buy**	140	E	E	E	E	VG
6	**Husqvarna** Mondo Max	170	E	VG	E	E	VG
7	**Husqvarna** 225L E-Tech	330	E	VG	VG	E	E
8	**Ryobi** 975r TrimmerPlus	195	VG	VG	E	G	VG
9	**Ryobi** 790r TrimmerPlus	160	VG	VG	VG	G	G
10	**Toro** 51920	200	VG	VG	G	G	G
11	**Sears Craftsman** Brushwacker 79501	170	VG	VG	G	G	G
12	**Toro** 51903	100	E	E	VG	VG	F
13	**Homelite** Easy Reach 20680	110	E	VG	VG	VG	F
14	**Sears Craftsman** Weedwacker 79856	100	G	VG	G	E	G
15	**Sears Craftsman** Weedwacker 79852	80	G	VG	G	E	G
16	**Weed Eater** FeatherLite SST	90	G	VG	G	E	G
17	**Weed Eater** FeatherLite	80	G	VG	G	E	G
18	**Homelite** TrimLite 20677	70	VG	VG	VG	VG	G
19	**McCulloch** MAC 2816	70	VG	VG	VG	VG	G
	CORDED MODELS						
20	**Ryobi** 132r TrimmerPlus	65	G	E	VG	E	G
21	**Toro** 51450	65	G	E	VG	E	G
22	**Sears Craftsman** Weedwacker 79914	50	G	VG	G	G	VG
23	**Weed Eater** Twist 'N Edge TE40	40	G	G	G	G	VG
24	**Weed Eater** Snap-N-Go SG14	40	G	G	VG	G	VG
25	**Weed Eater** XT110	40	F	VG	G	G	VG
26	**Black & Decker** GH400	50	F	G	G	G	E
27	**Black & Decker** ST3000	30	F	G	G	F	VG

Ratings continued

Key no.	Brand and model	Price	Overall score (0–100; P F G VG E)	Cut	Trim	Edge	Handling	Ease of use
	CORDED MODELS *continued*							
28	**Toro** 51231	$25		●	○	●	◒	○
29	**Weed Eater** ElectraLite EL8	20		◒	●	●	◒	○
30	**Black & Decker** ST1000	20		●	●	●	◒	○
	BATTERY-POWERED MODELS							
31	**Toro** 51559	105		◒	◒	●	◓	○
32	**Ryobi** 150r	95		◒	◒	●	○	○
33	**Weed Eater** HandyStik	70		○	●	●	◒	○

Details on the models

Weight is rounded to the nearest pound and includes a full spool of string (and, for gas models, a full fuel tank).

Gasoline models

1 Stihl FS-75 $200

• 11 lb. String resists breaking. **But:** Spool tricky to install. Lifetime warranty on drive shaft.

2 Echo GT-2000SB $180

• 11 lb. Head rotates for edging. String resists breaking. Split shaft. Lifetime warranty on drive shaft. **Similar model:** GT-2000, $150.

3 Echo SRM-2100 $230

• 12 lb. Straight shaft. Comfortable handles. Lifetime warranty on drive shaft. **Similar model:** SRM-2100SB, $260.

4 Ryobi 725r Trimmer Plus $100

• 13 lb. Head rotates for edging. Split shaft. **But:** Choke lever hard to move. **A CR Best Buy.**

5 Stihl FS-36 $140

• 12 lb. Comfortable handles. **But:** Spool tricky to install. Choke control confusing. Opaque fuel tank. **A CR Best Buy.**

6 Husqvarna Mondo Max $170

• 14 lb. Straight shaft. **But:** Spool tricky to install.

7 Husqvarna 225L E-Tech $330

• 16 lb. Straight shaft. Engine consistently started quickly. Mfr. claims engine is low-emission. Shoulder strap. **But:** Opaque fuel tank. **Similar model:** 225RS E-Tech, $350.

8 Ryobi 975r TrimmerPlus $195

• 17 lb. Head rotates for edging. 4-stroke engine. Straight, split shaft. Shoulder strap.

9 Ryobi 790r TrimmerPlus $160

• 14 lb. Head rotates for edging. Straight, split shaft. Shoulder strap. Comes with metal blade for clearing brush. But: Choke lever hard to move. More vibrations than most.

10 Toro 51920 $200

• 16 lb. 4-stroke engine. Shoulder strap. **But:** Taller users have to stoop.

11 Sears Craftsman Brushwacker 79501 $170

• 16 lb. Straight shaft. Shoulder strap. Comes with metal blade for clearing brush. 1-yr. warranty. **But:** Difficult to control while edging. Choke lever hard to move. More vibration than most. **Availability:** Discontinued but still available.

12 Toro 51903 $100

• 12 lb. No clutch. Taller users have to stoop. Choke lever hard to move. More vibration than most.

13 Homelite Easy Reach 20680 $110

• 12 lb. Straight shaft. **But:** No clutch. Uses precut strings; inconvenient for edging. **Similar model:** Versa Tool, $130.

14 Sears Craftsman Weedwacker 79856 $100

• 9 lb. Spool very easy to change. Straight shaft. 1-yr. warranty. **But:** No clutch. Only 1 cutting string. **Availability:** Discontinued.

15 Sears Craftsman Weedwacker 79852 $80

• 8 lb. Spool very easy to change. 1-yr. warranty. **But:** No clutch. Taller users have to stoop. Only 1 cutting string. **Availability:** Discontinued.

16 Weed Eater FeatherLite SST $90

• 9 lb. Spool very easy to change. Straight shaft. **But:** No clutch. Only 1 cutting string.

17 Weed Eater FeatherLite $80

• 8 lb. Spool very easy to change. **But:** No clutch. Taller users have to stoop. Only 1 cutting string.

18 Homelite TrimLite 20677 $70

• 11 lb. No clutch. Taller users have to stoop. Spool tricky to install.

19 McCulloch MAC 2816 $70

• 13 lb. String resists breaking. **But:** No clutch. Taller users have to stoop. Opaque fuel tank. **Availability:** Discontinued.

Corded models

20 Ryobi 132r Trimmer Plus $65

• 10 lb. Head rotates for edging. String resists breaking. Better balance than other electrics. Split shaft. 2 cutting strings.

21 Toro 51450 $65

• 8 lb. Better balance than other electrics. 2 cutting strings. **But:** Taller users have to stoop.

22 Sears Craftsman Weedwacker 79914 $50

• 5 lb. Head rotates for edging. Spool very easy to change. String resists breaking. 1-yr. warranty. **But:** Difficult to control while edging.

23 Weed Eater Twist 'N Edge TE40 $40

• 5 lb. Head rotates for edging. String resists breaking. Spool very easy to change. **But:** Difficult to control while edging. Taller users have to stoop.

24 Weed Eater Snap-N-Go SG14 $40

• 5 lb. Spool very easy to change. **But:** Taller users have to stoop.

25 Weed Eater XT110 $40

• 5 lb. Head rotates for edging. Spool very easy to change. String resists breaking.

26 Black & Decker GH400 $50

• 5 lb. Head rotates for edging. Automatic string feed. String resists breaking. **But:** Difficult to control while edging.

27 Black & Decker ST3000 $30

• 5 lb. String resists breaking. **But:** Taller users have to stoop.

28 Toro 51231 $25

• 4 lb. String resists breaking. **But:** Taller users have to stoop.

29 Weed Eater ElectraLite EL8 $20

• 4 lb. Spool very easy to change. String resists breaking. **But:** Taller users have to stoop.

30 Black & Decker ST1000 $20

• 4 lb. String resists breaking. **But:** Taller users have to stoop.

Battery-powered models

31 Toro 51559 $105

• 11 lb. String resists breaking. Battery runs about 30 min.

32 Ryobi 150r $95

• 11 lb. String resists breaking. Battery runs about 30 min.

33 Weed Eater HandyStik $70

• 10 lb. Spool very easy to change. **But:** Battery runs only about 15 min. Taller users have to stoop. On/off switch hard to operate. **Availability:** Discontinued but still available.

Ratings *Low-flush toilets*
& Recommendations

The tests behind the Ratings

Overall score summarizes performance in our tests. For **waste** removal, **solid** shows how well the toilet flushed away sponges, latex cylinders, and baby wipes—objects we used in the lab to simulate solid waste. **Liquid** shows the toilet's ability to flush liquids or finely dispersed solids. **Washdown** shows how well the toilet uses water to clean the sides of the bowl with each flush. **Soiling/odor** reflects the toilet's propensity to have odors linger, based on the surface area that's not covered by water. **Noise** is a measure of the loudest point of each flush. **Price** is the estimated average, based on a survey taken in early 1998.

Recommendations

The Gerber Ultra Flush, $270, **A CR Best Buy**, represents the best value and highest performance. It did an outstanding job of clearing waste and cleaning the bowl with each flush. Its biggest drawback is a noisy flush. The quieter Kohler Trocadero performed as well, but it costs a whopping $940. If you can't tolerate a noisy toilet, consider one of the higher-rated gravity-flush models like the Eljer Berkeley, $420, or the Mansfield Elderly, $150.

See report, page 163. Last time rated in CONSUMER REPORTS: May 1998.

Overall Ratings

E VG G F P

Listed in order of overall score

Key no.	Brand and model	Price	Overall score (0–100; P F G VG E)	Waste: SOLID	Waste: LIQUID	Washdown	Soiling/odor	Noise
	PRESSURE-ASSISTED MODELS							
1	**Gerber** Ultra Flush 21-302 **A CR Best Buy**	$270		E	E	VG	VG	F
2	**Crane** Economiser 3-804	230		VG	E	E	VG	F
3	**American Standard** Fontaine EL PA 2042.417	650		G	E	VG	VG	G
	GRAVITY-FLUSH MODELS							
4	**Eljer** Berkeley 081-1595	420		E	VG	VG	F	E
5	**Eljer** Patriot 091-1125	120		F	E	VG	F	VG
6	**American Standard** Cadet II EL 2174.139	145		F	G	E	F	VG
7	**Mansfield** Elderly 137-160	150		G	G	VG	F	E
8	**Gerber** New Aqua Saver 21-702	86		F	E	VG	F	G
9	**Universal-Rundle** Nostalgia 4065	185		F	E	G	G	E

Key no.	Brand and model	Price	Overall score (0–100; P F G VG E)	Waste: SOLID	Waste: LIQUID	Washdown	Soiling/odor	Noise
	GRAVITY-FLUSH MODELS							
10	**Kohler** Wellworth K-3422	$120		●	⊖	⊖	○	⊖
11	**Mansfield** Alto 130-160	75		●	⊖	○	◒	⊖
	PUMP-ASSISTED MODEL							
12	**Kohler** Trocadero Powerlite K-3437	940		⊖	⊖	⊖	⊖	⊖
	VACUUM-ASSISTED MODEL							
13	**Briggs** Vacuity 4200	225		⊖	●	⊖	○	⊖

Details on the models

Pressure-assisted models

1 Gerber Ultra Flush 21-302 $270

• 2-piece with round bowl • 27x20x28 in. Excellent solid- and liquid-waste removal. Has 5-yr. warranty on bowl, 2-yr. on pressure-assist mechanism. **But:** Dirt, hard water may clog rim outlets. Can splash when flushed. Noisy. **Recommendation:** Excellent despite some shortcomings. **A CR Best Buy**.

2 Crane Economiser 3-804 $230

• 2-piece with elongated bowl • 27x19x31 in. Has 5-yr. warranty on pressure-flush system and pressure-assist components, 2-yr. on bowl. **But:** Noisy. May splash when flushed. **Recommendation:** Very good overall—but some shortcomings.

3 American Standard Fontaine EL PA 2042.417 $650

• 1-piece with elongated bowl • 24x20x31 in. Set included. Has 1-yr. warranty on bowl, 2-yr. on pressure-assist mechanism. **But:** Flush button on top of tank difficult to use. **Recommendation:** Very good but pricey.

Gravity-flush models

4 Eljer Berkeley 081-1595 $420

• 1-piece with elongated bowl • 25x20x29 in. Best waste removal among gravity-flush models. Quiet. Seat included. Has 2-yr. warranty. **Recommendation:** Very good.

5 Eljer Patriot 091-1125 $120

• 2-piece with elongated bowl • 28x21x28 in. Has instructions for adjusting flush volume. Has 2-yr. warranty. **But:** Two samples required adjustments to fill to correct water level. **Similar models:** 091-1127, $180; 091-1135, $185. **Recommendation:** Good performance at a moderate price.

6 American Standard Cadet II EL 2174.139 $145

• 2-piece with elongated bowl • 29x19x30 in. Has instructions for adjusting flush volume. Has 1-yr. warranty. **But:** Takes special flapper valve; may use more water with standard valve. **Availability:** Discontinued. **Recommendation:** Good.

7 Mansfield Elderly 137-160 $150

• 2-piece with elongated bowl • 31x20x29 in. Taller than most; good for elderly and disabled people. Quiet. Has 5-yr. warranty. **But:** Requires special flapper valve; can't use standard parts. **Recommendation:** Good.

8 Gerber New Aqua Saver 21-702 $86

• 2-piece with round bowl • 29x20x27 in. Comes with instructions for adjusting flush volume. Has 2-yr. warranty on flush system, 5-yr. on bowl. **But:** Small water surface releases more odor. **Recommendation:** Good performance at a good price.

9 Universal-Rundle Nostalgia 4065 $185

• 2-piece with round bowl • 28x18x30 in.
Quiet. Has instructions for adjusting flush volume. Has 1-yr. warranty. **Recommendation:** Good, but there are better choices.

10 Kohler Wellworth K-3422 $120

• 2-piece with elongated bowl • 28x20x30 in.
Has instructions for adjusting flush volume. Has 1-yr. warranty. **But:** Poor solid-waste removal. Requires special flapper valve; can't use standard parts. **Similar models:** K-3422-RA, $150; K-3422-X, $255. **Recommendation:** There are better choices.

11 Mansfield Alto 130-160 $75

• 2-piece with round bowl • 28x20x26 in.
Has instructions for adjusting flush volume. Has 5-yr. warranty. **But:** Poor solid-waste removal. Takes special flapper valve; can't use standard parts. **Recommendation:** There are better choices.

Pump-assisted model

12 Kohler Trocadero Powerlite K-3437 $940

•1-piece with round bowl • 21x15x30 in.
Excellent solid- and liquid-waste removal. Seat included. Has 1-yr. warranty. **But:** Doesn't work if power goes out. Dirt, hard water may clog rim outlets. Electric water pump may require an electrician for installation. White only. **Recommendation:** Excellent but very pricey.

Vacuum-flush model

13 Briggs Vacuity 4200 $225

• 2-piece with elongated bowl • 30x19x29 in.
Quiet. Comes with instructions for adjusting flush volume. Has 5-yr. warranty. **But:** Removes liquid waste poorly; needs more than one flush. **Recommendation:** Very good overall.

Ratings *Vacuum cleaners*

& Recommendations

The tests behind the Ratings

Overall score is based mainly on results of our cleaning and convenience tests. **Cleaning** includes how well a machine cleans medium-pile **carpeting** and bare **floors. Ease of use** includes how easy it is to push a vacuum cleaner, maneuver it under a bed, change tools, and dispose of dirt. **Upkeep** is a judgment of how easy it is to perform simple fix-it jobs such as replacing a belt, brush, or headlamp bulb. We also tested each machine for particle **emissions;** people with asthma or allergies should choose a model with a high score for this attribute. **Price** is approximate retail.

Typical features for these models

• Onboard tools. • 20- to 30-foot power cord. • Carrying handle. • Two extension wands for reaching high places. • Manual rug-pile-height adjustment. **Uprights:** • Flexible hose attachment that's four to eight feet long. • Power nozzle with a rotating brush that can't be turned off. • Power cord with wraparound storage. **Canisters:** • Attachment for bare floors. • Detachable power nozzle with a rotating brush that can be turned off. • Retractable power cord. • Flexible hose that's 4 to 8 feet long. • Bag-change indicator. • Covered tools. • Suction control.• Motor-overload protection. • Ability to clean easily under furniture.

Recommendations

Every vacuum cleaner has its own peculiarities, as the Details on the models spell out. The canisters we tested are all very good. Uprights showed a greater range of performance. The Hoover Dirt Finder U6331-930, $340; Panasonic New Generation MC-V7395, $250, or Hoover WindTunnel Deluxe U5465-900, $280, are the best uprights under $350.

See report, page 165. Last time rated in CONSUMER REPORTS: March 1998.

Overall Ratings

E ⊜ VG ⊖ G ○ F ◒ P ●

Listed in order of overall score

Key no.	Brand and model	Price	Overall score 0–100 (P F G VG E)	Cleaning CARPET/ FLOORS	Ease of use	Up-keep	Emissions
	UPRIGHT MODELS						
1	**Hoover** Dirt Finder U6331-930	$340		⊜/⊖	⊖	⊜	⊜
2	**Kirby** G5	1,500		⊖/⊜	⊖	○	⊜

Ratings continued

Key no.	Brand and model	Price	Overall score (0–100; P F G VG E)	Cleaning CARPET/FLOORS	Ease of use	Up-keep	Emissions
	UPRIGHT MODELS *continued*						
3	**Panasonic** New Generation MC-V7395	$250		⊖/⊜	○	◒	⊜
4	**Kenmore** (Sears) 38512	230		○/⊜	⊖	◒	⊜
5	**Hoover** WindTunnel Deluxe U5465-900	280		⊜/⊖	⊖	◒	⊜
6	**Hoover** Encore Supreme U4271-930	90		⊖/⊖	○	⊖	⊜
7	**Electrolux** Epic 3500SR	650		○/⊜	⊖	[1]	⊖
8	**Sharp** EC-12TWT4	150		⊖/○	⊖	⊜	⊜
9	**Hoover** Dimension Supreme U5227-930	180		⊖/⊜	○	⊖	⊜
10	**Panasonic** Power Wave MC-V5710	100		⊖/⊖	⊖	○	⊖
11	**Fantom** Fury F10052	250		○/⊜	○	○	⊜
12	**Eureka** Bravo II The Boss Plus 7640BT	95		○/⊜	○	⊜	○
13	**Kenmore** (Sears) 37413	150		◒/⊜	⊖	⊜	⊖
14	**Sharp** EC-T4770	240		⊖/⊖	⊖	◒	⊜
15	**Eureka** Excalibur 6426AT	190		◒/⊜	○	⊜	⊖
16	**Sanyo** SCA111	250		◒/⊖	⊖	⊜	⊖
17	**Oreck** XL9200	340		○/⊜	○	○	⊖
18	**Windsor** Sensation SX2	390		◒/⊖	⊖	◒	⊖
19	**Bissell** Micro-Lock 35112	100		⊜/⊖	○	⊜	◒
	CANISTER MODELS						
20	**Miele** White Pearl S434i	800		○/⊜	⊖	[1]	⊜
21	**Electrolux** Epic 8000	900		○/⊜	⊖	[1]	⊖
22	**Eureka** Excalibur 6978A	500		⊖/⊜	⊖	◒	⊜
23	**Kenmore** (Sears) 27412	280		⊜/⊜	⊖	●	⊖
24	**Hoover** Powermax S3611	300		⊜/⊜	⊖	◒	◒

[1] *Manufacturer recommends against do-it-yourself maintenance.*

Details on the models

Weight is rounded to the nearest pound.

Upright models

1 Hoover Dirt Finder U6331-930 $340

Weight: 22 lb. Better than most on carpeting. A self-propeller switch makes it easy to push. Has a bag-change indicator, an extra-long cord, and on-board covered tools. The brush and agitator belt are easy to replace on your own if they break. 1-yr. warranty. **But:** Has only one extension wand. **Similar models:** U6311-930, $240; U6319-930, $300;

U6321-930, $300; U6323-930, $280; U6335-930, $350. **Availability:** Only through 12/98. **Recommendation:** A very good performer from one of the more reliable brands.

2 **Kirby G5** $1,500

Weight: 24 lb. One panelist called this the "Cadillac of vacuums." It's heavy and bulky, but a self-propeller option makes it easy to push. The dirtbag holds more than most, but changing it is somewhat difficult. Has suction control and a bare-floor attachment. The rotating brush can be turned off. Stronger hose suction than most. Better than most at edge-cleaning. 3-yr. warranty. **But:** No onboard tools, and changing tools is harder than most. Has less reach under furniture than most. **Availability:** Only through 12/98. **Recommendation:** A very good performer, but at a hefty price.

3 **Panasonic New Generation MC-V7395** $250

Weight: 17 lb. Quieter than most. The rotating brush can be turned off. The hose is easy to maneuver. Rug-pile-height adjustment is automatic. Has an extra-long crevice tool. 1-yr. limited warranty. **But:** The dirtbag holds less than most. **Recommendation:** A very good performer.

4 **Kenmore (Sears) 38512** $230

Weight: 19 lb. Quieter than most. The rotating brush can be turned off. Has suction control and an extra-long crevice tool. The easy-to-maneuver hose has stronger suction than most. 1-yr. limited warranty. **Similar model:** 38812, $230. **Availability:** Only through 12/98. **Recommendation:** A very good performer.

5 **Hoover WindTunnel Deluxe U5465-900** $280

Weight: 18 lb. Better than most on carpeting and at edge-cleaning. Has a bag-change indicator, an extra-long cord, and onboard covered tools. 1-yr. warranty. **But:** Rug-pile-height adjustment is difficult. **Similar model:** U5465-960, $300. **Availability:** Only through 12/98. **Recommendation:** A very good performer from one of the more reliable brands.

6 **Hoover Encore Supreme U4271-930** $90

Weight: 13 lb. 1-yr. warranty. **But:** Noisier than most. Changing the dirtbag is somewhat difficult. A short hose offers less flexibility. **Similar models:** U4293-930, $95; U4295-930, $100. **Availability:** Only through 12/98. **Recommendation:** A very good performer that's light, inexpensive, and from one of the more reliable brands.

7 **Electrolux Epic 3500SR** $650

Weight: 17 lb. Excellent design, according to our consultant. One of the few uprights that reaches easily under a bed. The dirtbag minimizes spillage when changed. Has suction control, motor-overload protection, a bag-change indicator, and a small power nozzle for stairs. The rotating brush can be turned off. 5-yr. warranty. **But:** No onboard tools. The dirtbag holds less than most. **Recommendation:** A very good performer from one of the more reliable brands, but expensive.

8 **Sharp EC-12TWT4** $150

Weight: 16 lb. Quieter than most. No tools needed to change the belt or brush. Has an extra-long crevice tool. Rug-pile-height adjustment is automatic. 1-yr. limited warranty. **But:** A short hose offers less flexibility, and the unit is unsteady when you clean high surfaces. **Recommendation:** A very good performer, and a good price.

9 **Hoover Dimension Supreme U5227-930** $180

Weight: 17 lb. Has a bag-change indicator and onboard covered tools. A long hose offers more flexibility. 1-yr. warranty. **But:** Weaker hose suction than most. Has only one extension wand. The dirtbag holds less than most. **Similar models:** U5223-930, $180; U5231-930, $200. **Availability:** Only through 12/98. **Recommendation:** A very good performer from one of the more reliable brands, but (6) is a better buy.

10 **Panasonic Power Wave MC-V5710** $100

Weight: 15 lb. Has an extra-long crevice tool. Rug-pile-height adjustment is automatic. 1-yr. limited warranty. **But:** A short hose offers less flexibility. No upholstery tool. Has only one extension wand. **Recommendation:** A very good performer and a very good price.

11 Fantom Fury F10052 $250

Weight: 18 lb. Has motor-overload protection and a bare-floor attachment. Tool-changing is particularly easy. 2-yr. limited warranty. **But:** Dirt collects in a plastic dust cup rather than a disposable bag—easy to install and remove, but messy. Has only one extension wand. **Similar model:** F10051, $245. **Availability:** Only through 9/98. **Recommendation:** A very good performer, but handling the dust cup adds to the chore.

12 Eureka Bravo II The Boss Plus 7640BT $95

Weight: 13 lb. Easier to carry and better at edge-cleaning than most. No tools needed to change the belt or brush. 1-yr. limited warranty. **But:** Noisier than most. Hose is stiffer than most. Changing the dirtbag is somewhat difficult. No headlamp. **Availability:** Discontinued. **Successor:** 7642AT, $95. **Recommendation:** A very good performer and a very good price.

13 Kenmore (Sears) 37413 $150

Weight: 16 lb. Hose is longer and easier to maneuver than most. Has an extra-long crevice tool. No tools needed to change the belt, brush, or bulb. Tool-changing is particularly easy. 1-yr. warranty. **But:** No carrying handle. **Availability:** Discontinued. **Recommendation:** A very good performer and a very good price.

14 Sharp EC-T4770 $240

Weight: 18 lb. Quieter than most. The rotating brush can be turned off. Has suction control, a bag-change indicator, and an extra-long crevice tool. Rug-pile-height adjustment is automatic. 1-yr. limited warranty. **But:** Has less reach under furniture than most. **Similar model:** EC-T4765, $230. **Availability:** Only through 12/98. **Recommendation:** A very good performer, but (8) is a better buy.

15 Eureka Excalibur 6426AT $190

Weight: 22 lb. The rotating brush can be turned off. Has suction control, a bag-change indicator, and an easy-to-maneuver hose. No tools needed to change the belt or brush. 1-yr. limited warranty. **But:** Has only one extension wand. The dirtbag holds less than most. **Availability:** Discontinued. **Successor:** 6426BT, $210. **Recommendation:** A very good performer.

16 Sanyo SCA111 $250

Weight: 16 lb. No tools needed to change the belt, brush, or bulb. Has an extra-long crevice tool. Rug-pile-height adjustment is automatic. 1-yr. limited warranty. **But:** A short hose offers less flexibility. **Availability:** Only through 12/98. **Similar model:** SC-A113. **Recommendation:** A very good performer.

17 Oreck XL9200 $340

Weight: 9 lb. Rug-pile-height adjustment is automatic. 3-yr. warranty. **But:** No attachments. Noisier than most. The dirtbag holds less than most, and changing it is somewhat difficult. **Recommendation:** A very good performer; lightweight, but pricey considering its limitations.

18 Windsor Sensation SX2 $390

Weight: 18 lb. Excellent design, according to our consultant. One of the few uprights that reaches easily under a bed. Quietest vac tested. Has motor-overload protection, a bag-change indicator, and an extra-long cord. Rug-pile-height adjustment is automatic. 3-yr. warranty. **But:** A short hose offers less flexibility. Hose suction is weaker than most. The dirtbag holds less than most. No headlamp. Has only one extension wand. **Similar models:** Kenmore Professional 31012, $350; Kenmore Professional 31015, $400. **Recommendation:** A very good performer, but pricier than some that do better.

19 Bissell Micro-Lock 35112 $100

Weight: 15 lb. No tools needed to change the belt or brush. A long hose offers more flexibility. 1-yr. warranty. **But:** Noisier than most. Changing the dirtbag is somewhat difficult. Weaker hose suction than most. Has only one extension wand. **Recommendation:** A good performer.

Canister models

20 Miele White Pearl S434i $800

Weight: 27 lb. Quieter than most. Has a radiator brush, a bag-change indicator, and a telescoping extension wand. 1-yr. limited warranty. **But:** The extension wand is heavy for cleaning high surfaces. No headlamp. **Availability:** Only through 12/98. **Recommendation:** A very good performer, but expensive.

21 Electrolux Epic 8000 $900

Weight: 25 lb. Excellent design, according to our consultant. Tool-changing is particularly easy. The dirtbag minimizes spillage when changed. Has an extra-long crevice tool and a small power nozzle for stairs. 5-yr. warranty. **But:** The extension wand doesn't lock in place and is heavy for cleaning high surfaces. Weaker hose suction than most. The dirtbag holds less than most. **Recommendation:** A very good, user-friendly performer, but expensive.

22 Eureka Excalibur 6978A $500

Weight: 22 lb. Quieter than most. Tool-changing is particularly easy. Easier to push than most. 1-yr. limited warranty. **But:** The cord is shorter than most. The dirtbag holds less than most. **Availability:** Only through 12/98. **Similar model:** 6978B. **Recommendation:** A very good performer, but expensive.

23 Kenmore (Sears) 27412 $280

Weight: 23 lb. Better than most on carpeting. Has a small power nozzle for stairs. Tool-changing is particularly easy. 1-yr. warranty. **But:** Noisiest canister tested. If the belt, bulb, or brush breaks, it's hard to replace the part yourself. **Similar models:** 27312, $260; 27512, $260. **Availability:** Discontinued. **Recommendation:** A very good performer, and inexpensive compared to other canisters.

24 Hoover Powermax S3611 $300

Weight: 22 lb. Better than most on carpeting. Rug-pile-height adjustment is automatic. 1-yr. warranty. **But:** The extension wand is heavy for cleaning high surfaces. **Similar models:** S3603-040, $260; S3613, $290. **Availability:** Only through 12/98. **Recommendation:** A very good performer.

Ratings *Whirlpool tubs*

& Recommendations

The tests behind the Ratings

Because so much depends on user preference, brands are listed alphabetically. Within brands, listed in order of panelists' **preference**. The panelists also judged tub **comfort**, the **force** of the jets, and **noise**. **Dimensions** are in order of length, width, height. **Weight** is for an empty tub. **Capacity** is minimum, with jets pointing down, and maximum, filled to the overflow drain. **Price** is approximate retail.

Recommendations

Consider the American Standard Luxury System II, $1,660, first. Panelists thought it spacious and comfortable. Also worth considering is The Jacuzzi Builder Luxura, $1,025. It got high marks from panelists even though the short interior and the back support can be uncomfortable.

See report, page 167. Last time rated in CONSUMER REPORTS: May 1998.

Details on the models

Brands are listed alphabetically within brands; within brands, listed in order of panelists' preference.

American Standard

Luxury System II Heritage 2801.128H $1,660

Preference ⊖ Comfort ⊖ Force ⊖ Noise ◒
• 60x32x22¼ in. • 120 lb. • Holds 25 to 63 gal. Acrylic. Drain on right. Spacious, comfortable. Has 2 rear, 2 front, and 2 side jets. 2-speed 1-hp motor with electronic control. **But:** On/off control at rear. **Similar model:** 2801.228H, $1,660 (drain on left).

Scala Renaissance System I 2660.018R $1,000

Preference ⊖ Comfort ⊖ Force ○ Noise ◒
• 60x32x20 in. • 87 lb. • Holds 31 to 56 gal. Acrylic. Left or right drain. Long and wide. Has 2 front and 4 side jets. 1-speed ¾-hp motor with pneumatic control. **But:** Steep angle for back support. On/off control at rear.

Cambridge System I 2461.028 $1,390

Preference ○ Comfort ○ Force ○ Noise ○
• 60x32x17¾ in. • 190 lb. • Holds 30 to 52 gal. Porcelain enamel on steel. Drain on right. Has 6 side jets. Comfortable angle for back support. 1-speed ¾-hp motor with pneumatic control. **But:** Short interior can be uncomfortable. On/off control at back. Hard to service pump. **Similar models:** 2460.028, $1,390; 2461.128, $1,410; and 2460.128, $1,410.

Jacuzzi

Builder Luxura 5 F942959 $1,025

Preference ⊖ Comfort ⊖ Force ⊖ Noise ○
• 60x32x20 in. • 92 lb. • Holds 39 to 58 gal. Acrylic. Drain on right. Has 2 front and 4 side jets. Controls are easy to reach and use; nozzles are easy to adjust. 1-speed 1½-hp motor with pneumatic control. **But:** Short interior can be uncomfortable. Steep angle for back support. **Similar model:** F941, $1,025.

Builder Vantage D441 $1,700

Preference ○ Comfort ○ Force ⊖ Noise ○
• 60x32x18½ in. • 92 lb., 175 lb. (with shower enclosure) • Holds 21 to 43 gal.
Acrylic. Drain on right. Comes with integral shower enclosure. Has 4 side jets. Comfortable angle for back support. Wide nozzles are easy to adjust. 1-speed 1½-hp motor with pneumatic control. **But:** Cramped, can be uncomfortable. Controls hard to reach. **Similar model:** D442, $1,600.

Designer Pulsar G076959 $2,100

Preference ○ Comfort ○ Force ⊖ Noise ○
• 60x32x20 in. • 92 lb. • 34 to 57 gal.
Acrylic. Drain on left. Has 2 rear, 2 front, and 2 side jets. Comfortable angle for back support. Wide nozzles are easy to adjust. 1-speed 2-hp motor with pneumatic control. **But:** Cramped, can be uncomfortable. Controls hard to reach. **Similar model:** G078, $2,000.

Kohler

System I Ellery 1273 $1,690

Preference ⊖ Comfort ⊖ Force ○ Noise ◒
• 60x32x20½ in. • 126 lb. • Holds 21 to 56 gal.
Acrylic. Drain on left. 2 rear and 3 side jets. Needs less water than others. Spacious. Easy-to-use controls. Nozzles swivel more than others. 1-speed ¾-hp motor with pneumatic control. **But:** Uneven massage sensation. Steep angle for back support. **Similar model:** 1274, $1,690.

System III Steeping Bath K-792-N $3,480

Preference ○ Comfort ⊖ Force ○ Noise ◒
• 60x36x20½ in. • 410 lb. • Holds 22 to 59 gal.
Cast iron. Drain on left or right. 2 front, 2 neck, and 4 side jets, which all need less water to operate than others. Wide and deep. Controls easy to use. Nozzles swivel more than others. Variable-speed 2-hp motor with electronic control. **But:** Hard to service pump. Short interior can be uncomfortable.

System II Mendota 514-H $1,730

Preference ○ Comfort ○ Force ○ Noise ◒
• 60x32x16½ in. • 450 lb. • Holds 26 to 44 gal.
Cast iron. Drain on right. 4 side jets. Easy-to-use controls. Nozzles swivel more than others. 2-speed 1-hp motor with electronic controls. **But:** Short and shallow, can be uncomfortable. Hard to service pump. **Similar model:** 513 H, $1,730.

Home office

CELL PHONES

Last CR report: September 1998
Ratings: page 236
Expect to pay: $0 to $500 or more

Cell phones are getting better. Compared with the handsets of less than a year ago, modern cell phones are slightly lighter and come with more features and battery choices.

Cell phone service is somewhat cheaper. Still, at between 30 cents and 60 cents per minute, calls are an expensive convenience. You're apt to pay far more over the course of a year for service than you do for the phone itself. We compared the costs of competing service plans in the 15 biggest cellular markets and found that the difference between the least and most expensive in the same city can be as much as $275 a year.

The deals are getting trickier, too. What you pay is a byproduct of the arcane rules of the plan you select. Your weekend calls may be free, but don't make "roaming" calls during "peak" hours, or your bill will soar. Drive a few feet outside an invisible perimeter that defines your "home" area, and a cellular call can suddenly jump from a dime to a dollar a minute. And you don't just pay for the calls you make; you'll often be charged for incoming calls. If you want to switch services before your contract expires, you may have to pay steep early-termination penalties.

Cellular-service providers try to make wireless appear less expensive by breaking the total cost into reasonable-looking pieces: a $19.95 monthly service charge, an allotment of minutes included as part of the basic plan, and extras like paging, e-mail, and voice mail—each costing a few dollars more per month. But those prices don't capture the full amount that will appear on your bill. The average new user now takes to the cellular airwaves for about 80 minutes per month, according to the Strategies Group, a wireless-industry consulting firm in Washington, D.C. For that airtime, you could pay $50 to $70 per month—or just $20 to $30.

What's available

Phone makers include Nokia, Motorola, Audiovox, Sony, NEC, Qualcomm, and Ericsson. Plans are offered by many companies, including AT&T wireless, regional Bell compaines, Cellular One, and GTE wireless.

Wireless marketers are pushing digital cellular and a variant called PCS (personal communications service) as the must-have technology. But it will be several years before there will be a big-enough network of antenna base stations to deliver the "100 percent digital" calling that companies like Sprint are selling today. For now, reasonably reliable digital connections are concentrated mainly in the cores of big metropolitan markets and along the major highways connecting them. Analog cellular, by contrast, covers 90 percent of the populated area of the 48 contiguous states.

The phones themselves may be thin and as light as four ounces, or bulkier and more than twice as heavy.

Analog phones. In addition to giving you true nationwide service, with coverage in rural and outlying areas, analog handsets are typically inexpensive or free with a calling plan. Battery talk time and standby time are generally half that of digital handsets.

Digital phones. There are currently three all-digital platforms (none of which is compatible with the others). In addition to reduced call "noise" and greater security against eavesdropping and theft of services, digital phones offer features like e-mail and headline news. But coverage is limited and spotty in many areas, and calls cut off abruptly when a signal is lost. For now, you can overcome the gaps with a dual-mode unit that combines analog and digital in a single handset. But dual-mode handsets are bigger and heavier than plain analog or digital models.

Key features

Don't assume that the battery offered with the phone in the store is your only option. There are several choices of battery size and chemistry—each offering different amounts of talk time and standby time. For the longest life between charges from a relatively compact energy source, look for a lithium-ion battery. Without recharging, it can power up a phone that hasn't been used for several months. Most of the models we bought came with a nickel-metal-hydride battery, a step up from the old standard nickel-cadmium power cells because you can keep it plugged in and recharging when you're not using the phone.

Some models come with an alkaline **battery adapter**—useful for when an emergency doesn't allow time to recharge. Models that have a **rapid charger** can replenish the battery in 1 or 2 hours in-

HOW TO COMPARE SERVICE COSTS

First **Compute the total annual cost of service.** Use this worksheet to estimate the cost of the service, your biggest expense when you buy cellular. From the service providers' rate sheets, fill in the basic monthly service charge; the per-minute charge for calls made during peak hours, off-peak hours, and while "roaming" outside your home area; and the number of minutes included at no charge each month in each category. If you aren't sure how you'll use your cell phone, assume you'll behave like an average user and make 80 minutes of calls per month—30 peak and 45 off-peak in your home area and 5 minutes "roaming." Use those figures to compute your total annual cost of service.

What you pay for service	Estimated minutes used	Nat'l avg.		Number of "free" minutes in plan		Per-minute charge*		Cost
During PEAK periods	☐	30 min.	−	☐	X	☐	=	☐ *Add*
During OFF-PEAK periods	☐	45 min.	−	☐	X	☐	=	☐ *Add*
While ROAMING	☐	5 min.	−	☐	X	☐	=	☐ *Add*

Basic monthly service charge	☐
Total MONTHLY cost of service	☐ *Multiply by 12*
Total ANNUAL cost of service	☐ *Add*
Price of the cell phone	☐
First-year cost of cellular	☐

Then **Add the price of the cell phone.** Use the Ratings to choose a handset with the performance and features you want.

Last **Which cell phone and plan to choose?** Shop for the lowest price. Our tests found that price is not related to performance. You can buy your handset from a local cellular service provider, electronics store, or other retailer; any of them can hook you up with the service plan you choose.

**If number of free minutes equals or exceeds your estimated need, enter zero; otherwise multiply the difference by the per-minute charge.*

stead of the 7 to 12 hours required by an ordinary "trickle" charger. An **automobile adapter** allows you to power the phone by plugging it into your car's cigarette lighter.

Instead of ringing, a phone with a **vibrating alert** can let you know discretely that you have an incoming call. **Any-key answer** lets you answer an incoming call by hitting any key, rather than a special send key.

Call timer keeps track of the time spent talking on the current call, as well as cumulatively. Some timers will beep at preset intervals.

Some **displays** are harder to read than others—check it yourself before you buy. An **alphanumeric directory** lets you store names as well as numbers.

A phone with **authentication** uses a system of secret codes to foil thieves who would steal your phone's electronic identification number, "clone" it, and fraudulently bill calls to you. Many phones have this feature, but not all cellular service providers support it yet. Check to see if yours does.

How to choose

Choose the plan first. To compare plans, collect rate information from the carriers that serve your area, take it home, and systematically work out what each plan will cost for the calls you're likely to make. Approximately 60 percent of personal calls on cell phones are made during evenings and weekends, the off-peak periods when rates are lowest. That still leaves a lot of peak-time calling, so don't assume you'll be talking only during the cheapest hours of the day. (The worksheet on page 221 can help.)

Choose a plan that suits your calling pattern. Your calls will cost less when made from within your "home" area other than during peak business hours. Remember, you don't have to choose a "home" area based on where you reside. Get a cell-phone number based on where you'll use the phone most, so those calls will be billed at the lower, home rate. Don't be seduced by offers of "free" weekend minutes if you need a phone mainly to stay in touch with your family or office during weekdays.

Consider a digital service plan. In the 15 markets we examined, a digital service plan turned out to be the least expensive option nearly three-fourths of the time. You'll have to get a dual-band phone to be certain of full coverage, however.

Performance differences. Our tests showed you don't have to pay a high price to get a high-quality handset. Most phones we tested had sufficient RF (radio frequency) sensitivity to "hear" signals sent out by the phone company's transmitters. And most handled "multipath" interferences well—these show up as static, crackling, or a rapid "pft-pft-pft" noise while you're moving.

What to spend. In our survey of 15 markets, the best or lowest monthly cost of service for 80 minutes of calls per month—30 minutes during peak hours, 45 minutes off-peak, and 5 minutes while roaming outside the less expensive "home" area—ranged from $19.95 to more than $40. Phones ranged from free to more than $500 with a service contract. You may be able to buy a phone without service, but you'd need to have a compelling reason to want a specific handset to be willing to pass up the low-cost one that comes with a service plan. Carriers don't reduce their calling-plan rates if you bring in your own phone, so buying a phone without service is like paying for it twice—once at the store and again through the monthly service charge.

COMPUTERS

Last CR report:* *June 1998
Expect to pay:* *$400 to $3,000

For several years now, the personal computer story has been short and sweet: faster and cheaper. More than one third of the computers now sold cost less than $1,000—and at last one as low as $400.

High-end models, in addition to the faster chips available, offer better graphics and access to other new technology, such as DVD, 56 K modems, USB "plug-and-play" peripherals, and flat-panel LCD monitors.

Family PC or office PC? Family computers come with educational, financial, and entertainment software, a sound system, and a modem. Many manufacturers also offer computers for the home office that are virtually identical to family machines but with more business software and less of a sound system. If you intend to use the computer primarily for work, a package like this is the better choice.

Macintosh or Windows? A PC running Windows and a Mac OS machine are comparable, though Macs still have the edge in ease of setting up and installing peripherals. If you use Windows at the office and a Mac at home you can transfer most files and documents from one system to the other. (It's easier to translate PC to Mac than vice versa.)

Desktop or notebook? A desktop computer gives you the most capability for the money. But it takes up precious room and is hard to move from place to place. If space or portability is important to you, a notebook computer may be a better choice, though you'll have to spend several thousand dollars extra to get the speed and memory that a low-end desktop model offers. Apple's new iMac puts most of the computer's works in a single box, and it's easier to move around.

Buy new or upgrade what you have? Upgrading your existing computer's memory, modem, or hard drive makes sense especially if the machine runs on a 166-MHz or faster Pentium processor. Even a new $1,000 machine will cost you more than a thorough upgrade and probably won't offer much of an edge in performance.

What's available

Compaq, Hewlett-Packard, Gateway, Packard-Bell, and IBM are the biggest brands of Windows machines. Apple is once again the only maker of Mac OS models.

Basic models. These machines are fine for basic computer tasks, like word processing, personal finance, web-surfing, online chat rooms, e-mail, record-keeping, drawing, desktop publishing, children's educational software, and most games. Some of the cheapest models may be hard to upgrade. Look for models with room for PCI plug-in expansion cards, memory upgrades, and video RAM.

What you'll spend: $800 to $1,200 (excluding monitor).

Basic equipment in this price class: • 300 to 333-MHz Pentium-class processor. • 64 MB of RAM, upgradable to 128 MB or more. • 4- to 6-GB hard drive. • 56 K V.90 fax-modem. • 24- to 32x CD-ROM drive. • At least one unused PCI slot (the most versatile kind of expansion slot), one free bay for an additional disk drive. • Sound system, which may lack the wavetable MIDI (music instrument digital interface) that provides realistic sound reproduction. • Speakers but no microphone. • Installed software, including basic word processing and spreadsheet, a banking program, a few games, and Internet sign-up kits.

Multimedia models. Move up to this category if high-quality graphics are important to you for games or Internet-surfing. These machines will handle the basics already mentioned, plus performance-oriented arcade games, musical entertainment, multimedia web sites.

What you'll spend: $1,200 to $1,800 (excluding monitor).

Basic equipment in this price class: • 350- to 400-MHz Pentium-class processor (Windows) or 266 MHz Power PC 750 (Mac OS). • 64 to 128 MB of RAM • A standard ATX main circuit board, which allows for upgrading. • 8-GB hard drive. • Accelerated (AGP) graphics (Windows), with at least 4 MB of video RAM. • 56 K fax-modem, which may have voice capability. • 32x CD-ROM or DVD drive. • Sound system with wavetable MIDI • Speakers and a microphone. • Three PCI expansion slots, two free bays or additional disk drives. • Installed software including full-fledged word processing and spreadsheet, a banking program, some games, and Internet sign-up kits.

Cutting-edge models. These machines handle the basic above, plus cutting-edge arcade games, serious music composing, surfing multimedia web sites, playing DVD software and movies, programming, developing your own multimedia web sites and video.

What you'll spend: $2,200 to $3,000 (excluding monitor).

Basic equipment in this price class: • 400 to 500 MHz Pentium II processor (Windows) or 300-MHz G3 processor (Mac OS). • 64 to 128 MB of SRAM. • A standard ATX main circuit board, which allows for upgrading. • 10-GB hard drive. • Accelerated (AGP) graphics (Windows), with at least 8 MB of video RAM. • 56 K V.90 fax-modem with voice capability. • DVD-ROM drive with hardware-based video decoder. • Sound system with wavetable MIDI. • Speakers with better sound quality, plus microphone. • Two or more PCI expansion slots, at least two free bays for additional disk drives. • Installed software including a suite of full office applications, a banking program, games, and Internet sign-up kits.

Key features

The standard **processor** for Windows machines has become the Pentium II, but many PCs are using chips from competitors like Cyprix or AMD. Intel itself has developed a cheaper line, Celeron. For Mac OS machines, the standard processor is the Power PC, with the new G3 series now the fastest chip available in home machines. These days, **memory** is fairly cheap. Buy at least 32 MB of RAM and 128 K of cache memory. The typical **hard drive** storage capacity now exceeds 4 gigabytes (GB), or about 4,000 MB. Many models offer a 6-GB or even a 10-GB hard drive.

To get the **better graphics** or **video** that accompany more-realistic action games or for multimedia web sites, you need at least 4 MB of video RAM and advanced graphics with 3-D acceleration. The wavetable MIDI, nearly standard, delivers very realistic sound—a plus for game aficionados and serious musicians.

A **CD-ROM drive** is now standard, along with a drive for 3½-inch diskettes (except for the iMac). Many models now come with a **DVD drive.** This component can play existing CD-ROMs and the newer DVD-ROMs, which hold a single movie or several gigabytes of data on a CD-sized disk.

A **monitor** typically must be purchased separately, which makes the hardware seem cheaper than it is. You may see a computer ad offering a complete bundle—for one price. Otherwise, unless you already own a monitor, plan on spending at least an additional $200 to $350 for a 15-inch monitor, $400 to $600 for one with a 17-inch display. (See the report on page 231.)

You can expect to get a **modem** rated for 56 kilobits per second. Such modems use a new industry standard, V.90, adopted in September 1998. Note that your Internet provider must upgrade to this standard for you to use it.

Expansion bays in Windows computers let you add more or newer drives. At least one empty bay should have front-panel access for removable disks. External drives can easily be added to a Mac with an SCSI or USB connector on the back panel. (The iMac uses USB ports.) **Expansion slots** allow the addition of PCI plug-in cards and most other add-ons, to allow for Ethernet connection and SCSI interface. **Universal serial bus (USB)** ports are now a standard feature that promises true cross-platform "plug and play" to make it easy to add printers, external hard drives, and other peripheral equipment. The latest ports, IEEE 1394 or "FireWire," promise extremely high-speed connections to multimedia devices.

How to choose

Performance differences. All the low-priced computers we tested performed everyday tasks—word processing, finances, and multimedia applications—as ably as the best computers we tested just a year ago. They should be good enough for all but the most demanding users. The higher-priced models also performed well, and include about $400 of useful software in addition to their speedier and more advanced hardware. The Power Macintosh G3/266 we tested features a fast chip and some key internal design changes that make it twice as fast as any other Mac we've tested.

What to spend. New computers should continue to leapfrog today's machines in price and performance for years to come. So for most people, it's not worth the money or effort to try to keep up with all the latest technology. You can keep costs down without sacrificing essential performance by buying only as much computer as you need now and choosing a design that lets you easily expand and upgrade critical components.

Many brands are sold at retail and also through mail-order catalogs or direct to consumers via the Internet. Retailers like Circuit City are now selling major brands such as Hewlett-Packard and Compaq through kiosks that let you custom-build your PC. Brands like Dell and Gateway are sold primarily by mail or at their own web sites. New models are introduced in spring and fall, so you may find good deals when the next crop of new models appears.

CORDLESS PHONES

Last CR report: *November 1998*
Ratings: *page 243*
Expect to pay: *$30 to $150*

Cordless phones now cost little more than corded models with comparable features. And cordless technology has improved sufficiently to make a cordless phone entirely suitable to be a home's primary—and secondary and tertiary—phone. (Because cordless phones require AC current, however, be sure to have at least one corded phone in the house in case the power goes out.)

What's available

Lucent, General Electric, Bell South, Uniden, and Sony are the big brands, accounting for around 70 percent of sales. The Lucent name is currently being phased out and replaced with the more familiar AT&T monicker. (Lucent is an AT&T spin-off company.)

Cordless phones are quieter than they were, thanks in large part to "compander" circuitry to reduce background noise and a larger number of channels (the more channels a phone uses, the less the chance of interference from neighbors' cordless phones, garage door openers, and the like).

A phone's frequency gives you an indication of its usable range. Only a few cordless phones that operate in the 43-49 MHz band use only 10 channels. More common in this band are models whose 25 channels reduce the chance of interference. Such phones can be used 100 to 400 feet from the base before the sound becomes noisy, according to our open-air tests, so they should provide noise-free operation throughout an apartment or modest-sized house (and perhaps also on its balcony or deck).

Cordless phones that use the **900-MHz** band are the best choices for a sizable home, especially if you want to talk at the farthest reaches of a fairly large yard. In our tests, 900-MHz phones could be used up to five times farther from the base than 43-49-MHz models. The longest ranges—upwards of 2,000 feet—were with digital **900-MHz models**. Digital models also have signals that make it extremely difficult to eavesdrop on your conversations.

Cordless phones of all these types can be bought with an **answering machine** built in, usually with digital (chip) message storage. Desirable features include a digital readout of the number of messages stored, the ability to scan back ("rewind") to hear part of the message, and, for large households, multiple mailboxes and memory larger than the 9 minutes or so some machines offer.

Key features

Many phone features are found on both corded and cordless models. A cordless phone, however, must contain a battery, making almost all cordless phones heavier than a corded phone to hold—6 to 11 ounces. Ideally, a **handset** should fit the contours of your face. Its earpiece should have rounded edges and a recessed center so it fits nicely over the middle of your ear, and the buttons on the keypad should be free of your jaw. The handsets of 900-MHz phones, which often mimic the easy-to-pocket design of cellular phones, frequently fall short of that ideal.

Look for **easy-to-use buttons**—ones that are large, with good spacing and decent contrast between the buttons and lettering and good tactile feedback. Phones with a **backlit keypad** are easier to use in the dark.

A **speakerphone** in the base lets you answer a call without the handset, allow others to participate in a conversation, or wait on hold without clamping the handset to your ear.

A **liquid crystal display** on the handset or base provides useful information such as the channel number, phone number dialed, speed-dial code, battery-strength indicator, or time you've been connected.

On most models, only the handset rings; a few phones have a **second ringer** in the base. That's generally a better alert than the standard flickering light.

Two keypads are helpful when negotiating a phone menu; the second keypad, mounted on the base, allows you to press keys without removing the handset to your ear. You can also dispense with the handset, if you want, and place calls using the second pad and the speakerphone.

Nondigital models sometimes **scramble** their signal, making them almost as safe from the casual busybody as a digital phone. That privacy comes at a price in sound quality, however. Scrambling made voices sound somewhat gritty and harsh in our tests.

All phones must be connected to household current and a telephone line. **Phone cords that unplug** from the base simplify repairs. The **battery** does require replacement every few years, which is typically a simple, do-it-yourself job. You can conserve battery power by pressing the "Battery Save" or "Power Off" buttons, but that deactivates the ringer. With a phone that has a **spare-battery charging** compartment in the base, you never have to return the handset to the base. When the battery in the handset runs down, you simply pop in the fresh one. Since cordless phones also require AC power, most are useless in a blackout. A few have backup alkaline batteries in case of power failure.

Caller ID displays the name and number of a caller, provided you subscribe to caller-ID services. Many phones with caller ID also allow you to see the name and number of another caller if you're already on the phone. **Two-line capability** is useful in homes that subscribe to on-line services. It also allows "conferencing" two callers in three-way connections.

How to choose

Performance differences. The basic choices are 43-49-MHz, 900-MHz analog, or 900-MHz digital spread spectrum (regular digital is now fading). All types are available with or without a built-in answering machine. The more channels, the lower the chance of interference—but the minimum 10 channels will suffice in many areas. Buy a 900-MHz phone primarily if you need exceptional range. Buy a digital version if you need very exceptional range and exceptional privacy—and you value total freedom from static.

What to spend. Our tests show that low-priced models within a type can offer fine performance; spending more mostly buys features. Extras that can drive up a phone's price include second-line capability ($25 to $50 more), caller ID, a liquid crystal display, a speakerphone, and dual keypads.

Sales (and advertising) peak in November and December. New cordless phones are usually introduced in the spring; summer can be a good time to find older models on sale.

Avoid tossing dead cordless-phone batteries into the trash. The spent cells in most cordless phones contain cadmium, a toxic metal that can contaminate landfills. Instead, bring the old batteries with you when buying replacements; most chains that sell replacement batteries, like Radio Shack, will forward the old cells to recyclers.

FAX MACHINES

***Last CR report:** September 1997*
***Expect to pay:** $200 to $800*

Fax machines do more than send and receive faxes. Indeed, many have become a different creature: a multifunction machine. Your buying decision will hinge on your budget, the space available, and what other equipment you own.

What's available

Leading brands include Brother, Sharp, and Panasonic. Hewlett-Packard and Samsung also make multifunction models.

Fax-only models send and receive faxes and make photocopies of documents. **Multifunction** machines also serve as printers for Windows computers (no multifunction models are available for Macintosh computers) and typically serve as a copier and scanner as well. Fax-only models cost anywhere between $200 and $400. Multifunction models cost $300 to $800.

Machines of both types print on either thermal or plain paper. The type of paper a machine uses doesn't affect the quality of the faxes it produces. Overall, neither plain paper nor thermal models produced better-looking faxes in our tests. A machine's paper stock does, however, affect how long its faxes last. Thermal-paper machines use a heated printhead that literally burns images into thin, heat-sensitive paper. Thermal paper yellows and fades over time, making it unsuitable for archiving.

For faxes that don't fade, you need a plain-paper machine. The best models, like computer printers, use either ink-jet or laser printing; all such machines are multifunction models. Most plain-paper fax-only models use a technology known as thermal transfer, in which a heated printhead sears images onto a continuous heat-sensitive film, which then transfers them to the paper.

Machines that use thermal technology—either thermal paper or thermal transfer printing—are relatively inexpensive to buy but relatively pricey to use. Expect paper-and-printing costs of about 6 to 8 cents per page, compared with 2 to 5 cents for models that use ink-jet or laser printing.

Key features

A data-transfer rate of 9.6 kbps (kilobits per second) is now the standard for all fax machines; 14.4 kbps handles faxes faster, but only if the receiving machine operates at the same rate.

How you connect your fax machine to the phone line is key. Most come with a **telephone handset**. If you decide to have your faxes share a phone line with voice calls, rather than adding a **second phone** line for them, you might want to take advantage of a telephone company service called **distinctive ringing**. For about $5 per month, two phone numbers can access your single line with different rings. You make the second number your fax "line" and let the machine pick up calls with that ring.

If you stay with a single phone line and a single ring, the fax machine can check for incoming faxes after a certain number of rings if you set its **fax/tel switch**. If you should pick up the phone before the fax machine and it's a fax transmission, most fax machines let you activate the fax by punching in a code like "999."

For occasions when no one answers the phone, most fax machines either include an **answering machine** or can send the call to an answering machine plugged into the fax machine. Typical features include **automatic message count**, **personal mailboxes**, **time-and-date stamp**, and **remote retrieval** of messages. Some machines include **caller ID**, which displays the number of the sender (or, for voice calls, the phone number of the caller) if you subscribe to your phone company's caller ID service. Models with **pager notification** can page you when a fax arrives.

Memory lets you store a number of fax pages—typically 20 to 30—that are received after the machine jams or its paper runs out. Memory also lets you create broadcast lists that allow you to automatically send a document to many machines after scanning it only once, and lets you use any other fax machine to retrieve faxes sent to your machine. The fax and telephone functions frequently share memory, but you can often elect to store only faxes or only voice calls. **Dual access** allows you to set a fax to transmit while the machine is receiving a fax or (with multifunctions) printing a document. **Error-correction mode (ECM)** helps the machine maintain high accuracy on a noisy line. **PC-fax** allows many functions of the fax machine to be controlled from a personal computer and lets the PC itself send faxes. An **output tray** holds faxed or printed pages and eliminates a paper heap on the floor or your desk.

Even fax-only models can be used as a **copier**—at about 30 seconds per page. But you can copy only what can be fed through their rollers—no copying books or fragile documents. Most machines allow you to order up multiple copies.

Most multifunctions also act as a **scanner,** letting you import text or images scanned by the machine into your computer. Photos—albeit only in black-and-white—can be used immediately by a graphics program. Text requires a two-stage process. After scanning, it has to be "read" by an **optical-character-recognition (OCR) program**, which is included with some multifunction models (it's under $100 bought separately).

Color faxing is only available on a limited basis as this book went to press, but some multifunction machines now print, scan, and copy in color.

How to choose

Performance differences. Fax transmission and reception is fairly similar across all models we've tested, fax-only and multifunction, but more expensive models are markedly better at printing than are low-priced ones, and they have more conveniences. The best printing of all came from a laser-printing model.

Most of the multifunction models tested were not up to the speed and versatility of the latest computer printers, which offer color capability as well. Nor were their copying and scanning abilities as robust as what dedicated home copiers and scanners provide.

What to spend. If you only send and receive faxes informally, a fax-only thermal-paper machine ($200 to $400) generally makes the best choice. For business use, a good fax-only machine that uses plain paper may be a better, if slightly bulkier, alternative. Consider a multifunction machine ($300 to $800) if you're short on space and can live with slightly lower quality printing than most dedicated printers provide.

Office-discount outlets often have broad selections at low prices. Retail office-supply dealers may provide better service. Prices at mail-order outlets can be low, but you can't look goods over before you buy. For mail-order sources, consult a computer magazine such as Computer Shopper.

COMPUTER DESKS

***Last CR report:** January 1997*
***Ratings:** page 248*
***Expect to pay:** $65 to $2,000*

In many households, the computer eventually acquires enough peripheral equipment that it must move from a corner of the kitchen table to a home of its own. You might consider tucking it into the fully assembled, solid wood, finely finished computer furniture sold in furniture stores, but those pieces can cost more than $2,000. Computer furniture you assemble yourself—sold by office-supply stores, home centers, home-furnishing stores, and catalogs—costs much less and is what most people buy for their workstation.

What's available

Ready-to-assemble computer furniture is designed to hold all the components of a desktop computer and, often, a printer. There are four basic configurations:

WHAT TO LOOK FOR IN AN ERGONOMIC CHAIR

In addition to being comfortable, a well-designed chair can help you adapt to a less-than-perfect setup. Although you can find office-type chairs priced as low as $25, you'll have to spend more to get basic ergonomic features:

- A lever to adjust seat height pneumatically
- A contoured backrest
- Adjustable armrests
- A five-wheel base that swivels

You can find such chairs in the same places you find computer desks—office furniture manufacturers, home-furnishings stores, and mass merchandisers, including the office superstores. "Contract" furniture makers supply furniture to corporate buyers but are increasingly available to home-office buyers as well.

Comfort is personal, so sit in a chair before you buy it. If, after you make a few adjustments, you still find that some contour hits you in the wrong place, or that the whole chair feels too big or small, then you're not likely to ever be very comfortable sitting in it. In our tests, we've found that first impressions of a chair's comfort correspond well to week-long impressions. Our tests also showed that no chair pleases everybody.

Cushioning should be soft enough that you don't feel pressure at points where your body hits the chair, but not so soft that you sink into the chair and can't move around freely.

When you sit back, there should be a few fingers to a fist's worth of space between the edge of the chair and the back of your knees so the seat doesn't cut off circulation to your lower legs. Too much space, and the chair won't support your thighs. If at the seat's lowest setting your feet aren't on the floor, the chair doesn't go low enough; if at the highest setting your knees angle up, it doesn't go high enough. Match the contours in the back of the chair to the natural curve of your spine by adjusting the backrest height or moving the lumbar support.

Desk with hutch. Most have a workspace of roughly 300 to 500 square inches, but they're shallower than the usual office desk. There's often a shelf for the printer (if not, it takes up desk space) and room for files and such. Price: about $200 to $300.

Armoire. These can pretend to be a china cabinet in a dining room or a free-standing closet in the bedroom. The desktop is usually smaller than on the desks. They usually have a printer shelf. Price: about $350 to $500.

Corner unit. These desks need lots of room. Most have a desktop of about 500 square inches. Some have a printer shelf. Price: about $200 to $300.

Cart. You can roll them around. Some have a hutch, which provides a rack for CDs and a bit of storage space for paperwork but limits the desktop to less than 150 square inches. They often have a printer shelf. Price: about $65 to $200.

Most computer furniture can't be adjusted to fit all family members equally well. You can create a more comfortable, versatile workstation with a plain large desk and a few other components:

Keyboard shelf. For $90 or so, you can buy a shelf mounted on a movable arm whose range of adjustments, in both height and angle, lets you put the keyboard where it should be. Buy a keyboard shelf large enough to fit a mouse, or one with an optional extension shelf, and separate soft, spongy wrist rest, available for less than $20 from most office-supply stores.

Monitor stand. Some have legs you adjust so the monitor is at the proper eye level. More elaborate stands mount on an arm that allows for easy adjustment of height and distance. Price: $40 to $200.

Copy stand. Anyone who does a lot of transcribing needs a copy stand that holds papers adjacent to and at the same height as the computer monitor. A stand costs as little as $15.

How to choose

Performance differences. Computer desk kits suffer all the problems bookshelves and entertainment centers do—they're heavy, complicated to assemble, and rarely bear much resemblance to an expensive furniture store piece.

What to spend. The most versatile workstation was one we designed, with an adjustable keyboard shelf and monitor stand. It cost less than $300, desk included.

MONITORS

Last CR report: June 1998
Ratings: page 240
Expect to pay: $200 to $1,000

Monitor prices have dropped so fast that 17-inch monitors now cost what 15-inch models used to, and 19-inch models now sell for less than $1,000.

The 14- and 15-inch monitor often offered with a new computer provides a screen size that's fine for common tasks like word processing. But to design graphics, play the newest computer games, or view multiple documents or extensive spreadsheets, that size might feel cramped.

What's available

Major computer makers—Apple, Compaq, IBM, Packard-Bell—all market their own brand of monitors. Other leading brands include NEC, Samsung, Sony, and View-Sonic.

Desktop monitors, like TV sets, come in sizes based on the diagonal measurement of the tube. Viewable image size (VIS)—the actual diagonal measurement of the screen image—is generally an inch or so less. Many manufacturers, complying with a voluntary standard established by the Consumer Electronics Manufacturers Association, a trade group, conspicuously state the VIS in product literature.

Compared with 15-inch monitors, 17-inch models provide about one-quarter to one-third more viewing area; the 19-inch screen, in fact, is almost big enough to fit an 8½ x 11-inch page of text at full size. With the increase in viewing area and the necessary software settings, you can either increase the size of a page or fit more document on the screen.

Flat-panel LCD monitors, which are similar to Notebook-computer displays, save space and energy. Though more expensive than conventional monitors, they continue to drop in price.

Key features

Resolution is the number of picture elements, or pixels, used to create the image. A resolution of 1,024 x 768, a popular mode for larger monitors, means there are 1,024 horizontal and 768 vertical pixels. A monitor can operate in several resolution modes. All else being equal, one operated at a higher resolution will show more detail.

Be wary of advertising that touts a monitor with a high resolution at a very low price. That high resolution may be achieved only by lowering the **refresh rate**—the number of times per second the image is redrawn on the tube, stated in hertz (Hz). The refresh rate largely determines the likelihood of flicker, the flashing reminiscent of silent films. The greater the resolution and the larger your monitor, the higher the refresh rate you'll need to avoid flicker. At a resolution of 1,024 x 768, we've found, 17- and 19-inch monitors can generally be used comfortably with a refresh rate of 75 Hz. But 85 Hz is preferable.

Before you upgrade to a bigger monitor, check either on-screen or in the manual to see that the **video card** in your computer can support the resolution, refresh rate, and number of colors you want to use. Your video card will need 2 megabytes (MB) or more of video memory to display 64,000 colors (adequate for general use) at a resolution of 1,024 x 768. It will need 4 MB or more to display 16.7 million colors (enough to view high-quality color photos) at the same resolution. Unless you have an older or very inexpensive computer, you should be able to increase the video memory or buy a new video card with more memory.

Dot pitch (or aperture-grill pitch) is the spacing between the colored dots or lines on the picture tube that create the image seen on the screen. A large dot pitch limits a monitor's ability to produce fine detail, but our tests show that other factors have a greater effect on image quality than small differences in dot pitch.

Larger monitors have more image control than 15-inch monitors. Most have **color temperature controls** to adjust the white tint so a picture seems richer in reds (warm) or blues (cool), and **red, green**, and **blue controls** to increase color intensity. They also have **geometric controls** to adjust the image to fill the screen and make corrections if, for example, the edges of documents are bulging or tilting. Some have a manual **demagnetizing control** to clear the screen of color splotches that sometimes appear if, say, you move loudspeakers too close while the monitor is on.

Monitors sold today typically operate in

the **plug-and-play** mode: When you start one up with a computer for the first time, you don't have to install software to get an adequate image. Some monitors come with driver software on a disk that you can use to fine-tune your display's setup. You can also download such software from the manufacturer's web site.

Most models comply with the Environmental Protection Agency's **Energy Star** program by automatically switching to lower-power modes if the computer isn't operated for a given amount of time.

How to choose

Decide on size. A 15-inch monitor is fine for word-processing tasks. If you work with graphics, with several documents open at once, or with large spreadsheets, a 17- or 19-inch monitor might be better. Still larger 20- and 21-inch monitors are tailored for professional use.

Performance differences. In our laboratory and panel tests, we found a fairly wide range in contrast (how well the screen shows the whitest white and blackest black in the image), clarity, distortion, and color. But all were at least good. You can make your own assessment in the store or at home. To do this, look at a page of text to see that the center and edges are bright and clear. And check a photo image to see that the colors look natural and the texture is appealing. Check also for quirks that may be distracting. We found that several monitors occasionally showed moiré—faint wavy lines or faint horizontal lines across the screen.

What to spend. Prices typically double for each jump in size. You'll pay about $200 to $350 for a 15-inch monitor, $300 to $600 for a 17-inch monitor, and $500 to $1,000 for a 19-inch monitor. Mail-order computer-makers offer good deals on monitors ordered with new computers.

Computer superstores like CompUSA and Computer City offer a wide selection and have flexible return policies. It's best to get a 30-day money-back guarantee and, if you order by mail, return-shipping-cost coverage. Be sure you have the accessories you need—including a Mac adapter if you have a Macintosh computer.

COMPUTER PRINTERS

Last CR report: *March 1998*
Expect to pay: *$100 to $450*

Unlike the computers they serve, most printers can't be upgraded. People usually get faster or more-detailed output by buying a new one. Fortunately, computer printers have dropped in price over the years while gaining steadily in speed and versatility. An important new use is to print your own photos. Advances in image-processing, ink, and new ways of applying it have allowed ink-jet printers to produce color photos that rival conventional ones from a photofinisher, if you use glossy photo paper.

What's available

Hewlett-Packard is the biggest brand in the printer market. Other brands include Canon, Epson, and Lexmark.

Most printers are made for Windows-based computers, but some can also be used with Macintosh computers.

Ink-jet printers, the only affordable color printers for home users, have a print head that deposits an ultrafine pattern of ink dots on the page. Ink-jet printers produce fairly crisp text on paper. They can also print greeting cards, banners, T-shirt iron-ons, words and images from web sites, and articles and images from CD-ROM encyclopedias. Several can even print photos that compare favorably with regular color prints. Price range: about $100 to $450.

Laser printers, reproducing a full page at a time much the way a photocopier does, can print crisp black-and-white text or graphics. Unless given more memory, lasers aren't well suited to printing photos, and the printers aimed at home use are strictly one-color machines. Color laser printers cost thousands. Price range for black-and-white home models: $200 to $400.

Key features

Most printers can deliver a **resolution** of 600 to 720 dots per inch (dpi), though some can print up to 1,440 dpi. But high resolution alone doesn't determine performance. Indeed, most of the time the printer won't even use the maximum dpi setting. For printing in the default mode on plain paper, most printers operate at 300 to 600 dpi.

Ink-jets use the microprocessor and **memory** in the computer to process data. The latest models are so fast partly because computers themselves have become more powerful, have faster extended-capabilities (ECP) printer ports, and contain much more memory than before.

The speed of a laser printer in printing complex graphics and photos can be improved by adding memory (4 megabytes costs about $40).

Another reason for faster printing is fast-drying **inks**. Ink-jet printers produce different hues by combining cyan (a greenish blue), magenta, and yellow inks from what's often termed a CMY cartridge, for the three ink colors. All ink-jets can use a separate black cartridge for printing text and black-and-white graphics. But only so-called CMYK models (K represents black) hold both color and black cartridges at the same time. Some cheaper printers hold only one cartridge at a time. Printing black means swapping the CMY cartridge for the black one, or using the CMY colors. Some ink-jets use yet another combination of cartridges just for reproducing color photos: black and a special photo cartridge containing six inks, or the CMY cartridge and a multiple-ink photo cartridge.

Laser printers use **toner** rather than ink. Sometimes, the toner cartridge and the print drum are one price. It's usually cheaper to replace just an empty toner cartridge.

Most models have a **paper feeder** that holds at least 100 sheets. Many have an **output tray** as well. Some have an **indicator light** to show when ink is low. Most can send and receive data through the **extended-capabilities port** found on new Windows computers.

All ink-jet printers can print **banners**; laser printers cannot.

How to choose

Performance differences. Until recently, laser printers held a clear advantage over ink-jets when it came to speed. Not any longer. The fastest ink-jets we tested are nearly as fast as some laser printers, at least for text. All the lasers produced excellent text, but then, that's their forte. The ink-jets were the clear standouts in printing graphics and photos. The best ink-jets printed deep blacks and colors with smooth gradations; the worst suffered from cruder shading and duller or paler colors. None of the laser printers matched the best ink-jets for printing photos.

We found little difference in quality

between the manufacturers' default printer settings and the high-quality or "best" printing modes when printing on copier paper. In general, the default settings provide the best mix of speed and quality. The high-quality modes may eliminate glitches like "banding" and rough textures in some prints, but they can slow printing considerably.

We compared text and graphics on both regular ink-jet paper and plain copier paper and saw no real quality differences.

What to spend. A color ink-jet printer is the most versatile choice, giving you color or black-and-white output. Laser printers' speed and economy make them well suited for printing lots of black-and-white text.

With either type, weigh the per-page printing costs, not just the purchase price. Printing great text, graphics, and photos can become a very costly habit. According to one estimate, most households with an ink-jet printer will use two to four ink cartridges a year. At $20 to $40 per cartridge, that can add up quickly.

In our tests, printing text averaged between 4 and 14 cents per page for ink-jets. Printing color graphics ranged from 18 cents to $1.40 each: photos cost from 90 cents to $3.80 (including the cost of the photo paper). A page of laser-printer text output cost 2 to 5 cents. You can keep routine printing costs down by using the printer's lower-quality "draft" mode. Generic ink cartridges and refill kits can also cut costs, but you may want to think twice before using them. The printer's warranty won't cover repairs if the off-brand cartridge damages the printer.

HOW TO USE THE RATINGS

- Read the Recommendations for information on specific models and general buying advice.
- Note how the rated products are listed—in order of performance and convenience, price, or alphabetically.
- The overall score graph gives the big picture in performance. Notes on features and performance for individual models are listed in the "Comments" column or "Details on the models."
- Use the key numbers to locate the details on each model.
- Before going to press, we verify model availability for most products with manufacturers. Some tested models listed in the Ratings may no longer be available. Discontinued models are noted in "Comments" or "Details on the models." Such models may still be available in some stores for part of 1999. Models indicated as successors should perform similarly to the tested models, according to the manufacturer. Features may vary.
- Models similar to the tested models, when they exist, are indicated in "Comments" or "Details on the models."
- The original date of publication is noted for each Ratings.

Ratings *Cellular phones*

& Recommendations

The tests behind the Ratings

Overall score is based on the quality of reception in analog mode, battery life, and ease of use. All compensated well for multipath interference. **Call setup** measures the signal level needed to establish a call connection. **Call maintenance** indicates the phone's ability to maintain an established call, generally requiring a lower signal level than a call setup. **Battery efficiency** indicates how little power is required to allow both **talk** time and **standby** time for incoming calls. **Ease of use** reflects our evaluation of various features: display legibility, keyboard layout and feel, ease of entering and recalling stored numbers, and portability.

Typical features for these models

• Authentication. • Ringer and earpiece volume controls. • Battery-strength indicator. • Audible keypad feedback. • DTMF keytone signalling. • 1 yr. parts-and-labor warranty. **Except as noted, all models:** Ability to store names as well as numbers. • Any-key answer. • One-touch dialing. • Caller ID. • Audible elapsed-talk timer.

Recommendations

First, shop for a service plan that suits your calling pattern. Then select a handset with the features that matter most to you. Some models that performed best in our tests—notably the Nokia 918+ and 252—were most basic. A compact lightweight, like the Motorola StarTAC 6500, may add convenience if you plan on carrying the phone in your pocket.

See report, page 219. Last time rated in CONSUMER REPORTS: September 1998.

Overall Ratings

E VG G F P

Listed in order of overall score

Key no.	Brand and model	Overall score (0–100; P F G VG E)	Call SETUP	Call MAINTENANCE	Battery efficiency TALK	Battery efficiency STANDBY	Ease of use
	ANALOG MODELS						
1	**Nokia** 918+		VG	G	VG	VG	VG
2	**Motorola** StarTAC 6500		VG	G	VG	VG	VG
3	**Nokia** 252		E	G	G	VG	VG
4	**Audiovox** MVX-470		VG	G	G	G	G
5	**Motorola** StarTAC 3000		G	F	VG	VG	G
6	**NEC** Talk Time MAX 960		VG	F	G	VG	VG

Key no.	Brand and model	Overall score (0–100; P F G VG E)	Call: Setup	Call: Maintenance	Battery efficiency: Talk	Battery efficiency: Standby	Ease of use
	ANALOG MODELS *continued*						
7	**Motorola** Profile/300 e*		⊖	○	⊜	⊖	○
8	**Ericsson** AH630		⊖	◒	⊖	⊜	○
9	**Motorola** MicroTAC/Piper e*		○	○	⊖	⊖	○
10	**Audiovox** MVX-507		◒	◒	○	○	○
	DUAL-MODE MODELS (ANALOG AND DIGITAL)						
11	**Sony** CM-B3200		○	⊖	⊜	⊜	⊖
12	**Qualcomm** QCP-820		⊜	◒	○	◒	⊖
13	**Audiovox** CDM-3000		⊖	◒	◒	◒	⊖
14	**Nokia** 2160i		○	○	○	⊖	⊖
15	**Ericsson** DH368vi		○	◒	○	⊖	⊖

Details on the models

Handset weight and battery information are based on the battery included with the tested models. **Price** with service is determined by a survey of cellular-service providers; without service is based on a poll of retailers in the 20 largest U.S. markets. **Availability** lists service providers and retailers offering the handsets in June 1998. **Digital platform** indicates which of several digital transmission formats—CDMA or TDMA, cellular or PCS—the listed handset uses.

Analog models

1 Nokia 918+

7x2x7/8 in. • 7 oz. • 600 mAh nickel-metal-hydride battery • 99 min. talk • 20 hr. standby
Price: $0-$150 with contract; $149-$309 without. **Recommendation:** Excellent overall reception purity. Among the best at handling multipath in hilly terrain. Among the best at setting up calls. Among the most efficient in battery use. **But:** Lacks caller ID. Lacks elapsed-talk timer. **Availability:** Service providers—Ameritech, AT&T Wireless, Bell Atlantic Mobile, BellSouth Mobility, Cellular One, Cellular One of San Francisco, GTE Wireless, Pacific Bell Mobile Services, Southwestern Bell; major retailers—Best Buy, Circuit City, Radio Shack, Staples, The Good Guys.

2 Motorola StarTAC 6500

4 3/4x2 3/8x1 in. • 4 oz. • 500 mAh nickel-metal-hydride battery • 67 min. talk • 13 hr. standby
Price: $199-$550 with contract; $349-$799 without. **Recommendation:** Excellent overall reception purity. Among the best at handling multipath in hilly terrain. Among the best at setting up calls. Among the most efficient in battery use. One of the lightest models tested. **But:** Display judged more difficult to read than most. Lacks caller ID. **Additional useful features:** Rapid charger included. Vibrating call alert. **Availablity:** Service providers—AirTouch, Ameritech, AT&T Wireless, BellSouth Mobility, Cellular One, Cellular One of San Francisco, GTE Wireless, Southwestern Bell; major retailers—Circuit City, J&R Music World, The Good Guys.

3 Nokia 252

6 5/8x1 7/8x1 in.• 6 oz. • 1,100 mAh nickel-cadmium battery • 132 min. talk • 32 hr. standby
Price: $49-$180 with contract; $249-$400 without. **Recommendation:** Among the best at setting up calls. One of the lightest models tested. **But:** Lacks elapsed-talk timer. **Availability:** Service providers—AirTouch, Cellular One, Cellular One of San Francisco, BellSouth Mobility, GTE Wireless, Southwestern Bell; major retailers—Best Buy,

Circuit City, Office Depot, Radio Shack, Staples, The Good Guys.

4 Audiovox MVX-470

7x2x1$\frac{3}{8}$ in.• 9 oz. • 1,200 mAh nickel-metal-hydride battery •127 min. talk • 25 hr. standby
Price: $0-$110 with contract; $320 without. **Recommendation:** Excellent overall reception purity. Among the best at handling multipath in hilly terrain. Among the best at setting up calls. **But:** Display judged more difficult to read than most. One of the heaviest. Lacks elapsed-talk timer. **Similar models:** MXV 440 and MXV 475. **Availability:** Service providers—AirTouch, Bell Atlantic, Cellular One, BellSouth Mobility, GTE Wireless; major retailer—The Good Guys.

5 Motorola StarTAC 3000

4$\frac{3}{4}$x2$\frac{3}{8}$x1 in. • 4 oz. • 500 mAh nickel-metal-hydride battery • 65 min. talk • 15 hr. standby
Price: $99-$280 with contract; $251-$499 without. **Recommendation:** Excellent overall reception purity. Among the best at handling multipath in hilly terrain. Among the most efficient in battery use. One of the lightest models tested. **But:** Display judged more difficult to read than most. Lacks alphanumeric directory. **Availability:** Service providers—AirTouch, AT&T Wireless, Cellular One, Cellular One of San Francisco, BellSouth Mobility, GTE Wireless, Southwestern Bell; major retailers—Best Buy, Circuit City, Radio Shack, Staples.

6 NEC Talk Time MAX 960

6$\frac{7}{8}$x1$\frac{7}{8}$x1$\frac{1}{8}$ in. • 8 oz. • 1,000 mAh nickel-cadmium battery • 113 min. talk • 30 hr. standby
Price: $79-$150 with contract. **Recommendation:** Excellent overall reception purity. Among the best at setting up calls. **Availability:** Service providers—Cellular One, Southwestern Bell. Discontinued but may still be available.

7 Motorola Profile/300 e*

6$\frac{3}{8}$x2$\frac{3}{8}$x1$\frac{3}{8}$ in. • 7 oz. • 500 mAh nickel-metal-hydride battery • 108 min. talk • 17 hr. standby
Price: $0-$130 with contract; $167-$300 without. **Recommendation:** Among the best at setting up calls. Among the most efficient in battery use. **But:** Display judged more difficult to read than most. Lacks alphanumeric directory. **Availability:** Service providers—AirTouch, Ameritech, AT&T Wireless, Bell Atlantic Mobile, Cellular One, Cellular One of San Francisco, BellSouth Mobility, GTE Wireless, Southwestern Bell.

8 Ericsson AH630

6$\frac{1}{2}$x2x1$\frac{1}{8}$ in. • 6 oz. • 500 mAh nickel-metal-hydride battery • 100 min. talk • 29 hr. standby
Price: $69-$119 with contract; $179-$399 without. **Recommendation:** One of the lightest models tested. Excellent overall reception purity. Among the best at setting up calls. Among the most efficient in battery use. **But:** Display judged more difficult to read than most. Lacks caller ID. Other useful feature: Claims to meet federal standards for compatibility with hearing aids. **Availability:** Service providers—AT&T Wireless, GTE Wireless, Southwestern Bell; major retailers—Best Buy, Office Depot, Staples, The Good Guys. Discontinued but may still be available.

9 Motorola MicroTAC/Piper e*

6$\frac{3}{8}$x2$\frac{3}{8}$x1$\frac{3}{8}$ in. • 7 oz. • 500 mAh nickel-metal-hydride battery • 80 min. talk •13 hr. standby
Price: $24-$160 with contract; $215-$245 without. **Recommendation:** Among the most efficient in battery use. **But:** Display judged more difficult to read than most. Lacks alphanumeric directory. **Availability:** Service providers—AirTouch, Ameritech, AT&T Wireless, Bell Atlantic Mobile, Cellular One, Cellular One of San Francisco, BellSouth Mobility, GTE Wireless, Southwestern Bell; major retailer—BJ's.

10 Audiovox MVX-507

6$\frac{1}{2}$x2$\frac{1}{4}$x1$\frac{1}{8}$ in. • 8 oz. • 1,200 mAh nickel-metal-hydride battery • 131 min. talk • 22 hr. standby
Price: $119 with contract. **Recommendation:** Excellent overall reception purity. **But:** Ability to establish a call judged only fair. Lacks any-key answer. **Similar model:** MVX506. **Availability:** Service provider—AirTouch.

Dual-mode models

11 Sony CM-B3200

6$\frac{1}{2}$x1$\frac{7}{8}$x1$\frac{1}{2}$ in. • 8 oz. • 1,200 mAh lithium-ion battery • 209 min. talk • 24 hr. standby
Price: $119-$409 with contract; $179-$249 without. **Recommendation:** Among the best at holding on to a call. Among the most efficient in battery use. **But:** Lacks any-key answer. **Digital**

platform: CDMA PCS. **Similar models:** CM-B1200 and CM-B2200. **Availability:** Service providers—Ameritech, Sprint.

12 Qualcomm QCP-820

6½x2⅛x1⅜ in. • 8 oz. • 1,200 mAh lithium-ion battery •129-min. talk • 15-hr. standby
Price: $129-$399 with contract; $399-$649 without. **Recommendation:** Excellent overall reception purity. Among the best at setting up calls. **Digital platform:** CDMA cellular. **Availability:** Service providers—AirTouch, Ameritech, Bell Atlantic Mobile.

13 Audiovox CDM-3000

6½x1¾x1⅜ in. • 9 oz. • 1,200 mAh nickel-metal-hydride battery • 109 min. talk • 14 hr. standby
Price: $150-$199 with contract; $349-$399 without. **Recommendation:** Excellent overall reception purity. Among the best at handling multipath in hilly terrain. Among the best at setting up calls. **But:** One of the heaviest. Other useful feature: Rapid charger included. **Digital platform:** CDMA cellular. **Similar model:** CDM-3000XL. **Availability:** Service providers—AirTouch, Bell Atlantic Mobile, GTE Wireless.

14 Nokia 2160i

6½x2¼x1¼ in. • 10 oz. • 1,100 mAh nickel-cadmium battery • 110 min. talk • 34 hr. standby
Price: $49-$250 with contract; $249-$500 without. **Recommendation:** Longest standby time among the tested models. **But:** One of the heaviest. Lacks elapsed-talk timer. Other useful feature: Vibrating call alert. **Digital platform:** TDMA cellular. **Availability:** Service providers—Aerial Communications, AirTouch, Ameritech, AT&T Wireless, Bell Atlantic Mobile, Cellular One, Cellular One of San Francisco, BellSouth Mobility, GTE Wireless, Pacific Bell Mobile Services, Southwestern Bell; major retailers—Best Buy, BJ's, Circuit City, OfficeMax, RadioShack, The Good Guys.

15 Ericsson DH368vi

7¾x2x1¼ in. • 6 oz. • 500 mAh nickel-metal-hydride battery • 63 min. talk • 12 hr. standby
Price: $49-$129 with contract; $300-$400 without. **Recommendation:** One of the lightest models tested. **But:** Poor at holding on to a call. Keypad judged only fair. Lacks any-key answer. Lacks one-touch dialing. Other useful features: Rapid charger included. **Digital platform:** TDMA cellular. **Availability:** Service providers—AT&T Wireless, Cellular One of San Francisco, Southwestern Bell. Discontinued but may still be available.

Ratings Computer monitors

& Recommendations

The tests behind the Ratings

Overall score is based mainly on the quality of the picture, but also includes how easy it is to use the controls and menus. We used both laboratory instruments and an expert panel to score **image quality,** which includes contrast, clarity, distortion, and color. **Ease of use** includes how easy the buttons and the on-screen menus are to read and use. We measured viewable image size **(VIS),** the diagonal measurement across the image, and found it consistent with manufacturers' claims. **Maximum resolution** is the highest number of pixels the screen can show at a flicker-free refresh rate of 85 Hz. **Price** is approximate retail.

Typical features for these models

• Horizontal and vertical size and position controls. • Brightness, contrast, and geometric controls. • Control for demagnetizing the screen. • Plug-and-play capability. • Comply with the government's Energy Star power-conservation program. • Comply with electromagnetic standards for low electromagnetic-field emissions. • Don't come with an adapter for using a Macintosh computer (you can request one from the manufacturer). • Don't tilt up and down easily. • 3-yr. warranty on parts, labor, and the tube.

Recommendations

The top six 17-inch monitors in the Ratings produced a good, crisp image. If you're willing to pay more for a good deal more screen space, any of the three 19-inch models we tested would be fine.

See report, page 231. Last time rated in CONSUMER REPORTS: June 1998.

Overall Ratings

E VG G F P

Listed in order of overall score

Key no.	Brand and model	Price	Overall score (0–100; P F G VG E)	Image quality	Ease of use	VIS	Maximum resolution
	17-INCH MONITORS						
1	**Sony** Multiscan CPD-200ES	$400		E	VG	16.0 in.	1024x768
2	**CTX** VL710	450		VG	E	15.7	1280x1024
3	**Panasonic** PanaSync S70	500		VG	G	16.0	1024x768
4	**ViewSonic** G771	400		VG	VG	16.0	1024x768
5	**Samsung** SyncMaster 700s	330		VG	G	15.7	1024x768
6	**NEC** MultiSync A700	430		VG	G	15.6	1024x768

Key no.	Brand and model	Price	Overall score (0–100; P F G VG E)	Image quality	Ease of use	VIS	Maximum resolution
	17-INCH MONITORS *continued*						
7	**MagInnovision** DJ700	$470		○	○	16.1	1024x768
8	**Hitachi** SuperScan Pro 620	450		○	⊖	15.9	1024x768
9	**Nokia** 447Za	500		○	⊖	16.0	1024x768
	19-INCH MONITORS						
10	**Sony** Multiscan GDM-400PS	850		⊖	⊖	18.0	1280x1024
11	**Hitachi** SuperScan Elite 751	800		⊖	○	18.0	1280x1024
12	**ViewSonic** G790	650		⊖	⊖	18.0	1280x1024

Details on the models

Height, width, and **depth** are rounded up to the nearest inch. **Dot pitch** (or aperture-grill pitch) is the manufacturer's measurement.

17-inch monitors

1 Sony Multiscan CPD-200ES $570
• 17x16x16 in. • Aperture-grill pitch: 0.25 mm
Image has a very smooth texture that gives photos natural edges. Driver software is supplied on disk. Screen contains two faint horizontal lines that may be distracting. Lacks manual control for demagnetizing the screen. 1-yr. warranty (shorter than most). **Recommendation:** Very good overall, but expensive.

2 CTX VL710 $450
• 18x16x17 in. • Dot pitch: 0.26 mm
Has control for reducing moiré patterns and for adjusting red, green, and blue color levels. Warranty is 3-yr. on parts and labor, 2-yr. on the tube (shorter than most). **Recommendation:** Very good overall, and a good value.

3 Panasonic PanaSync S70 $500
• 17x17x18 in. • Dot pitch: 0.27 mm
Driver software is supplied on disk. Has control for adjusting red, green, and blue color levels. **Recommendation:** Very good overall.

4 ViewSonic G771 $500
• 16x16x17 in. • Dot pitch: 0.27 mm
Driver software is supplied on disk. Has control for adjusting red, green, and blue color levels. **Availability:** Discontinued **Recommendation:** Very good overall.

5 Samsung SyncMaster 700s $450
• 17x17x17 in. • Dot pitch: 0.28 mm
On-screen menu can be hard to navigate. **Availability:** Discontinued. **Recommendation:** Very good overall.

6 NEC MultiSync A700 $550
• 17x16x17 in. • Dot pitch: 0.28 mm
Image has excellent contrast. Screen geometry needs adjustment after switching resolution mode. On-screen menu can be hard to navigate. **Recommendation:** Very good overall, but expensive.

7 MagInnovision DJ700 $470
• 17x16x17 in. • Dot pitch: 0.26 mm
Moiré patterns are occasionally noticeable. 3-yr. warranty on parts, 1-yr. on labor, 2-yr. on the tube (shorter than most). Lacks color controls. Power switch is inconvenient. **Recommendation:** Good overall.

8 Hitachi SuperScan Pro 620 $450
• 16x16x19 in. • Dot pitch: 0.24 mm
Image is lacking in contrast. Has control for adjusting red, green, and blue color levels. Moiré patterns are occasionally noticeable. **Recommendation:** Good overall.

9 Nokia 447Za $500

• 16x16x17 in. • Dot pitch: 0.27 mm

A multimedia monitor; includes speakers and microphone. Driver software is supplied on disk. Has control for reducing moiré patterns, which are occasionally noticeable. Image is lacking in contrast. Comes with a Mac adapter. Warranty is 3-yr. on parts and labor, 2-yr. on the tube (shorter than most). **Recommendation:** Good overall.

19-inch monitors

10 Sony Multiscan GDM-400PS $1,000

• 18x18x18 in. • Aperture-grill pitch: 0.25 mm

Image has excellent contrast and a very smooth texture that gives photos natural edges. Driver software is supplied on disk. Has control for reducing moiré patterns and for adjusting red, green, and blue color levels. Comes with a Mac adapter. Screen contains two faint horizontal and faint vertical lines that may be distracting. Screen geometry needs adjustment after switching resolution mode. **Recommendation:** Excellent overall.

11 Hitachi SuperScan Elite 751 $850

• 18x18x18 in. • Dot pitch: 0.22 mm

Image has excellent contrast and a texture that some users may prefer for reading text. Has control for reducing moiré patterns, which are occasionally noticeable, and for adjusting red, green, and blue color levels. Screen geometry needs adjustment after switching resolution mode. Front-panel controls are hard to read. **Recommendation:** Excellent overall.

12 ViewSonic G790 $900

• 18x18x18 in. • Dot pitch: 0.26 mm

Image has excellent contrast. Driver software is supplied on disk. Has control for reducing moiré patterns, which are occasionally noticeable, and for adjusting red, green, and blue color levels. Screen geometry needs adjustment after switching resolution mode. **Recommendation:** Excellent overall.

Ratings *Cordless phones*

& Recommendations

The tests behind the Ratings

Overall score is based mostly on speech clarity and convenience. **Ease of use** takes into account such factors as handset comfort and weight, how easy it is to use the keypad, how long you can talk between battery charges, and the presence of useful features. **Battery life** is based on how long a fully charged battery will permit you to talk before it becomes thoroughly drained. The best models could be used for around 14 hours; the worst, only around 5. For answerers, **answerer performance** combines message quality and convenience. **Price** is approximate retail.

Typical features for these models

• One-button redial of last number called. • "Flash" button to take a second call if you have call waiting. • Wall-mountable and tone/pulse switchable. • 1-yr. warranty. • 9 or 10 speed-dial keys to store and recall frequently called or emergency numbers. • Low-battery indicator. • Voice volume control. • Pager capability to track down misplaced handset or beep family member out of earshot.

Recommendations

Our tests revealed little relationship between price and performance. No phone we tested is less than good, but some of the best phones we tested are inexpensive, and some of the worst are very pricey. Unless you have special needs, a 43-49-MHz phone is probably your best choice. With a relatively long range and excellent speech quality, the Lucent (AT&T) 4336, $30, **A CR Best Buy,** should offer fine, no-frills performance throughout most homes and yards.

The best values among the 900 MHz models, which are the best choice for a large home, are the Southwestern Bell FF905, $70, and Lucent (AT&T) 9105, $80. If privacy is paramount, choose either of the digital models we tested—the GE 2-911SST, $105, or Sony SPP-SS950, $150, which is discontinued but has been replaced by the SPP-SS951, $140. If you're looking for a phone with an answerer, the GE 2-9790, $80, a 43-49-MHz model, is the best value of the three units.

See report, page 225. Last time rated in CONSUMER REPORTS: November 1998.

Overall Ratings

Key: E = Excellent, VG = Very good, G = Good, F = Fair, P = Poor

Listed in order of overall score

Key no.	Brand and model	Price	Overall score (0–100; P F G VG E)	Clarity	Ease of use	Battery life	Range
	43-49-MHZ MODELS						
1	**Lucent** 4336, **A CR Best Buy**	$30		E	G	VG	VG
2	**Uniden** XCI660	75		VG	VG	VG	G
3	**Bell South** 33007	60		VG	VG	G	VG
4	**GE** 2-9750	30		VG	G	G	G
5	**Cobra** CP-2530	140		G	G	G	G
	900-MHZ MODELS						
6	**Uniden** EXV 98	130		VG	VG	G	E
7	**Panasonic** KX-TCC912B	200		E	G	F	E
8	**Southwestern Bell** FF905	70		VG	G	F	E
9	**Lucent** 9105	80		E	G	G	E
10	**GE** 2-911SST	105		VG	G	F	E
11	**Radio Shack** ET-918	130		VG	G	G	E
12	**VTech** 912 ADLC	100		E	G	F	E
13	**Sony** SPP-SS950	150		VG	F	F	E
14	**GE** 2-9920	60		VG	F	F	E
	2 LINE 43-49-MHZ MODELS						
15	**Lucent** 7512	110		E	VG	VG	VG
16	**Sony** SPP-M100	120		E	VG	VG	VG

Overall Ratings of models with answerers

Key: E = Excellent, VG = Very good, G = Good, F = Fair, P = Poor

Listed in order of overall telephone score

Key no.	Brand and model	Price	Overall score (0–100; P F G VG E)	Phone performance: Clarity	Phone performance: Ease of use	Phone performance: Battery life	Phone performance: Range	Answerer performance
17	**Sony** SPP-A940 (900-MHz)	$175		E	G	G	E	G
18	**GE** 2-9790 (43-49-MHz)	80		VG	VG	VG	VG	G
19	**Lucent** 7720 (43-49-MHz)	140		VG	VG	F	G	VG

Details on the models

43-49-MHz models

1 Lucent (AT&T) 4336 $30

• 10 channels • 400-ft. range

A fine, if basic, phone with a long range for a 43-49-MHz model and a very comfortable handset. One of the best-sounding phones we tested. **But:** With only 10 channels, may occasionally be noisy in very crowded urban areas. Lacks voice volume control. Lacks pager to locate handset. **Recommendation:** Very good. **A CR Best Buy**.

2 Uniden XCI660 $75

• 25 channels • Liquid crystal display with capability for caller ID with call waiting • 200-ft. range

A full-featured model with a comfortable, curved handset with a lighted keypad and ringer volume control. 20 speed-dial numbers, more than most. **But:** Loudness dropped more than most when other extensions are in use. **Availability:** Discontinued, but may still be available in some stores. **Recommendation:** Very good, but a good value only if you subscribe to caller ID.

3 Bell South 33007 $60

• 25 channels • 400-ft. range

Very good sound, a long range for a 43-49-MHz model, and very convenient to use. Handset has lighted keypad. **But:** Lacks voice volume control. Loudness dropped more than most when other extensions are in use. **Recommendation:** Very good.

4 GE 2-9750 $30

• 25 channels • 200-ft. range

Fairly basic, like (1), though with niceties (pager, ringer-off control, and volume control on handset) that (1) lacks—and a better choice if airwaves are crowded. The lightest handset of all models tested (6 oz.). **But:** No modular phone jack on base; damaged cord hard to replace. **Similar models:** 2-9763, $30; 2-9752, $40. **Recommendation:** Good, and a very good value.

5 Cobra CP-2530 $140

• 25 channels • Liquid crystal display with caller ID capability, including caller ID with call waiting • 100-ft. range

The high price pays for features, including a backup battery in case of power failure, voice scrambling for improved privacy (which may degrade speech quality and cannot be switched off), 30 speed-dial numbers, and an antenna that's hidden inside the handset. **But:** Lowest range of all models tested. Imparted a hard-edged sound to speech. Handset heavy (11 oz.); must stand up to take charge. Lacks voice volume control. No modular phone jack on base; damaged cord hard to replace. **Recommendation:** OK and pricey.

900-Hz models

6 Uniden EXV 98 $130

• 40 channels • 1,300-ft. range

A solid performer. Has 30 speed-dial numbers, more than most. Speed-dial numbers can be activated by pressing a single digit, then speaking the person's name into the handset; the feature worked well in our tests, though it can recognize only a single user. Belt clip. **But:** Heavy handset (11-oz.). **Recommendation:** Very good, and the voice-activated dialing feature could be a boon to a disabled person.

7 Panasonic KX-TCC912B $200

• 30 channels • Speakerphone • Second keypad on base • Liquid crystal display with capability for caller ID with call waiting • 1,300-ft. range

One of the best-sounding phones tested, and rich in features, including lighted keypad on handset and spare battery-charger in base. Pager can function as intercom, enabling communication between base and handset. **But:** Among the worst models for battery life. Boxy handset doesn't sit comfortably against face and ear. **Similar model:** KX-TC911, $100, lacks caller-ID capability.

8 Southwestern Bell FF905 $70

• 40 channels • 1,100-ft. range

A basic 900-MHz model. Mute on handset. **But:** Among the worst models for battery life. Handset has flat profile; doesn't sit well against face and ear. **Similar model:** FF908, $65. **Recommendation:** Very good, and a very good value in a 900-MHz phone.

9 Lucent (AT&T) 9105 $80

• 10 channels • 1,200-ft. range
One of the best-sounding phones tested. Spare battery-charger built into base. Belt clip. **But:** Failed surge test; lightning strike could damage phone. **Recommendation:** Very good, and a very good value in a 900-MHz phone.

10 GE 2-911SST $105

• Digital transmission • 20 channels • 2,200-ft. (or more) range
Digital spread-spectrum technology offers exceptional range and privacy. Adjustable ringer. **But:** Among the worst models for battery life. Handset doesn't fit comfortably against face and ear. Hard-to-read labeling on buttons. Failed surge test; lightning strike could damage phone. **Similar model:** 2-913SST, approximately $130. **Recommendation:** Very good—and a very good value in a digital phone.

11 RadioShack ET-918 $130

• 40 channels • Headset jack • 1,300-ft. range
Has adjustable ringer. **But:** Hard-to-read labeling on buttons. **Recommendation:** Very good, but there are better values.

12 VTech 912 ADLC $100

• 10 channels • Liquid crystal display with capability for caller ID • 1,300-ft. range
One of the best-sounding phones tested. Spare battery-charger built into base. Voice volume control on handset. **But:** Among the worst models for battery life, and manufacturers' recommended recharging time is longer than for any other phone. Boxy, flat handset doesn't sit comfortably against face and ear. Failed surge test; lightning strike could damage phone. **Recommendation:** Very good, though with some notable shortcomings.

13 Sony SPP-SS950 $150

• Digital transmission • 20 channels • 2,200-ft. (or more) range
Digital spread-spectrum technology offers exceptional range and privacy. **But:** Among the worst models for battery life. Handset fairly heavy (10 oz.), and doesn't fit comfortably against face and ear. **Availability:** Discontinued. **Similar model:** SPP-SS951, $140. **Recommendation:** Very good, though (10) is a less expensive choice in a digital phone.

14 GE 2-9920 $60

• 30 channels • 1,100-ft. range
The least expensive 900-MHz phone tested. Mute button on handset. **But:** Among the worst models for battery life. Buttons are small, hard to read, and handset doesn't fit comfortably against face and ear. **Similar models:** 2-9921, $65; 2-9930, $100; and 2-9925, $115. **Recommendation:** Good, and a very good value in a 900-MHz phone.

Two-line 43-49-Hz models

15 Lucent (AT&T) 7512 $110

• 25 channels • Speakerphone • Second keypad on base • Mute button on handset • 300-ft. range
A fine performer—one of the best-sounding phones tested—and loaded with extras. Pager can function as intercom, enabling communication between base and handset. Allows three-way conferencing. 20 speed-dial numbers, more than most. **Recommendation:** Very good.

16 Sony SPP-M100 $120

• 25 channels • Mute button on handset • 400-ft. range
One of the best-sounding phones tested, with a long range for a 43-49-MHz model. Contoured handset is more comfortable than most and has large, legible buttons, though it is also fairly heavy (10 oz.). Allows three-way conferencing. **But:** Failed surge test; lightning strike could damage phone. **Availability:** Discontinued. **Similar model:** SPP-M502, $115. **Recommendation:** Very good.

Models with answerers

Message clarity reflects how pristine and natural messages sounded in the answerer's loudspeaker. Convenience takes into account ease of use and the presence of useful features. Memory is the maximum recording time for greeting and messages.

17 Sony SPP-A940 $175

• 900-MHz transmission • 10 channels • 1,100-ft. range • Messages ◒ • Convenience ⊖ • Memory 15.3 min.
One of the best-sounding phones tested. Answerer provides audible message alert and can quickly scan through message. Longer recording capacity than others. **But:** Handset fairly heavy (10 oz.), doesn't fit comfortably against

face and ear. Voices sounded a bit muffled on answerer playback. **Recommendation:** Very good as a phone and good as an answerer.

18 **GE 2-9790** $80

• 43-49-MHz transmission • 25 channels • 300-ft. range • Messages ○ • Convenience ⊖ • Memory 9.3 min.

Messages can be retrieved via handset. **But:** Lacks digital message counter. Clock must be reset even if power goes out for a mere 10 minutes. Can't replay only a portion of a message. **Recommendation:** Very good as a phone and good as an answerer, providing you don't get a lot of messages or crave a lot of features. Excellent value.

19 **Lucent (AT&T) 7720** $140

• 43-49-MHZ transmission • 25 channels • Speakerphone • Liquid crystal display with capability for caller ID with call waiting • 200-ft. range • Messages ○ • Convenience ◒ • Memory 9.3 min.

Base has battery backup in case of power failure. Pager can function as intercom, enabling communication between base and handset. Includes voice scrambling, which improved privacy; when scrambling is activated, voice quality degrades a little. Answerer provides audible message alert and can quickly scan through a message. Messages can be directed to one of two "mailboxes" and retrieved via handset. 20 speed-dial numbers, more than most. **But:** Among the worst models for battery life. Failed surge test; lightning strike could damage phone. **Recommendation:** Very good, both as a phone and an answerer; (17) is a better value.

Ratings *Computer furniture*

& Recommendations

The tests behind the Ratings

Overall score is based primarily on ergonomics; fit and finish, clarity of instructions, and ease of assembly were also scored. **Ergonomics** includes the monitor's position with regard to the viewer and the keyboard; the keyboard's height; the ability to use a mouse on the keyboard shelf; and leg room. The more adjustable the components, the better. **Fit** is how well the parts mesh when assembled; **finish**, how well laminates and veneers were applied. **Assembly** varies with the type of unit: Desks take longer than carts because more parts are involved. **Price** is approximate retail.

Typical features for these models

• Are particleboard covered with plastic laminate. • Fit a vertical CPU or wide horizontal CPU. • Have stationary printer shelf large enough to accommodate most printers. • Have room for a mouse on the keyboard shelf. • Have convenient, sturdy cam-bolt-and-lock fasteners. • Provide for at least adequate adjustment from monitor to eyes. • Lack height adjustments for monitor and keyboard. • Lack a copy shelf. • Have a 5- or 6-year warranty on defective parts.

Recommendations

Any of the high-rated pieces below are worth considering, as long as you make sure the one you take home is comfortable to work at. Among desks with a hutch, the top five were judged very good overall but aren't without drawbacks (see the Details on the models). Among the tested armoires, The Sauder 2649 would make the best choice (the Ikea Kavaljer has been discontinued). The O'Sullivan The Cockpit 61955 was the best in the corner-unit category. None of the carts earned better than a good rating; all have limited leg room and desktop space. The best of the lot are the top three; don't look any lower in the ratings.

See report, page 230. Last time rated in CONSUMER REPORTS: January 1998.

Overall Ratings

E VG G F P

Listed in order of overall score

Key no.	Brand and model	Price	Overall score (0–100; P F G VG E)	Ergonomics	Fit/finish	Assembly
	DESKS WITH HUTCH					
1	**Sauder** 2738 Heritage Hill	$300		G	VG/G	G
2	**Bush** 7902 Visions	200		G	VG/VG	G
3	**Sauder** 5637 Worthington	270		G	G/G	VG
4	**Ameriwood** Portfolio 33850	250		G	G/G	VG
5	**Bush** WC3401 Heritage Pine	200		G	G/G	VG
6	**IKEA** Kurs	250		G	VG/E	VG
7	**Bush** WC6402 Contours	300		G	VG/G	VG
8	**Sauder** 8437 Mission	240		G	G/VG	F
9	**O'Sullivan** Scandinavian 61933	200		F	G/G	G
	ARMOIRES					
10	**IKEA** Kavaljer	370		G	E/E	E
11	**Sauder** 2649 Monarch	490		G	G/VG	G
12	**Bush** WC3137 Hallmark	400		P	G/VG	VG
	CORNER UNITS					
13	**O'Sullivan** The Cockpit 61955	300		G	VG/G	F
14	**Bush** 3005C	200		F	G/G	VG
	CARTS					
15	**Bush** 7917 Visions (with hutch)	140		F	G/VG	VG
16	**O'Sullivan** 61222 (with hutch)	100		F	G/G	VG
17	**Ameriwood** Affordable 1317 (with hutch)	120		F	VG/G	VG
18	**Sauder** 5399 (with hutch)	140		F	F/G	G
19	**Bush** WC2806A Westwood	180		F	VG/E	E
20	**Sauder** 2799 Heritage Hill	120		F	G/G	VG
21	**O'Sullivan** 50118	65		P	G/G	VG
22	**Ameriwood** Affordable 2318	70		F	G/F	E

Details on the models

Measurements are HxWxD. We've listed finishes we tested; others may also be available.

Desks with hutch

1 Sauder 2738 Heritage Hill $300

• Traditional, cherry • 60x60x24 in.
CPU cabinet can be locked. **Recommendation:** Very good, and versatile for different computer hardware.

2 Bush 7902 Visions $200

• Contemporary, oak • 54x54x27 in.
Height of monitor shelf is adjustable, and both fit and finish are very good. **But:** Little room to adjust the monitor's distance, lacks printer shelf, won't fit a vertical CPU. And you'll need clearance on the left side of the unit to get at bookshelves. **Recommendation:** Very good, if you have a horizontal CPU.

3 Sauder 5637 Worthington $270

• Contemporary, oak • 57x60x25 in.
Separate printer cart and four monitor/keyboard configurations. **But:** Only one of the monitor/keyboard configurations aligns the two elements properly. Won't fit a vertical CPU. Doors and drawer fronts are hard to align and left large gaps. **Recommendation:** Very good, if you have a horizontal CPU.

4 Ameriwood Portfolio 33850 $250

• Contemporary, oak and black • 66x60x30 in.
No storage area for vertical CPU. Drawer fronts are hard to align and left large gaps. Flimsy hutch attachment makes assembled unit difficult to move. Coffee spill damaged finish. Defective-parts warranty only one year. **Recommendation:** Very good, with lots of working space.

5 Bush WC3401 Heritage Pine $200

• Contemporary, knotty pine • 57x53x23 in.
Lacks printer shelf. Keyboard shelf has no room for a mouse. Drawer fronts are hard to align and left large gaps. **Recommendation:** Very good, if you don't mind giving up work space to the printer.

6 IKEA Kurs $250

• Contemporary, pine veneer • 61x44x28 in.
Excellent fit, and lifetime warranty against quality defects. **But:** Desktop is smaller than that of other desks. Fairly high monitor shelf allows little distance adjustment. Won't fit a vertical CPU or a horizontal CPU wider than 18 inches. Won't fit a 17-inch monitor; even a 15-inch monitor fits poorly. Shallow printer shelf. Flimsy hutch attachment makes the assembled unit difficult to move. Poor instructions. **Availability:** Discontinued. **Recommendation:** Very good, but barely; looks better than it works.

7 Bush WC6402 Contours $300

• Contemporary, cherry and black • 54x53x29 in.
Height of monitor shelf adjustable, with difficulty. **But:** Lacks printer shelf. Little room to adjust monitor's distance. Won't fit a vertical CPU. You'll need clearance on the left side of the unit to get at bookshelves. Drawer fronts are hard to align and left large gaps. Coffee spill damaged finish. **Recommendation:** Very good, but barely, and not worth $100 more than (5).

8 Sauder 8437 Mission $240

• Mission style, fruitwood • 57x60x24 in.
Lacks printer shelf. Drawer fronts are hard to align and left large gaps. **Recommendation:** Very good, but barely.

9 O'Sullivan Scandinavian 61933 $200

• Contemporary, alder and black • 47x54x24 in.
Vertical CPU cabinet can be locked. **But:** Fairly high monitor shelf. When set up for left-handed user, ample leg room, but monitor isn't centered. For right-handed user, monitor is centered, but no leg room. Won't fit a horizontal CPU wider than 18 inches. Doors and drawer fronts are hard to align and left large gaps. **Recommendation:** Good, but others have fewer annoyances.

Armoires

10 IKEA Kavaljer $370

• Contemporary, pine veneer • 80x31x22 in.
Excellent fit and finish, and lifetime warranty against quality defects. **But:** Fairly high monitor shelf. Desktop smaller than that of other armoires. Won't fit a 17-inch monitor. Shallow printer shelf. Poor instructions. **Availability:** Discontinued. **Recommendation:** Very good.

11 Sauder 2649 Monarch $490

• Country, oak • 71x42x23 in.
Locks secure all doors. **But:** Requires extra room on sides to fully open cabinet doors and swing out work table and file drawer. You need to remove a bookshelf to make room for a vertical CPU. Overhanging desktop may block top of keyboard, especially if add-on wrist rest is used. **Recommendation:** Very good.

12 Bush WC3137 Hallmark $400

• Contemporary, oak • 74x47x21 in.
Height of monitor shelf adjustable. Locks secure all doors. **But:** Little room to adjust monitor's distance. Keyboard shelf has no room for mouse. You need to remove a bookshelf to make room for a vertical CPU. Little leg room. Little clearance above printer shelf. Doors are hard to align and left large gaps. **Availability:** Discontinued. **Recommendation:** Good overall, but ergonomic shortcomings.

Corner units

13 O'Sullivan The Cockpit 61955 $300

• Contemporary, alder and black • 54x48x48 in.
Height of monitor shelf adjustable. Has lighted copy shelf and keyboard whose angle can be adjusted. **But:** Keyboard tips only toward the user (up at the rear, instead of down), and unit won't fit a horizontal CPU wider than 18 inches. **Recommendation:** Very good overall.

14 Bush 3005C $200

• Contemporary, oak • 58x54x20 in.
Lacks printer shelf. Keyboard shelf has no room for mouse. Overhanging desktop may block upper portion of keyboard, especially if add-on wrist rest is used. Little clearance above printer on desktop. Doors hard to align and left large gaps. **Recommendation:** Good overall, but ergonomic shortcomings.

Carts

15 Bush 7917 Visions (with hutch) $140

• Contemporary, oak • 53x36x20 in.
Little leg room. **Recommendation:** Good.

16 O'Sullivan 61222 (with hutch) $100

• Contemporary, oak • 56x32x20 in.
Little leg room. **Recommendation:** Good.

17 Ameriwood Affordable 1317 (with hutch) $120

• Contemporary, light oak • 56x34x20 in.
Monitor shelf fairly high. Little leg room. Coffee spill damaged finish. Defective-parts warranty only one year. **Recommendation:** Good.

18 Sauder 5399 (with hutch) $140

• Contemporary, oak • 57x40x20 in.
Monitor shelf fairly high. Little leg room. **Recommendation:** Good, but there are better choices.

19 Bush WC2806A Westwood $180

• Contemporary, oak veneer • 30x36x20 in.
All wood. Excellent finish. **But:** Little leg room. **Recommendation:** Good, but pricey.

20 Sauder 2799 Heritage Hill $120

• Traditional, cherry • 30x35x20 in.
Excellent instructions. **But:** Little leg room. Only rear casters swivel, so it's hard to move sideways. **Recommendation:** Fair. Choose another.

21 O'Sullivan 50118 $65

• Contemporary, oak • 34x25x23 in.
Keyboard shelf has no room for mouse or add-on wrist rest. Won't fit a vertical CPU. Little leg room. **Availability:** Discontinued. **Recommendation:** Fair. Choose another.

22 Ameriwood Affordable 2318 $70

• Contemporary, black • 30x36x20 in.
Little leg room. Coffee spill damaged finish. Defective-parts warranty only one year. **Recommendation:** Fair. Choose another.

Autos

HOW TO BUY OR LEASE

Buying a car doesn't have to be an ordeal. If you do a little research and know what to expect, you can drive just as good a bargain as anyone else. Here are some tips to keep in mind:

Decide which models fit your needs. There are dozens of choices. The Ratings on page 271 and the previews of the 1999 models, starting on page 258, can help narrow your search for a new car. The lists on pages 275 to 278 can help you find a reliable used model. (For more on buying a used car, see page 256.) Consider more than one model so you have a fallback.

Know what the dealer paid. When you're buying a new car, having the invoice price gives you an advantage in negotiating a discount. Just as important, a detailed pricing report helps you make useful comparisons between the differently equipped cars you'll see on a dealer's lot. You can get price information from printed guides available at libraries, and from several World Wide Web sites, such as Kelley Blue Book and Edmund's. You can also get prices and customized model information for $12 from the Consumer Reports New Car Price Service (800-933-5555). See the back cover for more information.

Call several dealers. Find out what's available. If local dealers don't have the models you want, ask how long locating or special-ordering would take. And ask about the dealership's "document," "conveyance," or "processing" fee. This often-negotiable fee varies from zero to $300. It could swing you from one dealership to another.

Call your insurance agent. If you've been driving a nine-year-old car, you may not realize how much more insurance on a brand-new vehicle will cost.

Check out the car in the showroom. Visiting dealers will tell you how the car you want is typically equipped. Be flexible about optional equipment. You might find that a model with something you want—leather seats, say—also has something you don't want, such as a CD changer in the trunk. If you can live without the leather, you may find a car with other features that compensate.

Don't let on if you find your dream car. If you allow yourself to fall in love with a car—or grab an over-equipped model just because it's available now—you're apt to overpay. Tell the salesperson that you have invoice-price information and you're shopping around. Explain politely but firmly that whoever has the best price wins your business, and ask for the minimum markup over invoice the dealer will accept. Make it clear that you want an out-the-door price, minus taxes and registration fees. Once you get the dealer's best offer, say you'll be in touch if this is the best price you find—then leave.

What's a fair price? For a car left over from the previous model year, your target price shouldn't be much over invoice—it may even be below invoice if dealer rebates are in effect. For a brand-new model in high demand, the price might match the sticker. For most cars, 4 to 8 percent over invoice is reasonable.

If your trade-in is part of the deal, be realistic about its value. Determine what the vehicle is actually worth. To find the high end of your car's price range in your area, check classified ads, consult used-car price guides—available at libraries and on the Web—or get customized information from the Consumer Reports Used Car Price Service (800 422-1083). To establish the low end of the range, canvas the used-car department of local new-car dealers to see what they'd pay in a straight-out purchase. Have your car as clean as possible for an appraisal, then negotiate the trade-in separately from the new-car deal.

Online shopping

There are thousands of web sites devoted to automobiles.

Manufacturer sites, which supply the sort of information you'd find in a brochure—pictures, color choices, and specifications for the latest models—are basically glitzy advertising vehicles. You'll also find sticker prices, and sometimes links to local dealers, but little to aid comparison-shopping.

Dealer web sites, maintained by thousands of individual local dealers, are also fairly superficial. But they often give that dealership's various specials-of-the-week.

Online buying services such as Autobytel, Autostop, AutoVantage, Autoweb, and Carpoint promise to make car-shopping hassle-free by arranging for a discount price at a dealer near you. You wade through menus specifying your car and options preferences. The online service then E-mails, phones, or faxes you with a contact name at a local dealership.

Online services offer one great advantage—convenience. You don't have to leave home to glean vital information about prices, option packages, colors, and so forth.

In other respects, buying services are quite limited, and are only as good as the local dealer they happen to recommend. Since they can't tell you how cars in dealer stock are typically equipped, you can't know whether the car you select is mainstream or rare. What's more, the dealer they choose may be far from your home. You'll still have to visit in person to see what's actually available. And despite any promise of "guaranteed low prices," you must still shop around to find the best price available.

Leasing the smart way

This year, about one third of new cars, trucks, and minivans will be leased instead of bought.

Advantages of leasing include: less money down than for a loan on a comparable car; lower monthly payments;

and easy disposal of the car at the end of the lease term.

But a lease usually makes financial sense only if:

• You don't exceed the annual mileage allowance, typically 12,000 miles per year. Each additional mile costs from 10 to 25 cents—and can drive up costs quickly.

• You don't terminate the lease early—early termination may mean thousands of dollars in penalties.

• You keep your car in good shape—"excess wear and tear" charges at lease-end can be very expensive.

• You plan to trade in your car every two or three years anyway. If you keep a car for many years, you're usually better off buying it outright at the start.

Despite recent federal regulations making lease contract language more understandable, it can still be hard to compare one lease deal with another. Most egregious, the new law doesn't require the lease to disclose the "money factor"—analogous to an annual percentage rate—used to calculate the monthly payments.

Here are six steps to getting the best deal on a car lease:

• Negotiate the price as if you were buying the car. Make sure the agreed-upon price is the figure used to calculate the lease terms. Negotiate other aspects of a lease as well, such as the mileage limit, the down payment, and the purchase fee.

• If you have a trade-in, make sure its value is deducted from the "capitalized cost," or selling price.

• The four-digit "money factor" is roughly equivalent to a loan's annual percentage rate. To translate it into terms you can understand, multiply the money factor by 2,400.

• Make sure "excess wear and tear" is clearly defined, in writing.

• Purchase extra miles up front if you think you'll exceed the standard mileage allowance.

• Look for a "subvented" lease—one subsidized by the factory. Often promoted in full-page newspaper ads, subvented leases can be a good deal if you happen to want that particular vehicle.

Choosing the right options

Options vary by trim line—the model version designated GL, DL, and so on. They're often part of a package, called a "preferred equipment group" or "quick-order package." Sometimes it's hard to buy one single option without accepting a package of unrelated features. For instance, if you want to add the $550 antilock brakes to a Mazda Miata, you must buy a $2,330 "popular equipment" packages that includes cruise control, an upgraded sound system, power antenna, and power door locks.

Most of the cars on a dealer's lot come with one or another of those packages, installed at the factory. Don't confuse manufacturer's equipment with dealer "packs" —extra-cost add-ons put there by the dealer, not the factory, such as rustproofing, pinstripes, extra-dark window tinting, and paint and upholstery preservatives. These aren't worth the money.

Buying a used car

Late-model used cars may be the best automotive value. The reason: Someone else pays for the heaviest depreciation. When you buy a used car, reliability should be the main consideration. The lists on pages 276 to 278 can help you find a model likely to be reliable.

New-car dealers sell the most used cars, and generally offer the best-quality vehicles as well as the facilities to service them. You'll also get some sort of warranty. But expect these dealers to charge the highest prices.

"Factory certified" used cars are increasingly widespread. They're supposed to be carefully chosen by select new-car dealers and put through a long factory checklist to ensure top-notch condition. They generally come with a one-year factory warranty.

Cars from used-car dealers are usually a notch down in price. The trend in this market segment is toward superstores run by large national companies. Chains such as AutoNation and CarMax feature huge lots filled with clean late-model cars, usually at fixed, no-haggle prices. The stock is computerized, so you needn't trudge all across the lot. The salesperson can ask you about the type of vehicle you want and call up specific models on a computer in the office. Superstores tend to price competitively, but their prices aren't necessarily the lowest.

Of course, you can buy a car from a private owner. Though the price may be low, this kind of transaction gives you little recourse if the car isn't as represented.

However you buy the car, find out whether it's still covered under the factory warranty. If you buy from a new-car dealer who sells the same make, ask that the car's vehicle identification number (VIN) be run though the dealer's computer and a printout made of any warranty repairs that have been completed. The dealer can also check whether any repairs required by federal recalls have been done.

The car's overall condition should jibe with it's odometer reading. Signs of high mileage: excessive wear on the brake and accelerator pedals; brand-new pedal pads; a new set of tires or more than one brand of tires; a well-worn ignition key; worn or sagging driver's seat; frayed carpeting; a windshield scored by the wiper blades or pitted by debris.

When you find good prospect, take it to a mechanic for a thorough inspection—worth the $60 to $100 to avoid a clunker. Deduct the cost of any needed repairs from your offer, unless the seller agrees to make suitable repairs before you buy the car.

PREVIEWS OF THE 1999 CARS

Here, listed alphabetically by make and model, you'll find previews of the 1999 cars, minivans, sport-utility vehicles, and pickup trucks. Our comments are based on our assessment of manufacturers' specifications, and on road tests that pertain to this year's model (most models don't change significantly from year to year).

At the end of each entry, you'll find the date of the last full road test for that model published in CONSUMER REPORTS. These detailed reports are available at libraries or by fax or mail from our Consumer Reports by Request 24-hour service. To use the service, note the four-digit fax number at the end of the entry for the model or models you're interested in, then call 800 896-7788. from a touch-tone phone. The cost is $7.75 per report.

Predicted reliability is a judgment based on our Frequency-of-Repair data (see page 279). If a vehicle has been redesigned, only data for models relevant to the 1999 models are considered. New or recently redesigned models are marked "New." **Depreciation** predicts how well a new model will keep its value, based on the difference between it's original sticker price and the resale value after three years. As a group, sport-utility vehicles have the lowest depreciation rate. Pickup trucks also tend to hold their value. Large cars have a relatively high depreciation rate.

Throughout, ✔ indicates a model recommended by CONSUMER REPORTS; **NA** means data not available; ↑ means a model is promising.

Model	Predicted reliability	Depreciation	Comments
Acura CL	○	NA	This coupe is based on the previous generation Honda Accord. It is equipped with either a 2.3-liter Four or a 3.0-liter V6. Expect good handling and a refined, quiet ride. **Last report/fax: ——**
✔ Acura Integra ➡	⊜	○	An upscale relative of the Honda Civic. The standard engine provides more than adequate acceleration. The cabin feels a bit cramped and is somewhat noisy. **Last report/fax: August 97/9597**
✔ Acura RL	⊜	○	Acura's flagship sedan is quiet, spacious, and refined, though rather bland. It handles well and delivers a smooth, quiet ride. Not as well rounded as the BMW 5-Series or Mercedes E-Class. **Last report/fax: November 96/9513**
Acura SLX	NA	NA	A rebadged Isuzu Trooper. We rated the 1996-1997 SLX Not Acceptable because of its tendency to roll over. Outdated and overpriced. **Last report/fax: ——**
Acura TL	⊜	○	This upscale midsized sedan was redesigned for 1999. It is based on the current Honda Accord, with a sprightly and quiet 3.2-liter V6. Expect sound handling, a comfortable ride, and good reliability. **Last report/fax: ——**
✔ Audi A4	○	⊖	The A4 rides firmly and handles precisely and nimbly. The rear seat is very tight. Audi's all-wheel-drive Quattro feature is a worthwhile option. **Last report/fax: ——**
✔ Audi A6	⊖	○	Audi's midsized sedan was redesigned and much improved for 1998. Has a supple ride, competent handling, and comfortable and supportive seats. Also available as a wagon and with all-wheel-drive. **Last report/fax: October 98/9803**
Audi A8	NA	NA	Audi's top-of-the-line A8 is a full-sized luxury car that competes with the BMW 7-Series, Mercedes S-Class, and Lexus LS400. It doesn't ride as well as those, but the available all-wheel-drive Quattro feature is unique in that class. **Last report/fax: ——**

Model	Predicted reliability	Depreciation	Comments
BMW 3-Series	⊖	⊖	The 3-Series sedans are all-new for 1999. They're a bit larger, and the cabin feels less confining. Both engines are now smooth Sixes. Expect nimble handling and a taut, comfortable ride. **Last report/fax: ——**
BMW 318ti	NA	⊖	The 318ti is the "entry level" BMW. Side-impact air bags are standard. This rear-wheel-drive hatchback coupe is fun to drive, with precise handling, tenacious tire grip, plus a firm but comfortable ride. **Last report/fax: ——**
✔ BMW 5-Series	○	⊖	Embodies pure precision. These superbly designed rear-wheel-drive luxury sports sedans handle nimbly and responsively. The ride is supple and quiet, with extremely comfortable, supportive seats. **Last report/fax: November 96/9513**
BMW 740i	NA	○	The top-of-the-line 7-Series BMW competes with the world's premier luxury sedans. The 740i handles superbly for a car its size. Important standard safety items include an anti-skid system as well as front side and head-level air bags. **Last report/fax: ——**
✔ BMW Z3	○	○	This roadster handles sharply, but when pushed too hard, the rear end can suddenly slide out. The interior is cramped. A 2.5-liter Six replaced the 1.9-liter Four for 1999. A high-performance, 240-hp M version is available. **Last report/fax: August 98/9686**
Buick Century	○	◒	The Century feels like old technology. The ride is quiet and soft, at least at low speeds, but bumpy roads easily upset its composure. The front bench seat is roomy, but the soft seats offer little support. **Last report/fax: October 97/9618**
Buick LeSabre	○	○	A quiet, softly sprung freeway cruiser. Expect the LeSabre to handle sloppily and its body to lean sharply in turns. An optional firmer suspension helps. **Last report/fax: January 96/9447**
Buick Park Avenue	◒	◒	Buick's top-of-the-line sedan rides and handles well. Acceleration is effortless in the Ultra. The interior is roomy and quiet, and the seats are comfortable. Reliability has fallen off of late. **Last report/fax: June 98/9672**
Buick Regal	◒	◒	This car rides well at low speeds, its V6 accelerates adequately, and the automatic transmission is very smooth. The cabin is quiet. The seats feel soft at first but grow less comfortable on longer rides. **Last report/fax: January 98/9644**
Buick Riviera	○	◒	This big and clumsy coupe will be discontinued at the end of the 1998 model year. **Last report/fax: ——**
Cadillac Catera	◒	NA	Yields nothing in performance to competing sports sedans, but reliability has been a problem. It accelerates briskly and has a firm, well-controlled ride. The front seats are large and supportive, and three adults easily fit in the rear. **Last report/fax: March 97/9558**
✔ Cadillac DeVille	○	◒	This big, plush freeway cruiser handles well for such a large car, and it offers plenty of power and a mostly compliant ride. The control layout is inconvenient. **Last report/fax: June 98/9672**
Cadillac Eldorado	●	◒	This luxury coupe comes with lots of high-tech equipment. The front seat is roomy. The rear seat is fairly comfortable for two, but access is awkward. **Last report/fax: ——**
Cadillac Escalade	NEW	NA	The Escalade is really a rebadged Chevrolet Tahoe. Virtues include a powerful engine and a smooth-shifting transmission plus a very spacious interior. But don't expect competent handling or anything but abysmal fuel economy. **Last report/fax: ——**
Cadillac Seville	○	◒	Positioned as an alternative to European and Japanese luxury sedans. The Seville was redesigned for 1998. It is powered by the sophisticated Northstar V8. It has a tight rear seat for the class. **Last report/fax: ——**
Chevrolet Astro	●	○	Can haul lots of cargo or tow a heavy trailer. Offers all-wheel drive. Handles ponderously and rides uncomfortably. Seriously outclassed by all modern minivan designs. The GMC Safari is similar. **Last report/fax: July 96/9489**

Model	Predicted reliability	Depreciation	Comments
Chevrolet Blazer	◒	○	The Blazer offers generous cargo room, a decent powertrain, and a tolerable ride. But handling and reliability have been subpar. **Last report/fax: May 98/9661**
Chevrolet Camaro	●	○	Similar to the Pontiac Firebird, this muscle car is really too bulky to be nimble. Traction control is a worthy option on V8-powered models. The ride is uncomfortable. Reliability has been poor. **Last report/fax: ——**
Chevrolet Cavalier	— ◒	○	Rough roads make the body bounce. The front seats feel comfortable on short trips but are fatiguing on long journeys. The rear seat is barely adequate. Reliability has fallen below average in our latest survey. **Last report/fax: January 97/9539**
Chevrolet Corvette	◒	○	Redesigned for 1997, the new Corvette comes as a coupe, convertible, or hardtop. Though very fast and responsive, the Corvette is really more about thrust than driving finesse. **Last report/fax: August 98/9686**
✔ Chevrolet Lumina	⊖	◒	Does most things adequately but unexceptionally. Ride and handling are acceptable. Controls and displays are generally well designed. The front seats are thinly padded; the rear seat is uncomfortable. **Last report/fax: February 97/9549**
Chevrolet Malibu	●	NA	Positioned as a lower-priced alternative to a Honda Accord or Toyota Camry. But it's less refined than those two. Handles soundly. The ride is firm. Reliability has not held up well in its second year. **Last report/fax: May 97/9572**
Chevrolet Metro	⊖	◒	This undesireable car—a close copy of the Suzuki Swift hatchback—is smaller than other small cars. It's also greatly underpowered. The ride is choppy, noisy, and uncomfortable. **Last report/fax: ——**
Chevrolet Monte Carlo	○	○	This coupe handles sloppily and rides stiffly. The cabin has plenty of room up front, but the cloth seats feel lumpy and lack support. The rear seat is uncomfortable and hard to access. **Last report/fax: ——**
✔ Chevrolet Prizm	○	◒	Rides comfortably and gets excellent fuel economy. Acceleration is brisk. The front seats are firm and supportive. A standard front stabilizer bar has balanced the Prizm's once subpar handling. **Last report/fax: March 98/9657**
Chevrolet S-Series	●	○	The compact S-Series and its sibling, the GMC Sonoma, ride stiffly and lean a lot in corners. The cabin is quiet. The V6 accelerates well. **Last report/fax: December 98/9805**
Chevrolet Silverado	NEW	⊖	The Silverado, a full-sized pickup, was redesigned for 1999 and much improved. The engines are more powerful but less thirsty, and the optional four-wheel-drive system is now full-time. The GMC Sierra is similar. **Last report/fax: ——**
Chevrolet Suburban	◒	⊜	One of the largest SUVs offered. The Chevy and its GMC twin can seat as many as nine or tow a heavy trailer. Selectable full-time four-wheel drive is optional. **Last report/fax: ——**
Chevrolet Tahoe	●	⊖	This big SUV's virtues include a cavernous interior, a powerful engine, and a smooth-shifting transmission. But it's also heavy, clumsy, and an expensive gas-guzzler. A form of full-time four-wheel drive is optional. **Last report/fax: October 96/9508**
Chevrolet Tracker	NEW	◒	The redesigned Tracker uses an old-school body-on-frame design that hardly lends itself to a good ride or crisp handling. It's similar to the Suzuki Vitara. **Last report/fax: ——**
Chevrolet Venture	◒	NA	This minivan offers a useful left-side sliding door and a powered right-side door. The front seats are comfortable, but middle-row and third-row seats are too low. Performed poorly in offset front crash tests. **Last report/fax: July 97/9589**

Model	Predicted reliability	Depreciation	Comments
Chrysler 300M	NEW	NA	This sedan is new for 1999. It's a roomy, upscale sibling of the Dodge Intrepid and Chrysler Concorde. Powered by the same new 3.5-liter V6 as the LHS. **Last report/fax: ——**
Chrysler Cirrus	○	○	Offers a well-designed interior with a relatively roomy rear seat. But the ride is only so-so. Handling is sound. Front seats are fairly comfortable. This car is quickly becoming outdated. **Last report/fax: October 97/9618**
✔ Chrysler Concorde	⊖	○	Redesigned for 1998. Basically a middling car. It handles fairly nimbly, and the ride is supple. Both engines lack refinement. Road noise is constant. Access is a chore. **Last report/fax: July 98/9673**
Chrysler LHS	NEW	NA	New for 1999, this is Chrysler's largest sedan. It comes with interesting interior touches. The standard engine is a new 253-hp V6. **Last report/fax: ——**
Chrysler Sebring	●	○	This sporty coupe's handling is competent. Front seats provide quite good support, though the rear seat is tight for three adults. Some minor controls are poorly placed. **Last report/fax: ——**
Chrysler Sebring Convertible	●	○	Stylish but mediocre. The ride is jittery. Handles predictably but not crisply. The V6 is a better choice than the Four. **Last report/fax: August 97/5598**
Chrysler Town & Country	◒	○	The extended-length minivan is similar to the Dodge Grand Caravan and Plymouth Grand Voyager. They convert easily from people-carrier to cargo-hauler. Less reliable than Chysler's short-wheelbase models. **Last report/fax: July 97/9589**
Daewoo Lanos	NEW	NA	About the size of a Hyundai Accent but a lot cruder, less nimble, and more cramped. The engine is a 1.6-liter Four. Like other Daewoos, this car is priced competitively and comes well equipped. **Last report/fax: ——**
Daewoo Leganza	NEW	NA	A basically middling car. It competes in price and size with cars like the Pontiac Grand Am and Ford Contour. Ride and handling are unremarkable. **Last report/fax: ——**
Daewoo Nubira	NEW	NA	Offers more equipment and a lower price than most comparable models. Engine performance is strong. Interior ergonomics are OK, and ride and handling are competitive. **Last report/fax: ——**
Dodge Avenger	●	○	This sporty coupe is better equipped with the V6 than with the noisy Four. Handling is competent. Front seats provide good support, but the rear is a tight fit for three. **Last report/fax: ——**
✔ Dodge Caravan	○	○	This minivan performs well overall. The 3.3-liter V6 is the engine of choice. Reaching the rearmost seat takes agility. Reliability has been spotty. **Last report/fax: July 96/9489**
✔ Dodge Dakota	○	◒	Handles nimbly for a truck. It feels stable and predictable during hard cornering. The ride is jarring. The skimpy rear bench in extended-cab versions supposedly seats three, but leg room is scant. **Last report/fax: July 97/5591**
Dodge Durango	○	NA	The Durango offers three rows of seats, although the third row is not much fun. The front seats are reasonably comfortable. The ride is stiff and choppy. The V8 guzzles fuel but doesn't give much oomph. **Last report/fax: May 98/9661**
Dodge Grand Caravan	◒	○	This long-wheelbase minivan rides quietly and handles nimbly. The front seats are fairly comfortable. A second, left-side sliding door is a handy option. Less reliable than Chysler's short-wheelbase models. **Last report/fax: July 97/9589**
✔ Dodge Intrepid	⊖	◒	Redesigned for 1998. A large and stylish car with overall middling performance. Handling is nimble; the ride is steady. The 2.7-liter V6 is noisy and transmits vibration to the cabin. Access is a chore. **Last report/fax: July 98/9673**

Model	Predicted reliability	Depreciation	Comments
Dodge Neon —	○	○	Has a relatively roomy interior. The stronger of the two four-cylinder engines is fairly sprightly when it's mated to the five-speed manual transmission. Handling is predictable; the ride is harsh. Reliability has improved of late. **Last report/fax: March 96/9457**
Dodge Ram 1500	●	⊜	This pickup's bulk takes a toll on acceleration and fuel economy. Handling is ponderous but predictable. The front seats are comfortable except for insufficient lower-back support. There is generous storage room. **Last report/fax: September 96/9499**
Dodge Stratus	◒	○	Offers a roomy and nicely designed interior. The ride is jiggly. Handling is competent. The optional V6 provides lively acceleration. The front seats are fairly comfortable. This car is quickly becoming outdated. **Last report/fax: October 97/9618**
✔ Ford Contour —	○	◒	This European-feeling sedan provides nimble handling with a firm, supple ride. The front seats are comfortable; the rear is a little cramped. **Last report/fax: August 96/9493**
✔ Ford Crown Victoria	○	○	A big, quiet, comfortable-riding large sedan. Handling is not bad for a car this large. Braking and emergency handling are fairly good. Rear leg room is skimpier than you might expect. The Mercury Grand Marquis is similar. **Last report/fax: July 98/9673**
✔ Ford Escort —	⊜	NA	The wagon offers respectable cargo space for its size. Cornering is fairly nimble, but the ride feels stiff and choppy, and the cabin is a little noisy. Rear leg room is tight. The front seats are supportive. **Last report/fax: September 97/9603**
✔ Ford Expedition	○	NA	This SUV is based on the F-150 pickup truck. Without a full load of cargo, the ride is firm and a bit jiggly. Seating is roomy and quite comfortable. The optional third-row seat is supposed to hold three, but it's cramped. **Last report/fax: June 97/9575**
✔ Ford Explorer	○	⊜	This midsized SUV offers a roomy interior. Handles soundly and steers nicely. The ride is stiff on bumpy roads and a little jiggly even on the highway. The SOHC V6 is the engine to choose. **Last report/fax: June 97/9575**
✔ Ford F-150	⊜	○	The F-150 feels relatively nimble for a big truck. The ride is composed and fairly quiet. Extended-cab models include a handy four-door configuration. **Last report/fax: September 96/9499**
Ford Mustang	●	○	For 1999, this old-fashioned muscle car is getting its first significant change since its 1994 redesign. This might make the Mustang feel more sporty. The previous model lacked excitement. **Last report/fax: ——**
✔ Ford Ranger	○	○	Redesigned for 1998, this pickup was substantially improved. Handling is good; the seat padding is too thin. The "super cab" models offer ample storage space as well as four doors. **Last report/fax: December 98/9805**
✔ Ford Taurus	○	◒	This is a roomy, comfortable, quiet sedan. Handling is nimble. Choose the more powerful V6. The front seats are supportive. The rear bench seat can hold three adults comfortably. **Last report/fax: January 96/9447**
Ford Windstar	NEW	○	This minivan rides smoothly and quietly. A low floor eases loading. It offers a left-side sliding door for 1999. The seats are comfortable. Not as spacious as that of GM's and Chrysler's bigger vans. **Last report/fax: ——**
GMC Jimmy	◒	○	The Jimmy offers generous cargo room and a decent powertrain. The ride is tolerable. But handling and reliability have been subpar. **Last report/fax: May 98/9661**
GMC Safari	●	○	This minivan can haul lots of cargo or tow a heavy trailer. Offers optional all-wheel drive. But feels far more like a truck than a car. Handles ponderously. **Last report/fax: July 96/9489**

Model	Predicted reliability	Depreciation	Comments
GMC Sierra	NEW	⊖	The Sierra, a full-sized pickup, was redesigned for 1999 and much improved. The engines are more powerful but less thirsty, and the optional four-wheel-drive system is now full-time. The Chevrolet Silverado is similar. **Last report/fax: ——**
GMC Sonoma	●	◒	The compact GMC Sonoma and its sibling, the Chevy S-Series pickup, ride stiffly and lean a lot in corners. On the plus side, the cabin is quiet and the 4.3-liter V6 accelerates well enough. **Last report/fax: December 98/9805**
GMC Suburban	◒	⊜	One of the largest SUVs offered. Can seat as many as nine or tow a heavy trailer. Selectable full-time four-wheel drive is optional. **Last report/fax: ——**
GMC Yukon	●	⊖	This SUV's cargo bay is almost as roomy as a minivan's. Selectable full-time four-wheel drive is optional. Rides relatively well for a truck. The spacious cabin is generally quiet. **Last report/fax: October 96/9508**
✔ Honda Accord	⊜	○	Handles fairly nimbly, but the cabin is not as quiet as it could be. The front seats are comfortable for most people. The 1998 redesign made this sedan bigger. The V6 is responsive; the Four is more economical. **Last report/fax: February 98/9651**
✔ Honda CR-V	⊜	NA	This small SUV offers permanent all-wheel-drive. The ride is car-like, but handling is just OK. Acceleration is sluggish. The seats are reasonably comfortable, but the driving position is tiring. **Last report/fax: November 97/9622**
✔ Honda Civic	⊜	⊖	One of the best small cars on the market. Glides surefootedly through twists and turns, and delivers a comfortable ride. Fuel economy is top-notch. **Last report/fax: March 96/9457**
Honda Odyssey	⊜	○	The brand-new Odyssey is much larger than last year's, and has a sprightly V6. Instead of swing-out doors it has left- and right-side sliding rear doors, and a clever third-row bench seat that stows into the floor. **Last report/fax: ——**
Honda Passport	NA	○	This is an old-school, truck-based SUV made by Isuzu. The ride is busy and jittery. Handling is sluggish. The front seats are well shaped but too low. The rear seat is low, too, but there's ample head and knee room. **Last report/fax: May 98/9661**
✔ Honda Prelude	⊜	○	This is a good-handling coupe. It's powered by a strong 2.3-liter Four. It offers an automatic transmission that can be shifted manually as well as a sophisticated limited-slip differential that improves tire grip during hard turns. **Last report/fax: ——**
Hyundai Accent	NA	◒	The Accent scores fairly well among the very smallest models. The ride is choppy but relatively quiet. The rear seat is a bit tight for tall people. Its 92-hp, 1.5-liter Four accelerates adequately. Antilock brakes can be hard to find. **Last report/fax: ——**
Hyundai Elantra	NA	◒	Fits between the smaller Hyundai Accent and the midsized Hyundai Sonata. Expect nimble handling. The ride is jittery . The front seats are supportive. The rear seat feels hard, but it's relatively roomy. **Last report/fax: January 97/9539**
Hyundai Sonata	NEW	◒	The midsized Sonata was redesigned for 1999. It has a revised independent suspension and the choice of a Four or a V6. In general, Hyundais have improved somewhat with each generation, but we haven't yet tested the new one. **Last report/fax: ——**
Hyundai Tiburon	NA	NA	This sporty coupe has a lot going for it, provided you can fit in the cramped cockpit. It handles crisply and competently. The seats are reasonably well shaped but very firm and mounted low. The rear seat is tiny. **Last report/fax: August 97/9597**
Infiniti G20	⊜	◒	The redesigned G20, Infiniti's entry-level car, is about the same size as a Ford Contour. It's less nimble and less comfortable than the old one. It also feels underpowered. **Last report/fax: ——**

Model	Predicted reliability	Depreciation	Comments
✔ Infiniti I30	⊜	◒	Essentially a Nissan Maxima with extra sound-deadening material and a more plush interior. A smooth V6 is this car's best feature. The interior is roomy. The ride is unexceptional; handling is adequate. **Last report/fax: February 96/9456**
✔ Infiniti Q45	⊜	●	This is Nissan's flagship sedan. It's positioned to compete against other luxury models from Lexus and Mercedes-Benz. But this car has struggled against its competitors, and depreciation is high. **Last report/fax: ——**
✔ Infiniti QX4	⊜	NA	A Nissan Pathfinder with delusions of grandeur. Cargo space and payload are quite modest. The front seats are comfortable; the rear seat, much less so. Handling is secure but unimpressive. Outstanding reliability. **Last report/fax: September 98/9695**
Isuzu Amigo	NA	NA	This is a small-sized two-door SUV with a partial canvas top covering the rear seats and cargo area. It shares its V6 with the Rodeo. But don't expect this old-style, truck-based vehicle to be more than a beach-buggy. **Last report/fax: ——**
Isuzu Hombre	NA	NA	Essentially Chevrolet's compact S-Series pickup with slightly different sheet metal. Offers an extended cab and optional four-wheel drive. **Last report/fax: ——**
✔ Isuzu Oasis	⊜	○	The Oasis is a clone of the previous-generation Honda Odyssey. It's a smallish van with swing-out rear doors. The engine is just adequate, ride and handling are good, and the controls are simple. **Last report/fax: ——**
Isuzu Rodeo	NA	○	This is an old-school, truck-based SUV: The ride is busy and jittery. Handling is sluggish. The front seats are well shaped but too low. The rear seat is low, too, but there's ample head and knee room. **Last report/fax: May 98/9661**
Isuzu Trooper	NA	NA	We have rated the 1995-1997 Trooper Not Acceptable because of its rollover propensity in our tests. It's a big ungainly SUV, dated and overpriced for what you get. **Last report/fax: ——**
Jaguar XJ8	NA	◒	One of the fanciest luxury sedans. The ride is one of the best in the world. Accommodations are tight. For a roomier back seat, consider the extended-wheelbase L model. **Last report/fax: ——**
Jeep Cherokee	●	○	A very trucklike SUV. It's a good off-roader but pitches and rocks even on good roads. Finding a comfortable driving position is a challenge. The rear seats are cramped. Cargo space is only so-so. **Last report/fax: November 97/9622**
Jeep Grand Cherokee	NEW	NA	The Grand Cherokee was redesigned for 1999 but looks much like the old one. Jeep improved the suspension and four-wheel-drive system, and a new V8 is now optional. This should be quite competitive in its class. **Last report/fax: ——**
Jeep Wrangler	◒	⊜	The smallest and crudest Jeep. The ride is hard and noisy; the handling, primitive. Popular with off-roaders despite a below average reliability record. The driving position is unpleasant. **Last report/fax: November 97/9622**
Kia Sephia	NA	NA	A small Korean-built sedan, it's powered by a 1.8-liter Four. Remains to be seen whether it catches on in the competitive and declining small-car market. **Last report/fax: ——**
Kia Sportage	NA	NA	A small trucklike sport-utility vehicle, the Sportage is among the cheaper SUVs on the market. Offers only a part-time four-wheel-drive system. It is not as sophisticated or up-to-date as the Toyota RAV4, Honda CR-V, or Subaru Forester. **Last report/fax: ——**
Land Rover Discovery	NEW	○	The redesigned Discovery grew a little longer and now offers a forward-facing third-row seat. The engine is a little stronger, too. It will need to have improved a lot to compete with the best in this class. **Last report/fax: ——**

Model	Predicted reliability	Depreciation	Comments
Land Rover Range Rover	NA	○	This upscale SUV comes with all sorts of luxury-car amenities. It also includes a sophisticated all-wheel-drive system and air suspension. Provides standard front side-impact air bags and safety-belt pretensioners. **Last report/fax: ——**
✔ Lexus ES300	⊜	○	The ES300 and its cheaper, less lavish cousin, the Toyota Camry, are well-designed sedans. Side air bags are standard. Exceptionally quiet inside. The front seats are supportive. The rear is crowded for three adults. **Last report/fax: March 97/9558**
✔ Lexus GS300	○	○	Redesigned for 1998 with an improved powertrain and a lower price. Handling is competent but unexceptional. The front seats are very comfortable. The rear is adequate for two adults but tight for three. **Last report/fax: October 98/9803**
✔ Lexus LS400	⊖	○	This flagship of Toyota's upscale Lexus division is one of the world's finest luxury sedans. The ride is very comfortable, but handling is not so crisp. Has a superquiet interior. Side air bags are standard. **Last report/fax: ——**
Lexus LX470	NA	NA	Revamped for 1998. This luxury-priced SUV is based on the big, imposing Toyota Land Cruiser. It has a height-adjustable suspension and a fancy interior. Full-time four-wheel drive ensures good traction. Five adults can fit comfortably. **Last report/fax: ——**
✔ Lexus RX300	⊖	NA	The RX300 is a mild-mannered hybrid of car and truck—a unit-body SUV based on the Lexus ES300. Easy and pleasant enough to drive. Handling is sound but unremarkable. Rides comfortably and quietly. **Last report/fax: September 98/9695**
✔ Lexus SC300/SC400	⊜	○	This luxury coupe emphasizes both slick refinement and crisp performance. The SC300 comes with a spirited Six. The SC400 has a powerful V8. The front seats offer generally fine accommodations. The rear is better left uninhabited. **Last report/fax: ——**
Lincoln Continental	○	●	Aspires to compete with the finest luxury models, but falls short of world standards. Has a muscular V8 that accelerates with gusto. But ride, noise isolation, and general feel are run-of-the-mill. **Last report/fax: November 96/9513**
Lincoln Navigator	○	NA	If this fancy SUV is like the Expedition, expect sound handling but terrible fuel economy. Its selectable all-wheel-drive system can be left permanently engaged. **Last report/fax: ——**
✔ Lincoln Town Car	○	◓	The last of the domestic rear-wheel-drive luxury cruisers. The ride is very smooth, and handling is quite good. The front seats are soft but poorly shaped. The rear seats three with ease. The trunk is very large. **Last report/fax: June 98/9672**
Mazda 626	○	◓	Only a so-so performer. Ride and handling are both mediocre. New height adjustment should improve the low driving position. The rear seat is roomy. V6 versions are far better than the four-cylinder models. **Last report/fax: February 98/9651**
✔ Mazda B-Series	○	○	A compact Ford Ranger pickup with a Mazda badge. Handling is quite good for a truck, but the ride is stiff and jiggly. The 4.0-liter V6 accelerates adequately. Consider the rear seats a place for cargo rather than people. **Last report/fax: December 98/9805**
✔ Mazda MX-5 Miata	⊜	○	Redesigned for 1999, the Miata retained its zesty performance, nimble handling, and precise and direct steering. The interior remains cramped for tall people, and lots of road and engine noise intrudes into the cabin. **Last report/fax: August 98/9686**
✔ Mazda Millenia	⊖	◓	Sensible design makes this a comfortable sedan. The suspension soaks up bumps with quiet aplomb. The front seats are comfortable but low; the rear seat can hold two adults comfortably. Price was reduced for 1999. **Last report/fax: ——**
Mazda Protegé	⊖	○	Mazda's good entry-level small car was redesigned for 1999. Inside, it's a little smaller but still roomy. The standard engine is a good deal stronger than the middling powertrain in the old car. **Last report/fax: ——**

	Model	Predicted reliability	Depreciation	Comments
✔	Mercedes-Benz C-Class	○	⊖	A competent package but not cheap: You can easily drop $40,000 on a C280 by including only a few options. The ride is taut; handling is very capable. **Last report/fax: March 97/9558**
	Mercedes-Benz CLK	NA	NA	A coupe version of the C-Class sedan that's styled to look like the larger E-Class. The two rear seats are reasonably hospitable for a coupe. The base engine is a good-performing V6. It handles well and is fast, frugal, and comfortable. **Last report/fax: ——**
✔	Mercedes-Benz E-Class	○	⊜	Combines spirited acceleration with acceptable fuel economy and precise handling with a luxurious ride. The seats and driving position are first-class. Side air bags and traction control are standard. **Last report/fax: November 96/9513**
	Mercedes-Benz M-Class	●	NA	Our top-rated SUV, but first-year reliability has been disappointing. Rides and handles well. Lots of room for people or cargo. The seats are comfortable, too. An optional V8 engine is new for 1999. **Last report/fax: September 98/9695**
	Mercedes-Benz SLK	NA	NA	This two-seat convertible is a thoroughly modern design. An electrically retractable hardtop (that folds and stows itself in the trunk when lowered) makes this convertible feel almost as solid as a fixed-roof coupe. **Last report/fax: ——**
	Mercury Cougar	NEW	NA	The new 1999 Cougar is a front-drive hatchback coupe based on the Ford Contour/Mercury Mystique. The V6 is crisp but doesn't feel very powerful. Handling is nimble; the ride is tight and controlled. **Last report/fax: ——**
✔	Mercury Grand Marquis	○	○	If you want a big, quiet, comfortable-riding large sedan for the least money, look no further. Handling is not bad for a car this large, although the steering is a bit light. Braking and emergency handling are fairly good. **Last report/fax: July 98/9673**
✔	Mercury Mountaineer	○	○	A rebadged Ford Explorer that seeks to compete in the ranks of upscale SUVs. The ride is stiff; handling is sound. Fuel economy is mediocre. The front seats are supportive. Cargo room is generous. **Last report/fax: September 98/9695**
✔	Mercury Mystique	○	◒	This sedan has a distinctly sporty flavor and drives like a good, agile European car. The ride is firm but well controlled. Choose the 2.5-liter V6 over the noisy 2.0-liter Four. The front seats are comfortable; the rear feels cramped. **Last report/fax: October 97/9618**
✔	Mercury Sable	○	◒	This sedan is comfortable and quiet, and handles soundly. Opt for the Duratec V6 engine over the older Vulcan V6. The front seats are supportive. The rear bench seat can hold three adults comfortably, but access is difficult. **Last report/fax: February 97/9549**
✔	Mercury Tracer	⊖	◒	This small car corners fairly nimbly. The ride feels choppy but remains composed in bumpy turns. Noise from the engine and road creeps into the cabin. The front seats are small but supportive; the rear seat is cramped. **Last report/fax: January 97/9539**
	Mercury Villager	NEW	○	The Villager and similar Nissan Quest were redesigned for 1999. They have grown larger, and offer a more powerful engine and a second, left-side sliding door. Both should be competitive in this class. **Last report/fax: ——**
	Mitsubishi 3000GT	NA	◒	This sports car is too heavy and wide to feel nimble. And its rear seat is just for show. The VR-4 model delivers fierce acceleration, exceptionally short stops, and good cornering grip. Other versions are far less costly but less interesting. **Last report/fax: ——**
	Mitsubishi Diamante	NA	●	This sedan competes with other midluxury models such as the Infiniti I30, Lexus ES300, and Mazda Millenia. Power comes from a 210-hp V6. Antilock brakes and a remote keyless-entry system are standard. **Last report/fax: ——**
	Mitsubishi Eclipse	●	○	This sporty car is available as a convertible and a coupe. It's an old design. Turbocharged versions are very quick but expensive. The Eclipse comes with either front-wheel or all-wheel drive. The rear seat is almost unusable. **Last report/fax: ——**

Model	Predicted reliability	Depreciation	Comments
Mitsubishi Galant	NEW	◒	Redesigned for 1999. Mitsubishi is trying to set it apart from the crowd with a more stylish, less restrained design. It offers a new V6. Generally generic transportation. **Last report/fax: ——**
Mitsubishi Mirage	NA	◒	This is a capable small car. It handles securely and predictably, and its ride is supple. The interior feels airy and spacious. The front seats are supportive and roomy enough; the rear seat is cramped. **Last report/fax: January 97/9539**
Mitsubishi Montero	NA	○	This SUV is seriously outdated and feels ponderous in normal driving. The selectable four-wheel-drive system can remain permanently engaged. The middle seat provides decent space for two adults. **Last report/fax: ——**
Mitsubishi Montero Sport	NA	NA	Compared to most other existing SUVs, the Montero Sport is very trucklike. Common road bumps deliver stiff, rubbery kicks, and even the highway ride is jittery. Handling is rather cumbersome. **Last report/fax: June 97/9575**
✔ Nissan Altima	⊖	◒	This sedan is a cheaper alternative to the Honda Accord and Toyota Camry but falls a notch below those cars. Neither the ride nor the handling are very good. The seats are uncomfortable; the cabin is noisy. **Last report/fax: February 98/9651**
Nissan Frontier	NA	NA	This compact pickup truck is fairly crude. Antilock brakes are standard with four-wheel-drive models, but only rear ABS comes with two-wheel-drive versions. **Last report/fax: ——**
✔ Nissan Maxima	⊜	○	This sedan's best features are a strong, refined V6 and a roomy interior with lots of head room. While the car remains competent, the ride is just so-so, and handling is only adequate. The seats aren't especially comfortable. **Last report/fax: January 98/9644**
✔ Nissan Pathfinder	○	⊖	This midsized SUV has a good ride and handles securely. Cargo space isn't as commodious as in some other SUVs in this class. The V6 accelerates adequately, but it's noisy. The four-wheel drive is only a part-time system. **Last report/fax: October 96/9508**
Nissan Quest	NEW	○	The Nissan Quest and similar Mercury Villager were redesigned for 1999. They have grown larger, and offer a more powerful engine and a second, left-side sliding door. Both should be competitive in this class. **Last report/fax: ——**
✔ Nissan Sentra	⊖	◒	Falls a notch or two below the best small cars on the market, such as the Honda Civic and Mazda Protegé ES. The ride is satisfactory on most roads. The front seats provide adequate support, but the rear seat is cramped. **Last report/fax: ——**
Oldsmobile 88	○	◒	This large sedan is a rather old design. It's quiet and softly sprung. The Regency nominally seats six, but only five comfortably. It will be discontinued at the end of the 1998 model year. **Last report/fax: ——**
Oldsmobile Alero	NEW	NA	Oldsmobile's entry-level sedan and coupe, the Alero is new this year. It's a cousin of the Pontiac Grand Am, with which it shares many parts. Styling is up-to-date. The V6 is a better choice than the Four. **Last report/fax: ——**
Oldsmobile Aurora	◒	◒	The Aurora is Oldsmobile's flagship sedan. A powerful V8 is its best feature. The ride, handling, and braking are all so-so. The cockpit feels claustrophobic. **Last report/fax: June 98/9672**
Oldsmobile Bravada	○	○	This is an upscale version of the Chevrolet Blazer and GMC Jimmy. Standard equipment includes permanent all-wheel drive—though without a low range. Ride and handling are both so-so. **Last report/fax: ——**
Oldsmobile Cutlass	●	NA	A well-rounded sedan overall, but needs a little more polish to join competing models. The ride is jittery on good roads. Handling is sound. The interior is spacious. Reliability has not held up well in its second year. **Last report/fax: October 97/9618**

Model	Predicted reliability	Depreciation	Comments
✔ Oldsmobile Intrigue	○	NA	This is a solid performer. The interior is well-designed. It rides well on most roads. The front seats are comfortable; the rear seat is fairly accommodating but head room is limited. **Last report/fax: January 98/9644**
Oldsmobile Silhouette	◒	○	This minivan offers a useful, left-side sliding door and a powered right-side door. The front seats are comfortable, but middle-row and third-row seats are too low. Performed poorly in offset front crash tests. **Last report/fax: July 97/9589**
Plymouth Breeze	◒	◒	This midsized sedan has a spacious interior. The ride is jittery. The handling is sound but not crisp. The 2.0-liter Four is noisy and underpowered. **Last report/fax: August 96/9493**
Plymouth Grand Voyager	◒	○	This long-wheelbase minivan rides quietly, handles fairly nimbly, and converts easily from people-carrier to roomy cargo-hauler. A second, left-side sliding door is a handy option. Less reliable than Chysler's short-wheelbase models. **Last report/fax: July 97/9589**
Plymouth Neon	○	○	This small car has a relatively roomy interior. The four-cylinder engine sounds harsh. Handles predictably. The front seats are generally comfortable, and three adults can fit in the rear. Reliability has improved of late. **Last report/fax: May 96/9471**
✔ Plymouth Voyager	○	○	This minivan performs well overall. It rides quietly, handle nimbly, and converts easily from people-carrier to cargo-hauler. A second, left-side sliding door is either standard or optional, depending on the trim line. **Last report/fax: July 96/9489**
Pontiac Bonneville	○	○	Pontiac's largest sedan has changed little over the years. The optional firm suspension and touring tires improve handling markedly. The front seats are comfortable; the rear seat is roomy for three adults. **Last report/fax: ——**
Pontiac Firebird	●	○	Even though this car aspires to be sporty, it's too bulky to be nimble, and the ride is uncomfortable. Traction control is a worthy option on V8-powered models. Reliability has been poor. **Last report/fax: ——**
Pontiac Grand Am	NEW	◒	The Grand Am was redesigned for 1999. Handling is adequate but not very crisp. The ride is still unremarkable. Wind noise is quite pronounced. The V6 is a better choice than the adequate but noisy Four. **Last report/fax: ——**
✔ Pontiac Grand Prix	○	○	This is the sportiest of a clan that includes the Buick Century, Buick Regal, and Oldsmobile Intrigue. The front seats are reasonably comfortable. The rear seat is spacious. The ride is not as comfortable as it should be. **Last report/fax: February 97/9549**
Pontiac Montana	◒	◒	This minivan offers a useful, left-side sliding door and a powered right-side door. The front seats are comfortable, but middle-row and third-row seats are too low. Performed poorly in offset front crash tests. **Last report/fax: July 97/9589**
Pontiac Sunfire	◒	○	The Sunfire and the Chevrolet Cavalier are cousins. The front seats feel comfortable on short trips, but thin padding makes them fatiguing on long journeys. Reliability has fallen below average in our latest survey. **Last report/fax: May 96/9471**
⬆ Porsche Boxster	NA	NA	The Boxster is everything a sports car should be. Plus, with two trunks, it's almost practical. Handling and braking are superb, and the ride is firm but not too punishing. Lowering the top is very easy. **Last report/fax: August 98/9686**
Saab 9-3	⊖	○	This quirky sedan is available in both three- and five-door variations. Ride amd handling are nothing special. Really a four-passenger car; three in the rear is one too many. The hatchback design provides ample storage space. **Last report/fax: ——**
Saab 9-5	NEW	NA	Replaced the aging Saab 9000. It's competent and very pleasant to drive. Front seats are very comfortable; two adults can ride comfortably in the rear. A station-wagon debuts in the spring. **Last report/fax: October 98/9803**

Model	Predicted reliability	Depre-ciation	Comments
Saturn	⊖	⊖	One of the few domestic lines that manages to appeal to import-buyers. But the cars themselves have been pretty unremarkable. Accommodations and controls are inferior, and the four-cylinder engine is still coarse. **Last report/fax: March 98/9657**
✔ Saturn SC	○	⊖	Holds its own with other sporty coupes. Accelerates well and handles responsively. The body doesn't lean much in turns. The ride is a little unsettled but on a par with many other small cars. Uncomfortable front seats. **Last report/fax: August 97/9597**
✔ Subaru Forester	⊜	NA	One of the best car-SUV hybrids. It has a tall and roomy cargo compartment and a fairly good, compliant ride. It has an effective all-wheel-drive system and a responsive automatic transmission. The rear seat is cramped. **Last report/fax: May 98/9661**
✔ Subaru Impreza	⊜	○	The least expensive all-wheel-drive model on the market. The ride is relatively good. The front seats provide good support; the rear is cramped. The wagon isn't the roomiest in its class, but it is nimble and fun. **Last report/fax: September 97/9603**
✔ Subaru Legacy	⊖	○	Feels almost as agile as a European sports sedan. Permanent all-wheel drive is a plus. The ride is firm but supple. The front seats are comfortable; the rear is roomy. The wagon is a reasonable alternative to an SUV. **Last report/fax: May 97/9572**
Suzuki Esteem	NA	◒	Suzuki's first foray into the mainstream sedan market. Falls short in ride, quietness, and powertrain smoothness. It accelerates well enough. The seats are fairly comfortable. A small wagon model is also available. **Last report/fax: March 96/9457**
Suzuki Swift	⊖	◒	This hatchback is one of the smallest and lightest cars on the road. It is too sluggish and clumsy to nip neatly through city traffic. The ride is choppy and noisy. The rear seat holds just two. **Last report/fax: ——**
Suzuki Vitara	NEW	○	A new and improved version of the basically dreadful Sidekick. Its old-school design doesn't really lend itself to a good ride or crisp handling. The Grand Vitara has a V6. The Vitara is also sold as the Chevrolet Tracker. **Last report/fax: ——**
✔ Toyota 4Runner	⊖	⊜	Among the better SUVs. The 3.4-liter V6 is the engine of choice. The driving position is too low. Selectable full-time four-wheel-drive is available only in the top-of-the-line Limited model. **Last report/fax: October 96/9508**
✔ Toyota Avalon	⊜	○	Essentially a well-equipped pre-1997 Camry with an extra-roomy rear seat and trunk. The V6 is powerful and economical; the cabin is quiet. The front seats are large and comfortable. **Last report/fax: July 98/9673**
✔ Toyota Camry	⊜	○	A fine car overall. The ride is quiet and compliant. Handling is secure and predictable. The seats are fairly comfortable, and the rear is roomy. The optional V6 delivers plenty of thrust; fuel economy is slighlty better with the Four. **Last report/fax: May 97/9572**
✔ Toyota Camry Solara	⊜	NA	The new-for-1999 Camry Solara tries to offer a more indulgent choice for those who don't need a four-door sedan. Expect a good ride and sound handling. **Last report/fax: ——**
✔ Toyota Celica	⊜	⊖	This model has changed little over the years but still continues to offer a balanced combination of good handling, fuel economy, and reliability. The car responds quickly to its steering, and the tires grip well. The front seats offer good support. **Last report/fax: ——**
✔ Toyota Corolla	⊖	○	One of the first economy cars to offer side air bags. Rides comfortably. The front seats are nicely shaped and supportive. A standard front stabilizer bar has balanced the Corolla's subpar handling in the lower-trim lines. **Last report/fax: March 98/9657**
Toyota Land Cruiser	NA	⊜	Revamped for 1998, this is a big, expensive SUV. It sports a 4.7-liter V8 and independent front suspension. The interior offers lots of cargo room. Full-time four-wheel-drive is standard. **Last report/fax: ——**

Model	Predicted reliability	Depreciation	Comments
✔ Toyota RAV4	⊜	⊜	Competes successfully with other car-based small SUVs, such as the Subaru Forester and Honda CR-V. Nimble handling makes the RAV4 fun to drive. Small but supportive front seats. **Last report/fax: November 97/9622**
✔ Toyota Sienna	⊜	○	Our highest-rated recommended minivan. Rides quietly and handles competently. Front- and middle-row seats are comfortable. The rearmost seat is well padded. Has both left-side and right-side sliding doors. **Last report/fax: March 98/5662**
Toyota Tacoma	⊖	○	The compact Tacoma pickup truck rides uncomfortably and handles ponderously. Acceleration is adequate. The seats are low and flat. **Last report/fax: December 98/9805**
Volkswagen EuroVan	NEW	NA	After a four-year absence, the Eurovan returns to the US with a more powerful engine and updated controls. The seats are firm and comfortable, but the driving position is still awkward. Its singular advantage is a cavernous interior. **Last report/fax: ——**
✔ Volkswagen Golf	○	⊖	A redesigned model appears in early 1999. The responsive 2.0-liter Four and easy-shifting manual transmission perform well together. The ride is supple. The front seats offer good, firm support. **Last report/fax: May 96/9471**
Volkswagen Jetta	NEW	⊖	VW's best-selling sedan is all new for 1999. Positioned as an upmarket small car, it boasts a host of thoughtful details and a European driving experience. **Last report/fax: ——**
⬆ Volkswagen New Beetle	NA	NA	Bears a vague resemblance to the car VW scrapped more than two decades ago. Handling and ride are good. The front seats are supportive; the rear is cramped. **Last report/fax: November 98/5804**
✔ Volkswagen Passat	⊖	○	Redesigned and greatly improved. Roomy and comfortable inside. Handles precisely; delivers a firm yet supple ride. The interior appointments have a quality feel. All-wheel-drive is available with the wagon. **Last report/fax: February 98/9651**
Volvo C70	NA	NA	This is a coupe based on the Volvo S70 sedan. The turbocharged, 236-hp Five doesn't feel very responsive unless it's revved a lot. Choose the 190-hp engine instead. **Last report/fax: ——**
✔ Volvo S70/V70	⊖	○	The S70 sedan and V70 wagon handle and brake well, and in GLT trim this car is fast. The interior is spacious and the seats are large and comfortable. The ride is stiff, though. Works best as a wagon. **Last report/fax: October 98/9803**
Volvo S80	NEW	NA	Volvo's new flagship is a stylish front-wheel-drive sedan with lots of room inside. The engine is a lively straight Six with or without a turbocharger. It should compete well with the best in this class. **Last report/fax: ——**

RATINGS OF THE 1999 CARS

The Ratings include only cars for which we have recent test results. To earn our recommendation—marked by a ✔—a model must perform well in our tests and have been at least average in reliability. New models that perform well but whose reliability we can't yet predict are marked promising (↑). Twins and triplets—essentially similar models sold under different nameplates—are grouped in the charts below; each is marked with a ■. Typically, we've tested only one of these models. **Fuel usage** is overall mpg, based on our own tests in a range of driving conditions. **Tested model** notes the trim line, engine, and drivetrain of the model tested—items that can affect specific test results.

Model	Overall score 0–100	Overall mpg	Tested model
SMALL SEDANS			
✔ Honda Civic		31 mpg	LX 1.6 Four; auto 4
Mitsubishi Mirage		27	LS 1.8 Four; auto 4
✔ Toyota Corolla		30	CE 1.8 Four; auto 4
✔ Chevrolet Prizm		31	Base 1.8 Four; auto 4
✔ ■ Ford Escort		28	LX 2.0 Four; auto 4
✔ ■ Mercury Tracer		28	Ford Escort LX 2.0 Four; auto 4
Hyundai Elantra		25	GLS 1.8 Four; auto 4
■ Chevrolet Cavalier		26	LS 2.2 Four; auto 4
■ Pontiac Sunfire		26	Chevrolet Cavalier LS 2.2 Four; auto 4
Suzuki Esteem		29	GLX 1.6 Four; auto 4
Saturn		29	SL2 1.9 Four; auto 4
Dodge/Plymouth Neon		26	Highline 2.0 Four; auto 3
FAMILY SEDANS			
Volkswagen Passat		24	GLS 4 1.8 Four Turbo; auto 5
✔ Toyota Camry		25/23	LE 2.2 Four/3.0 V6; auto 4
✔ Honda Accord		23	EX 3.0 V6; auto 4
✔ Mercury Mystique		22	LS 2.5 V6; auto 4
✔ Honda Accord		25	EX 2.3 Four; auto 4
✔ Subaru Legacy		24	L 2.2 Four; auto 4
■ Oldsmobile Cutlass		24	GLS 3.1 V6; auto 4
■ Chevrolet Malibu		24	Base 2.4 Four; auto 4
Oldsmobile Intrigue		20	GL 3.8 V6; auto 4
✔ Nissan Maxima		23	GXE 3.0 V6; auto 4
✔ Pontiac Grand Prix		21	SE 3.8 V6; auto 4

Model	Overall score (0–100)	Overall mpg	Tested model
FAMILY SEDANS *continued*			
✔ ▪ Ford Taurus		21 mpg	LX 3.0 V6; auto 4
✔ ▪ Mercury Sable		22	GS 3.0 V6; auto 4
✔ Ford Contour		24	GL 2.0 Four; auto 4
▪ Chrysler Cirrus		22	LXi 2.5 V6; auto 4
▪ Dodge Stratus		22	Chrysler Cirrus LXi 2.5 V6; auto 4
Plymouth Breeze		23	2.0 Four; auto 4
✔ Nissan Altima		25	GXE 2.4 Four; auto 4
✔ Chevrolet Lumina		22	LS 3.1 V6; auto 4
Mazda 626		24	LX 2.0 Four; auto 4
Buick Regal		21	LS 3.8 V6; auto 4
Buick Century		22	Limited 3.1 V6; auto 4
UPSCALE SEDANS			
✔ Audi A6		20	Quattro 2.8 V6; auto 5
✔ Lexus ES300		22	3.0 V6; auto 4
✔ Mercedes-Benz C280		24	2.8 Six; auto 5
Cadillac Catera		20	3.0 V6; auto 4
Saab 9-5		23	2.3 Four Turbo; auto 4
✔ Volvo S70		21	GLT 2.4 Five turbo; auto 4
✔ Infiniti I30		23	3.0 V6; auto 4
STATION WAGONS			
✔ Volvo V70		21	GLT 2.4 Five turbo; auto 4
✔ Subaru Legacy		21	GT 2.5 Four; auto 4
✔ ▪ Ford Taurus		20	LX 3.0 V6; auto 4
✔ ▪ Mercury Sable		20	Ford Taurus LX 3.0 V6; auto 4
✔ Subaru Legacy		21	Outback 2.5 Four; auto 4
✔ Subaru Impreza		23	Outback Sport 2.2 Four; auto 4
✔ ▪ Ford Escort		25	LX 2.0 Four; auto 4
✔ ▪ Mercury Tracer		25	Ford Escort LX 2.0 Four; auto 4
LARGE SEDANS			
✔ Toyota Avalon		23	XL 3.0 V6; auto 4
✔ Buick Park Avenue		21	Ultra 3.8 V6 supercharged; auto 4
Chrysler Concorde		21	LXi 3.2 V6; auto 4
✔ Dodge Intrepid		22	Base 2.7 V6; auto 4
Lincoln Continental		18	4.6 V8; auto 4

Model	Overall score (0–100)	Overall mpg	Tested model
✔ ■ Ford Crown Victoria		19 mpg	Mercury Grand Marquis GS 4.6 V8; auto 4
✔ ■ Mercury Grand Marquis		19	GS 4.6 V8; auto 4
Oldsmobile Aurora		19	4.0 V8; auto 4
Buick LeSabre		20	Custom 3.8 V6; auto 4
▶ **LUXURY SEDANS**			
✔ Mercedes-Benz E320		22	3.2 V6; auto 5
✔ BMW 528i		20	2.8 Six; auto 4
✔ Lexus GS300		23	3.0 Six; auto 5
✔ Acura RL		20	3.5 V6; auto 4
✔ Lincoln Town Car		19	Executive 4.6 V8; auto 4
✔ Cadillac DeVille		20	Base 4.6 V8; auto 4
▶ **SPORTS CARS**			
⬆ Porsche Boxster		24	2.5 Six; man 5
Chevrolet Corvette		20	5.7 V8; auto 4
✔ BMW Z3		24	2.8 Six; man 5
✔ Mazda MX-5 Miata		27	1.8 Four; man 5
▶ **SMALL COUPES**			
⬆ Volkswagen New Beetle		29	2.0 Four; man 5
✔ Volkswagen Golf GTI		27	2.0 Four; man 5
✔ Acura Integra Coupe		31	LS 1.8 Four; man 5
✔ Honda Civic Coupe		34	EX 1.6 Four; man 5
Hyundai Tiburon		27	FX 2.0 Four; man 5
✔ Saturn SC		28	SC2 1.9 Four; man 5
■ Chevrolet Cavalier		25	Pontiac Sunfire GT 2.4 Four; man 5
■ Pontiac Sunfire		25	GT 2.4 Four; man 5
Dodge/Plymouth Neon		26	Sport 2.0 Four; man 5
▶ **MINIVANS**			
■ Chrysler Town & Country		18	Plymouth Grand Voyager SE 3.3 V6; auto 4
■ Dodge Grand Caravan		18	Plymouth Grand Voyager SE 3.3 V6; auto 4
■ Plymouth Grand Voyager		18	SE 3.3 V6; auto 4
✔ Toyota Sienna		19	LE 3.0 V6; auto 4
✔ ■ Dodge Caravan		19	LE 3.3 V6; auto 4
✔ ■ Plymouth Voyager		19	Dodge Caravan LE 3.3 V6; auto 4
■ Chevrolet Venture		19	LS 3.4 V6; auto 4
■ Oldsmobile Silhouette		19	Chevrolet Venture LS 3.4 V6; auto 4
■ Pontiac Montana		18	3.4 V6; auto 4

Model	Overall score (0–100)	Overall mpg	Tested model
MINIVANS *continued*			
■ Chevrolet Astro		15 mpg	GMC Safari SLE 4.3 V6; auto 4
■ GMC Safari		15	SLE 4.3 V6; auto 4
SMALL SPORT-UTILITY VEHICLES			
✔ Subaru Forester		22	S 2.5 Four; auto 4
✔ Toyota RAV4		22	2.0 Four; auto 4
✔ Honda CR-V		24	EX 2.0 Four; auto 4
Jeep Cherokee		16	Sport 4.0 Six; auto 4
Jeep Wrangler		15	Sahara 4.0 Six; auto 3
SPORT-UTILITY VEHICLES			
Mercedes-Benz ML320		19	3.2 V6; auto 5
✔ Lexus RX300		19	3.0 V6; auto 4
✔ ■ Ford Explorer		16	XLT 4.0 V6; auto 5
✔ ■ Mercury Mountaineer		16	4.0 V6; auto 5
✔ Toyota 4Runner		18	SR5 3.4 V6; auto 4
✔ Ford Expedition		13	XLT 4.6 V8; auto 4
✔ ■ Nissan Pathfinder		15	LE 3.3 V6; auto 4
✔ ■ Infiniti QX4		16	3.3 V6; auto 4
■ Chevrolet Blazer		15	LT 4.3 V6; auto 4
■ GMC Jimmy		15	Chevrolet Blazer LT 4.3 V6; auto 4
Mitsubishi Montero Sport		18	LS 3.0 V6; auto 4
■ Honda Passport		18	Isuzu Rodeo S 3.2 V6; auto 4
■ Isuzu Rodeo		18	S 3.2 V6; auto 4
■ Chevrolet Tahoe		13	LS 5.7 V8; auto 4
■ GMC Yukon		13	Chevrolet Tahoe LS 5.7 V8; auto 4
Dodge Durango		13	SLT Plus 5.2 V8; auto 4
COMPACT PICKUP TRUCKS—EXTENDED CAB 4WD			
Ford Ranger		18	XLT 4.0 V6; man 5
Mazda B-Series		18	Ford Ranger XLT 4.0 V6; man 5
■ Chevrolet S-10		17	LS 4.3 V6; man 5
■ GMC Sonoma		17	Chevrolet S-10 LS 4.3 V6; man 5
Toyota Tacoma		19	SR5 3.4 V6; man 5
PICKUP TRUCKS—EXTENDED CAB 2WD			
✔ Ford F-150		16	XLT 4.6 V8; auto 4
✔ Dodge Dakota		16	SLT 3.9 V6; auto 4
Dodge Ram 1500		13	Laramie SLT 5.2 V8; auto 4

BEST & WORST USED CARS

Overall, used cars are less of a gamble than they once were. Better engineering, design, and manufacturing have drastically reduced once-common problems like body rust and water leakage. Still, some cars are significantly more reliable than others. That's what these lists detail. Derived from the reliability summaries, they include 1990 through 1997 models that showed better-than-average or worse-than-average reliability.

Most 1997 cars were less than six months old when our readers reported on them for the 1997 survey and are considered too new for these lists.

Problems with the engine, engine cooling, transmission, clutch, driveline, and body rust have been weighted more heavily than other problems. Prices in the "reliable" list are average as of mid-1998 in the East for a car with average mileage, air-conditioning, and cassette stereo sound system. Luxury cars were priced with leather upholstery, sunroof, and CD player.

We've assumed an automatic transmission for all but sporty cars. Throughout, 2WD means two-wheel drive; 4WD is all- or four-wheel drive.

Once you've narrowed your search to a particular model, check the model's reliability and Frequency-of-Repair chart for details on exactly where trouble may lie.

RELIABLE USED CARS

Listed alphabetically by price.

Less than $6,000

ACURA Integra '90-91
BUICK LeSabre '90-91
EAGLE Summit Wagon 2WD '92
FORD Ranger Pickup 2WD '93
GEO Metro, '93-94 , '96 • Prizm, '93 • Tracker, '91, '93
HONDA Accord '90-91 • Civic, '90-92 • CRX, '90-91 • Prelude, '90
INFINITI G20 '91
LEXUS ES250 '90
MAZDA 626 '90 • MX-5 Miata, '90 • Pickup 2WD, '90-92 • Protegé, '94
MITSUBISHI Galant '90-92 • Montero, '90
NISSAN 240SX '90-91 • Altima, '93 • Maxima, '90 • Pickup 2WD, '90 [2], '91-92 • Sentra, '91-94 • Stanza, '91-92
OLDSMOBILE 98 '90
PLYMOUTH Colt Vista Wagon '92
SUZUKI Sidekick '91, '93
TOYOTA Camry '90-91 • Celica, '90 • Corolla, '90-93 • Paseo, '92 • Pickup 2WD, '90-92 • Tercel, '91-94
VOLVO 240 Series '90 • 740 Series, '90

$6,000-$8,000

ACURA Integra '92 • Legend, '90 [2]
BUICK Electra Park Avenue '90
CADILLAC DeVille '90
EAGLE Summit Wagon 2WD '93
GEO Prizm '94-95
HONDA Accord '92-93 • Civic, '93-94 • Civic del Sol, '93 • Prelude, '91-92

INFINITI G20 '92
LEXUS ES250 '91
MAZDA MX-5 Miata '91-92 • Pickup 2WD, '93 • Protegé, '95
MITSUBISHI Diamante '92
NISSAN 240SX '92-93 • Altima, '94 • Maxima, '91, '92 [2] • Pickup 2WD, '93-94
PLYMOUTH Colt Vista Wagon '93
SUBARU Impreza '93 • Legacy, '91-92
TOYOTA Camry '92 • Celica, '91-92 • Corolla, '94 • MR2, '91 • Pickup 2WD, '93 • Pickup 4WD, 90-'92 • Tercel, '95-96
VOLVO 740 Series '91

$8,000-$10,000

ACURA Integra '93-'94 • Legend, '91 • Vigor, '92
GEO Prizm '96
HONDA Accord '94 • Civic, '95 • Prelude, '93
INFINITI G20 '93
MAZDA MX-5 Miata '93 • Protegé, '96
NISSAN 200SX '95 • Altima, '95 • Maxima, '93 • Pathfinder 4WD, '90 • Pickup 2WD, '94
SUBARU Legacy '93-94
TOYOTA Camry '93-94 • Celica, '93 • Corolla, '95-96 • Pickup 2WD, '95 • Pickup 4WD, '93-94 • Previa, '91-92 • T100 Pickup 2WD, '93 • Tacoma Pickup 2WD, '95
VOLVO 940 Series '91

$10,000-$12,000

ACURA Integra '95 • Legend, '92
BUICK Regal '96
CHEVROLET Lumina '96
HONDA Accord '95 • Civic, '96 • Civic del Sol, '95
INFINITI G20 '94
MAZDA 626 '96 • MX-5 Miata, '94
MITSUBISHI Diamante '94
NISSAN Altima '96 • Maxima, '94 • Pathfinder 4WD, '92 • Pickup 2WD, '96
SUBARU Impreza '95-96 • Legacy, '94
TOYOTA Camry '95 • Celica, '94 • Pickup 4WD, '95 • Previa, '93 • Tacoma Pickup 2WD, '96

$12,000-$15,000

ACURA Integra '96 • Legend, '93
HONDA Accord '96 • Prelude, '95
INFINITI G20 '95-96 • J30, '93
LEXUS ES300 '92-93 • LS400, '90-91
MAZDA MX-5 Miata '95-96
NISSAN Maxima '95 [2] • Pathfinder 4WD, '93
OLDSMOBILE 88 '96
SUBARU Legacy '95-96
TOYOTA Camry '96 • Celica, '95 • Previa, '94 • RAV4, '96 • T100 Pickup 2WD,'95 • T100 Pickup 4WD,'95
VOLVO 850 '93

$15,000-$20,000

ACURA Legend '94-95 • TL, '96
BMW 3-Series '94
HONDA Odyssey '95-96
INFINITI I30 '96 • J30, '94-95 • Q45, '94
ISUZU Oasis '96
LEXUS ES300 '94 • GS300, '93 • LS400, '92 • SC300/SC400, '92
MAZDA Millenia '95-96
NISSAN Maxima '96
OLDSMOBILE 98 '96
TOYOTA 4Runner 4WD '94-95 • Avalon, '95-96 • Celica, '96 • Previa, '95
VOLVO 850 '95

$20,000-$25,000

AUDI A4 '96 [1] • A6, '95-96
BMW 3-Series '95
LEXUS ES300 '95-96 • GS300, '94 • LS400, '93 • SC300/SC400, '93
MERCEDES-BENZ E-Class 6 cyl. '94
TOYOTA 4Runner 2WD '96
VOLVO 850 '96

$25,000 and up

ACURA RL '96
BMW 5-Series '95
LEXUS LS400 '94-96 • SC300/SC400, '95
MERCEDES-BENZ C-Class '96 • E-Class 6 cyl., '95

Throughout, "2WD" means two-wheel drive; "4WD" is all- or four-wheel drive.
1 *Manual transmission only.*
2 *Automatic transmission only.*

USED CARS TO AVOID

BUICK Roadmaster '96 • Skylark '90

CADILLAC Eldorado '96 • Seville '92-93

CHEVROLET Astro '93-94, '96 • S-10 Blazer '90-94 • Blazer '95-96 • K-Blazer '93 • Tahoe '96 • Camaro V6 '95 • Camaro V8 '94-96 • Caprice '96 • Cavalier '91-92, '94, '96 • Corsica, Beretta '90, '92-93 • Lumina APV Van '90-93, '96 • Monte Carlo '95-96 • C1500 Pickup '96 • K1500 Pickup '95-96 • S-10 Pickup 4 '91, '95-96 • S-10 Pickup V6 2WD '94, '96 • S-10 Pickup V6 4WD '90-96 • Sportvan V8 '91-96 • Suburban '90-94

CHRYSLER Cirrus '95-96 • Concorde '93-94 • LeBaron Coupe/Convertible '90-95 • New Yorker Fifth Avenue '93 • New Yorker, LHS '94-95 • Sebring V6 '95-96 • Town & Country '90-94, '96

DODGE Avenger V6 '95-96 • Caravan 4 '93-94, '96 • Caravan V6 2WD '90-93 • Grand Caravan 4 '96 • Grand Caravan V6 '90-94, '96 • Dakota Pickup 2WD '96 • Dakota Pickup 4WD '91-96 • Dynasty V6 '92-93 • Intrepid '93-95 • Monaco '90-91 • Neon '95-96 • Ram 1500 Pickup 4WD '94-96 • Ram Van/Wagon B150 '90-91, '93-96 • Shadow '91-92, '94 • Stratus '95-96

EAGLE Premier V6 '90-91 • Talon '94-96 • Vision '93-95

FORD Aerostar '90-92, '95-96 • Bronco V8 '90-96 • Bronco II '90 • Club Wagon, Van '90-94, '96 • Contour '95 • Explorer '91-92 • F-150 Pickup 4WD '90-96 • Mustang '92, '94, '96 • Probe '91 • Ranger Pickup 4WD '90-92, '95 • Taurus '90-93, '96 • Taurus SHO '90-95 • Tempo '90-94 • Thunderbird '94, '96 • Windstar '95

GEO Storm '90-92

GMC S-15 Jimmy '90-94 • Jimmy '95-96 • Yukon '93, '96 • S-15 Sonoma Pickup 4 '91, '95-96 • S-15 Sonoma Pickup V6 2WD '94, '96 • S-15 Sonoma Pickup V6 4WD '90-96 • Safari '93-94, '96 • Sierra C1500 Pickup '96 • Sierra K1500 Pickup '95-96 • Suburban '90-94

HONDA Passport V6 '94, '96

HYUNDAI Excel '90-91

ISUZU Rodeo V6 '93-94, '96

JEEP Cherokee '90, '96 • Grand Cherokee '93 •

Wrangler '90-95

LINCOLN Continental '90-93, '95 • Mark VIII '93

MAZDA 626 '94 • MX-6 '93 • Navajo 4WD '91 • Pickup 4WD '95

MERCURY Cougar '94, '96 • Mystique '95 • Sable '90-93, '96 • Topaz '90-94 • Villager '96

MITSUBISHI Eclipse '94-96

NISSAN Pathfinder 4WD '96 • Pickup 4WD '95 • Quest '96

OLDSMOBILE Achieva '93 • Bravada '94 • Cutlass Calais 4 '90-91 • Cutlass Supreme '94-96 • 98 '92 • Silhouette '90-93, '96

PLYMOUTH Laser '94 • Neon '95-96 • Sundance '91-92, '94 • Voyager 4 '93-94, '96 • Voyager V6 2WD '90-93 • Grand Voyager 4 '96 • Grand Voyager V6 '90-94, '96

PONTIAC Firebird V6 '95 • Firebird V8 '94-96 • Grand Am '90-94, '96 • Grand Prix '90-96 • Sunbird '91-92, '94 • Sunfire '96 • Trans Sport '90-93, '96

SAAB 900 '94-95 • 9000 '91-93, '95

SUBARU Loyale '90-92

VW Golf, GTI, Golf III '90-92 • Jetta, Jetta III '90-92

VOLVO 960 Series '95

FOR THE MOST RECENT PRODUCT RATINGS

See the monthly issues of Consumer Reports magazine. Or check out Consumer Reports Online at *www.ConsumerReports.org* for the latest ratings of autos, appliances, electronic gear, yard equipment and more.

AUTO RELIABILITY

CONSUMER REPORTS rates auto reliability by asking its readers for their real-life experiences. Because we've been collecting those experiences every year for more than 40 years, we know some makes and models are far more dependable than others. We've also seen auto reliability improve greatly overall.

In our most recent survey, readers told us about troubles with more than 575,000 cars, minivans, pickup trucks, and sport-utility vehicles. We ask for "serious" problems only—ones that are expensive to repair, put the car out of commission for a time, or cause a safety problem—that occurred in the last year.

Sorting the data by make, model, and year gives us a snapshot of each model's history (see the Frequency-of-Repair charts that start on page 281). Combining that history with our test knowledge lets us confidently predict the reliability of this year's models (see the previews on page 258). Other findings include:

- On average, cars with a Japanese nameplate are more reliable than European makes, which are more reliable than American makes. These differences, true for many years, are now narrowing, particularly with newer models.
- In general, the cars most likely to be trouble-free are from the three major Japanese manufacturers—Honda/Acura, Toyota/Lexus, and Nissan/Infiniti.
- Some manufacturers have greatly improved their cars in recent years. For instance, newer Subarus and Isuzus rank higher overall in reliability than did these makers' 1990 to 1994 models. Volkswagen has also improved its products—a good thing, since older Volkswagens are the most troublesome of any make.
- New sport-utility vehicles and trucks are much more reliable than before.
- The worst, most troublesome 1997 models overall were the redesigned GM minivans—the Chevrolet Venture, Oldsmobile Silhouette, and Pontiac Trans Sport triplets, which had a problem rate of 71 per 100 cars.

How to read the charts

The Frequency-of-Repair charts on the following pages distill the results of our 1997 Annual Questionnaire. Behind all the symbols in these charts lie real problems experienced by real people. The charts show at a glance which of a car's systems suffered a serious problem in the survey year. The symbols on these charts are on an absolute scale, from ◉ (2 percent or fewer vehicles suffered a problem) to ● (nearly 15 percent or more—sometimes a lot more).

Any car, as it ages, is likely to need some repair. But due to the quality of the parts, the nature of the design, or the production-line craftsmanship, some models suffer problems at a rate far lower or higher than what one might expect from aging alone. To assess how good or bad an older model might be and identify its problem areas, you need to compare its trouble rates with the overall average for that model year.

The chart for "the average model" on the next page shows which systems, overall, will most likely deteriorate as the car ages. (Not surprisingly, brakes wear out a lot.) The adjacent column details what each trouble spot includes.

In assessing individual cars, look at the column for the specific model year you're considering. A black mark in a model's record doesn't mean all such cars will suffer a problem, but it means that this model will probably have more than its share.

Trouble spots

Trouble rates for "the average model" show how some problems can be expected to increase as the car ages. Use this chart to see how the model and year you're considering compares with the overall average and whether its problems are excessive for its age.

The Average Model — TROUBLE SPOTS

90	91	92	93	94	95	96	97	TROUBLE SPOTS
○	○	○	⊖	⊖	⊖	⊜	⊜	Engine
◒	○	○	⊖	⊖	⊖	⊜	⊜	Cooling
○	○	⊖	⊖	⊖	⊖	⊖	⊜	Fuel
◒	◒	○	○	⊖	⊖	⊖	⊜	Ignition
○	○	○	○	○	⊖	⊖	⊜	Auto. trans.
⊖	⊖	⊖	⊜	⊜	⊜	⊜	⊜	Man. trans.
○	○	○	⊖	⊖	⊖	⊜	⊜	Clutch
◒	◒	◒	◒	○	○	⊖	⊖	Electrical
◒	◒	○	○	⊖	⊖	⊜	⊜	A/C
○	○	○	⊖	⊖	⊖	⊖	⊜	Suspension
●	●	●	◒	◒	○	⊖	⊜	Brakes
◒	◒	○	⊖	⊜	⊜	⊜	⊜	Exhaust
○	⊖	⊖	⊜	⊜	⊜	⊜	⊜	Body rust
◒	◒	○	⊖	⊖	⊖	⊖	⊜	Paint/trim
◒	◒	○	○	○	◒	○	⊖	Integrity
●	◒	◒	◒	◒	◒	○	⊖	Hardware

Key to problem rates

- ⊜ 2.0% or less
- ⊖ 2.0% to 5.0%
- ○ 5.0% to 9.3%
- ◒ 9.3% to 14.8%
- ● More than 14.8%

Overall average

Engine Pistons, rings, valves, block, heads, bearings, camshafts, gaskets, turbocharger, cam belts and chains, oil pump.

Cooling Radiator, heater core, water pump, thermostat, hoses, plumbing.

Fuel Fuel injection, computer and sensors, fuel pump, tank, emissions controls.

Ignition Starter, alternator, battery, spark plugs, coil, distributor, electronic ignition, sensors and modules, timing.

Transmission Transaxle, gear selector and linkage, coolers and lines.

Clutch Lining, pressure plate, release bearing, linkage and hydraulics.

Electrical Horn, switches, controls, lights, radio and sound system, power accessories, wiring.

Air conditioning Compressor, condenser, evaporator, expansion valves, hoses, dryer, fans, electronics.

Suspension Linkage, power-steering gear, pump, coolers and lines, alignment and balance, springs and torsion bars, ball joints, bushings, shocks and struts, electronic or air suspension.

Brakes Hydraulic system, linings, discs and drums, power boost, antilock system, parking brake and linkage.

Exhaust Manifold, muffler, catalytic converter, pipes.

Body rust Corrosion, pitting, perforation.

Paint/trim Fading, discoloring, chalking, peeling, cracking; loose trim, moldings, outside mirrors.

Integrity Seals, weather stripping, air and water leaks, wind noise, rattles and squeaks.

Hardware Window, door, seat mechanisms; locks, safety belts, sunroof, glass, wipers.

Acura CL	90	91	92	93	94	95	96	97
Engine								⊜
Cooling								⊜
Fuel								⊜
Ignition								⊜
Auto. trans.								⊜
Man. trans.								⊜
Clutch								⊜
Electrical								⊜
A/C								⊜
Suspension								⊜
Brakes								⊜
Exhaust								⊜
Body rust								⊜
Paint/trim								⊜
Integrity								○
Hardware								○

Acura Integra	90	91	92	93	94	95	96	97
Engine	⊖	⊖	⊖	⊜	⊜	⊜	⊜	
Cooling	⊖	○	⊖	⊖	⊜	⊜	⊜	
Fuel	⊜	⊜	⊜	⊜	⊜	⊜	⊜	
Ignition	⊖	⊖	○	⊖	⊜	⊜	⊜	
Auto. trans.	⊖	⊜	⊜	⊜	⊖	⊜	⊜	
Man. trans.	⊜	⊜	⊜	⊜	⊜	⊜	⊜	
Clutch	○	⊖	○	⊖	⊜	⊜	⊜	
Electrical	○	○	○	⊖	⊖	⊖	⊖	
A/C	○	⊖	⊖	○	⊖	⊜	⊜	
Suspension	○	⊜	⊖	⊜	⊜	⊜	⊜	
Brakes	◒	○	◒	○	○	⊖	⊜	
Exhaust	●	◒	●	◒	⊜	⊜	⊜	
Body rust	⊖	⊜	⊜	⊜	⊜	⊜	⊜	
Paint/trim	○	⊖	⊖	⊖	⊖	⊖	⊜	
Integrity	◒	○	○	○	○	○	⊖	
Hardware	○	○	○	⊖	○	⊖	⊖	

Acura Legend	90	91	92	93	94	95	96	97
Engine	⊖	⊜	⊜	⊜	⊜	⊜		
Cooling	○	◒	○	⊖	⊜	⊜		
Fuel	⊖	⊜	⊜	⊜	⊜	⊜		
Ignition	○	⊖	⊖	⊖	⊜	⊜		
Auto. trans.	⊖	⊖	⊖	⊖	⊜	⊜		
Man. trans.	⊜	*	*	*	*	*		
Clutch	●	*	*	*	*	*		
Electrical	◒	◒	○	○	◒	⊖		
A/C	○	⊖	○	⊜	⊜	⊜		
Suspension	○	⊖	⊖	⊜	⊜	⊜		
Brakes	●	●	◒	⊖	○	⊜		
Exhaust	○	⊜	⊜	⊜	⊜	⊜		
Body rust	⊖	⊜	⊜	⊜	⊜	⊜		
Paint/trim	⊖	⊖	⊖	⊜	⊜	⊜		
Integrity	○	○	○	○	⊖	○		
Hardware	○	◒	○	○	○	⊖		

Acura RL	90	91	92	93	94	95	96	97
Engine							⊜	Insufficient data
Cooling							⊜	
Fuel							⊜	
Ignition							⊜	
Auto. trans.							⊖	
Man. trans.								
Clutch								
Electrical							⊖	
A/C							⊜	
Suspension							⊜	
Brakes							⊜	
Exhaust							⊜	
Body rust							⊜	
Paint/trim							⊜	
Integrity							⊖	
Hardware							⊜	

Acura TL	90	91	92	93	94	95	96	97
Engine							⊜	⊜
Cooling							⊜	⊜
Fuel							⊜	⊜
Ignition							⊜	⊜
Auto. trans.							⊜	⊜
Man. trans.								
Clutch								
Electrical							⊖	⊜
A/C							⊜	⊜
Suspension							⊜	⊜
Brakes							⊖	⊜
Exhaust							⊜	⊜
Body rust							⊜	⊜
Paint/trim							⊖	⊜
Integrity							⊖	⊖
Hardware							⊖	⊖

Audi 100, A6	90	91	92	93	94	95	96	97
Engine	Insufficient data	Insufficient data	◒	Insufficient data	Insufficient data	⊜	⊜	Insufficient data
Cooling			◒			⊜	⊜	
Fuel			○			⊜	⊖	
Ignition			⊖			⊖	⊜	
Auto. trans.			○			*	⊜	
Man. trans.			*			*		
Clutch			*			*		
Electrical			○			◒	◒	
A/C			○			⊜	⊖	
Suspension			⊖			⊜	⊜	
Brakes			●			⊜	⊜	
Exhaust			⊜			⊜	⊜	
Body rust			⊜			⊜	⊜	
Paint/trim			⊜			⊜	⊖	
Integrity			⊜			⊖	⊜	
Hardware			⊖			⊖	○	

Audi A4	90	91	92	93	94	95	96	97
Engine							⊜	⊜
Cooling							⊜	⊜
Fuel							⊜	⊜
Ignition							⊜	⊜
Auto. trans.							○	*
Man. trans.							⊜	*
Clutch							⊜	*
Electrical							◒	⊖
A/C							⊜	⊜
Suspension							⊖	⊜
Brakes							⊖	⊜
Exhaust							⊜	⊜
Body rust							⊜	⊜
Paint/trim							⊜	⊜
Integrity							⊖	⊜
Hardware							○	⊖

BMW 3-Series	90	91	92	93	94	95	96	97
Engine	Insufficient data	●	○	⊖	⊜	⊜	⊜	⊜
Cooling		◒	◒	○	⊖	⊜	⊜	⊜
Fuel		◒	○	○	⊖	⊖	⊖	⊜
Ignition		○	○	⊖	⊖	⊜	⊖	⊜
Auto. trans.		*	⊖	⊖	⊜	⊜	⊜	*
Man. trans.		⊖	⊖	⊖	⊜	⊖	⊜	*
Clutch		⊜	⊖	○	⊜	⊖	⊜	*
Electrical		●	●	◒	◒	○	○	⊜
A/C		◒	◒	⊖	⊖	⊜	⊜	⊜
Suspension		○	○	⊖	⊜	⊜	⊜	⊜
Brakes		●	○	◒	⊖	⊖	⊖	⊜
Exhaust		○	⊖	⊖	⊜	⊜	⊜	⊜
Body rust		⊖	⊜	⊜	⊜	⊜	⊜	⊜
Paint/trim		⊖	⊖	⊖	⊜	⊜	⊜	⊜
Integrity		○	○	○	○	⊖	○	⊜
Hardware		●	●	◒	◒	○	○	⊜

BMW 5-Series

Trouble spots	90	91	92	93	94	95	96	97
Engine	◒	Insufficient data	⊖	Insufficient data	○	⊜	Insufficient data	⊜
Cooling	●		◒		⊖	⊜		⊜
Fuel	⊖		○		⊜	⊖		⊜
Ignition	⊖		○		⊜	⊜		⊜
Auto. trans.	*		*		○	⊜		⊜
Man. trans.	*		*		*	*		*
Clutch	*		*		*	*		*
Electrical	●		●		○	○		○
A/C	◒		◒		⊜	⊖		⊜
Suspension	○		◒		○	⊜		⊜
Brakes	◒		◒		○	⊖		⊜
Exhaust	◒		⊖		⊜	⊜		⊜
Body rust	⊜		⊜		⊜	⊜		⊜
Paint/trim	○		⊖		⊖	⊜		⊜
Integrity	⊖		○		⊖	⊖		○
Hardware	○		◒		○	⊖		○

BMW Z3

Trouble spots	90	91	92	93	94	95	96	97
Engine							Insufficient data	⊜
Cooling								⊜
Fuel								⊜
Ignition								⊜
Auto. trans.								*
Man. trans.								*
Clutch								*
Electrical								⊖
A/C								⊜
Suspension								⊜
Brakes								⊜
Exhaust								⊜
Body rust								⊖
Paint/trim								⊜
Integrity								○
Hardware								⊖

Buick Century

Trouble spots	90	91	92	93	94	95	96	97
Engine	○	⊖	⊖	⊜	⊖	⊖	⊜	Insufficient data
Cooling	◒	●	○	○	⊖	⊖	⊜	
Fuel	○	○	⊖	⊜	⊖	⊖	⊖	
Ignition	◒	◒	◒	⊖	○	⊜	⊖	
Auto. trans.	⊖	⊖	⊖	⊖	⊖	⊖	⊜	
Man. trans.								
Clutch								
Electrical	◒	○	○	○	○	⊖	○	
A/C	○	○	⊖	○	⊖	⊖	⊜	
Suspension	○	○	○	⊖	⊖	⊖	⊜	
Brakes	●	●	●	●	●	◒	○	
Exhaust	●	●	●	◒	○	⊜	⊜	
Body rust	○	◒	○	⊜	⊖	⊖	⊜	
Paint/trim	◒	◒	○	○	○	⊖	⊖	
Integrity	◒	○	○	○	◒	○	◒	
Hardware	◒	◒	○	○	◒	◒	○	

Buick Electra, Park Ave. & Ultra

Trouble spots	90	91	92	93	94	95	96	97
Engine	⊖	⊖	⊖	⊖	⊖	⊖	⊜	⊜
Cooling	○	○	○	○	⊖	⊜	⊜	⊜
Fuel	○	⊖	⊖	⊖	⊜	⊜	⊜	⊜
Ignition	●	●	●	●	○	⊖	⊜	⊜
Auto. trans.	○	⊖	⊖	⊖	⊖	⊖	⊖	⊜
Man. trans.								
Clutch								
Electrical	●	●	●	●	◒	●	◒	○
A/C	◒	◒	◒	◒	○	○	⊜	⊖
Suspension	⊖	○	○	○	⊖	⊖	⊖	⊜
Brakes	●	●	●	◒	○	⊖	⊖	⊖
Exhaust	⊖	⊜	⊜	⊖	⊜	⊖	⊜	⊜
Body rust	⊖	○	⊖	⊜	⊜	⊜	⊜	⊜
Paint/trim	◒	○	○	⊜	⊖	⊜	⊜	⊖
Integrity	◒	◒	○	◒	○	○	○	⊜
Hardware	◒	●	◒	●	●	●	○	○

Buick LeSabre

Trouble spots	90	91	92	93	94	95	96	97
Engine	⊖	⊖	⊖	⊖	⊖	⊖	⊜	⊜
Cooling	◒	○	◒	○	⊖	⊜	⊜	⊜
Fuel	○	○	⊖	⊖	⊖	⊖	⊖	⊜
Ignition	●	●	◒	◒	○	⊖	⊖	⊜
Auto. trans.	⊖	⊖	⊖	○	⊖	⊖	⊖	⊜
Man. trans.								
Clutch								
Electrical	◒	◒	◒	◒	○	○	○	⊖
A/C	◒	◒	◒	○	⊖	○	⊜	⊖
Suspension	⊖	○	○	⊖	⊖	⊖	⊖	⊜
Brakes	●	●	●	●	○	○	⊖	⊖
Exhaust	⊖	⊜	⊖	○	⊜	⊜	⊖	⊜
Body rust	○	○	⊖	⊜	⊜	⊜	⊜	⊜
Paint/trim	◒	○	◒	○	⊖	⊖	⊜	⊜
Integrity	○	○	◒	◒	○	○	○	⊖
Hardware	○	◒	◒	◒	◒	○	○	⊖

Buick Regal

Trouble spots	90	91	92	93	94	95	96	97
Engine	◒	⊖	⊖	⊖	○	⊖	⊜	Insufficient data
Cooling	◒	○	○	○	⊖	⊜	⊜	
Fuel	◒	○	⊖	⊖	⊜	⊜	⊜	
Ignition	●	◒	◒	○	⊖	⊜	⊜	
Auto. trans.	○	⊖	⊖	⊖	⊖	⊖	⊖	
Man. trans.								
Clutch								
Electrical	●	●	◒	◒	●	○	○	
A/C	◒	◒	○	○	⊖	⊖	⊜	
Suspension	◒	○	○	⊖	⊖	⊖	⊜	
Brakes	●	●	●	●	●	◒	○	
Exhaust	⊖	⊜	⊖	⊖	⊜	⊜	⊜	
Body rust	⊖	⊖	⊖	⊜	⊜	⊜	⊜	
Paint/trim	◒	○	⊖	⊖	⊖	⊖	⊜	
Integrity	◒	○	○	◒	◒	○	○	
Hardware	●	◒	◒	○	●	○	○	

Buick Riviera

Trouble spots	90	91	92	93	94	95	96	97
Engine	Insufficient data	Insufficient data	Insufficient data	Insufficient data		○	⊜	Insufficient data
Cooling						⊖	⊖	
Fuel						⊖	⊜	
Ignition						⊖	⊖	
Auto. trans.						⊖	⊖	
Man. trans.								
Clutch								
Electrical						●	●	
A/C						○	⊖	
Suspension						⊖	⊖	
Brakes						○	⊜	
Exhaust						⊜	⊖	
Body rust						⊜	⊜	
Paint/trim						⊖	⊜	
Integrity						◒	◒	
Hardware						●	○	

Buick Roadmaster

Trouble spots	90	91	92	93	94	95	96	97
Engine		Insufficient data	⊖	⊖	⊖	⊖	⊜	
Cooling			◒	○	⊜	⊜	⊜	
Fuel			⊖	⊜	⊖	⊜	⊖	
Ignition			○	○	○	⊖	⊜	
Auto. trans.			○	⊜	⊖	⊖	⊖	
Man. trans.								
Clutch								
Electrical			●	◒	◒	◒	○	
A/C			●	◒	⊖	⊜	⊖	
Suspension			⊖	○	○	○	○	
Brakes			◒	◒	○	⊖	⊖	
Exhaust			⊖	⊜	⊜	⊜	⊜	
Body rust			⊖	⊜	⊜	⊜	⊜	
Paint/trim			●	○	○	⊖	⊖	
Integrity			○	○	◒	●	●	
Hardware			◒	◒	◒	●	●	

Key: ⊜ ⊖ ○ ◒ ● Few ← Problems → Many

* Insufficient data

Buick Skylark

TROUBLE SPOTS	90	91	92	93	94	95	96	97
Engine	◒	○	⊖	⊖	⊖	⊖	⊜	
Cooling	○	◒	●	○	⊜	⊜	⊜	
Fuel	◒	○	○	○	⊖	⊜	⊖	
Ignition	●	●	○	○	⊖	⊖	⊖	
Auto. trans.	◒	○	⊖	⊖	⊜	⊖	⊜	
Man. trans.								
Clutch								
Electrical	●	◒	◒	○	○	○	○	Insufficient data
A/C	●	⊖	◒	○	⊖	○	⊜	
Suspension	◒	○	◒	○	⊖	○	⊜	
Brakes	●	●	●	●	●	●	○	
Exhaust	●	●	○	⊖	⊜	⊜	⊜	
Body rust	●	●	⊖	⊖	⊜	⊜	⊜	
Paint/trim	●	●	◒	⊖	⊖	⊖	⊖	
Integrity	●	◒	◒	◒	○	⊖	◒	
Hardware	●	◒	◒	◒	◒	◒	○	

Cadillac Brougham, Fleetwood (RWD)

TROUBLE SPOTS	90	91	92	93	94	95	96	97
Engine	○	○		⊖	⊖			
Cooling	◒	○		◒	⊖			
Fuel	○	⊖		⊖	⊖			
Ignition	◒	◒		○	○			
Auto. trans.	○	○		⊖	⊖			
Man. trans.								
Clutch								
Electrical	◒	●	Insufficient data	●	◒	Insufficient data	Insufficient data	
A/C	●	○		◒	⊖			
Suspension	○	◒		○	○			
Brakes	◒	●		◒	◒			
Exhaust	○	○		⊜	⊜			
Body rust	○	⊖		⊖	⊖			
Paint/trim	◒	○		●	◒			
Integrity	◒	○		◒	◒			
Hardware	◒	●		●	◒			

Cadillac Catera

TROUBLE SPOTS	90	91	92	93	94	95	96	97
Engine								⊜
Cooling								⊜
Fuel								⊜
Ignition								⊜
Auto. trans.								⊜
Man. trans.								
Clutch								
Electrical								○
A/C								⊜
Suspension								⊜
Brakes								⊖
Exhaust								⊜
Body rust								⊜
Paint/trim								○
Integrity								○
Hardware								⊖

Cadillac DeVille, Concours (FWD)

TROUBLE SPOTS	90	91	92	93	94	95	96	97
Engine	○	◒	◒	○	⊖	⊖	⊖	⊜
Cooling	○	○	◒	⊖	⊜	⊜	⊜	⊜
Fuel	◒	◒	◒	○	⊖	⊖	⊖	⊖
Ignition	○	◒	○	⊖	⊖	⊖	⊜	⊜
Auto. trans.	⊖	○	⊖	○	⊖	⊜	⊖	⊖
Man. trans.								
Clutch								
Electrical	●	◒	◒	○	◒	◒	○	○
A/C	◒	●	◒	◒	○	⊖	⊖	⊖
Suspension	⊖	○	○	●	○	○	⊖	⊜
Brakes	●	●	●	●	○	○	⊖	⊖
Exhaust	○	⊖	⊖	⊖	⊜	⊜	⊜	⊜
Body rust	⊖	⊜	⊖	⊜	⊜	⊜	⊜	⊜
Paint/trim	⊖	⊖	⊖	⊖	⊖	⊖	⊖	⊖
Integrity	○	⊖	○	○	⊖	○	○	○
Hardware	◒	○	○	○	●	◒	○	○

Cadillac Eldorado

TROUBLE SPOTS	90	91	92	93	94	95	96	97
Engine	○		○		⊖	⊖	⊖	
Cooling	◒		○		⊜	⊜	⊖	
Fuel	○		○		⊖	⊖	⊖	
Ignition	◒		○		◒	⊖	⊖	
Auto. trans.	○		⊖		⊜	⊖	⊖	
Man. trans.								
Clutch								
Electrical	●	Insufficient data	●	Insufficient data	◒	◒	◒	Insufficient data
A/C	●		◒		○	○	○	
Suspension	○		●		⊖	⊜	⊖	
Brakes	●		●		○	⊖	○	
Exhaust	⊖		⊖		⊜	⊜	⊜	
Body rust	⊖		⊖		⊜	⊜	⊜	
Paint/trim	⊖		⊖		⊖	⊖	○	
Integrity	⊖		●		◒	●	●	
Hardware	◒		●		●	●	○	

Cadillac Seville

TROUBLE SPOTS	90	91	92	93	94	95	96	97
Engine	◒	◒	◒	○	⊖	⊖	⊖	⊜
Cooling	◒	◒	◒	○	⊖	⊜	⊜	⊜
Fuel	○	○	⊖	○	⊖	⊖	⊖	⊜
Ignition	◒	○	○	○	○	⊖	⊖	⊜
Auto. trans.	⊖	⊖	○	○	⊖	⊖	⊖	⊜
Man. trans.								
Clutch								
Electrical	●	●	◒	◒	●	◒	◒	◒
A/C	●	●	●	◒	○	⊖	⊖	⊖
Suspension	○	◒	◒	◒	⊖	⊖	⊖	⊜
Brakes	●	●	●	◒	⊖	⊖	⊜	⊖
Exhaust	⊖	○	⊖	⊜	⊜	⊜	⊜	⊜
Body rust	⊜	⊜	⊜	⊜	⊜	⊜	⊜	⊜
Paint/trim	⊖	⊖	○	⊖	⊖	⊖	⊖	○
Integrity	○	○	◒	◒	◒	○	○	◒
Hardware	◒	○	◒	◒	●	●	◒	⊖

Chevrolet Astro Van

TROUBLE SPOTS	90	91	92	93	94	95	96	97
Engine	○	○	○	○	⊖	⊖	⊜	⊜
Cooling	◒	⊖	⊖	⊖	⊖	⊜	⊖	⊜
Fuel	⊖	⊖	⊖	○	○	○	⊖	○
Ignition	◒	◒	◒	●	○	⊖	⊖	⊖
Auto. trans.	○	○	⊖	○	⊖	⊖	⊖	⊖
Man. trans.								
Clutch								
Electrical	●	●	◒	●	●	○	○	⊖
A/C	◒	◒	○	○	◒	⊖	⊖	⊖
Suspension	◒	◒	◒	◒	○	○	⊖	⊖
Brakes	●	●	●	●	●	◒	○	⊜
Exhaust	◒	◒	○	◒	⊖	⊜	⊖	⊜
Body rust	⊖	⊖	⊖	⊜	⊖	⊜	⊜	⊜
Paint/trim	●	●	◒	◒	○	⊖	⊖	⊖
Integrity	●	●	●	●	●	●	●	◒
Hardware	●	●	●	●	●	◒	●	◒

Chevrolet Blazer, K-Blazer, Tahoe

TROUBLE SPOTS	90	91	92	93	94	95	96	97
Engine				○	⊖	⊖	⊖	⊜
Cooling				●	⊖	⊜	⊜	⊜
Fuel				⊖	⊖	⊖	⊖	⊖
Ignition				○	⊖	○	⊜	⊜
Auto. trans.				○	⊖	⊜	⊖	⊜
Man. trans.				*	*	*		
Clutch				*	*	*		
Electrical	Insufficient data	Insufficient data	Insufficient data	●	○	○	○	⊖
A/C				○	○	⊖	⊖	⊜
Suspension				○	⊖	○	⊖	⊖
Brakes				●	◒	◒	○	⊜
Exhaust				◒	⊖	⊜	⊜	⊜
Body rust				○	⊜	⊜	⊜	⊜
Paint/trim				○	⊖	⊖	⊜	⊜
Integrity				○	○	◒	○	⊖
Hardware				◒	◒	◒	○	⊖

Chevrolet C1500 Pickup

TROUBLE SPOTS	90	91	92	93	94	95	96	97
Engine	○	⊖	⊖	⊖	⊖	⊖	⊖	⊜
Cooling	○	○	⊖	⊖	⊖	⊜	⊖	⊜
Fuel	⊖	⊖	⊖	⊖	⊖	⊜	⊖	⊖
Ignition	◒	◒	◒	○	⊖	⊖	⊖	⊜
Auto. trans.	○	○	◒	⊖	⊖	⊜	⊖	⊜
Man. trans.	⊖	○	⊖	*	*	⊖	*	*
Clutch	◒	●	◒	*	*	◒	*	*
Electrical	◒	◒	◒	○	○	○	⊖	⊖
A/C	○	◒	○	⊖	○	⊖	⊖	⊜
Suspension	○	○	○	⊖	⊖	⊖	○	○
Brakes	◒	◒	○	○	○	⊖	○	⊜
Exhaust	●	●	◒	○	⊖	⊜	⊖	⊜
Body rust	⊖	⊜	⊜	⊜	⊜	⊜	⊜	⊜
Paint/trim	●	◒	◒	○	⊖	⊖	⊖	⊜
Integrity	○	○	○	○	○	○	○	○
Hardware	○	◒	◒	○	○	○	◒	○

Chevrolet Camaro V8

TROUBLE SPOTS	90	91	92	93	94	95	96	97
	Insufficient data		Insufficient data	Insufficient data				Insufficient data
Engine		○			○	◒	◒	
Cooling		◒			○	⊖	⊜	
Fuel		●			⊖	⊖	⊖	
Ignition		●			◒	○	⊜	
Auto. trans.		*			⊜	⊜	*	
Man. trans.		*			*	*	*	
Clutch		*			*	*	*	
Electrical		◒			◒	●	◒	
A/C		○			⊖	○	⊜	
Suspension		○			⊖	⊖	⊖	
Brakes		◒			◒	○	⊖	
Exhaust		◒			⊜	⊖	⊜	
Body rust		⊜			⊜	⊜	⊜	
Paint/trim		●			⊖	⊖	○	
Integrity		●			●	●	◒	
Hardware		●			●	◒	◒	

Chevrolet Caprice

TROUBLE SPOTS	90	91	92	93	94	95	96	97
Engine	○	⊖	⊖	⊜	⊖	⊜	⊜	
Cooling	●	○	○	⊖	⊖	⊖	⊜	
Fuel	○	⊖	⊖	⊜	⊖	⊖	⊖	
Ignition	◒	◒	◒	○	◒	○	⊜	
Auto. trans.	○	⊖	⊖	⊖	⊖	○	⊖	
Man. trans.								
Clutch								
Electrical	◒	●	●	◒	●	●	○	
A/C	○	●	◒	○	⊖	⊖	⊖	
Suspension	○	○	◒	○	◒	○	○	
Brakes	●	●	●	○	◒	○	⊖	
Exhaust	●	●	⊜	⊜	⊜	⊜	⊜	
Body rust	●	⊖	⊜	⊜	⊜	⊜	⊜	
Paint/trim	●	●	○	⊖	⊖	⊖	○	
Integrity	○	◒	⊖	○	◒	○	◒	
Hardware	◒	●	◒	◒	●	◒	○	

Chevrolet Cavalier

TROUBLE SPOTS	90	91	92	93	94	95	96	97
Engine	◒	◒	○	○	○	○	⊖	⊜
Cooling	●	●	◒	○	○	⊖	⊖	⊜
Fuel	○	○	⊖	⊖	⊖	⊖	⊖	⊜
Ignition	●	●	●	◒	◒	⊖	⊖	⊖
Auto. trans.	⊖	⊖	⊖	⊖	⊖	⊖	⊖	⊜
Man. trans.	*	⊖	*	*	*	*	⊖	⊖
Clutch	*	⊖	*	*	*	*	○	⊜
Electrical	◒	●	◒	◒	◒	◒	◒	⊖
A/C	●	◒	○	○	○	⊜	⊜	⊜
Suspension	◒	○	○	○	⊖	⊖	⊖	⊖
Brakes	●	●	●	●	●	◒	○	⊖
Exhaust	◒	○	⊖	⊖	⊖	⊖	⊖	⊜
Body rust	●	◒	◒	○	○	⊜	⊜	⊜
Paint/trim	●	●	◒	○	○	⊖	⊖	⊜
Integrity	●	●	◒	◒	●	◒	●	○
Hardware	◒	◒	●	◒	◒	◒	○	⊖

Chevrolet Corsica, Beretta

TROUBLE SPOTS	90	91	92	93	94	95	96	97
Engine	◒	◒	○	⊖	⊖	⊖	⊜	
Cooling	●	●	●	◒	⊜	⊖	⊖	
Fuel	◒	○	○	⊖	⊖	⊜	⊖	
Ignition	●	●	●	◒	○	⊖	⊜	
Auto. trans.	○	⊖	⊖	⊖	⊜	⊖	⊜	
Man. trans.	*	*	*	*	*	*	*	
Clutch	*	*	*	*	*	*	*	
Electrical	●	◒	●	◒	◒	○	⊖	
A/C	◒	◒	◒	○	⊖	⊖	⊖	
Suspension	○	○	○	◒	○	⊜	⊖	
Brakes	●	●	●	●	●	●	○	
Exhaust	●	○	⊖	⊜	⊜	⊜	⊜	
Body rust	◒	○	⊜	⊜	⊖	⊜	⊜	
Paint/trim	●	●	●	○	○	⊖	⊖	
Integrity	●	◒	●	●	●	◒	◒	
Hardware	●	◒	◒	○	●	○	◒	

Chevrolet K1500 Pickup

TROUBLE SPOTS	90	91	92	93	94	95	96	97
Engine	○	⊖	⊖	⊖	○	⊖	⊖	⊜
Cooling	◒	○	○	⊖	⊖	⊜	⊜	⊜
Fuel	⊖	⊖	⊖	⊖	⊖	⊜	⊖	⊜
Ignition	●	●	◒	○	⊖	⊖	⊜	⊜
Auto. trans.	◒	◒	◒	⊖	⊖	⊖	⊖	⊜
Man. trans.	*	⊖	⊖	*	*	⊖	*	*
Clutch	*	◒	○	*	*	○	*	*
Electrical	◒	◒	●	○	○	○	○	⊖
A/C	○	○	⊖	⊖	⊖	⊖	⊜	⊜
Suspension	○	○	○	⊖	⊖	⊖	⊖	⊖
Brakes	◒	◒	◒	○	○	○	○	⊖
Exhaust	●	●	◒	◒	⊜	⊖	⊜	⊜
Body rust	○	⊖	⊜	⊖	⊜	⊜	⊜	⊜
Paint/trim	●	◒	○	◒	⊖	⊖	⊖	⊜
Integrity	◒	○	◒	○	○	○	○	⊖
Hardware	◒	○	◒	○	◒	◒	◒	⊖

Chevrolet Lumina

TROUBLE SPOTS	90	91	92	93	94	95	96	97
Engine	◒	○	○	⊖	⊖	⊖	⊜	⊜
Cooling	◒	○	○	⊖	⊜	⊜	⊜	⊜
Fuel	◒	○	⊖	○	⊜	⊜	⊖	⊜
Ignition	●	●	●	●	○	⊖	⊖	⊜
Auto. trans.	○	○	○	⊖	⊖	⊖	⊖	⊜
Man. trans.		*	*	*				
Clutch		*	*	*				
Electrical	◒	○	◒	○	◒	○	⊖	⊖
A/C	◒	○	○	⊖	⊖	⊖	⊜	⊜
Suspension	◒	○	⊖	⊖	⊜	⊖	⊖	⊜
Brakes	●	●	●	●	●	◒	⊖	⊜
Exhaust	⊖	⊖	⊖	⊜	⊜	⊜	⊜	⊜
Body rust	○	⊖	⊜	⊜	⊜	⊜	⊜	⊜
Paint/trim	●	◒	○	⊖	⊖	⊖	⊖	⊖
Integrity	●	◒	◒	◒	○	○	○	⊜
Hardware	●	◒	◒	○	◒	◒	○	⊖

Chevrolet Lumina APV Van

TROUBLE SPOTS	90	91	92	93	94	95	96	97
Engine	⊖	○	⊖	⊖	⊖	⊖	⊜	
Cooling	●	●	●	○	⊖	⊖	⊜	
Fuel	⊖	⊖	⊖	○	⊖	⊜	⊖	
Ignition	●	◒	◒	●	○	⊖	⊜	
Auto. trans.	⊖	○	○	○	⊖	⊜	⊖	
Man. trans.								
Clutch								
Electrical	●	●	●	◒	○	◒	○	
A/C	◒	◒	○	○	⊖	⊖	⊖	
Suspension	○	◒	◒	○	⊖	⊖	⊖	
Brakes	●	●	●	●	◒	○	⊖	
Exhaust	◒	⊜	⊖	⊖	⊜	⊜	⊜	
Body rust	⊜	⊜	⊜	⊖	⊜	⊜	⊜	
Paint/trim	●	●	○	○	⊖	○	○	
Integrity	●	◒	○	◒	◒	◒	●	
Hardware	●	●	●	●	●	●	◒	

⊜ ⊖ ○ ◒ ●

Few ← Problems → Many

*

Insufficient data

Chevrolet Malibu V6	90	91	92	93	94	95	96	97
Engine								⊜
Cooling								⊜
Fuel								⊜
Ignition								⊜
Auto. trans.								⊜
Man. trans.								
Clutch								
Electrical								○
A/C								⊖
Suspension								⊖
Brakes								○
Exhaust								⊜
Body rust								⊜
Paint/trim								⊖
Integrity								○
Hardware								⊜

Chevrolet Monte Carlo	90	91	92	93	94	95	96	97
Engine						○	○	Insufficient data
Cooling						⊖	⊜	
Fuel						⊜	○	
Ignition						⊖	○	
Auto. trans.						⊖	⊖	
Man. trans.								
Clutch								
Electrical						◒	○	
A/C						⊖	⊖	
Suspension						⊖	⊖	
Brakes						●	○	
Exhaust						⊜	⊜	
Body rust						⊜	⊜	
Paint/trim						○	○	
Integrity						◒	◒	
Hardware						●	○	

Chevrolet S-10 Blazer, Blazer	90	91	92	93	94	95	96	97
Engine	○	○	○	◒	○	○	○	⊜
Cooling	◒	○	◒	○	⊖	⊜	⊜	⊜
Fuel	○	○	◒	●	◒	◒	○	⊖
Ignition	◒	◒	◒	◒	○	○	⊖	⊜
Auto. trans.	○	⊖	⊖	○	○	⊖	⊖	⊜
Man. trans.	*	*	*	*	*	*	*	*
Clutch	*	*	*	*	*	*	*	*
Electrical	●	●	◒	●	◒	◒	○	⊖
A/C	◒	○	○	⊖	⊖	⊖	⊖	⊜
Suspension	◒	◒	◒	◒	○	⊖	⊖	⊜
Brakes	●	●	●	●	●	●	○	⊖
Exhaust	●	●	○	○	⊜	⊜	⊜	⊜
Body rust	●	●	○	○	○	⊜	⊜	⊜
Paint/trim	●	●	●	◒	○	○	⊖	⊜
Integrity	●	●	●	●	●	●	○	○
Hardware	●	●	◒	●	◒	●	○	⊖

Chevrolet S-10 Pickup V6 (2WD)	90	91	92	93	94	95	96	97
Engine	○	⊖	○	⊖	⊖	⊖	○	⊜
Cooling	◒	◒	⊖	⊖	⊖	⊜	⊖	⊜
Fuel	○	⊖	⊖	⊖	○	○	○	⊜
Ignition	◒	○	○	○	○	○	⊖	⊜
Auto. trans.	*	⊖	⊜	⊜	⊖	⊜	⊖	⊜
Man. trans.	*	⊖	⊜	⊖	*	⊖	*	*
Clutch	*	○	◒	○	*	⊖	*	*
Electrical	●	◒	○	○	◒	◒	⊖	⊖
A/C	*	○	⊖	⊖	○	⊖	⊖	⊜
Suspension	⊖	⊖	○	⊖	○	⊖	⊖	⊜
Brakes	◒	○	◒	◒	●	◒	○	⊜
Exhaust	●	◒	◒	○	⊖	⊜	⊜	⊜
Body rust	●	◒	○	○	⊜	⊜	⊜	⊜
Paint/trim	●	●	●	◒	○	○	⊖	⊖
Integrity	●	◒	○	○	○	◒	◒	○
Hardware	◒	◒	○	○	◒	◒	○	○

Chevrolet S-10 Pickup V6 (4WD)	90	91	92	93	94	95	96	97
Engine	Insufficient data	⊖	○	Insufficient data	○	○	○	Insufficient data
Cooling		○	◒		○	⊖	⊖	
Fuel		⊖	○		○	⊖	⊖	
Ignition		●	◒		○	○	⊖	
Auto. trans.		○	*		⊖	⊖	⊜	
Man. trans.		*	*		*	*	*	
Clutch		*	*		*	*	*	
Electrical		◒	○		●	◒	⊖	
A/C		⊖	*		⊖	⊜	⊖	
Suspension		◒	◒		○	⊖	○	
Brakes		◒	●		●	●	○	
Exhaust		●	◒		⊖	⊜	⊜	
Body rust		●	◒		⊜	⊖	⊜	
Paint/trim		●	●		○	○	⊖	
Integrity		●	○		◒	●	●	
Hardware		◒	◒		◒	◒	○	

Chevrolet Sportvan V8	90	91	92	93	94	95	96	97
Engine	○	⊖	○	○	○	⊖	Insufficient data	Insufficient data
Cooling	●	●	○	⊖	⊖	⊖		
Fuel	⊖	⊜	○	⊜	⊖	⊖		
Ignition	◒	◒	○	◒	○	○		
Auto. trans.	⊖	●	◒	○	⊖	⊖		
Man. trans.								
Clutch								
Electrical	◒	◒	◒	●	●	◒		
A/C	●	◒	◒	◒	◒	◒		
Suspension	◒	◒	◒	○	○	⊖		
Brakes	●	●	●	●	●	●		
Exhaust	●	◒	◒	○	⊜	⊖		
Body rust	◒	◒	⊖	○	⊖	⊖		
Paint/trim	●	●	◒	◒	○	◒		
Integrity	◒	●	◒	●	●	●		
Hardware	●	●	◒	●	●	●		

Chevrolet Suburban	90	91	92	93	94	95	96	97
Engine	○	○	○	⊖	⊖	⊜	⊜	⊜
Cooling	●	◒	●	●	⊜	⊜	⊜	⊜
Fuel	⊖	⊖	⊖	⊜	⊖	⊜	⊖	⊜
Ignition	●	●	◒	○	○	⊖	⊖	⊜
Auto. trans.	◒	●	◒	○	⊖	⊖	⊖	⊜
Man. trans.	*							
Clutch	*							
Electrical	●	◒	◒	◒	◒	◒	○	⊖
A/C	●	◒	○	○	◒	○	⊖	⊜
Suspension	◒	○	○	○	⊖	⊖	⊖	⊖
Brakes	●	●	●	●	●	◒	○	○
Exhaust	◒	●	○	○	⊖	⊜	⊜	⊜
Body rust	◒	○	⊖	⊖	⊜	⊜	⊜	⊜
Paint/trim	●	●	◒	○	⊖	⊖	⊜	⊜
Integrity	●	●	●	◒	◒	○	○	⊖
Hardware	●	●	◒	●	◒	●	◒	⊖

Chevrolet Venture Van (ext.)	90	91	92	93	94	95	96	97
Engine								⊜
Cooling								⊜
Fuel								⊖
Ignition								⊖
Auto. trans.								⊜
Man. trans.								
Clutch								
Electrical								○
A/C								⊖
Suspension								⊖
Brakes								⊖
Exhaust								⊖
Body rust								⊜
Paint/trim								○
Integrity								◒
Hardware								●

Chrysler Cirrus

TROUBLE SPOTS	90	91	92	93	94	95	96	97
Engine						⊖	⊖	⊜
Cooling						⊜	⊜	⊜
Fuel						⊖	⊖	⊜
Ignition						⊖	⊖	⊖
Auto. trans.						⊖	⊖	⊜
Man. trans.								
Clutch								
Electrical						◒	○	⊖
A/C						◒	⊜	⊜
Suspension						◒	○	⊜
Brakes						●	○	⊜
Exhaust						⊜	⊜	⊜
Body rust						⊜	⊜	⊜
Paint/trim						●	⊖	⊜
Integrity						●	◒	⊖
Hardware						◒	○	⊖

Chrysler Concorde

TROUBLE SPOTS	90	91	92	93	94	95	96	97
Engine				○	⊖	⊜	⊜	⊜
Cooling				○	⊖	⊖	⊜	⊜
Fuel				○	⊖	⊖	⊜	⊜
Ignition				○	⊖	⊖	⊖	⊜
Auto. trans.				◒	●	○	⊖	⊖
Man. trans.								
Clutch								
Electrical				●	◒	○	⊖	⊜
A/C				●	●	●	⊖	⊖
Suspension				○	○	⊖	⊖	⊜
Brakes				●	●	○	⊖	⊜
Exhaust				⊜	⊜	⊜	⊜	⊜
Body rust				⊜	⊜	⊜	⊜	⊜
Paint/trim				⊖	⊖	⊖	⊜	⊜
Integrity				○	◒	○	⊖	⊖
Hardware				●	○	○	⊖	⊖

Chrysler LeBaron Coupe & Conv.

TROUBLE SPOTS	90	91	92	93	94	95	96	97
Engine	●	◒	○	⊖	○	○		
Cooling	◒	◒	○	⊖	⊖	⊖		
Fuel	○	◒	○	○	○	⊖		
Ignition	◒	◒	○	○	⊖	⊖		
Auto. trans.	●	●	●	◒	○	⊖		
Man. trans.	*	*	*	*				
Clutch	*	*	*	*				
Electrical	●	●	●	◒	●	◒		
A/C	◒	○	◒	●	⊖	⊖		
Suspension	○	⊖	⊖	⊖	○	○		
Brakes	●	◒	●	◒	⊖	⊖		
Exhaust	⊖	●	◒	⊜	⊜	⊜		
Body rust	⊖	⊜	⊜	⊜	⊜	⊜		
Paint/trim	●	◒	○	◒	○	⊖		
Integrity	●	●	●	●	●	●		
Hardware	●	●	●	●	●	●		

Chrysler LeBaron Sedan

TROUBLE SPOTS	90	91	92	93	94	95	96	97
Engine	◒	◒	◒	○	⊖			
Cooling	●	○	○	○	⊖			
Fuel	○	○	○	○	○			
Ignition	◒	○	○	⊖	⊖			
Auto. trans.	●	◒	○	◒	◒			
Man. trans.								
Clutch								
Electrical	◒	○	◒	○	○			
A/C	◒	◒	○	●	◒			
Suspension	◒	○	○	○	⊖			
Brakes	●	◒	◒	○	⊖			
Exhaust	⊖	●	●	⊜	⊜			
Body rust	○	⊖	⊖	⊖	⊖			
Paint/trim	◒	◒	○	⊖	○			
Integrity	○	○	○	○	○			
Hardware	◒	○	○	○	○			

Chrysler New Yorker, LHS

TROUBLE SPOTS	90	91	92	93	94	95	96	97
Engine					⊖	⊜	⊜	⊖
Cooling					⊖	⊖	⊖	⊜
Fuel					○	⊖	⊜	⊜
Ignition					○	⊖	⊜	⊜
Auto. trans.					●	○	⊖	⊖
Man. trans.								
Clutch								
Electrical					◒	○	○	⊖
A/C					●	◒	⊖	⊜
Suspension					○	○	⊖	⊜
Brakes					●	◒	⊖	⊜
Exhaust					⊜	⊜	⊜	⊜
Body rust					⊜	⊜	⊜	⊜
Paint/trim					⊖	⊖	⊜	⊜
Integrity					◒	○	○	⊜
Hardware					◒	○	○	⊜

Chrysler Sebring Convertible

TROUBLE SPOTS	90	91	92	93	94	95	96	97
Engine							⊜	⊜
Cooling							⊜	⊜
Fuel							⊜	⊜
Ignition							⊖	⊜
Auto. trans.							⊖	⊜
Man. trans.								
Clutch								
Electrical							◒	○
A/C							⊜	⊜
Suspension							⊖	⊜
Brakes							○	⊜
Exhaust							⊜	⊜
Body rust							⊜	⊜
Paint/trim							⊖	⊖
Integrity							◒	○
Hardware							◒	⊖

Chrysler Sebring V6

TROUBLE SPOTS	90	91	92	93	94	95	96	97
Engine						⊖	⊜	
Cooling						⊜	⊜	
Fuel						○	⊖	
Ignition						◒	○	
Auto. trans.						○	⊖	
Man. trans.						*		
Clutch						*		Insufficient data
Electrical						◒	◒	
A/C						⊜	⊖	
Suspension						⊖	⊖	
Brakes						●	○	
Exhaust						⊜	⊖	
Body rust						⊖	⊜	
Paint/trim						◒	○	
Integrity						●	●	
Hardware						●	●	

Chrysler Town & Country (ext.)

TROUBLE SPOTS	90	91	92	93	94	95	96	97
Engine	◒	○	◒	○	⊖	⊜	⊜	⊜
Cooling	●	◒	○	○	⊖	⊖	⊖	⊜
Fuel	◒	○	○	○	⊖	⊖	○	⊜
Ignition	◒	◒	◒	○	⊖	⊖	⊜	⊜
Auto. trans.	●	●	●	●	●	○	⊖	⊜
Man. trans.								
Clutch								
Electrical	◒	●	●	◒	◒	○	◒	○
A/C	●	○	○	●	○	⊖	⊖	⊜
Suspension	◒	◒	◒	○	○	○	⊖	⊜
Brakes	●	●	●	●	◒	○	◒	⊖
Exhaust	⊖	●	◒	⊜	⊜	⊜	⊜	⊜
Body rust	○	⊖	⊖	⊜	⊜	⊜	⊜	⊜
Paint/trim	●	◒	○	○	○	⊖	⊖	⊖
Integrity	●	◒	◒	◒	◒	◒	◒	○
Hardware	●	●	●	●	●	●	◒	○

⊜ ⊖ ○ ◒ ●
Few ← **Problems** → Many

*
Insufficient data

Dodge Avenger V6 — TROUBLE SPOTS	90	91	92	93	94	95	96	97
Engine						⊖	⊜	Insufficient data
Cooling						⊜	⊜	
Fuel						○	⊜	
Ignition						◒	○	
Auto. trans.						○	⊖	
Man. trans.						*		
Clutch						*		
Electrical						◒	◒	
A/C						⊜	⊖	
Suspension						⊖	⊖	
Brakes						●	○	
Exhaust						⊜	⊖	
Body rust						⊖	⊜	
Paint/trim						◒	○	
Integrity						●	●	
Hardware						●	●	

Dodge Caravan V6 — TROUBLE SPOTS	90	91	92	93	94	95	96	97
Engine	●	◒	◒	○	⊖	⊖	⊖	⊜
Cooling	◒	◒	○	○	⊖	⊜	⊜	⊜
Fuel	◒	○	○	⊖	⊖	⊖	○	⊜
Ignition	○	○	○	○	⊖	⊜	⊜	⊜
Auto. trans.	●	●	●	◒	◒	○	⊖	⊜
Man. trans.								
Clutch								
Electrical	◒	◒	●	◒	○	○	○	⊖
A/C	◒	○	○	●	○	⊖	⊖	⊜
Suspension	○	○	○	○	○	⊖	⊖	⊜
Brakes	●	●	●	●	◒	○	◒	⊖
Exhaust	⊖	●	◒	⊜	⊜	⊖	⊜	⊜
Body rust	○	⊖	⊖	⊜	⊜	⊜	⊜	⊜
Paint/trim	●	◒	○	⊖	⊖	⊖	⊖	⊜
Integrity	●	●	◒	◒	◒	◒	○	○
Hardware	●	●	◒	◒	◒	◒	◒	○

Dodge Colt, Colt Wagon (2WD) — TROUBLE SPOTS	90	91	92	93	94	95	96	97
Engine	●	◒	○	⊖	Insufficient data			
Cooling	○	⊖	⊖	⊖				
Fuel	○	⊖	⊖	⊖				
Ignition	○	○	○	○				
Auto. trans.	⊖	○	◒	◒				
Man. trans.	⊖	⊖	⊖	○				
Clutch	○	○	○	⊜				
Electrical	○	○	⊖	○				
A/C	○	◒	○	⊖				
Suspension	◒	⊖	○	○				
Brakes	◒	◒	◒	◒				
Exhaust	⊖	⊖	⊜	⊜				
Body rust	○	⊖	⊜	⊖				
Paint/trim	◒	◒	○	○				
Integrity	●	◒	◒	◒				
Hardware	●	◒	◒	●				

Dodge Dakota Pickup (2WD) — TROUBLE SPOTS	90	91	92	93	94	95	96	97
Engine	○	○	○	○	○	⊖	⊖	⊜
Cooling	◒	◒	○	○	⊖	⊜	⊜	⊜
Fuel	○	○	○	○	○	⊖	○	⊜
Ignition	◒	◒	◒	○	⊖	⊖	⊖	⊜
Auto. trans.	●	◒	◒	○	◒	○	◒	⊖
Man. trans.	*	*	*	*	*	*	*	*
Clutch	*	*	*	*	*	*	*	*
Electrical	◒	◒	◒	◒	○	○	◒	⊖
A/C	◒	◒	⊖	⊖	○	⊖	⊜	⊜
Suspension	○	○	⊖	⊖	○	⊖	⊖	⊜
Brakes	●	●	●	●	◒	◒	○	⊜
Exhaust	○	●	●	⊖	⊜	⊜	⊜	⊜
Body rust	○	○	⊖	⊖	⊖	⊜	⊜	⊜
Paint/trim	●	◒	●	◒	○	⊖	○	⊜
Integrity	◒	○	○	○	◒	○	◒	○
Hardware	◒	○	⊖	○	○	○	○	⊖

Dodge Dakota Pickup (4WD) — TROUBLE SPOTS	90	91	92	93	94	95	96	97
Engine	Insufficient data	Insufficient data	◒	⊖	⊖	⊜	⊖	⊜
Cooling			○	○	⊜	⊖	⊖	⊜
Fuel			○	○	⊜	○	◒	⊜
Ignition			◒	⊖	○	○	⊖	⊜
Auto. trans.			◒	●	○	○	◒	⊖
Man. trans.			*	*	*	*	*	*
Clutch			*	*	*	*	*	*
Electrical			◒	◒	○	○	◒	⊖
A/C			⊖	○	○	⊜	⊜	⊜
Suspension			○	○	○	⊖	⊜	⊖
Brakes			●	●	○	○	⊖	⊖
Exhaust			●	⊖	⊜	⊜	⊜	⊜
Body rust			⊖	⊜	⊜	⊖	⊖	⊜
Paint/trim			●	○	⊖	○	⊖	⊜
Integrity			○	◒	○	◒	●	⊖
Hardware			⊖	◒	○	○	○	⊜

Dodge Dynasty V6 — TROUBLE SPOTS	90	91	92	93	94	95	96	97
Engine	◒	○	◒	○				
Cooling	◒	○	○	○				
Fuel	○	○	○	⊜				
Ignition	●	◒	◒	○				
Auto. trans.	●	●	●	●				
Man. trans.								
Clutch								
Electrical	●	◒	●	◒				
A/C	◒	○	●	●				
Suspension	◒	○	○	○				
Brakes	●	●	◒	◒				
Exhaust	⊖	●	●	⊖				
Body rust	○	⊖	⊖	⊜				
Paint/trim	◒	○	◒	⊖				
Integrity	◒	○	◒	◒				
Hardware	◒	○	◒	○				

Dodge Grand Caravan V6 — TROUBLE SPOTS	90	91	92	93	94	95	96	97
Engine	◒	○	◒	○	⊖	⊜	⊜	⊜
Cooling	●	◒	○	○	⊖	⊖	⊖	⊜
Fuel	◒	○	○	○	⊖	⊖	○	⊜
Ignition	◒	◒	◒	○	⊖	⊖	⊜	⊜
Auto. trans.	●	●	●	●	●	○	⊖	⊜
Man. trans.								
Clutch								
Electrical	◒	●	●	◒	◒	○	◒	○
A/C	●	○	○	●	○	⊖	⊖	⊜
Suspension	◒	◒	◒	○	○	○	⊖	⊜
Brakes	●	●	●	●	◒	○	◒	⊖
Exhaust	⊖	●	◒	⊜	⊜	⊜	⊜	⊜
Body rust	○	⊖	⊖	⊜	⊜	⊜	⊜	⊜
Paint/trim	●	◒	○	○	○	⊖	⊖	⊖
Integrity	●	◒	◒	◒	◒	◒	◒	○
Hardware	●	●	●	●	●	●	◒	○

Dodge Intrepid — TROUBLE SPOTS	90	91	92	93	94	95	96	97
Engine				○	⊖	⊖	⊜	⊜
Cooling				○	⊖	⊖	⊖	⊜
Fuel				○	⊖	⊖	⊜	⊜
Ignition				○	○	⊖	⊜	⊜
Auto. trans.				◒	●	◒	⊖	⊖
Man. trans.								
Clutch								
Electrical				●	◒	○	○	⊖
A/C				●	●	◒	⊖	⊜
Suspension				◒	○	○	⊖	⊜
Brakes				●	●	◒	⊖	⊜
Exhaust				⊖	⊜	⊜	⊜	⊜
Body rust				⊖	⊜	⊜	⊜	⊜
Paint/trim				●	◒	○	⊖	⊖
Integrity				●	●	●	◒	○
Hardware				●	◒	◒	○	⊖

Dodge Neon

TROUBLE SPOTS	90	91	92	93	94	95	96	97
Engine						○	⊖	⊜
Cooling						⊜	⊖	⊜
Fuel						○	⊖	⊜
Ignition						○	⊖	⊜
Auto. trans.						⊜	⊖	⊜
Man. trans.						⊖	⊜	*
Clutch						⊜	⊜	*
Electrical						◒	◒	⊜
A/C						○	⊜	⊜
Suspension						⊖	⊖	⊜
Brakes						●	○	⊜
Exhaust						⊖	⊜	⊜
Body rust						⊜	⊜	⊜
Paint/trim						○	⊖	⊜
Integrity						●	◒	○
Hardware						◒	◒	⊜

Dodge Ram Pickup (2WD)

TROUBLE SPOTS	90	91	92	93	94	95	96	97
Engine					⊖	⊖	⊖	⊜
Cooling					⊖	⊜	⊜	⊜
Fuel					○	⊖	⊖	⊜
Ignition					○	⊖	⊜	⊜
Auto. trans.					○	⊖	⊖	⊖
Man. trans.					*	*	*	*
Clutch					*	*	*	*
Electrical					◒	○	○	⊖
A/C	Insufficient data	Insufficient data	Insufficient data	Insufficient data	⊖	⊖	⊖	⊜
Suspension					◒	◒	○	⊖
Brakes					○	◒	○	⊖
Exhaust					⊖	⊖	⊜	⊜
Body rust					⊖	⊜	⊜	⊜
Paint/trim					○	⊖	⊖	⊖
Integrity					○	○	○	⊖
Hardware					◒	⊖	⊖	⊜

Dodge Ram Pickup (4WD)

TROUBLE SPOTS	90	91	92	93	94	95	96	97
Engine					⊖	⊖	⊖	⊜
Cooling					⊜	⊖	⊜	⊜
Fuel					○	○	⊖	⊜
Ignition					⊖	⊖	⊖	⊖
Auto. trans.					◒	◒	○	○
Man. trans.					*	*	*	*
Clutch					*	*	*	*
Electrical					○	○	○	⊖
A/C	Insufficient data	Insufficient data	Insufficient data	Insufficient data	⊖	⊖	⊖	⊜
Suspension					◒	●	⊖	⊖
Brakes					●	◒	○	⊖
Exhaust					⊜	⊜	⊜	⊜
Body rust					⊜	⊜	⊜	⊖
Paint/trim					⊖	⊖	○	⊖
Integrity					○	◒	○	⊖
Hardware					◒	○	⊖	⊜

Dodge Ram Van B150

TROUBLE SPOTS	90	91	92	93	94	95	96	97
Engine	⊜		⊖		⊜	⊜	⊜	
Cooling	◒		○		⊖	⊜	⊜	
Fuel	○		○		⊖	⊖	⊖	
Ignition	○		○		○	⊖	⊖	
Auto. trans.	●		◒		○	⊖	⊖	
Man. trans.	*		*					
Clutch	*		*					
Electrical	●		◒		○	○	◒	
A/C	●	Insufficient data	○	Insufficient data	⊖	○	⊖	Insufficient data
Suspension	○		○		○	○	⊖	
Brakes	●		◒		◒	◒	⊖	
Exhaust	○		◒		⊜	⊜	⊜	
Body rust	◒		⊖		○	⊜	⊜	
Paint/trim	●		◒		○	○	○	
Integrity	●		●		●	●	●	
Hardware	●		○		●	◒	◒	

Dodge Shadow

TROUBLE SPOTS	90	91	92	93	94	95	96	97
Engine	●	◒	◒	○	⊖			
Cooling	●	◒	○	⊖	⊖			
Fuel	◒	◒	◒	⊖	○			
Ignition	●	○	◒	○	⊖			
Auto. trans.	○	○	○	○	○			
Man. trans.	*	*	*	*	*			
Clutch	*	*	*	*	*			
Electrical	●	●	◒	◒	◒			
A/C	●	●	◒	●	◒			
Suspension	○	○	○	⊖	⊖			
Brakes	●	●	◒	○	○			
Exhaust	⊖	●	●	⊜	⊜			
Body rust	◒	○	○	○	⊖			
Paint/trim	●	●	●	◒	○			
Integrity	◒	●	◒	◒	●			
Hardware	◒	◒	○	○	◒			

Dodge Spirit

TROUBLE SPOTS	90	91	92	93	94	95	96	97
Engine	◒	◒	◒	○	⊖	○		
Cooling	●	○	○	○	⊖	⊖		
Fuel	○	○	○	○	○	⊖		
Ignition	◒	○	○	⊖	⊖	⊖		
Auto. trans.	●	◒	○	◒	◒	⊖		
Man. trans.	*	*	*	*				
Clutch	*	*	*	*				
Electrical	◒	○	◒	○	○	○		
A/C	◒	◒	○	●	◒	○		
Suspension	◒	○	○	○	⊖	⊖		
Brakes	●	◒	◒	○	⊖	⊖		
Exhaust	⊖	●	●	⊜	⊜	⊜		
Body rust	○	⊖	⊖	⊖	⊖	⊜		
Paint/trim	◒	◒	○	⊖	○	○		
Integrity	○	○	○	○	○	◒		
Hardware	◒	○	○	○	○	◒		

Dodge Stealth (2WD)

TROUBLE SPOTS	90	91	92	93	94	95	96	97
Engine		⊖	○	⊖	⊜			
Cooling		○	⊖	⊖	⊜			
Fuel		⊜	⊜	⊜	⊜			
Ignition		○	○	⊖	○			
Auto. trans.		*	*	*	*			
Man. trans.		*	*	*	*			
Clutch		*	*	*	*			
Electrical		◒	●	◒	○			
A/C		○	⊜	⊖	⊖	Insufficient data	Insufficient data	
Suspension		⊖	○	○	⊜			
Brakes		○	○	◒	⊖			
Exhaust		⊜	⊜	⊜	⊜			
Body rust		⊜	⊜	⊜	⊜			
Paint/trim		◒	○	◒	○			
Integrity		◒	◒	○	○			
Hardware		●	◒	◒	◒			

Dodge Stratus

TROUBLE SPOTS	90	91	92	93	94	95	96	97
Engine						⊖	⊖	⊜
Cooling						⊜	⊜	⊜
Fuel						⊖	⊖	⊜
Ignition						⊖	⊖	⊖
Auto. trans.						⊖	⊖	⊜
Man. trans.						*	*	*
Clutch						*	*	*
Electrical						◒	○	⊖
A/C						◒	⊖	⊜
Suspension						◒	○	⊜
Brakes						●	○	⊜
Exhaust						⊜	⊜	⊜
Body rust						⊜	⊜	⊜
Paint/trim						●	⊖	⊜
Integrity						●	◒	⊖
Hardware						◒	○	⊖

⊜ ⊖ ○ ◒ ●
Few ◄— Problems —► Many

*
Insufficient data

Eagle Summit (except Wagon)

Trouble spots	90	91	92	93	94	95	96	97
Engine	●	◒	○	⊖	Insufficient data	Insufficient data	Insufficient data	
Cooling	○	⊖	⊖	⊖				
Fuel	○	⊖	⊖	⊖				
Ignition	○	○	○	○				
Auto. trans.	⊖	○	◒	◒				
Man. trans.	⊖	⊖	⊖	○				
Clutch	○	○	○	⊜				
Electrical	○	○	⊖	○				
A/C	○	◒	○	⊜				
Suspension	◒	⊖	○	○				
Brakes	◒	◒	◒	◒				
Exhaust	⊖	⊖	⊜	⊜				
Body rust	○	⊖	⊜	⊖				
Paint/trim	◒	◒	○	○				
Integrity	●	◒	◒	◒				
Hardware	●	◒	◒	●				

Eagle Talon

Trouble spots	90	91	92	93	94	95	96	97
Engine	●	◒	◒	○	◒	○	⊖	Insufficient data
Cooling	○	○	⊖	○	⊖	⊖	⊜	
Fuel	⊖	○	○	⊖	⊜	◒	○	
Ignition	○	◒	◒	○	⊖	○	○	
Auto. trans.	○	◒	◒	*	*	⊖	*	
Man. trans.	○	○	○	○	*	⊖	*	
Clutch	○	○	○	○	*	⊖	*	
Electrical	◒	◒	◒	◒	○	●	◒	
A/C	○	⊖	⊜	○	○	⊖	⊜	
Suspension	○	⊖	⊖	⊖	⊖	⊖	○	
Brakes	◒	◒	◒	◒	○	◒	○	
Exhaust	⊖	⊖	○	⊖	⊜	⊜	⊖	
Body rust	⊜	⊖	⊖	⊖	⊖	⊜	⊜	
Paint/trim	◒	◒	●	○	◒	○	⊖	
Integrity	◒	◒	◒	◒	●	●	◒	
Hardware	●	●	●	◒	●	●	●	

Eagle Vision

Trouble spots	90	91	92	93	94	95	96	97
Engine				○	⊖	⊖	⊖	Insufficient data
Cooling				◒	⊖	⊜	⊜	
Fuel				○	⊖	⊖	⊜	
Ignition				◒	○	⊜	⊖	
Auto. trans.				◒	◒	◒	○	
Man. trans.								
Clutch								
Electrical				●	◒	○	⊖	
A/C				●	●	●	⊖	
Suspension				○	○	○	⊜	
Brakes				●	◒	○	⊜	
Exhaust				⊜	⊜	⊜	⊜	
Body rust				⊜	⊜	⊜	⊖	
Paint/trim				⊖	⊖	⊖	⊜	
Integrity				●	●	◒	○	
Hardware				●	◒	◒	○	

Ford Aerostar Van

Trouble spots	90	91	92	93	94	95	96	97
Engine	◒	◒	○	⊖	⊖	⊖	⊜	Insufficient data
Cooling	●	●	◒	⊖	⊖	⊜	⊜	
Fuel	○	⊖	⊖	⊖	⊖	⊖	⊜	
Ignition	◒	◒	○	○	⊖	⊖	⊖	
Auto. trans.	◒	○	○	⊖	⊖	⊖	⊜	
Man. trans.	*	*	*	*	*			
Clutch	*	*	*	*	*			
Electrical	●	●	●	◒	◒	○	○	
A/C	●	●	●	◒	⊖	⊖	⊖	
Suspension	●	◒	◒	○	○	○	○	
Brakes	●	●	●	●	●	●	○	
Exhaust	●	●	●	○	⊜	⊜	⊜	
Body rust	●	○	⊖	⊜	⊜	⊜	⊜	
Paint/trim	◒	○	⊖	⊖	⊖	⊖	○	
Integrity	●	◒	◒	◒	◒	◒	◒	
Hardware	●	●	◒	●	◒	◒	○	

Ford Bronco V8

Trouble spots	90	91	92	93	94	95	96	97
Engine	●	Insufficient data	Insufficient data	○	⊜	⊜	⊜	
Cooling	◒			⊖	⊖	⊜	⊜	
Fuel	●			○	○	⊖	⊖	
Ignition	●			○	⊖	⊖	⊖	
Auto. trans.	◒			○	*	○	⊖	
Man. trans.	*			*	*	*	*	
Clutch	*			*	*	*	*	
Electrical	●			○	●	○	○	
A/C	◒			⊖	⊖	⊜	⊖	
Suspension	○			○	◒	○	⊖	
Brakes	●			●	●	●	◒	
Exhaust	●			○	⊖	⊜	⊜	
Body rust	●			⊖	⊜	⊖	⊖	
Paint/trim	●			○	○	○	⊖	
Integrity	●			◒	●	●	◒	
Hardware	●			○	◒	◒	◒	

Ford Club Wagon, Van

Trouble spots	90	91	92	93	94	95	96	97
Engine	◒	◒	○	⊖	⊖	⊜	⊖	Insufficient data
Cooling	◒	●	○	○	○	⊜	⊖	
Fuel	◒	◒	●	○	○	⊖	⊖	
Ignition	◒	○	◒	⊖	⊖	⊜	⊖	
Auto. trans.	○	◒	◒	○	⊖	⊜	⊖	
Man. trans.								
Clutch								
Electrical	●	●	◒	◒	◒	○	○	
A/C	●	●	●	●	◒	⊖	○	
Suspension	●	◒	●	●	●	◒	○	
Brakes	●	◒	●	●	●	●	◒	
Exhaust	●	●	●	◒	⊖	⊜	⊜	
Body rust	●	●	⊖	⊜	⊖	⊜	⊜	
Paint/trim	●	◒	⊖	○	○	⊖	⊖	
Integrity	●	●	○	○	○	○	○	
Hardware	●	◒	◒	◒	◒	○	◒	

Ford Contour

Trouble spots	90	91	92	93	94	95	96	97
Engine						⊖	⊜	⊜
Cooling						⊖	⊜	⊜
Fuel						◒	○	⊖
Ignition						⊖	⊖	⊖
Auto. trans.						○	⊜	⊜
Man. trans.						⊜	⊜	*
Clutch						⊜	⊜	*
Electrical						◒	○	○
A/C						⊖	⊜	⊜
Suspension						○	⊖	⊖
Brakes						◒	⊖	⊖
Exhaust						⊜	⊜	⊜
Body rust						⊜	⊜	⊜
Paint/trim						○	⊖	⊜
Integrity						◒	○	○
Hardware						◒	◒	○

Ford Crown Victoria, LTD Crown Victoria

Trouble spots	90	91	92	93	94	95	96	97
Engine	○	○	⊖	⊜	⊜	⊜	⊜	⊜
Cooling	◒	○	⊜	⊜	⊜	⊜	⊜	⊜
Fuel	○	○	○	⊖	⊖	⊖	⊖	⊜
Ignition	◒	◒	●	◒	⊖	⊖	⊖	⊜
Auto. trans.	○	○	◒	●	●	○	⊖	⊜
Man. trans.								
Clutch								
Electrical	●	●	◒	◒	○	◒	○	⊖
A/C	●	◒	◒	⊖	⊖	⊖	⊜	⊜
Suspension	○	○	⊖	⊖	⊖	⊖	○	⊜
Brakes	●	●	●	●	◒	◒	○	⊖
Exhaust	●	●	◒	⊜	⊜	⊜	⊜	⊜
Body rust	○	○	⊜	⊜	⊜	⊜	⊜	⊜
Paint/trim	◒	○	○	⊖	⊖	⊖	⊖	⊖
Integrity	○	○	○	○	○	○	○	⊖
Hardware	●	●	●	◒	○	○	○	⊖

Ford Escort

TROUBLE SPOTS	90	91	92	93	94	95	96	97
Engine	◒	○	⊖	⊖	⊖	⊜	⊜	⊜
Cooling	◒	◒	○	⊖	⊖	⊜	⊜	⊜
Fuel	●	○	○	⊖	⊜	⊜	⊖	⊜
Ignition	●	◒	○	○	⊖	⊖	⊖	⊜
Auto. trans.	◒	○	○	⊖	⊖	⊖	⊖	⊜
Man. trans.	⊖	⊜	⊖	⊜	⊜	⊜	⊜	⊜
Clutch	○	○	○	○	⊖	⊜	⊜	⊜
Electrical	●	●	◒	○	○	○	○	⊖
A/C	●	●	○	⊖	⊖	⊖	⊖	⊜
Suspension	◒	○	○	⊖	⊖	⊖	⊖	⊜
Brakes	●	●	◒	◒	◒	⊖	⊜	⊜
Exhaust	○	⊖	⊖	⊜	⊜	⊜	⊜	⊜
Body rust	◒	○	⊜	⊜	⊜	⊜	⊜	⊜
Paint/trim	◒	◒	○	⊖	⊖	⊖	⊖	⊜
Integrity	●	◒	◒	○	○	○	○	⊖
Hardware	◒	◒	◒	◒	○	○	○	⊖

Ford Expedition (4WD)

TROUBLE SPOTS	90	91	92	93	94	95	96	97
Engine								⊜
Cooling								⊜
Fuel								⊜
Ignition								⊜
Auto. trans.								⊜
Man. trans.								
Clutch								
Electrical								⊖
A/C								⊖
Suspension								⊖
Brakes								⊜
Exhaust								⊜
Body rust								⊜
Paint/trim								⊜
Integrity								⊖
Hardware								⊖

Ford Explorer

TROUBLE SPOTS	90	91	92	93	94	95	96	97
Engine		◒	◒	⊖	⊜	⊜	⊜	⊜
Cooling		●	○	⊖	⊖	⊖	⊜	⊜
Fuel		○	⊖	⊖	⊖	⊖	⊖	⊜
Ignition		○	○	⊖	⊖	⊜	⊜	⊜
Auto. trans.		○	○	⊜	⊜	⊖	⊜	⊜
Man. trans.		◒	◒	○	⊖	⊖	⊜	*
Clutch		◒	◒	○	○	⊖	⊖	*
Electrical		◒	○	○	○	◒	○	⊖
A/C		●	●	○	⊖	⊖	⊜	⊜
Suspension		●	◒	○	○	○	⊖	⊜
Brakes		●	●	●	●	⊖	⊜	⊜
Exhaust		●	●	○	○	⊜	⊜	⊜
Body rust		◒	⊖	⊜	⊜	⊜	⊜	⊜
Paint/trim		◒	○	⊖	○	⊖	⊖	⊜
Integrity		○	○	○	⊖	○	○	⊖
Hardware		◒	◒	○	◒	○	○	⊖

Ford F150 Pickup (2WD)

TROUBLE SPOTS	90	91	92	93	94	95	96	97
Engine	○	○	⊖	⊖	⊖	⊖	⊜	⊜
Cooling	○	○	○	⊖	⊖	⊖	⊜	⊜
Fuel	◒	●	◒	○	⊖	⊖	⊜	⊜
Ignition	●	◒	○	○	⊖	⊖	⊖	⊜
Auto. trans.	◒	◒	○	○	○	⊖	⊖	⊜
Man. trans.	⊖	⊖	⊖	⊖	⊖	⊖	⊖	⊜
Clutch	○	○	◒	◒	◒	◒	○	⊜
Electrical	◒	◒	◒	○	◒	○	⊖	⊖
A/C	◒	◒	○	⊖	⊖	⊖	⊜	⊜
Suspension	◒	○	⊖	○	○	○	⊜	⊖
Brakes	●	●	●	●	●	●	⊖	⊜
Exhaust	●	●	●	○	⊜	⊜	⊜	⊜
Body rust	◒	○	⊖	⊖	⊜	⊜	⊜	⊜
Paint/trim	●	●	◒	○	⊖	⊖	⊖	⊜
Integrity	◒	○	○	○	○	○	○	⊖
Hardware	◒	◒	◒	◒	○	○	⊜	⊖

Ford F150 Pickup (4WD)

TROUBLE SPOTS	90	91	92	93	94	95	96	97
Engine	◒	◒	○	⊖	⊖	⊜	⊜	⊜
Cooling	◒	○	○	⊖	⊖	⊜	⊜	⊜
Fuel	●	●	○	○	⊖	⊖	⊜	⊜
Ignition	●	◒	◒	○	⊖	⊖	⊜	⊜
Auto. trans.	●	◒	○	○	○	○	○	⊜
Man. trans.	○	⊖	○	○	⊜	⊖	*	⊜
Clutch	◒	◒	○	●	◒	○	*	⊜
Electrical	●	◒	◒	◒	◒	○	⊖	⊖
A/C	◒	○	○	⊖	⊖	⊜	⊜	⊜
Suspension	◒	◒	◒	○	○	○	○	⊖
Brakes	●	●	●	●	●	●	⊖	⊜
Exhaust	●	●	●	●	⊜	⊜	⊜	⊜
Body rust	●	○	○	⊖	⊜	⊜	⊜	⊜
Paint/trim	●	●	◒	○	⊖	⊖	⊜	⊖
Integrity	◒	○	◒	○	○	○	○	⊖
Hardware	●	◒	●	○	⊖	○	○	⊖

Ford Festiva

TROUBLE SPOTS	90	91	92	93	94	95	96	97
Engine	○	○	Insufficient data	⊜				
Cooling	⊜	⊖		⊖				
Fuel	○	⊖		⊖				
Ignition	○	⊖		○				
Auto. trans.	*	*		*				
Man. trans.	⊜	⊜		⊜				
Clutch	○	⊜		⊖				
Electrical	●	○		◒				
A/C	*	*		*				
Suspension	○	⊖		⊖				
Brakes	●	●		●				
Exhaust	●	●		●				
Body rust	○	○		⊖				
Paint/trim	○	○		○				
Integrity	◒	●		◒				
Hardware	◒	●		●				

Ford Mustang

TROUBLE SPOTS	90	91	92	93	94	95	96	97
Engine	○	○	⊜	⊖	⊜	⊖	⊜	Insufficient data
Cooling	◒	○	⊖	⊖	⊜	⊜	⊜	
Fuel	○	○	○	⊖	⊜	⊖	⊜	
Ignition	○	◒	◒	○	○	⊖	⊖	
Auto. trans.	◒	○	○	○	●	○	⊖	
Man. trans.	○	*	*	*	⊖	○	⊖	
Clutch	◒	*	*	*	⊖	⊜	⊖	
Electrical	◒	◒	○	◒	○	○	○	
A/C	●	●	◒	○	○	⊖	⊜	
Suspension	◒	○	○	◒	○	⊖	○	
Brakes	○	◒	●	◒	◒	○	⊖	
Exhaust	◒	◒	◒	⊖	⊖	⊜	⊜	
Body rust	○	⊖	⊖	⊖	⊜	⊜	⊜	
Paint/trim	●	◒	●	●	○	○	⊖	
Integrity	●	●	●	●	◒	◒	◒	
Hardware	●	●	●	●	◒	○	○	

Ford Probe

TROUBLE SPOTS	90	91	92	93	94	95	96	97
Engine	○	○	⊖	⊖	⊖	⊜	⊜	Insufficient data
Cooling	◒	◒	○	⊖	⊜	⊜	⊜	
Fuel	○	○	○	○	⊖	⊜	⊜	
Ignition	◒	○	⊖	◒	○	⊖	⊜	
Auto. trans.	○	⊖	⊜	⊖	⊖	*	*	
Man. trans.	⊜	*	*	⊖	⊜	⊜	*	
Clutch	⊜	*	*	⊖	⊜	⊜	*	
Electrical	●	●	◒	◒	◒	◒	⊖	
A/C	●	●	◒	⊖	⊖	⊜	⊜	
Suspension	○	○	○	○	⊖	○	⊜	
Brakes	●	●	●	◒	◒	⊖	⊖	
Exhaust	●	◒	◒	○	⊖	⊜	⊜	
Body rust	⊖	⊖	⊖	⊜	⊜	⊖	⊜	
Paint/trim	◒	◒	●	○	○	○	○	
Integrity	●	●	●	●	●	●	◒	
Hardware	●	●	●	●	◒	◒	◒	

⊜ ⊖ ○ ◒ ●
Few ◄— Problems —► Many

* Insufficient data

Ford Ranger Pickup (2WD)	90	91	92	93	94	95	96	97
Engine	◒	○	○	⊖	⊜	⊜	⊜	⊜
Cooling	◒	○	○	⊖	⊖	⊖	⊜	⊜
Fuel	○	⊖	⊖	⊜	⊖	⊖	⊖	⊜
Ignition	◒	○	○	⊖	⊖	⊖	⊜	⊜
Auto. trans.	⊖	○	⊖	⊖	⊖	○	⊜	⊖
Man. trans.	○	⊖	⊖	⊜	⊖	⊜	⊜	⊜
Clutch	◒	○	○	⊖	⊖	⊖	⊜	⊜
Electrical	○	○	⊖	⊖	○	●	○	⊖
A/C	●	●	◒	⊖	⊖	⊖	⊜	⊜
Suspension	⊖	⊖	⊖	⊖	⊖	⊖	⊖	⊖
Brakes	●	◒	○	◒	◒	○	⊖	⊖
Exhaust	●	◒	◒	○	⊖	⊜	⊜	⊜
Body rust	○	⊖	⊖	⊜	⊜	⊜	⊜	⊜
Paint/trim	●	◒	○	⊖	⊖	⊖	⊖	⊖
Integrity	○	○	○	⊖	⊖	⊖	⊖	⊜
Hardware	○	○	○	⊖	⊖	◒	⊖	⊖

Ford Ranger Pickup (4WD)	90	91	92	93	94	95	96	97
Engine	●	○	○	⊖	⊖	⊖	⊜	⊜
Cooling	◒	○	⊖	⊖	⊖	⊖	⊖	⊜
Fuel	○	⊖	⊖	⊖	⊖	○	⊖	⊖
Ignition	◒	○	○	⊜	⊖	○	⊜	⊜
Auto. trans.	○	*	*	⊜	⊖	⊖	⊜	⊖
Man. trans.	⊖	○	○	○	⊖	⊜	⊜	*
Clutch	●	◒	○	◒	○	⊖	⊖	*
Electrical	○	○	○	○	○	●	○	⊜
A/C	●	●	●	⊖	⊖	⊜	⊖	⊜
Suspension	○	○	○	○	⊖	○	○	⊜
Brakes	●	●	●	●	◒	◒	⊖	⊜
Exhaust	●	●	◒	◒	⊖	⊜	⊜	⊜
Body rust	◒	⊖	○	⊜	⊜	⊜	⊜	⊜
Paint/trim	◒	◒	◒	⊖	⊖	⊖	⊖	⊖
Integrity	○	◒	◒	⊖	⊖	○	⊖	⊖
Hardware	○	○	●	○	⊖	◒	⊖	⊜

Ford Taurus	90	91	92	93	94	95	96	97
Engine	○	○	○	○	⊖	⊜	⊜	⊜
Cooling	●	◒	●	◒	◒	⊖	⊖	⊜
Fuel	◒	○	○	○	⊖	⊖	⊖	⊜
Ignition	●	○	○	○	⊖	⊖	⊖	⊜
Auto. trans.	◒	●	○	⊖	○	⊖	○	⊖
Man. trans.								
Clutch								
Electrical	●	◒	◒	●	◒	○	○	⊖
A/C	●	●	◒	◒	⊖	⊖	⊜	⊜
Suspension	●	●	◒	◒	○	⊖	◒	⊖
Brakes	●	●	●	●	○	⊖	○	⊖
Exhaust	⊖	⊖	⊖	⊜	⊜	⊜	⊜	⊜
Body rust	●	◒	⊖	⊜	⊜	⊜	⊜	⊜
Paint/trim	◒	◒	○	⊖	⊖	⊖	⊖	⊜
Integrity	◒	◒	◒	◒	◒	●	●	⊖
Hardware	◒	◒	◒	◒	◒	○	◒	⊜

Ford Taurus SHO	90	91	92	93	94	95	96	97
Engine	⊖	○	⊖	⊖	⊜	⊖	Insufficient data	Insufficient data
Cooling	●	●	●	◒	○	○		
Fuel	○	○	○	○	○	○		
Ignition	◒	◒	◒	●	○	○		
Auto. trans.				◒	○	○		
Man. trans.	*	*	⊖	*	*	*		
Clutch	*	*	●	*	*	*		
Electrical	●	●	◒	●	●	○		
A/C	●	●	●	◒	○	⊖		
Suspension	◒	●	○	◒	○	⊖		
Brakes	●	●	●	●	○	⊖		
Exhaust	⊖	○	⊜	⊜	⊜	⊜		
Body rust	◒	◒	⊖	⊜	⊜	⊜		
Paint/trim	◒	◒	⊖	⊖	⊖	⊖		
Integrity	●	◒	◒	◒	●	●		
Hardware	◒	○	◒	◒	○	○		

Ford Tempo	90	91	92	93	94	95	96	97
Engine	◒	◒	○	○	○			
Cooling	◒	◒	◒	○	○			
Fuel	●	◒	○	◒	○			
Ignition	●	●	◒	○	⊖			
Auto. trans.	○	⊖	○	⊖	○			
Man. trans.	*	*	*	*	*			
Clutch	*	*	*	*	*			
Electrical	●	●	◒	◒	◒			
A/C	●	●	○	○	○			
Suspension	●	◒	○	○	○			
Brakes	●	●	●	●	●			
Exhaust	●	●	●	●	○			
Body rust	◒	○	⊖	⊖	⊜			
Paint/trim	●	●	◒	○	○			
Integrity	◒	◒	◒	◒	◒			
Hardware	●	●	●	●	●			

Ford Thunderbird	90	91	92	93	94	95	96	97
Engine	○	○	⊖	⊖	⊜	⊜	⊜	⊜
Cooling	◒	○	○	⊖	⊜	⊖	⊜	⊜
Fuel	○	○	○	⊖	⊖	⊖	○	⊜
Ignition	◒	◒	◒	○	⊖	⊖	○	⊜
Auto. trans.	○	○	⊖	⊖	●	○	○	⊖
Man. trans.	*	*	*	*	*	*		
Clutch	*	*	*	*	*	*		
Electrical	●	●	◒	●	◒	○	○	⊜
A/C	●	●	◒	○	○	⊖	○	⊜
Suspension	○	○	○	⊖	○	○	○	○
Brakes	●	●	●	●	●	●	●	⊖
Exhaust	⊖	⊖	⊖	⊜	⊜	⊜	⊜	⊜
Body rust	○	○	⊖	⊖	⊜	⊜	⊜	⊜
Paint/trim	●	●	◒	●	⊖	⊖	⊖	⊜
Integrity	●	◒	◒	○	◒	○	◒	○
Hardware	●	●	●	●	◒	○	○	⊖

Ford Windstar Van	90	91	92	93	94	95	96	97
Engine						⊖	⊜	⊜
Cooling						⊖	⊜	⊜
Fuel						⊖	⊖	⊜
Ignition						⊖	⊜	⊖
Auto. trans.						○	⊖	⊜
Man. trans.								
Clutch								
Electrical						●	◒	○
A/C						⊖	⊖	⊜
Suspension						○	⊖	⊜
Brakes						●	○	⊖
Exhaust						⊜	⊜	⊜
Body rust						⊜	⊜	⊜
Paint/trim						⊖	⊖	⊜
Integrity						◒	○	⊖
Hardware						●	◒	○

Geo Metro	90	91	92	93	94	95	96	97
Engine	○	○	○	⊖	⊖	⊜	⊜	Insufficient data
Cooling	⊖	⊖	⊖	⊜	⊜	⊜	⊜	
Fuel	○	⊖	⊖	⊜	⊜	⊖	⊜	
Ignition	○	○	◒	⊖	⊖	⊜	⊖	
Auto. trans.	*	*	⊖	*	*	*	*	
Man. trans.	⊖	○	⊖	⊜	⊜	⊜	*	
Clutch	⊖	⊖	⊖	⊖	⊜	⊜	*	
Electrical	○	○	◒	◒	○	◒	○	
A/C	●	●	⊖	○	○	●	○	
Suspension	○	⊖	⊖	⊖	⊖	⊖	⊜	
Brakes	●	◒	◒	○	○	⊖	⊜	
Exhaust	●	●	●	◒	⊖	⊜	⊜	
Body rust	○	○	⊖	⊜	⊜	⊜	⊜	
Paint/trim	◒	○	⊖	⊖	⊜	⊖	⊖	
Integrity	●	●	●	○	○	○	⊖	
Hardware	●	●	●	●	◒	◒	○	

Geo Prizm

Trouble spots	90	91	92	93	94	95	96	97
Engine	⊖	⊖	⊖	⊖	⊜	⊜	⊜	⊜
Cooling	◒	○	⊖	⊜	⊜	⊜	⊜	⊜
Fuel	⊜	⊜	⊜	⊜	⊜	⊜	⊜	⊜
Ignition	○	◒	◒	○	⊖	⊜	⊜	⊜
Auto. trans.	⊖	⊜	⊖	⊜	⊜	⊜	⊜	*
Man. trans.	⊜	*	*	⊜	⊜	⊜	⊜	*
Clutch	⊜	*	*	⊖	⊜	⊜	⊜	*
Electrical	○	◒	◒	○	○	⊖	⊖	⊜
A/C	⊖	⊖	⊖	⊜	⊜	⊜	⊜	⊜
Suspension	○	○	⊖	⊜	⊜	⊖	⊜	⊜
Brakes	◒	◒	◒	⊖	⊖	⊜	⊜	⊜
Exhaust	●	●	●	⊖	⊜	⊜	⊜	⊜
Body rust	◒	○	⊖	⊜	⊜	⊜	⊜	⊜
Paint/trim	◒	◒	○	⊖	⊖	⊖	⊜	⊜
Integrity	●	◒	○	⊖	○	○	⊖	⊖
Hardware	●	●	●	●	◒	○	⊖	○

Geo Tracker

Trouble spots	90	91	92	93	94	95	96	97
Engine	○	⊖	⊜	⊖	⊖	⊜	⊖	Insufficient data
Cooling	⊖	⊖	⊖	⊖	⊖	⊜	⊜	
Fuel	◒	⊖	⊖	⊜	⊖	⊖	⊜	
Ignition	○	○	○	○	○	○	⊜	
Auto. trans.	*	*	*	*	*	⊜	⊖	
Man. trans.	*	*	*	*	⊜	⊖	⊜	
Clutch	*	*	*	*	⊖	⊖	⊜	
Electrical	◒	◒	◒	○	○	○	○	
A/C	*	*	*	○	⊖	⊖	⊖	
Suspension	⊖	⊜	○	⊖	⊜	⊜	⊜	
Brakes	●	●	●	○	○	⊖	○	
Exhaust	●	●	◒	○	⊜	⊜	⊜	
Body rust	◒	⊖	⊜	⊖	⊜	⊖	⊜	
Paint/trim	○	⊖	○	⊜	⊜	⊖	⊖	
Integrity	◒	◒	◒	◒	●	◒	○	
Hardware	●	◒	●	○	◒	◒	○	

GMC Jimmy, Yukon

Trouble spots	90	91	92	93	94	95	96	97
Engine	Insufficient data	Insufficient data	Insufficient data	○	⊖	⊖	⊖	⊜
Cooling				●	⊖	⊜	⊜	⊜
Fuel				⊖	⊖	⊖	⊖	⊖
Ignition				○	⊜	○	⊜	⊜
Auto. trans.				○	⊖	⊜	⊖	⊜
Man. trans.				*	*	*		
Clutch				*	*	*		
Electrical				●	○	○	○	⊖
A/C				○	○	⊖	⊖	⊜
Suspension				○	⊖	○	⊖	⊖
Brakes				●	◒	◒	○	⊜
Exhaust				◒	⊖	⊜	⊜	⊜
Body rust				○	⊜	⊜	⊜	⊜
Paint/trim				○	⊖	⊖	⊖	⊜
Integrity				○	○	◒	○	⊖
Hardware				◒	◒	◒	○	⊖

GMC S-15 Jimmy, Jimmy

Trouble spots	90	91	92	93	94	95	96	97
Engine	○	○	○	◒	○	○	○	⊜
Cooling	◒	○	◒	○	⊖	⊜	⊜	⊜
Fuel	○	○	◒	●	◒	◒	○	⊖
Ignition	◒	◒	◒	◒	○	○	⊖	⊜
Auto. trans.	○	⊖	⊖	○	○	⊖	⊖	⊜
Man. trans.	*	*	*	*	*	*	*	*
Clutch	*	*	*	*	*	*	*	*
Electrical	●	●	◒	●	◒	◒	○	⊖
A/C	◒	○	○	⊖	⊖	⊖	⊖	⊜
Suspension	◒	◒	◒	◒	○	⊖	⊖	⊜
Brakes	●	●	●	●	●	●	○	⊖
Exhaust	●	●	○	○	⊜	⊜	⊜	⊜
Body rust	●	●	○	○	○	⊜	⊜	⊜
Paint/trim	●	●	●	◒	○	○	⊖	⊜
Integrity	●	●	●	●	●	●	○	○
Hardware	●	●	◒	●	◒	●	○	⊖

GMC S-15 Sonoma Pickup V6 (2WD)

Trouble spots	90	91	92	93	94	95	96	97
Engine	○	⊖	○	⊖	⊖	⊖	○	⊜
Cooling	◒	◒	⊖	⊖	⊖	⊜	⊖	⊜
Fuel	○	⊖	⊖	⊖	○	○	○	⊜
Ignition	◒	○	○	○	○	○	⊜	⊜
Auto. trans.	*	⊖	⊜	⊜	⊖	⊜	⊖	⊜
Man. trans.	*	⊖	⊜	⊖	*	⊖	*	*
Clutch	*	○	◒	○	*	⊖	*	*
Electrical	●	◒	○	○	◒	◒	⊖	⊖
A/C	*	○	⊖	⊖	○	⊖	⊖	⊜
Suspension	⊖	⊖	○	⊖	○	⊖	⊖	⊜
Brakes	◒	○	◒	◒	●	◒	○	⊜
Exhaust	●	◒	◒	○	⊖	⊜	⊜	⊜
Body rust	●	◒	○	○	⊜	⊜	⊜	⊜
Paint/trim	●	●	●	◒	○	○	⊖	⊖
Integrity	●	◒	○	○	○	◒	◒	○
Hardware	◒	◒	○	○	◒	◒	○	○

GMC S-15 Sonoma Pickup V6 (4WD)

Trouble spots	90	91	92	93	94	95	96	97
Engine	Insufficient data	⊖	○	Insufficient data	○	○	○	Insufficient data
Cooling		○	◒		○	⊜	⊖	
Fuel		⊖	○		○	⊜	⊖	
Ignition		●	◒		○	○	⊖	
Auto. trans.		○	*		⊖	⊖	⊜	
Man. trans.		*	*		*	*	*	
Clutch		*	*		*	*	*	
Electrical		◒	○		●	◒	⊖	
A/C		⊖	*		⊖	⊜	⊖	
Suspension		◒	◒		○	⊖	○	
Brakes		◒	●		●	●	○	
Exhaust		●	◒		⊖	⊜	⊜	
Body rust		●	◒		⊜	⊖	⊜	
Paint/trim		●	●		○	○	⊖	
Integrity		●	○		◒	●	●	
Hardware		◒	◒		◒	◒	○	

GMC Safari Van

Trouble spots	90	91	92	93	94	95	96	97
Engine	○	○	○	○	⊖	⊖	⊜	⊜
Cooling	◒	⊖	⊖	⊖	⊖	⊜	⊖	⊜
Fuel	⊖	⊖	⊖	○	○	○	⊖	○
Ignition	◒	◒	◒	●	○	⊖	⊖	⊖
Auto. trans.	○	○	⊖	○	⊖	⊖	⊖	⊖
Man. trans.								
Clutch								
Electrical	●	●	◒	●	●	○	○	⊖
A/C	◒	◒	○	○	◒	⊖	⊖	⊖
Suspension	◒	◒	◒	◒	○	○	⊜	⊜
Brakes	●	●	●	●	●	◒	○	⊜
Exhaust	◒	◒	○	◒	⊖	⊜	⊖	⊜
Body rust	⊖	⊖	⊖	⊜	⊖	⊜	⊜	⊜
Paint/trim	●	●	◒	◒	○	⊖	⊖	⊖
Integrity	●	●	●	●	●	●	●	◒
Hardware	●	●	●	●	●	◒	●	◒

GMC Sierra C1500 Pickup

Trouble spots	90	91	92	93	94	95	96	97
Engine	○	⊖	⊖	⊖	⊖	⊖	⊖	⊜
Cooling	○	○	⊖	⊖	⊖	⊜	⊖	⊜
Fuel	⊖	⊖	⊖	⊖	⊖	⊜	⊖	⊖
Ignition	◒	◒	◒	○	⊖	⊖	⊖	⊜
Auto. trans.	○	○	◒	⊖	⊖	⊜	⊖	⊜
Man. trans.	⊖	○	⊖	*	*	⊖	*	*
Clutch	◒	●	◒	*	*	◒	*	*
Electrical	◒	◒	◒	○	○	○	⊖	⊖
A/C	○	◒	○	⊖	○	⊖	⊖	⊜
Suspension	○	○	○	⊖	⊖	⊖	○	○
Brakes	◒	◒	○	○	○	⊖	○	⊜
Exhaust	●	●	◒	○	⊖	⊜	⊖	⊜
Body rust	⊖	⊜	⊜	⊜	⊜	⊜	⊜	⊜
Paint/trim	●	◒	◒	○	⊖	⊖	⊖	⊜
Integrity	○	○	○	○	○	○	○	○
Hardware	○	◒	◒	○	○	○	◒	○

⊜ ⊖ ○ ◒ ●
Few ◄— **Problems** —► Many

*
Insufficient data

GMC Sierra K1500 Pickup

TROUBLE SPOTS	90	91	92	93	94	95	96	97
Engine	○	⊜	⊖	⊖	○	⊜	⊖	⊜
Cooling	◒	○	○	⊖	⊖	⊜	⊜	⊜
Fuel	⊖	⊖	⊖	⊖	⊖	⊜	⊖	⊜
Ignition	●	●	◒	○	⊖	⊖	⊜	⊜
Auto. trans.	◒	◒	◒	⊖	⊖	⊖	⊖	⊜
Man. trans.	*	⊖	⊖	*	*	⊖	*	*
Clutch	*	◒	○	*	*	○	*	*
Electrical	◒	◒	●	○	○	○	○	⊖
A/C	○	○	⊖	⊖	⊖	⊖	⊜	⊜
Suspension	○	○	○	⊖	⊖	⊖	⊖	⊖
Brakes	◒	◒	◒	○	○	○	○	⊖
Exhaust	●	●	◒	◒	⊜	⊖	⊜	⊜
Body rust	○	⊖	⊜	⊖	⊜	⊜	⊜	⊜
Paint/trim	●	◒	○	◒	⊜	⊖	⊖	⊜
Integrity	◒	○	◒	○	○	○	○	⊖
Hardware	◒	○	◒	○	◒	◒	◒	⊖

GMC Suburban

TROUBLE SPOTS	90	91	92	93	94	95	96	97
Engine	○	○	○	⊖	⊖	⊜	⊜	⊜
Cooling	●	◒	●	●	⊖	⊜	⊜	⊖
Fuel	⊖	⊖	⊖	⊜	⊖	⊜	⊖	⊜
Ignition	●	●	◒	○	○	⊖	⊖	⊜
Auto. trans.	◒	●	◒	○	⊖	⊖	⊖	⊜
Man. trans.	*							
Clutch	*							
Electrical	●	◒	◒	◒	◒	◒	○	⊖
A/C	●	◒	○	○	◒	○	⊖	⊜
Suspension	◒	○	○	○	⊖	⊖	⊖	⊖
Brakes	●	●	●	●	●	◒	○	○
Exhaust	◒	●	○	○	⊖	⊜	⊜	⊜
Body rust	◒	○	⊖	⊖	⊜	⊜	⊜	⊜
Paint/trim	●	●	◒	○	⊖	⊖	⊜	⊜
Integrity	●	●	●	◒	◒	○	○	⊖
Hardware	●	●	◒	●	◒	●	◒	⊖

Honda Accord

TROUBLE SPOTS	90	91	92	93	94	95	96	97
Engine	⊖	⊖	⊖	⊜	⊜	⊜	⊜	⊜
Cooling	⊖	⊖	⊖	⊜	⊜	⊜	⊜	⊜
Fuel	⊜	⊜	⊜	⊜	⊜	⊜	⊜	⊜
Ignition	○	○	⊖	⊜	⊜	⊜	⊜	⊜
Auto. trans.	⊖	⊖	⊖	⊜	⊜	⊜	⊜	⊜
Man. trans.	⊜	⊜	⊜	⊜	⊜	⊜	⊜	⊜
Clutch	○	⊖	⊜	⊜	⊜	⊜	⊜	⊜
Electrical	○	○	⊖	⊖	⊖	⊖	⊖	⊜
A/C	○	○	○	⊖	○	⊖	⊜	⊜
Suspension	○	⊖	⊖	⊜	⊜	⊜	⊜	⊜
Brakes	◒	◒	○	⊖	○	⊖	⊖	⊜
Exhaust	◒	○	○	⊖	⊜	⊜	⊜	⊜
Body rust	○	⊖	⊜	⊜	⊜	⊜	⊜	⊜
Paint/trim	⊖	⊖	⊖	⊜	⊖	⊖	⊖	⊜
Integrity	○	○	○	○	○	⊖	⊖	⊜
Hardware	◒	◒	◒	○	○	○	⊖	⊜

Honda Civic

TROUBLE SPOTS	90	91	92	93	94	95	96	97
Engine	○	⊖	⊖	⊜	⊜	⊜	⊜	⊜
Cooling	○	⊖	⊖	⊜	⊜	⊜	⊜	⊜
Fuel	⊖	⊜	⊜	⊜	⊜	⊖	⊜	⊜
Ignition	◒	○	○	⊖	⊜	⊜	⊜	⊜
Auto. trans.	⊖	⊖	⊜	⊜	⊜	⊜	⊜	⊜
Man. trans.	⊖	⊜	⊜	⊜	⊜	⊜	⊜	⊜
Clutch	○	⊖	⊜	⊜	⊜	⊜	⊜	⊜
Electrical	○	⊖	⊖	⊜	⊖	⊖	⊖	⊜
A/C	◒	◒	⊖	⊖	◒	○	⊖	⊜
Suspension	○	⊖	⊖	⊖	⊜	⊜	⊜	⊜
Brakes	●	●	○	⊖	⊖	⊖	○	⊜
Exhaust	●	●	◒	⊖	⊜	⊜	⊜	⊜
Body rust	○	⊖	⊜	⊜	⊜	⊜	⊜	⊜
Paint/trim	⊖	⊖	○	⊖	⊖	⊖	⊖	⊜
Integrity	◒	◒	○	⊖	⊖	⊖	○	⊖
Hardware	◒	○	○	⊖	⊖	⊖	○	⊖

Honda Civic del Sol

TROUBLE SPOTS	90	91	92	93	94	95	96	97
Engine				⊜	⊜	⊜	Insufficient data	Insufficient data
Cooling				⊜	⊜	⊜		
Fuel				⊜	⊜	⊜		
Ignition				⊜	⊜	⊜		
Auto. trans.				*	*	*		
Man. trans.				⊜	*	*		
Clutch				⊖	*	*		
Electrical				⊜	⊜	⊖		
A/C				⊖	*	*		
Suspension				⊜	⊜	⊜		
Brakes				⊖	⊜	⊜		
Exhaust				⊜	⊜	⊜		
Body rust				⊜	⊜	⊜		
Paint/trim				⊖	○	⊖		
Integrity				●	●	●		
Hardware				◒	●	○		

Honda CR-V

TROUBLE SPOTS	90	91	92	93	94	95	96	97
Engine								⊜
Cooling								⊜
Fuel								⊜
Ignition								⊜
Auto. trans.								○
Man. trans.								
Clutch								
Electrical								⊜
A/C								⊜
Suspension								⊜
Brakes								⊜
Exhaust								⊜
Body rust								⊜
Paint/trim								⊜
Integrity								⊜
Hardware								⊜

Honda CRX

TROUBLE SPOTS	90	91	92	93	94	95	96	97
Engine	○	⊜						
Cooling	⊜	⊖						
Fuel	⊖	⊜						
Ignition	◒	○						
Auto. trans.	*	*						
Man. trans.	⊜	⊖						
Clutch	⊖	○						
Electrical	⊖	⊖						
A/C	◒	○						
Suspension	⊖	⊖						
Brakes	◒	○						
Exhaust	●	●						
Body rust	○	⊜						
Paint/trim	○	⊖						
Integrity	○	◒						
Hardware	◒	◒						

Honda Odyssey

TROUBLE SPOTS	90	91	92	93	94	95	96	97
Engine						⊜	⊜	⊜
Cooling						⊜	⊜	⊜
Fuel						⊜	⊜	⊜
Ignition						⊜	⊜	⊜
Auto. trans.						⊜	⊜	⊜
Man. trans.								
Clutch								
Electrical						⊖	⊜	⊜
A/C						⊖	⊜	⊜
Suspension						⊖	⊜	⊜
Brakes						⊖	⊜	⊜
Exhaust						⊜	⊜	⊜
Body rust						⊜	⊜	⊜
Paint/trim						⊜	⊜	⊜
Integrity						⊜	⊜	⊜
Hardware						○	⊜	⊜

Honda Passport V6

TROUBLE SPOTS	90	91	92	93	94	95	96	97
Engine					◒	○	○	Insufficient data
Cooling					⊖	⊜	◒	
Fuel					⊖	⊜	○	
Ignition					⊖	⊖	⊖	
Auto. trans.					⊜	⊖	○	
Man. trans.					*	*	*	
Clutch					*	*	*	
Electrical					○	◒	◒	
A/C					⊖	⊜	⊖	
Suspension					⊖	⊖	⊖	
Brakes					⊜	⊖	⊖	
Exhaust					⊜	⊜	⊜	
Body rust					○	⊜	⊖	
Paint/trim					○	○	⊜	
Integrity					◒	◒	◒	
Hardware					●	●	◒	

Honda Prelude

TROUBLE SPOTS	90	91	92	93	94	95	96	97
Engine	○	○	⊜	⊜	Insufficient data	⊜	Insufficient data	Insufficient data
Cooling	⊖	○	⊜	⊜		⊜		
Fuel	⊖	⊖	⊜	⊜		⊜		
Ignition	⊖	⊖	⊖	⊖		⊜		
Auto. trans.	*	*	⊜	*		*		
Man. trans.	⊜	⊜	⊜	*		*		
Clutch	○	◒	⊖	*		*		
Electrical	○	○	⊖	○		⊖		
A/C	◒	○	⊖	⊜		○		
Suspension	○	⊖	⊖	⊜		⊜		
Brakes	◒	◒	⊜	⊖		⊖		
Exhaust	○	○	○	⊜		⊜		
Body rust	⊜	⊜	⊖	⊜		⊜		
Paint/trim	⊖	○	○	○		⊜		
Integrity	⊖	○	◒	⊖		○		
Hardware	○	◒	○	○		◒		

Hyundai Excel

TROUBLE SPOTS	90	91	92	93	94	95	96	97
Engine	●	●	Insufficient data	Insufficient data	Insufficient data			
Cooling	◒	◒						
Fuel	◒	○						
Ignition	○	◒						
Auto. trans.	*	*						
Man. trans.	*	*						
Clutch	*	*						
Electrical	◒	◒						
A/C	*	*						
Suspension	◒	●						
Brakes	●	◒						
Exhaust	●	●						
Body rust	◒	◒						
Paint/trim	●	◒						
Integrity	●	◒						
Hardware	●	◒						

Infiniti G20

TROUBLE SPOTS	90	91	92	93	94	95	96	97
Engine		⊖	⊜	⊜	⊜	⊜	⊜	
Cooling		⊜	⊜	⊜	⊜	⊜	⊜	
Fuel		⊖	⊖	⊖	⊖	⊜	⊜	
Ignition		○	⊖	⊖	⊜	⊜	⊜	
Auto. trans.		○	⊜	⊜	⊜	⊜	⊖	
Man. trans.		*	*	⊖	*	⊜	⊖	
Clutch		*	*	○	*	⊖	⊜	
Electrical		◒	○	○	○	⊖	⊜	
A/C		◒	○	⊖	⊜	⊜	⊜	
Suspension		○	⊖	⊖	⊖	⊜	⊖	
Brakes		○	○	⊜	⊖	⊜	⊜	
Exhaust		⊖	⊖	⊜	⊜	⊜	⊜	
Body rust		⊜	⊜	⊜	⊜	⊜	⊜	
Paint/trim		○	⊖	⊖	⊜	⊜	⊜	
Integrity		⊖	○	⊖	⊖	⊖	⊖	
Hardware		●	●	○	○	⊖	⊖	

Infiniti I30

TROUBLE SPOTS	90	91	92	93	94	95	96	97
Engine							⊜	⊜
Cooling							⊜	⊜
Fuel							⊜	⊜
Ignition							⊜	⊜
Auto. trans.							⊜	⊜
Man. trans.							*	*
Clutch							*	*
Electrical							⊖	⊜
A/C							⊜	⊜
Suspension							⊜	⊜
Brakes							⊜	⊜
Exhaust							⊜	⊜
Body rust							⊜	⊜
Paint/trim							⊜	⊜
Integrity							⊖	⊜
Hardware							⊖	⊜

Infiniti J30

TROUBLE SPOTS	90	91	92	93	94	95	96	97
Engine				⊖	⊜	⊜	Insufficient data	Insufficient data
Cooling				⊜	⊜	⊜		
Fuel				⊜	⊖	⊜		
Ignition				⊖	⊖	⊜		
Auto. trans.				⊖	⊖	⊜		
Man. trans.								
Clutch								
Electrical				○	○	⊜		
A/C				○	⊖	⊖		
Suspension				⊜	⊜	⊜		
Brakes				⊖	⊖	⊖		
Exhaust				⊜	⊜	⊜		
Body rust				⊜	⊜	⊜		
Paint/trim				⊜	○	⊖		
Integrity				⊖	○	⊖		
Hardware				◒	○	⊖		

Infiniti Q45

TROUBLE SPOTS	90	91	92	93	94	95	96	97
Engine	Insufficient data	○	⊖	Insufficient data	⊜	Insufficient data	Insufficient data	Insufficient data
Cooling		○	⊖		⊜			
Fuel		○	○		⊖			
Ignition		⊜	⊖		⊖			
Auto. trans.		○	◒		⊜			
Man. trans.								
Clutch								
Electrical		●	○		○			
A/C		○	○		⊖			
Suspension		⊖	○		◒			
Brakes		●	●		○			
Exhaust		⊜	⊜		⊜			
Body rust		⊖	⊖		⊖			
Paint/trim		⊜	⊖		⊖			
Integrity		○	⊖		⊜			
Hardware		●	◒		⊖			

Isuzu Oasis

TROUBLE SPOTS	90	91	92	93	94	95	96	97
Engine							⊜	⊜
Cooling							⊜	⊜
Fuel							⊜	⊜
Ignition							⊜	⊜
Auto. trans.							⊜	⊜
Man. trans.								
Clutch								
Electrical							⊜	⊜
A/C							⊜	⊜
Suspension							⊜	⊜
Brakes							⊜	⊜
Exhaust							⊜	⊜
Body rust							⊜	⊜
Paint/trim							⊜	⊜
Integrity							⊜	⊜
Hardware							⊜	⊜

⊜ ⊖ ○ ◒ ●
Few ← **Problems** → Many

* Insufficient data

Isuzu Rodeo V6

Trouble spots	90	91	92	93	94	95	96	97
Engine		Insufficient data	○	◒	◒	○	○	Insufficient data
Cooling			◒	⊜	⊖	⊜	◒	
Fuel			⊜	⊜	⊖	⊜	○	
Ignition			⊖	○	⊖	⊖	⊖	
Auto. trans.			*	*	⊜	⊖	○	
Man. trans.			*	*	*	*	*	
Clutch			*	*	*	*	*	
Electrical			◒	◒	○	◒	◒	
A/C			*	*	⊖	⊜	⊖	
Suspension			⊜	⊖	⊖	⊖	⊖	
Brakes			◒	○	⊖	⊖	⊖	
Exhaust			○	⊜	⊜	⊜	⊜	
Body rust			⊖	○	○	⊖	⊖	
Paint/trim			◒	●	○	○	⊜	
Integrity			◒	●	◒	◒	◒	
Hardware			●	●	●	●	◒	

Isuzu Trooper

Trouble spots	90	91	92	93	94	95	96	97
Engine	●	○	○	⊖	○	⊜	⊜	Insufficient data
Cooling	◒	○	⊜	⊜	⊜	⊜	⊜	
Fuel	⊖	⊖	⊖	⊖	⊜	⊖	⊜	
Ignition	○	⊖	⊖	⊖	⊖	⊜	⊜	
Auto. trans.	*	*	*	*	○	⊜	*	
Man. trans.	○	⊖	*	*	*	*	*	
Clutch	◒	●	*	*	*	*	*	
Electrical	⊖	○	●	○	○	⊜	⊖	
A/C	◒	◒	⊖	⊖	⊖	⊖	⊜	
Suspension	⊖	○	⊖	⊜	⊖	⊜	⊜	
Brakes	●	●	○	⊜	⊖	⊜	⊜	
Exhaust	●	●	◒	⊜	⊖	⊖	⊜	
Body rust	●	◒	⊜	⊜	⊖	⊜	⊜	
Paint/trim	○	◒	⊜	○	○	⊖	⊜	
Integrity	◒	○	⊜	⊖	○	○	⊖	
Hardware	◒	◒	◒	○	○	○	⊖	

Jeep Cherokee, Wagoneer

Trouble spots	90	91	92	93	94	95	96	97
Engine	◒	○	○	⊖	⊖	⊖	⊜	Insufficient data
Cooling	●	◒	○	○	⊖	⊖	⊜	
Fuel	◒	○	⊖	⊖	⊜	⊜	⊖	
Ignition	◒	○	⊖	⊖	⊖	⊖	⊖	
Auto. trans.	○	○	⊖	⊖	⊖	⊖	⊖	
Man. trans.	*	*	*	*	*	*	*	
Clutch	*	*	*	*	*	*	*	
Electrical	●	◒	○	◒	◒	○	○	
A/C	◒	○	⊖	⊖	⊖	⊖	⊖	
Suspension	○	○	○	⊖	⊖	⊖	⊜	
Brakes	●	●	●	◒	○	○	○	
Exhaust	●	●	●	⊜	⊜	⊜	⊜	
Body rust	○	⊖	⊖	⊜	⊜	⊜	⊜	
Paint/trim	●	◒	○	○	○	○	○	
Integrity	●	◒	●	◒	◒	◒	◒	
Hardware	●	◒	○	○	◒	○	◒	

Jeep Grand Cherokee

Trouble spots	90	91	92	93	94	95	96	9[illegible]
Engine				○	⊖	⊖	⊜	[illegible]
Cooling				○	⊖	⊖	⊜	[illegible]
Fuel				⊖	⊖	⊜	⊖	[illegible]
Ignition				○	○	⊖	⊖	[illegible]
Auto. trans.				○	○	○	○	[illegible]
Man. trans.				*	*	*		
Clutch				*	*	*		
Electrical				◒	◒	○	◒	[illegible]
A/C				●	◒	◒	⊖	[illegible]
Suspension				○	⊖	⊖	⊖	[illegible]
Brakes				●	◒	○	⊖	[illegible]
Exhaust				⊖	⊜	⊜	⊜	[illegible]
Body rust				⊖	⊖	⊜	⊜	[illegible]
Paint/trim				○	⊜	⊜	⊖	[illegible]
Integrity				◒	○	○	○	[illegible]
Hardware				◒	○	○	○	[illegible]

Jeep Wrangler

Trouble spots	90	91	92	93	94	95	96	97
Engine	Insufficient data	○	○	○	⊖	⊖	Insufficient data	⊜
Cooling		○	◒	○	⊖	⊖		⊜
Fuel		◒	⊜	◒	⊖	⊜		⊜
Ignition		◒	⊖	○	○	○		⊜
Auto. trans.		*	*	*	*	*		*
Man. trans.		*	*	⊖	⊖	⊜		⊖
Clutch		*	*	○	⊖	⊜		⊜
Electrical		○	◒	◒	◒	◒		⊖
A/C		*	*	*	*	*		⊜
Suspension		○	⊜	⊜	⊜	⊖		⊜
Brakes		◒	◒	○	⊖	⊖		⊜
Exhaust		●	◒	○	●	○		⊜
Body rust		○	●	○	○	○		⊜
Paint/trim		⊖	◒	◒	○	○		⊜
Integrity		●	●	◒	●	●		⊖
Hardware		●	●	●	●	●		⊖

Lexus ES250, ES300

Trouble spots	90	91	92	93	94	95	96	97
Engine	○	○	⊜	⊖	⊜	⊜	⊜	⊜
Cooling	○	○	⊖	○	⊜	⊜	⊜	⊜
Fuel	⊜	⊖	⊜	⊜	⊜	⊜	⊜	⊜
Ignition	⊖	⊖	⊖	⊖	⊜	⊜	⊜	⊜
Auto. trans.	○	○	⊖	⊖	⊜	⊜	⊜	⊜
Man. trans.	*	*	*	*				
Clutch	*	*	*	*				
Electrical	○	○	○	⊖	⊖	⊖	⊜	⊜
A/C	○	⊖	⊖	⊜	⊜	⊜	⊜	⊜
Suspension	◒	◒	⊖	⊖	⊖	⊜	⊜	⊜
Brakes	◒	●	○	⊖	⊖	⊜	⊜	⊜
Exhaust	⊜	⊜	⊜	⊜	⊜	⊜	⊜	⊜
Body rust	⊜	⊖	⊜	⊜	⊜	⊜	⊜	⊜
Paint/trim	○	○	⊖	⊜	⊜	⊜	⊜	⊜
Integrity	⊖	○	⊖	⊖	⊖	○	⊖	⊖
Hardware	●	●	○	⊖	⊖	⊖	⊖	⊜

Lexus GS300

Trouble spots	90	91	92	93	94	95	96	97
Engine				⊖	⊜	Insufficient data	Insufficient data	Insufficient data
Cooling				⊜	⊜			
Fuel				⊜	⊜			
Ignition				⊖	⊜			
Auto. trans.				⊜	⊜			
Man. trans.								
Clutch								
Electrical				○	⊖			
A/C				⊜	⊜			
Suspension				⊖	⊖			
Brakes				○	⊖			
Exhaust				⊜	⊜			
Body rust				⊜	⊜			
Paint/trim				⊖	⊜			
Integrity				○	⊖			
Hardware				○	⊖			

Lexus LS400

Trouble spots	90	91	92	93	94	95	96	97
Engine	⊜	⊜	⊜	⊜	⊜	⊜	⊜	⊜
Cooling	⊜	⊜	⊜	⊜	⊜	⊜	⊜	⊜
Fuel	⊜	⊜	⊜	⊜	⊜	⊖	⊜	⊜
Ignition	⊖	⊖	⊜	⊖	⊜	⊖	⊜	⊜
Auto. trans.	⊜	⊜	⊜	⊜	⊜	⊖	⊜	⊜
Man. trans.								
Clutch								
Electrical	○	○	⊖	⊖	⊖	○	⊖	⊖
A/C	◒	◒	○	⊜	⊜	⊖	⊜	⊜
Suspension	◒	◒	○	⊜	⊖	⊖	⊜	⊜
Brakes	○	○	○	⊖	◒	○	⊖	⊜
Exhaust	⊜	⊜	⊜	⊜	⊜	⊜	⊜	⊜
Body rust	⊜	⊜	⊜	⊜	⊜	⊜	⊜	⊜
Paint/trim	⊜	⊜	⊜	⊜	⊜	⊜	⊜	⊜
Integrity	⊖	⊖	⊜	⊖	⊖	⊖	⊖	⊖
Hardware	○	⊖	⊖	⊖	⊖	⊖	○	⊖

Lexus SC300/SC400

TROUBLE SPOTS	90	91	92	93	94	95	96	97
Engine			⊜	⊜	Insufficient data	⊜	Insufficient data	Insufficient data
Cooling			⊜	⊜		⊜		
Fuel			⊜	⊜		⊜		
Ignition			⊜	⊜		⊜		
Auto. trans.			⊜	⊜		⊖		
Man. trans.			*	*		*		
Clutch			*	*		*		
Electrical			○	○		⊖		
A/C			⊖	⊖		⊖		
Suspension			⊖	⊜		⊖		
Brakes			⊖	⊜		⊜		
Exhaust			⊜	⊜		⊜		
Body rust			⊜	⊜		⊜		
Paint/trim			⊖	⊖		○		
Integrity			⊖	⊖		⊖		
Hardware			○	○		⊖		

Lincoln Continental

TROUBLE SPOTS	90	91	92	93	94	95	96	97
Engine	●	●	●	○	○	⊜	⊜	⊜
Cooling	◒	○	○	○	⊖	⊜	⊜	⊖
Fuel	○	○	⊖	⊖	⊖	○	⊜	⊖
Ignition	●	◒	○	○	⊖	○	⊖	⊜
Auto. trans.	◒	●	○	○	⊖	⊖	○	⊜
Man. trans.								
Clutch								
Electrical	●	●	●	●	◒	●	◒	○
A/C	●	●	●	●	◒	⊖	⊜	⊜
Suspension	●	●	●	◒	○	◒	○	○
Brakes	●	●	●	●	○	○	⊖	⊜
Exhaust	⊖	⊖	⊖	⊜	⊜	⊜	⊜	⊜
Body rust	⊖	⊜	⊜	⊜	⊜	⊜	⊜	⊜
Paint/trim	◒	◒	⊖	⊖	⊖	⊖	⊜	⊜
Integrity	○	◒	○	◒	○	◒	○	⊖
Hardware	●	●	●	◒	●	◒	○	⊖

Lincoln Mark VII, Mark VIII

TROUBLE SPOTS	90	91	92	93	94	95	96	97
Engine	⊖	Insufficient data	Insufficient data	⊖	⊜	⊖	⊜	Insufficient data
Cooling	○			○	⊜	⊜	⊖	
Fuel	○			⊖	⊜	⊖	⊖	
Ignition	◒			○	○	⊜	⊜	
Auto. trans.	◒			●	◒	⊖	⊜	
Man. trans.								
Clutch								
Electrical	●			●	◒	◒	◒	
A/C	●			⊖	⊖	⊜	⊜	
Suspension	●			◒	⊖	⊜	○	
Brakes	●			●	○	○	◒	
Exhaust	◒			⊜	⊜	⊜	⊜	
Body rust	◒			⊜	⊜	⊜	⊜	
Paint/trim	●			⊖	⊜	⊖	⊜	
Integrity	○			○	⊖	◒	○	
Hardware	●			◒	○	○	○	

Lincoln Town Car

TROUBLE SPOTS	90	91	92	93	94	95	96	97
Engine	○	⊖	⊖	⊖	⊜	⊜	⊜	⊜
Cooling	○	⊜	⊜	⊜	⊜	⊜	⊜	⊜
Fuel	◒	○	○	⊖	⊖	⊜	⊖	⊜
Ignition	◒	●	◒	○	⊜	⊖	⊖	⊜
Auto. trans.	○	⊖	◒	●	◒	○	⊖	⊖
Man. trans.								
Clutch								
Electrical	●	●	●	◒	○	○	○	⊖
A/C	◒	●	◒	○	⊖	⊖	⊜	⊜
Suspension	◒	○	⊖	○	⊖	⊖	○	⊖
Brakes	●	●	●	●	○	◒	⊖	⊜
Exhaust	◒	○	⊜	⊜	⊜	⊜	⊜	⊜
Body rust	⊖	⊜	⊜	⊜	⊜	⊜	⊜	⊜
Paint/trim	○	○	⊖	⊖	⊖	⊜	⊜	⊜
Integrity	○	○	⊖	○	○	○	○	⊖
Hardware	●	●	●	◒	◒	○	○	○

Mazda 323

TROUBLE SPOTS	90	91	92	93	94	95	96	97
Engine	○	○	⊖	Insufficient data	Insufficient data			
Cooling	○	○	⊖					
Fuel	⊖	⊖	⊜					
Ignition	○	⊖	⊜					
Auto. trans.	*	*	*					
Man. trans.	⊜	⊜	*					
Clutch	⊖	⊖	*					
Electrical	◒	○	○					
A/C	◒	◒	*					
Suspension	○	○	⊖					
Brakes	●	◒	◒					
Exhaust	●	●	●					
Body rust	○	⊖	⊖					
Paint/trim	◒	○	○					
Integrity	◒	●	●					
Hardware	◒	●	◒					

Mazda 626

TROUBLE SPOTS	90	91	92	93	94	95	96	97
Engine	○	○	○	○	○	⊖	⊜	⊜
Cooling	○	○	⊖	⊜	⊜	⊜	⊜	⊜
Fuel	⊖	⊖	○	⊖	○	⊜	⊜	⊜
Ignition	⊖	⊖	⊖	◒	◒	⊖	⊜	⊜
Auto. trans.	○	⊖	○	○	◒	⊖	⊖	⊜
Man. trans.	⊜	⊜	*	⊖	⊜	⊜	⊖	*
Clutch	⊖	⊖	*	⊖	⊜	⊜	⊖	*
Electrical	◒	◒	⊖	◒	◒	○	⊖	⊜
A/C	◒	○	○	○	⊖	⊜	⊜	⊜
Suspension	○	○	○	○	○	⊖	⊜	⊜
Brakes	●	●	●	◒	◒	⊖	⊖	⊜
Exhaust	●	◒	◒	○	⊜	⊜	⊜	⊜
Body rust	⊖	⊜	⊖	⊜	⊜	⊜	⊜	⊜
Paint/trim	○	◒	○	○	○	○	⊖	⊜
Integrity	◒	◒	◒	●	●	◒	○	⊖
Hardware	◒	◒	◒	●	●	○	○	⊖

Mazda 929

TROUBLE SPOTS	90	91	92	93	94	95	96	97
Engine	○	◒	○	⊖	Insufficient data	Insufficient data		
Cooling	○	○	◒	⊖				
Fuel	○	⊖	⊖	⊜				
Ignition	◒	○	○	⊖				
Auto. trans.	◒	◒	○	○				
Man. trans.								
Clutch								
Electrical	◒	○	◒	●				
A/C	○	⊖	○	○				
Suspension	○	○	⊜	⊖				
Brakes	●	●	◒	●				
Exhaust	●	●	○	○				
Body rust	⊖	⊜	⊜	⊜				
Paint/trim	○	○	○	⊖				
Integrity	○	⊖	○	○				
Hardware	●	◒	●	●				

Mazda Millenia

TROUBLE SPOTS	90	91	92	93	94	95	96	97
Engine						⊖	⊜	Insufficient data
Cooling						⊜	⊜	
Fuel						⊖	⊜	
Ignition						○	⊜	
Auto. trans.						⊜	⊜	
Man. trans.								
Clutch								
Electrical						○	○	
A/C						⊖	⊜	
Suspension						⊖	⊜	
Brakes						⊜	⊜	
Exhaust						⊜	⊜	
Body rust						⊜	⊜	
Paint/trim						⊖	⊜	
Integrity						⊖	⊖	
Hardware						○	⊖	

⊜ ⊖ ○ ◒ ●
Few ← **Problems** → Many

* Insufficient data

Trouble spots	Mazda MPV Van V6 (2WD) 90	91	92	93	94	95	96	97
					Insufficient data	Insufficient data	Insufficient data	Insufficient data
Engine	●	●	◒	●				
Cooling	◒	◒	◒	⊜				
Fuel	⊖	⊖	○	⊖				
Ignition	○	○	○	⊖				
Auto. trans.	◒	○	○	⊖				
Man. trans.	*							
Clutch	*							
Electrical	○	◒	○	○				
A/C	●	○	○	⊖				
Suspension	○	○	○	⊖				
Brakes	●	●	●	⊖				
Exhaust	◒	◒	⊖	⊜				
Body rust	⊜	⊖	⊜	⊜				
Paint/trim	○	○	○	⊜				
Integrity	⊖	⊖	⊖	⊖				
Hardware	◒	◒	○	○				

Trouble spots	Mazda MX-5 Miata 90	91	92	93	94	95	96	97
								Insufficient data
Engine	⊖	⊖	⊖	⊖	⊖	⊜	⊜	
Cooling	⊖	⊜	⊜	⊜	⊜	⊜	⊜	
Fuel	⊜	⊜	⊜	⊜	⊖	⊜	⊜	
Ignition	⊖	⊖	○	⊖	◒	⊖	⊜	
Auto. trans.		*	*	*	*	*	*	
Man. trans.	⊜	⊜	⊜	⊜	⊜	⊖	⊜	
Clutch	○	◒	⊖	⊜	⊜	⊜	⊜	
Electrical	○	○	◒	○	○	⊖	⊖	
A/C	⊖	⊖	⊜	⊖	⊖	⊜	⊜	
Suspension	⊜	⊜	⊜	⊜	⊖	⊖	⊜	
Brakes	⊖	○	○	⊜	⊜	⊖	⊜	
Exhaust	⊜	⊖	⊜	⊜	⊜	⊜	⊜	
Body rust	⊜	⊜	⊜	⊜	⊜	⊜	⊜	
Paint/trim	◒	○	○	⊖	⊖	⊖	⊖	
Integrity	○	○	○	○	○	◒	⊖	
Hardware	○	◒	◒	⊖	○	⊜	⊖	

Trouble spots	Mazda MX-6 90	91	92	93	94	95	96	97
			Insufficient data			Insufficient data	Insufficient data	Insufficient data
Engine	○	○		○	⊖			
Cooling	⊖	⊖		⊜	⊖			
Fuel	⊖	⊖		○	⊖			
Ignition	⊖	⊖		◒	○			
Auto. trans.	*	*		⊖	*			
Man. trans.	⊜	*		⊜	*			
Clutch	⊖	*		⊖	*			
Electrical	◒	◒		◒	○			
A/C	◒	○		○	○			
Suspension	○	○		○	⊜			
Brakes	◒	●		○	○			
Exhaust	●	◒		○	⊜			
Body rust	○	⊜		⊜	⊜			
Paint/trim	◒	●		◒	○			
Integrity	●	●		●	●			
Hardware	●	●		●	●			

Trouble spots	Mazda B-Series Pickup (2WD) 90	91	92	93	94	95	96	97
Engine	○	○	○	⊖	⊜	⊜	⊜	⊜
Cooling	⊖	⊖	⊖	⊖	⊖	⊖	⊜	⊜
Fuel	⊖	⊖	⊖	⊖	⊖	⊖	⊖	⊜
Ignition	⊖	⊖	⊖	⊖	⊖	⊖	⊜	⊜
Auto. trans.	⊜	*	*	*	⊖	○	⊜	⊖
Man. trans.	⊜	⊜	⊖	⊜	⊖	⊜	⊜	⊜
Clutch	○	⊖	⊖	⊖	⊖	⊖	⊜	⊜
Electrical	○	⊖	⊖	⊖	○	●	○	⊖
A/C	◒	○	◒	○	⊖	⊖	⊜	⊜
Suspension	⊖	⊖	⊖	⊜	⊖	⊖	⊖	⊖
Brakes	●	◒	◒	○	◒	○	⊖	⊖
Exhaust	●	●	●	◒	⊖	⊜	⊜	⊜
Body rust	◒	⊖	○	⊖	⊜	⊜	⊜	⊜
Paint/trim	◒	○	⊖	⊖	⊖	⊖	⊖	⊖
Integrity	○	○	⊖	○	⊖	⊖	⊖	⊜
Hardware	○	⊖	⊖	⊖	⊖	◒	⊖	⊖

Trouble spots	Mazda B-Series Pickup (4WD) 90	91	92	93	94	95	96	97
	Insufficient data	Insufficient data	Insufficient data	Insufficient data				
Engine					⊖	⊖	⊜	⊜
Cooling					⊜	⊖	⊖	⊜
Fuel					⊖	○	⊖	⊖
Ignition					⊖	○	⊜	⊜
Auto. trans.					⊜	⊖	⊜	⊖
Man. trans.					⊖	⊜	⊜	*
Clutch					○	⊖	⊖	*
Electrical					○	●	○	⊜
A/C					⊖	⊜	⊖	⊜
Suspension					⊜	○	○	⊜
Brakes					◒	◒	⊖	⊜
Exhaust					⊖	⊜	⊜	⊜
Body rust					⊜	⊜	⊜	⊜
Paint/trim					⊖	⊖	⊖	⊖
Integrity					⊖	○	⊖	⊖
Hardware					⊖	◒	⊖	⊜

Trouble spots	Mazda Protegé 90	91	92	93	94	95	96	97
Engine	○	○	⊖	⊖	⊖	⊜	⊜	⊜
Cooling	◒	○	⊖	⊖	⊜	⊜	⊜	⊜
Fuel	⊖	⊖	⊖	⊖	⊖	⊜	⊜	⊖
Ignition	○	⊖	○	○	⊖	⊖	⊜	⊜
Auto. trans.	○	⊖	⊜	⊜	⊖	⊖	⊜	⊜
Man. trans.	⊜	⊖	⊜	⊜	⊜	⊜	⊖	*
Clutch	⊖	⊖	⊖	⊖	⊜	⊜	⊜	*
Electrical	◒	○	◒	○	○	●	○	○
A/C	◒	⊖	○	○	⊖	⊜	⊜	⊜
Suspension	○	⊖	○	⊖	⊜	⊖	⊜	⊜
Brakes	◒	●	●	◒	○	⊖	⊖	⊜
Exhaust	●	●	◒	○	⊖	⊜	⊜	⊜
Body rust	○	⊖	⊜	⊜	⊜	⊜	⊜	⊜
Paint/trim	◒	◒	○	⊖	⊖	⊖	⊖	⊜
Integrity	○	○	○	○	○	○	⊖	○
Hardware	◒	◒	◒	◒	◒	○	⊖	⊖

Trouble spots	Mercedes-Benz C-Class 90	91	92	93	94	95	96	97
Engine					○	⊖	⊜	⊜
Cooling					⊜	⊜	⊜	⊜
Fuel					⊖	⊖	⊖	⊜
Ignition					⊖	⊖	⊖	⊜
Auto. trans.					⊜	○	⊜	⊜
Man. trans.								
Clutch								
Electrical					◒	●	○	⊖
A/C					○	○	⊖	○
Suspension					⊜	⊜	⊜	⊜
Brakes					◒	○	⊜	⊜
Exhaust					⊜	⊜	⊜	⊜
Body rust					⊜	⊜	⊜	⊜
Paint/trim					⊜	⊜	⊜	⊜
Integrity					⊖	⊖	⊖	⊜
Hardware					●	◒	⊜	⊖

Trouble spots	Mercedes-Benz E-Class 6 90	91	92	93	94	95	96	97
			Insufficient data	Insufficient data				
Engine	○	●			○	⊖	⊖	⊜
Cooling	●	●			⊖	⊜	⊜	⊜
Fuel	○	⊖			⊜	⊜	⊖	⊜
Ignition	⊖	⊖			⊜	⊜	⊜	⊖
Auto. trans.	⊖	⊖			⊜	⊖	⊜	⊖
Man. trans.								
Clutch								
Electrical	●	◒			⊖	○	○	⊜
A/C	●	◒			⊖	⊖	⊜	⊖
Suspension	⊖	⊖			⊜	⊖	⊜	⊜
Brakes	○	○			○	⊖	⊖	⊜
Exhaust	⊖	⊖			⊜	⊜	⊜	⊜
Body rust	⊜	⊖			⊜	⊜	⊜	⊜
Paint/trim	⊖	⊜			⊖	⊜	⊖	⊜
Integrity	⊖	⊖			⊜	⊜	○	⊜
Hardware	◒	◒			⊖	⊖	⊖	⊜

Mercury Cougar

Trouble spots	90	91	92	93	94	95	96	97
Engine	○	○	⊖	⊖	⊜	⊜	⊜	⊜
Cooling	◒	○	○	⊖	⊜	⊖	⊜	⊜
Fuel	○	○	○	⊖	⊖	⊖	○	⊜
Ignition	◒	◒	◒	○	⊖	⊖	○	⊜
Auto. trans.	○	○	⊜	⊖	●	○	○	⊖
Man. trans.	*							
Clutch	*							
Electrical	●	●	◒	●	◒	○	○	⊜
A/C	●	●	◒	○	○	⊖	○	⊜
Suspension	○	○	○	⊖	○	○	○	○
Brakes	●	●	●	●	●	●	●	⊖
Exhaust	⊖	⊖	⊖	⊜	⊜	⊜	⊜	⊜
Body rust	○	○	⊖	⊖	⊜	⊜	⊜	⊜
Paint/trim	●	●	◒	●	⊖	⊖	⊖	⊜
Integrity	●	◒	◒	○	◒	○	◒	○
Hardware	●	●	●	●	◒	○	○	⊖

Mercury Grand Marquis

Trouble spots	90	91	92	93	94	95	96	97
Engine	○	○	⊖	⊜	⊜	⊜	⊜	⊜
Cooling	◒	○	⊜	⊜	⊜	⊜	⊜	⊜
Fuel	○	○	○	⊖	⊖	⊖	⊜	⊜
Ignition	◒	◒	●	◒	⊖	⊖	⊖	⊜
Auto. trans.	○	○	◒	●	●	○	⊖	⊜
Man. trans.								
Clutch								
Electrical	●	●	◒	◒	○	◒	○	⊖
A/C	●	◒	◒	⊖	⊖	⊖	⊜	⊜
Suspension	○	○	⊖	⊖	⊖	⊖	○	⊜
Brakes	●	●	●	●	◒	◒	○	⊖
Exhaust	●	●	◒	⊜	⊜	⊜	⊜	⊖
Body rust	○	○	⊜	⊜	⊜	⊜	⊜	⊜
Paint/trim	◒	○	○	⊖	⊖	⊖	⊖	⊖
Integrity	○	○	○	○	○	○	○	⊖
Hardware	●	●	●	◒	○	○	○	⊖

Mercury Mountaineer

Trouble spots	90	91	92	93	94	95	96	97
Engine								⊜
Cooling								⊜
Fuel								⊜
Ignition								⊜
Auto. trans.								⊜
Man. trans.								
Clutch								
Electrical								⊖
A/C								⊜
Suspension								⊜
Brakes								⊜
Exhaust								⊜
Body rust								⊜
Paint/trim								⊜
Integrity								⊖
Hardware								⊖

Mercury Mystique

Trouble spots	90	91	92	93	94	95	96	97
Engine						⊖	⊜	⊜
Cooling						⊖	⊜	⊜
Fuel						◒	○	⊖
Ignition						⊖	⊖	⊖
Auto. trans.						○	⊜	⊜
Man. trans.						⊜	⊜	*
Clutch						⊜	⊜	*
Electrical						◒	○	○
A/C						⊖	⊜	⊜
Suspension						○	⊖	⊖
Brakes						◒	⊖	⊖
Exhaust						⊜	⊜	⊜
Body rust						⊜	⊜	⊜
Paint/trim						○	⊖	⊜
Integrity						◒	○	○
Hardware						◒	◒	○

Mercury Sable

Trouble spots	90	91	92	93	94	95	96	97
Engine	◒	○	○	○	⊖	⊜	⊜	⊜
Cooling	●	●	◒	○	○	⊖	⊜	⊜
Fuel	◒	○	○	○	⊖	⊖	⊖	⊜
Ignition	●	○	◒	○	⊖	⊖	⊖	⊜
Auto. trans.	◒	●	○	○	○	⊜	○	⊜
Man. trans.								
Clutch								
Electrical	●	◒	●	●	○	○	○	⊖
A/C	●	●	◒	◒	○	⊖	⊖	⊜
Suspension	●	●	●	◒	○	⊖	○	⊖
Brakes	●	●	●	●	○	⊜	⊖	⊜
Exhaust	⊖	⊖	⊖	⊜	⊜	⊜	⊜	⊜
Body rust	●	○	⊖	⊜	⊜	⊜	⊜	⊜
Paint/trim	●	◒	○	⊖	⊜	⊖	⊖	⊜
Integrity	◒	◒	◒	◒	●	●	●	⊖
Hardware	●	●	◒	◒	○	○	◒	⊖

Mercury Topaz

Trouble spots	90	91	92	93	94	95	96	97
Engine	◒	◒	○	○	○			
Cooling	◒	◒	◒	○	○			
Fuel	●	◒	○	◒	○			
Ignition	●	●	◒	○	⊖			
Auto. trans.	○	⊖	○	⊖	○			
Man. trans.	*	*	*	*	*			
Clutch	*	*	*	*	*			
Electrical	●	●	◒	◒	◒			
A/C	●	●	○	○	○			
Suspension	●	◒	○	○	○			
Brakes	●	●	●	●	●			
Exhaust	●	●	●	●	○			
Body rust	◒	○	⊖	⊖	⊜			
Paint/trim	●	●	◒	○	○			
Integrity	◒	◒	◒	◒	◒			
Hardware	●	●	●	●	●			

Mercury Tracer

Trouble spots	90	91	92	93	94	95	96	97
Engine		○	⊖	⊖	⊖	⊜	⊜	⊜
Cooling		◒	○	⊜	⊖	⊜	⊜	⊜
Fuel		○	○	⊖	⊜	⊜	⊖	⊜
Ignition		◒	○	○	⊖	⊖	⊖	⊜
Auto. trans.		○	○	⊖	⊖	⊖	⊖	⊜
Man. trans.		⊜	⊖	⊜	⊜	⊜	⊜	⊜
Clutch		○	○	○	⊖	⊜	⊜	⊜
Electrical		●	◒	○	○	○	○	⊖
A/C		●	○	⊖	⊖	⊖	⊖	⊜
Suspension		○	○	⊖	⊖	⊖	⊖	⊜
Brakes		●	◒	◒	◒	⊖	⊜	⊜
Exhaust		⊖	⊖	⊜	⊜	⊜	⊜	⊜
Body rust		○	⊖	⊜	⊜	⊜	⊜	⊜
Paint/trim		◒	○	⊖	⊖	⊖	⊖	⊜
Integrity		◒	◒	○	○	○	○	⊖
Hardware		◒	◒	◒	○	○	○	⊖

Mercury Villager Van

Trouble spots	90	91	92	93	94	95	96	97
Engine				⊖	⊖	○	○	⊜
Cooling				⊖	⊖	⊜	⊜	⊜
Fuel				⊖	⊖	⊖	⊜	⊜
Ignition				⊖	⊖	⊖	⊜	⊜
Auto. trans.				⊖	⊜	⊜	⊜	⊜
Man. trans.								
Clutch								
Electrical				●	◒	●	◒	○
A/C				○	○	⊖	⊖	⊜
Suspension				○	⊖	⊖	⊖	⊖
Brakes				◒	◒	◒	⊖	⊜
Exhaust				●	⊖	⊜	⊜	⊜
Body rust				⊜	⊜	⊜	⊜	⊜
Paint/trim				⊖	⊖	⊖	⊜	⊜
Integrity				◒	○	◒	◒	○
Hardware				●	◒	●	◒	○

⊜ ⊖ ○ ◒ ●
Few ◄— **Problems** —► Many

* Insufficient data

TROUBLE SPOTS	Mitsubishi 3000GT (2WD) 90	91	92	93	94	95	96	97
Engine		⊖	○	⊖	⊜			
Cooling		○	⊖	⊖	⊜			
Fuel		⊜	⊜	⊜	⊜			
Ignition		○	○	⊖	○			
Auto. trans.		*	*	*	*			
Man. trans.		*	*	*	*			
Clutch		*	*	*	*	Insufficient data	Insufficient data	Insufficient data
Electrical		◒	●	◒	○			
A/C		○	⊜	⊖	⊖			
Suspension		⊜	○	○	⊜			
Brakes		○	○	◒	⊖			
Exhaust		⊜	⊜	⊜	⊜			
Body rust		⊜	⊜	⊜	⊜			
Paint/trim		◒	○	◒	○			
Integrity		◒	◒	○	○			
Hardware		●	◒	◒	◒			

TROUBLE SPOTS	Mitsubishi Diamante 90	91	92	93	94	95	96	97
Engine			○	⊖	⊖			
Cooling			⊖	⊖	⊜			
Fuel			⊖	⊜	⊜			
Ignition			⊖	⊖	⊖			
Auto. trans.			⊖	●	⊖			
Man. trans.								
Clutch						Insufficient data	Insufficient data	Insufficient data
Electrical			○	◒	○			
A/C			⊖	⊖	⊖			
Suspension			⊖	⊖	⊖			
Brakes			●	◒	○			
Exhaust			⊜	⊜	⊜			
Body rust			⊜	⊜	⊜			
Paint/trim			⊖	⊖	○			
Integrity			⊖	○	⊖			
Hardware			○	○	◒			

TROUBLE SPOTS	Mitsubishi Eclipse 90	91	92	93	94	95	96	97
Engine	●	◒	◒	○	◒	○	⊖	
Cooling	○	○	⊖	○	⊖	⊖	⊜	
Fuel	⊖	○	○	⊖	⊜	◒	○	
Ignition	○	◒	◒	○	⊖	○	○	
Auto. trans.	○	◒	◒	*	*	⊖	*	
Man. trans.	○	○	○	○	*	⊖	*	
Clutch	○	○	○	○	*	⊖	*	Insufficient data
Electrical	◒	◒	◒	◒	○	●	◒	
A/C	○	⊖	⊜	○	○	⊖	⊜	
Suspension	○	⊖	⊖	⊖	⊖	⊖	○	
Brakes	◒	◒	◒	◒	○	◒	○	
Exhaust	⊖	⊖	○	⊖	⊜	⊜	⊜	
Body rust	⊜	⊖	⊖	⊖	⊖	⊜	⊜	
Paint/trim	◒	◒	●	○	◒	○	⊖	
Integrity	◒	◒	◒	◒	●	●	◒	
Hardware	●	●	●	◒	●	●	●	

TROUBLE SPOTS	Mitsubishi Galant 90	91	92	93	94	95	96	97
Engine	◒	○	○		⊖	⊜	⊖	⊖
Cooling	○	⊖	⊖		⊜	⊜	⊜	⊜
Fuel	⊖	○	⊜		⊜	⊜	⊖	⊜
Ignition	○	○	⊖		○	⊖	⊖	⊜
Auto. trans.	○	○	⊖		⊖	⊖	⊖	○
Man. trans.	*	*	*		*	*	*	*
Clutch	*	*	*	Insufficient data	*	*	*	*
Electrical	○	⊖	⊜		◒	⊖	⊖	⊖
A/C	○	⊖	⊖		⊖	⊖	⊖	⊜
Suspension	○	○	⊖		○	○	⊖	⊜
Brakes	●	●	○		◒	●	○	⊜
Exhaust	⊖	⊜	⊖		⊜	⊜	⊜	⊜
Body rust	⊜	⊖	⊜		⊜	⊜	⊜	⊜
Paint/trim	○	○	○		⊖	⊖	⊖	⊜
Integrity	○	⊖	○		○	◒	◒	⊜
Hardware	○	⊖	○		●	◒	◒	⊖

TROUBLE SPOTS	Mitsubishi Mirage 90	91	92	93	94	95	96	97
Engine	●	◒	○	⊖				
Cooling	○	⊖	⊖	⊖				
Fuel	○	⊖	⊖	⊖				
Ignition	○	○	○	○				
Auto. trans.	⊖	○	◒	◒				
Man. trans.	⊖	⊖	⊖	○				
Clutch	○	○	○	⊜	Insufficient data	Insufficient data	Insufficient data	Insufficient data
Electrical	○	○	⊖	○				
A/C	○	◒	○	⊖				
Suspension	◒	⊖	○	○				
Brakes	◒	◒	◒	◒				
Exhaust	⊖	⊖	⊜	⊜				
Body rust	○	⊜	⊜	⊖				
Paint/trim	◒	◒	○	○				
Integrity	●	◒	◒	◒				
Hardware	●	◒	◒	●				

TROUBLE SPOTS	Nissan 200SX 90	91	92	93	94	95	96	97
Engine						⊖	⊜	
Cooling						⊜	⊜	
Fuel						○	⊖	
Ignition						⊜	⊜	
Auto. trans.						*	*	
Man. trans.						*	*	
Clutch						*	*	Insufficient data
Electrical						⊖	⊖	
A/C						⊜	⊖	
Suspension						○	⊖	
Brakes						⊖	⊖	
Exhaust						⊖	⊜	
Body rust						⊜	⊜	
Paint/trim						⊖	⊖	
Integrity						⊜	⊖	
Hardware						○	○	

TROUBLE SPOTS	Nissan 240SX 90	91	92	93	94	95	96	97
Engine	○	⊖	⊖	⊖				
Cooling	⊖	⊜	⊜	⊜				
Fuel	○	○	⊖	⊜				
Ignition	○	⊖	○	⊖				
Auto. trans.	*	*	*	*				
Man. trans.	⊖	⊜	*	*				
Clutch	◒	○	*	*	Insufficient data	Insufficient data	Insufficient data	Insufficient data
Electrical	◒	○	○	⊖				
A/C	○	⊖	⊖	⊖				
Suspension	⊖	⊖	⊖	⊖				
Brakes	●	●	○	○				
Exhaust	●	◒	⊖	⊜				
Body rust	○	⊖	⊜	⊜				
Paint/trim	○	⊖	⊖	⊖				
Integrity	○	⊖	⊖	○				
Hardware	●	◒	⊖	○				

TROUBLE SPOTS	Nissan Altima 90	91	92	93	94	95	96	97
Engine				⊖	⊖	⊜	⊜	⊜
Cooling				⊜	⊜	⊜	⊜	⊜
Fuel				⊖	⊜	⊖	⊖	⊜
Ignition				⊖	⊖	⊖	⊜	⊜
Auto. trans.				⊜	⊖	⊖	⊜	⊜
Man. trans.				⊜	⊜	⊖	*	*
Clutch				○	⊜	⊜	*	*
Electrical				◒	○	○	○	⊖
A/C				○	⊖	⊖	⊜	⊜
Suspension				⊖	⊖	⊖	⊜	⊜
Brakes				◒	○	○	⊖	⊜
Exhaust				⊖	⊜	⊜	⊜	⊜
Body rust				⊜	⊜	⊜	⊜	⊜
Paint/trim				○	⊖	⊖	⊖	⊜
Integrity				⊖	⊖	○	○	⊖
Hardware				○	⊖	○	○	○

Nissan Maxima

TROUBLE SPOTS	90	91	92	93	94	95	96	97
Engine	⊖	⊖	○	⊖	⊜	⊜	⊜	⊜
Cooling	⊖	⊖	⊜	⊜	⊜	⊜	⊜	⊜
Fuel	○	○	○	⊖	⊖	⊖	⊖	⊜
Ignition	○	○	⊖	⊖	⊜	⊖	⊜	⊜
Auto. trans.	○	⊖	⊜	⊖	⊖	⊜	⊜	⊜
Man. trans.	◒	⊖	⊖	*	*	⊜	⊜	*
Clutch	◒	◒	◒	*	*	○	⊜	*
Electrical	●	◒	○	○	○	⊖	⊖	⊖
A/C	⊖	⊖	⊖	⊖	⊜	⊜	⊜	⊜
Suspension	⊖	⊖	⊖	⊖	⊜	⊜	⊜	⊜
Brakes	●	●	●	◒	○	⊖	⊜	⊜
Exhaust	◒	○	⊖	⊜	⊜	⊜	⊜	⊜
Body rust	⊖	⊖	⊖	⊜	⊜	⊜	⊜	⊜
Paint/trim	○	○	⊖	⊖	⊖	⊖	⊖	⊖
Integrity	⊖	⊖	⊖	⊖	⊖	⊖	⊖	⊜
Hardware	●	◒	◒	◒	○	⊖	⊖	⊜

Nissan Pathfinder (4WD)

TROUBLE SPOTS	90	91	92	93	94	95	96	97
Engine	⊜	⊖	⊜	⊜	⊜	⊖	⊜	⊜
Cooling	⊖	⊜	⊖	⊜	⊜	⊜	⊜	⊜
Fuel	⊖	○	○	⊜	⊖	⊜	⊖	⊜
Ignition	⊖	○	⊜	⊜	○	⊜	⊜	⊜
Auto. trans.	●	●	○	⊜	⊖	⊜	⊜	⊜
Man. trans.	*	⊜	⊜	⊜	*	○	*	*
Clutch	*	○	⊜	⊜	*	◒	*	*
Electrical	◒	◒	◒	◒	◒	○	○	⊖
A/C	○	⊖	⊖	⊖	⊖	⊜	⊜	⊜
Suspension	○	○	○	⊖	○	⊖	◒	⊜
Brakes	○	◒	◒	○	○	⊖	⊜	⊜
Exhaust	●	●	○	⊖	⊜	⊜	⊜	⊜
Body rust	○	○	○	⊜	⊖	⊜	⊜	⊜
Paint/trim	○	⊖	⊖	⊜	⊖	⊖	⊖	⊜
Integrity	○	◒	○	○	○	○	◒	⊖
Hardware	●	●	○	○	◒	○	○	⊖

Nissan Pickup (2WD)

TROUBLE SPOTS	90	91	92	93	94	95	96	97
Engine	⊜	⊜	⊖	⊖	⊖	⊖	⊜	Insufficient data
Cooling	⊖	⊖	⊜	⊜	⊜	⊜	⊜	
Fuel	⊜	⊖	⊜	⊖	⊖	⊖	⊖	
Ignition	○	○	○	⊖	⊖	⊜	⊜	
Auto. trans.	○	◒	*	⊖	⊜	⊜	*	
Man. trans.	⊖	⊖	⊜	⊜	⊜	⊖	⊜	
Clutch	●	○	○	⊖	○	◒	⊜	
Electrical	○	○	○	○	○	○	○	
A/C	○	○	⊖	⊖	⊖	⊖	⊜	
Suspension	⊖	⊖	○	⊖	○	⊖	⊖	
Brakes	○	○	○	⊖	⊜	⊜	⊜	
Exhaust	●	●	◒	⊜	⊜	⊜	⊜	
Body rust	◒	○	⊖	⊖	⊖	⊜	⊜	
Paint/trim	●	●	○	⊖	⊜	⊖	⊖	
Integrity	○	○	○	⊖	○	○	○	
Hardware	●	◒	⊜	⊖	○	○	⊖	

Nissan Quest Van

TROUBLE SPOTS	90	91	92	93	94	95	96	97
Engine				⊖	⊖	○	○	⊜
Cooling				⊖	⊖	⊜	⊜	⊜
Fuel				⊖	⊖	⊖	⊜	⊜
Ignition				⊖	⊖	⊖	⊜	⊜
Auto. trans.				⊖	⊜	⊜	⊜	⊜
Man. trans.								
Clutch								
Electrical				●	◒	●	◒	○
A/C				○	○	⊖	⊖	⊜
Suspension				○	⊖	⊖	⊖	⊖
Brakes				◒	◒	◒	⊖	⊜
Exhaust				●	⊖	⊜	⊜	⊜
Body rust				⊜	⊜	⊜	⊜	⊜
Paint/trim				⊖	⊖	⊖	⊜	⊜
Integrity				◒	○	◒	◒	○
Hardware				●	◒	●	◒	○

Nissan Sentra

TROUBLE SPOTS	90	91	92	93	94	95	96	97
Engine	◒	⊖	⊖	⊜	⊜	⊜	⊜	⊜
Cooling	⊖	⊖	⊖	⊜	⊜	⊜	⊜	⊜
Fuel	⊖	○	○	⊖	⊖	⊖	⊖	⊜
Ignition	◒	○	○	⊜	⊖	⊖	⊜	⊜
Auto. trans.	○	○	⊖	⊖	⊖	⊖	○	*
Man. trans.	⊜	⊜	⊖	⊜	⊜	⊜	⊜	*
Clutch	○	○	○	⊜	⊜	⊖	⊜	*
Electrical	○	○	○	○	○	◒	○	⊖
A/C	○	○	⊖	⊖	⊖	⊜	⊜	⊖
Suspension	○	⊖	⊖	⊖	⊜	⊜	⊜	⊜
Brakes	●	●	●	●	◒	○	⊖	⊜
Exhaust	◒	◒	⊖	⊖	⊜	⊜	⊜	⊜
Body rust	◒	⊖	⊜	⊖	⊜	⊜	⊜	⊜
Paint/trim	●	◒	○	○	⊖	○	⊜	⊜
Integrity	◒	◒	○	○	○	○	○	⊖
Hardware	●	◒	○	○	○	○	○	⊖

Nissan Stanza

TROUBLE SPOTS	90	91	92	93	94	95	96	97
Engine	○	○	⊖					
Cooling	⊖	⊖	⊜					
Fuel	○	○	○					
Ignition	○	○	○					
Auto. trans.	◒	⊖	⊖					
Man. trans.	○	⊖	*					
Clutch	●	◒	*					
Electrical	○	○	○					
A/C	◒	○	⊖					
Suspension	⊖	○	⊖					
Brakes	●	●	●					
Exhaust	◒	⊖	⊜					
Body rust	○	⊖	⊜					
Paint/trim	○	◒	○					
Integrity	◒	○	⊖					
Hardware	○	◒	○					

Oldsmobile 88

TROUBLE SPOTS	90	91	92	93	94	95	96	97
Engine	⊖	⊖	⊖	⊖	○	⊖	⊜	⊜
Cooling	◒	○	◒	◒	⊖	⊜	⊜	⊜
Fuel	○	○	⊖	⊖	⊖	⊖	⊜	⊜
Ignition	●	●	●	◒	◒	⊖	⊖	⊜
Auto. trans.	○	⊖	⊖	○	⊖	⊖	⊜	⊜
Man. trans.								
Clutch								
Electrical	●	◒	●	◒	◒	◒	○	○
A/C	●	◒	◒	○	⊖	⊖	⊜	⊜
Suspension	○	○	○	⊖	⊖	⊖	⊖	⊖
Brakes	●	●	●	●	○	○	⊜	⊖
Exhaust	⊖	⊜	⊜	⊖	⊜	⊖	⊜	⊜
Body rust	○	⊖	⊜	⊜	⊜	⊜	⊜	⊜
Paint/trim	◒	◒	○	⊖	○	⊖	⊜	⊖
Integrity	○	⊖	○	○	◒	◒	◒	○
Hardware	○	●	◒	◒	●	●	○	⊖

Oldsmobile 98

TROUBLE SPOTS	90	91	92	93	94	95	96	97
Engine	⊖	⊜	○	⊜	○	⊖	⊖	
Cooling	○	○	◒	○	⊖	⊜	⊜	
Fuel	◒	⊖	⊖	⊜	⊖	⊖	⊜	
Ignition	●	●	●	◒	◒	⊖	⊖	
Auto. trans.	⊖	⊖	⊖	⊜	⊖	⊖	⊜	
Man. trans.								
Clutch								
Electrical	●	●	●	●	●	●	◒	
A/C	◒	●	●	○	○	○	⊖	
Suspension	○	⊖	○	⊖	⊖	⊖	⊖	
Brakes	●	●	●	●	○	○	⊖	
Exhaust	⊖	⊜	⊖	⊖	⊜	⊜	⊜	
Body rust	⊜	⊜	⊜	⊜	⊜	⊜	⊜	
Paint/trim	○	⊖	○	⊜	⊖	⊖	⊜	
Integrity	○	○	◒	◒	○	○	○	
Hardware	◒	●	●	◒	●	●	○	

⊜ ⊖ ○ ◒ ●
Few ◄— **Problems** —► Many

* Insufficient data

Oldsmobile Achieva

TROUBLE SPOTS	90	91	92	93	94	95	96	97
Engine			◒	○	⊖	Insufficient data	Insufficient data	Insufficient data
Cooling			◒	○	⊖			
Fuel			⊖	○	⊜			
Ignition			◒	○	⊖			
Auto. trans.			⊜	○	⊖			
Man. trans.			*	*	*			
Clutch			*	*	*			
Electrical			◒	●	◒			
A/C			⊖	⊜	⊖			
Suspension			○	◒	⊜			
Brakes			●	●	●			
Exhaust			⊜	⊖	⊜			
Body rust			⊜	⊜	⊜			
Paint/trim			●	○	○			
Integrity			◒	●	◒			
Hardware			●	●	●			

Oldsmobile Aurora

TROUBLE SPOTS	90	91	92	93	94	95	96	97
Engine						⊖	⊖	⊜
Cooling						⊖	⊜	⊜
Fuel						⊖	⊖	⊜
Ignition						⊖	⊜	⊜
Auto. trans.						⊖	⊜	⊖
Man. trans.								
Clutch								
Electrical						◒	◒	●
A/C						○	⊖	⊖
Suspension						⊖	⊖	⊜
Brakes						⊖	⊖	⊖
Exhaust						⊜	⊜	⊜
Body rust						⊜	⊜	⊖
Paint/trim						⊖	⊖	⊖
Integrity						◒	◒	⊖
Hardware						●	⊖	⊖

Oldsmobile Bravada

TROUBLE SPOTS	90	91	92	93	94	95	96	97
Engine		Insufficient data	Insufficient data	Insufficient data	⊖		⊜	Insufficient data
Cooling					⊖		⊜	
Fuel					◒		⊖	
Ignition					○		⊜	
Auto. trans.					⊖		⊜	
Man. trans.								
Clutch								
Electrical					◒		⊜	
A/C					⊜		⊜	
Suspension					◒		⊜	
Brakes					●		○	
Exhaust					⊜		⊜	
Body rust					⊜		⊜	
Paint/trim					○		⊜	
Integrity					◒		⊖	
Hardware					⊖		⊜	

Oldsmobile Cutlass

TROUBLE SPOTS	90	91	92	93	94	95	96	97
Engine								⊜
Cooling								⊜
Fuel								⊜
Ignition								⊜
Auto. trans.								⊜
Man. trans.								
Clutch								
Electrical								○
A/C								⊖
Suspension								⊖
Brakes								○
Exhaust								⊜
Body rust								⊜
Paint/trim								⊖
Integrity								○
Hardware								⊜

Oldsmobile Cutlass Ciera

TROUBLE SPOTS	90	91	92	93	94	95	96	97
Engine	○	⊖	⊖	⊖	⊖	⊖	⊜	
Cooling	◒	●	◒	○	⊖	⊜	⊜	
Fuel	○	○	⊖	○	⊖	⊜	⊜	
Ignition	◒	◒	◒	○	⊖	⊜	⊜	
Auto. trans.	⊖	⊖	⊖	⊜	⊖	⊜	⊖	
Man. trans.								
Clutch								
Electrical	○	◒	⊖	○	○	○	○	
A/C	○	○	⊖	○	⊖	⊖	⊖	
Suspension	○	○	○	○	⊖	○	⊖	
Brakes	●	●	●	●	●	◒	○	
Exhaust	●	●	●	◒	○	⊜	⊜	
Body rust	◒	○	○	⊖	⊖	⊜	⊜	
Paint/trim	◒	◒	○	⊖	⊖	⊖	⊖	
Integrity	◒	◒	○	○	◒	○	○	
Hardware	◒	◒	○	○	◒	○	○	

Oldsmobile Cutlass Supreme

TROUBLE SPOTS	90	91	92	93	94	95	96	97
Engine	◒	○	⊖	⊖	○	⊖	⊖	⊜
Cooling	◒	○	○	⊖	⊜	⊖	⊜	⊜
Fuel	○	○	⊖	○	⊖	⊜	⊖	⊖
Ignition	●	●	●	●	◒	⊖	⊖	⊜
Auto. trans.	○	○	○	⊖	○	⊖	⊖	⊜
Man. trans.	*	*	*					
Clutch	*	*	*					
Electrical	●	●	●	◒	●	◒	○	○
A/C	●	◒	◒	○	⊖	⊖	⊜	⊖
Suspension	○	◒	○	⊖	⊖	⊖	⊖	⊜
Brakes	●	●	●	●	●	◒	○	⊜
Exhaust	○	⊖	⊖	⊜	⊜	⊜	⊜	⊜
Body rust	⊖	⊖	⊜	⊜	⊜	⊜	⊖	⊜
Paint/trim	●	●	○	○	○	◒	○	⊖
Integrity	◒	◒	◒	◒	◒	◒	◒	◒
Hardware	●	●	●	●	●	●	◒	⊖

Oldsmobile Silhouette Van (ext.)

TROUBLE SPOTS	90	91	92	93	94	95	96	97
Engine								⊜
Cooling								⊜
Fuel								⊖
Ignition								⊖
Auto. trans.								⊜
Man. trans.								
Clutch								
Electrical								○
A/C								⊖
Suspension								⊖
Brakes								⊖
Exhaust								⊖
Body rust								⊜
Paint/trim								○
Integrity								◒
Hardware								●

Oldsmobile Silhouette Van (reg.)

TROUBLE SPOTS	90	91	92	93	94	95	96	97
Engine	⊖	○	⊖	⊖	⊖	⊖	⊜	⊜
Cooling	●	●	●	○	⊖	⊖	⊜	⊜
Fuel	⊖	⊖	⊖	○	⊖	⊜	⊖	⊖
Ignition	●	◒	◒	●	○	⊖	⊜	⊖
Auto. trans.	⊖	○	○	○	⊖	⊜	⊖	⊜
Man. trans.								
Clutch								
Electrical	●	●	●	◒	○	◒	○	○
A/C	◒	◒	○	○	⊖	⊖	⊖	⊖
Suspension	○	◒	◒	○	⊖	⊖	⊖	⊖
Brakes	●	●	●	●	◒	○	⊖	⊖
Exhaust	◒	⊜	⊖	⊖	⊜	⊜	⊜	⊖
Body rust	⊜	⊜	⊜	⊖	⊜	⊜	⊜	⊜
Paint/trim	●	●	○	○	⊖	○	○	○
Integrity	●	◒	○	◒	◒	◒	●	◒
Hardware	●	●	●	●	●	●	◒	●

Plymouth Acclaim

Trouble spots	90	91	92	93	94	95	96	97
Engine	◒	◒	◒	○	⊖	○		
Cooling	●	○	○	○	⊖	⊖		
Fuel	○	○	○	○	○	⊖		
Ignition	◒	○	○	⊖	⊖	⊖		
Auto. trans.	●	◒	○	◒	◒	⊖		
Man. trans.	*	*	*	*	*	*		
Clutch	*	*	*	*	*	*		
Electrical	◒	○	◒	○	○	○		
A/C	◒	◒	○	●	◒	○		
Suspension	◒	○	○	○	⊖	⊖		
Brakes	●	◒	◒	○	⊖	⊖		
Exhaust	⊖	●	●	⊜	⊜	⊜		
Body rust	○	⊖	⊖	⊖	⊖	⊜		
Paint/trim	◒	◒	○	⊖	○	○		
Integrity	○	○	○	○	○	◒		
Hardware	◒	○	○	○	○	◒		

Plymouth Breeze

Trouble spots	90	91	92	93	94	95	96	97
Engine							⊜	
Cooling							⊜	
Fuel							⊜	
Ignition							⊖	
Auto. trans.							*	
Man. trans.							*	
Clutch							*	
Electrical							○	Insufficient data
A/C							⊜	
Suspension							⊖	
Brakes							○	
Exhaust							⊜	
Body rust							⊜	
Paint/trim							⊖	
Integrity							◒	
Hardware							○	

Plymouth Grand Voyager Van V6

Trouble spots	90	91	92	93	94	95	96	97
Engine	◒	○	◒	○	⊖	⊜	⊜	⊜
Cooling	●	◒	○	○	⊖	⊖	⊖	⊜
Fuel	◒	○	○	○	⊜	⊖	○	⊜
Ignition	◒	◒	◒	○	⊖	⊖	⊜	⊜
Auto. trans.	●	●	●	●	●	○	⊖	⊜
Man. trans.								
Clutch								
Electrical	◒	●	●	◒	◒	○	◒	○
A/C	●	○	○	●	○	⊖	⊖	⊜
Suspension	◒	◒	◒	○	○	○	⊖	⊜
Brakes	●	●	●	●	◒	○	◒	⊖
Exhaust	⊖	●	◒	⊜	⊜	⊜	⊜	⊜
Body rust	○	⊖	⊖	⊜	⊜	⊜	⊜	⊜
Paint/trim	●	◒	○	○	○	⊖	⊖	⊖
Integrity	●	◒	◒	◒	◒	◒	◒	○
Hardware	●	●	●	●	●	●	◒	○

Plymouth Laser

Trouble spots	90	91	92	93	94	95	96	97
Engine	●	◒	◒	○	◒			
Cooling	○	○	⊖	○	⊖			
Fuel	⊜	○	○	⊖	⊜			
Ignition	○	◒	◒	○	⊖			
Auto. trans.	○	◒	◒	*	*			
Man. trans.	○	○	○	○	*			
Clutch	○	○	○	○	*			
Electrical	◒	◒	◒	◒	○			
A/C	○	⊖	⊜	○	○			
Suspension	○	⊖	⊖	⊖	⊖			
Brakes	◒	◒	◒	◒	○			
Exhaust	⊖	⊖	○	⊖	⊜			
Body rust	⊜	⊖	⊖	⊖	⊖			
Paint/trim	◒	◒	●	○	◒			
Integrity	◒	◒	◒	◒	●			
Hardware	●	●	●	◒	●			

Plymouth Neon

Trouble spots	90	91	92	93	94	95	96	97
Engine						○	⊖	⊜
Cooling						⊜	⊖	⊜
Fuel						○	⊖	⊜
Ignition						○	⊖	⊜
Auto. trans.						⊖	⊖	⊜
Man. trans.						⊖	⊜	*
Clutch						⊜	⊜	*
Electrical						◒	◒	⊜
A/C						○	⊖	⊖
Suspension						⊖	⊖	⊜
Brakes						●	○	⊜
Exhaust						⊖	⊜	⊜
Body rust						⊜	⊜	⊜
Paint/trim						○	⊖	⊜
Integrity						●	◒	○
Hardware						◒	◒	⊜

Plymouth Sundance

Trouble spots	90	91	92	93	94	95	96	97
Engine	●	◒	◒	○	⊖			
Cooling	●	◒	○	⊖	⊖			
Fuel	◒	◒	◒	⊖	○			
Ignition	●	○	◒	○	⊖			
Auto. trans.	○	○	○	○	○			
Man. trans.	*	*	*	*	*			
Clutch	*	*	*	*	*			
Electrical	●	●	◒	◒	◒			
A/C	●	●	◒	●	◒			
Suspension	○	○	○	⊖	⊖			
Brakes	●	●	◒	○	○			
Exhaust	⊖	●	●	⊜	⊖			
Body rust	◒	○	○	○	⊖			
Paint/trim	●	●	●	◒	○			
Integrity	◒	●	◒	◒	●			
Hardware	◒	◒	○	○	◒			

Plymouth Voyager Van V6

Trouble spots	90	91	92	93	94	95	96	97
Engine	●	◒	◒	○	⊖	⊖	⊖	⊜
Cooling	◒	◒	○	○	⊖	⊜	⊜	⊜
Fuel	◒	○	○	⊖	⊖	⊖	○	⊜
Ignition	○	○	○	○	⊖	⊜	⊜	⊜
Auto. trans.	●	●	●	◒	◒	○	⊖	⊜
Man. trans.								
Clutch								
Electrical	◒	◒	●	◒	○	○	○	⊖
A/C	◒	○	○	●	○	⊖	⊖	⊜
Suspension	○	○	○	○	○	⊖	⊖	⊜
Brakes	●	●	●	●	◒	○	◒	⊖
Exhaust	⊖	●	◒	⊜	⊜	⊖	⊜	⊜
Body rust	○	⊖	⊖	⊜	⊜	⊜	⊜	⊜
Paint/trim	●	◒	○	⊖	⊖	⊖	⊖	⊜
Integrity	●	●	◒	◒	◒	◒	○	○
Hardware	●	●	◒	◒	◒	◒	◒	○

Pontiac Bonneville

Trouble spots	90	91	92	93	94	95	96	97
Engine	⊖	⊖	⊖	⊖	⊖	⊖	⊜	⊜
Cooling	◒	○	○	◒	⊖	⊜	⊜	⊜
Fuel	◒	○	⊖	⊖	⊖	⊖	⊜	⊜
Ignition	●	●	●	◒	◒	⊖	⊜	⊜
Auto. trans.	⊖	⊖	⊖	⊖	⊖	⊖	⊜	⊜
Man. trans.								
Clutch								
Electrical	●	●	●	●	◒	◒	◒	○
A/C	◒	◒	◒	○	○	⊖	⊜	⊜
Suspension	○	○	○	⊖	⊖	⊖	⊖	⊖
Brakes	●	●	●	●	○	⊖	⊖	⊜
Exhaust	⊜	⊜	⊖	⊖	⊜	⊖	⊖	⊜
Body rust	○	○	⊜	⊜	⊖	⊖	⊜	⊜
Paint/trim	◒	○	◒	⊖	⊖	⊖	⊖	⊜
Integrity	○	○	◒	○	◒	◒	◒	○
Hardware	◒	●	●	●	●	◒	○	⊖

⊜ ⊖ ○ ◒ ●

Few ◄— Problems —► Many

*

Insufficient data

Trouble Spots	Pontiac Firebird V8 90	91	92	93	94	95	96	97
Engine	Insufficient data	○	Insufficient data	Insufficient data	○	◒	◒	Insufficient data
Cooling		◒			○	⊖	⊜	
Fuel		●			⊖	⊖	⊖	
Ignition		●			◒	○	⊜	
Auto. trans.		*			⊜	⊜	*	
Man. trans.		*			*	*	*	
Clutch		*			*	*	*	
Electrical		◒			◒	●	◒	
A/C		○			⊖	○	⊜	
Suspension		○			⊖	⊖	⊖	
Brakes		◒			◒	○	⊖	
Exhaust		◒			⊜	⊖	⊜	
Body rust		⊜			⊜	⊜	⊜	
Paint/trim		●			⊖	⊖	○	
Integrity		●			●	●	◒	
Hardware		●			●	◒	◒	

Trouble Spots	Pontiac Grand Am 90	91	92	93	94	95	96	97
Engine	●	●	◒	○	⊖	⊖	⊖	⊜
Cooling	●	◒	●	◒	⊖	⊜	⊜	⊜
Fuel	◒	○	○	○	⊖	⊜	⊖	⊜
Ignition	●	●	◒	○	○	⊖	⊜	⊜
Auto. trans.	◒	○	⊖	⊖	⊖	⊖	⊖	⊜
Man. trans.	*	*	*	*	*	*	*	*
Clutch	*	*	*	*	*	*	*	*
Electrical	◒	○	●	●	◒	◒	◒	⊖
A/C	○	◒	○	○	⊖	⊖	⊜	⊜
Suspension	◒	◒	○	○	○	⊖	⊖	⊖
Brakes	●	●	●	●	●	●	○	⊜
Exhaust	●	●	⊖	⊜	⊜	⊜	⊜	⊜
Body rust	●	●	⊖	⊖	⊜	⊜	⊜	⊜
Paint/trim	●	●	◒	◒	⊖	⊖	⊖	⊖
Integrity	●	●	●	●	◒	◒	◒	⊖
Hardware	●	●	●	●	◒	●	◒	⊖

Trouble Spots	Pontiac Grand Prix 90	91	92	93	94	95	96	97
Engine	◒	◒	○	○	○	⊖	⊖	⊜
Cooling	◒	●	◒	○	⊖	⊖	⊜	⊜
Fuel	◒	◒	○	⊖	⊖	⊜	⊖	⊜
Ignition	●	●	●	●	○	⊖	⊖	⊜
Auto. trans.	◒	○	⊖	○	⊖	○	⊖	⊜
Man. trans.	*	*	*	*				
Clutch	*	*	*	*				
Electrical	●	●	●	◒	●	◒	◒	⊖
A/C	◒	●	○	⊖	⊖	⊖	⊖	⊜
Suspension	◒	○	⊖	⊖	⊖	⊖	⊖	⊜
Brakes	●	●	●	●	●	●	○	⊜
Exhaust	⊖	⊜	⊜	⊜	⊜	⊜	⊜	⊜
Body rust	○	⊖	⊖	⊖	⊜	⊜	⊜	⊜
Paint/trim	●	◒	○	○	⊖	○	○	⊜
Integrity	◒	◒	◒	◒	◒	◒	●	○
Hardware	●	●	●	●	●	◒	◒	⊖

Trouble Spots	Pontiac Sunbird 90	91	92	93	94	95	96	97
Engine	◒	◒	○	○	○			
Cooling	●	●	◒	○	○			
Fuel	○	○	⊖	⊖	⊖			
Ignition	●	●	●	◒	◒			
Auto. trans.	⊖	⊖	⊖	⊖	⊖			
Man. trans.	*	⊖	*	*	*			
Clutch	*	⊖	*	*	*			
Electrical	◒	●	◒	◒	◒			
A/C	●	◒	○	○	○			
Suspension	◒	○	○	○	⊖			
Brakes	●	●	●	●	●			
Exhaust	◒	○	⊖	⊖	⊖			
Body rust	●	◒	◒	○	○			
Paint/trim	●	●	◒	○	○			
Integrity	●	●	◒	◒	●			
Hardware	◒	◒	●	◒	◒			

Trouble Spots	Pontiac Sunfire 90	91	92	93	94	95	96	97
Engine						○	⊖	⊜
Cooling						⊖	⊖	⊜
Fuel						⊖	⊖	⊜
Ignition						⊖	⊖	⊖
Auto. trans.						⊖	⊖	⊜
Man. trans.						*	⊖	⊖
Clutch						*	○	⊜
Electrical						◒	◒	⊖
A/C						⊜	⊜	⊜
Suspension						⊖	⊖	⊖
Brakes						◒	○	⊖
Exhaust						⊖	⊖	⊜
Body rust						⊜	⊜	⊜
Paint/trim						⊖	⊖	⊜
Integrity						◒	●	○
Hardware						◒	○	⊖

Trouble Spots	Pontiac Trans Sport Van (ext.) 90	91	92	93	94	95	96	97
Engine								⊜
Cooling								⊜
Fuel								⊖
Ignition								⊖
Auto. trans.								⊜
Man. trans.								
Clutch								
Electrical								○
A/C								⊖
Suspension								⊖
Brakes								⊖
Exhaust								⊖
Body rust								⊜
Paint/trim								○
Integrity								◒
Hardware								●

Trouble Spots	Pontiac Trans Sport Van (reg.) 90	91	92	93	94	95	96	97
Engine	⊖	○	⊖	⊖	⊖	⊖	⊜	⊜
Cooling	●	●	●	○	⊖	⊖	⊜	⊜
Fuel	⊖	⊖	⊖	○	⊖	⊜	⊖	⊖
Ignition	●	◒	◒	●	○	⊖	⊜	⊖
Auto. trans.	⊖	○	○	○	⊖	⊜	⊖	⊜
Man. trans.								
Clutch								
Electrical	●	●	●	◒	○	◒	○	○
A/C	◒	◒	○	○	⊖	⊖	⊖	⊖
Suspension	○	◒	◒	○	⊖	⊖	⊖	⊖
Brakes	●	●	●	●	◒	○	⊖	⊖
Exhaust	◒	⊜	⊖	⊖	⊜	⊜	⊜	⊖
Body rust	⊜	⊜	⊜	⊖	⊜	⊜	⊜	⊜
Paint/trim	●	●	○	○	⊖	○	○	○
Integrity	●	◒	○	◒	◒	◒	●	◒
Hardware	●	●	●	●	●	●	◒	●

Trouble Spots	Saab 900 90	91	92	93	94	95	96	97
Engine	◒	◒	◒	Insufficient data	◒	⊖	⊖	Insufficient data
Cooling	●	●	◒		◒	○	⊜	
Fuel	○	⊖	⊖		⊖	⊖	⊜	
Ignition	○	○	○		○	○	⊖	
Auto. trans.	*	*	*		○	⊖	⊜	
Man. trans.	*	*	*		○	⊖	⊜	
Clutch	*	*	*		○	⊖	⊜	
Electrical	●	●	◒		◒	●	◒	
A/C	●	●	◒		○	○	⊖	
Suspension	○	⊖	⊖		○	○	⊖	
Brakes	◒	●	◒		○	○	⊖	
Exhaust	●	●	○		○	⊖	⊜	
Body rust	⊖	⊜	⊜		⊜	⊜	⊜	
Paint/trim	○	○	○		⊖	⊖	⊜	
Integrity	○	◒	◒		○	◒	○	
Hardware	◒	○	◒		◒	◒	◒	

Saab 9000

Trouble spots	90	91	92	93	94	95	96	97
Engine	Insufficient data	●	●	◒	Insufficient data	○	Insufficient data	Insufficient data
Cooling		●	●	◒		◒		
Fuel		○	○	○		⊖		
Ignition		○	◒	●		⊖		
Auto. trans.		*	*	*		*		
Man. trans.		*	*	*		*		
Clutch		*	*	*		*		
Electrical		●	●	●		●		
A/C		◒	○	⊖		⊖		
Suspension		○	⊜	⊖		⊖		
Brakes		◒	○	◒		⊜		
Exhaust		●	◒	◒		⊜		
Body rust		⊖	⊖	⊜		⊜		
Paint/trim		⊖	⊖	⊖		⊜		
Integrity		◒	○	⊖		○		
Hardware		◒	○	○		○		

Saturn SC Coupe

Trouble spots	90	91	92	93	94	95	96	97
Engine		Insufficient data	◒	○	○	⊖	⊜	⊜
Cooling			○	○	⊖	⊜	⊜	⊜
Fuel			⊖	⊜	⊖	⊜	⊖	⊖
Ignition			◒	○	○	⊖	⊖	⊜
Auto. trans.			⊜	○	⊖	○	⊜	⊜
Man. trans.			⊜	⊜	⊜	⊜	⊜	⊜
Clutch			⊖	○	⊖	⊜	⊜	⊜
Electrical			◒	○	○	○	○	⊜
A/C			○	⊜	⊜	⊜	⊜	⊜
Suspension			⊖	⊖	⊜	⊜	⊜	⊖
Brakes			◒	◒	◒	◒	⊖	⊜
Exhaust			⊜	⊖	⊜	⊜	⊜	⊜
Body rust			⊜	⊜	⊜	⊜	⊜	⊜
Paint/trim			⊖	○	⊖	⊖	⊖	⊜
Integrity			◒	◒	○	◒	○	⊖
Hardware			●	◒	◒	◒	○	⊖

Saturn SL Sedan, SW Wagon

Trouble spots	90	91	92	93	94	95	96	97
Engine		◒	◒	○	○	⊖	⊜	⊜
Cooling		○	⊖	⊖	⊜	⊜	⊜	⊜
Fuel		○	⊖	⊖	⊖	⊖	⊖	⊜
Ignition		◒	◒	○	○	⊖	⊖	⊜
Auto. trans.		○	⊖	⊖	○	⊖	⊜	⊜
Man. trans.		⊜	⊜	⊜	⊜	⊖	⊜	⊜
Clutch		⊖	⊖	⊖	⊖	⊜	⊜	⊜
Electrical		○	○	⊖	⊖	○	○	⊖
A/C		○	○	⊖	⊜	⊜	⊜	⊜
Suspension		⊖	⊜	⊖	⊜	⊜	⊜	⊜
Brakes		●	◒	●	◒	◒	○	⊜
Exhaust		⊖	⊖	⊜	⊜	⊜	⊜	⊜
Body rust		⊖	⊜	⊜	⊜	⊜	⊜	⊜
Paint/trim		○	⊖	⊜	⊜	⊜	⊜	⊜
Integrity		◒	◒	◒	○	◒	○	⊖
Hardware		●	●	◒	○	⊖	○	⊖

Subaru Impreza

Trouble spots	90	91	92	93	94	95	96	97
Engine				⊜	Insufficient data	⊜	⊜	⊜
Cooling				⊜		⊜	⊜	⊜
Fuel				⊜		⊖	⊜	⊜
Ignition				⊖		⊖	⊜	⊜
Auto. trans.				⊖		⊜	⊜	⊜
Man. trans.				⊜		*	⊜	*
Clutch				⊖		*	⊜	*
Electrical				⊖		⊖	⊖	⊖
A/C				⊖		⊜	⊜	⊜
Suspension				⊖		⊜	⊜	⊜
Brakes				○		⊜	⊖	⊖
Exhaust				⊜		⊜	⊜	⊜
Body rust				⊜		⊜	⊜	⊜
Paint/trim				⊜		⊜	⊖	⊜
Integrity				⊖		○	○	⊖
Hardware				⊖		⊖	⊜	⊖

Subaru Legacy

Trouble spots	90	91	92	93	94	95	96	97
Engine	⊖	⊖	⊖	⊖	⊜	⊜	⊜	⊜
Cooling	○	⊖	⊜	⊜	⊜	⊜	⊜	⊜
Fuel	⊖	⊖	⊜	⊜	⊖	⊖	⊜	⊜
Ignition	⊖	⊖	⊖	⊖	⊖	○	⊜	⊜
Auto. trans.	○	○	⊜	⊜	⊜	⊜	⊜	⊜
Man. trans.	⊖	⊖	⊜	⊜	⊜	⊜	⊜	⊜
Clutch	◒	○	○	○	○	⊖	⊖	⊜
Electrical	○	○	⊖	⊖	○	○	⊖	⊖
A/C	◒	○	○	⊜	⊜	⊜	⊜	⊜
Suspension	○	◒	⊖	⊖	⊖	⊜	⊜	⊜
Brakes	●	●	●	◒	○	⊖	⊖	⊜
Exhaust	⊖	⊖	⊜	⊜	⊜	⊜	⊜	⊜
Body rust	◒	⊖	⊖	⊜	⊜	⊜	⊜	⊜
Paint/trim	○	○	○	⊖	⊖	⊜	⊖	⊜
Integrity	◒	○	○	○	⊖	⊜	⊖	⊜
Hardware	●	●	◒	○	○	⊖	○	⊖

Subaru Loyale

Trouble spots	90	91	92	93	94	95	96	97
Engine	●	●	●	◒	Insufficient data			
Cooling	●	◒	○	○				
Fuel	○	⊖	⊖	○				
Ignition	○	⊖	⊖	⊖				
Auto. trans.	*	*	○	*				
Man. trans.	*	⊜	⊜	*				
Clutch	*	◒	◒	*				
Electrical	◒	○	◒	⊖				
A/C	●	⊖	○	⊖				
Suspension	○	⊖	⊖	⊖				
Brakes	●	◒	◒	○				
Exhaust	●	●	◒	⊖				
Body rust	●	◒	○	⊖				
Paint/trim	●	⊖	○	⊖				
Integrity	●	○	◒	○				
Hardware	◒	◒	○	○				

Suzuki Sidekick

Trouble spots	90	91	92	93	94	95	96	97
Engine	○	⊖	⊜	⊖	⊖	⊜	⊖	Insufficient data
Cooling	⊖	⊖	⊖	⊖	⊖	⊜	⊜	
Fuel	◒	⊖	⊖	⊜	⊖	⊖	⊜	
Ignition	○	○	○	○	○	○	⊜	
Auto. trans.	*	*	*	*	*	⊜	⊖	
Man. trans.	*	*	*	*	⊜	⊖	⊜	
Clutch	*	*	*	*	⊖	⊖	⊜	
Electrical	◒	◒	◒	○	○	○	○	
A/C	*	*	*	○	⊖	⊖	⊖	
Suspension	⊖	⊜	○	⊖	⊜	⊜	⊜	
Brakes	●	●	●	○	○	⊖	○	
Exhaust	●	●	◒	○	⊜	⊜	⊜	
Body rust	◒	⊖	⊜	⊖	⊜	⊖	⊜	
Paint/trim	○	⊖	○	⊜	⊜	⊖	⊖	
Integrity	◒	◒	◒	◒	●	◒	○	
Hardware	●	◒	●	○	◒	◒	○	

Suzuki Swift

Trouble spots	90	91	92	93	94	95	96	97
Engine	○	○	○	⊖	⊖	⊜	⊜	Insufficient data
Cooling	⊖	⊖	⊖	⊜	⊜	⊜	⊜	
Fuel	○	⊖	⊖	⊜	⊜	⊖	⊜	
Ignition	○	○	◒	⊖	⊖	⊜	⊖	
Auto. trans.	*	*	⊖	*	*	*	*	
Man. trans.	⊖	○	⊖	⊜	⊜	⊖	*	
Clutch	⊖	⊖	⊖	⊖	⊜	⊜	*	
Electrical	○	○	◒	◒	○	◒	○	
A/C	●	●	⊖	○	○	●	○	
Suspension	○	⊖	⊖	⊖	⊖	⊖	⊜	
Brakes	●	◒	◒	○	○	⊖	⊜	
Exhaust	●	●	●	◒	⊖	⊜	⊜	
Body rust	○	○	⊜	⊜	⊜	⊜	⊜	
Paint/trim	◒	○	⊖	⊖	⊜	⊖	⊖	
Integrity	●	●	●	○	○	○	⊖	
Hardware	●	●	●	●	◒	◒	○	

⊜ ⊖ ○ ◒ ●
Few ◄— Problems —► Many

* Insufficient data

Toyota 4Runner (2WD)

Trouble spots	90	91	92	93	94	95	96	97
Engine	Insufficient data	Insufficient data	Insufficient data	Insufficient data	Insufficient data	Insufficient data	⊖	⊜
Cooling							⊜	⊜
Fuel							⊜	⊜
Ignition							⊜	⊜
Auto. trans.							⊜	⊜
Man. trans.							★	★
Clutch							★	★
Electrical							⊖	⊜
A/C							⊜	⊜
Suspension							⊖	⊜
Brakes							⊖	⊜
Exhaust							⊜	⊜
Body rust							⊜	⊜
Paint/trim							⊜	⊜
Integrity							⊖	⊖
Hardware							⊖	⊖

Toyota 4Runner (4WD)

Trouble spots	90	91	92	93	94	95	96	97
Engine	◒	●	●	◒	⊖	⊖	◒	⊜
Cooling	○	○	◒	⊖	⊖	⊜	⊖	⊜
Fuel	⊜	⊜	⊖	⊜	⊜	⊜	⊜	⊜
Ignition	○	⊖	⊖	⊖	⊜	⊖	⊜	⊜
Auto. trans.	⊖	⊖	⊖	⊜	⊜	⊜	⊜	⊜
Man. trans.	⊖	⊖	⊜	⊜	⊜	⊜	⊜	★
Clutch	◒	◒	○	○	○	⊖	⊜	★
Electrical	◒	◒	⊖	⊖	⊖	⊖	⊖	⊜
A/C	●	◒	○	⊜	⊜	⊜	⊜	⊜
Suspension	⊖	○	⊖	⊖	⊖	⊖	⊖	⊜
Brakes	◒	◒	○	◒	○	⊖	⊜	⊜
Exhaust	◒	○	○	⊖	⊜	⊜	⊜	⊜
Body rust	○	⊖	○	⊖	⊜	⊜	⊜	⊜
Paint/trim	⊖	⊖	⊜	⊖	⊖	⊖	⊜	⊜
Integrity	○	○	⊖	⊖	⊖	○	⊖	⊖
Hardware	◒	◒	○	⊖	⊖	⊖	⊖	⊜

Toyota Avalon

Trouble spots	90	91	92	93	94	95	96	97
Engine						⊜	⊜	⊜
Cooling						⊜	⊜	⊜
Fuel						⊜	⊜	⊜
Ignition						⊜	⊜	⊜
Auto. trans.						⊜	⊜	⊜
Man. trans.								
Clutch								
Electrical						○	○	⊜
A/C						⊜	⊜	⊜
Suspension						⊜	⊖	⊜
Brakes						⊖	⊖	⊜
Exhaust						⊜	⊜	⊜
Body rust						⊜	⊜	⊜
Paint/trim						⊜	⊖	⊜
Integrity						●	◒	⊖
Hardware						○	○	⊖

Toyota Camry

Trouble spots	90	91	92	93	94	95	96	97
Engine	○	⊖	⊖	⊜	⊜	⊜	⊜	⊜
Cooling	⊖	⊖	⊖	⊜	⊜	⊜	⊜	⊜
Fuel	⊖	⊜	⊜	⊜	⊜	⊜	⊜	⊜
Ignition	○	○	⊖	⊜	⊜	⊜	⊜	⊜
Auto. trans.	⊖	⊖	⊜	⊜	⊜	⊜	⊜	⊜
Man. trans.	⊖	⊜	⊜	⊜	⊜	⊜	⊜	★
Clutch	○	⊖	⊖	⊜	⊜	⊜	⊜	★
Electrical	○	◒	○	⊖	⊖	⊖	⊖	⊜
A/C	⊖	⊖	○	⊜	⊜	⊜	⊜	⊜
Suspension	⊖	⊖	⊖	⊖	⊖	⊖	⊜	⊜
Brakes	◒	●	○	○	⊖	⊖	⊖	⊜
Exhaust	●	⊖	⊖	⊜	⊜	⊜	⊜	⊜
Body rust	◒	○	⊜	⊜	⊜	⊜	⊜	⊜
Paint/trim	○	⊖	⊖	⊖	⊖	⊜	⊜	⊜
Integrity	○	⊖	⊖	⊖	⊖	⊖	⊖	⊖
Hardware	○	○	○	○	⊖	⊖	⊖	⊖

Toyota Celica

Trouble spots	90	91	92	93	94	95	96	97
Engine	⊖	⊖	⊖	⊖	⊜	⊜	⊜	Insufficient data
Cooling	○	⊜	⊖	⊜	⊜	⊜	⊜	
Fuel	⊖	⊜	⊜	⊜	⊜	⊜	⊜	
Ignition	○	⊖	⊖	⊖	⊜	⊖	⊜	
Auto. trans.	⊜	⊖	⊜	★	⊜	★	★	
Man. trans.	⊜	⊜	⊜	★	⊜	★	★	
Clutch	○	⊜	○	★	⊜	★	★	
Electrical	◒	◒	○	○	⊜	○	⊜	
A/C	●	●	◒	⊖	⊜	⊖	⊜	
Suspension	⊖	⊖	⊜	⊜	⊖	⊜	⊖	
Brakes	○	○	○	○	⊜	⊖	⊖	
Exhaust	⊖	⊖	⊜	⊜	⊜	⊜	⊜	
Body rust	⊖	⊜	⊜	⊜	⊜	⊜	⊜	
Paint/trim	○	○	○	⊖	⊜	⊖	⊜	
Integrity	○	○	○	○	⊖	○	⊖	
Hardware	○	○	◒	◒	○	○	⊖	

Toyota Corolla

Trouble spots	90	91	92	93	94	95	96	97
Engine	⊖	⊖	⊖	⊜	⊜	⊜	⊜	⊜
Cooling	○	○	⊖	⊜	⊜	⊜	⊜	⊜
Fuel	⊖	⊜	⊜	⊜	⊜	⊜	⊜	⊜
Ignition	○	◒	◒	○	⊖	⊜	⊜	⊜
Auto. trans.	⊖	⊖	⊜	⊜	⊜	⊜	⊜	⊜
Man. trans.	⊜	⊜	⊜	⊜	⊜	⊜	⊜	★
Clutch	⊖	○	○	⊜	⊜	⊜	⊜	★
Electrical	○	◒	○	○	○	○	⊖	⊖
A/C	○	⊖	⊖	⊖	⊜	⊜	⊜	⊜
Suspension	⊖	⊖	⊖	⊜	⊜	⊖	⊜	⊜
Brakes	◒	◒	○	○	⊖	⊖	⊜	⊜
Exhaust	●	●	●	⊜	⊜	⊜	⊜	⊜
Body rust	○	○	⊖	⊜	⊜	⊜	⊜	⊜
Paint/trim	○	⊖	⊖	⊖	⊖	⊖	⊜	⊜
Integrity	○	○	○	○	⊖	⊖	⊖	⊖
Hardware	◒	◒	◒	◒	◒	○	⊖	⊖

Toyota Cressida

Trouble spots	90	91	92	93	94	95	96	97
Engine	●	◒	Insufficient data					
Cooling	◒	◒						
Fuel	⊖	⊖						
Ignition	○	◒						
Auto. trans.	⊖	⊖						
Man. trans.								
Clutch								
Electrical	○	⊖						
A/C	●	●						
Suspension	○	⊖						
Brakes	●	●						
Exhaust	⊖	⊖						
Body rust	⊖	⊖						
Paint/trim	⊜	⊖						
Integrity	⊖	⊖						
Hardware	○	○						

Toyota Pickup (2WD)

Trouble spots	90	91	92	93	94	95	96	97
Engine	○	○	⊖	⊜	⊖	⊜		
Cooling	○	◒	○	○	⊖	⊜		
Fuel	⊜	⊜	⊜	⊜	⊜	⊜		
Ignition	⊖	⊖	⊜	⊖	⊖	⊜		
Auto. trans.	⊖	⊖	○	⊜	⊜	★		
Man. trans.	⊜	⊜	⊜	⊜	⊖	★		
Clutch	○	⊖	⊖	○	⊖	★		
Electrical	⊖	⊖	⊖	⊖	⊖	⊖		
A/C	○	⊖	⊖	⊖	⊜	⊖		
Suspension	⊖	⊖	⊖	⊖	⊖	⊖		
Brakes	◒	◒	○	○	⊖	⊖		
Exhaust	○	○	⊜	⊜	⊜	⊜		
Body rust	○	⊖	⊜	⊜	⊜	⊜		
Paint/trim	⊖	⊖	⊖	⊖	⊖	⊜		
Integrity	⊖	⊖	⊖	⊖	○	○		
Hardware	⊖	⊖	⊖	○	○	○		

Toyota Pickup (4WD)

TROUBLE SPOTS	90	91	92	93	94	95	96	97
Engine	◒	◒	○	⊖	⊖	⊖		
Cooling	○	◒	○	○	⊜	⊜		
Fuel	⊖	⊖	⊜	⊖	⊜	⊖		
Ignition	⊖	⊖	⊖	⊜	⊖	⊖		
Auto. trans.	*	*	*	*	*	*		
Man. trans.	⊖	⊖	⊜	⊖	⊜	⊜		
Clutch	○	○	○	⊖	⊖	⊖		
Electrical	⊖	○	⊖	⊖	⊖	⊖		
A/C	○	⊖	⊜	⊖	⊜	*		
Suspension	⊖	○	⊖	⊖	⊖	○		
Brakes	◒	○	○	⊖	⊖	⊖		
Exhaust	●	◒	○	⊖	⊖	⊜		
Body rust	○	○	⊜	⊖	⊖	⊜		
Paint/trim	⊖	⊖	⊖	⊖	⊖	⊜		
Integrity	⊖	⊖	⊖	⊖	○	⊖		
Hardware	○	○	○	⊖	⊖	○		

Toyota Previa Van

TROUBLE SPOTS	90	91	92	93	94	95	96 (Insufficient data)	97 (Insufficient data)
Engine		⊖	⊜	⊜	⊜	⊜		
Cooling		⊖	⊜	⊜	⊜	⊜		
Fuel		⊜	⊜	⊜	⊜	⊜		
Ignition		◒	○	⊖	⊜	⊜		
Auto. trans.		⊜	⊜	⊜	⊜	⊜		
Man. trans.		*	*	*				
Clutch		*	*	*				
Electrical		◒	◒	⊖	⊖	○		
A/C		●	◒	⊖	⊖	⊜		
Suspension		○	⊖	⊜	⊖	⊖		
Brakes		◒	◒	◒	○	◒		
Exhaust		⊖	⊜	⊜	⊜	⊖		
Body rust		⊜	⊜	⊜	⊜	⊜		
Paint/trim		⊖	⊖	⊜	⊜	⊜		
Integrity		○	⊖	○	⊖	⊖		
Hardware		◒	○	○	○	○		

Toyota RAV4

TROUBLE SPOTS	90	91	92	93	94	95	96	97
Engine							⊜	⊜
Cooling							⊜	⊜
Fuel							⊜	⊜
Ignition							⊜	⊜
Auto. trans.							⊖	⊜
Man. trans.							⊜	⊜
Clutch							⊜	⊜
Electrical							⊜	⊜
A/C							⊜	⊜
Suspension							⊜	⊜
Brakes							⊜	⊜
Exhaust							⊜	⊜
Body rust							⊜	⊜
Paint/trim							⊜	⊜
Integrity							⊖	⊖
Hardware							⊖	⊜

Toyota T100 Pickup (2WD)

TROUBLE SPOTS	90	91	92	93	94 (Insufficient data)	95	96	97 (Insufficient data)
Engine				○		⊖	⊖	
Cooling				⊖		⊜	⊜	
Fuel				⊜		⊜	⊜	
Ignition				⊜		⊜	⊜	
Auto. trans.				*		⊜	○	
Man. trans.				*		*	*	
Clutch				*		*	*	
Electrical				⊖		⊖	⊖	
A/C				*		⊜	⊜	
Suspension				⊖		⊖	⊖	
Brakes				⊖		⊜	⊜	
Exhaust				⊜		⊜	⊜	
Body rust				⊖		⊜	⊜	
Paint/trim				⊜		⊜	⊖	
Integrity				⊜		○	⊖	
Hardware				○		○	⊖	

Toyota T100 Pickup (4WD)

TROUBLE SPOTS	90	91	92	93 (Insufficient data)	94 (Insufficient data)	95	96	97 (Insufficient data)
Engine						⊖	◒	
Cooling						⊜	⊖	
Fuel						⊜	⊜	
Ignition						⊜	⊜	
Auto. trans.						⊜	⊜	
Man. trans.						*	*	
Clutch						*	*	
Electrical						⊖	⊜	
A/C						⊜	⊜	
Suspension						⊖	⊖	
Brakes						○	⊖	
Exhaust						⊜	⊜	
Body rust						⊜	⊜	
Paint/trim						⊜	⊖	
Integrity						⊖	⊖	
Hardware						○	○	

Toyota Tacoma Pickup (2WD)

TROUBLE SPOTS	90	91	92	93	94	95	96	97 (Insufficient data)
Engine						⊜	⊜	
Cooling						⊜	⊜	
Fuel						⊜	⊜	
Ignition						⊜	⊜	
Auto. trans.						⊜	⊜	
Man. trans.						⊜	⊜	
Clutch						⊜	⊜	
Electrical						⊖	⊖	
A/C						⊜	⊜	
Suspension						●	○	
Brakes						⊖	⊜	
Exhaust						⊜	⊜	
Body rust						⊜	⊜	
Paint/trim						⊖	⊖	
Integrity						◒	⊖	
Hardware						○	⊖	

Toyota Tacoma Pickup (4WD)

TROUBLE SPOTS	90	91	92	93	94	95	96	97
Engine						⊖	⊖	⊜
Cooling						⊖	⊜	⊜
Fuel						⊜	⊜	⊜
Ignition						⊜	⊜	⊜
Auto. trans.						*	*	*
Man. trans.						⊜	⊖	*
Clutch						⊜	⊜	*
Electrical						⊖	⊖	⊜
A/C						⊜	⊜	⊜
Suspension						◒	○	⊜
Brakes						○	⊖	⊜
Exhaust						⊜	⊜	⊜
Body rust						⊜	⊜	⊜
Paint/trim						⊖	⊖	⊜
Integrity						◒	○	⊖
Hardware						⊖	⊖	⊜

Toyota Tercel

TROUBLE SPOTS	90	91	92	93	94	95	96	97 (Insufficient data)
Engine	◒	○	⊖	⊖	⊜	⊜	⊜	
Cooling	○	○	⊖	○	⊖	⊜	⊜	
Fuel	◒	⊜	⊜	⊜	⊜	⊜	⊜	
Ignition	◒	⊖	⊖	⊖	⊜	⊜	⊜	
Auto. trans.	⊖	⊖	⊜	⊜	⊜	⊖	*	
Man. trans.	⊜	⊜	⊜	⊜	⊜	*	*	
Clutch	○	⊖	⊖	⊜	⊜	*	*	
Electrical	○	○	○	⊜	⊖	⊜	⊜	
A/C	○	◒	○	○	⊖	⊜	⊜	
Suspension	○	⊜	⊜	⊜	⊜	⊖	⊜	
Brakes	●	○	◒	⊖	⊖	⊜	⊜	
Exhaust	●	○	⊖	⊖	⊜	⊜	⊜	
Body rust	◒	⊜	⊜	⊜	⊜	⊜	⊜	
Paint/trim	○	○	○	○	⊖	⊖	○	
Integrity	○	○	○	⊖	⊖	◒	⊖	
Hardware	○	○	○	⊖	⊖	○	⊖	

⊜ ⊖ ○ ◒ ●
Few ← **Problems** → Many

* Insufficient data

TROUBLE SPOTS	Volkswagen Golf, GTI, Golf III 90	91	92	93	94	95	96	97
Engine	◒	◒	◒		⊖	⊖	⊜	⊜
Cooling	●	●	○		⊖	⊜	⊜	⊜
Fuel	◒	◒	◒		○	○	⊖	⊜
Ignition	◒	◒	◒		○	○	⊖	⊜
Auto. trans.	*	*	*		○	○	○	*
Man. trans.	⊖	⊖	⊖		⊖	⊜	⊜	⊖
Clutch	○	○	○	Insufficient data	⊖	⊜	⊜	⊜
Electrical	●	●	●		◒	●	◒	⊖
A/C	●	◒	○		○	⊖	⊜	⊜
Suspension	◒	○	○		⊜	⊖	⊖	⊜
Brakes	●	◒	◒		○	⊖	⊜	⊜
Exhaust	●	●	●		⊖	⊜	⊜	⊜
Body rust	○	⊖	⊖		⊖	⊜	⊜	⊜
Paint/trim	◒	○	○		○	○	⊖	⊖
Integrity	◒	●	◒		○	○	○	⊖
Hardware	●	●	●		●	●	◒	⊖

TROUBLE SPOTS	Volkswagen Jetta, Jetta III 90	91	92	93	94	95	96	97
Engine	◒	◒	◒		⊖	⊖	⊜	⊜
Cooling	●	●	○		⊖	⊜	⊜	⊜
Fuel	◒	◒	◒		○	○	⊖	⊜
Ignition	◒	◒	◒		○	○	⊖	⊜
Auto. trans.	*	*	*		○	○	○	*
Man. trans.	⊖	⊖	⊖		⊖	⊜	⊜	⊖
Clutch	○	○	○	Insufficient data	⊖	⊜	⊜	⊜
Electrical	●	●	●		◒	●	◒	⊖
A/C	●	◒	○		○	⊖	⊜	⊜
Suspension	◒	○	○		⊜	⊖	⊖	⊜
Brakes	●	◒	◒		○	⊖	⊜	⊜
Exhaust	●	●	●		⊖	⊜	⊜	⊜
Body rust	○	⊖	⊖		⊖	⊜	⊜	⊜
Paint/trim	◒	○	○		○	○	⊖	⊖
Integrity	◒	●	◒		○	○	○	⊖
Hardware	●	●	●		●	●	◒	⊖

TROUBLE SPOTS	Volkswagen Passat 90	91	92	93	94	95	96	97
Engine						⊜	⊜	
Cooling						⊖	⊜	
Fuel						⊖	⊜	
Ignition						⊖	⊜	
Auto. trans.						*	*	
Man. trans.						*	*	
Clutch	Insufficient data	Insufficient data	Insufficient data	Insufficient data	Insufficient data	*	*	Insufficient data
Electrical						◒	⊖	
A/C						⊖	⊜	
Suspension						⊜	⊜	
Brakes						⊜	⊖	
Exhaust						⊜	⊜	
Body rust						⊜	⊜	
Paint/trim						⊜	⊜	
Integrity						⊖	⊖	
Hardware						◒	◒	

TROUBLE SPOTS	Volvo 240 Series 90	91	92	93	94	95	96	97
Engine	⊖	⊖	⊜	⊖				
Cooling	○	○	◒	○				
Fuel	○	○	⊖	⊖				
Ignition	○	○	○	○				
Auto. trans.	○	⊖	⊖	⊖				
Man. trans.	*	*	*	*				
Clutch	*	*	*	*				
Electrical	●	●	●	●				
A/C	●	○	○	○				
Suspension	⊖	⊖	○	⊖				
Brakes	●	●	●	●				
Exhaust	●	◒	○	○				
Body rust	⊜	⊜	⊜	⊜				
Paint/trim	○	○	○	⊜				
Integrity	○	○	○	○				
Hardware	○	◒	◒	○				

TROUBLE SPOTS	Volvo 740 Series 90	91	92	93	94	95	96	97
Engine	○	○	◒					
Cooling	○	○	◒					
Fuel	◒	○	○					
Ignition	○	○	○					
Auto. trans.	⊖	⊜	⊜					
Man. trans.	*	*						
Clutch	*	*						
Electrical	◒	◒	◒					
A/C	○	○	○					
Suspension	⊖	⊖	○					
Brakes	●	●	◒					
Exhaust	◒	○	◒					
Body rust	⊜	⊜	⊜					
Paint/trim	⊖	⊖	⊖					
Integrity	○	○	○					
Hardware	◒	◒	◒					

TROUBLE SPOTS	Volvo 850 Series 90	91	92	93	94	95	96	97
Engine				⊖	⊖	⊜	⊜	⊜
Cooling				⊜	⊖	⊜	⊜	⊜
Fuel				⊖	⊖	⊖	⊜	⊜
Ignition				○	○	⊖	⊜	⊜
Auto. trans.				○	⊜	⊖	⊜	⊜
Man. trans.				⊖	⊖	⊜	⊜	*
Clutch				○	⊜	⊜	⊜	*
Electrical				◒	◒	◒	○	⊖
A/C				○	○	⊖	⊜	⊜
Suspension				○	⊖	⊜	⊜	⊜
Brakes				⊖	○	⊖	○	⊜
Exhaust				⊜	⊜	⊜	⊜	⊜
Body rust				⊜	⊜	⊜	⊜	⊜
Paint/trim				⊖	○	⊖	⊜	⊜
Integrity				○	◒	○	⊖	⊜
Hardware				◒	◒	○	⊖	⊖

TROUBLE SPOTS	Volvo 940 Series 90	91	92	93	94	95	96	97
Engine		⊖	⊖	○	⊖	⊜		
Cooling		◒	◒	◒	○	⊜		
Fuel		⊖	⊖	⊖	⊖	⊖		
Ignition		⊖	⊖	⊖	⊖	○		
Auto. trans.		⊖	⊜	⊖	⊖	◒		
Man. trans.								
Clutch								
Electrical		◒	◒	○	◒	○		
A/C		⊖	◒	○	○	⊜		
Suspension		○	⊖	⊖	⊖	⊖		
Brakes		◒	◒	◒	◒	○		
Exhaust		⊖	○	⊖	⊖	⊜		
Body rust		⊜	⊜	⊜	⊜	⊜		
Paint/trim		⊖	⊖	⊖	⊖	⊜		
Integrity		○	○	○	○	○		
Hardware		◒	◒	◒	○	○		

TROUBLE SPOTS	Volvo 960 Series 90	91	92	93	94	95	96	97
Engine						⊖	⊜	⊜
Cooling						⊖	⊜	⊜
Fuel						⊖	⊜	⊜
Ignition						○	⊖	⊖
Auto. trans.						◒	⊜	⊜
Man. trans.								
Clutch								
Electrical			Insufficient data	Insufficient data	Insufficient data	◒	○	⊖
A/C						○	⊖	⊜
Suspension						◒	⊖	⊜
Brakes						◒	○	⊜
Exhaust						⊜	⊜	⊜
Body rust						⊜	⊜	⊜
Paint/trim						⊖	⊖	⊜
Integrity						○	○	⊜
Hardware						●	○	⊖

TIRES

Last CR report: November 1998
Ratings: pages 310 & 312
Expect to pay: $30 to $140

How responsively your car, SUV, or minivan handles and how smoothly it rides depend largely on its tires. So when it's time to replace them, it's also a chance to significantly improve your vehicle.

No tire does everything perfectly, however. Tire makers usually emphasize one characteristic or another for each of their lines. Some tires grip especially well on dry or wet roads. Others really bite into snow. Still others deliver crisp steering response or give a smooth ride.

What's available

The leading U.S. tire manufacturers are Goodyear, Michelin (which markets tire lines under the Uniroyal and B.F. Goodrich names) and Firestone (which also uses the Bridgestone name). Since these companies dominate the tire market, these are the brands you're most likely to find. You'll also find more tire variants—many with shared characteristics between types—as manufacturers vie for new market niches. Here are the major categories:

All-season tires. Standard equipment on most sedans, these moderately priced tires are also the most popular replacements. They're designed to handle most conditions reasonably well—including wet and dry pavement and light snow—though they emphasize a comfortable, quiet ride. Typical prices range from $65 to $95 apiece.

Touring-performance tires. A step up in price—and one of the types covered in the Ratings—these are also the ultimate compromise. They provide all-weather performance but with an emphasis on cornering and braking. The best ones we tested did nearly everything well, though the trade-off is shorter tread life. Typical prices: $75 to $105.

Sport-performance tires. These tires are the priciest by far. They deliver maximum handling and grip at the expense of tread life and all-season performance. They also tend to ride harshly and noisily. Expect to pay $85 and up.

Light-truck tires. They're designed for SUVs, vans, and light pickups. Though usually slanted toward general road use, some are aimed at off-road driving. Figure on paying from $75 to $125.

Winter tires. That's the new name for snow tires (and the second type covered in the Ratings). Their deep, chunky tread is still the best in heavy snow, and their rubber is formulated for traction on ice. But their sharp-edged, widely spaced tread blocks may make them noisy and skittish on dry pavement. If you need winter tires, plan on using them during winter months. Typical prices: $60 to $105.

Key features

Look at any tire's sidewall, and you'll see a multipart designation; "P185/70R14 87S" is typical. These codes are key to buying tires that fit your car or truck and deliver the performance you want. Here's what the codes mean:

Size. The P signifies the vehicle type—P for passenger-car tire (some light-truck tires have LT instead). The next three digits are the tire's cross-section width in millimeters: 185 mm. Then comes the "aspect ratio"—the ratio of sidewall height to cross-section width. The 70 means the sidewall height is 70 percent—about 130 mm in a tire 185 mm wide. (Performance tires tend to have a relatively low sidewall height that provides better steering response—and a harder ride). The R means a radial tire (virtually the only design sold today). The next two digits represent the diameter of the wheel on which the tire fits, in inches.

Load index and speed rating. A three-figure code like "87S" is typical. The 87 is a numerical code associated with the maximum load a tire can carry. And the S is the speed rating. It specifies the top speed the tire can sustain. For typical passenger tires, speed ratings start with Q (99 mph) and S (112 mph) and include T (118 mph), U (124 mph), H (130 mph), and V (150 mph)—along with W, Y and ZR, which run from 150+ to more than 186 mph. While that may sound like gross overkill, tires with a high speed rating also tend to deliver better handling at legal speeds. But they aren't for everyone.

- Most all-season tires are usually rated S or T.
- Touring-performance tires typically have an H rating or better, while sport-performance tires are usually rated V and above.
- Most winter tires carry a Q speed rating, though some are now available with higher ratings.

Still other codes on the tire provide other information worth considering:

Tread-wear rating. This three-digit index number, developed by the government, compares a tire's tread life with that of a "reference tire" graded at 100. A tire with a tread-wear index of 450 (relatively high) would seem to last three times as long as one with an index of 150 (quite low). But tire makers assign these numbers without outside verification so view them somewhat skeptically.

Traction and temperature. These are scores for government-specified tests for stopping on a wet surface and resisting overheating. AA is the best for traction, and A is the best for temperature; C worst. Look for at least A in traction, B in temperature.

Date of manufacture. The Department of Transportation serial number on every tire looks something like this: DOT M6 RV T1HR 498. The last three digits are a date code indicating the week and year the tire was made—in this case, the 49th week of 1998. Don't buy a tire that's more than a couple of years old; the rubber may have hardened or even begun to crack.

How to choose

What to spend. Mail-order houses usually offer the best prices and selection, plus a knowledgeable staff; just remember that shipping and mounting are extra. Tire dealers can come close on price and selection. Service stations and car dealers generally have the smallest selection and highest prices, while warehouse clubs tend to stock economy tires.

Shopping tips. Start by matching the tire type with your vehicle and driving conditions. Usually, it's best to stick with the tire category that came with the vehicle. The same holds for size and speed rating; if your car's original tires had an H rating, so should the replacements. Refer to your car's owner manual or the tire-size placecard, usually on the door sill. And don't put too much stock on treadwear warranties, which can top 80,000 miles. You'll usually get only a prorated amount based on usable tread left. And because most warranties don't cover road hazards, you may end up with nothing.

Ratings *Performance tires*

& Recommendations

The tests behind the Ratings

We tested touring-performance tires in size P205/60R15, common on midsized sedans. These tires would probably score relatively similarly in other sizes from 185/60R14 to 225/60R16. The Goodyear Eagle GT+4 is actually an all-season tire with a T speed rating (it came on our test car, a 1998 Mercury Mystique). The ten others, popular touring-performance tires, all have an H speed rating. We tested each tire in sets of four. **Braking** and **cornering** were measured on dry (first score) and wet (second score) pavement. **Prices** are approximate retail.

Recommendations

For all-weather use, it's hard to beat the Michelin Energy MXV4. It did especially well in dry braking, cornering, handling, resistance to hydroplaning, and ride comfort, and it gripped well in snow. The Dunlop D60 A2 with JLB is a CR Best Buy—a set of four may be as much as $200 cheaper than the top-rated Michelins. The Dunlop excelled in dry braking and handling, but it was noisy on coarse pavement. The next six tires in the Ratings all performed very well in our tests. If you choose one of those, pick one that scores well in the attributes most important to you.

See report, page 308. Last time rated in CONSUMER REPORTS: March 1998.

Overall Ratings

E VG G F P

Listed in order of overall score

Key no.	Brand and model	Price	Overall score (P F G VG E)	Braking DRY/WET	Cornering DRY/WET	Emerg. handling	Ride	Snow
1	**Michelin** Energy MXV4	$126		E/VG	VG/G	E	VG	E
2	**Dunlop** D60 A2 with JLB	76		E/E	E/G	E	VG	G
3	**Goodyear** Eagle GT+4	108		E/VG	VG/G	E	VG	F
4	**Pirelli** P6000 SportVeloce	100		E/E	VG/G	E	G	P
5	**BF Goodrich** Touring T/A HR4	78		VG/VG	E/G	VG	VG	VG
6	**General** XP 2000 H4	70		VG/VG	G/G	E	VG	VG
7	**Yokohama** Avid H4	77		E/E	G/G	G	G	P
8	**Goodyear** Eagle LS	133		VG/VG	VG/G	VG	VG	E
9	**Bridgestone** Turanza H	98		VG/VG	F/P	VG	VG	G
10	**Firestone** Firehawk Touring LH	96		G/G	G/P	G	VG	E
11	**Cooper** Cobra GTH	73		VG/E	G/P	VG	P	P

Details on the models

Braking distance is the average for stopping on dry pavement from 60 mph on wet pavement at 40 mph with anti-lock brakes (ABS) and without. We tested **hydroplaning** by driving through a curve over water, increasing speed until the tires started to slide. **Rolling resistance** is a measure of how easily a tire rolls. **Tread-wear rating** is an index number ranging from 300 to 400.

1 Michelin Energy MXV4 $126

A fine all-around performance compromise. Excellent for summer and winter, but expensive. Excellent emergency handling. Braking: at 60 mph on dry pavement, 138 ft.; at 40 mph on wet pavement with ABS, 74 ft., and without ABS, 91 ft. Hydroplaning:⊖. Noise: ⊖/○. Rolling resistance: ⊖. Tread-wear rating: 340. Warranty, miles: none.

2 Dunlop D60 A2 with JLB $76

Sporty, and excellent overall. Braking: at 60 mph on dry pavement, 134 ft.; at 40 mph on wet pavement with ABS, 72 ft., and without ABS, 88 ft. Hydroplaning: ⊖. Noise: ⊖/◒. Rolling resistance: ○. Tread-wear rating: 320. Warranty, miles: 45,000. A CR Best Buy.

3 Goodyear Eagle GT+4 $108

Very good in regions with no snow. Braking: at 60 mph on dry pavement, 136 ft.; at 40 mph on wet pavement with ABS, 74 ft., and without ABS, 91 ft. Hydroplaning: ⊖. Noise: ⊖/○. Rolling resistance: ⊖. Tread-wear rating: 240. Warranty, miles: none.

4 Pirelli P6000 SportVeloce $100

Very good for regions with no snow. Braking: at 60 mph on dry pavement, 136 ft.; at 40 mph on wet pavement with ABS, 71 ft., and without ABS, 86 ft. Hydroplaning: ⊖. Noise: ⊖/○. Rolling resistance: ○. Tread-wear rating: 320. Warranty, miles: 50,000.

5 BF Goodrich Touring T/A HR4 $78

Consistently very good in all weather. Braking: at 60 mph on dry pavement, 141 ft.; at 40 mph on wet pavement with ABS, 75 ft., and without ABS, 90 ft. Hydroplaning: ⊖. Noise: ⊖/○. Rolling resistance: ⊖. Tread-wear rating: 380. Warranty, miles: none.

6 General XP2000 H4 $70

A very good all-around performer. Braking at 60 mph on dry pavement, 142 ft.; at 40 mph on wet pavement with ABS, 76 ft., and without ABS, 87 ft. Hydroplaning: ⊖. Noise: ⊖/○. Rolling resistance: ○. Tread-wear rating: 360.Warranty, miles: 45,000.

7 Yokohama Avid H4 $77

Very good for regions with no snow. Braking at 60 mph on dry pavement, 136 ft.; at 40 mph on wet pavement with ABS, 70 ft, and without ABS, 88 ft. Hydroplaning: ⊖. Noise: ⊖/◒. Rolling resistance: ⊖. Tread-wear rating: 360. Warranty, miles: 45,000.

8 Goodyear Eagle LS $133

Very good in snow, but expensive. Braking at 60 mph on dry pavement, 144 ft.; at 40 mph on wet pavement with ABS, 74 ft., and without ABS, 94. Hydroplaning: ⊖. Noise: ⊖/○. Rolling resistance: ⊖. Tread-wear rating: 360. Warranty, miles: none.

9 Bridgestone Turanza H $98

Good but not great. Emphasizes comfort over sportiness. Braking at 60 mph on dry pavement, 144 ft.; at 40 mph on wet pavement with ABS, 73 ft., and without ABS, 96 ft. ABS. Hydroplaning: ○. Noise: ⊖/◒. Rolling resistance: ⊖. Tread-wear rating: 300. Warranty, miles: 50,000.

10 Firestone Firehawk Touring LH $96

A good tire, with the best snow traction in the group. Braking at 60 mph on dry pavement, 150 ft.; at 40 mph on wet pavement with ABS, 80 ft., and without ABS, 92 ft. Hydroplaning: ○. Noise: ⊖/○. Rolling resistance: ⊖. Tread-wear rating: 400. Warranty, miles: 60,000.

11 Cooper Cobra GTH $73

Good for regions with no snow. Braking at 60 mph on dry pavement,142 ft.; at 40 mph on wet pavement with ABS, 72 ft., and without ABS, 88 ft. Hydroplaning: ⊖. Noise: ○/●. Rolling resistance: ⊖. Tread-wear rating: 400. Warranty, miles: 45,000.

Ratings *Winter tires*

& Recommendations

The tests behind the Ratings

We tested size 205/60R15, which is appropriate for our test car, a 1998 Mercury Mystique LS and also fits many other popular compact and midsized cars. For these winter tires, performance in other sizes should be comparable with that of the size we tested. We also included the Firestone Firehawk Touring LH, which is not a winter tire but nevertheless scored highest in its group in the snow-traction tests we reported on in March 1998. Most of the winter tires we tested have a "Q" speed rating, indicating that they can safely sustain speeds up to 99 mph. The Firestone Winterfire's "T" rating is good up to 118 mph; the Firestone Firehawk's "H" rating is good up to 130 mph. We tested each tire in sets of four. **Price** is the estimated average, based on a national survey.

Recommendations

For mild winter conditions, an all-season tire should suffice. The Firestone Firehawk Touring LH, $89, gave the best traction in snow among the 10 touring-performance tires we tested for our March 1998 report. But it was humbled by all seven winter tires in this group. The Michelin XM+S Alpin, $94, gave the best overall performance—very good wet and dry braking, competent cornering and handling, and excellent snow traction. For the very best winter traction, the best choices are the Dunlop Graspic HS-1, $74, and the Yokohama Guardex 600, $89, both of which excelled in braking on ice.

See report, page 308. Last time rated in CONSUMER REPORTS: November 1998.

Overall Ratings

E VG G F P

Listed in order of overall score

Key no.	Brand and model	Price	Overall score 0–100 (P F G VG E)	Snow traction	Braking DRY/WET/ICE	Cornering DRY/WET	Emergency handling
1	**Michelin** XM+S Alpin	$94		E	G/VG/G	VG/G	G
2	**Bridgestone** Blizzak WS-15	100		VG	G/F/E	G/F	F
3	**Firestone** Firehawk Touring LH	89		F	VG/VG/F	G/G	VG
4	**Pirelli** Winter Ice Asimmetrico	104		G	G/G/VG	G/F	G
5	**Firestone** Winterfire	66		VG	G/G/G	F/P	P
6	**Dunlop** Graspic HS-1	74		VG	F/F/E	F/P	G
7	**Yokohama** Guardex 600	89		E	F/P/E	G/P	P
8	**Cooper** Weather-Master XGR	59		G	F/F/E	VG/P	F

Details on the models

Braking tests were from 60 mph on dry pavement, 40 mph on wet pavement, and 15 mph on ice. Some vehicles don't have an antilock brake system (ABS), so we ran all our braking tests on wet pavement and on ice with the ABS working and again with the ABS disabled. We tested **hydroplaning** by driving repeatedly through a mild curve over a pool of water about 10 mm deep, increasing speed until the car started to slip to the side. We evaluated **ride comfort** and **noise** on both smooth and coarse roads. **Rolling resistance** is a measure of how easily the tires roll.

1 **Michelin XM+S Alpin** $94

Excellent overall, especially well balanced. Excellent snow traction. Braking: at 60 mph on dry pavement, 154 ft.; at 40 mph on wet pavement with ABS, 79 ft., and without ABS, 94 ft.; at 15 mph on ice with ABS, 55 ft., and without ABS, 67 ft. Hydroplaning: ⊖. Comfort: ○. Noise (smooth/coarse): ⊜/◒. Rolling resistance: ⊖.

2 **Bridgestone Blizzak WS-15** $100

Very good for winter, but don't delay changing to conventional tires in the spring. Braking: at 60 mph on dry pavement, 156 ft.; at 40 mph on wet pavement with ABS, 86 ft., and without ABS, 108 ft.; at 15 mph on ice with ABS, 43 ft., and without ABS, 59 ft. Hydroplaning: ⊜. Comfort: ⊖. Noise (smooth/coarse): ⊜/○. Rolling resistance: ○.

3 **Firestone Firehawk Touring LH** $89

A touring tire, not in the same league with winter tires on snow and ice. Braking: at 60 mph on dry pavement, 140 ft.; at 40 mph on wet pavement with ABS, 75 ft., and without ABS, 93 ft.; at 15 mph on ice with ABS, 61 ft., and without ABS, 75 ft. Hydroplaning: ⊖. Comfort: ⊖. Noise (smooth/coarse): ⊖/◒. Rolling resistance: ⊖.

4 **Pirelli Winter Ice Asimmetrico** $104

Very good all-weather performer, but expensive. Stiff outer tread is said to improve handling of heavier cars. Braking: at 60 mph on dry pavement,153 ft.; at 40 mph on wet pavement with ABS, 82 ft., and without ABS, 99 ft.; at 15 mph on ice with ABS, 45 ft., and without ABS, 64 ft. Hydroplaning: ⊖. Comfort: ○. Noise (smooth/coarse): ⊖/○. Rolling resistance: ⊖.

5 **Firestone Winterfire** $66

Very good overall. The only tire in this group that can be studded, but we don't recommend studs and we tested this tire without them. Braking: at 60 mph on dry pavement, 151 ft.; at 40 mph on wet pavement with ABS, 83 ft., and without ABS, 102 ft.; at 15 mph on ice with ABS, 51 ft., and without ABS, 66 ft. Hydroplaning: ⊖. Comfort: ○. Noise (smooth/coarse): ⊖/○. Rolling resistance: ⊖.

6 **Dunlop Graspic HS-1** $74

A good tire at a good price. Impressive winter performance, but marginal grip on dry and wet pavement. Braking: at 60 mph on dry pavement, 160 ft.; at 40 mph on wet pavement with ABS, 87 ft., and without ABS, 108 ft.; at 15 mph on ice with ABS, 42 ft., and without ABS, 58 ft. Hydroplaning: ⊖. Comfort: ◒. Noise (smooth/coarse): ⊖/◒. Rolling resistance: ⊜.

7 **Yokohama Guardex** $89

Excellent in winter conditions; a good tire if you drive a lot on snow and ice. Among the worst in braking and cornering on wet pavement. Braking: at 60 mph on dry pavement, 160 ft.; at 40 mph on wet pavement with ABS, 91 ft., and without ABS, 104 ft.; at 15 mph on ice with ABS, 43 ft., and without ABS, 58 ft. Hydroplaning: ○. Comfort: ○. Noise (smooth/coarse): ⊖/○. Rolling resistance: ⊖.

8 **Cooper Weather-Master XGR** $59

A good tire overall. But unless most of your driving is on icy roads, there are better choices. Among the best in this group in braking on ice and in resistance to hydroplaning. Braking: at 60 mph on dry pavement, 161 ft.; at 40 mph on wet pavement with ABS, 86 ft., and without ABS, 103 ft.; at 15 mph on ice with ABS, 42 ft., and without ABS, 58 ft. Hydroplaning: ⊜. Comfort: ◒. Noise (smooth/coarse): ⊜/○. Rolling resistance: ○.

CAR BATTERIES

Last CR report: *October 1998*
Ratings: *page 316*
Expect to pay: *$50 to $100*

When your car battery gives up the ghost, you want a new one that will last for years and will start your car in all kinds of weather. Just be sure your old battery is really dead by checking it at the first sign of slow starting. See that its terminals are clean and its cables securely attached. If they are—and the charging system is working properly—a mechanic can check the battery's condition by performing a "load test" to determine whether it's still in good shape and worth keeping.

What's available

Most batteries are made by Exide (which makes most *DieHards*), Johnson Controls (*AutoZone*, *Eveready*, *Interstate*, and *Motorcraft*), and ACDelco (batteries sold under that name, and some *DieHards*). Look for a battery appropriate for your car. You'll find the right specs for your vehicle in the owner's manual or in a catalog at an auto-parts store. The two most crucial specs:

Group size. This number denotes a battery's length, width, height, and terminal type (they can be posts on top, bolt holes on the side, or both for dual-terminal batteries). Batteries within a given group have the same dimensions and the terminals in the same place. What's more, some vehicles can accommodate more than one size battery. You'll find the group size on the battery.

CCA. This stands for cold-cranking amps—a measure of a battery's ability to start a car in cold weather, when thickened engine oil and slowed chemical reactions make starting hardest. CCAs denote how much current the battery can deliver to the starter motor for at least 30 seconds at 0° F. Again, check your owner's manual or a store catalog for the CCA that's right for your vehicle, then match it to the one on the battery. And don't get confused by ads that misleadingly tout a battery's **CA**, for cranking amps. Similar to cold-cranking amps, CA is measured at 32° instead of 0°—and is typically much higher than a battery's CCA. The battery industry says the CA ratings can keep people who live in hot climates from buying more cold-cranking amps than they need. We say the higher CA ratings are merely confusing—ignore them and go by CCA.

Key considerations

Batteries vary in other important ways:

Reserve capacity. This figure indicates how many minutes your car might run using only the energy stored in the battery—say, if the alternator fails. Reserve capacity ranged between 1¼ and 2 hours in the batteries we tested. But because it's usually not on the battery, you need to check the product literature.

Freshness. The fresher a car battery is when you buy it, the better. But manufacturers seldom make it easy to tell when a battery was made. You must decipher a code found on most batteries (on an attached sticker or stamped on the case). The information you need is usually in the first two characters—one a letter and one a digit. Most codes start with the letter, which represents the month: A for January, B for February, and so forth. The digit denotes the year—9 for 1999. So A-9 stands for

January 1999. The catch: Some of those dates are postdated.

Warranty. These, like CA ratings and date codes, can sound better than they are. You'll see two numbers: one for the total warranty period (usually five to seven years), and another, shorter time for the free-replacement period (usually three months to two years). The free-replacement period is key; once it's up, if the battery fails, you get only a prorated credit toward a new battery.

How to choose

Performance differences. Our tests of batteries regularly show wide variation between brands. And, except for the *DieHards*, batteries of the same brand varied greatly in performance. Buy the the right group size for your vehicle; a battery too small may vibrate excessively, which can shorten its life.

What to spend. Not every brand comes in every CCA level, so you may need to go a bit above it to get the brand you want. But steer clear of batteries with a CCA rating below the one specified for your vehicle and those rated 200 amps or higher. Other factors being equal, batteries with a higher CCA often cost more and are more fragile, so they have a shorter life.

Buy a battery with the longest reserve capacity you can find. If the figure isn't on the battery—and it often isn't—ask at the store or check the product literature. Should your car's charging system fail, a longer capacity can mean the difference between driving to safety and getting stuck in the breakdown lane.

Shopping tips. Here are some other things to keep in mind:

- Buy the freshest battery you can. Look for a date code that indicates the battery has been shipped from the factory within the last three months or so. While batteries don't age precipitously until they're about six months old, they may sit in factory storage for weeks before they're shipped.
- Don't be swayed by a generous total warranty period. Instead, choose the battery with the longest free-replacement period you can find.
- Where you buy a battery can also affect choice, price, and convenience—notably whether you install the battery yourself or have the seller handle the job.

Auto service centers include Goodyear, Firestone, Sears, and Pep Boys, among others. Service is often fast and expert. Those service centers tend to have a large, fresh inventory and relatively low prices. And they handle the installation. Stores that sell batteries, like Wal-Mart, Kmart, Target and Trak Auto, may have the lowest prices, but only some will install the battery for you. Service stations and tire and tuneup shops offer local convenience and comprehensive service. But they're usually shy on choices. And because they do less business than the other outlets, batteries may not be fresh. Auto dealers know your vehicle best, which is why they're your first choice for cars and trucks still under warranty. But because dealers are expensive, they're probably your last resort for older vehicles.

Ratings *Car batteries*
& Recommendations

The tests behind the Ratings

Overall score is based on our tests of cold-cranking performance and reserve capacity. **Claimed CCA** is the manufacturer's rating of the cold-cranking amps the battery can deliver. **Cold cranking** is how well each battery measured up in our tests. **Reserve capacity** is an indication of how long a battery can keep the engine running without help from the alternator. **Warranty** shows for how long the manufacturer will **replace** the battery free of charge, plus the **overall** prorated period of coverage–a much less useful figure. **Price** is the estimated average, based on a national survey.

Recommendations

Most of the rated batteries performed very well; you won't go wrong with any but the lowest rated. In group size 24 (for many Chrysler, Honda, Nissan, Toyota, and older GM cars), the clear champ was the AutoZone Duralast 24-DS, $50. In group size 58 (for many Chrysler, Ford, and Mazda cars), the DieHard Gold 37158, $83—designed for warm climates—bested the others, including its cold-climate brandmate. Best in group size 34/78—a "universal size" battery that, in some cars, can replace sizes 23, 24, 27, 46, 74, 76, and 77, in addition to 34 and 78—was the Interstate Mega-tron MTPlus-78DT, $89. It was discontinued after our tests but may still be available.

See report, page 314. Last time rated in CONSUMER REPORTS: October 1998.

Overall Ratings

E ⊜ VG ⊖ G ○ F ◒ P ●

Listed in order of overall score

Brand and model	Price	Overall score (0–100; P F G VG E)	Claimed CCA	Cold cranking	Reserve capacity	Warranty REPLACE/OVERALL
GROUP SIZE 24						
AutoZone Duralast 24-DS [1]	$50		600	⊜	⊜	24/72 mo.
DieHard WeatherHandler 36524 (Sears)	65		560	⊜	⊜	12/60
Exide Nascar Select 24T-84N	75		675	○	⊜	24/84
ACDelco Professional 24-7YR	64		660	○	⊜	24/84
GROUP SIZE 58						
DieHard Gold 37158 (Sears)	83		490	⊜	⊖	24/84
Napa 7558	63		440	⊜	○	18/75
DieHard WeatherHandler 36458 (Sears)	65		540	⊖	○	12/60

Brand and model	Price	Overall score (0–100; P F G VG E)	Claimed CCA	Cold cranking	Reserve capacity	Warranty REPLACE/OVERALL
GROUP SIZE 58 *continued*						
Interstate Mega-tron MT-58 [1]	$63		540	⊖	○	18/60 mo.
Exide Nascar Select 58-84N	85		500	⊖	○	24/84
Motorcraft Silver BXT-58 [1]	65		540	○	○	24/84
ACDelco Professional 58-6YR	60		560	○	◒	18/72
GROUP SIZE 34/78						
Interstate Mega-tron MTPlus-78DT [1] [2]	89		900	⊜	⊜	18/60
DieHard Gold 37090 (Sears)	84		875	○	⊜	24/84
DieHard Silver 36290 (Sears)	75		800	○	⊜	18/72
Exide Nascar Select 78DT-84NS	90		875	○	⊜	24/84
AutoZone Duralast 34DT-DGS [1]	70		800	○	⊜	24/84
Everstart Extreme DT-1 (Wal-Mart)	60		725	○	⊜	24/84
ACDelco Professional 78DT-7YR	70		850	○	⊖	24/84

[1] *Requires periodic addition of water.* [2] *Discontinued, but may still be available.*

Other good batteries Below are high-rated batteries from previous reports. Prices are approximate retail.

Group size 75 (all Saturns and many GM cars)
- ACDelco Maintenance Free 75-60, $58
- Interstate Mega-tron MT-75, $83
- Everstart 75-5 (Wal-Mart), $30
- DieHard WeatherHandler 36475 (Sears), $67

Group size 26/70 (replaces 21-27, 34, 35, 46, 70-78, 85, 86)
- ACDelco Maintenance Free 70DT-60, $62
- DieHard Silver 36280 (Sears), $77

Group size 24 (many Chrysler, Honda, Nissan, Toyota, and older GM cars)
- Motorcraft Silver Series BXT-24F, $64
- ACDelco Maintenance Free 24-60, $62
- Everstart 24-5 (Wal-Mart), $30
- Interstate 24-50, $61
- DieHard WeatherHandler 36424 (Sears), $67

Product recalls

Products ranging from child safety seats to chain saws are recalled when there are safety defects. Various federal agencies—the Consumer Product Safety Commission (CPSC), the National Highway Traffic Safety Administration, the U.S. Coast Guard, and the Food and Drug Administration—monitor consumer complaints and injuries and, when there's a problem, issue a recall.

However, the odds of your hearing about an unsafe product are slim. Manufacturers are reluctant to issue a recall in the first place because they can be costly. And getting the word out to consumers can be haphazard.

A selection of the most far-reaching recalls appear monthly in consumer reports. The following pages gather together a year's worth of recalls published in the November 1996 through October 1997 issues of Consumer Reports. For the latest information, see the current issue of the magazine.

If you wish to report an unsafe product or get recall information, call the CPSC's hotline, 800 638-2772.

Recall notices about your automobile can be obtained from a new-car dealer or by calling the NHTSA hotline at 800 424-9393. Questions about food and drugs are handled by the FDA's Office of Consumer Affairs, 301 827-4420.

You can better assure yourself of getting a recall notice by returning the warranty cards that come with many products.

Children's products

Activity Block Sets

Rods on one of blocks could break and release small hollow cylinders that could choke child.

Products: 4,000 block sets sold 5/97-6/98 for $7 or $8 in East and Midwest at Cook Brothers, Johnny's Toys, Meijer, and Ocean State Job Lot stores. Set consists of four colorful plastic blocks and plastic shape sorters. One block has beeper, one has clicker dial, another has mirror, and fourth has rollers—hollow plastic cylinders—on plastic rods. Toy came in multicolored window box labeled, in part, "QUALITY FunKids TOYS . . . Activity Blocks . . . ITEM NO. 38329 . . . T.S. TOYS . . . MADE IN CHINA."

What to do: Return toy to store for refund

Oscar Mayer Wienermobile pedal car

Decals contain excessive lead, which is toxic if ingested.

Products: 16,000 pedal cars shaped like hot dog, distributed 6/95-5/98 as supermarket promotions. A few were also sold by mail order. The car, geared toward children ages 3 to 7, about 46 inches long.

What to do: Call 800 433-9361 to order replacement decals.

Toy saxophone distributed with kids' Adventure Meals at Arby's restaurants

Small keys and part of mouthpiece could come off and choke child.

Products: 220,000 toys distributed 1/98-3/98. Orange-plastic toy is nine inches long and has four white finger-operated keys and white mouthpiece.

What to do: Return toy to Arby's for free replacement toy.

Baseball Striker and Softball Striker training aids

When struck with bat, ball can fly off cable and seriously injure user or bystanders.

Products: 12,000 products sold 1/94-4/98 at sporting goods stores for $50 to $70. Device, used for batter's warm-up, consists of metal extending arm with cable attached to molded polyurethane baseball or softball. Device fastens to chain-link fence. Version made by Hollywood Bases has painted extending arm; version made by Schutt Mfg. has plated arm. Maker's name is on each product.

What to do: Return training aid to store for refund.

Step 2 Big Storage toy chest

Lid could collapse on child's head or neck.

Products: 350,000 toy chests, sold 2/92-11/97 by Kmart, Toys 'R' Us, and other retailers for about $40. Chest, made of white plastic with blue lid and red handles, is 33 inches long, 19 inches wide, and 23 inches high. "Step 2" logo is on front, just below lid. Model number 7211 or 7511 is on packaging.

What to do: Call 800 347-8372 for repair kit that prevents lid from closing fully unless it's closed by an adult.

Graco infant carriers and carrier/swings

Seat handle could unlock and let infant fall out.

Products: 564,000 products made 8/1/93 to 8/31/97, including model numbers: 1300, 1301, 1310, 1350, 1501, 1502, 1530, 1723, 2788, 5510, 8108, and 36264. Model number and date of manufacture are on label under seat or under top of swing. Carrier seat was sold separately for about $30 or as part of Graco Carrier/ Swing set for about $100.

What to do: Call 800 281-3676 for repair kit and instructions.

Baskets of Bubbles child's craft set sold at Toys 'R' Us

If soap is melted in microwave oven according to instructions, pieces could catch fire.

Products: 4,000 craft sets sold 11/97-12/97 for about $15. Toy, for ages 12 and older, is for making baskets of small glycerin soaps in various shapes, sizes, and colors. Kit includes disks of colored, scented soap, which must be cut and melted in measuring cup. It also includes plastic molds and two baskets to hold finished product. Sets are labeled "Arts & Crafts by Alex . . . Baskets of Bubbles."

What to do: Return crafts set to Toys "R" Us for refund.

J. Mason infant carrier

Handle could break and allow carrier to fall.

Products: 18,200 white plastic carriers with fabric seat pad and matching removable canopy, sold 4/96-8/97 at Kmart, Rose, and State Enterprises stores for about $20. Fabric came in three designs: multicolored (pink, white, blue, and green) with geometric pattern; light blue with white squiggly lines; and light blue with pink and purple patterns. "J. MASON" is imprinted on handle. "MADE IN U.S.A." is imprinted on bottom of carrier, which also bears red sticker that reads, "Warning Do Not Use As A Car Seat."

What to do: Call 800 242-1922 for replacement carrier.

Plush "Pajama" bears

Eyes could come off and choke child.

Products: 8,000 stuffed toy bears distributed 10/95-5/97 at amusements parks, including Busch Gardens in Tampa, Fla., Dutch Wonderland in Lancaster, Pa., and Play Day Amusements in Seaside Heights, N.J. Twelve-inch version is white with brown eyes and pink nose and mouth. It's dressed in one-piece floral-print pajamas (gray and mint green or yellow and peach) with ruffled collar and elastic cuffs; paws have same print pattern as pajama. Thirteen-inch version is also white, but with black nose and eyes. It's dressed in one-piece pajamas with muticolored fish or dinosaur design and white collar with red bow; ears have same print pattern as pajamas. Sewn-in label says "Nadel & Sons Toy Corp. . . . Made in China."

What to do: For $5 refund plus postage, call 800 234-4697.

"Hot Pet Car" battery-powered toy

Small pieces could break off and choke child.

Products: 4,400 toys sold 4/97-5/97, mostly in Los Angeles area, for about $3. Red car is 8 inches long, 3½ in. wide, and 5 in. high. Driver is yellow dog with orange ears wearing purple bow and using cellular phone. When toy is turned on, wheels turn crookedly, and toy plays music and sound effects. Pressing spare tire in trunk also activates sound effects. Decals say "YAHOO!" and "NO. 1." Toy came in green box labeled "HOT PET CAR" and "I.C. SOUND." Model number, HK-736, is on sides of box.

What to do: Call 888 898-9296 toll-free for refund.

Francisca full-sized wooden cribs sold through J.C. Penney catalog

Spindles could come off side rails, creating spaces large enough to trap child's head and cause strangulation or to allow child to slip through and fall out.

Products: 6000 cribs, models 343-3935 and 343-4065, sold 8/96-4/97 for $200. Crib came in hardwood or cherry finish. Model number is on bottom of mattress support.

What to do: Return crib to nearest J.C. Penney store for refund or replacement.

Various wooden and metal bunk beds

Openings in top bunk could trap child's head.

Products: Bunk beds made by following companies: Heartland Furniture Mfg., Oklahoma City (wooden beds, models 200, 204, 220, 240, 241, 247, 260, 261,264, 265, 270, 3015, 3046, and 4098, distributed 11/95-5/97 in Okla. and Tex.); Kidron Woodcraft, Apple Creek, Ohio (wooden bed, model 215, distributed '92-97 in Ill. and Ohio); Rosalco Inc., Jeffersonville, Ind. (3-in-1 metal beds, models 3246, 3276, and 3286, distributed '93-97 nationwide, phone 812 284-0022); Springhill Woodcrafters, Greensburg, Pa. (wooden beds, models 92 and 1013, distributed '91-97 in Ohio, Md., and Pa., phone 412 834-3037); Temple Pine Furniture, Temple, Ga. (wooden bed, model 124, distributed '94-97 in Ga. and Tenn., phone 770 562-5910). Since 11/94, more than 514,500 bunk beds from 36 companies have been recalled with similar hazards. To be safe, all bunk beds should have guard rails on both sides of top bunk, and all spaces between guard rail and bed frame and in headboard and footboard should be less than 3½ inches.

What to do: Call manufacturer—or, with Heartland or Kidron, contact retailer—for free replacement guard rail, retrofit kit, or instructions to help eliminate hazard. If you are unsure of manufacturer or have other questions, call Consumer Product Safety Commission (see phone number below). Additional safeguard: Don't let children under age 6 sleep in top bunk.

Halcyon WaterSpring Dex Wipe Warmer electric heating pad for baby wipes

Device could overheat, melt, and catch fire.

Products: 536,000 warmers sold 1/94-12/96 for about $10 to $15. Warmer, 27 inches long and 3½ inches wide, wraps around disposable plastic container. It has white cloth cover with pink, blue, yellow, and green handprints, and Velcro fasteners. Tan or off-white plastic warmer unit beneath cloth has white sticker with model number WW-01. Warmer came in mostly purple box labeled "Dex Products Wipe Warmer, A must for every nursery!" in white print. Warmers sold after 12/96 with red bar across top of white label on warmer unit are not subject to recall.

What to do: Call 888 735-5585 toll-free for refund or free replacement.

Fisher-Price Little People Roadside Rescue toy vehicle set

Back of police car could break into small parts and choke child.

Products: 17,000 toys sold since 2/97 for $8. Set consists of white and blue plastic police car, yellow tow truck, red passenger car, three toy people (mechanic, driver, police officer), two orange traffic cones, red stop sign, and yellow yield sign. Only police car is subject to recall. Vehicle set came in box labeled, in part, "Fisher-Price Little People Roadside Rescue . . . Ages 1½ - 5 yrs . . . 72394."

What to do: Call 888 407-6479 for police-car replacement .

Playskool "Weebles" tractor

Plunger on top could break off and choke child.

Products: 116,000 toys sold since 1/96 for $13. Plastic tractor is mostly yellow with blue wheels and red plunger. Trailer is mostly red with blue wheels. Farm-girl spins when you press plunger. Item number 5242 is on bottom of tractor.

What to do: Call 888 377-3335 for free replacement.

Brio wooden clown stacking toy

Clown's small hat could choke child.

Products: 79,000 toys sold '77 to 9/97 at specialty stores and by mail order for about $19. Clown is 9 inches high and consists of 12 brightly colored pieces, including base. When pieces are stacked, toy forms clown figure with yellow cone-shaped hat. "BRIO . . . MADE IN SWEDEN" is stamped on bottom of base. Toy came in red, white, and yellow cardboard package that includes pictures of toy, model number 30130, and words "BRIO . . . CLOWN. " Latest version, which isn't being recalled, has redesigned hat and comes in box that says "CONTAINS NEW HAT DESIGN."

What to do: Mail hat to Brio Corp., N120 W18485 Freistadt Rd., Germantown, Wisc. 53022, for replacement toy and postage.

Clock tambourine toy

Small pieces could break off and choke child.

Products: 20,400 toys sold 6/95-6/97 at discount stores for about $1. Toy is shaped like clock dial with multicolored numbers and hands and with feet and handle. Blue sticker in center shows sun, moon, clouds, musical notes, and stars. Metal noisemakers are visible through slots in back. Toy is 7¾ inches high and 1 inch thick; dial is 5¾ inches in diameter.

What to do: Mail toy to STK International Inc., 2602 E. 37th St., Vernon, Calif. 90058 for refund for toy and postage.

Minnie Mouse nautical outfits for infant and toddler girls

Small cloth loop on bow around neckline could come off and choke child.

Products: 29,400 outfits sold 11/95-4/96 for $10-$14. Outfits came in four styles: Knit dress with leggings (style 16500); infant dress (style 18500); toddler dress (style 19500); and short set (style 17214H). Short set features beach scene with Minnie Mouse on front. Other garments have embroidered appliqué of Minnie Mouse on front. All outfits have long sailor tie at neckline, held together with small beige fabric loop that says "Minnie Mouse" in red letters. Label in short set says, in part: "Catton Brothers...60% Cotton/40% Polyester...Made in Hong Kong...." Labels in other garments say, in part: "MICKEY' STUFF for kids ...Catton Brothers...70% Cotton/30% Polyester ...Made in Thailand...."

What to do: Return garments to store for refund. For more information, call 800 357-6343.

Children's pullover hooded anorak windbreakers sold at GapKids stores

Paint on zipper pull contains excessive lead, which is toxic to children if ingested.

Products: 127,800 spring/summer nylon windbreakers sold 1/98-6/2/98. Jacket bears "Made in Russia" label and came in white, yellow, pink, light blue, purple, red, navy, green, and multicolored, in various children's sizes. Jacket comes with zippered travel pouch. Windbreakers sold before 1/98 are not subject to recall.

What to do: Return jacket and travel pouch to GapKids store for refund.

Household products

Grand Sequoia folding lawn chair

Could collapse.

Products: 5,000 plastic chairs, in green, white, or taupe, sold 1/98-6/98 for about $40. Chairs were sold at stores, such as Sears and Costco. Chair is five-position folding recliner with extra-wide seat measuring about 22 inches. "Model 2068" is embossed on underside of seat. Chair, made by Bemis Mfg. Co., was sold under Grand Sequoia brand name.

What to do: Return chair to store for refund.

Ekco 12-inch skillets sold at Kmart and Walmart

Handle could break or bend and spill hot contents.

Products: 16,800 Endura and Eterna skillets. Walmart sold Endura skillets 9/97-5/98 at for about $26. Kmart sold Eterna skillets 4/98-5/98 for about $30. Both products are stainless steel; Endura pans ha ve non-stick cooking surface. "EKCO Eterna" is embossed on bottom of Eterna pans. Also, Endura and Eterna pans both have "EKCO Housewares, Inc., 18/10 Stainless Steel, Made in China" embossed on bottom.

What to do: Return pan to store for refund.

Weil-McLain GV model gas boilers

Could produce carbon monoxide, which is deadly.

Products: 8,500 boilers, equipped with certain White-Rodgers model 36C98-303 gas-control valves, sold 6/96-11/97 by heating/cooling companies and contractors for about $1,500 to $3,000. Suspect boilers bear date code 9621 through 9723. Date code and model number are on control valve, at front and center of boiler under jacket. Also recalled are all GV boilers (about 1,000 in all) installed at locations 7,000 feet or more above sea level. These units have "WEIL-MCLAIN GOLD GV" on jacket. They were installed 6/90-1/98.

What to do: Call 800 625-5249. If boiler is involved, company will arrange for adjustment of valve's pressure setting.

Cadet and Encore in-wall electric heaters

Limit switch could spark and pose fire hazard.

Products: 190,000 heaters installed '85-92 in homes in Calif., Idaho, Mont., Ore., Wash., and Wyo. (About 2,000 Encore units were sold nationwide at Ace Hardware, Builders Square, Fred Meyer, Home Base, and Menards stores for $100 to $200.) Heaters have model number beginning with FW, FX, LX, or ZA followed by three digits, as well as one or two black plastic limit switches, which look like small black disc with wires attached. (Heaters with white ceramic switch casing aren't being recalled.) Model number is on label on front of internal heater assembly. To identify unit, first disconnect power supply to heater or fuse box. Then remove grill (with Cadet or Encore name) and screw at top of heater assembly.

What to do: Call 800 567-2613 to arrange for replacement of limit switch or switches.

General Electric "Heavy-Duty Grounding Triple Tap" that converts single electrical outlet into triple outlets

Inadequate grounding poses serious shock hazard.

Products: 50,000 outlet converters sold 9/97-1/98 for $3 to $4. Outlet converters are ivory, orange, or green plastic and are about four inches long and one inch wide. GE logo is on one side of converter; "15A-125V . . . CURRENT TAP . . . MADE IN CHINA" is on other side. Silver "UL" label also appears on converter.

What to do: Call 800 729-4399 for instructions on returning converter for free replacement.

Sears back-massage cushion

Motor inside could overheat and burn user or start fire.

Products: 183,000 Sears Health Essentials Back Massaging System with Heat cushions, made by Conair and sold 2/97-3/98 at Sears stores and through Sears catalog for about $30. Padded black cushion is about 21 inches long and 17 inches wide. Handheld controller says "Health Essentials" in front and "Sears SR4503" on back.

What to do: Return cushion to any Sears store for refund.

Ralph Lauren Thoroughbred candles

Could emit excessively high flame, posing fire hazard.

Products: 1,222 candles sold 9/95-4/98 at department stores like Bloomingdale's and Saks Fifth Avenue and specialty stores such as Polo for about $30. Yellow wax candles are in silver holder with saddle-brown leather sleeve. Candle came in multicolored brown and green paisley box with clear front cover and green ribbon. Tag attached to package shows horse-and-rider scene. Item code number RLT027 also appears on box.

What to do: Return candle to store for refund.

Duracraft, DeLonghi, and Honeywell portable electric ceramic heaters and humidifiers

Could overheat and cause fire.

Products: 1.6 million Duracraft Heat Express heaters, models CZ-303, CZ-304, CZ-308, CZ-318, and CZ-319, sold 1/89-3/98 for $50 to $75; 8,000 DeLonghi heaters, model CER-1, sold 1/89-12/90; and 150,000 Duracraft model DH-950 Moisture Select and Honeywell model HCW-3040 Moisture Select humidifers sold 5/95-3/98 for about $50 to $80. All have model number at bottom. Heaters are rated at1500 watts and are black, with control knobs on top or front. "Heat Express" and either "Duracraft" or "DeLonghi" are on front panel. Humidifiers are white and have clear water tank holding about two gallons. Control knobs and two output vents are on top. "Duracraft" or "Honeywell" appears between vents.

What to do: Call 800 632-9498 to learn how to get free replacement.

Ryobi and Sears Craftsman oscillating detail sanders

If left plugged in, sander could go on unexpectedly and create fire hazard.

Products: 1.2 million sanders, including Ryobi model DS 1000 and Craftsman models 315.11600 and 315.11639, made 5/93-4/97 and sold for $35-$40. Model number and brand name are on plate on side of sander. Serial number or date code is along bottom edge of plate. Serial numbers of affected Ryobi sanders end in digits 9318 through 9718. Affected Craftsman models bear date code A4001 through A9717. Handheld tools are blue or black, 11 inches long, and weigh 1.6 lbs. Sanding arm extends forward and down from front end, and sanding head is triangular.

What to do: Call Ryobi at 800 867-9624 for free repair or replacement. Meanwhile, unplug sander when it's not in use.

Relaxor Deep Knead Shiatsu back massagers

Motor could overheat, and pose fire hazard.

Products: 15,000 back massagers sold 10/97-12/97 at specialty stores including Brookstone, Nordic Track, Sharper Image for $200 to $260. Massagers came in two sizes: "seat topper," which is 46 inches long and 20 inches wide; and "seat lounger," 69¼ inches long and 20⅛ inches wide. Both are covered in solid black or gray tweed fabric. "Relaxor" is printed on front, and elastic straps attach massager to chair. If front of control wand has words "Deep Knead" and back of wand has model number JDK46H and serial numbers from 000001 to 020000, massager is subject to recall.

What to do: Call 800 771-5792 for instructions on getting free replacement.

Takka Pasta and Dough and Pasta Express pasta machines

If safety cutoff switch on lid fails to operate when user's hand is in mixing bowl, machine could crush or sever fingers.

Products: 50,000 machines sold '89-92 at department stores, warehouse clubs, and by mail order for $90 to $200. Recall involves Takka model X1000 and Pasta Express models X2000, X3000, and X4000. Only models bearing serial numbers 78209 or lower are subject to recall. Model and serial number are on label on bottom of machine. Front says "Pasta Express by CTC" or "Takka Pasta and Dough by CTC." Machines are beige or white, and some have chrome-plated front panel.

What to do: Call Creative Technologies Corp. at 800 449-3040 for free replacement lid.

Circulon whisk for use with nonstick cookware

Pin that secures whisk to handle could come off and fall into food.

Products: 60,300 black plastic whisks sold 2/96-12/97 at department and specialty stores for about $8. Whisk is about 13½ inches long, with "CIRCULON" imprinted on handle.

What to do: Return whisk to store for refund, or call 800 326-3933 to return whisk to company and select free kitchen tool.

Wrought-iron "Gables" patio rocking chair sold at Kmart stores

If assembled improperly, chair could collapse.

Products: 148,000 chairs with green textured finish, sold 9/96-8/97 as part of five-piece patio set for $250. Set includes 54-inch oval table and four high-back spring-rocker chairs. Item number 21-34-59 and UPC code 018866001024 appear on hang tags on set.

What to do: Check four bolts under seat. Bolts toward front, closer to rocker coil, should protrude about 1⁄16 inch; bolts toward back should screw fully into holes. Be sure all are tight. Call Compex International at 800 288-0918 for further repair information, or return entire set to nearest Kmart for refund.

Frigidaire, Gibson, Tappan, and White-Westinghouse gas ranges

Oven-burner assemblies could leak gas and cause fire, or explosion.

Products: 23,000 ranges sold 6/97-10/97 for $200 to $450. Affected ranges have 10-digit model number and 10-digit serial number. First six digits of model number are:
970-33 (serial numbers VF72808400 to VF73714402)
FGF333 (VF71205887 to VF73713122)
GGF333 (VF72303525 to VF73310146)
MGF300 (VF72105043 to VF73712212)
MGF311 (VF72010854 to VF73510650)
MGF316 (VF72912839 to VF73711672)
MGF324 (VF71906196 to VF73712362)
MGF331 (VF72007660 TO VF73802057)
MGF345 (VF72104790 to VF73712419)
TGF330 (VF72504892 to VF73404575)
TGF332 (VF72104950 to VF73713181)
TGF334 (VF2008614 to VF73714892)
TGF335 (VF72204981 to VF73810667).
Identifying numbers are under top cover on left wall or in oven or broiler drawer on right side.

What to do: Call 800 724-7519 for inspection and, if necessary, repair. If you smell gas or hear a leak, turn off oven immediately, open windows and door, and call gas company.

Envirotech plastic floor and desktop fans

Pose fire and shock hazards.

Products: 780,000 three-speed oscillating fans sold 1/97-6/97 at Ace Hardware, All American Home Centers, BJ's Wholesale Club, Hechinger's, Home Base, Marc's, Menard's, Rose's Stores, and Supply One for $15 to $35. Fans are 8, 9, 12, 16, and 18 inches high, and are labeled "Envirotech." Recalled fans bear following model numbers: FB-102H, FBD-208, FBD-612, FC-071A, FC-0171A, FC-1071A, FCP-167J, FD-12SD, FD-122L, FD-125J, FD-164J, FS-124J, FS-161J, FS-164J, and FS-181J. Model number is on silver label on bottom of base. Fan came in multicolored box that read, in part: "Envirotech . . . Made in China." Plastic enclosure is extremely flammable, and power cord can come apart and expose live electrical parts. Also, Underwriters Laboratories (UL) mark on fans is counterfeit.

What to do: Return fan to store for refund.

Husqvarna gasoline-powered hedge trimmer

Screws attaching gearcase to crankcase can loosen, allowing internal parts to fly out.

Products: 1,800 hedge trimmers, about 41 inches long, sold 2/97-9/97 for about $400. Model number 225H and Husqvarna name are printed on top of orange engine casing. Serial number is on plate on bottom of engine near handle; recalled hedge trimmers bear serial numbers 6500001 through 7330009.

What to do: Return trimmer to nearest Husqvarna dealer for inspection, repair, or replacement. For name of nearest dealer, call 800 438-7297.

"Super Power" extension cords in various lengths

Pose fire and electrocution hazards.

Products: 115,300 extension cords, in 6-, 9-, 12-, 15-, and 20-foot lengths, sold 10/96-12/96 at discount stores mostly in Fla., N.Y., and N.C. for $1 to $4. Cords are white or brown, have double wires, three outlets, and one plug. Receptacle is labeled, in part, "Rated for 125 volts . . . For indoor use only." Cords came in red, white, and black cardboard sleeve labeled, in part, "SUPER POWER EXTENSION CORD . . . MADE IN CHINA." Last five digits of UPC code range from 70027 to 70036.

What to do: Return extension cord to store for refund.

Lennox Pulse furnaces

Corrosion in heat exchanger could allow deadly carbon monoxide gas to escape.

Products: Lennox Pulse furnaces installed before 1990. Furnaces have model number beginning with G14 or GSR14. Remove front door and look for identification stickers, which usually appear on inside cabinet wall on left side. Pulse furnaces can be identifed by name on door. (Pulse 21 furnaces were made after 1990 and aren't part of inspection program, but should still be inspected annually.)

What to do: Have model and serial number on hand when you call Lennox at 800 537-4341 for free inspection. If necessary, company will replace heat exchanger or give $400 rebate toward new furnace. If other work is required, you may have to pay some repair costs.

Black & Decker Spacemaker Optima under-the-cabinet toaster

Food can catch fire. If food flames up and automatic door opens, flames could spread to cabinet.

Products: 224,000 toasters, model T1000, Type I Spacemaker Optima Horizontal Toaster sold for $50-$69. Affected models bear date codes 402 through 504 (2/94-4/95), which appear on outside of plug prong. Model number T1000 TY I is on back of toaster. "Black & Decker . . . Spacemaker . . . Horizontal Toaster . . . Optima" is imprinted on door. To right of door is control knob with pastry and toaster setting from 1 through 5, button labeled "START," and button labeled "OPEN." Toasters without "OPEN" button are not affected by recall.

What to do: Disconnect power cord, cut off plug, and mail it to Black & Decker Toaster Recall, 6 Armstrong Rd., Shelton, Conn. 06484, for free replacement Spacemaker toaster or $40 coupon toward the purchase of another Black & Decker product from the company's catalog. (Note that choice of free toaster is new option, not available in original terms of recall.)

Sling Garden Chairs sold at Kmart stores

Could collapse and amputate occupant's fingers.

Products: 205,000 chairs sold 2/97-9/97 nationwide for about $13. Chair has white metal frame and striped vinyl seat in following color combinations: royal blue and white, navy and white, orange and lime, lime and orange, and hunter green and white. Color of armrests matches seat. Chair is about 34 inches high and 22 inches wide. White label on back of chair says "MADE IN CHINA," and hang tag says "SLING GARDEN CHAIR . . . KMART."

What to do: Return chair to store for refund.

Deluxe Grill Rocks replacement briquettes

When heated in gas grill, rocks could break apart and fly out of grill, burning or injuring bystanders.

Products: 4,200 packages of briquettes sold 1/98-4/98 at Wal-Mart stores for about $10. Briquettes are reddish brown and shaped like pyramids. Each package contains about 54 pieces. Package reads, in part, "GRILL Care gourmet series . . . DELUXE GRILL ROCKS . . . Continually cleans as you cook—virtually maintenance free." Wording on package is in English, French, and Spanish. Recalled briquettes were made by CharmBrik & Stone Inc. in Mexico. Deluxe Grill Rocks identified as being made in U.S. are not being recalled.

What to do: Return briquettes to store for refund, or call 800 668-5323 for information on returning product using company's overnight-mail account.

NuTone ceiling exhaust fan and light unit

Poses electric shock hazard when change bulb.

Products: 500,000 units sold 6/96-7/97 at store chains and hardware stores for $60 to $75. Model numbers 663LN, 663LNB, 663LNMP, 669L, 669LB, VF305C, and VF307C are being recalled. NuTone name and model number are on installation instructions. Unit is wired to remote wall switch; white grille protrudes from ceiling in shallow "V" shape. Grille is 12¼ inches long and 10¾ inches wide, with white light lens at center and air-intake vent on each side. NuTone fans with larger grill or fluorescent lights are not affected.

What to do: Call 800 273-1124 for free repair kit and instructions.

Mares Corp. Guardian scuba-dive computer

Could fail and cause diver to suffer from decompression sickness.

Products: 1,200 wrist- or hose-mounted computers, used to keep track of dive time, depth, and other scuba measurements, sold 1/97-8/97 at Mares dive shops for about $400. Computer, which resembles digital wristwatch, is black and gray with yellow buttons and is about 3 inches square. "Mares" and "Guardian" are written on frame of computer around screen.

What to do: Return computer to authorized Mares dealer for free replacement.

"Lava Java" microwavable beverage mugs

Could catch fire or split open and spew hot liquid into microwave oven.

Products: 44,000 14-ounce gray, green, or burgundy plastic mugs, sold 7/96-1/97 at stores such as Wal-Mart and Stein Mart and in Veterans Administration Hospital canteens for about $10. Mugs are 5¾ inches high with 5-inch-wide black bottom and 3½-inch-wide black top. "Lava Java" is printed in top, side, and base and instructions are imprinted on base. "MICROCORE TM" is printed on top of straight-shaped handle. Mugs with curved handle lacking "MICROCORE TM" imprint are not being recalled.

What to do: For refund, return mug to store, or call 800 283-7887 for prepaid mailer to ship mug to company.

AC adapters for HiNote VP500 Series notebook computers

Connecter pins could break off AC adapter and remain in power cord, creating shock hazard.

Products: 20,000 adapters packaged with computer or sold separately 9/96-8/97. Adapter is gray and measures 4 inches long and 2¼ inches wide, with 4-foot power cord. Part number 30-47941-01 Rev. A01 or 30-47941 Rev. B01 appears on bar-code label.

What to do: Call 800 550-4741 for replacement.

Dell A/C adapters for Latitude LM notebook computers and port replicators

Connector pins could break off and remain in power cord, posing shock hazard.

Products: 233,000 adapters sold 6/96-10/97 with computer and port replicator or separately for about $39. (Port replicator is docking station used to connect notebook computer to external monitor and keyboard.) Black adapter is 4 inches long and 2¼ inches wide, and has one permanently attached and one detachable power cord. Bottom of adapter says, in part: "DELL . . . MADE IN TAIWAN," and carries "DP/N" bar code whose first eight digits are "00097689" or "00099500." Among 00099500 adapters, only those with A00, A01, A02, or A03 at far right of bar code are being recalled.

What to do: Call 800 715-1483 for free replacement.

Cars

'98 Volkswagen Beetle

Electrical wiring could abrade from contact with battery tray, disable fuel injection, stall engine, and start engine-compartment fire.

Models: 8,500 cars made 1/98-5/98.

What to do: Have dealer install modified battery tray, and inspect, properly route, and secure wiring.

'96-97 Subaru Legacy and Outback

Suspension could fail, causing loss of control.

Models: 29,442 vehicles made 6/96-9/96.

What to do: Have dealer inspect and, if necessary, replace front-suspension support brackets.

'95-98 Nissan Sentra and 200SX

Windshield wipers could fail.

Models: 512,387 cars made 11/94-12/97.

What to do: Have dealer modify wiper-linkage assembly to keep out moisture.

'95 Cadillac (various models)

Air bag could deploy when it shouldn't and cause loss of control.

Models: 102,627 Concours, DeVille, Eldorado, and Seville models made 4/94-2/95.

What to do: Have dealer seal electronic module under driver's seat to keep out moisture.

'98 Mitsubishi Spyder and Eclipse

Engine speed may not drop to idle when driver releases accelerator pedal.

Models: 20,974 cars made 7/97-1/98.

What to do: Have dealer trim dashboard-panel pad to clear throttle cable.

'99 Mazda Miata

Fuel-injector harness could contact engine manifold and blow fuse, stalling the engine.

Models: 8,000 cars made 11/97-3/98.

What to do: Have dealer reroute and, if necessary, replace injector harness.

'95 Chrysler Cirrus and Dodge Stratus

Rear safety belts could fail in crash.

Models: 91,544 cars made 7/94-5/95.

What to do: Have dealer inspect and, if necessary, reposition outboard floor attachment for rear belts.

'96 Buick, Chevrolet, Oldsmobile, and Pontiac cars

Interior lamps could come on unexpectedly, startling driver and increasing risk of crash.

Models: 249,420 cars made 4/95-1/96, including Buick Skylark, Chevrolet Beretta and Cavalier, Oldsmobile Achieva, and Pontiac Grand Am and Sunfire.

What to do: Have dealer check and, if necessary, replace light-control module.

'98 Acura CL and Honda Accord

Vehicle could roll away even when shifter is in park.

Models: 33,966 cars made 9/97-1/98.

What to do: Have dealer install collar on transmission parking pawl.

'98 Cadillac DeVille

Instead of buckling in crash, hood could penetrate windshield, increasing risk of injury to occupants.

Models: 14,423 cars made 9/97-11/97.

What to do: Have dealer replace hood hinge-pivot bolts.

'95-96 Ford Contour and Mercury Mystique

In cars with traction control, engine may not slow to idle when driver removes foot from accelerator.

Models: 38,000 cars made 4/94-8/96.

What to do: Have dealer replace throttle cable.

'98 Ford Mustang GT

Fuel system could leak, creating fire hazard.

Models: 8,300 V8 models made 8/4/97-10/31/97.

What to do: Have dealer replace fuel rail.

'95-97 Chrsyler, Dodge, and Plymouth models

Ball joints in front suspension could corrode and fail, causing loss of steering control.

Models: 599,000 cars, including '95-97 Chrysler Cirrus, Dodge Stratus, and Plymouth Breeze, and '96-97 Chrysler Sebring convertibles.

What to do: Have dealer inspect and, if necessary, replace ball-joints.

'97 Toyota Camry

In extremely cold climates, icing could disable brake vacuum assist, increasing pedal effort and lengthening stopping distances.

Models: 18,746 cars registered in the following states: Alaska, Colo., Idaho, Ill., Iowa, Kan., Me., Mich., Minn., Mont., Neb., Nev., N.H., N.Y., N.D., S.D., Vt., Wisc., and Wyo.

What to do: Have dealer install redesigned brake vacuum hose.

'95-97 Audi (various models)

Driver's-side air bag could deploy suddenly, possibly causing injury.

Models: 39,300 cars made 7/94-9/96, including Audi 90, Cabriolet, A4, A6, and A8. In low humidity, static electricity could trigger air bag when driver touches steering wheel.

What to do: Have dealer install ground wire on driver's-side air bag.

'89-93 Audi (various models)

While car is being driven, air bag could deploy suddenly, possibly causing loss of control.

Models: 54,800 cars made 9/88-7/93, including Audi 80, 90, 100, 200, V8, Coupe, and S4.

What to do: Have dealer replace air bag's sensor control module.

'95 Dodge and Plymouth Neon

Driver could lose steering control if car runs over object that strikes underbody.

Models: 375,000 cars made 1/94-8/95.

What to do: Have dealer install new steering-column coupler.

'97 Lexus ES300, Toyota Avalon, and Toyota Camry

In extreme cold, icing could disable brakes' power assist. Brakes would then require more distance and much greater pedal pressure to stop car.

Models: 18,746 cars made 7/96-2/97 and originally sold or currently registered in Alaska, Colo., Idaho, Ill., Iowa, Kan., Me., Mich., Minn., Mont., Neb., Nev., N.H., N.Y., N.D., S.D., Vt., Wisc., and Wyo.

What to do: Have dealer install redesigned brake vacuum hose. Owners of cars in other states who drive in extremely cold weather should also ask dealer for redesigned hose.

'97 Saturn SC1 and SC2
If front safety belts are repeatedly pulled out very quickly, belt could fail.

Models: 26,135 cars made 5/96-11/96.

What to do: Have dealer replace driver's and front passenger's safety belts.

'92-93 Ford Thunderbird and Mercury Cougar
Fuel hose could chafe, leak, and cause fire.

Models: 134,500 cars made 8/91-9/93 and originally sold or currently registered in Conn., Del., Ill., Ind., Iowa, Ky., Me., Md., Mass., Mich., Minn., Mo., N.H., N.J., N.Y., Ohio, Pa., R.I., Vt., Washington D.C., W. Va., and Wisc.

What to do: Have dealer install protective plastic shields around fuel hoses and, if necessary, replace damaged hoses.

'94-98 Bentley and Rolls-Royce
Brake fluid could leak from hose, reducing brake effectiveness.

Models: 1,621 cars made 5/93-6/97, including Bentley Azure, Brooklands, Continental, Turbo R, and Turbo RL; and Rolls-Royce Corniche IV and S, Flying Spur, Silver Dawn, Silver Spirit, and Silver Spur.

What to do: Have dealer reposition hydraulic brake hoses to prevent abrasion and replace any damaged hoses.

'96-97 Saturn SL
Steering could fail.

Models: 14,580 cars with manual steering made 12/95-6/96.

What to do: Have dealer replace steering-gear assembly.

'95-97 BMW 740i, 740iL, and 750iL
Front springs could break and cause loss of control.

Models: 29,000 cars made 9/94-8/96.

What to do: Have dealer replace front springs and lower spring mounts.

'95 Ford Escort and Mercury Tracer
Plastic fuel tank could crack and cause fire hazard.

Models: 69,100 cars built 4/95-10/95 and originally sold or currently registered in Ala., Ariz., Ark., Calif., Fla., Ga., Hawaii, La., Miss., Nev., Okla., S.C., and Tex.

What to do: Have dealer remove spacer block between fuel tank and its heat shield.

'92-95 Mazda MX3
Road salt could corrode front suspension spring. If spring breaks, it could puncture tire.

Models: 25,000 cars made 8/91-8/94 and registered in Conn., Del., Ill., Ind., Iowa, Me., Md., Mass., Mich., Minn., N.H., N.J., N.Y., Ohio, Pa., R.I., Vt., Washington D.C., W. Va., and Wisc.

What to do: Have dealer install guard assembly to keep broken suspension spring from contacting and puncturing tire.

Sport-utility vehicles, trucks, vans

'98 Isuzu Amigo
Rear safety belts might not provide adequate protection in crash.

Models: 3,044 sport-utility vehicles made 12/97-3/98.

What to do: Have dealer install rear safety-belt anchor bolts.

'98 Dodge Ram
Safety belts might not protect adequately in crash.

Models: 4,200 pickup trucks made 4/98.

What to do: Have dealer replace front outer safety-belt buckles.

'97-98 Ford F-150 and F-250 pickups, and Ford Expedition and Lincoln Navigator sport-utility vehicles
Wheels could come off.

Models: 1,520,000 pickups made 12/95-4/98 and sport-utility vehicles made 5/96-4/98.

What to do: Have dealer inspect wheel studs and replace lug nuts.

'98 Nissan Frontier
Safety belts could be severed in frontal crash.

Models: 20,000 pickup trucks, with bucket seats, made 9/97-1/98. Sharp metal edge of seatback-recliner lever could sever safety belt.

What to do: Have dealer replace plastic handle on reclining lever to keep belt from slipping between seat and lever.

'98 Nissan Frontier
Shifter could inadvertently be moved out of park, allowing vehicle to roll away.

Models: 3,000 pickup trucks with automatic transmission, made 10/97-12/97.

What to do: Have dealer inspect and, if necessary, replace transmission-control assembly.

'97-98 Ford Explorer and Mercury Mountaineer
Fuel hose could pose fire hazard during jump-starting.

Models: 320,000 V6-powered sport-utility vehicles made 8/96-2/98. If ground cable is attached to fuel-line bracket near battery during jump-starting, fuel hose could act as a ground, overheat, and leak.

What to do: Have dealer install warning label on fuel-line bracket advising against its use as jump-start ground. Dealer will also replace bolt in alternator bracket to provide convenient ground for jump-starting.

'91-93 Mazda Navajo
Sunroof could fly off while vehicle is moving.

Models: 23,000 sport-utility vehicles made 2/90-12/92.

What to do: If Mazda hasn't sent you an instruction booklet outlining proper removal and installation of sunroof, plus warning label to affix to latch knob of sunroof, call 800 222-5500.

'94-98 Land Rover Discovery and '95 Range Rover
Cruise-control wiring could abrade from contact with steering components and trigger air bag.

Models: 54,488 sport-utility vehicles made 12/93-12/97.

What to do: Have dealer install fusible link to protect steering-wheel rotary coupler from overheating.

'91-93 Ford Explorer with detachable sunroof
If sunroof is installed incorrectly, it could fly off while vehicle is moving.

Models: 185,000 sport-utility vehicles made 1/90-1/93.

What to do: Ford will provide instruction booklet that thoroughly outlines proper procedures for removal, storage, and installation, plus warning label to affix to sunroof's latch knob. If you haven't received these, call 800 392-3673.

'98 Chrysler, Dodge, and Plymouth minivans with built-in child safety seat
Seat may not restrain child adequately in crash.

Models: 25,900 minivans made 11/97, including Chrysler Town & Country, Dodge Caravan and Grand Caravan, and Plymouth Voyager and Grand Voyager.

What to do: Have dealer inspect and, if necessary, reroute seat's harness webbing.

'98 Dodge Durango
Wiring in engine compartment could overheat and cause fire.

Models: 25,000 sport-utility vehicles made 9/97-1/98.

What to do: Have dealer inspect and, if necessary, tighten wiring connection.

97-98 Mercury Villager. Battery could rupture and cause fire or prevent engine from starting.

Models: 4,945 minivans made 8/28/97-9/24/97.

What to do: Have dealer inspect and, if needed, replace battery.

'98 Ford Ranger pickup
Fuel hose could leak, creating fire hazard.

Models: 2,600 V6 pickup trucks made 8/5/97-9/19/97.

What to do: Have dealer install extra clip to keep hose away from hot exhaust manifold.

'94-96 Dodge Ram pickup trucks
Fuel could leak from tank and create fire hazard.

Models: 497,000 pickup trucks. Hazard exists when fuel tank is full and when truck is parked on slope or weather is hot.

What to do: Have dealer replace fuel-tank valve.

'97-98 Ford F-150 and F-250 pickup trucks and '97-98 Ford Expedition and '98 Lincoln Navigator sport-utility vehicles
Insulation on battery cable could chafe against body panel in trunk and eventually wear away. Short circuit could cause loss of electrical power and create fire hazard.

Models: 866,000 vehicles made11/95-9/97.

What to do: Have dealer reposition and, if necessary, replace main battery cable.

'96-97 Chevrolet S10 and GMC Sonoma pickup trucks
Front brake hose could chafe against left side of engine oil pan, leak, and reduce stopping ability.

Models: 146,851 light pickups, with V6 engine, made 3/95-8/96.

What to do: Have dealer check brake-hose clearance and, if necessary, install extra brake-hose clip and replace hose.

'97-98 Ford F-150 and F-250 pickup trucks and '97-98 Ford Expedition and Lincoln Navigator sport-utility vehicles
Transmission shifter could jam or indicate wrong gear position. Either condition could result in unintended vehicle movement.

Models: 973,000 vehicles made 11/95 to 8/97.

What to do: Have dealer inspect and, if necessary, replace shift cable. Also, have dealer install retention strap.

'91-93 Chrysler, Dodge, and Plymouth minivans
Safety belts could fail in crash.

Models: 1.1 million minivans made 8/90-3/93, including '91-93 Chrysler Town & Country, Dodge Caravan and Grand Caravan, and Plymouth Voyager and Grand Voyager.

What to do: Have dealer install cover-retaining clip on stalk-mounted buckles and replace anchor-retaining clip on right side of center rear belt.

'96 Ford Explorer and '97 Mercury Mountaineer
Raised liftgate could drop and injure anyone underneath.

Models: 2,200 sport-utility vehicles made 6/96.

What to do: Have dealer reinforce liftgate's gas-cylinder bracket with two pop rivets.

Motorcycles & bicycles

'94-96 BMW R1100RSL motorcycles

If motorcycle is stationary and engine is left running at speed above normal idle, exhaust system could overheat, creating fire hazard.

Models: 1,275 motorcycles made 6/93-5/96.

What to do: If BMW hasn't sent you warning label for motorcycle and insert for owner's manual, contact dealer or call 800 831-1117.

'97 Suzuki TL1000SV motorcycle

When front wheel hits bump, rider could lose control.

Models: 2,935 motorcycles made 6/97.

What to do: Have dealer install steering-damper kit.

Cannondale C-Sole bicycling shoes

Cleats could come off and allow foot to slip off pedal.

Products: 15,000 pairs of cycling shoes sold by Cannondale bicycle dealers early '97-4/97 for $60 to $80. Multicolored shoes come in adult-sizes. Cleats are installed by dealer.

What to do: Return shoes to Cannondale dealer for free installation of thin metal backing plate under each insole for firmer attachment of cleats. For name of nearest dealer, call 800-245-3872.

'95-98 GT Speed Series and Robinson bicycle frames

Frame could break, causing loss of control.

Products: 10,000 bicycles and frame kits sold 11/94-2/98 , including '95-98 XL and XXL GT Speed Series, Speed Series Team, and Speed Series Cruiser, and '97-98 Robinson Pro, Pro XL, Pro 24, and Amtrac. Model name is on frame. Bikes sold for about $600 to $1,450; frame kits for $300 to $450.

What to do: Take bike to nearest authorized GT dealer for free frame replacement. For location of dealer, call 800 743-3248.

Child safety seats

Fisher-Price Safe Embrace safety seats

Shoulder-harness locking mechanism may malfunction, compromising protection in a crash.

Products: 55,000 "Safe Embrace" convertible child safety seats, manufactured from May 19, 1997 through March 29, 1998. Product comes with a tether that secures the top of the seat to the car's rear shelf or cargo area (see CONSUMER REPORTS, July 1998).

What to do: Call Fisher-Price at 800 355-8882 for a free replacement harness-adjuster (consumers who had registered the seat with Fisher-Price will automatically receive one). It's OK to continue using the seat until the new adjuster arrives, but inspect the seat each time that it's used to be sure the harness belts stay locked in place.

Evenflo Two-In-One booster car seats

Seatback could separate from base in crash, increasing likelihood of injury to child.

Products: 32,000 child seats with cloth pad, designed for children weighing 22 to 65 pounds. Recalled seats were made 1/7/98-3/20/98 and have six-digit model number starting with 636 or 637. Date of manufacture and model number are on label on backrest. Seats are plastic with cloth pad.

What to do: Call 800 985-7328 for free replacement seat.

Evenflo On My Way infant car seats/carriers

When used as carrier, seat could flip forward and toss infant to the ground.

Products: 800,000 seats made12/15/95-7/27/97 and sold since 1/96. Model 492 "Travel System" includes stroller; model 207 doesn't. Model number and date of manufacture are on bottom of seat. Seats were sold since 1/96.

What to do: Call 800 203-2138 for free repair kit, which includes redesigned latch buttons. Until seat is repaired, continue using it in car, but don't lift it with the carrying handle.

Evenflo Sidekick child booster seat

May not adequately restrain child in crash.

Products: 35,856 booster seats, with model numbers beginning with 244, made 4/23/96-5/20/97. Model number and date of manufacture appear on label on seat shell. Hazard exists only when seat is used with its shield. Shield is necessary when booster is secured only with lap belt. Evenflo advises owners to use Sidekick without shield in seat equipped with lap-and-shoulder belt. Safety note: Don't use safety seat in car's front seat.

What to do: Evenflo will give partial refund if you can use booster seat in seating position with lap-and-shoulder belt, and full refund if you use booster seat in seating position equipped only with lap belt. Call 800 233-5921 for refund.

Kolcraft Secure-Fit and Performa infant safety seats

After crash, buckle may require too much pressure to release, making it hard to remove child. Also, shield pads on 1000 Performa seats don't meet federal flammability standard and could catch fire.

Products: 159,400 safety seats made 1/96-7/97. Date of manufacture appears on label on seat shell.

What to do: Call 800 453-7673 for free replacement buckle, tools, and installation instructions. Company will also provide new shield pad cover, if necessary.

STATEMENT OF OWNERSHIP, MANAGEMENT, AND CIRCULATION
(Required by 39 U.S.C. 3685)

1. Publication Title: Consumer Reports. 2. Publication No: 0010-7174. 3. Filing Date: September 21, 1998. 4. Issue Frequency: Monthly, except two issues in December. 5. No. of Issues Published Annually: 13. 6. Annual Subscription Price: $24.00. 7. Complete Mailing Address of Known Office of Publication: 101 Truman Avenue, Yonkers, New York 10703-1057. 8. Complete Mailing Address of Headquarters or General Business Office of Publisher: 101 Truman Avenue, Yonkers, New York 10703-1057. 9. Full Names and Complete Mailing Addresses of Publisher, Editor, and Managing Editor. Publisher: Consumers Union of United States, Inc., 101 Truman Avenue, Yonkers, New York 10703-1057. President: Rhoda H. Karpatkin; Editor: Julia Kagan; Executive Editor: Eileen Denver. 10. Owner: (If the publication is published by a nonprofit organization, its name and address must be stated.) Full Name: Consumers Union of United States, Inc., a nonprofit organization. Complete Mailing Address: 101 Truman Avenue, Yonkers, New York 10703-1057. 11. Known Bondholders, Mortgagees, and Other Security Holders Owning or Holding 1 Percent or More of Total Amount of Bonds, Mortgages, or Other Securities. If none, so state: None. 12. For Completion by Nonprofit Organizations Authorized to Mail at Special Rates: The purpose, function, and nonprofit status of this organization and the exempt status for federal income tax purposes has not changed during preceding 12 months.

15. Extent and Nature of Circulation:

	Average no. copies each issue during past 12 mo.	Actual no. copies of single issue published nearest to filing date
A. Total no. of copies (net press run)	5,151,353	5,078,529
B. Paid and/or requested circulation		
1. Sales through dealers, carriers, street vendors, counter sales (not mailed)	126,319	102,972
2. Paid or requested mail subscriptions (include advertisers'proof copies/exchange copies)	4,762,101	4,745,115
C. Total paid and/or requested circulation (sum of 15b(1) and 15b(2))	4,888,420	4,848,087
D. Free distribution by mail (samples, complimentary, and other free)	11,140	2,250
E. Free distribution outside the mail	16,254	17,643
F. Total free distribution (sum of 15c and 15e)	27,394	19,893
G. Total distribution (sum of 15 and 15f)	4,915,814	4,867,980
H. Copies not distributed		
1. Office use, leftovers, spoiled	16,238	13,576
2. Return from news agents	219,301	196,973
I. TOTAL (sum of 15g, 15h(1) and 15h(2)	5,151,353	5,078,529
J. Percent paid and/or requested circulation	99.44%	99.59%

17. I certify that the statements made by me above are correct and complete.

Louis J. Milani, Senior Director, Strategic Marketing and Business Affairs

Manufacturer & brand locator

Phone numbers and web addresses to help you track down information about a product or manufacturer. Web addresses are given when a functioning one exists at press time. Alphabetically, by brand.

A

Ace	630 990-6522	www.acehardware.com
Acer	800 733-2237	www.acer.com/aac
Acoustic Research	707 748-5930	—
Action Lane	888 367-5263	www.action-lane.com
Acura	800 862-2872	www.acura.com
Admiral	800 688-9920	www.maytag.com
Advent	800 225-9847	—
Agfa	888 988-2432	www.agfa.com
Aiwa	800 289-2492	www.aiwa.com
Alcoa	800 962-6973	www.alcoahomes.com
Allison	606 236-8298	—
Alside	800 922-6009	www.alside.com
Altec Lansing	800 258-3288	www.altecmm.com
Amana	800 843-0304	www.amana.com
American Sensors	800 387-4219	www.madi.com
American Standard	800 524-9797	www.americanstandard.com
Ameriwood	800 253-2093	www.ameriwood.com
AmerTac	914 352-2400	—
Ametek	800 645-5427	www.plymouthwater.com
Amtico	800 268-4260	www.amtico.com
Amway	800 544-7167	www.amway.com
Apple	800 538-9696	www.apple.com
Ariens	800 678-5443	www.ariens.com
Armstrong (flooring)	800 233-3823	www.armstrong.com
Armstrong (heating)	419 483-4840,ext. 2362	—
Ashland-Davis	800 231-1614	www.ashland-davis.com
Asko	800 367-2444	www.askousa.com
AST	800 876-4278	www.ast.com
AT&T	800 222-3111	www.att.com

Atlas	800 478-0258	www.atlasroofing.com
Audi	800 822-2834	www.audiusa.com
Audiovox	800 229-1235	www.audiovox.com

B

B.F. Goodrich	800 847-3435	www.bfgoodrichtires.com
B.I.C.	800 348-6492	www.ameriwood.com
Bassett (bedding)	941 676-6061	www.bassettfurniture.com
Bassett (recliners)	540 629-6405	www.bassettfurniture.com
Beaulieu/Coronet	800 227-7211	www.beaulieu-usa.com
Behr	800 854-0133	www.behrpaint.com
Bell	800 456-2355	www.bellsports.com
Bell South	800 338-1694	www.bellsouth.com
Benjamin Moore	Contact local store	—
Berkline	888 777-3843	www.berkline.com
Betty Crocker	800 688-8782	—
Bianchi	510 264-1001	www. bianchi.it
Bissell	800 237-7691	www.bissell.com
Black & Decker	800 544-6986	www.blackanddecker.com
BMW	800 831-1117	www.bmwusa.com
Boca	561 241-8088	www.bocaresearch.com
Bosch (appliances)	800 944-2904	www.boschappliances.com
Bosch (tools, East Coast)	888 394-4646	www.boschtools.com
Bosch (tools, West Coast)	888 648-7278	www.boschtools.com
Bose	800 444-2673	www.bose.com
Boston Acoustics	800 246-7767	www.bostonacoustics.com
Brainerd	800 652-7277	www.libertyhardware.com
Braun	800 272-8611	www.braun.de
Breadman	800 233-9054	www.breadman.com
Bridgestone	800 706-8473	www.bridgestone-firestone.com
Briggs	800 888-4458	—
Brita	800 442-7482	—
Brother (fax machines, fax-modems)	800 284-4329	www.brother.com
Brother (printers)	877 284-3238	www.brother.com
Bruce	800 722-4647	www.brucehardwoodfloors.com
Bryant	800 468-7253	www.bryant.com
Buick	800 521-7300	www.buick.com
Bunn	800 637-8606	www.bunnomatic.com
Bush	800 727-2874	www.bushfurniture.com

C

Cadillac	800 458-8006	www.cadillac.com
Cambridge Soundworks	800 367-4434	www.hifi.com
Canon (camcorders, cameras, faxes)	800 828-4040	www.usa.canon.com
Canon (copiers)	800 652-2666	www.usa.canon.com
Canon (printers)	800 848-4123	www.ccsi.canon.com
Carpet Magic	800 784-3628	www.rugdoctor.com

Carpet One	800 227-7381	www.carpet1.com
CarpetMax	770 590-9369	www.carpetmax.com
Carrier	800 227-7437	www.carrier.com
Casablanca	888 227-2178	—
Casio	800 962-2746	www.casio.com
Celotex	800 544-7533	www.celotex.com
Certain Teed	800 233-8990	www.certainteed.com
Cerwin Vega	805 584-9332	www.cerwin-vega.com
Char-Broil	800 241-7548	www.grilllovers.com
Chevrolet	800 222-1020	www.chevrolet.com
Chrysler	800 992-1997	www.chryslercars.com
Cobra	773 889-3087	www.cobraelec.com
Coleman	800 241-7548	www.grilllovers.com
Comfortmaker	931 270-4128	www.icpusa.com
Compaq	800 345-1518	www.compaq.com
Congoleum	800 274-3266	www.congoleum.com
Cooper	800 854-6288	www.coopertire.com
Costar	800 432-5599	www.qqinc.com
Craftsman (Sears)	Contact local store	www.sears.com
Crane	800 877-6678	—
Creative Labs	800 998-1000	www.creativelabs.com
CTX	800 888-2120	www.ctxintl.com
Cub Cadet	800 528-1009	—
Cuisinart	800 726-0190	www.cuisinart.com
Culligan	888 285-5442	—
CyberMax	800 443-9868	—

D

Dal-Tile	800 933-8453	www.dtile.com
Dazey	800 557-4825	www.rivco.com
DCM	800 878-8463	www.dcmspeakers.com
Delco	800 223-3526	www.acdelco.com
Dell	800 879-3355	www.dell.com
DeLonghi	800 322-3848	www.delonghi-products.com
Denon	973 575-7810	www.denon.com
DeWalt	800 433-9258	www.dewalt.com
Diamond	800 468-5846	www.diamondmm.com
Diamondback	805 484-4450	www.diamondback.com
DieHard (Sears)	Contact local store	www.sears.com
DirecTV	800 347-3288	www.directtv.com
Dirt Devil	800 321-1134	www.dirtdevil.com
Dish Network	800 333-3474	www.dishnetwork.com
Dixon	800 264-6075	—
Dodge	800 992-1997	www.4adodge.com
Domco	800 248-5574	www.domco.com
DSS Satellite TV	Call local dealer	—
Ducane	800 382-2637	www.ducane.com
Dunlop	800 548-4714	www.dunloptire.com
Dutch Boy	800 828-5669	www.roombyroom.com

E

Eagle Electric	800 441-3177	www.eagle-electric.com
Echo	800 432-3246	—
Echostar	800 333-3474	www.dishnetwork.com
Ecko	847 678-8600	—
Ecowater	800 869-2837	www.ecowater.com
Electrolux	800 243-9078	www.electroluxusa.com
Eljer	800 423-5537	—
Elk	972 851-0400	www.elkcorp.com
Emerson (air conditioners)	217 342-3901	www.fedders.com
Emerson (ceiling fans)	800 237-6511	www.emersonfans.com
Emerson (microwaves, VCRs)	972 884-2350	—
Encon	817 927-5100	—
Englander	800 837-5337	www.englandersleep.com
Enzone	800 448-0535	www.enzoneusa.com
Epson	800 463-7766	www.epson.com
Equator	800 935-1955	www.equatorappl.com
Ericsson	800 374-2776	www.ericsson.com
Estro	800 933-7876	www.saeco-usa.com
Eureka	800 282-2886	www.eureka.com
Everpure	800 323-7873	www.everpure.com
EverStart	888 387-8278	—

F

Fantom	800 668-9600	www.fantom.com
Fasco	800 288-5588	www.rivco.com
Fedders	217 342-3901	www.fedders.com
Firestone	800 706-8473	www.bridgestone-firestone.com
First Alert	800 323-9005	www.firstalert.com
First Years	800 533-6708	—
Fisher (CD players)	800 421-5013	www.audvidfisher.com
Fisher (minisystems, receivers)	800 421-5013	www.sanyousa.com
Fisher-Price	800 432-5437	www.fisher-price.com
Flexsteel	800 685-7632	www.flexsteel.com
Ford	800 392-3673	www.fordusa.com
Franklin	601 456-4286	www.franklincorp.com
Friedrich	210 225-2000	—
Frigidaire	800 374-4432	www.frigidaire.com
Frigidaire (dishwashers)	800 944-9044	www.frigidaire.com
Fuji	800 800-3854	www.fujifilm. com

G

GAF	800 840-0497	www.gaf.com
Gaggia	201 939-2555	—
Gateway	800 846-2000	www.gateway.com
GE Saf-T-Gard	800 833-4933	—
Gem	516 273-2230	—

General	800 847-3349	www.generaltire.com
General Electric (TVs)	800 447-1700	www.home-electronics.net
General Electric (appliances, air conditioners)	800 626-2000	www.ge.com
Genie	800 654-3643	—
Georgia-Pacific	800 839-2588	www.gapac.com
Gerber (child-proofing products)	800 443-7237	www.gerber.com
Gerber (toilets)	847 675-6570	www.gerberonline.com
Gerry	800 525-2472	—
Giant	800 874-4268	—
Gibson	800 374-4432	—
Giro	800 969-4476	www.giro.com
Glacier Pure	617 568-1305	—
GLI	630 705-1000	—
Glidden	800 221-4100	www.ici.com
Global Village	800 736-4821	www.globalvillage.com
GMC	800 462-8782	www.gmc.com
Goldstar	800 243-0000	www.lgeus.com
Goodyear	800 466-3932	www.goodyear.com
GS Roofing	800 999-5150	www.gsroof.com
GT	800-743-3248	www.gtbicycles.com

H

Hamilton Beach	800 851-8900	www.hambeach.com
Hampton Bay (Home Depot)	Contact local store	www.homedepot.com
Harbor Breeze	800 527-1292	—
Hayes	770 441-1617	www.hayes.com/support/status/
Heil	931 270-4128	www.icpusa.com
Heartland	800 432-7801	www.heart-land.com
Hewlett-Packard (digital cameras)	888 474-3867	www.hp.com
Hewlett-Packard (scanners)	800 722-6538	www.hp.com
Hewlett-Packard (computers)	800 724-6631	www.hp.com
Hewlett-Packard (copiers, printers, fax machines, fax-modems)	800 752-0900	www.hp.com
Hitachi (monitors)	800 441-4832	www.nsa-hitachi.com
Hitachi (TVs, VCRs)	800 448-2244	www.hitachi.com
Home Depot	800 553-3199	www.homedepot.com
Home Water	800 547-3944	www.homewater.com
Honda (cars)	310 783-2000	www.honda.com
Honda (mowers)	800 426-7701	www.honda.com
Hoover	800 944-9200	www.hoovercompany.com
Hotpoint	800 626-2000	www.hotpoint.com
Huffy	800 872-2453	www.huffy.com
Hunter	800 448-6837	www.hunterfans.com
Husqvarna	800 487-5962	www.husqvarna.com
Hyundai	800 633-5151	www.hyundai.com

I

IBM	800 426-7235	www.ibm.com
Ikea	610 834-0180	www.ikea.com
IKO	888 456-7663	www.iko.com
Image	800 722-2504	www.imageind.com
Infiniti (cars)	800 662-6200	www.infiniti-usa.com
Infinity (speakers)	800 553-3332	—
Iomega	800 697-8833	www.iomega.com
Isuzu	310 699-0500	www.isuzu.com

J

J.C. Penney	Contact local store	www.jcpenney.com
Jacuzzi	800 288-4002	www.jacuzzi.com
Jaguar	800 544-4767	www.jaguar.com
Janitrol (heating)	713 861-2500, ext. 290	—
JBL	800 336-4525	—
Jeep	800 992-1997	www.jeep.com
Jenn-Air	800 688-1100	www.jennair.com
John Deere	800 537-8233	www.deere.com
Joyce Chen	978 671-9500	www.joycechen.com
JVC	800 252-5722	www.jvc.com

K

Karastan	800 234-1120	www.karastan.com
Kelly-Springfield	800 592-3267	www.kelly-springfield.com
Kenmore (Sears)	Call local store	www.kenmore.com
Kent	800 245-3123	—
Kenwood	800 536-9663	www.kenwoodusa.com
Kidco	847 970-9100	www.kidcoinc.com
KinderGard	800 255-2634, ext. 222	www.mace.com
Kinetico	800 944-9283	www.kinetico.com
King Koil	800 888-6070	www.kingkoil.com
Kirby	800 494-8586	www.kirby.com
KitchenAid (large appliances)	800 422-1230	www.kitchenaid.com
KitchenAid (countertop appliances)	800 541-6390	—
Kmart	Call local store	www.kmart.com
Kodak (cameras)	800 242-2424	www.kodak.com
Kodak (digital cameras, scanners)	800 235-6325	www.kodak.com
Kohler	800 456-4537	www.kohlerco.com
Konica	800 756-6422	www.konica.com
Krups	800 526-5377	—
Kubota (mowers)	310 370-3370	—
Kubota (tractors, riding mowers)	888 458-2682, ext. 900	—

L

La-Z-Boy	800 625-3246	www.lazyboy.com
Lasko	800 394-3267	www.laskoproducts.com
Lawn Chief	800 800-7310	www.mtdproducts.com
Lawn-Boy	800 526-6937, ext. 4003	www.lawn-boy.com
Lennox	800 953-6669	www.lennox.com
Leviton's	800 367-5424	www.leviton.com
Lexmark	800 539-6275	www.lexmark.com
Lexus	800 872-5398	www.lexus.com
Lifesaver	800 654-9677	www.kidde.com
Lincoln	800 392-3673	www.lincolnvehicles.com
Logitech	800 231-7717	www.logitech.com
Lucent	800 222-3111	www.lucent.com

M

Macurco	303 781-4062	www.macurco.com
MAG	800 827-3998	www.maginnovision.com
Magic Chef	800 688-1120	—
MagInnovision	800 827-3998	www.maginnovision.com
Magna	800 551-0032	—
Magnavox (TVs)	800 531-0039	www.philipsmagnavox.com
Magnavox (VCRs)	423 475-8869	www.philipsmagnavox.com
Makita	800 462-5482	—
Malarkey	800 545-1191	www.malarkey-rfg.com
Mannington	800 356-6787	www.mannington.com
Mansfield	419 938-1352	—
Marantz	630 307-3100	www.marantz.com
Mastic	800 627-8426	www.mastic.com
Maxim	800 233-9054	www.salton-maxim.com
Maytag	800 688-9900	www.maytag.com
Mazda	800 222-5500	www.mazda.com
McCulloch	800 423-6302	—
Melitta	800 451-1694	www.melitta.com
Mercedes-Benz	800 222-0100	www.mercedes.com
Mercury	800 392-3673	www.mercuryvehicles.com
Michelin	800 847-3435	www.michelin.com
Micron	800 438-3343	www.micron.com
Microtek	800 654-4160	www.microtekusa.com
Miele (dishwashers)	800 688-1120	www.miele.com
Miele (vacs)	800 694-4868	www.miele.com
Miele (washers)	800 843-7231	www.miele.com
Miller & Kreisel	310 204-2854	www.mksound.com
Milwaukee	800 729-3878	www.mil-electric-tool.com
Minolta	201 825-4000	www.minolta.com
Mitsubishi (TVs)	800 332-2119	www.mitsubishi.com
Mitsubishi (cars)	800 222-0037	www.mitsucars.com
Mohawk	800 266-4295	www.mohawkcarpet.com
Mongoose	800 257-0662	www.mongoose.com

Montgomery Ward	800 695-3553	—
Motorcraft	800 392-3673	www.motorcraft.com
Motorola (phones)	800 331-6456	www.startac.com
Motorola (computers)	800 759-1107	www.mot.com
Motorola (pagers)	800 548-9954	www.mot.com
Mr. Coffee	800 672-6333	—
MTD	800 800-7310	www.mtdproducts.com
Munsey	800 235-2853	www.munseypro.com
Muratec	972 364-3350	www.muratec.com
Murray (bikes, mowers)	800 251-8007	www.murrayinc.com
Murray (tractors, riding mowers)	800 224-8940	www.murrayinc.com
Mustek	949 788-3600	www.mustek.com

N

Nafco	800 248-5574	www.domco.com
Nanao	800 800-5202	www.eizo.com
NEC (CD-ROMs, monitors, computers)	800 632-4636	www.nec.com
NEC (cell phones)	800 225-5664	www.nec.com
NEC (pagers)	800 421-2141	www.nec.com
NEC (printers)	800 632-4650	www.nec.com
NHT	800 648-9993	www.recoton.com
Nighthawk	800 880-6788	www.kidde.com or www.kiddesafety.com
Nikon (digital cameras, scanners)	800 526-4566	www.nikon.com
Nikon (cameras)	800 645-6687	www.nikon.com
Nilfisk	800 645-3475	www.nilfisk-advance.com
Nissan	800 647-7261	www.nissanmotors.com
Nokia (cell phones)	888 665-4228	www.nokia.com
Nokia (monitors)	800 296-6542	www.nokia.com
NordicWare	800 328-4310	www.nordicware.com

O

O'Sullivan	800 327-9782	www.osullivan.com
Okidata	800 654-3282	www.okidata.com
Oldsmobile	800 442-6537	www.oldsmobile.com
Olympus (digital cameras, scanners)	888 553-4448	www.olympus.com
Olympus (cameras)	800 221-3000	www.olympus.com
Omni	800 937-6664	www.omnifilter.com
Onkyo	201 825-7950	www.onkyo.co.jp
Optimus (Radio Shack)	Contact local store	www.radioshack.com
Oreck	800 989-3535	www.oreck.com
Orion	800 289-0981	www.orion-audio.com
Oster	800 597-5978	—
Osterizer	800 528-7713	—
Owens Corning	800 438-7465	www.owenscorning.com

P

Pacific	800 666-8813	—
Packard Bell	800 733-5858	www.packardbell.com
Panasonic (digital cameras)	800 222-4213	www.panasonic.com
Panasonic (breadmakers)	800 871-5279	www.panasonic.com
Panasonic (computer backups,monitors, printers)	800 742-8086	www.panasonic.com
Panasonic (phones, VCRs)	800 211-7262	www.panasonic.com
Pentax	800 877-0155	www.pentax.com
Perstorp Pergo	800 337-3746	www.pergo.com
Phase Technology	904 777-0700	www.phasetech.com
Philips Magnavox	800 531-0039	www.philipsmagnavox.com
Pillsbury	800 858-3277	—
Pinnacle (N.Y.)	516 576-9052	www.pinnacle-speakers.com
Pinnacle (out of N.Y.)	800 346-2863	www.pinnacle-speakers.com
Pioneer	800 746-6337	www.pioneerelectronics.com
Pirelli	800 327-2442	www.pirelli.com
Pittsburgh	800 441-9695	www.ppg.com
Plymouth	800 992-1997	www.chryslerplymouth.com
Polaroid	800 343-5000	www.polaroid.com
Polk Audio	800 377-7655	www.polkaudio.com
Pollenex	800 767-6020	—
Pontiac	800 762-2737	www.pontiac.com
Porsche	800 545-8039	www.porsche.com
Porter Cable	800 321-9443	www.porter-cable.com
Pratt & Lambert	800 289-7728	—
Presto	715 839-2209	www.presto-net.com
Primestar	800 774-6378	www.primestar.com
Pro-Action	800 288-4280	www.pro-action.com
Proctor-Silex	800 851-8900	www.hambeach.com
PTI	800 515-0074	www.pti.com
PUR	800 665-9787	www.pur.com

Q

Qualcomm	800 349-4188	www.qualcomm.com
Quasar	800 222-4213	www.panasonic.com
Queen	Call local dealer	www.queencarpet.com

R

Radio Shack	800 843-7422	www.radioshack.com
Rainbow	800 852-8569	www.rainbow.com
Rainsoft	800 860-7638	www.rainsoft.com
Raleigh	800 222-5527	—
RCA	800 336-1900	www.rca.com
Regal (breadmakers, food processors)	800 313-8807	www.regalware.com
Regal (coffee makers)	414 626-2121	www.regalware.com
Regina	800 847-8336	—
Restonic	800 898-6075	www.restonic.com

Ricoh	800 225-1899	www.ricoh.com
Rinse 'N Vac	800 784-3628	www.rugdoctor.com
Rival	800 557-4825	www.rivco.com
Roadmaster (kids' bikes)	800 626-2811	—
Roadmaster (mountain bikes)	618 393-2991	—
Rollerblade	800 232-7655	www.rollerblade.com
Roper	616 973-7113	www.roperappliances.com
Ross	800 338-7677	—
Royal (building products)	800 387-2789	www.royplas.com
Royce Union	800 888-2453	—
Rug Doctor	800 784-3628	www.rugdoctor.com
Ruud	800 848-7883	—
Ryobi	800 345-8746	www.ryobi.com

S

S&S Mills	800 241-4013	—
Saab	800 955-9007	www.saabcars.com
Sabre	800 533-1377	www.deere.com
Safety 1st	800 723-3065	—
Safety Source Mericon	800 327-3534	www.safetysource.com
Samsung (cameras)	800 762-7746 ext. 198.	www.samsung.com
Samsung (monitors, fax machines, TVs, VCRs, microwave ovens)	800 767-4675	www.samsung.com
Sanyo	818 998-7322	www.sanyo.usa
Saturn	800 553-6000	www.saturn.com
Sauder	800 537-8560	www.sauder.com
Schwinn	800 724-9466	www.schwinn.com
Scotts	800 646-8442	www.scottscompany.com
Seagate	800 626-6637	www.seagate.com
Sears	Contact local store	www.sears.com
Serta	630 285-9300	www.serta.com
Seymour	800 457-9881	—
Shaklee	800 742-5533	www.shaklee.com
Sharp	800 237-4277	www.sharp-usa.com
Shaw	800 441-7429	www.greatfloors.com
Sherwin-Williams	800 474-3794	www.sherwin.com
Sherwood	800 962-3203	www.sherwoodusa.com
Shop Vac	717 321-7056	www.shopvac.com
Signet	905 474-9129	—
Simmons	800 746-6667	www.simmons.com
Simplicity	800 987-5296	www.simplicitymfg.com
Singer (vacuum cleaners)	800 237-7691	www.bissell.com
Singer (sewing machines)	800 877-7762	www.talktous@singerco.com
Skil	773 286-7330	www.skiltools.com
Snapper	800 762-7737	www.snapper.com
Sony (CD players, camcorders, digital cameras, phones, monitors, receivers, TVs, VCRs)	800 222-7669	www.sony.com

Sony (computers)	800 476-6972	www.sony.com
Southwestern	800 255-8480	www.swbell.com
Southwestern Bell	800 366-0937	www.subfreedom-phone.com
Specialized	408 779-6229	www.specialized.com
Speed Queen	800 843-0304	www.amana.com
Stanton Carpet	800 452-4474	www.stantoncarpet.com
Stihl	800 467-8445	www.stihlusa.com
Storm	888 438-3279	www.stormtech.com
Subaru	800 782-2783	www.subaru.com
Sunbeam (frypans, woks, food processors)	800 597-5978	www.sunbeam.com
Sunbeam (grills)	800 641-2100	www.sunbeam.com
Sunbeam (toasters, toaster-ovens)	800 831-9678	www.sunbeam.com
Sunbeam (blenders)	800 528-7713	www.sunbeam.com
Supra	800 727-8772	www.supra.com
Suzuki	714 996-7040	www.suzuki.com
Swatch	800 879-2824	www.swatch-art.com
Symphonic	201 288-2063	www.funai-corp.com
SyQuest	800 245-2278	www.syquest.com

T

T-Fal	800 395-8325	www.t-fal.com
Tamko	800 218-2656	www.tamko.com
Tappan	800 374-4432	—
Tarkett	800 367-8275	www.tarkettna.com
Technics (receivers, CD players)	800 211-7262	www.panasonic.com
Technics (speakers)	800 222-4213	www.panasonic.com
Teledyne	800 525-2774	www.waterpik.com
Tempstar	931 270-4306	www.icpusa.com
Texas Instrument	800 336-5236	www.ti.com
Therapedic	908 561-6000	www.therapedic.com
Thermos	800 241-7548	www.grilllovers.com
Toastmaster	800 947-3744	www.toastmaster.com
Toro	800 348-2424	www.toro.com
Toshiba (computers)	800 457-7777	www.toshiba.com
Toshiba (TVs)	800 631-3811	www.toshiba.com
Toyota	800 331-4331	www.toyota.com
Trane	Call local dealer	www.trane.com
Trek	800 369-8735	www.trekbikes.com
Troy-Bilt	800 437-8686	www.troybilt.com
Tru-Test	800 874-8494	www.tru-test.com

U

U.S. Robotics	800 342-5877	www.3com.com
Umax	800 562-0311	www.umax.com
Uniden	800 297-1023	www.uniden.com
Universal-Rundle	800 955-0316	www.universal-rundle.com
U. S. Satellite Broadcasting	800 204-8772	www.ussb.com

V

Van Dijk Carpet	800 222-9005	—
Variflex	800 327-0821	www.conquest.com/variflex
Verlo	800 229-8957	www.verlo.com
ViewSonic	800 888-8583	www.viewsonic.com
Visioneer	800 787-7007	www.visioneer.com
Vivitar	800 421-2381	www.vivitar.com
Volkswagen	800 822-8987	www.vw.com
Volvo	800 458-1552	www.volvo.com
VTech	800 624-5688	www.vtech.com

W

Wal-Mart	800 925-6278	www.wal-mart.com
Waring	800 492-7464	—
Weber	800 999-3237	www.weberbbq.com
Weed Eater	800 554-6723	www.weedeater.com
West Bend	414 334-2311	www.westbend.com
Whirlpool	800 253-1301	www.whirlpool.com
White	800 949-4483	www.mtdproducts.com
White-Westinghouse	800 374-4432	www.frigidaire.com
Windmere	800 582-0179	www.windmere.com
Windsor	800 444-7654	www.windsorind.com
World	800 241-4900	—
Wolverine	888 838-8100	www.vinylsiding.com

X

Xerox	800 832-6979	www.xerox.com

Y

Yamaha	800 492-6242	www.yamaha.com
Yard Machine	800 800-7310	www.mtdproducts.com
Yard-Man	800 800-7310	www.mtdproducts.com
Yashica	800 526-0266	www.yashica.com
Yokohama	800 366-8473	www.yokohamatire.com

Z

Zenith	847 391-8752	www.zenith.com
Zojirushi	800 733-6270	www.zojirushi.com
Zoom	800 631-3116	www.zoomtel.com

Indexes

8-YEAR INDEX TO CONSUMER REPORTS

This index indicates when the last full report on a given subject was published in CONSUMER REPORTS. It goes back as far as 1991. Note: Beginning with Volume 61 (January 1996), CONSUMER REPORTS stopped using continuous pagination throughout each volume year. From January 1996 forward, each issue begins on page 1. **Bold type** indicates Ratings reports or brand-name discussions; *italic type* indicates corrections, followups, or Updates. Some reports are available by fax or mail from our **Reports by Request** 24-hour service. To order a report, note the fax number at the left of the entry and call 800 896-7788 from a touch-tone phone. (No code or an * means a report is not available by fax.) You can use a credit card. Reports typically are $7.75.

A

D

R

S

BUYING GUIDE INDEX

This index covers all the reports, brand-name Ratings' charts, and repair histories in this year's Buying Guide. To find the last full report published in CONSUMER REPORTS, see the eight-year guide that starts on page 347.

Canada Extra

HOW TO USE THE CANADA EXTRA

The Ratings you'll find in this new sixteen-page section list some of the same products included in Ratings reports elsewhere in this book, but with a difference: The products listed here are those that, according to the manufacturers, are sold in Canada. You can use this section in either of two ways: Start with the main Ratings, find several products you like, and turn to this section to find whether they're sold—and for what price—in Canada. Or start here, find products sold in Canada whose price and overall score you like, and read more about them in the main report and full Ratings chart.

We've tried to make it easier to compare products in the main Ratings to products in the Canadian lists by using the same key numbers (in Ratings that use them) in both. In the Ratings of air conditioners, for example, the Carrier model listed first in this section has key number 6, because it appears sixth in the main Ratings on page 169.

In most cases, the prices we list here are the approximate retail in Canadian dollars. We used the exchange rate that was in effect at the time of the original publication. And we include, when it's available, the manufacturer's phone number, so you can call to get information on a model you can't find in the stores.

ROOM AIR CONDITIONERS

Report begins on page 146; Ratings on page 169

Fewer than half the tested air conditioners are sold in Canada; in one cooling capacity group, you have only a single model to choose from. And we can't help you much with prices; only Whirlpool and Panasonic were able to pass along the Canadian selling prices for all the tested air conditioners. NA indicates information not available.

Within size groups, listed in order of overall score

Key no.	Brand and model	Price	Overall score	Manufacturer's phone number
			0–100 (P F G VG E)	
	5,000 TO 5,800 BTU/HR. MODELS			
6	**Carrier** UCA051B	NA		800 227-7437
7	**Friedrich** Q-star SQ05J10	NA		NA
	6,000 TO 6,600 BTU/HR. MODELS			
13	**Gibson** Panorama GAB067F7B	NA		NA
14	**Friedrich** Q-star SQ06J10	NA		NA
15	**Carrier** VisionAire LCA061P	NA		800 227-7437
	7,000 TO 7,800 BTU/HR. MODELS			
17	**Panasonic** CW-806TK	$600		905 624-5505
20	**Friedrich** Q-star SQ07J10	NA		NA
	8,000 TO 8,600 BTU/HR. MODELS			
21	**Friedrich** Quietmaster Electronic SS08J10A	NA		NA
23	**Whirlpool** DesignerStyle YACQ082XD	550		800 461-5681
24	**Carrier** Siesta Series TCA081P	NA		800 227-7437
25	**Fedders** Portable Series A3Q08F2BG	NA		800 661-0131
26	**Carrier** Siesta Series TCA081D	NA		800 227-7437
27	**Frigidaire** Custom Series FAC083W7A	NA		NA
	9,100 TO 9,200 BTU/HR. MODEL			
32	**Friedrich** Quietmaster Electronic SS09J10A	NA		NA
	10,000 TO 10,500 BTU/HR. MODELS			
33	**Friedrich** Quietmaster Electronic SS10J10A	NA		NA
35	**Whirlpool** DesignerStyle YACQ102XD	625		800 461-5681
36	**White-Westinghouse** Continental Series WAL103Y1A	NA		NA
37	**Carrier** Siesta Series TCA101D	NA		800 227-7437
	11,500 TO 12,000 BTU/HR. MODELS			
38	**Friedrich** Quietmaster Electronic SS12J10A	NA		NA
39	**Gibson** Air Sweep GAX128Y1A	NA		NA
42	**Fedders** Regency Series A3J12E2AG	NA		800 661-0131
43	**Whirlpool** DesignerStyle YACQ122XD	715		800 461-5681

AUTO BATTERIES

Report begins on page 314; Ratings on page 316

Half the batteries we tested this time are sold in Canada, including four models each in groups sizes 58 and 34/78. In group size 24, the selection is limited to one model. An * indicates list price; NA, information not available.

Within sizes, listed in order of overall score

Brand and model	Price	Overall score (0–100: P F G VG E)	Manufacturer's phone number
GROUP SIZE 24			
ACDelco Professional 24-7YR	$95		NA
GROUP SIZE 58			
DieHard WeatherHandler 50658 (Sears) (cold)	80		Contact local Sears store
Interstate Mega-tron MT-58 [1]	96		800 843-0200
Motorcraft Silver WETBXT-58 [1]	89*		800 561-3673
ACDelco Professional 58-6YR	100		NA
GROUP SIZE 34/78			
Interstate Mega-tron MTPlus-78DT [1] [2]	132		800 843-0200
DieHard Gold 50078 (Sears) (cold)	100		Contact local Sears store
Eveready DT-LTV (Wal-Mart)	NA		NA
ACDelco Professional 78DT-7YR	121		NA

[1] *Requires periodic addition of water.*
[2] *Discontinued, but may still be available.*

HOW TO USE THE RATINGS

- Read the Recommendations for information on specific models and general buying advice.
- Note how the rated products are listed—in order of performance and convenience, price, or alphabetically.
- The overall score graph gives the big picture in performance. Notes on features and performance for individual models are listed in the "Comments" column or "Details on the models."
- Use the key numbers to locate the details on each model.
- Before going to press, we verify model availability for most products with manufacturers. Some tested models listed in the Ratings may no longer be available. Discontinued models are noted in "Comments" or "Details on the models." Such models may still be available in some stores for part of 1999. Models indicated as successors should perform similarly to the tested models, according to the manufacturer. Features may vary.
- Models similar to the tested models, when they exist, are indicated in "Comments" or "Details on the models."
- The original date of publication is noted for each Ratings.

CAMCORDERS

Report begins on page 39; Ratings on page 61

All the tested camcorders, like most electronic products we tested, are sold in Canada. An * indicates list price; NA, information not available.

Within types, listed in order of overall score

Key no.	Brand and model	Price	Overall score	Manufacturer's phone number
			0 100 P F G VG E	
	DIGITAL CAMCORDERS			
1	**Sony** DCR-PC10	$3,500*		416 499-1414
2	**Panasonic** PV-DV710	3,200		905 624-5505
	ANALOG CAMCORDERS			
3	**Sony** CCD-TRV65	1,100*		416 499-1414
4	**Panasonic** PV-D408K	800		905 624-5505
5	**Panasonic** PV-L608K	1,000		905 624-5505
6	**Sony** CCD-TRV25	1,000*		416 499-1414
7	**Sharp** VL-E665U	NA		NA
8	**Hitachi** VM-E540A	700*		905 821-4445
9	**JVC** GR-AX930C	NA		NA
10	**RCA** Pro-V730	800*		NA
11	**Sony** CCD-TR67	800*		416 499-1414
12	**JVC** GR-AX430C	NA		NA
13	**Canon** ES970	NA		NA

CELLULAR PHONES

Report begins on page 219; Ratings on page 236

All but three of the tested cell phones are available in Canada. But as in the U.S., it makes sense to shop first for cellular service, since a cell phone tends to be less expensive when bought bundled with a service plan.

While hundreds of carriers compete to provide Americans with cellular phone service, the Canadian market is highly concentrated. Two services command more than 90 percent of the market: Cantel/ATT, an alliance between Canadian telecommunications giant Rogers Communications and U.S. telecommunications giant AT&T, and Mobility Canada, which provides service (at varying rates) through cellular subsidiaries of the country's 15 regional telephone companies, from Newtel in Newfoundland to BCTel in British Columbia and from NorthwestTel in the Territories to Bell in Ontario and Quebec. Two other providers, Clearnet and FIDO/Microcell, mostly provide digital service to subscribers in major cities. (As in the U.S., Canadian digital service is consistently dependable only in urban areas.)

In a growing retail trend, you can buy a cell phone bundled with service not only from the carrier but from such stores as Canadian Tire and The Future Shop. The "cell phone in a box" packages sold by these retailers include both the phone and a service plan, which can sometimes be activated with a phone call.

In addition, a decision by the Canadian Radio-Telecommunications Commission has opened the way for the regional Mobility partners to market cellular service bundled with residential service at the same retail outlets (previously, consumers could not get information on Mobility services at residential phone centres). In response, Bell Canada has launched a *SimplyOne* service that integrates residential and cellular service; all calls ring first on your home phone, then are transferred to your cell phone if they go unanswered. Other Mobility members are expected to offer similar services soon.

NA indicates information not available.

Within types, listed in order of overall score

Key no.	Brand and model	Price	Overall score (0–100: P F G VG E)	Manufacturer's phone number
	ANALOG MODELS			
1	**Nokia** 918+	$69-$199		888 226-6542
2	**Motorola** StarTAC-6500	NA		800 461-4575
3	**Nokia** 252	99-199		888 226-6542
4	**Audiovox** MVX-470	169-199		905 712-9299
5	**Motorola** StarTAC-3000	NA		800 461-4575
6	**NEC** Talk Time MAX 960	NA		905 795-3500
7	**Motorola** Profile 300 e*	NA		800 461-4575
8	**Ericsson** AH630	0-29		800 661-4201
9	**Motorola** 650e	NA		800 461-4575
	DUAL-MODE MODELS (ANALOG AND DIGITAL)			
11	**Sony** (Clearnet) CM-B1207CNTO	NA		888 253-2763
12	**Qualcomm** QCP-820	NA		619 651-4029
13	**Audiovox** CDM-3000	649-699		905 712-9299
14	**Nokia** 2160i	99-199		888 226-6542

COMPACT CAMERAS

Report begins on page 41; Ratings on page 64

Your choice in compact cameras can be determined by the kind of pictures you want to take, the amount of money you want to spend, and whether you prefer 35mm or the new APS format. Your choice isn't limited by geography; as the chart here shows, all of the rated cameras are available in Canada. NA indicates information not available.

Within types, listed in order of overall score

Key no.	Brand and model	Price	Overall score	Focal length(s)	Manufacturer's phone number
			0 — 100 (P F G VG E)		
	35mm MODELS				
1	**Olympus** LT Zoom 105	$449		38-105 mm	800 387-0437
2	**Canon** Sure Shot 105 Zoom	350		38-105	800 652-2666
3	**Ricoh** RZ10 5SF (zoom)	NA		38-10	514 338-3838
4	**Leica** Mini 3 [1]	300		32	905 940-9262
5	**Fujifilm** DL-290 Zoom	280		38-90	800 263-5018
6	**Pentax** Espio 90MC	320		38-90	905 625-4930
7	**Samsung** Maxima Evoca 115	330		38-115	800 268-4987
8	**Yashica** Microtec Zoom 90	279		38-90	732 560-0060
	APS MODELS				
9	**Kodak** Advantix 3700ix	255		24	800 465-6325
10	**Canon** Elph 490Z (zoom)	700		22.5-90	800 795-2666
11	**Konica** Super Big Mini BM-S100	235		28	800 268-7722
12	**Nikon** Nuvis 125 i (zoom)	430		30-100	905 625-9910
13	**Fujifilm** Fotonex 400ix Zoom	550		25-100	800 263-5018
14	**Minolta** Vectis 40 (zoom)	500		30-120	201 825-4000
15	**Minox** CD 25 [1]	180		25	905 940-9262

[1] *Available only through 12/98, according to the manufacturer.*

COMPUTER MONITORS

Report begins on page 231; Ratings on page 240

All but two of the 17- and 19-inch monitors we tested are sold in Canada, most at prices comparable with those in the U.S. An * indicates list price; NA, information not available.

Within sizes, listed in order of overall score

Key no.	Brand and model	Price	Overall score	Manufacturer's phone number
			0 100 P F G VG E	
	17-INCH MONITORS			
1	**Sony** Multiscan CPD-200ES	$815		416 499-1414
2	**CTX** VL710	NA		NA
3	**Panasonic** PanaSync S70	700*		905 624-5505
6	**NEC** MultiSync A700	710		800 632-4662
7	**MagInnovision** DJ700	670		800 827-3998
8	**Hitachi** SuperScan Pro 620	700*		905 821-4545
9	**Nokia** 447Za	NA		NA
	19-INCH MONITORS			
10	**Sony** Multiscan GDM-400PS	1,430		416 499-1414
11	**Hitachi** SuperScan Elite 751	1,300*		905 821-4545
12	**ViewSonic** G790	1,310*		800 888-8583

DISHWASHERS

Report begins on page 96; Ratings on page 113

All but a few of the tested dishwashers are available in Canada. An * indicates list price; NA, information not available.

Listed in order of overall score

Key no.	Brand and model	Price	Overall score	Manufacturer's phone number
			0 — 100 (P F G VG E)	
1	**Kenmore** (Sears) Dirt Sensor 1595	$700		Contact local store
2	**Kenmore** (Sears) QuietGuard 7738 [1]	600		Contact local store
3	**Kenmore** (Sears) Dirt Sensor 1583	600		Contact local store
4	**Frigidaire** Gallery FDB949GF	750		905 565-9200
5	**Kenmore** (Sears) QuietGuard 1568 **A CR Best Buy** [1]	500		Contact local store
6	**Maytag** Quiet Plus II MDB6000A	690		800 688-2002
7	**GE** Profile Performance GSD4911X	730		800 361-3400
9	**Asko** 1585	1,205*		NA
10	**KitchenAid** Whisper Quiet Ultima Superba KUDS24SE	1,000		800 461-5681
11	**Maytag** Quiet Pack MDB4000A	590		800 688-2002
12	**Asko** 1375	870*		NA
16	**KitchenAid** Quiet Scrub KUDI24SE	800		800 461-5681
18	**GE** Profile Quiet Power GSD4310X	650		800 361-3400
20	**Frigidaire** Ultra Quiet II Precision Wash FDB635RF	550		905 565-9200
21	**Magic Chef** Tri Power Wash System DU6500	590		800 688-1120

[1] *Available only through 12/98, according to the manufacturer.*

GAS GRILLS

Report begins on page 149; Ratings on page 189

About half of the tested barbecue grills are sold in Canada, including five of the models we specifically recommend.

Listed in order of overall score

Key no.	Brand and model	Price	Overall score (0–100: P F G VG E)	Manufacturer's phone number
1	**Weber** Genesis 1000	$800		800 265-2150
2	**Weber** Spirit 500	600		800 265-2150
3	**Ducane** 1504SHLPE	720		800 382-2637
4	**Sunbeam** Grillmaster AG850C	660		800 667-8623
6	**Coleman** Powerhouse Plus 4868862	370		800 241-7548
8	**Sunbeam** Grillmaster AG455EP	300		800 667-8623
12	**Sunbeam** Grillmaster AG540EPB	260		800 667-8623

PUSH-TYPE LAWN MOWERS

Report begins on page 155; Ratings on page 192

About half the mowers we tested are sold in Canada, including the two highest-rated mowers of each type we tested. An * indicates list price; NA, information not available.

Within types, listed in order of overall score

Key no.	Brand and model	Price	Weight	Overall score (0–100: P F G VG E)	Manufacturer's phone number
	HYBRID MOWERS (REAR-BAGGING, SIDE-DISCHARGE)				
1	**John Deere** JS60	$485	34 kg.		800 537-8233
2	**Sabre** M10 by John Deere	445	34		800 537-8233
5	**Murray** Select 20456X31	275	28		800 661-6662
6	**Snapper** MR215014B	NA	29		888 477-8650
	REAR-BAGGING MOWERS				
7	**Yard Machines** by MTD 11A-428C	330	27		800 668-1238
8	**Yard Machines** by MTD 11A-413A	270	25		800 668-1238
11	**Murray** 20406X83	230	25		800 661-6662

Ratings continued

CANADA EXTRA

Key no.	Brand and model	Price	Weight	Overall score (0–100; P F G VG E)	Manufacturer's phone number
	SIDE-DISCHARGE MOWERS *continued*				
12	**Honda** Harmony II HRS216PDC	$490*	29 kg.		416 284-8110
13	**Yard-Man** By MTD 11A-106C501	300	27		800 668-1238
14	**Sears** Craftsman 36802	270	25		Contact local Sears store
15	**Yard Machines** by MTD 11A-021C	145	20		800 668-1238
18	**Yard Machines** by MTD 11A-084A	230	25		800 668-1238
19	**Murray** 22405X83	200	27		800 661-6662

THREE-PIECE LOUDSPEAKER SETS

Report begins on page 51; Ratings on page 72

All but two of the tested three-piece speaker sets are available in Canada. With plenty of choices, you should have no trouble finding a set whose sound and specifications match your needs. Note that all the prices listed in the chart are manufacturers' list prices. None of the manufacturers we contacted was able to estimate an actual selling price.

Listed in order of overall performance

Key no.	Brand and model	List price (bass/sat.)	Overall performance (P F G VG E)	Manufacturer's phone number
1	**Bose** Acoustimass-5 Series II [1]	$1,000		800 465-2673
2	**Cambridge Soundworks** Ensemble III, **A CR Best Buy**	500		800 367-4434
3	**Yamaha** YST-SW150 (bass)	600		416 298-1311
4	**NHT** SW1P (bass), SuperZero (satellite)	1,000 (700/300)		514 631-6448
6	**Bose** Acoustimass-3 Series III	700		800 465-2673
7	**Polk Audio** RM3300	1,200		800 377-7655
8	**Acoustic Research** S8HO (bass), The Edge (satellite)	900 (500/400)		800 732-6866
9	**Boston Acoustics** Micro90	1,200		978 538-5000
10	**Infinity** BU-1 (bass), Reference 2000.1 (satellite)	700 (400/300)		800 567-3275

[1] *Available only through 12/98, according to the manufacturer.*

SNOW THROWERS

Report begins on page 160; Ratings on page 199

About half the snow throwers we tested are sold in Canada, generally at comparable prices. Sears reports that none of its U.S. models are sold in Canada. But both top-rated snow throwers are available in Canada: the two-stage *Toro 824 Power Shift*, $1949, and the single-stage *John Deere TRS21*, $739, A CR Best Buy. (Canadian winters are a compelling reason to choose the extra snow-clearing power of a two-stage machine. Single-stage models bog down in anything beyond about 15 to 20 cm of snow.) NA indicates information not available.

Within types, listed in order of overall score

Key no.	Brand and model	Price	Overall score (0–100: P F G VG E)	Manufacturer's phone number
	TWO-STAGE MODELS			
1	**Toro** 824 Power Shift	$1,949		800 544-5364
3	**MTD** E640F **A CR Best Buy**	1,070		800 668-1238
8	**Troy-Bilt** 42010	1,600		800 225-3585
9	**Toro** 622 Power Throw	1,240		800 544-5364
10	**Simplicity** 860E	2,050		800 987-5296
11	**John Deere** 826D	1,670		NA
14	**Simplicity** 555M	1,430		800 987-5296
	SINGLE-STAGE MODELS			
16	**John Deere** TRS21 **A CR Best Buy**	740		NA
17	**Honda** HS62C5	1,125		West: 604 278-7121; Central: 416 299-3400; Quebec: 514 655-6161; Atlantic: 902 468-4116
18	**Toro** CCR3000GTS	1,000		800 544-5364
20	**MTD** 140	500		800 668-1238
23	**Snapper** LE317R	580		800 762-7737

Key no.	Brand and model	Price	Overall score	Manufacturer's phone number
	NOT ACCEPTABLE *This model lacks a deadman safety control for its auger.*			
26	**Toro** CCR Powerlite	550	**Not scored**	800 544-5364

STRING TRIMMERS

Report begins on page 161; Ratings on page 204

The 24 trimmers that are available in Canada include two CR Best Buys, the eight highest-rated gas models, and the top-rated corded electric. While two of the four battery-powered trimmers aren't sold in Canada, we didn't find much to recommend about any of the battery models anyway.

Within types, listed in order of overall score

Key no.	Brand and model	Price	Overall score	Manufacturer's phone number
			0 100 P F G VG E	
	GASOLINE MODELS			
1	**Stihl** FS-75	$260		800 267-8445
2	**Echo** GT-2000SB	305		800 720-1358
3	**Echo** SRM-2100	360		800 720-1358
4	**Ryobi** 725r TrimmerPlus **A CR Best Buy**	160		800 265-6778
5	**Stihl** FS-36 **A CR Best Buy**	150		800 267-8445
6	**Husqvarna** Mondo Max	260		604 444-4676
7	**Husqvarna** 225L E-Tech	420		604 444-4676
8	**Ryobi** 990r TrimmerPlus	340		800 265-6778
13	**Homelite** Easy Reach 20680	160		800 363-5715
14	**Sears Craftsman** Weedwacker 51736	130		Contact local Sears store
16	**Weed Eater** FeatherLite SST	125		800 554-6723
17	**Weed Eater** FeatherLite	90		800 554-6723
18	**Homelite** TrimLite 20677	130		800 363-5715
19	**McCulloch** MAC 2816	140*		800 556-3634
	CORDED MODELS			
20	**Ryobi** 132r TrimmerPlus	115		800 265-6778
23	**Weed Eater** Twist 'N Edge TE40	55		800 554-6723
24	**Weed Eater** Snap-N-Go SG14	55		800 554-6723
25	**Weed Eater** XT110	45		800 554-6723
26	**Black & Decker** GH400	75		800 544-6986
27	**Black & Decker** ST3000	50		800 544-6986
29	**Weed Eater** ElectraLite EL8	35		800 554-6723
30	**Black & Decker** ST1000	25		800 544-6986
	BATTERY-POWERED MODELS			
32	**Ryobi** 150r	150		800 265-6778
34	**Black & Decker** CST1000	145		800 544-6986

TOURING-PERFORMANCE TIRES

Report begins on page 308; Ratings on page 310

All the tires we tested for this report, and the ones from two previous reports that we checked on, are sold in Canada. The per-tire prices listed here are calculated from the average selling prices in the U.S., manufacturers didn't provide actual Canadian selling prices. NA indicates information not available.

Listed in order of overall score

Key no.	Brand and model	Price	Overall score	Manufacturer's phone number
			P F G VG E	
1	**Michelin** Energy MXV4	$180		800 461-8473
2	**Dunlop** D60 A2 with JLB **A CR Best Buy**	110		800 263-1302
3	**Goodyear** Eagle GT+4	155		800 387-3288
4	**Pirelli** P6000 SportVeloce	145		514 331-4330
5	**BF Goodrich** Touring T/A HR4	110		800 461-8473
6	**General** XP 2000 H4	100		800 461-1776
7	**Yokohama** Avid H4	110		800 661-4033
8	**Goodyear** Eagle LS	190		800 387-3288
9	**Bridgestone** Turanza H	140		NA
10	**Firestone** Firehawk Touring LH	140		NA
11	**Cooper** Cobra GTH	105		800 854-6288

TOASTERS & OVENS

Report begins on page 107; Ratings on page 129

Only a handful of toasters from our tests can't be found on Canadian shelves. The top-rated four-slice toaster and the top-rated oven/broiler are among the missing, but all of the top-five two-slice toasters are sold in Canada. NA indicates information not available.

Within types, listed in order of overall score

Key no.	Brand and model	Price	Overall score	Manufacturer's phone number
			0 100 P F G VG E	
	TWO-SLICE TOASTERS			
1	**Cuisinart** CPT-60C	$105		800 472-7606
2	**Sunbeam** 3802	40		800 667-8623
3	**KitchenAid** 4KTT251	110		800 461-5681
4	**Black & Decker** T270	40		800 465-6070
5	**Cuisinart** CPT-30C	60		800 472-7606

Ratings continued

Key no.	Brand and model	Price	Overall score	Manufacturer's phone number
			0 100 / P F G VG E	
	TWO-SLICE TOASTERS *continued*			
7	**Proctor-Silex** C22425	$30		800 267-2826
8	**Krups** 155	40		NA
10	**Toastmaster** B1021	40		800 947-3744
11	**Proctor-Silex** C22415	35		800 267-2826
12	**Toastmaster** B1035	40		800 947-3744
14	**Proctor-Silex** C22205	20		800 267-2826
15	**Rival** TT9215	15		800 363-3479
	FOUR-SLICE TOASTERS			
17	**Proctor-Silex** C24415	55		800 267-2826
18	**Rival** TT9415	35		800 363-3479
19	**Toastmaster** D1050	40		800 947-3744
20	**Black & Decker** TS443	70		800 465-6070
	TOASTER-OVEN/BROILERS			
22	**Black & Decker** TRO400 **A CR Best Buy**	70		800 465-6070
23	**DeLonghi** XU-23STD	150		888 335-6644
24	**Toastmaster** 316	60		800 947-3744

LOW-FLUSH TOILETS

Report begins on page 163; Ratings on page 208

The top-rated pressure-assisted toilet and all of the gravity-flush toilets we tested are sold in Canada. Briggs, manufacturer of the one vacuum-assisted model, says its products will be sold in Canada beginning later this year. An * indicates list price; NA, information not available.

Within types, listed in order of overall score

Key no.	Brand and model	Price	Overall score	Dimensions	Manufacturer's phone number
			0 100 / P F G VG E		
	PRESSURE-ASSISTED MODEL				
1	**Gerber** Ultra Flush 21-302	NA		70x52x71 cm.	847 675-6570
	GRAVITY-FLUSH MODELS				
4	**Eljer** Berkeley 081-1595	$707		64x52x75	905 564-0616
5	**Eljer** Patriot 091-1125	184		71x53x71	905 564-0616
6	**American Standard** Cadet II EL 2174.139	294*		74x48x76	800 524-9797
7	**Mansfield** Elderly 137-160	130*		80x51x73	NA
8	**Gerber** New Aqua Saver 21-702	NA		74x52x69	847 675-6570
9	**Universal-Rundle** Nostalgia 4065	300		74x46x76	NA
10	**Kohler** Wellworth K-3422	252		71x51x76	800 964-5590
11	**Mansfield** Alto 130-160	250*		72x51x67	NA

VACUUM CLEANERS

Report begins on page 165; Ratings on page 211

Only a few of the tested upright and canister vacuum cleaners are available in Canada. An * indicates list price; NA, information not available.

Within types, listed in order of overall score

Key no.	Brand and model	Price	Overall score	Manufacturer's phone number
			0 100 P F G VG E	
	UPRIGHT MODELS			
2	**Kirby** G5	NA		216 529-6208
4	**Kenmore** (Sears) 38512	$400		Contact local store
7	**Electrolux** Epic 3500SR	720		800 668-0763
8	**Sharp** EC-12TWT4	200		800 370-6744
10	**Panasonic** Power Wave MC-V5710	230		905 624-5505
14	**Sharp** EC-T4770	300		800 567-4277
18	**Windsor** Sensation SX2	800		800 444-7654
19	**Bissell** Micro-Lock 3511C	150*		800 263-2535
	CANISTER MODELS			
21	**Electrolux** Epic 8000	1,020		800 668-0763

WASHING MACHINES

Report begins on page 108; Ratings on page 133

About half the tested washing machines are sold in Canada, including five of the six front-loader models. An * indicates list price; NA, information not available.

Within types, listed in order of overall score

Key no.	Brand and model	Price	Overall score	Manufacturer's phone number
			0 100 P F G VG E	
	FRONT-LOADING MODELS			
3	**Miele** W1918	$2,300		NA
4	**Maytag** MAH3000A	NA		800 688-2002
5	**Equator** EZ3600C	1,500		NA
6	**Asko** 11505	NA		800 367-2444

Ratings continued

Key no.	Brand and model	Price	Overall score	Manufacturer's phone number
			0 100 P F G VG E	
	TOP-LOADING MODELS *continued*			
9	**GE** Profile Performance WPSP4170	$750		NA
14	**Whirlpool** LSL9244E	690*		800 461-5681
16	**Maytag** LAT9706AA	NA		800 688-2002
19	**Whirlpool** YLSR5233E	650*		NA
20	**Maytag** LAT9406AA	NA		800 688-2002
22	**White-Westinghouse** MWS445RF	570		905 565-9200
23	**Frigidaire** FWS645GF	650		905 565-9200
25	**Magic Chef** W227L	NA		905 565-9200
26	**White-Westinghouse** MWX645RE	580		905 565-9200

WHIRLPOOL TUBS

Report begins on page 167; Ratings on page 216

Six of the nine tested whirlpool tubs are sold in Canada, including the model in each brand group that our panelists preferred most: the American Standard Luxury System II, the Jacuzzi Builder Luxura, and the Kohler System II Ellery. Besides listing Canadian prices and manufacturers' phone numbers, we've converted the tubs' specifications to metric measurements. An * indicates list price.

Within brands, listed in order of panelists' preference

Brand and model	Price	Height	Weight	Capacity	Manufacturer's phone number
American Standard Luxury System II Heritage 2801.128H	$2,292*	57 cm.	55 kg.	93–237 L.	800 524-9797
American Standard Scala System I Renaissance 2660.018R	1,940*	51	40	115–211	800 524-9797
Jacuzzi Builder Luxura 5 L016H (F942959)	1,150	51	42	148–218	800 387-6926
Kohler System I Ellery K-1273-J1-0 (1273)	3,252	52	57	78–214	800 964-5590
Kohler System III Steeping Bath K-792-J3-0 (K-792-N)	5,601	52	186	83–223	800 964-5590
Kohler System II Mendota K-514-J3-0 (514-H)	3,350	42	205	97–165	800 964-5590